# Auditing and Reporting

# 2009–10

# Supplement

Extant at 30 April 2009

# Auditing and Reporting

# 2009–10

## Supplement

Extant at 30 April 2009

### General Editor
*John Selwood*

**Wolters Kluwer (UK) Limited**
145 London Road
Kingston upon Thames
Surrey KT2 6SR
Tel: 0844 561 8166
Fax: 020 8547 2638
Email: customerservices@cch.co.uk
www.cch.co.uk

**Disclaimer**

This publication is sold with the understanding that neither the publisher nor the authors, with regard to this publication, are engaged in rendering legal or professional services. The material contained in this publication neither purports, nor is intended to be, advice on any particular matter.

Although this publication incorporates a considerable degree of standardisation, subjective judgment by the user, based on individual circumstances, is indispensable. This publication is an 'aid' and cannot be expected to replace such judgment.

Neither the publisher nor the authors can accept any responsibility or liability to any person, whether a purchaser of this publication or not, in respect of anything done or omitted to be done by any such person in reliance, whether sole or partial, upon the whole or any part of the contents of this publication.

**Telephone Helpline Disclaimer Notice**

Where purchasers of this publication also have access to any Telephone Helpline Service operated by Wolters Kluwer (UK), then Wolters Kluwer's total liability to contract, tort (including negligence, or breach of statutory duty) misrepresentation, restitution or otherwise with respect to any claim arising out of its acts or alleged omissions in the provision of the Helpline Service shall be limited to the yearly subscription fee paid by the Claimant.

**British Library Cataloguing-in-Publication Data**

A catalogue record for this book is available from the British Library.

Typeset by YHT Ltd, London
Printed and bound in Italy by Legoprint-Lavis (TN)

# Contents

# Proposed Clarified International Standards on Auditing (UK and Ireland)

## Contents

# Consultation Paper

# Proposed Clarified International Standards on Auditing (UK and Ireland)

## INVITATION TO COMMENT

Following a prior consultation, the Auditing Practices Board (APB) announced in early March 2009 its decision to update UK and Irish auditing standards for the new, clarified, International Standards on Auditing (Clarity ISAs) recently finalised by the International Auditing and Assurance Standards Board (IAASB) following completion of the 'Clarity Project'.

APB is now issuing for public comment exposure drafts of a revised Statement of the Scope and Authority of APB Pronouncements, 33 proposed 'clarified' International Standards on Auditing (UK and Ireland) (ISAs (UK and Ireland)) and a 'clarified' International Standard on Quality Control (UK and Ireland) 1 (ISQC (UK and Ireland) 1). When finalised, these standards will replace the existing ISAs (UK and Ireland) and ISQC (UK and Ireland) 1 with effect for audits of financial statements for periods ending on or after 15 December 2010.

To assist commentators APB has prepared this Consultation Paper to:

- Summarise the views of respondents to APB's October 2008 consultation on whether APB should adopt the clarified ISAs and, if so, when; and
- Explain APB's approach to including the proposed supplementary requirements and guidance that are specific to the UK and Ireland.

Over the last three years APB, and its SME Audit and Public Sector sub-committees, have invested many hours in preparing responses to the draft Clarity ISAs when they were exposed. The IAASB has also received many responses to their exposure drafts from other respondents based in the UK and Ireland. The IAASB has responded to comments received and their due process has been overseen by the Public Interest Oversight Board. This exercise has been very beneficial and has led to important changes in the final standards. In particular most of APB's recommendations for improvement have been accepted and, as a result, APB is able to reduce significantly the number of supplementary requirements now needed in the ISAs (UK and Ireland).

Having previously consulted on the adoption of the Clarity ISAs, in this consultation, APB is seeking views on the proposed APB supplementary requirements and guidance to be retained, and specifically responses to the questions asked in Section 3 below, rather than general views from commentators on the underlying IAASB Clarity ISAs.

APB would prefer to receive letters of comment in an electronic form that facilitates 'copy and paste': these may be sent by e-mail to **k.billing@frc-apb.org.uk.** If this is not possible, please send letters of comment to:

**Keith Billing**
**Project Director**
**The Auditing Practices Board**
**5<sup>th</sup> Floor**
**Aldwych House**

**71-91 Aldwych**
**London WC2B 4HN**

Letters of comment should be sent so as to be received no later than *22 July 2009.*
All comments will be regarded as being on the public record, unless otherwise
requested and will be posted to APB's website soon after receipt.

# 1. Reasons for Updating the Existing Auditing Standards

This Section sets out the background to APB's proposal to update the current UK    1
and Irish auditing standards and provides feedback on the prior consultation that
sought views on that proposal.

In 2004 APB made the strategic decision to base UK and Irish auditing standards on    2
ISAs, supplemented with additional standards and guidance where necessary to
maintain the requirements of the previous UK and Irish auditing standards.

One of the reasons for adopting ISAs was to benefit efficiently from future    3
improvements in them. The IAASB has recently completed an important project to
reformat the ISAs. This, so called, 'Clarity Project' was undertaken with international regulatory support in order to improve the understandability of the ISAs and
make them more compatible with regulatory frameworks, including the EC's Statutory Audit Directive.

In parallel with the Clarity Project, ISAs on important topics such as auditing    4
groups, estimates (including fair values) and related party transactions have been
revised and improved to reflect the latest developments and thinking.

As the revisions and other improvements that have been made are designed to    5
improve audit quality and the Clarity Project has been undertaken primarily to
improve the understandability of the ISAs, APB believes that it is appropriate to
introduce these new standards in the UK and Ireland as soon as is practicable.

## Feedback on Consultation on Updating the Existing UK and Irish Auditing Standards

In October 2008 APB published a Consultation Paper seeking views on whether UK    6
and Irish auditing standards should be updated for the new international auditing
standards[1]. The Consultation Paper outlined the main differences between the current ISAs (UK and Ireland) and the Clarity ISAs issued by the IAASB and
considered the possible impact on auditors' procedures and the cost of audits.

APB asked for comments on whether the Clarity ISAs should be adopted, whether    7
the same standards should apply to all audits, and when the new standards should be
adopted.

## Responses to the consultation

There were 18 formal responses to the Consultation Paper[2]. In these, the interests of    8
smaller practitioners were largely represented by comments from the accountancy
bodies to which they belong, with one, brief, response received directly from a
smaller firm. To obtain further views, the ICAEW and the Irish Institutes held
meetings with practitioners and others specifically to discuss the Consultation Paper
at these meetings there was good representation from the small practitioner
community.

---

[1] *The Consultation Paper is available to view in the Publications/Exposure Drafts section of the APB's website (www.frc.org.uk/apb/publications/exposure.cfm) together with copies of the responses received.*

[2] *Responses were received from 5 accountancy bodies, 4 public sector bodies, 8 audit firms and 1 organisation representing preparers of financial statements.*

9   Both the formal responses to the Consultation Paper and the clear consensus from the meetings held demonstrated very strong support for implementing the Clarity ISAs for all calendar 2010 audits. A summary of the responses to the key elements of the consultation is given below.

*Should the Clarity ISAs be adopted?*

10   Overall there was very strong support for the adoption of the Clarity ISAs, with many emphasising why they thought it important to do so, including:

- The benefits of the clarification of the requirements and guidance in increasing the understandability of the standards;
- The appropriateness of improving requirements in the areas of auditing estimates, related parties and group audits;
- The importance for firms that operate globally of the harmonisation of standards internationally; and
- Maintaining the UK's position as a leader in audit quality.

> **APB's Conclusion**
> APB concluded that it should proceed with updating the existing UK and Irish auditing standards to adopt the Clarity ISAs as soon as practicable.

*Should the same standards apply to all audits?*

11   There was clear support for this view from respondents, with strong arguments expressed in favour of applying the same standards to all audits, effective from the same date, including:

- Views that the implementation of dual standards is not practical and would lead to confusion for companies, investors and auditors in understanding the nature of an audit.
- Beliefs that different standards would create two tiers of audit, compromising perceptions of the value of a smaller entity audit and leading to the audit profession becoming more stratified.
- Expectation that having more than one set of standards would result in additional costs for those firms which would audit under both sets of auditing standards.

12   Throughout the Clarity Project APB has been conscious of the impact that the new standards might have on smaller audits. APB's SME audit sub-committee was heavily involved in helping APB respond to exposure drafts and achieve important changes in the final standards.

13   In its October 2008 Consultation Paper APB provided some information about the possible costs of adopting the Clarity ISAs. APB's view is that, particularly for smaller audits, any cost impact can be minimised if there is effective training and support provided to audit firms. Whilst training is not part of APB's remit, APB has been liaising with the accountancy bodies on this and is committed to providing appropriate support to them.

APB also notes that the International Federation of Accountants (IFAC), under the **14** auspices of which the IAASB operates, has published a policy position[3] supporting a single set of auditing standards. IFAC concluded that it "believes that high quality auditing standards should be capable of being applied to the audits of the financial statements of entities of all sizes. This enables a consistent level of assurance to be associated with the word "audit" and allows users to make decisions in the light of a common understanding about the reliability of the financial statements."

---

**APB's conclusion**

APB concluded that the updated auditing standards should be applicable to audits of entities of all sizes, effective from the same date.

---

*Timing of adoption*

While a few respondents believed there may be some merit in allowing further time **15** for smaller entities to adopt the new standards, the clear majority of respondents supported adopting the standards in line with the IAASB timetable (i.e. audits of periods beginning on or after 15 December 2009). This was considered important so as to avoid the UK and Ireland lagging behind other countries in applying the best standards available.

Practitioners from smaller firms who attended the meetings described in paragraph 8 **16** were comfortable with applying the ISAs for calendar 2010 audits and this approach is considered feasible by organisations who provide training and support to smaller firms.

Some respondents suggested that the effective date should be for periods ending on **17** or after 15 December 2010 rather than for periods commencing on or after 15 December 2009. For most entities this will not actually be a difference but it would serve to exclude 'short accounting periods' which would otherwise need to be audited before new systems and training are in place.

---

**APB's conclusion**

APB concluded that the new ISAs (UK and Ireland) should be effective in the UK and Ireland for audits of periods ending on after 15 December 2010. Excluding 'short accounting periods' avoids accelerating the timetable for updating audit materials and training audit personnel, which may be particularly beneficial for smaller audit firms and organisations that support them.

---

*Other important matters*

APB's supplementary material

Several commentators expressed the view that APB 'pluses' should only reflect **18** additional requirements arising from UK and Irish specific laws and regulations. Their rationale was that APB 'pluses' would undermine some of the benefits of international harmonisation in standards. They also anticipated the adoption of the ISAs within the EU and the possibility that this would be achieved in a manner that

---

[3] *IFAC Policy Position 2, "IFAC's Support for a Single Set of Auditing Standards: Implications for Audits of Small and Medium-sized Entities," September 2008.*

would preclude supplementary audit procedures or requirements, other than those that stem from specific national legal requirements relating to the scope of statutory audits[4].

19    APB is planning to retain some supplementary requirements specific to the UK and Ireland. In this context it should be noted that:

- All of the proposed supplementary requirements are in the current ISAs (UK and Ireland); APB is not proposing any new 'pluses';
- Changes in the Clarity ISAs mean that there will be a significant reduction in the number of supplementary requirements that are in the current ISAs (UK and Ireland) (see paragraph 33); and
- Most of the supplementary requirements to be retained relate to compliance with UK and Irish specific law or regulation; only 5 relate to audit quality.

20    If, and when, the EC adopts the ISAs APB will review what action it needs to take in relation to its supplementary material (it is expected that all regulatory pluses will be retained). Until that time it believes that it is appropriate to retain the proposed 5 supplementary requirements relating to audit quality set out in the exposure drafts.

### Guidance for smaller entities

21    Nine commentators advocated updating or developing new guidance to assist the application of the standards to the audits of smaller entities. In particular it was suggested that Practice Note 26, "Guidance for Smaller Entity Audit Documentation," could helpfully be updated.

22    APB has concluded that it will update Practice Note 26 and include additional documentation examples on other aspects of an audit in addition to those currently included for audit planning and risk assessment.

23    APB is also giving consideration as to how best to communicate the main changes in the new standards to assist with the implementation of them.

---

[4] *The EC Statutory Audit Directive provides the basis for the adoption of the ISAs within the EU; Article 26.3 sets out a framework for dealing with differences from national standards. The EC has yet to make a decision as to whether to adopt the ISAs and further discussion can be expected as to how Article 26.3 would apply in practice.*

## 2. The Structure of the Proposed Clarified Standards

Reflecting the underlying IAASB standards, the proposed clarified ISAs (UK and   **24**
Ireland) and ISQC (UK and Ireland) 1 now have a new structure, in which infor-
mation is presented in separate sections: Introduction, Objective, Definitions,
Requirements, and Application and Other Explanatory Material.

### *Introduction*

Introductory material may include information regarding the purpose, scope, and   **25**
subject matter of the standard, in addition to the responsibilities of the auditors and
others in the context in which the standard is set.

### *Objective*

Each standard contains a clear statement of the objective of the auditor in the audit   **26**
area addressed by that standard. Paragraph 21 of proposed clarified ISA (UK and
Ireland) 200, "Overall Objectives of the Independent Auditor and the Conduct of an
Audit in Accordance with International Standards on Auditing," requires:

> "To achieve the overall objectives of the auditor, the auditor shall use the
> objectives stated in relevant ISAs (UK and Ireland) in planning and performing
> the audit, having regard to the interrelationships among the ISAs (UK and
> Ireland), to:
> (a) Determine whether any audit procedures in addition to those required by
>     the ISAs (UK and Ireland) are necessary in pursuance of the objectives
>     stated in the ISAs (UK and Ireland); and
> (b) Evaluate whether sufficient appropriate audit evidence has been obtained."

### *Definitions*

For greater understanding of the standards, applicable terms have been defined in   **27**
each standard.

### *Requirements*

Each objective is supported by clearly stated requirements. Requirements are always   **28**
expressed by the phrase "the auditor shall."

### *Application and Other Explanatory Material*

The application and other explanatory material explains more precisely what a   **29**
requirement means or is intended to cover, or includes examples of procedures that
may be appropriate under given circumstances. Proposed clarified ISA (UK and
Ireland) 200, paragraph A59, explains that "While such guidance does not in itself
impose a requirement, it is relevant to the proper application of the requirements of
an ISA (UK and Ireland)."

### APB Supplementary Material

When APB adopted the ISAs in 2004, it supplemented them with additional stan-   **30**
dards and guidance where necessary to maintain the requirements and meaning of

the previous UK and Irish auditing standards. In the current standards supplementary APB requirements and guidance are identified with grey highlighting.

31   Many of the supplementary requirements and guidance in the current ISAs (UK and Ireland) have been rendered unnecessary by the improvements made to the ISAs as part of the Clarity Project and the revisions of particular ISAs.

### Requirements

32   The criteria APB has used for keeping supplementary requirements are that they either relate to UK and Irish legal/regulatory requirements or are still considered important for audit quality (and are not covered by the IAASB requirements in the Clarity ISAs).

33   Excluding ISA (UK and Ireland) 700, which has been reviewed and revised in a separate project, this has resulted in the following proposed changes in the total number of supplementary requirements:

| Number of supplementary requirements in current ISAs (UK and Ireland) | Number of supplementary requirements rendered unnecessary by the Clarity Project and revision of particular ISAs | Legal/Regulatory supplementary requirements to be kept | Proposed audit quality supplementary requirements to be kept |
|---|---|---|---|
| 61 | 39 | 17 | 5 |

34   An analysis of the reasons why APB has decided to retain some of the current supplementary requirements is attached to each of the Exposure Drafts.

35   13 of the legal/regulatory supplementary requirements are in proposed clarified ISA (UK and Ireland) 250, Section B, "The Auditor's Right and Duty to Report to Regulators in the Financial Sector," and proposed clarified ISA (UK and Ireland) 720, Section B, "The Auditor's Statutory reporting Responsibility in relation to Directors' Reports."

36   The other 4 legal/regulatory supplementary requirements are:

| Proposed clarified ISA (UK and Ireland) | Legal/regulatory plus |
|---|---|
| 250 Section A Consideration of Laws and Regulations in an Audit of Financial Statements | 2 requirements that relate (i) to the obligations to report money laundering offences, and (ii) the need to fulfil statutory duties to report non-compliances with law and regulations to the appropriate authority as soon as practicable. (paragraphs 15-1 and 28-1) |

| 402 Audit Considerations Relating to Entities Using Service Organisations | Requiring the auditor to assess whether an entity's arrangements with a service organisation affect the auditor's legal or regulatory reporting responsibilities in relation to the entity's accounting records. (paragraph 9(e)) |
|---|---|
| 570 Going Concern | Requiring the auditor to disclose in the auditor's report if the period considered by those charged with governance in assessing going concern is less than one year from the date of approval of the financial statement and those charged with governance have not disclosed that fact themselves. (paragraph 17-2) |

The proposed audit quality supplementary requirements are: 37

| Proposed clarified ISA (UK and Ireland) | Audit quality plus |
|---|---|
| 450 Evaluation of misstatements | Requiring the auditor to seek to obtain a written representation from those charged with governance that explains their reasons for not correcting misstatements brought to their attention by the auditor. (paragraph 14-1) |
| 510 Opening balances | Extending the requirements relating to opening balances on initial engagements to all audits. (paragraph 3) |
| 570 Going concern | Requiring the auditor to plan and perform procedures specifically designed to identify any material matters which could indicate concern about the entity's ability to continue as a going concern. (paragraph 13-2) |
| | Requiring the auditor to document the extent of the auditor's concern (if any) about the entity's ability to continue as a going concern. (paragraph 17-1) |
| 720 A Other information | Requiring the auditor to consider including an "Other Matters" paragraph in the auditor's report when an amendment is necessary in the other information and the entity refuses to make the amendment. (paragraph 16-1) |

*Guidance*

The criteria APB has used for keeping supplementary guidance that has not been covered in the Clarity ISAs is that: 38

- It supports a proposed retained supplementary requirement; or
- It provides other guidance relating to legal/regulatory matters (for example, to refer to relevant sections of the UK Companies Act 2006); or
- It provides other guidance that is still considered helpful to achieving audit quality (for example, in relation to going concern considerations).

Application of these criteria results in a significant reduction in the amount of supplementary guidance. APB is satisfied that guidance not to be carried forward relates to matters that are adequately addressed in the Clarity ISAs or other APB guidance such as Bulletins and Practice Notes. 39

## ISAs (UK and Ireland) 250 (Law and Regulations) and 720 (Other Information)

40  These two standards both have a 'Section B'. In effect, these are complete supplementary standards addressing legal and regulatory requirements (reporting to regulators and reporting on the consistency of the directors' report with the financial statements).

41  These supplementary standards have been reformatted to match the Clarity format (i.e. stating an objective and having separate sections for requirements and application material). However, present tense guidance in the current standards has not been eliminated. APB believes it more appropriate to address any present tense guidance at such a time as the standards need to be revised for other reasons such as a change in related regulatory requirements.

# 3. Specific Questions on APB's Proposals

APB is not seeking views on the adoption of the Clarity ISAs and the imple-   **42**
mentation date of the proposed clarified ISAs (UK and Ireland). These important
matters were addressed in the October 2008 Consultation Paper and APB's position
is described in Section 1 above. APB is seeking views on the proposed supplementary
requirements and guidance and specifically:

Q1  Do you agree with the criteria APB has applied for deciding to retain:
 (a)  Supplementary requirements
 (b)  Supplementary guidance?
  If not, please give your reasons and explain what criteria you would apply.
Q2  Are there any particular proposed audit quality supplementary requirements
 and guidance that you are believe are not necessary to retain? If yes, please
 identify them and give your reasons.
Q3  Do you believe that the proposed supplementary requirements and guidance are
 clearly expressed? If not, please explain how they could be improved.
Q4  Are there any particular current audit quality supplementary requirements and
 guidance that APB has not proposed to retain that you believe should be? If so,
 please identify them and give your reasons.

# The Auditing Practices Board – Scope and Authority of Pronouncements (revised)

## Contents

This statement describes the scope and authority of the Auditing Practices Board's (APB's) pronouncements applicable to engagements relating to financial periods ending on or after 15 December 2010For engagements relating to financial periods ending before 15 December 2010, see the previous edition of this Statement which is available on the APB website and is also included in the printed volume of APB's "Standards and Guidance 2009"..

# Introduction

The objectives of the Auditing Practices Board, which is a constituent body of the Financial Reporting Council[1], are to:   **1**

- Establish Auditing Standards which set out the basic principles and essential procedures with which external auditors in the United Kingdom and the Republic of Ireland are required to comply;
- Issue guidance on the application of Auditing Standards in particular circumstances and industries and timely guidance on new and emerging issues;
- Establish Standards and related guidance for accountants providing assurance services where they relate to activities that are reported in the public domain, and are therefore within the "public interest";
- Establish Ethical Standards in relation to the independence, objectivity and integrity of external auditors and those providing assurance services;
- Participate in the development of any legislative or regulatory initiatives which affect the conduct of auditing and assurance services, both domestically and internationally; and
- Contribute to efforts to advance public understanding of the roles and responsibilities of external auditors and the providers of assurance services including the sponsorship of research.

The Auditing Practices Board discharges its responsibilities through a Board ('the APB'), comprising individuals who are eligible for appointment as company auditors and those who are not so eligible. Those who are eligible for appointment as company auditors may not exceed 40% of the APB by number.   **2**

The Nomination Committee of the Financial Reporting Council appoints members of the Board.   **3**

# Nature and Scope of APB Pronouncements

APB pronouncements include:   **4**

- 'Quality control standards' for firms that perform audits of financial statements, reports in connection with investment circulars and other assurance engagements,
- A framework of fundamental principles which APB expects to guide the conduct of auditors (see Appendix 2),
- 'Engagement standards' for audits of financial statements, reports in connection with investment circulars and other assurance engagements, and
- Guidance for auditors of financial statements, reporting accountants acting in connection with an investment circular and auditors involved in other assurance engagements.

The structure of APB pronouncements is shown in Appendix 1.

Auditors and reporting accountants should not claim compliance with APB standards unless they have complied fully with all of those standards relevant to an engagement.   **5**

---

[1] *Information about the Financial Reporting Council (FRC) and its structure, including its operating bodies, can be found on the FRC's web site (www.frc.org.uk).*

6    APB quality control standards and Auditing Standards for audits of financial statements include objectives for the auditor, together with requirements[2] and related guidance. It is necessary to have an understanding of the entire text of a Standard, including its guidance content, to understand its objectives and to apply its requirements properly. Further explanation of the scope, authority and structure of the Auditing Standards are set out in International Standard on Auditing (UK and Ireland) (ISA (UK and Ireland)) 200, "Overall Objectives of the Independent Auditor and the Conduct of an Audit in Accordance with International Standards on Auditing (UK and Ireland)."

7    APB engagement standards for reporting accountants acting in connection with an investment circular and auditors involved in other assurance engagements contain basic principles and essential procedures (identified in bold type lettering[3]) together with related guidance. The basic principles and essential procedures are to be understood and applied in the context of the explanatory and other material that provide guidance for their application. It is therefore necessary to consider the whole text of a Standard to understand and apply the basic principles and essential procedures.

8    APB Ethical Standards for auditors and reporting accountants contain requirements (identified in bold type lettering) together with related guidance.

9    In 2009 APB adopted the new, clarified, International Standard on Quality Control 1 (ISQC 1) and International Standards on Auditing (ISAs), issued by the International Auditing and Assurance Standards Board[4] (IAASB) for application to audits of financial statements for periods ending on or after 15 December 2010. Where necessary APB has augmented the international standards with additional requirements and guidance to: address specific UK and Irish legal and regulatory requirements; and to maintain requirements and guidance of previous UK and Irish auditing standards that are, in APB's view, important for audit quality. This additional material is clearly differentiated from the original text of the international standards by the use of grey shading.

10   APB has not at this time adopted ISA 700 "Forming an Opinion and Reporting on Financial Statements." APB has instead issued ISA (UK and Ireland) 700, "The Auditor's Report on Financial Statements" which addresses the requirements of company law and also provides for a more concise auditor's report, reflecting feedback to APB consultations. The main effect of this is that the form of UK and Ireland auditor's reports may not be exactly aligned with the precise format of auditor's reports required by ISA 700 issued by the IAASB. However, ISA (UK and Ireland) 700 has been designed to ensure that compliance with it will not preclude the auditor from being able to assert compliance with the ISAs issued by the IAASB[5].

11   The ISAs and ISQC 1 as issued by the IAASB, require compliance with 'relevant ethical requirements' which are described, in the application material, as ordinarily

---

[2] *The level of authority of the text in requirements paragraphs is identified by use of the expression "the auditor shall ...".*

[3] *The level of authority of the text in these paragraphs is identified by use of the expression "the auditor should ...".*

[4] *IAASB is a committee of the International Federation of Accountants (IFAC). The IAASB's constitution and due process is described in its 'Preface to the international standards on Quality Control, Auditing, Assurance and Related Services'.*

[5] *See ISA (UK and Ireland) 700, paragraph 5.*

comprising Parts A and B of the IFAC Code of Ethics for Professional Accountants (the IFAC Code[6]) related to an audit of financial statements together with national requirements that are more restrictive. The ISAs (UK and Ireland) and ISQC (UK and Ireland) 1 have supplementary material that makes clear that auditors in the UK and Ireland are subject to ethical requirements from two sources: the Ethical Standards for Auditors established by APB concerning the integrity, objectivity and independence of the auditor, and the ethical pronouncements established by the auditor's relevant professional body. ISQC (UK and Ireland) 1 also has supplementary material that makes clear that the APB Ethical Standard for Reporting Accountants applies to all engagements that are subject to APB Standards for Investment Reporting and involve investment circulars in which a report from the reporting accountant is to be published.

APB has sought to ensure that the Ethical Standards for auditors and reporting **12** accountants adhere to the principles of the IFAC Code. APB is not aware of any significant instances where the relevant parts of the IFAC Code are more restrictive than the Ethical Standards[7].

## Standards and Guidance for Audits of Financial Statements

The Auditors' Code, which is set out as Appendix 2, provides a framework of **13** fundamental principles which encapsulate the concepts that govern the conduct of audits and underlie APB's ethical and auditing standards.

APB engagement standards for audits of financial statements, which comprise APB **14** Ethical Standards for Auditors and International Standards on Auditing (UK and Ireland), apply to auditors carrying out:

● Statutory audits of companies in accordance with the Companies Acts[8];
● Audits of financial statements of entities in accordance with other UK or Irish legislation e.g. building societies, credit unions, friendly societies, pension funds, charities and registered social landlords;
● Public sector audits in the UK, including those carried out either on behalf of the national audit agencies or under contract to those agencies. (The standards governing the conduct and reporting of the audit of financial statements are a matter for the national audit agencies to determine. However, the heads of the national audit agencies[9] in the UK have chosen to adopt APB's engagement standards and quality control standards for audits as the basis of their approach to the audit of financial statements);

---

[6] *The IFAC Code is included in the IFAC "Handbook of International Auditing, Assurance, and Ethics Pronouncements" and can be downloaded free of charge from the publications section of the IAASB web site (www.ifac.org/IAASB).*

[7] *Should auditors wish to state that an audit has been conducted in compliance with ISAs as issued by IAASB they will need to ensure that they have complied with the relevant parts of the IFAC Code.*

[8] *Companies Act 2006 in the UK and the Companies Acts 1963 – 2003 in the Republic of Ireland.*

[9] *National audit agencies in the UK are the National Audit Office (for the Comptroller and Auditor General), the Welsh Audit Office (for the Auditor General for Wales), the Audit Commission, Audit Scotland (for the Auditor General for Scotland and the Accounts Commission) and the Northern Ireland Audit Office (for the Comptroller and Auditor General (Northern Ireland)).*

- Other audits performed by audit firms registered with the members of the Consultative Committee of Accountancy Bodies (CCAB)[10] unless the nature of the engagement requires the use of other recognised auditing standards; and
- Other audits where audit firms not registered with members of the CCAB elect, or are required by contract, to perform the work in accordance with UK or Irish auditing standards.

15   APB also issues guidance to auditors of financial statements in the form of Practice Notes and Bulletins. Practice Notes and Bulletins are persuasive rather than pre-scriptive and are indicative of good practice. Practice Notes assist auditors in applying APB engagement standards to particular circumstances and industries and Bulletins provide timely guidance on new or emerging issues. Auditors should be aware of and consider Practice Notes applicable to the engagement. Auditors who do not consider and apply the guidance included in a relevant Practice Note should be prepared to explain how the basic principles and essential procedures in APB stan-dards have been complied with.

16   APB also issues consultative documents, briefing papers and research studies to stimulate public debate and comment.

## Standards and Guidance for Reporting Accountants Acting in Connection With an Investment Circular

17   APB engagement standards apply to reporting accountants when carrying out engagements involving investment circulars intended to be issued in connection with a securities transaction governed wholly or in part by the laws and regulations of the United Kingdom or the Republic of Ireland. They comprise APB Ethical Standards for Reporting Accountants (ESRA) and Standards for Investment Reporting (SIRs).

## Statements of Standards for Reporting Accountants

18   APB also issues standards and guidance for accountants on assurance engagements closely related to an audit of the financial statements. This includes the International Standard on Reporting Engagements (ISRE) (UK and Ireland) 2410, "Review of Interim Financial Information Performed by the Independent Auditor of the Entity." ISRE (UK and Ireland) 2410 adopts the text of ISRE 2410 issued by the IAASB and, as with ISAs (UK and Ireland), APB has added a relatively small amount of supplementary material (highlighted with grey shading) in order to clarify certain matters (for example in relation to the rules and regulations implementing the requirements of the European Transparency Directive applicable to UK and Irish listed companies) and to perpetuate existing APB guidance that remains pertinent. APB's other pronouncements on assurance engagements take the form of Bulletins (e.g. the auditor's statement on summary financial statements).

# Authority of APB Pronouncements

19   In order to be eligible for appointment in the UK as auditors of companies, or of any of the other entities which require their auditors to be eligible for appointment as auditors under section 1212 of the Companies Act 2006, persons must be registered

---

[10] *Members of CCAB are The Institute of Chartered Accountants in England & Wales, The Institute of Chartered Accountants of Scotland, The Institute of Chartered Accountants in Ireland, The Association of Chartered Certified Accountants, The Chartered Institute of Management Accountants and The Chartered Institute of Public Finance and Accountancy.*

with a Recognised Supervisory Body (RSB)[11] recognised under that Act and must be eligible for appointment under the rules of that RSB. The Companies Act 2006 requires RSBs to have rules and practices as to the technical standards to be applied in company audit work and the manner in which those standards are to be applied in practice. Each RSB is also required to have arrangements in place for the effective monitoring and enforcement of compliance with those standards.

In the Republic of Ireland legislative requirements concerning qualifications for appointment as auditor and recognition of bodies[12] of accountants are contained in the Companies Act, 1990 as amended by the Companies (Auditing and Accounting) Act 2003. This Act requires bodies of accountants to have satisfactory rules and practices as to technical and other standards. The Act also empowers the Irish Auditing and Accounting Supervisory Authority to revoke or suspend recognition or authorisation of a body of accountants or individual auditor. **20**

The members of the CCAB have undertaken to adopt APB standards and guidance developed by APB within three months of promulgation by APB of such Standards and guidance. In the Republic of Ireland, accountancy bodies which are not members of the CCAB but which are also recognised bodies for the supervision of auditors may choose to require their members to comply with APB standards. **21**

Apparent failures by auditors to comply with APB standards are liable to be investigated by the relevant accountancy body. Auditors who do not comply with auditing standards when performing company or other audits make themselves liable to regulatory action which may include the withdrawal of registration and hence of eligibility to perform company audits. **22**

All relevant APB pronouncements and in particular auditing standards are likely to be taken into account when the adequacy of the work of auditors is being considered in a court of law or in other contested situations. **23**

The nature of APB standards and associated guidance requires professional accountants to exercise professional judgment in applying them. Where, in exceptional circumstances, auditors and reporting accountants judge it necessary to depart from a basic principle or essential procedure that is relevant in the circumstances of the engagement, the auditor or reporting accountant documents how the alternative procedures performed achieve the objective of the engagement and, unless otherwise clear, the reasons for the departure. **24**

## Development of APB Pronouncements

Before publishing or amending its standards or Practice Notes APB publishes an exposure draft on its website and sends a copy of the exposure draft to the members of the CCAB and to other parties. **25**

[11] *The Institute of Chartered Accountants in England & Wales, The Institute of Chartered Accountants of Scotland, The Institute of Chartered Accountants in Ireland, the Association of Authorised Public Accountants and The Association of Chartered Certified Accountants are Recognised Supervisory Bodies for the purpose of regulating auditors in the UK.*

[12] *The Institute of Chartered Accountants in Ireland, the Institute of Certified Public Accountants in Ireland, the Institute of Incorporated Public Accountants, The Association of Chartered Certified Accountants, The Institute of Chartered Accountants in England and Wales and The Institute of Chartered Accountants in Scotland are "Recognised Bodies" in the Republic of Ireland.*

**26**    APB's aim is to allow three months for representations to be made on draft standards and Practice Notes. Where the draft standards are based on international standards APB intends to co-ordinate its exposure process with that of IAASB.

**27**    Where exposure drafts would cause changes to be made to other previously issued publications, any such consequential changes will also be exposed for comment and published simultaneously. Representations received on exposure drafts will be given full and proper consideration by APB, and will be available for public inspection.

**28**    Bulletins and other publications may be developed without the full process of consultation and exposure used for APB standards and Practice Notes. However, in the development of such documents, and before publication, APB will decide the means by which it will obtain external views on them.

**29**    Each year APB considers its priorities and consults on its proposed work programme with interested parties.

# **Appendix 1**

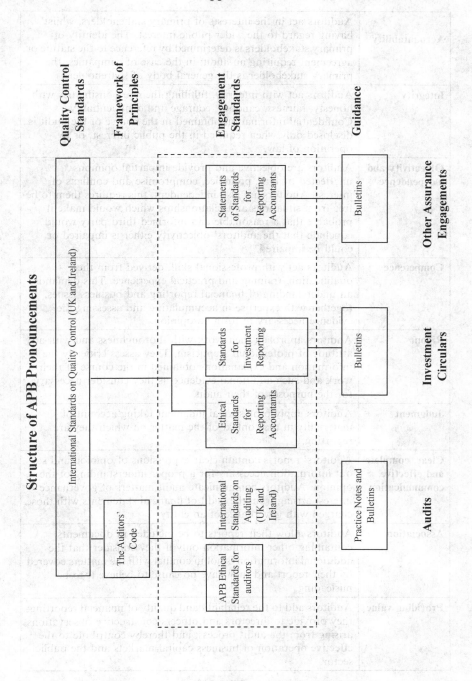

**Structure of APB Pronouncements**

# Appendix 2 – The Auditors' Code

| | |
|---|---|
| **Accountability** | Auditors act in the interests of primary stakeholders, whilst having regard to the wider public interest. The identity of primary stakeholders is determined by reference to the statute or agreement requiring an audit: in the case of companies, the primary stakeholder is the general body of shareholders. |
| **Integrity** | Auditors act with integrity, fulfilling their responsibilities with honesty, fairness, candour, courage and confidentiality. Confidential information obtained in the course of the audit is disclosed only when required in the public interest, or by operation of law. |
| **Objectivity and independence** | Auditors are objective and provide impartial opinions unaffected by bias, prejudice, compromise and conflicts of interest. Auditors are also independent, this requires them to be free from situations and relationships which would make it probable that a reasonable and informed third party would conclude that the auditors' objectivity either is impaired or could be impaired. |
| **Competence** | Auditors act with professional skill, derived from their qualification, training and practical experience. This demands an understanding of financial reporting and business issues, together with expertise in accumulating and assessing the evidence necessary to form an opinion. |
| **Rigour** | Auditors approach their work with thoroughness and with an attitude of professional scepticism. They assess critically the information and explanations obtained in the course of their work and such additional evidence as they consider necessary for the purposes of their audit. |
| **Judgment** | Auditors apply professional judgment taking account of materiality in the context of the matter on which they are reporting. |
| **Clear, complete and effective communication** | Auditors' reports contain clear expressions of opinion and set out information necessary for a proper understanding of the opinion. Auditors communicate audit matters of governance interest arising from the audit of financial statements with those charged with governance of an entity. |
| **Association** | Auditors allow their reports to be included in documents containing other information only if they consider that the additional information is not in conflict with the matters covered by their report and they have no cause to believe it to be misleading. |
| **Providing value** | Auditors add to the reliability and quality of financial reporting; they provide to directors and officers constructive observations arising from the audit process; and thereby contribute to the effective operation of business capital markets and the public sector. |

# Proposed Clarified International Standard on Quality Control (UK and Ireland) 1

# Quality control for firms that perform audits and reviews of financial statements, and other assurance and related services engagements

*(Effective as of 15 December 2010)*

# Contents

International Standard on Quality Control (UK and Ireland) (ISQC (UK and Ireland)) 1, "Quality Control for Firms that Perform Audits and Reviews of Financial Statements, and Other Assurance and Related Services Engagements" should be read in conjunction with ISA (UK and Ireland) 200, "Overall Objectives of the Independent Auditor and the Conduct of an Audit in Accordance with International Standards on Auditing (UK and Ireland)."

# Introduction

## Scope of this ISQC (UK and Ireland)

This International Standard on Quality Control (UK and Ireland) (ISQC (UK and Ireland)) deals with a firm's responsibilities for its system of quality control for audits and reviews of financial statements, and other assurance and related services engagements. This ISQC (UK and Ireland) is to be read in conjunction with relevant ethical requirements.    **1**

Other pronouncements of the International Auditing and Assurance Standards Board (IAASB) set out additional standards and guidance on the responsibilities of firm personnel regarding quality control procedures for specific types of engagements. ISA (UK and Ireland) 220,[1] for example, deals with quality control procedures for audits of financial statements.    **2**

A system of quality control consists of policies designed to achieve the objective set out in paragraph 11 and the procedures necessary to implement and monitor compliance with those policies.    **3**

## Authority of this ISQC (UK and Ireland)

This ISQC (UK and Ireland) applies to all firms of professional accountants in respect of audits and reviews of financial statements, and other assurance and related services engagements. The nature and extent of the policies and procedures developed by an individual firm to comply with this ISQC (UK and Ireland) will depend on various factors such as the size and operating characteristics of the firm, and whether it is part of a network.    **4**

This ISQC (UK and Ireland) contains the objective of the firm in following the ISQC (UK and Ireland), and requirements designed to enable the firm to meet that stated objective. In addition, it contains related guidance in the form of application and other explanatory material, as discussed further in paragraph 8, and introductory material that provides context relevant to a proper understanding of the ISQC (UK and Ireland), and definitions.    **5**

The objective provides the context in which the requirements of this ISQC (UK and Ireland) are set, and is intended to assist the firm in:    **6**

- Understanding what needs to be accomplished; and
- Deciding whether more needs to be done to achieve the objective.

The requirements of this ISQC (UK and Ireland) are expressed using "shall."    **7**

Where necessary, the application and other explanatory material provides further explanation of the requirements and guidance for carrying them out. In particular, it may:    **8**

- Explain more precisely what a requirement means or is intended to cover.
- Include examples of policies and procedures that may be appropriate in the circumstances.

While such guidance does not in itself impose a requirement, it is relevant to the proper application of the requirements. The application and other explanatory

---

[1] ISA (UK and Ireland) 220, "Quality Control for an Audit of Financial Statements."

material may also provide background information on matters addressed in this ISQC (UK and Ireland). Where appropriate, additional considerations specific to public sector audit organizations or smaller firms are included within the application and other explanatory material. These additional considerations assist in the application of the requirements in this ISQC (UK and Ireland). They do not, however, limit or reduce the responsibility of the firm to apply and comply with the requirements in this ISQC (UK and Ireland).

9    This ISQC (UK and Ireland) includes, under the heading "Definitions," a description of the meanings attributed to certain terms for purposes of this ISQC (UK and Ireland). These are provided to assist in the consistent application and interpretation of this ISQC (UK and Ireland), and are not intended to override definitions that may be established for other purposes, whether in law, regulation or otherwise. The Glossary of Terms[1a] relating to International Standards issued by the IAASB in the *Handbook of International Standards on Auditing, Assurance, and Ethics Pronouncements* published by IFAC includes the terms defined in this ISQC (UK and Ireland). It also includes descriptions of other terms found in this ISQC (UK and Ireland) to assist in common and consistent interpretation and translation.

## Effective Date

10    Systems of quality control in compliance with this ISQC (UK and Ireland) are required to be established by 15 December 2010.

# Objective

11    The objective of the firm is to establish and maintain a system of quality control to provide it with reasonable assurance that:
    (a)  The firm and its personnel comply with professional standards and applicable legal and regulatory requirements; and
    (b)  Reports issued by the firm or engagement partners are appropriate in the circumstances.

# Definitions

12    In this ISQC (UK and Ireland), the following terms have the meanings attributed below:

    (a)  Date of report – The date selected by the practitioner to date the report.
    (b)  Engagement documentation – The record of work performed, results obtained, and conclusions the practitioner reached (terms such as "working papers" or "workpapers" are sometimes used).
    (c)  Engagement partner[2] – The partner or other person in the firm who is responsible for the engagement and its performance, and for the report that is issued on behalf of the firm, and who, where required, has the appropriate authority from a professional, legal or regulatory body.
    (d)  Engagement quality control review – A process designed to provide an objective evaluation, on or before the date of the report, of the significant judgments the

---

[1a] *The APB's Glossary of Terms defines terms used in the ISAs (UK and Ireland). It is based on the Glossary of Terms issued by the IAASB.*

[2] *"Engagement partner," "partner," and "firm" should be read as referring to their public sector equivalents where relevant.*

engagement team made and the conclusions it reached in formulating the report. The engagement quality control review process is for audits of financial statements of listed entities, and those other engagements, if any, for which the firm has determined an engagement quality control review is required.

(e) Engagement quality control reviewer – A partner, other person in the firm, suitably qualified external person, or a team made up of such individuals, none of whom is part of the engagement team, with sufficient and appropriate experience and authority to objectively evaluate the significant judgments the engagement team made and the conclusions it reached in formulating the report.

(f) Engagement team –All partners and staff performing the engagement, and any individuals engaged by the firm or a network firm who perform procedures on the engagement. This excludes external experts engaged by the firm or a network firm.

(g) Firm – A sole practitioner, partnership or corporation or other entity of professional accountants.

(h) Inspection – In relation to completed engagements, procedures designed to provide evidence of compliance by engagement teams with the firm's quality control policies and procedures.

(i) Listed entity – An entity whose shares, stock or debt are quoted or listed on a recognized stock exchange, or are marketed under the regulations of a recognized stock exchange or other equivalent body.

(j) Monitoring – A process comprising an ongoing consideration and evaluation of the firm's system of quality control, including a periodic inspection of a selection of completed engagements, designed to provide the firm with reasonable assurance that its system of quality control is operating effectively.

(k) Network firm – A firm or entity that belongs to a network.

(l) Network – A larger structure:
  (i) That is aimed at cooperation, and
  (ii) That is clearly aimed at profit or cost-sharing or shares common ownership, control or management, common quality control policies and procedures, common business strategy, the use of a common brand name, or a significant part of professional resources.

(m) Partner – Any individual with authority to bind the firm with respect to the performance of a professional services engagement.

(n) Personnel – Partners and staff.

(o) Professional standards – IAASB Engagement Standards, as defined in the IAASB's *Preface to the International Standards on Quality Control, Auditing, Review, Other Assurance and Related Services*, and relevant ethical requirements.

(p) Reasonable assurance – In the context of this ISQC (UK and Ireland), a high, but not absolute, level of assurance.

(q) Relevant ethical requirements – Ethical requirements to which the engagement team and engagement quality control reviewer are subject, which ordinarily comprise Parts A and B of the International Federation of Accountants' *Code of Ethics for Professional Accountants* (IFAC Code) together with national requirements that are more restrictive.

Auditors in the UK and Ireland are subject to ethical requirements from two sources: the Ethical Standards for Auditors established by APB concerning the integrity, objectivity and independence of the auditor, and the ethical pronouncements established by the auditor's relevant professional body. The APB is not aware of any significant instances where the relevant parts of the IFAC Code of Ethics are more restrictive than the Ethical Standards for Auditors.

> The APB Ethical Standard for Reporting Accountants applies to all engagements:
>
> - that are subject to the requirements of the Standards for Investment Reporting (SIRs), and
> - which are in connection with an investment circular in which a report from the reporting accountant is to be published.

   (r)  Staff – Professionals, other than partners, including any experts the firm employs.

   (s)  Suitably qualified external person – An individual outside the firm with the competence and capabilities to act as an engagement partner, for example a partner of another firm, or an employee (with appropriate experience) of either a professional accountancy body whose members may perform audits and reviews of historical financial information, or other assurance or related services engagements, or of an organization that provides relevant quality control services.

# Requirements

## Applying, and Complying with, Relevant Requirements

13    Personnel within the firm responsible for establishing and maintaining the firm's system of quality control shall have an understanding of the entire text of this ISQC (UK and Ireland), including its application and other explanatory material, to understand its objective and to apply its requirements properly.

14    The firm shall comply with each requirement of this ISQC (UK and Ireland) unless, in the circumstances of the firm, the requirement is not relevant to the services provided in respect of audits and reviews of financial statements, and other assurance and related services engagements. (Ref: Para. A1)

15    The requirements are designed to enable the firm to achieve the objective stated in this ISQC (UK and Ireland). The proper application of the requirements is therefore expected to provide a sufficient basis for the achievement of the objective. However, because circumstances vary widely and all such circumstances cannot be anticipated, the firm shall consider whether there are particular matters or circumstances that require the firm to establish policies and procedures in addition to those required by this ISQC (UK and Ireland) to meet the stated objective.

## Elements of a System of Quality Control

16    The firm shall establish and maintain a system of quality control that includes policies and procedures that address each of the following elements:

   (a)  Leadership responsibilities for quality within the firm.
   (b)  Relevant ethical requirements.
   (c)  Acceptance and continuance of client relationships and specific engagements.
   (d)  Human resources.
   (e)  Engagement performance.
   (f)  Monitoring.

The firm shall document its policies and procedures and communicate them to the firm's personnel. (Ref: Para. A2-A3) **17**

## Leadership Responsibilities for Quality within the Firm

The firm shall establish policies and procedures designed to promote an internal culture recognizing that quality is essential in performing engagements. Such policies and procedures shall require the firm's chief executive officer (or equivalent) or, if appropriate, the firm's managing board of partners (or equivalent) to assume ultimate responsibility for the firm's system of quality control. (Ref: Para. A4-A5) **18**

The firm shall establish policies and procedures such that any person or persons assigned operational responsibility for the firm's system of quality control by the firm's chief executive officer or managing board of partners has sufficient and appropriate experience and ability, and the necessary authority, to assume that responsibility. (Ref: Para. A6) **19**

## Relevant Ethical Requirements

The firm shall establish policies and procedures designed to provide it with reasonable assurance that the firm and its personnel comply with relevant ethical requirements. (Ref: Para. A7-A10) **20**

### *Independence*

The firm shall establish policies and procedures designed to provide it with reasonable assurance that the firm, its personnel and, where applicable, others subject to independence requirements (including network firm personnel) maintain independence where required by relevant ethical requirements. Such policies and procedures shall enable the firm to: **21**

(a) Communicate its independence requirements to its personnel and, where applicable, others subject to them; and
(b) Identify and evaluate circumstances and relationships that create threats to independence, and to take appropriate action to eliminate those threats or reduce them to an acceptable level by applying safeguards, or, if considered appropriate, to withdraw from the engagement, where withdrawal is permitted by law or regulation. (Ref: Para. A10)

Such policies and procedures shall require: **22**

(a) Engagement partners to provide the firm with relevant information about client engagements, including the scope of services, to enable the firm to evaluate the overall impact, if any, on independence requirements;
(b) Personnel to promptly notify the firm of circumstances and relationships that create a threat to independence so that appropriate action can be taken; and
(c) The accumulation and communication of relevant information to appropriate personnel so that:
  (i) The firm and its personnel can readily determine whether they satisfy independence requirements;
  (ii) The firm can maintain and update its records relating to independence; and
  (iii) The firm can take appropriate action regarding identified threats to independence that are not at an acceptable level. (Ref: Para. A10)

23   The firm shall establish policies and procedures designed to provide it with reason-able assurance that it is notified of breaches of independence requirements, and to enable it to take appropriate actions to resolve such situations. The policies and procedures shall include requirements for:

(a)   Personnel to promptly notify the firm of independence breaches of which they become aware;

(b)   The firm to promptly communicate identified breaches of these policies and procedures to:

(i)    The engagement partner who, with the firm, needs to address the breach; and

(ii)   Other relevant personnel in the firm and, where appropriate, the network, and those subject to the independence requirements who need to take appropriate action; and

(c)   Prompt communication to the firm, if necessary, by the engagement partner and the other individuals referred to in subparagraph (b)(ii) of the actions taken to resolve the matter, so that the firm can determine whether it should take further action. (Ref: Para. A10)

24   At least annually, the firm shall obtain written confirmation of compliance with its policies and procedures on independence from all firm personnel required to be independent by relevant ethical requirements. (Ref: Para. A10-A11)

25   The firm shall establish policies and procedures:

(a)   Setting out criteria for determining the need for safeguards to reduce the familiarity threat to an acceptable level when using the same senior personnel on an assurance engagement over a long period of time; and

(b)   Requiring, for audits of financial statements of listed entities, the rotation of the engagement partner and the individuals responsible for engagement quality control review, and where applicable, others subject to rotation requirements, after a specified period in compliance with relevant ethical requirements. (Ref: Para. A10, A12-A17)

### Acceptance and Continuance of Client Relationships and Specific Engagements

26   The firm shall establish policies and procedures for the acceptance and continuance of client relationships and specific engagements, designed to provide the firm with reasonable assurance that it will only undertake or continue relationships and engagements where the firm:

(a)   Is competent to perform the engagement and has the capabilities, including time and resources, to do so; (Ref: Para. A18, A23)

(b)   Can comply with relevant ethical requirements; and

(c)   Has considered the integrity of the client, and does not have information that would lead it to conclude that the client lacks integrity. (Ref: Para. A19-A20, A23)

27   Such policies and procedures shall require:

(a)   The firm to obtain such information as it considers necessary in the circum-stances before accepting an engagement with a new client, when deciding whether to continue an existing engagement, and when considering acceptance of a new engagement with an existing client. (Ref: Para. A21, A23)

(b) If a potential conflict of interest is identified in accepting an engagement from a new or an existing client, the firm to determine whether it is appropriate to accept the engagement.
(c) If issues have been identified, and the firm decides to accept or continue the client relationship or a specific engagement, the firm to document how the issues were resolved.

The firm shall establish policies and procedures on continuing an engagement and **28** the client relationship, addressing the circumstances where the firm obtains information that would have caused it to decline the engagement had that information been available earlier. Such policies and procedures shall include consideration of:

(a) The professional and legal responsibilities that apply to the circumstances, including whether there is a requirement for the firm to report to the person or persons who made the appointment or, in some cases, to regulatory authorities; and
(b) The possibility of withdrawing from the engagement or from both the engagement and the client relationship. (Ref: Para. A22-A23)

## Human Resources

The firm shall establish policies and procedures designed to provide it with reason- **29** able assurance that it has sufficient personnel with the competence, capabilities, and commitment to ethical principles necessary to:

(a) Perform engagements in accordance with professional standards and applicable legal and regulatory requirements; and
(b) Enable the firm or engagement partners to issue reports that are appropriate in the circumstances. (Ref: Para. A24-A29)

### *Assignment of Engagement Teams*

The firm shall assign responsibility for each engagement to an engagement partner **30** and shall establish policies and procedures requiring that:

(a) The identity and role of the engagement partner are communicated to key members of client management and those charged with governance;
(b) The engagement partner has the appropriate competence, capabilities, and authority to perform the role; and
(c) The responsibilities of the engagement partner are clearly defined and communicated to that partner. (Ref: Para. A30)

The firm shall also establish policies and procedures to assign appropriate personnel **31** with the necessary competence, and capabilities to:

(a) Perform engagements in accordance with professional standards and applicable legal and regulatory requirements; and
(b) Enable the firm or engagement partners to issue reports that are appropriate in the circumstances. (Ref: Para. A31)

## Engagement Performance

The firm shall establish policies and procedures designed to provide it with reason- **32** able assurance that engagements are performed in accordance with professional standards and applicable legal and regulatory requirements, and that the firm or the engagement partner issue reports that are appropriate in the circumstances. Such policies and procedures shall include:

(a)  Matters relevant to promoting consistency in the quality of engagement performance; (Ref: Para. A32-A33)
(b)  Supervision responsibilities; and (Ref: Para. A34)
(c)  Review responsibilities. (Ref: Para. A35)

33    The firm's review responsibility policies and procedures shall be determined on the basis that work of less experienced team members is reviewed by more experienced engagement team members.

### Consultation

34    The firm shall establish policies and procedures designed to provide it with reasonable assurance that:

(a)  Appropriate consultation takes place on difficult or contentious matters;
(b)  Sufficient resources are available to enable appropriate consultation to take place;
(c)  The nature and scope of, and conclusions resulting from, such consultations are documented and are agreed by both the individual seeking consultation and the individual consulted; and
(d)  Conclusions resulting from consultations are implemented. (Ref: Para. A36-A40)

### Engagement Quality Control Review

35    The firm shall establish policies and procedures requiring, for appropriate engagements, an engagement quality control review that provides an objective evaluation of the significant judgments made by the engagement team and the conclusions reached in formulating the report. Such policies and procedures shall:

(a)  Require an engagement quality review for all audits of financial statements of listed entities;
(b)  Set out criteria against which all other audits and reviews of historical financial information and other assurance and related services engagements shall be evaluated to determine whether an engagement quality control review should be performed; and (Ref: Para. A41)
(c)  Require an engagement quality control review for all engagements, if any, meeting the criteria established in compliance with subparagraph (b).

36    The firm shall establish policies and procedures setting out the nature, timing and extent of an engagement quality control review. Such policies and procedures shall require that the engagement report not be dated until the completion of the engagement quality control review. (Ref: Para. A42-A43)

37    The firm shall establish policies and procedures to require the engagement quality control review to include:

(a)  Discussion of significant matters with the engagement partner;
(b)  Review of the financial statements or other subject matter information and the proposed report;
(c)  Review of selected engagement documentation relating to significant judgments the engagement team made and the conclusions it reached; and
(d)  Evaluation of the conclusions reached in formulating the report and consideration of whether the proposed report is appropriate. (Ref: Para. A44)

For audits of financial statements of listed entities, the firm shall establish policies **38** and procedures to require the engagement quality control review to also include consideration of the following:

(a)   The engagement team's evaluation of the firm's independence in relation to the specific engagement;
(b)   Whether appropriate consultation has taken place on matters involving differences of opinion or other difficult or contentious matters, and the conclusions arising from those consultations; and
(c)   Whether documentation selected for review reflects the work performed in relation to the significant judgments and supports the conclusions reached. (Ref: Para. A45-A46)

*Criteria for the Eligibility of Engagement Quality Control Reviewers*

The firm shall establish policies and procedures to address the appointment of **39** engagement quality control reviewers and establish their eligibility through:

(a)   The technical qualifications required to perform the role, including the necessary experience and authority; and (Ref: Para. A47)
(b)   The degree to which an engagement quality control reviewer can be consulted on the engagement without compromising the reviewer's objectivity. (Ref: Para. A48)

The firm shall establish policies and procedures designed to maintain the objectivity **40** of the engagement quality control reviewer. (Ref: Para. A49-A51)

The firm's policies and procedures shall provide for the replacement of the engage- **41** ment quality control reviewer where the reviewer's ability to perform an objective review may be impaired.

*Documentation of the Engagement Quality Control Review*

The firm shall establish policies and procedures on documentation of the engagement **42** quality control review which require documentation that:

(a)   The procedures required by the firm's policies on engagement quality control review have been performed;
(b)   The engagement quality control review has been completed on or before the date of the report; and
(c)   The reviewer is not aware of any unresolved matters that would cause the reviewer to believe that the significant judgments the engagement team made and the conclusions it reached were not appropriate.

**Differences of Opinion**

The firm shall establish policies and procedures for dealing with and resolving dif- **43** ferences of opinion within the engagement team, with those consulted and, where applicable, between the engagement partner and the engagement quality control reviewer. (Ref: Para. A52-A53)

Such policies and procedures shall require that: **44**

(a)   Conclusions reached be documented and implemented; and
(b)   The report not be dated until the matter is resolved.

### Engagement Documentation

Completion of the Assembly of Final Engagement Files

**45**    The firm shall establish policies and procedures for engagement teams to complete the assembly of final engagement files on a timely basis after the engagement reports have been finalized. (Ref: Para. A54-A55)

*Confidentiality, Safe Custody, Integrity, Accessibility and Retrievability of Engagement Documentation*

**46**    The firm shall establish policies and procedures designed to maintain the confidentiality, safe custody, integrity, accessibility and retrievability of engagement documentation. (Ref: Para. A56-A59)

*Retention of Engagement Documentation*

**47**    The firm shall establish policies and procedures for the retention of engagement documentation for a period sufficient to meet the needs of the firm or as required by law or regulation. (Ref: Para. A60-A63)

## Monitoring

### Monitoring the Firm's Quality Control Policies and Procedures

**48**    The firm shall establish a monitoring process designed to provide it with reasonable assurance that the policies and procedures relating to the system of quality control are relevant, adequate, and operating effectively. This process shall:

(a)    Include an ongoing consideration and evaluation of the firm's system of quality control including, on a cyclical basis, inspection of at least one completed engagement for each engagement partner;

(b)    Require responsibility for the monitoring process to be assigned to a partner or partners or other persons with sufficient and appropriate experience and authority in the firm to assume that responsibility; and

(c)    Require that those performing the engagement or the engagement quality control review are not involved in inspecting the engagements. (Ref: Para. A64-A68)

### Evaluating, Communicating and Remedying Identified Deficiencies

**49**    The firm shall evaluate the effect of deficiencies noted as a result of the monitoring process and determine whether they are either:

(a)    Instances that do not necessarily indicate that the firm's system of quality control is insufficient to provide it with reasonable assurance that it complies with professional standards and applicable legal and regulatory requirements, and that the reports issued by the firm or engagement partners are appropriate in the circumstances; or

(b)    Systemic, repetitive or other significant deficiencies that require prompt corrective action.

The firm shall communicate to relevant engagement partners and other appropriate    **50**
personnel deficiencies noted as a result of the monitoring process and recommendations for appropriate remedial action. (Ref: Para. A69)

Recommendations for appropriate remedial actions for deficiencies noted shall    **51**
include one or more of the following:

(a)  Taking appropriate remedial action in relation to an individual engagement or
     member of personnel;
(b)  The communication of the findings to those responsible for training and pro-
     fessional development;
(c)  Changes to the quality control policies and procedures; and
(d)  Disciplinary action against those who fail to comply with the policies and
     procedures of the firm, especially those who do so repeatedly.

The firm shall establish policies and procedures to address cases where the results of    **52**
the monitoring procedures indicate that a report may be inappropriate or that
procedures were omitted during the performance of the engagement. Such policies
and procedures shall require the firm to determine what further action is appropriate
to comply with relevant professional standards and legal and regulatory requirements and to consider whether to obtain legal advice.

The firm shall communicate at least annually the results of the monitoring of its    **53**
system of quality control to engagement partners and other appropriate individuals
within the firm, including the firm's chief executive officer or, if appropriate, its
managing board of partners. This communication shall be sufficient to enable the
firm and these individuals to take prompt and appropriate action where necessary in
accordance with their defined roles and responsibilities. Information communicated
shall include the following:

(a)  A description of the monitoring procedures performed.
(b)  The conclusions drawn from the monitoring procedures.
(c)  Where relevant, a description of systemic, repetitive or other significant defi-
     ciencies and of the actions taken to resolve or amend those deficiencies.

Some firms operate as part of a network and, for consistency, may implement some    **54**
of their monitoring procedures on a network basis. Where firms within a network
operate under common monitoring policies and procedures designed to comply with
this ISQC (UK and Ireland), and these firms place reliance on such a monitoring
system, the firm's policies and procedures shall require that:

(a)  At least annually, the network communicate the overall scope, extent and results
     of the monitoring process to appropriate individuals within the network firms;
     and
(b)  The network communicate promptly any identified deficiencies in the system of
     quality control to appropriate individuals within the relevant network firm or
     firms so that the necessary action can be taken,

in order that engagement partners in the network firms can rely on the results of the
monitoring process implemented within the network, unless the firms or the network
advise otherwise.

### Complaints and Allegations

The firm shall establish policies and procedures designed to provide it with reason-    **55**
able assurance that it deals appropriately with:

(a)  Complaints and allegations that the work performed by the firm fails to comply with professional standards and applicable legal and regulatory requirements; and

(b)  Allegations of non-compliance with the firm's system of quality control.

As part of this process, the firm shall establish clearly defined channels for firm personnel to raise any concerns in a manner that enables them to come forward without fear of reprisals. (Ref: Para. A70)

56   If during the investigations into complaints and allegations, deficiencies in the design or operation of the firm's quality control policies and procedures or non-compliance with the firm's system of quality control by an individual or individuals are identified, the firm shall take appropriate actions as set out in paragraph 51. (Ref: Para. A71-A72)

## Documentation of the System of Quality Control

57   The firm shall establish policies and procedures requiring appropriate documentation to provide evidence of the operation of each element of its system of quality control. (Ref: Para. A73-A75)

58   The firm shall establish policies and procedures that require retention of documentation for a period of time sufficient to permit those performing monitoring procedures to evaluate the firm's compliance with its system of quality control, or for a longer period if required by law or regulation.

59   The firm shall establish policies and procedures requiring documentation of complaints and allegations and the responses to them.

***

# Application and Other Explanatory Material

## Applying, and Complying with, Relevant Requirements

### *Considerations Specific to Smaller Firms* (Ref: Para. 14)

A1   This ISQC (UK and Ireland) does not call for compliance with requirements that are not relevant, for example, in the circumstances of a sole practitioner with no staff. Requirements in this ISQC (UK and Ireland) such as those for policies and procedures for the assignment of appropriate personnel to the engagement team (see paragraph 31), for review responsibilities (see paragraph 33), and for the annual communication of the results of monitoring to engagement partners within the firm (see paragraph 53) are not relevant in the absence of staff.

## Elements of a System of Quality Control (Ref: Para. 17)

A2   In general, communication of quality control policies and procedures to firm personnel includes a description of the quality control policies and procedures and the objectives they are designed to achieve, and the message that each individual has a personal responsibility for quality and is expected to comply with these policies and procedures. Encouraging firm personnel to communicate their views or concerns on quality control matters recognizes the importance of obtaining feedback on the firm's system of quality control.

*Considerations Specific to Smaller Firms*

Documentation and communication of policies and procedures for smaller firms may    **A3**
be less formal and extensive than for larger firms.

## Leadership Responsibilities for Quality within the Firm

*Promoting an Internal Culture of Quality* (Ref: Para. 18)

The firm's leadership and the examples it sets significantly influence the internal    **A4**
culture of the firm. The promotion of a quality-oriented internal culture depends on
clear, consistent and frequent actions and messages from all levels of the firm's
management that emphasize the firm's quality control policies and procedures, and
the requirement to:

(a) Perform work that complies with professional standards and applicable legal
    and regulatory requirements; and
(b) Issue reports that are appropriate in the circumstances.

Such actions and messages encourage a culture that recognizes and rewards high
quality work. These actions and messages may be communicated by, but are not
limited to, training seminars, meetings, formal or informal dialogue, mission statements, newsletters, or briefing memoranda. They may be incorporated in the firm's
internal documentation and training materials, and in partner and staff appraisal
procedures such that they will support and reinforce the firm's view on the importance of quality and how, practically, it is to be achieved.

Of particular importance in promoting an internal culture based on quality is the    **A5**
need for the firm's leadership to recognize that the firm's business strategy is subject
to the overriding requirement for the firm to achieve quality in all the engagements
that the firm performs. Promoting such an internal culture includes:

(a) Establishment of policies and procedures that address performance evaluation,
    compensation, and promotion (including incentive systems) with regard to its
    personnel, in order to demonstrate the firm's overriding commitment to quality;
(b) Assignment of management responsibilities so that commercial considerations
    do not override the quality of work performed; and
(c) Provision of sufficient resources for the development, documentation and sup-
    port of its quality control policies and procedures.

*Assigning Operational Responsibility for the Firm's System of Quality Control* (Ref:
Para. 19)

Sufficient and appropriate experience and ability enables the person or persons    **A6**
responsible for the firm's system of quality control to identify and understand quality
control issues and to develop appropriate policies and procedures. Necessary
authority enables the person or persons to implement those policies and procedures.

## Relevant Ethical Requirements

*Compliance with Relevant Ethical Requirements* (Ref: Para. 20)

A7    The IFAC Code[2a] establishes the fundamental principles of professional ethics, which include:

    (a)  Integrity;
    (b)  Objectivity;
    (c)  Professional competence and due care;
    (d)  Confidentiality; and
    (e)  Professional behavior.

A8    Part B of the IFAC Code[2a] illustrates how the conceptual framework is to be applied in specific situations. It provides examples of safeguards that may be appropriate to address threats to compliance with the fundamental principles and also provides examples of situations where safeguards are not available to address the threats.

A9    The fundamental principles are reinforced in particular by:

- The leadership of the firm;
- Education and training;
- Monitoring; and
- A process for dealing with non-compliance.

*Definition of "Firm," "Network" and "Network Firm" (Ref: Para. 20-25)*

A10    The definitions of "firm," "network" or "network firm" in relevant ethical requirements may differ from those set out in this ISA (UK and Ireland). For example, the IFAC Code[3] defines the "firm" as:

    (i)  A sole practitioner, partnership or corporation of professional accountants;
    (ii)  An entity that controls such parties through ownership, management or other means; and
    (iii)  An entity controlled by such parties through ownership, management or other means.

The IFAC Code also provides guidance in relation to the terms "network" and "network firm."

In complying with the requirements in paragraphs 20-25, the definitions used in the relevant ethical requirements apply in so far as is necessary to interpret those ethical requirements.

*Written Confirmation (Ref: Para. 24)*

A11    Written confirmation may be in paper or electronic form. By obtaining confirmation and taking appropriate action on information indicating non-compliance, the firm demonstrates the importance that it attaches to independence and makes the issue current for, and visible to, its personnel.

---

[2a]  *See paragraph 12(q). Auditors and reporting accountants in the UK and Ireland are subject to ethical requirements from two sources: the Ethical Standards established by APB, and the ethical pronouncements established by the auditor's relevant professional body. The APB is not aware of any significant instances where the relevant parts of the IFAC Code of Ethics are more restrictive than the APB Ethical Standards.*

[3]  *"IFAC Code of Ethics for Professional Accountants."* See footnote 2a.

*Familiarity Threat ( Ref: Para. 25)*

The IFAC Code[2a] discusses the familiarity threat that may be created by using the   **A12**
same senior personnel on an assurance engagement over a long period of time and
the safeguards that might be appropriate to address such threats.

Determining appropriate criteria to address familiarity threat may include matters   **A13**
such as:

- The nature of the engagement, including the extent to which it involves a matter of public interest; and
- The length of service of the senior personnel on the engagement.

Examples of safeguards include rotating the senior personnel or requiring an
engagement quality control review.

The IFAC Code[2a] recognizes that the familiarity threat is particularly relevant in the   **A14**
context of financial statement audits of listed entities. For these audits, the IFAC
Code requires the rotation of the key audit partner[4] after a pre-defined period,
normally no more than seven years[4a], and provides related standards and guidance.
National requirements may establish shorter rotation periods.

*Considerations specific to public sector audit organizations*

Statutory measures may provide safeguards for the independence of public sector   **A15**
auditors. However, threats to independence may still exist regardless of any statutory
measures designed to protect it. Therefore, in establishing the policies and procedures required by paragraphs 20-25, the public sector auditor may have regard to the
public sector mandate and address any threats to independence in that context.

Listed entities as referred to in paragraphs 25 and A14 are not common in the public   **A16**
sector. However, there may be other public sector entities that are significant due to
size, complexity or public interest aspects, and which consequently have a wide range
of stakeholders. Therefore, there may be instances when a firm determines, based on
its quality control policies and procedures, that a public sector entity is significant for
the purposes of expanded quality control procedures.

In the public sector, legislation may establish the appointments and terms of office of   **A17**
the auditor with engagement partner responsibility. As a result, it may not be possible to comply strictly with the engagement partner rotation requirements envisaged
for listed entities. Nonetheless, for public sector entities considered significant, as
noted in paragraph A16, it may be in the public interest for public sector audit
organizations to establish policies and procedures to promote compliance with the
spirit of rotation of engagement partner responsibility.

---

[4] *IFAC Code, Definitions. See footnote 2a.*

[4a] *APB Ethical Standard 3, "Long Association With The Audit Engagement," requires that, save for particular circumstances described therein, no one should act as audit engagement partner or as independent partner for a listed company for a continuous period longer than 5 years.*

## Acceptance and Continuance of Client Relationships and Specific Engagements

*Competence, Capabilities, and Resources* (Ref: Para. 26(a))

A18   Consideration of whether the firm has the competence, capabilities, and resources to undertake a new engagement from a new or an existing client involves reviewing the specific requirements of the engagement and the existing partner and staff profiles at all relevant levels, and including whether:

* Firm personnel have knowledge of relevant industries or subject matters;
* Firm personnel have experience with relevant regulatory or reporting requirements, or the ability to gain the necessary skills and knowledge effectively;
* The firm has sufficient personnel with the necessary competence and capabilities;
* Experts are available, if needed;
* Individuals meeting the criteria and eligibility requirements to perform engagement quality control review are available, where applicable; and
* The firm is able to complete the engagement within the reporting deadline.

*Integrity of Client* (Ref: Para. 26(c))

A19   With regard to the integrity of a client, matters to consider include, for example:

* The identity and business reputation of the client's principal owners, key management, and those charged with its governance.
* The nature of the client's operations, including its business practices.
* Information concerning the attitude of the client's principal owners, key management and those charged with its governance towards such matters as aggressive interpretation of accounting standards and the internal control environment.
* Whether the client is aggressively concerned with maintaining the firm's fees as low as possible.
* Indications of an inappropriate limitation in the scope of work.
* Indications that the client might be involved in money laundering or other criminal activities.
* The reasons for the proposed appointment of the firm and non-reappointment of the previous firm.
* The identity and business reputation of related parties.

The extent of knowledge a firm will have regarding the integrity of a client will generally grow within the context of an ongoing relationship with that client.

A20   Sources of information on such matters obtained by the firm may include the following:

* Communications with existing or previous providers of professional accountancy services to the client in accordance with relevant ethical requirements, and discussions with other third parties.
* Inquiry of other firm personnel or third parties such as bankers, legal counsel and industry peers.
* Background searches of relevant databases.

### Continuance of Client Relationship (Ref: Para. 27(a))

Deciding whether to continue a client relationship includes consideration of significant matters that have arisen during the current or previous engagements, and their implications for continuing the relationship. For example, a client may have started to expand its business operations into an area where the firm does not possess the necessary expertise.

**A21**

### Withdrawal (Ref: Para. 28)

Policies and procedures on withdrawal from an engagement or from both the engagement and the client relationship address issues that include the following:

**A22**

- Discussing with the appropriate level of the client's management and those charged with its governance the appropriate action that the firm might take based on the relevant facts and circumstances.
- If the firm determines that it is appropriate to withdraw, discussing with the appropriate level of the client's management and those charged with its governance withdrawal from the engagement or from both the engagement and the client relationship, and the reasons for the withdrawal.
- Considering whether there is a professional, legal or regulatory requirement for the firm to remain in place, or for the firm to report the withdrawal from the engagement, or from both the engagement and the client relationship, together with the reasons for the withdrawal, to regulatory authorities.
- Documenting significant matters, consultations, conclusions and the basis for the conclusions.

### Considerations Specific to Public Sector Audit Organizations (Ref: Para. 26-28)

In the public sector, auditors may be appointed in accordance with statutory procedures. Accordingly, certain of the requirements and considerations regarding the acceptance and continuance of client relationships and specific engagements as set out paragraphs 26-28 and A18-A22 may not be relevant. Nonetheless, establishing policies and procedures as described may provide valuable information to public sector auditors in performing risk assessments and in carrying out reporting responsibilities.

**A23**

## Human Resources (Ref: Para. 29)

Personnel issues relevant to the firm's policies and procedures related to human resources include, for example:

**A24**

- Recruitment.
- Performance evaluation.
- Capabilities, including time to perform assignments.
- Competence.
- Career development.
- Promotion.
- Compensation.
- The estimation of personnel needs.

Effective recruitment processes and procedures help the firm select individuals of integrity who have the capacity to develop the competence and capabilities necessary to perform the firm's work and possess the appropriate characteristics to enable them to perform competently.

**A25**   Competence can be developed through a variety of methods, including the following:

- Professional education.
- Continuing professional development, including training.
- Work experience.
- Coaching by more experienced staff, for example, other members of the engagement team.
- Independence education for personnel who are required to be independent.

**A26**   The continuing competence of the firm's personnel depends to a significant extent on an appropriate level of continuing professional development so that personnel maintain their knowledge and capabilities. Effective policies and procedures emphasize the need for continuing training for all levels of firm personnel, and provide the necessary training resources and assistance to enable personnel to develop and maintain the required competence and capabilities.

**A27**   The firm may use a suitably qualified external person, for example, when internal technical and training resources are unavailable.

**A28**   Performance evaluation, compensation and promotion procedures give due recognition and reward to the development and maintenance of competence and commitment to ethical principles. Steps a firm may take in developing and maintaining competence and commitment to ethical principles include:

- Making personnel aware of the firm's expectations regarding performance and ethical principles;
- Providing personnel with evaluation of, and counseling on, performance, progress and career development; and
- Helping personnel understand that advancement to positions of greater responsibility depends, among other things, upon performance quality and adherence to ethical principles, and that failure to comply with the firm's policies and procedures may result in disciplinary action.

### Considerations Specific to Smaller Firms

**A29**   The size and circumstances of the firm will influence the structure of the firm's performance evaluation process. Smaller firms, in particular, may employ less formal methods of evaluating the performance of their personnel.

### Assignment of Engagement Teams

*Engagement Partners (Ref: Para. 30)*

**A30**   Policies and procedures may include systems to monitor the workload and availability of engagement partners so as to enable these individuals to have sufficient time to adequately discharge their responsibilities.

*Engagement Teams (Ref: Para. 31)*

**A31**   The firm's assignment of engagement teams and the determination of the level of supervision required, include for example, consideration of the engagement team's:

- Understanding of, and practical experience with, engagements of a similar nature and complexity through appropriate training and participation;
- Understanding of professional standards and legal and regulatory requirements;

- Technical knowledge and expertise, including knowledge of relevant information technology;
- Knowledge of relevant industries in which the clients operate;
- Ability to apply professional judgment; and
- Understanding of the firm's quality control policies and procedures.

## Engagement Performance

### *Consistency in the Quality of Engagement Performance* (Ref: Para. 32(a))

The firm promotes consistency in the quality of engagement performance through its **A32** policies and procedures. This is often accomplished through written or electronic manuals, software tools or other forms of standardized documentation, and industry or subject matter-specific guidance materials. Matters addressed may include:

- How engagement teams are briefed on the engagement to obtain an understanding of the objectives of their work.
- Processes for complying with applicable engagement standards.
- Processes of engagement supervision, staff training and coaching.
- Methods of reviewing the work performed, the significant judgments made and the form of report being issued.
- Appropriate documentation of the work performed and of the timing and extent of the review.
- Processes to keep all policies and procedures current.

Appropriate teamwork and training assist less experienced members of the engagement team to clearly understand the objectives of the assigned work.   **A33**

### *Supervision* (Ref: Para. 32(b))

Engagement supervision includes the following:   **A34**

- Tracking the progress of the engagement;
- Considering the competence and capabilities of individual members of the engagement team, whether they have sufficient time to carry out their work, whether they understand their instructions and whether the work is being carried out in accordance with the planned approach to the engagement;
- Addressing significant matters arising during the engagement, considering their significance and modifying the planned approach appropriately; and
- Identifying matters for consultation or consideration by more experienced engagement team members during the engagement.

### *Review* (Ref: Para. 32(c))

A review consists of consideration of whether:   **A35**

- The work has been performed in accordance with professional standards and applicable legal and regulatory requirements;
- Significant matters have been raised for further consideration;
- Appropriate consultations have taken place and the resulting conclusions have been documented and implemented;
- There is a need to revise the nature, timing and extent of work performed;
- The work performed supports the conclusions reached and is appropriately documented;
- The evidence obtained is sufficient and appropriate to support the report; and

- The objectives of the engagement procedures have been achieved.

***Consultation*** (Ref: Para. 34)

**A36**   Consultation includes discussion at the appropriate professional level, with individuals within or outside the firm who have specialized expertise.

**A37**   Consultation uses appropriate research resources as well as the collective experience and technical expertise of the firm. Consultation helps to promote quality and improves the application of professional judgment. Appropriate recognition of consultation in the firm's policies and procedures helps to promote a culture in which consultation is recognized as a strength and encourages personnel to consult on difficult or contentious matters.

**A38**   Effective consultation on significant technical, ethical and other matters within the firm, or where applicable, outside the firm can be achieved when those consulted:

- are given all the relevant facts that will enable them to provide informed advice; and
- have appropriate knowledge, seniority and experience,

and when conclusions resulting from consultations are appropriately documented and implemented.

**A39**   Documentation of consultations with other professionals that involve difficult or contentious matters that is sufficiently complete and detailed contributes to an understanding of:

- The issue on which consultation was sought; and
- The results of the consultation, including any decisions taken, the basis for those decisions and how they were implemented.

*Considerations Specific to Smaller Firms*

**A40**   A firm needing to consult externally, for example, a firm without appropriate internal resources, may take advantage of advisory services provided by:

- Other firms;
- Professional and regulatory bodies; or
- Commercial organizations that provide relevant quality control services.

Before contracting for such services, consideration of the competence and capabilities of the external provider helps the firm to determine whether the external provider is suitably qualified for that purpose.

**Engagement Quality Control Review**

*Criteria for an Engagement Quality Control Review (Ref: Para. 35(b))*

**A41**   Criteria for determining which engagements other than audits of financial statements of listed entities are to be subject to an engagement quality control review may include, for example:

- The nature of the engagement, including the extent to which it involves a matter of public interest.

- The identification of unusual circumstances or risks in an engagement or class of engagements.
- Whether laws or regulations require an engagement quality control review.

*Nature, Timing and Extent of the Engagement Quality Control Review (Ref: Para. 36-37)*

The engagement report is not dated until the completion of the engagement quality control review. However, documentation of the engagement quality control review may be completed after the date of the report.   A42

Conducting the engagement quality control review in a timely manner at appropriate stages during the engagement allows significant matters to be promptly resolved to the engagement quality control reviewer's satisfaction on or before the date of the report.   A43

The extent of the engagement quality control review may depend, among other things, on the complexity of the engagement, whether the entity is a listed entity, and the risk that the report might not be appropriate in the circumstances. The performance of an engagement quality control review does not reduce the responsibilities of the engagement partner.   A44

*Engagement Quality Control Review of a Listed Entity (Ref: Para. 38)*

Other matters relevant to evaluating the significant judgments made by the engagement team that may be considered in an engagement quality control review of an audit of financial statements of a listed entity include:   A45

- Significant risks identified during the engagement and the responses to those risks.
- Judgments made, particularly with respect to materiality and significant risks.
- The significance and disposition of corrected and uncorrected misstatements identified during the engagement.
- The matters to be communicated to management and those charged with governance and, where applicable, other parties such as regulatory bodies.

These other matters, depending on the circumstances, may also be applicable for engagement quality control reviews for audits of the financial statements of other entities as well as reviews of financial statements and other assurance and related services engagements.

*Considerations specific to public sector audit organizations*

Although not referred to as listed entities, as described in paragraph A16, certain public sector entities may be of sufficient significance to warrant performance of an engagement quality control review.   A46

**Criteria for the Eligibility of Engagement Quality Control Reviewers**

*Sufficient and Appropriate Technical Expertise, Experience and Authority (Ref: Para. 39(a))*

What constitutes sufficient and appropriate technical expertise, experience and authority depends on the circumstances of the engagement. For example, the   A47 engagement quality control reviewer for an audit of the financial statements of a listed entity is likely to be an individual with sufficient and appropriate experience and authority to act as an audit engagement partner on audits of financial statements of listed entities.

*Consultation with the Engagement Quality Control Reviewer (Ref: Para. 39(b))*

**A48**    The engagement partner may consult the engagement quality control reviewer during the engagement, for example, to establish that a judgment made by the engagement partner will be acceptable to the engagement quality control reviewer. Such consultation avoids identification of differences of opinion at a late stage of the engagement and need not compromise the engagement quality control reviewer's eligibility to perform the role. Where the nature and extent of the consultations become significant the reviewer's objectivity may be compromised unless care is taken by both the engagement team and the reviewer to maintain the reviewer's objectivity. Where this is not possible, another individual within the firm or a suitably qualified external person may be appointed to take on the role of either the engagement quality control reviewer or the person to be consulted on the engagement.

*Objectivity of the Engagement Quality Control Reviewer (Ref: Para. 40)*

**A49**    The firm is required to establish policies and procedures designed to maintain objectivity of the engagement quality control reviewer. Accordingly, such policies and procedures provide that the engagement quality control reviewer:

- Where practicable, is not selected by the engagement partner;
- Does not otherwise participate in the engagement during the period of review;
- Does not make decisions for the engagement team; and
- Is not subject to other considerations that would threaten the reviewer's objectivity.

*Considerations specific to smaller firms*

**A50**    It may not be practicable, in the case of firms with few partners, for the engagement partner not to be involved in selecting the engagement quality control reviewer. Suitably qualified external persons may be contracted where sole practitioners or small firms identify engagements requiring engagement quality control reviews. Alternatively, some sole practitioners or small firms may wish to use other firms to facilitate engagement quality control reviews. Where the firm contracts suitably qualified external persons, the requirements in paragraphs 39-41 and guidance in paragraphs A47-A48 apply.

*Considerations specific to public sector audit organizations*

**A51**    In the public sector, a statutorily appointed auditor (for example, an Auditor General, or other suitably qualified person appointed on behalf of the Auditor General) may act in a role equivalent to that of engagement partner with overall responsibility for public sector audits. In such circumstances, where applicable, the selection of the engagement quality control reviewer includes consideration of the need for independence from the audited entity and the ability of the engagement quality control reviewer to provide an objective evaluation.

**Differences of Opinion** (Ref: Para. 43)

Effective procedures encourage identification of differences of opinion at an early    **A52**
stage, provide clear guidelines as to the successive steps to be taken thereafter, and
require documentation regarding the resolution of the differences and the implementation of the conclusions reached.

Procedures to resolve such differences may include consulting with another practi-    **A53**
tioner or firm, or a professional or regulatory body.

**Engagement Documentation**

*Completion of the Assembly of Final Engagement Files (Ref: Para. 45)*

Law or regulation may prescribe the time limits by which the assembly of final    **A54**
engagement files for specific types of engagement is to be completed. Where no such
time limits are prescribed in law or regulation, paragraph 45 requires the firm to
establish time limits that reflect the need to complete the assembly of final engagement files on a timely basis. In the case of an audit, for example, such a time limit
would ordinarily not be more than 60 days after the date of the auditor's report.

Where two or more different reports are issued in respect of the same subject matter    **A55**
information of an entity, the firm's policies and procedures relating to time limits for
the assembly of final engagement files address each report as if it were for a separate
engagement. This may, for example, be the case when the firm issues an auditor's
report on a component's financial information for group consolidation purposes
and, at a subsequent date, an auditor's report on the same financial information for
statutory purposes.

*Confidentiality, Safe Custody, Integrity, Accessibility and Retrievability of
Engagement Documentation (Ref: Para. 46)*

Relevant ethical requirements establish an obligation for the firm's personnel to    **A56**
observe at all times the confidentiality of information contained in engagement
documentation, unless specific client authority has been given to disclose information, or there is a legal or professional duty to do so. Specific laws or regulations may
impose additional obligations on the firm's personnel to maintain client confidentiality, particularly where data of a personal nature are concerned.

Whether engagement documentation is in paper, electronic or other media, the    **A57**
integrity, accessibility or retrievability of the underlying data may be compromised if
the documentation could be altered, added to or deleted without the firm's knowledge, or if it could be permanently lost or damaged. Accordingly, controls that the
firm designs and implements to avoid unauthorized alteration or loss of engagement
documentation may include those that:

- Enable the determination of when and by whom engagement documentation
  was created, changed or reviewed;
- Protect the integrity of the information at all stages of the engagement, especially when the information is shared within the engagement team or
  transmitted to other parties via the Internet;
- Prevent unauthorized changes to the engagement documentation; and
- Allow access to the engagement documentation by the engagement team and
  other authorized parties as necessary to properly discharge their responsibilities.

A58    Controls that the firm designs and implements to maintain the confidentiality, safe custody, integrity, accessibility and retrievability of engagement documentation may include the following:

- The use of a password among engagement team members to restrict access to electronic engagement documentation to authorized users.
- Appropriate back-up routines for electronic engagement documentation at appropriate stages during the engagement.
- Procedures for properly distributing engagement documentation to the team members at the start of the engagement, processing it during engagement, and collating it at the end of engagement.
- Procedures for restricting access to, and enabling proper distribution and con-fidential storage of, hardcopy engagement documentation.

A59    For practical reasons, original paper documentation may be electronically scanned for inclusion in engagement files. In such cases, the firm's procedures designed to maintain the integrity, accessibility, and retrievability of the documentation may include requiring the engagement teams to:

- Generate scanned copies that reflect the entire content of the original paper documentation, including manual signatures, cross-references and annotations;
- Integrate the scanned copies into the engagement files, including indexing and signing off on the scanned copies as necessary; and
- Enable the scanned copies to be retrieved and printed as necessary.

There may be legal, regulatory or other reasons for a firm to retain original paper documentation that has been scanned.

*Retention of Engagement Documentation (Ref: Para. 47)*

A60    The needs of the firm for retention of engagement documentation, and the period of such retention, will vary with the nature of the engagement and the firm's circum-stances, for example, whether the engagement documentation is needed to provide a record of matters of continuing significance to future engagements. The retention period may also depend on other factors, such as whether local law or regulation prescribes specific retention periods for certain types of engagements, or whether there are generally accepted retention periods in the jurisdiction in the absence of specific legal or regulatory requirements.

A61    In the specific case of audit engagements, the retention period would ordinarily be no shorter than five years from the date of the auditor's report, or, if later, the date of the group auditor's report.[4b]

---

[4b] *In the UK and Republic of Ireland this requirement is applied having regard to specific requirements of the Audit Regulations.*
*Audit Regulation 3.08b states that "A Registered Auditor must keep all audit working papers which auditing standards require for a period of at least six years. The period starts with the end of the accounting period to which the papers relate."*
*Audit Regulation 7.06 states that "In carrying out its responsibilities under regulation 7.03, the Registration Committee, any sub-committee, the secretariat, or a monitoring unit may, to the extent necessary for the review of a firm's audit work or how it is complying or intends to comply with these regulations, require a Registered Auditor or an applicant for registration to provide any information, held in whatsoever form (including elec-tronic), about the firm or its clients and to allow access to the firm's systems and personnel."*
*The Audit Regulations referred to above were originally published in December 1995 and updated in June 2005 (Audit News 40).*

Procedures that the firm adopts for retention of engagement documentation include **A62**
those that enable the requirements of paragraph 47 to be met during the retention
period, for example to:

- Enable the retrieval of, and access to, the engagement documentation during the
  retention period, particularly in the case of electronic documentation since the
  underlying technology may be upgraded or changed over time;
- Provide, where necessary, a record of changes made to engagement documentation after the engagement files have been completed; and
- Enable authorized external parties to access and review specific engagement
  documentation for quality control or other purposes.

*Ownership of engagement documentation*

Unless otherwise specified by law or regulation, engagement documentation is the **A63**
property of the firm. The firm may, at its discretion, make portions of, or extracts
from, engagement documentation available to clients, provided such disclosure does
not undermine the validity of the work performed, or, in the case of assurance
engagements, the independence of the firm or its personnel.

## Monitoring

### *Monitoring the Firm's Quality Control Policies and Procedures* (Ref: Para. 48)

The purpose of monitoring compliance with quality control policies and procedures **A64**
is to provide an evaluation of:

- Adherence to professional standards and legal and regulatory requirements;
- Whether the system of quality control has been appropriately designed and
  effectively implemented; and
- Whether the firm's quality control policies and procedures have been appropriately applied, so that reports that are issued by the firm or engagement
  partners are appropriate in the circumstances.

Ongoing consideration and evaluation of the system of quality control include **A65**
matters such as the following:

- Analysis of:
  - New developments in professional standards and legal and regulatory
    requirements, and how they are reflected in the firm's policies and proce-
    dures where appropriate;
  - Written confirmation of compliance with policies and procedures on
    independence;
  - Continuing professional development, including training; and
  - Decisions related to acceptance and continuance of client relationships and
    specific engagements.
- Determination of corrective actions to be taken and improvements to be made
  in the system, including the provision of feedback into the firm's policies and
  procedures relating to education and training.
- Communication to appropriate firm personnel of weaknesses identified in the
  system, in the level of understanding of the system, or compliance with it.
- Follow-up by appropriate firm personnel so that necessary modifications are
  promptly made to the quality control policies and procedures.

Inspection cycle policies and procedures may, for example, specify a cycle that spans **A66**
three years. The manner in which the inspection cycle is organized, including the

timing of selection of individual engagements, depends on many factors, such as the following:

- The size of the firm.
- The number and geographical location of offices.
- The results of previous monitoring procedures.
- The degree of authority both personnel and offices have (for example, whether individual offices are authorized to conduct their own inspections or whether only the head office may conduct them).
- The nature and complexity of the firm's practice and organization.
- The risks associated with the firm's clients and specific engagements.

A67    The inspection process includes the selection of individual engagements, some of which may be selected without prior notification to the engagement team. In determining the scope of the inspections, the firm may take into account the scope or conclusions of an independent external inspection program. However, an independent external inspection program does not act as a substitute for the firm's own internal monitoring program.

*Considerations Specific to Smaller Firms*

A68    In the case of small firms, monitoring procedures may need to be performed by individuals who are responsible for design and implementation of the firm's quality control policies and procedures, or who may be involved in performing the engagement quality control review. A firm with a limited number of persons may choose to use a suitably qualified external person or another firm to carry out engagement inspections and other monitoring procedures. Alternatively, the firm may establish arrangements to share resources with other appropriate organizations to facilitate monitoring activities.

*Communicating Deficiencies* (Ref: Para. 50)

A69    The reporting of identified deficiencies to individuals other than the relevant engagement partners need not include an identification of the specific engagements concerned, although there may be cases where such identification may be necessary for the proper discharge of the responsibilities of the individuals other than the engagement partners.

*Complaints and Allegations*

*Source of Complaints and Allegations (Ref: Para. 55)*

A70    Complaints and allegations (which do not include those that are clearly frivolous) may originate from within or outside the firm. They may be made by firm personnel, clients or other third parties. They may be received by engagement team members or other firm personnel.

*Investigation Policies and Procedures (Ref: Para. 56)*

A71    Policies and procedures established for the investigation of complaints and allegations may include for example, that the partner supervising the investigation:

- Has sufficient and appropriate experience;
- Has authority within the firm; and
- Is otherwise not involved in the engagement.

The partner supervising the investigation may involve legal counsel as necessary.

*Considerations specific to smaller firms*

It may not be practicable, in the case of firms with few partners, for the partner   **A72**
supervising the investigation not to be involved in the engagement. These small firms
and sole practitioners may use the services of a suitably qualified external person or
another firm to carry out the investigation into complaints and allegations.

## Documentation of the System of Quality Control (Ref: Para. 57)

The form and content of documentation evidencing the operation of each of the   **A73**
elements of the system of quality control is a matter of judgment and depends on a
number of factors, including the following:

- The size of the firm and the number of offices.
- The nature and complexity of the firm's practice and organization.

For example, large firms may use electronic databases to document matters such as
independence confirmations, performance evaluations and the results of monitoring
inspections.

Appropriate documentation relating to monitoring includes, for example:   **A74**

- Monitoring procedures, including the procedure for selecting completed
  engagements to be inspected.
- A record of the evaluation of:
  - Adherence to professional standards and applicable legal and regulatory
    requirements;
  - Whether the system of quality control has been appropriately designed and
    effectively implemented; and
  - Whether the firm's quality control policies and procedures have been
    appropriately applied, so that reports that are issued by the firm or
    engagement partners are appropriate in the circumstances.
- Identification of the deficiencies noted, an evaluation of their effect, and the
  basis for determining whether and what further action is necessary.

### Considerations Specific to Smaller Firms

Smaller firms may use more informal methods in the documentation of their systems   **A75**
of quality control such as manual notes, checklists and forms.

# Addendum

*This addendum provides a summary of APB's rationale for retaining or excluding in the proposed clarified ISQC (UK and Ireland) the supplementary material in the existing ISQC (UK and Ireland). It is provided for information and does not form part of the proposed clarified ISQC (UK and Ireland).*

*The Consultation Paper published with the exposure drafts explains the general approach used by the APB for determining whether current supplementary material should be proposed to be retained.*

## Analysis of proposed treatment of current APB supplementary material in current ISQC (UK and Ireland) 1

### Requirements

There are no supplementary requirements in the current ISQC (UK and Ireland) 1

### Guidance

There is very little supplementary guidance in the current ISQC (UK and Ireland) 1 most of which relates to references to ethical matters, with an additional reference to the Glossary of Terms. These have been addressed where relevant in the proposed clarified standard (see paragraph 12(q) and footnotes 1a, 2a and 4a).

# Proposed Clarified International Standard on Auditing (UK and Ireland) 200

# Overall objectives of the independent auditor and the conduct of an audit in accordance with International Standards on Auditing (UK and Ireland)

*(Effective for audits of financial statements for periods ending on or after 15 December 2010)*

## Contents

# Introduction

## Scope of this ISA (UK and Ireland)

1   This International Standard on Auditing (UK and Ireland) (ISA (UK and Ireland)) deals with the independent auditor's overall responsibilities when conducting an audit of financial statements in accordance with ISAs (UK and Ireland). Specifically, it sets out the overall objectives of the independent auditor, and explains the nature and scope of an audit designed to enable the independent auditor to meet those objectives. It also explains the scope, authority and structure of the ISAs (UK and Ireland), and includes requirements establishing the general responsibilities of the independent auditor applicable in all audits, including the obligation to comply with the ISAs (UK and Ireland). The independent auditor is referred to as "the auditor" hereafter.

2   ISAs (UK and Ireland) are written in the context of an audit of financial statements by an auditor. They are to be adapted as necessary in the circumstances when applied to audits of other historical financial information. ISAs (UK and Ireland) do not address the responsibilities of the auditor that may exist in legislation, regulation or otherwise in connection with, for example, the offering of securities to the public[1a]. Such responsibilities may differ from those established in the ISAs (UK and Ireland). Accordingly, while the auditor may find aspects of the ISAs (UK and Ireland) helpful in such circumstances, it is the responsibility of the auditor to ensure compliance with all relevant legal, regulatory or professional obligations.

## An Audit of Financial Statements

3   The purpose of an audit is to enhance the degree of confidence of intended users in the financial statements. This is achieved by the expression of an opinion by the auditor on whether the financial statements are prepared, in all material respects, in accordance with an applicable financial reporting framework. In the case of most general purpose frameworks, that opinion is on whether the financial statements are presented fairly, in all material respects, or give a true and fair view in accordance with the framework. An audit conducted in accordance with ISAs (UK and Ireland) and relevant ethical requirements enables the auditor to form that opinion. (Ref: Para. A1)

4   The financial statements subject to audit are those of the entity, prepared by management of the entity with oversight from those charged with governance[1b]. ISAs (UK and Ireland) do not impose responsibilities on management or those charged with governance and do not override laws and regulations that govern their responsibilities. However, an audit in accordance with ISAs (UK and Ireland) is conducted on the premise that management and, where appropriate, those charged with governance have acknowledged certain responsibilities that are fundamental to the conduct of the audit. The audit of the financial statements does not relieve management or those charged with governance of their responsibilities. (Ref: Para. A2-A11)

---

[1a] *In the UK and Ireland, standards and guidance for accountants undertaking engagements in connection with an investment circular are set out in APB's Statements of Investment Circular Reporting Standards (SIRS)*

[1b] *In the UK and Ireland, those charged with governance are responsible for the preparation of the financial statements. For corporate entities, directors have a collective responsibility; those charged with governance of other types of entity may also have a collective responsibility established in applicable law or regulation or under the terms of their appointment.*

As the basis for the auditor's opinion, ISAs (UK and Ireland) require the auditor to   **5**
obtain reasonable assurance about whether the financial statements as a whole are
free from material misstatement, whether due to fraud or error. Reasonable assurance is a high level of assurance. It is obtained when the auditor has obtained
sufficient appropriate audit evidence to reduce audit risk (i.e., the risk that the
auditor expresses an inappropriate opinion when the financial statements are
materially misstated) to an acceptably low level. However, reasonable assurance is
not an absolute level of assurance, because there are inherent limitations of an audit
which result in most of the audit evidence on which the auditor draws conclusions
and bases the auditor's opinion being persuasive rather than conclusive. (Ref: Para.
A28-A52)

The concept of materiality is applied by the auditor both in planning and performing   **6**
the audit, and in evaluating the effect of identified misstatements on the audit and of
uncorrected misstatements, if any, on the financial statements.[1] In general, misstatements, including omissions, are considered to be material if, individually or in
the aggregate, they could reasonably be expected to influence the economic decisions
of users taken on the basis of the financial statements. Judgments about materiality
are made in the light of surrounding circumstances, and are affected by the auditor's
perception of the financial information needs of users of the financial statements, and
by the size or nature of a misstatement, or a combination of both. The auditor's
opinion deals with the financial statements as a whole and therefore the auditor is not
responsible for the detection of misstatements that are not material to the financial
statements as a whole.

The ISAs (UK and Ireland) contain objectives, requirements and application and   **7**
other explanatory material that are designed to support the auditor in obtaining
reasonable assurance. The ISAs (UK and Ireland) require that the auditor exercise
professional judgment and maintain professional skepticism throughout the planning and performance of the audit and, among other things:

- Identify and assess risks of material misstatement, whether due to fraud or
  error, based on an understanding of the entity and its environment, including
  the entity's internal control.
- Obtain sufficient appropriate audit evidence about whether material misstatements exist, through designing and implementing appropriate responses to the
  assessed risks.
- Form an opinion on the financial statements based on conclusions drawn from
  the audit evidence obtained.

The form of opinion expressed by the auditor will depend upon the applicable   **8**
financial reporting framework and any applicable law or regulation. (Ref: Para. A12-
A13)

The auditor may also have certain other communication and reporting responsi-   **9**
bilities to users, management, those charged with governance, or parties outside the
entity, in relation to matters arising from the audit. These may be established by the
ISAs (UK and Ireland) or by applicable law or regulation.[2]

[1] ISA (UK and Ireland) 320, "Materiality in Planning and Performing an Audit" and ISA (UK and Ireland)
450, "Evaluation of Misstatements Identified during the Audit."

[2] See, for example, ISA (UK and Ireland) 260, "Communication with Those Charged with Governance;" and
paragraph 43 of ISA (UK and Ireland) 240, "The Auditor's Responsibilities Relating to Fraud in an Audit of
Financial Statements."

**Effective Date**

10   This ISA (UK and Ireland) is effective for audits of financial statements for periods ending on or after 15 December 2010.

## Overall Objectives of the Auditor

11   In conducting an audit of financial statements, the overall objectives of the auditor are:

(a)   To obtain reasonable assurance about whether the financial statements as a whole are free from material misstatement, whether due to fraud or error, thereby enabling the auditor to express an opinion on whether the financial statements are prepared, in all material respects, in accordance with an applicable financial reporting framework; and

(b)   To report on the financial statements, and communicate as required by the ISAs (UK and Ireland), in accordance with the auditor's findings.

12   In all cases when reasonable assurance cannot be obtained and a qualified opinion in the auditor's report is insufficient in the circumstances for purposes of reporting to the intended users of the financial statements, the ISAs (UK and Ireland) require that the auditor disclaim an opinion or withdraw (or resign)[3] from the engagement, where withdrawal is possible under applicable law or regulation.

## Definitions

13   For purposes of the ISAs (UK and Ireland), the following terms have the meanings attributed below:

(a)   Applicable financial reporting framework – The financial reporting framework adopted by management and, where appropriate, those charged with governance in the preparation of the financial statements that is acceptable in view of the nature of the entity and the objective of the financial statements, or that is required by law or regulation.

The term "fair presentation framework" is used to refer to a financial reporting framework that requires compliance with the requirements of the framework and:

(i)   Acknowledges explicitly or implicitly that, to achieve fair presentation of the financial statements, it may be necessary for management to provide disclosures beyond those specifically required by the framework; or

(ii)   Acknowledges explicitly that it may be necessary for management to depart from a requirement of the framework to achieve fair presentation of the financial statements. Such departures are expected to be necessary only in extremely rare circumstances.

The term "compliance framework" is used to refer to a financial reporting framework that requires compliance with the requirements of the framework, but does not contain the acknowledgements in (i) or (ii) above.

(b)   Audit evidence – Information used by the auditor in arriving at the conclusions on which the auditor's opinion is based. Audit evidence includes both information contained in the accounting records underlying the financial statements and other information. For purposes of the ISAs (UK and Ireland):

---

[3] *In the ISAs (UK and Ireland), only the term "withdrawal" is used.*

(i) Sufficiency of audit evidence is the measure of the quantity of audit evidence. The quantity of the audit evidence needed is affected by the auditor's assessment of the risks of material misstatement and also by the quality of such audit evidence.

(ii) Appropriateness of audit evidence is the measure of the quality of audit evidence; that is, its relevance and its reliability in providing support for the conclusions on which the auditor's opinion is based.

(c) Audit risk – The risk that the auditor expresses an inappropriate audit opinion when the financial statements are materially misstated. Audit risk is a function of the risks of material misstatement and detection risk.

(d) Auditor – "Auditor" is used to refer to the person or persons conducting the audit, usually the engagement partner or other members of the engagement team, or, as applicable, the firm. Where an ISA (UK and Ireland) expressly intends that a requirement or responsibility be fulfilled by the engagement partner, the term "engagement partner" rather than "auditor" is used. "Engagement partner" and "firm" are to be read as referring to their public sector equivalents where relevant.

(e) Detection risk – The risk that the procedures performed by the auditor to reduce audit risk to an acceptably low level will not detect a misstatement that exists and that could be material, either individually or when aggregated with other misstatements.

(f) Financial statements – A structured representation of historical financial information, including related notes, intended to communicate an entity's economic resources or obligations at a point in time or the changes therein for a period of time in accordance with a financial reporting framework. The related notes ordinarily comprise a summary of significant accounting policies and other explanatory information. The term "financial statements" ordinarily refers to a complete set of financial statements as determined by the requirements of the applicable financial reporting framework, but can also refer to a single financial statement.

(g) Historical financial information – Information expressed in financial terms in relation to a particular entity, derived primarily from that entity's accounting system, about economic events occurring in past time periods or about economic conditions or circumstances at points in time in the past.

(h) Management – The person(s) with executive responsibility for the conduct of the entity's operations. For some entities in some jurisdictions, management includes some or all of those charged with governance, for example, executive members of a governance board, or an owner-manager.

In the UK and Ireland, depending on the nature and circumstances of the entity, management may include some or all of those charged with governance (e.g. executive directors). Management will not normally include non-executive directors.

(i) Misstatement – A difference between the amount, classification, presentation, or disclosure of a reported financial statement item and the amount, classification, presentation, or disclosure that is required for the item to be in accordance with the applicable financial reporting framework. Misstatements can arise from error or fraud.

Where the auditor expresses an opinion on whether the financial statements are presented fairly, in all material respects, or give a true and fair view, misstatements also include those adjustments of amounts, classifications, presentation, or disclosures that, in the auditor's judgment, are necessary for the financial statements to be presented fairly, in all material respects, or to give a true and fair view.

(j)   Premise, relating to the responsibilities of management and, where appropriate, those charged with governance, on which an audit is conducted – That management and, where appropriate, those charged with governance have acknowledged and understand that they have the following responsibilities that are fundamental to the conduct of an audit in accordance with ISAs (UK and Ireland). That is, responsibility:

   (i)   For the preparation of the financial statements in accordance with the applicable financial reporting framework, including where relevant their fair presentation;

   (ii)  For such internal control as management and, where appropriate, those charged with governance determine is necessary to enable the preparation of financial statements that are free from material misstatement, whether due to fraud or error; and

   (iii) To provide the auditor with:

      a.   Access to all information of which management and, where appropriate, those charged with governance are aware that is relevant to the preparation of the financial statements such as records, documentation and other matters;

      b.   Additional information that the auditor may request from management and, where appropriate, those charged with governance for the purpose of the audit; and

      c.   Unrestricted access to persons within the entity from whom the auditor determines it necessary to obtain audit evidence.

   In the case of a fair presentation framework, (i) above may be restated as "for the preparation and *fair* presentation of the financial statements in accordance with the financial reporting framework," or "for the preparation of financial statements *that give a true and fair view* in accordance with the financial reporting framework."

   The "premise, relating to the responsibilities of management and, where appropriate, those charged with governance, on which an audit is conducted" may also be referred to as the "premise."

(k)  Professional judgment – The application of relevant training, knowledge and experience, within the context provided by auditing, accounting and ethical standards, in making informed decisions about the courses of action that are appropriate in the circumstances of the audit engagement.

(l)   Professional skepticism – An attitude that includes a questioning mind, being alert to conditions which may indicate possible misstatement due to error or fraud, and a critical assessment of audit evidence.

(m) Reasonable assurance – In the context of an audit of financial statements, a high, but not absolute, level of assurance.

(n)  Risk of material misstatement – The risk that the financial statements are materially misstated prior to audit. This consists of two components, described as follows at the assertion level:

   (i)   Inherent risk – The susceptibility of an assertion about a class of transaction, account balance or disclosure to a misstatement that could be material, either individually or when aggregated with other misstatements, before consideration of any related controls.

   (ii)  Control risk – The risk that a misstatement that could occur in an assertion about a class of transaction, account balance or disclosure and that could be material, either individually or when aggregated with other misstatements, will not be prevented, or detected and corrected, on a timely basis by the entity's internal control.

(o)  *Those charged with governance* – The person(s) or organization(s) (e.g., a corporate trustee) with responsibility for overseeing the strategic direction of the entity and obligations related to the accountability of the entity. This includes overseeing the financial reporting process. For some entities in some jurisdictions, those charged with governance may include management personnel, for example, executive members of a governance board of a private or public sector entity, or an owner-manager.

In the UK and Ireland, those charged with governance include the directors (executive and non-executive) of a company or other body, the members of an audit committee where one exists, the partners, proprietors, committee of management or trustees of other forms of entity, or equivalent persons responsible for directing the entity's affairs and preparing its financial statements.

# Requirements

## Ethical Requirements Relating to an Audit of Financial Statements

The auditor shall comply with relevant ethical requirements, including those pertaining to independence, relating to financial statement audit engagements. (Ref: Para. A14-A17)   **14**

## Professional Skepticism

The auditor shall plan and perform an audit with professional skepticism recognizing that circumstances may exist that cause the financial statements to be materially misstated. (Ref: Para. A18-A22)   **15**

## Professional Judgment

The auditor shall exercise professional judgment in planning and performing an audit of financial statements. (Ref: Para. A23-A27)   **16**

## Sufficient Appropriate Audit Evidence and Audit Risk

To obtain reasonable assurance, the auditor shall obtain sufficient appropriate audit evidence to reduce audit risk to an acceptably low level and thereby enable the auditor to draw reasonable conclusions on which to base the auditor's opinion. (Ref: Para. A28-A52)   **17**

## Conduct of an Audit in Accordance with ISAs (UK and Ireland)

### Complying with ISAs (UK and Ireland) Relevant to the Audit

The auditor shall comply with all ISAs (UK and Ireland) relevant to the audit. An ISA (UK and Ireland) is relevant to the audit when the ISA (UK and Ireland) is in effect and the circumstances addressed by the ISA (UK and Ireland) exist. (Ref: Para. A53-A57)   **18**

The auditor shall have an understanding of the entire text of an ISA (UK and Ireland), including its application and other explanatory material, to understand its objectives and to apply its requirements properly. (Ref: Para. A58-A66)   **19**

**20**    The auditor shall not represent compliance with ISAs (UK and Ireland) in the auditor's report unless the auditor has complied with the requirements of this ISA and all other ISAs (UK and Ireland) relevant to the audit.

### Objectives Stated in Individual ISAs (UK and Ireland)

**21**    To achieve the overall objectives of the auditor, the auditor shall use the objectives stated in relevant ISAs (UK and Ireland) in planning and performing the audit, having regard to the interrelationships among the ISAs (UK and Ireland), to: (Ref: Para. A67-A69)

(a)    Determine whether any audit procedures in addition to those required by the ISAs (UK and Ireland) are necessary in pursuance of the objectives stated in the ISAs (UK and Ireland); and (Ref: Para. A70)

(b)    Evaluate whether sufficient appropriate audit evidence has been obtained. (Ref: Para. A71)

### Complying with Relevant Requirements

**22**    Subject to paragraph 23, the auditor shall comply with each requirement of an ISA (UK and Ireland) unless, in the circumstances of the audit:

(a)    The entire ISA (UK and Ireland) is not relevant; or

(b)    The requirement is not relevant because it is conditional and the condition does not exist. (Ref: Para. A72-A73)

**23**    In exceptional circumstances, the auditor may judge it necessary to depart from a relevant requirement in an ISA (UK and Ireland). In such circumstances, the auditor shall perform alternative audit procedures to achieve the aim of that requirement. The need for the auditor to depart from a relevant requirement is expected to arise only where the requirement is for a specific procedure to be performed and, in the specific circumstances of the audit, that procedure would be ineffective in achieving the aim of the requirement. (Ref: Para. A74)

### Failure to Achieve an Objective

**24**    If an objective in a relevant ISA (UK and Ireland) cannot be achieved, the auditor shall evaluate whether this prevents the auditor from achieving the overall objectives of the auditor and thereby requires the auditor, in accordance with the ISAs (UK and Ireland), to modify the auditor's opinion or withdraw from the engagement (where withdrawal is possible under applicable law or regulation). Failure to achieve an objective represents a significant matter requiring documentation in accordance with ISA (UK and Ireland) 230. [4] (Ref: Para. A75-A76)

***

---

[4] ISA (UK and Ireland) 230, "Audit Documentation," paragraph 8(c).

# Application and Other Explanatory Material

## An Audit of Financial Statements

*Scope of the Audit* (Ref: Para. 3)

The auditor's opinion on the financial statements deals with whether the financial   **A1**
statements are prepared, in all material respects, in accordance with the applicable
financial reporting framework. Such an opinion is common to all audits of financial
statements. The auditor's opinion therefore does not assure, for example, the future
viability of the entity nor the efficiency or effectiveness with which management has
conducted the affairs of the entity. In some jurisdictions, however, applicable law or
regulation may require auditors to provide opinions on other specific matters, such
as the effectiveness of internal control, or the consistency of a separate management
report with the financial statements. While the ISAs (UK and Ireland) include
requirements and guidance in relation to such matters to the extent that they are
relevant to forming an opinion on the financial statements, the auditor would be
required to undertake further work if the auditor had additional responsibilities to
provide such opinions.

*Preparation of the Financial Statements* (Ref: Para. 4)

Law or regulation may establish the responsibilities of management and, where   **A2**
appropriate, those charged with governance in relation to financial reporting.
However, the extent of these responsibilities, or the way in which they are described,
may differ across jurisdictions. Despite these differences, an audit in accordance with
ISAs (UK and Ireland) is conducted on the premise that management and, where
appropriate, those charged with governance have acknowledged and understand that
they have responsibility:

(a) For the preparation of the financial statements in accordance with the applic-
    able financial reporting framework, including where relevant their fair
    presentation;
(b) For such internal control as management and, where appropriate, those charged
    with governance determine is necessary to enable the preparation of financial
    statements that are free from material misstatement, whether due to fraud or
    error; and
(c) To provide the auditor with:
    (i)   Access to all information of which management and, where appropriate,
          those charged with governance are aware that is relevant to the preparation
          of the financial statements such as records, documentation and other
          matters;
    (ii)  Additional information that the auditor may request from management
          and, where appropriate, those charged with governance for the purpose of
          the audit; and
    (iii) Unrestricted access to persons within the entity from whom the auditor
          determines it necessary to obtain audit evidence.

The preparation of the financial statements by management and, where appropriate,   **A3**
those charged with governance requires:

• The identification of the applicable financial reporting framework, in the context of any relevant laws or regulations.
• The preparation of the financial statements in accordance with that framework.

- The inclusion of an adequate description of that framework in the financial statements.

The preparation of the financial statements requires management to exercise judgment in making accounting estimates that are reasonable in the circumstances, as well as to select and apply appropriate accounting policies. These judgments are made in the context of the applicable financial reporting framework.

A4   The financial statements may be prepared in accordance with a financial reporting framework designed to meet:

- The common financial information needs of a wide range of users (i.e., "general purpose financial statements"); or
- The financial information needs of specific users (i.e., "special purpose financial statements").

A5   The applicable financial reporting framework often encompasses financial reporting standards established by an authorized or recognized standards setting organization, or legislative or regulatory requirements. In some cases, the financial reporting framework may encompass both financial reporting standards established by an authorized or recognized standards setting organization and legislative or regulatory requirements. Other sources may provide direction on the application of the applicable financial reporting framework. In some cases, the applicable financial reporting framework may encompass such other sources, or may even consist only of such sources. Such other sources may include:

- The legal and ethical environment, including statutes, regulations, court decisions, and professional ethical obligations in relation to accounting matters;
- Published accounting interpretations of varying authority issued by standards setting, professional or regulatory organizations;
- Published views of varying authority on emerging accounting issues issued by standards setting, professional or regulatory organizations;
- General and industry practices widely recognized and prevalent; and
- Accounting literature.

Where conflicts exist between the financial reporting framework and the sources from which direction on its application may be obtained, or among the sources that encompass the financial reporting framework, the source with the highest authority prevails.

A6   The requirements of the applicable financial reporting framework determine the form and content of the financial statements. Although the framework may not specify how to account for or disclose all transactions or events, it ordinarily embodies sufficient broad principles that can serve as a basis for developing and applying accounting policies that are consistent with the concepts underlying the requirements of the framework.

A7   Some financial reporting frameworks are fair presentation frameworks, while others are compliance frameworks. Financial reporting frameworks that encompass primarily the financial reporting standards established by an organization that is authorized or recognized to promulgate standards to be used by entities for preparing general purpose financial statements are often designed to achieve fair presentation, for example, International Financial Reporting Standards (IFRSs) issued by the International Accounting Standards Board (IASB).

A8   The requirements of the applicable financial reporting framework also determine what constitutes a complete set of financial statements. In the case of many frameworks, financial statements are intended to provide information about the financial position, financial performance and cash flows of an entity. For such frameworks, a complete set of financial statements would include a balance sheet; an income statement; a statement of changes in equity; a cash flow statement; and related notes. For some other financial reporting frameworks, a single financial statement and the related notes might constitute a complete set of financial statements:

- For example, the International Public Sector Accounting Standard (IPSAS), "Financial Reporting Under the Cash Basis of Accounting" issued by the International Public Sector Accounting Standards Board states that the primary financial statement is a statement of cash receipts and payments when a public sector entity prepares its financial statements in accordance with that IPSAS.
- Other examples of a single financial statement, each of which would include related notes, are:
  - Balance sheet.
  - Statement of income or statement of operations.
  - Statement of retained earnings.
  - Statement of cash flows.
  - Statement of assets and liabilities that does not include owner's equity.
  - Statement of changes in owners' equity.
  - Statement of revenue and expenses.
  - Statement of operations by product lines.

ISA (UK and Ireland) 210 establishes requirements and provides guidance on determining the acceptability of the applicable financial reporting framework.[5] ISA 800 deals with special considerations when financial statements are prepared in accordance with a special purpose framework.[6]   **A9**

Because of the significance of the premise to the conduct of an audit, the auditor is required to obtain the agreement of management and, where appropriate, those charged with governance that they acknowledge and understand that they have the responsibilities set out in paragraph A2 as a precondition for accepting the audit engagement.[7]   **A10**

*Considerations Specific to Audits in the Public Sector*

The mandates for audits of the financial statements of public sector entities may be broader than those of other entities. As a result, the premise, relating to management's responsibilities, on which an audit of the financial statements of a public sector entity is conducted may include additional responsibilities, such as the responsibility for the execution of transactions and events in accordance with law, regulation or other authority[8].   **A11**

[5] *ISA (UK and Ireland) 210, "Agreeing the Terms of Audit Engagements," paragraph 6(a).*

[6] *ISA 800, "Special Considerations—Audits of Financial Statements Prepared in Accordance with Special Purpose Frameworks," paragraph 8.*
*ISA 800 has not been promulgated by the APB for application in the UK and Ireland.*

[7] *ISA (UK and Ireland) 210 , paragraph 6(b).*

[8] *See paragraph A57.*

*Form of the Auditor's Opinion* (Ref: Para. 8)

A12    The opinion expressed by the auditor is on whether the financial statements are prepared, in all material respects, in accordance with the applicable financial reporting framework. The form of the auditor's opinion, however, will depend upon the applicable financial reporting framework and any applicable law or regulation. Most financial reporting frameworks include requirements relating to the presentation of the financial statements; for such frameworks, *preparation* of the financial statements in accordance with the applicable financial reporting framework includes *presentation*.

A13    Where the financial reporting framework is a fair presentation framework, as is generally the case for general purpose financial statements, the opinion required by the ISAs (UK and Ireland) is on whether the financial statements are presented fairly, in all material respects, or give a true and fair view. Where the financial reporting framework is a compliance framework, the opinion required is on whether the financial statements are prepared, in all material respects, in accordance with the framework. Unless specifically stated otherwise, references in the ISAs (UK and Ireland) to the auditor's opinion cover both forms of opinion.

**Ethical Requirements Relating to an Audit of Financial Statements** (Ref: Para. 14)

A14    The auditor is subject to relevant ethical requirements, including those pertaining to independence, relating to financial statement audit engagements. Relevant ethical requirements ordinarily comprise Parts A and B of the International Federation of Accountants' *Code of Ethics for Professional Accountants* (the IFAC Code) related to an audit of financial statements together with national requirements that are more restrictive.

A14-1    Auditors in the UK and Ireland are subject to ethical requirements from two sources: the Ethical Standards for Auditors established by APB concerning the integrity, objectivity and independence of the auditor, and the ethical pronouncements established by the auditor's relevant professional body. The APB is not aware of any significant instances where the relevant parts of the IFAC Code of Ethics are more restrictive than the Ethical Standards for Auditors.

A15    Part A of the IFAC Code establishes the fundamental principles of professional ethics relevant to the auditor when conducting an audit of financial statements and provides a conceptual framework for applying those principles. The fundamental principles with which the auditor is required to comply by the IFAC Code are:

(a)  Integrity;
(b)  Objectivity;
(c)  Professional competence and due care;
(d)  Confidentiality; and
(e)  Professional behavior.

Part B of the IFAC Code illustrates how the conceptual framework is to be applied in specific situations.

A16    In the case of an audit engagement it is in the public interest and, therefore, required by the IFAC Code, that the auditor be independent of the entity subject to the audit. The IFAC Code describes independence as comprising both independence of mind and independence in appearance. The auditor's independence from the entity safe-guards the auditor's ability to form an audit opinion without being affected by influences that might compromise that opinion. Independence enhances the auditor's ability to act with integrity, to be objective and to maintain an attitude of profes-sional skepticism.

International Standard on Quality Control (ISQC) 1[9]), or national requirements that are at least as demanding,[10] deal with the firm's responsibilities to establish and maintain its system of quality control for audit engagements. ISQC 1 sets out the responsibilities of the firm for establishing policies and procedures designed to provide it with reasonable assurance that the firm and its personnel comply with relevant ethical requirements, including those pertaining to independence.[11] ISA (UK and Ireland) 220 sets out the engagement partner's responsibilities with respect to relevant ethical requirements. These include remaining alert, through observation and making inquiries as necessary, for evidence of non-compliance with relevant ethical requirements by members of the engagement team, determining the appro-priate action if matters come to the engagement partner's attention that indicate that members of the engagement team have not complied with relevant ethical require-ments, and forming a conclusion on compliance with independence requirements that apply to the audit engagement.[12] ISA (UK and Ireland) 220 recognizes that the engagement team is entitled to rely on a firm's system of quality control in meeting its responsibilities with respect to quality control procedures applicable to the individual audit engagement, unless information provided by the firm or other parties suggests otherwise.    **A17**

## Professional Skepticism (Ref: Para. 15)

Professional skepticism includes being alert to, for example:    **A18**

- Audit evidence that contradicts other audit evidence obtained.
- Information that brings into question the reliability of documents and responses to inquiries to be used as audit evidence.
- Conditions that may indicate possible fraud.
- Circumstances that suggest the need for audit procedures in addition to those required by the ISAs (UK and Ireland).

Maintaining professional skepticism throughout the audit is necessary if the auditor is, for example, to reduce the risks of:    **A19**

- Overlooking unusual circumstances.
- Over generalizing when drawing conclusions from audit observations.
- Using inappropriate assumptions in determining the nature, timing, and extent of the audit procedures and evaluating the results thereof.

Professional skepticism is necessary to the critical assessment of audit evidence. This includes questioning contradictory audit evidence and the reliability of documents and responses to inquiries and other information obtained from management and those charged with governance. It also includes consideration of the sufficiency and    **A20**

---

[9] *International Standard on Quality Control (ISQC) 1, "Quality Control for Firms that Perform Audits and Reviews of Financial Statements, and Other Assurance and Related Services Engagements."*

[10] *See ISA (UK and Ireland) 220, "Quality Control for an Audit of Financial Statements," paragraph 2.*

[11] *(ISQC (UK and Ireland) 1, paragraphs 20-24.*

[12] *ISA (UK and Ireland) 220, paragraphs 9-11.*

appropriateness of audit evidence obtained in the light of the circumstances, for example in the case where fraud risk factors exist and a single document, of a nature that is susceptible to fraud, is the sole supporting evidence for a material financial statement amount.

A21   The auditor may accept records and documents as genuine unless the auditor has reason to believe the contrary. Nevertheless, the auditor is required to consider the reliability of information to be used as audit evidence.[13] In cases of doubt about the reliability of information or indications of possible fraud (for example, if conditions identified during the audit cause the auditor to believe that a document may not be authentic or that terms in a document may have been falsified), the ISAs (UK and Ireland) require that the auditor investigate further and determine what modifications or additions to audit procedures are necessary to resolve the matter.[14]

A22   The auditor cannot be expected to disregard past experience of the honesty and integrity of the entity's management and those charged with governance. Nevertheless, a belief that management and those charged with governance are honest and have integrity does not relieve the auditor of the need to maintain professional skepticism or allow the auditor to be satisfied with less-than-persuasive audit evidence when obtaining reasonable assurance.

## Professional Judgment (Ref: Para. 16)

A23   Professional judgment is essential to the proper conduct of an audit. This is because interpretation of relevant ethical requirements and the ISAs (UK and Ireland) and the informed decisions required throughout the audit cannot be made without the application of relevant knowledge and experience to the facts and circumstances. Professional judgment is necessary in particular regarding decisions about:

- Materiality and audit risk.
- The nature, timing, and extent of audit procedures used to meet the requirements of the ISAs (UK and Ireland) and gather audit evidence.
- Evaluating whether sufficient appropriate audit evidence has been obtained, and whether more needs to be done to achieve the objectives of the ISAs (UK and Ireland) and thereby, the overall objectives of the auditor.
- The evaluation of management's judgments in applying the entity's applicable financial reporting framework.
- The drawing of conclusions based on the audit evidence obtained, for example, assessing the reasonableness of the estimates made by management in preparing the financial statements.

A24   The distinguishing feature of the professional judgment expected of an auditor is that it is exercised by an auditor whose training, knowledge and experience have assisted in developing the necessary competencies to achieve reasonable judgments.

A25   The exercise of professional judgment in any particular case is based on the facts and circumstances that are known by the auditor. Consultation on difficult or contentious matters during the course of the audit, both within the engagement team and between the engagement team and others at the appropriate level within or outside

---

[13] *ISA (UK and Ireland) 500, "Audit Evidence," paragraphs 7-9.*

[14] *ISA (UK and Ireland) 240, paragraph 13; ISA (UK and Ireland) 500, paragraph 11; and ISA (UK and Ireland) 505, "External Confirmations," paragraphs 10-11, and 16.*

the firm, such as that required by ISA (UK and Ireland) 220,[15] assist the auditor in making informed and reasonable judgments.

Professional judgment can be evaluated based on whether the judgment reached reflects a competent application of auditing and accounting principles and is appropriate in the light of, and consistent with, the facts and circumstances that were known to the auditor up to the date of the auditor's report.  **A26**

Professional judgment needs to be exercised throughout the audit. It also needs to be appropriately documented. In this regard, the auditor is required to prepare audit documentation sufficient to enable an experienced auditor, having no previous connection with the audit, to understand the significant professional judgments made in reaching conclusions on significant matters arising during the audit.[16] Professional judgment is not to be used as the justification for decisions that are not otherwise supported by the facts and circumstances of the engagement or sufficient appropriate audit evidence.  **A27**

## Sufficient Appropriate Audit Evidence and Audit Risk (Ref: Para. 5 and 17)

### Sufficiency and Appropriateness of Audit Evidence

Audit evidence is necessary to support the auditor's opinion and report. It is cumulative in nature and is primarily obtained from audit procedures performed during the course of the audit. It may, however, also include information obtained from other sources such as previous audits (provided the auditor has determined whether changes have occurred since the previous audit that may affect its relevance to the current audit[17]) or a firm's quality control procedures for client acceptance and continuance. In addition to other sources inside and outside the entity, the entity's accounting records are an important source of audit evidence. Also, information that may be used as audit evidence may have been prepared by an expert employed or engaged by the entity. Audit evidence comprises both information that supports and corroborates management's assertions, and any information that contradicts such assertions. In addition, in some cases, the absence of information (for example, management's refusal to provide a requested representation) is used by the auditor, and therefore, also constitutes audit evidence. Most of the auditor's work in forming the auditor's opinion consists of obtaining and evaluating audit evidence.  **A28**

The sufficiency and appropriateness of audit evidence are interrelated. Sufficiency is the measure of the quantity of audit evidence. The quantity of audit evidence needed is affected by the auditor's assessment of the risks of misstatement (the higher the assessed risks, the more audit evidence is likely to be required) and also by the quality of such audit evidence (the higher the quality, the less may be required). Obtaining more audit evidence, however, may not compensate for its poor quality.  **A29**

Appropriateness is the measure of the quality of audit evidence; that is, its relevance and its reliability in providing support for the conclusions on which the auditor's opinion is based. The reliability of evidence is influenced by its source and by its nature, and is dependent on the individual circumstances under which it is obtained.  **A30**

---

[15] *ISA (UK and Ireland) 220, paragraph 18.*

[16] *ISA (UK and Ireland) 230, paragraph 8.*

[17] *ISA (UK and Ireland) 315, "Identifying and Assessing the Risks of Material Misstatement through Understanding the Entity and Its Environment," paragraph 9.*

A31  Whether sufficient appropriate audit evidence has been obtained to reduce audit risk to an acceptably low level, and thereby enable the auditor to draw reasonable conclusions on which to base the auditor's opinion, is a matter of professional judgment. ISA (UK and Ireland) 500 and other relevant ISAs (UK and Ireland) establish additional requirements and provide further guidance applicable through- out the audit regarding the auditor's considerations in obtaining sufficient appropriate audit evidence.

### Audit Risk

A32  Audit risk is a function of the risks of material misstatement and detection risk. The assessment of risks is based on audit procedures to obtain information necessary for that purpose and evidence obtained throughout the audit. The assessment of risks is a matter of professional judgment, rather than a matter capable of precise measurement.

A33  For purposes of the ISAs (UK and Ireland), audit risk does not include the risk that the auditor might express an opinion that the financial statements are materially misstated when they are not. This risk is ordinarily insignificant. Further, audit risk is a technical term related to the process of auditing; it does not refer to the auditor's business risks such as loss from litigation, adverse publicity, or other events arising in connection with the audit of financial statements.

### Risks of Material Misstatement

A34  The risks of material misstatement may exist at two levels:

- The overall financial statement level; and
- The assertion level for classes of transactions, account balances, and disclosures.

A35  Risks of material misstatement at the overall financial statement level refer to risks of material misstatement that relate pervasively to the financial statements as a whole and potentially affect many assertions.

A36  Risks of material misstatement at the assertion level are assessed in order to deter- mine the nature, timing, and extent of further audit procedures necessary to obtain sufficient appropriate audit evidence. This evidence enables the auditor to express an opinion on the financial statements at an acceptably low level of audit risk. Auditors use various approaches to accomplish the objective of assessing the risks of material misstatement. For example, the auditor may make use of a model that expresses the general relationship of the components of audit risk in mathematical terms to arrive at an acceptable level of detection risk. Some auditors find such a model to be useful when planning audit procedures.

A37  The risks of material misstatement at the assertion level consist of two components: inherent risk and control risk. Inherent risk and control risk are the entity's risks; they exist independently of the audit of the financial statements.

A38  Inherent risk is higher for some assertions and related classes of transactions, account balances, and disclosures than for others. For example, it may be higher for complex calculations or for accounts consisting of amounts derived from accounting estimates that are subject to significant estimation uncertainty. External circum- stances giving rise to business risks may also influence inherent risk. For example, technological developments might make a particular product obsolete, thereby causing inventory to be more susceptible to overstatement. Factors in the entity and its environment that relate to several or all of the classes of transactions, account balances, or disclosures may also influence the inherent risk related to a specific assertion. Such factors may include, for example, a lack of sufficient working capital to continue operations or a declining industry characterized by a large number of business failures.

Control risk is a function of the effectiveness of the design, implementation and maintenance of internal control by management to address identified risks that threaten the achievement of the entity's objectives relevant to preparation of the entity's financial statements. However, internal control, no matter how well designed and operated, can only reduce, but not eliminate, risks of material misstatement in the financial statements, because of the inherent limitations of internal control. These include, for example, the possibility of human errors or mistakes, or of controls being circumvented by collusion or inappropriate management override. Accordingly, some control risk will always exist. The ISAs (UK and Ireland) provide the conditions under which the auditor is required to, or may choose to, test the operating effectiveness of controls in determining the nature, timing and extent of substantive procedures to be performed.[18]      **A39**

The ISAs (UK and Ireland) do not ordinarily refer to inherent risk and control risk separately, but rather to a combined assessment of the "risks of material misstatement." However, the auditor may make separate or combined assessments of inherent and control risk depending on preferred audit techniques or methodologies and practical considerations. The assessment of the risks of material misstatement may be expressed in quantitative terms, such as in percentages, or in non-quantitative terms. In any case, the need for the auditor to make appropriate risk assessments is more important than the different approaches by which they may be made.      **A40**

ISA (UK and Ireland) 315 establishes requirements and provides guidance on identifying and assessing the risks of material misstatement at the financial statement and assertion levels.      **A41**

*Detection Risk*

For a given level of audit risk, the acceptable level of detection risk bears an inverse relationship to the assessed risks of material misstatement at the assertion level. For example, the greater the risks of material misstatement the auditor believes exists, the less the detection risk that can be accepted and, accordingly, the more persuasive the audit evidence required by the auditor.      **A42**

Detection risk relates to the nature, timing, and extent of the auditor's procedures that are determined by the auditor to reduce audit risk to an acceptably low level. It is therefore a function of the effectiveness of an audit procedure and of its application by the auditor. Matters such as:      **A43**

- adequate planning;
- proper assignment of personnel to the engagement team;
- the application of professional scepticism; and
- supervision and review of the audit work performed,

assist to enhance the effectiveness of an audit procedure and of its application and reduce the possibility that an auditor might select an inappropriate audit procedure, misapply an appropriate audit procedure, or misinterpret the audit results.

[18] *ISA (UK and Ireland) 330, "The Auditor's Reponses to Assessed Risks," paragraphs 7-17.*

**A44**    ISA (UK and Ireland) 300[19] and ISA (UK and Ireland) 330 establish requirements and provide guidance on planning an audit of financial statements and the auditor's responses to assessed risks. Detection risk, however, can only be reduced, not eliminated, because of the inherent limitations of an audit. Accordingly, some detection risk will always exist.

### Inherent Limitations of an Audit

**A45**    The auditor is not expected to, and cannot, reduce audit risk to zero and cannot therefore obtain absolute assurance that the financial statements are free from material misstatement due to fraud or error. This is because there are inherent limitations of an audit, which result in most of the audit evidence on which the auditor draws conclusions and bases the auditor's opinion being persuasive rather than conclusive. The inherent limitations of an audit arise from:

- The nature of financial reporting;
- The nature of audit procedures; and
- The need for the audit to be conducted within a reasonable period of time and at a reasonable cost.

### The Nature of Financial Reporting

**A46**    The preparation of financial statements involves judgment by management in applying the requirements of the entity's applicable financial reporting framework to the facts and circumstances of the entity. In addition, many financial statement items involve subjective decisions or assessments or a degree of uncertainty, and there may be a range of acceptable interpretations or judgments that may be made. Consequently, some financial statement items are subject to an inherent level of variability which cannot be eliminated by the application of additional auditing procedures. For example, this is often the case with respect to certain accounting estimates. Nevertheless, the ISAs (UK and Ireland) require the auditor to give specific consideration to whether accounting estimates are reasonable in the context of the applicable financial reporting framework and related disclosures, and to the qualitative aspects of the entity's accounting practices, including indicators of possible bias in management's judgments.[20]

### The Nature of Audit Procedures

**A47**    There are practical and legal limitations on the auditor's ability to obtain audit evidence. For example:

- There is the possibility that management or others may not provide, intentionally or unintentionally, the complete information that is relevant to the preparation of the financial statements or that has been requested by the auditor. Accordingly, the auditor cannot be certain of the completeness of

---

[19] *ISA (UK and Ireland) 300, "Planning an Audit of Financial Statements."*

[20] *ISA (UK and Ireland) 540, "Auditing Accounting Estimates, Including Fair Value Accounting Estimates, and Related Disclosures," and ISA 700, "Forming an Opinion and Reporting on Financial Statements," paragraph 12.*
*The APB has not promulgated ISA 700 as issued by the IAASB for application in the UK and Ireland. In the UK and Ireland the applicable auditing standard is ISA (UK and Ireland) 700, "The Auditor's Report on Financial Statements." Paragraph 8 of ISA (UK and Ireland) 700 includes requirements equivalent to those in paragraph 12 of ISA 700.*

information, even though the auditor has performed audit procedures to obtain assurance that all relevant information has been obtained.

- Fraud may involve sophisticated and carefully organized schemes designed to conceal it. Therefore, audit procedures used to gather audit evidence may be ineffective for detecting an intentional misstatement that involves, for example, collusion to falsify documentation which may cause the auditor to believe that audit evidence is valid when it is not. The auditor is neither trained as nor expected to be an expert in the authentication of documents.
- An audit is not an official investigation into alleged wrongdoing. Accordingly, the auditor is not given specific legal powers, such as the power of search, which may be necessary for such an investigation.

*Timeliness of Financial Reporting and the Balance between Benefit and Cost*

The matter of difficulty, time, or cost involved is not in itself a valid basis for the auditor to omit an audit procedure for which there is no alternative or to be satisfied with audit evidence that is less than persuasive. Appropriate planning assists in making sufficient time and resources available for the conduct of the audit. Notwithstanding this, the relevance of information, and thereby its value, tends to diminish over time, and there is a balance to be struck between the reliability of information and its cost. This is recognized in certain financial reporting frameworks (see, for example, the IASB's "Framework for the Preparation and Presentation of Financial Statements"). Therefore, there is an expectation by users of financial statements that the auditor will form an opinion on the financial statements within a reasonable period of time and at a reasonable cost, recognizing that it is impracticable to address all information that may exist or to pursue every matter exhaustively on the assumption that information is in error or fraudulent until proved otherwise.  **A48**

Consequently, it is necessary for the auditor to:  **A49**

- Plan the audit so that it will be performed in an effective manner;
- Direct audit effort to areas most expected to contain risks of material misstatement, whether due to fraud or error, with correspondingly less effort directed at other areas; and
- Use testing and other means of examining populations for misstatements.

In light of the approaches described in paragraph A49, the ISAs (UK and Ireland) contain requirements for the planning and performance of the audit and require the auditor, among other things, to:  **A50**

- Have a basis for the identification and assessment of risks of material misstatement at the financial statement and assertion levels by performing risk assessment procedures and related activities;[21] and
- Use testing and other means of examining populations in a manner that provides a reasonable basis for the auditor to draw conclusions about the population.[22]

[21] *ISA (UK and Ireland) 315, paragraphs 5-10.*

[22] *ISA (UK and Ireland) 330; ISA (UK and Ireland) 500; ISA 520, "Analytical Procedures;" and ISA (UK and Ireland) 530, "Audit Sampling."*

*Other Matters that Affect the Inherent Limitations of an Audit*

**A51**   In the case of certain assertions or subject matters, the potential effects of the inherent limitations on the auditor's ability to detect material misstatements are particularly significant. Such assertions or subject matters include:

- Fraud, particularly fraud involving senior management or collusion. See ISA (UK and Ireland) 240 for further discussion.
- The existence and completeness of related party relationships and transactions. See ISA (UK and Ireland) 550[23] for further discussion.
- The occurrence of non-compliance with laws and regulations. See ISA (UK and Ireland) 250[24] for further discussion.
- Future events or conditions that may cause an entity to cease to continue as a going concern. See ISA (UK and Ireland) 570[25] for further discussion.

Relevant ISAs (UK and Ireland) identify specific audit procedures to assist in mitigating the effect of the inherent limitations.

**A52**   Because of the inherent limitations of an audit, there is an unavoidable risk that some material misstatements of the financial statements may not be detected, even though the audit is properly planned and performed in accordance with ISAs (UK and Ireland). Accordingly, the subsequent discovery of a material misstatement of the financial statements resulting from fraud or error does not by itself indicate a failure to conduct an audit in accordance with ISAs (UK and Ireland). However, the inherent limitations of an audit are not a justification for the auditor to be satisfied with less-than-persuasive audit evidence. Whether the auditor has performed an audit in accordance with ISAs is determined by the audit procedures performed in the circumstances, the sufficiency and appropriateness of the audit evidence obtained as a result thereof and the suitability of the auditor's report based on an evaluation of that evidence in light of the overall objectives of the auditor.

## Conduct of an Audit in Accordance with ISAs (UK and Ireland)

*Nature of the ISAs (UK and Ireland)* (Ref: Para. 18)

**A53**   The ISAs (UK and Ireland), taken together, provide the standards for the auditor's work in fulfilling the overall objectives of the auditor. The ISAs (UK and Ireland) deal with the general responsibilities of the auditor, as well as the auditor's further considerations relevant to the application of those responsibilities to specific topics.

**A54**   The scope, effective date and any specific limitation of the applicability of a specific ISA (UK and Ireland) is made clear in the ISA (UK and Ireland). Unless otherwise stated in the ISA (UK and Ireland), the auditor is permitted to apply an ISA (UK and Ireland) before the effective date specified therein.

**A55**   In performing an audit, the auditor may be required to comply with legal or regulatory requirements in addition to the ISAs (UK and Ireland). The ISAs (UK and Ireland) do not override law or regulation that governs an audit of financial statements. In the event that such law or regulation differs from the ISAs (UK and

---

[23] *ISA (UK and Ireland) 550, "Related Parties."*

[24] *ISA (UK and Ireland) 250, "Consideration of Laws and Regulations in an Audit of Financial Statements."*

[25] *ISA (UK and Ireland) 570, "Going Concern."*

Ireland), an audit conducted only in accordance with law or regulation will not automatically comply with ISAs (UK and Ireland).

The auditor may also conduct the audit in accordance with both ISAs (UK and Ireland) and auditing standards of a specific jurisdiction or country. In such cases, in addition to complying with each of the ISAs (UK and Ireland) relevant to the audit, it may be necessary for the auditor to perform additional audit procedures in order to comply with the relevant standards of that jurisdiction or country.   **A56**

*Considerations Specific to Audits in the Public Sector*

The ISAs (UK and Ireland) are relevant to engagements in the public sector. The public sector auditor's responsibilities, however, may be affected by the audit mandate, or by obligations on public sector entities arising from law, regulation or other authority (such as ministerial directives, government policy requirements, or resolutions of the legislature), which may encompass a broader scope than an audit of financial statements in accordance with the ISAs (UK and Ireland). These additional responsibilities are not dealt with in the ISAs (UK and Ireland). They may be dealt with in the pronouncements of the International Organization of Supreme Audit Institutions or national standard setters, or in guidance developed by government audit agencies.   **A57**

*Contents of the ISAs (UK and Ireland)* (Ref: Para. 19)

In addition to objectives and requirements (requirements are expressed in the ISAs (UK and Ireland) using "shall"), an ISA (UK and Ireland) contains related guidance in the form of application and other explanatory material. It may also contain introductory material that provides context relevant to a proper understanding of the ISA (UK and Ireland), and definitions. The entire text of an ISA (UK and Ireland), therefore, is relevant to an understanding of the objectives stated in an ISA (UK and Ireland) and the proper application of the requirements of an ISA (UK and Ireland).   **A58**

Where necessary, the application and other explanatory material provides further explanation of the requirements of an ISA (UK and Ireland) and guidance for carrying them out. In particular, it may:   **A59**

- Explain more precisely what a requirement means or is intended to cover.
- Include examples of procedures that may be appropriate in the circumstances.

While such guidance does not in itself impose a requirement, it is relevant to the proper application of the requirements of an ISA (UK and Ireland). The application and other explanatory material may also provide background information on matters addressed in an ISA (UK and Ireland).

Appendices form part of the application and other explanatory material. The purpose and intended use of an appendix are explained in the body of the related ISA (UK and Ireland) or within the title and introduction of the appendix itself.   **A60**

Introductory material may include, as needed, such matters as explanation of:   **A61**

- The purpose and scope of the ISA (UK and Ireland), including how the ISA (UK and Ireland) relates to other ISAs (UK and Ireland).
- The subject matter of the ISA (UK and Ireland).
- The respective responsibilities of the auditor and others in relation to the subject matter of the ISA (UK and Ireland).
- The context in which the ISA (UK and Ireland) is set.

A62   An ISA (UK and Ireland) may include, in a separate section under the heading "Definitions," a description of the meanings attributed to certain terms for purposes of the ISAs (UK and Ireland). These are provided to assist in the consistent application and interpretation of the ISAs (UK and Ireland), and are not intended to override definitions that may be established for other purposes, whether in law, regulation or otherwise. Unless otherwise indicated, those terms will carry the same meanings throughout the ISAs (UK and Ireland). The Glossary of Terms relating to International Standards issued by the International Auditing and Assurance Standards Board in the *Handbook of International Auditing, Assurance, and Ethics Pronouncements* published by IFAC contains a complete listing of terms defined in the ISAs (UK and Ireland). It also includes descriptions of other terms found in ISAs (UK and Ireland) to assist in common and consistent interpretation and translation.

A63   When appropriate, additional considerations specific to audits of smaller entities and public sector entities are included within the application and other explanatory material of an ISA (UK and Ireland). These additional considerations assist in the application of the requirements of the ISA (UK and Ireland) in the audit of such entities. They do not, however, limit or reduce the responsibility of the auditor to apply and comply with the requirements of the ISAs (UK and Ireland).

*Considerations Specific to Smaller Entities*

A64   For purposes of specifying additional considerations to audits of smaller entities, a "smaller entity" refers to an entity which typically possesses qualitative characteristics such as:

   (a)   Concentration of ownership and management in a small number of individuals (often a single individual – either a natural person or another enterprise that owns the entity provided the owner exhibits the relevant qualitative characteristics); and
   (b)   One or more of the following:
      (i)   Straightforward or uncomplicated transactions;
      (ii)   Simple record-keeping;
      (iii)   Few lines of business and few products within business lines;
      (iv)   Few internal controls;
      (v)   Few levels of management with responsibility for a broad range of controls; or
      (vi)   Few personnel, many having a wide range of duties.

These qualitative characteristics are not exhaustive, they are not exclusive to smaller entities, and smaller entities do not necessarily display all of these characteristics.

A65   The considerations specific to smaller entities included in the ISAs (UK and Ireland) have been developed primarily with unlisted entities in mind. Some of the considerations, however, may be helpful in audits of smaller listed entities.

A66   The ISAs (UK and Ireland) refer to the proprietor of a smaller entity who is involved in running the entity on a day-to-day basis as the "owner-manager."

**Objectives Stated in Individual ISAs (UK and Ireland)** (Ref: Para. 21)

A67   Each ISA (UK and Ireland) contains one or more objectives which provide a link between the requirements and the overall objectives of the auditor. The objectives in individual ISAs (UK and Ireland) serve to focus the auditor on the desired outcome of the ISA (UK and Ireland), while being specific enough to assist the auditor in:

- Understanding what needs to be accomplished and, where necessary, the appropriate means of doing so; and
- Deciding whether more needs to be done to achieve them in the particular circumstances of the audit.

Objectives are to be understood in the context of the overall objectives of the auditor stated in paragraph 11 of this ISA (UK and Ireland). As with the overall objectives of the auditor, the ability to achieve an individual objective is equally subject to the inherent limitations of an audit.  **A68**

In using the objectives, the auditor is required to have regard to the interrelationships among the ISAs (UK and Ireland). This is because, as indicated in paragraph A53, the ISAs (UK and Ireland) deal in some cases with general responsibilities and in others with the application of those responsibilities to specific topics. For example, this ISA (UK and Ireland) requires the auditor to adopt an attitude of professional skepticism; this is necessary in all aspects of planning and performing an audit but is not repeated as a requirement of each ISA (UK and Ireland). At a more detailed level, ISA (UK and Ireland) 315 and ISA (UK and Ireland) 330 contain, among other things, objectives and requirements that deal with the auditor's responsibilities to identify and assess the risks of material misstatement and to design and perform further audit procedures to respond to those assessed risks, respectively; these objectives and requirements apply throughout the audit. An ISA (UK and Ireland) dealing with specific aspects of the audit (for example, ISA (UK and Ireland) 540) may expand on how the objectives and requirements of such ISAs (UK and Ireland) as ISA (UK and Ireland) 315 and ISA (UK and Ireland) 330 are to be applied in relation to the subject of the ISA (UK and Ireland) but does not repeat them. Thus, in achieving the objective stated in ISA (UK and Ireland) 540, the auditor has regard to the objectives and requirements of other relevant ISAs (UK and Ireland).  **A69**

*Use of Objectives to Determine Need for Additional Audit Procedures (Ref: Para. 21(a))*

The requirements of the ISAs (UK and Ireland) are designed to enable the auditor to achieve the objectives specified in the ISAs (UK and Ireland), and thereby the overall objectives of the auditor. The proper application of the requirements of the ISAs (UK and Ireland) by the auditor is therefore expected to provide a sufficient basis for the auditor's achievement of the objectives. However, because the circumstances of audit engagements vary widely and all such circumstances cannot be anticipated in the ISAs (UK and Ireland), the auditor is responsible for determining the audit procedures necessary to fulfill the requirements of the ISAs (UK and Ireland) and to achieve the objectives. In the circumstances of an engagement, there may be particular matters that require the auditor to perform audit procedures in addition to those required by the ISAs (UK and Ireland) to meet the objectives specified in the ISAs (UK and Ireland).  **A70**

*Use of Objectives to Evaluate Whether Sufficient Appropriate Audit Evidence Has Been Obtained (Ref: Para. 21(b))*

The auditor is required to use the objectives to evaluate whether sufficient appropriate audit evidence has been obtained in the context of the overall objectives of the auditor. If as a result the auditor concludes that the audit evidence is not sufficient and appropriate, then the auditor may follow one or more of the following approaches to meeting the requirement of paragraph 21(b):  **A71**

- Evaluate whether further relevant audit evidence has been, or will be, obtained as a result of complying with other ISAs (UK and Ireland);
- Extend the work performed in applying one or more requirements; or
- Perform other procedures judged by the auditor to be necessary in the circumstances.

Where none of the above is expected to be practical or possible in the circumstances, the auditor will not be able to obtain sufficient appropriate audit evidence and is required by the ISAs (UK and Ireland) to determine the effect on the auditor's report or on the auditor's ability to complete the engagement.

### Complying with Relevant Requirements

*Relevant Requirements (Ref: Para. 22)*

A72   In some cases, an ISA (UK and Ireland) (and therefore all of its requirements) may not be relevant in the circumstances. For example, if an entity does not have an internal audit function, nothing in ISA (UK and Ireland) 610[26] is relevant.

A73   Within a relevant ISA (UK and Ireland), there may be conditional requirements. Such a requirement is relevant when the circumstances envisioned in the requirement apply and the condition exists. In general, the conditionality of a requirement will either be explicit or implicit, for example:

- The requirement to modify the auditor's opinion if there is a limitation of scope[27] represents an explicit conditional requirement.
- The requirement to communicate significant deficiencies in internal control identified during the audit to those charged with governance,[28] which depends on the existence of such identified significant deficiencies; and the requirement to obtain sufficient appropriate audit evidence regarding the presentation and disclosure of segment information in accordance with the applicable financial reporting framework,[29] which depends on that framework requiring or permitting such disclosure, represent implicit conditional requirements.

In some cases, a requirement may be expressed as being conditional on applicable law or regulation. For example, the auditor may be required to withdraw from the audit engagement, *where withdrawal is possible under applicable law or regulation*, or the auditor may be required to do something, *unless prohibited by law or regulation*. Depending on the jurisdiction, the legal or regulatory permission or prohibition may be explicit or implicit.

---

[26] *ISA (UK and Ireland) 610, "Using the Work of Internal Auditors."*

[27] *ISA (UK and Ireland) 705, "Modifications to the Opinion in the Independent Auditor's Report," paragraph 13.*

[28] *ISA (UK and Ireland) 265, "Communicating Deficiencies in Internal Control to Those Charged with Governance and Management," paragraph 9.*

[29] *ISA (UK and Ireland) 501, "Audit Evidence—Specific Considerations for Selected Items," paragraph 13.*

*Departure from a Requirement (Ref: Para. 23)*

ISA (UK and Ireland) 230 establishes documentation requirements in those excep-     **A74**
tional circumstances where the auditor departs from a relevant requirement.[30] The
ISAs (UK and Ireland) do not call for compliance with a requirement that is not
relevant in the circumstances of the audit.

**Failure to Achieve an Objective** (Ref: Para. 24)

Whether an objective has been achieved is a matter for the auditor's professional     **A75**
judgment. That judgment takes account of the results of audit procedures performed
in complying with the requirements of the ISAs (UK and Ireland), and the auditor's
evaluation of whether sufficient appropriate audit evidence has been obtained and
whether more needs to be done in the particular circumstances of the audit to achieve
the objectives stated in the ISAs (UK and Ireland). Accordingly, circumstances that
may give rise to a failure to achieve an objective include those that:

- Prevent the auditor from complying with the relevant requirements of an ISA
  (UK and Ireland).
- Result in its not being practicable or possible for the auditor to carry out the
  additional audit procedures or obtain further audit evidence as determined
  necessary from the use of the objectives in accordance with paragraph 21, for
  example due to a limitation in the available audit evidence.

Audit documentation that meets the requirements of ISA (UK and Ireland) 230 and     **A76**
the specific documentation requirements of other relevant ISAs (UK and Ireland)
provides evidence of the auditor's basis for a conclusion about the achievement of
the overall objectives of the auditor. While it is unnecessary for the auditor to
document separately (as in a checklist, for example) that individual objectives have
been achieved, the documentation of a failure to achieve an objective assists the
auditor's evaluation of whether such a failure has prevented the auditor from
achieving the overall objectives of the auditor.

[30] *ISA (UK and Ireland) 230, paragraph 12.*

# Addendum

*This addendum provides a summary of APB's rationale for retaining or excluding in the proposed clarified ISA (UK and Ireland) the supplementary requirements in the existing ISA (UK and Ireland). It also sets out the supplementary guidance material in the existing ISA (UK and Ireland) that APB considers is not necessary to retain in light of the improvements in the underlying Clarity ISAs issued by the IAASB as part of the Clarity Project. It is provided for information and does not form part of the proposed clarified ISA (UK and Ireland).*

*The Consultation Paper published with the exposure drafts explains the general approach used by the APB for determining whether current supplementary material should be proposed to be retained.*

## Analysis of proposed treatment of existing APB supplementary material in current ISA (UK and Ireland) 200

Note that underlying ISA 200 has been revised as well as redrafted in the IAASB Clarity Project.

## Requirements

| APB supplementary requirement | Is it covered in substance in the Clarity ISA? | Should it be retained? |
|---|---|---|
| 4-1.  **In the UK and Ireland the relevant ethical pronouncements with which the auditor should comply are the APB's Ethical Standards and the ethical pronouncements relating to the work of auditors issued by the auditor's relevant professional body.** | – The requirement in the revised ISA (para 14) is that auditors shall comply with 'relevant ethical requirements'. In the application material (para A14), this stated to ordinarily comprise parts A and B of IFAC Code plus more restrictive national requirements). | ✗ But guidance has been added explaining the regulatory position in the UK and Ireland (i.e. APB and professional bodies ethical requirements apply).  **A14-1** |

## Guidance

The following guidance in current ISA (UK and Ireland) 200 has not been carried forward to the proposed clarified standard.

| Current paragraph reference (*Italic text is from IAASB for context*) |
|---|
| 1-1. This ISA (UK and Ireland) uses the terms 'those charged with governance' and 'management'. The term 'governance' describes the role of persons entrusted with the supervision, control and direction of an entity. Ordinarily, those charged with governance are accountable for ensuring that the entity achieves its objectives, and for the quality of its financial reporting and reporting to interested parties. Those charged with governance include management only when they perform such functions. |
| 1-3. 'Management' comprises those persons who perform senior managerial functions. |
| 2-1. The "applicable financial reporting framework" comprises those requirements of accounting standards, law and regulations applicable to the entity that determine the form and content of its financial statements |
| 7-1. Although the basic principles of auditing are the same in the public and the private sectors, the auditor of a public service body often has wider objectives and additional duties and statutory responsibilities, laid down in legislation, directives or codes of practice. |
| 9. *An auditor cannot obtain absolute assurance because there are inherent limitations in an audit that affect the auditor's ability to detect material misstatements. These limitations result from factors such as:*<br>• The impracticality of examining all items within a class of transactions or account balance.<br>• The possibility of collusion or misrepresentation for fraudulent purposes. |
| 9-1. The view given in financial statements is itself based on a combination of fact and judgment and, consequently, cannot be characterized as either 'absolute' or 'correct'. A degree of imprecision is inevitable in the preparation of all but the simplest of financial statements because of inherent uncertainties and the need to use judgment in making accounting estimates and selecting appropriate accounting policies. |

# Proposed Clarified International Standard on Auditing (UK and Ireland) 210

## Agreeing the terms of audit engagements

*(Effective for audits of financial statements for periods ending on or after 15 December 2010)*

## Contents

International Standard on Auditing (UK and Ireland) (ISA (UK and Ireland)) 210, "Agreeing the Terms of Audit Engagements" should be read in conjunction with ISA (UK and Ireland) 200, "Overall Objectives of the Independent Auditor and the Conduct of an Audit in Accordance with International Standards on Auditing (UK and Ireland)."

# Introduction

## Scope of this ISA (UK and Ireland)

This International Standard on Auditing (UK and Ireland) (ISA (UK and Ireland)) **1** deals with the auditor's responsibilities in agreeing the terms of the audit engagement with management and, where appropriate, those charged with governance. This includes establishing that certain preconditions for an audit, responsibility for which rests with management and, where appropriate, those charged with governance, are present. ISA (UK and Ireland) 220[1] deals with those aspects of engagement acceptance that are within the control of the auditor. (Ref: Para. A1)

## Effective Date

This ISA (UK and Ireland) is effective for audits of financial statements for periods **2** ending on or after 15 December 2010.

# Objective

The objective of the auditor is to accept or continue an audit engagement only when **3** the basis upon which it is to be performed has been agreed, through:

(a) Establishing whether the preconditions for an audit are present; and
(b) Confirming that there is a common understanding between the auditor and management and, where appropriate, those charged with governance of the terms of the audit engagement.

# Definitions

For purposes of the ISAs (UK and Ireland), the following term has the meaning **4** attributed below:

Preconditions for an audit – The use by management[1a] of an acceptable financial reporting framework in the preparation of the financial statements and the agreement of management and, where appropriate, those charged with governance to the premise[2] on which an audit is conducted.

For the purposes of this ISA (UK and Ireland), references to "management" should **5** be read hereafter as "management and, where appropriate, those charged with governance."

---

[1] *ISA (UK and Ireland) 220, "Quality Control for an Audit of Financial Statements."*

[1a] *In the UK and Ireland those charged with governance are responsible for the preparation of the financial statements.*

[2] *ISA (UK and Ireland) 200, "Overall Objectives of the Independent Auditor and the Conduct of an Audit in Accordance with International Standards on Auditing," paragraph 13.*

# Requirements

## Preconditions for an Audit

6   In order to establish whether the preconditions for an audit are present, the auditor shall:

(a)   Determine whether the financial reporting framework to be applied in the preparation of the financial statements is acceptable; and (Ref: Para. A2-A10)

(b)   Obtain the agreement of management that it acknowledges and understands its responsibility: (Ref: Para A11-A14, A20)

   (i)   For the preparation of the financial statements in accordance with the applicable financial reporting framework, including where relevant their fair presentation; (Ref: Para. A15)

   (ii)   For such internal control as management determines is necessary to enable the preparation of financial statements that are free from material misstatement, whether due to fraud or error; and (Ref: Para. A16-A19)

   (iii)   To provide the auditor with[2a]:

   a.   Access to all information of which management is aware that is relevant to the preparation of the financial statements such as records, documentation and other matters;

   b.   Additional information that the auditor may request from management for the purpose of the audit; and

   c.   Unrestricted access to persons within the entity from whom the auditor determines it necessary to obtain audit evidence.

### *Limitation on Scope Prior to Audit Engagement Acceptance*

7   If management or those charged with governance impose a limitation on the scope of the auditor's work in the terms of a proposed audit engagement such that the auditor believes the limitation will result in the auditor disclaiming an opinion on the financial statements, the auditor shall not accept such a limited engagement as an audit engagement, unless required by law or regulation to do so.

### *Other Factors Affecting Audit Engagement Acceptance*

8   If the preconditions for an audit are not present, the auditor shall discuss the matter with management. Unless required by law or regulation to do so, the auditor shall not accept the proposed audit engagement:

(a)   If the auditor has determined that the financial reporting framework to be applied in the preparation of the financial statements is unacceptable, except as provided in paragraph 19; or

(b)   If the agreement referred to in paragraph 6(b) has not been obtained.

## Agreement on Audit Engagement Terms

9   The auditor shall agree the terms of the audit engagement with management or those charged with governance, as appropriate[2b]. (Ref: Para. A21)

---

[2a] *Sections 499 and 500 of the Companies Act 2006 set legal requirements in relation to the auditor's right to obtain information. For the Republic of Ireland, relevant requirements are set out in Section 193(3), Companies Act 1990.*

[2b] *In the UK and Ireland the terms of the audit engagement are agreed with those charged with governance.*

Subject to paragraph 11, the agreed terms of the audit engagement shall be recorded   **10**
in an audit engagement letter or other suitable form of written agreement and shall
include: (Ref: Para. A22-A25)

(a) The objective and scope of the audit of the financial statements;
(b) The responsibilities of the auditor;
(c) The responsibilities of management;
(d) Identification of the applicable financial reporting framework for the preparation of the financial statements; and
(e) Reference to the expected form and content of any reports to be issued by the
 auditor and a statement that there may be circumstances in which a report may
 differ from its expected form and content.

If law or regulation prescribes in sufficient detail the terms of the audit engagement   **11**
referred to in paragraph 10, the auditor need not record them in a written agreement,
except for the fact that such law or regulation applies and that management
acknowledges and understands its responsibilities as set out in paragraph 6(b). (Ref:
Para. A22, A26-A27)

If law or regulation prescribes responsibilities of management similar to those   **12**
described in paragraph 6(b), the auditor may determine that the law or regulation
includes responsibilities that, in the auditor's judgment, are equivalent in effect to
those set out in that paragraph. For such responsibilities that are equivalent, the
auditor may use the wording of the law or regulation to describe them in the written
agreement. For those responsibilities that are not prescribed by law or regulation
such that their effect is equivalent, the written agreement shall use the description in
paragraph 6(b). (Ref: Para. A26)

## Recurring Audits

On recurring audits, the auditor shall assess whether circumstances require the terms   **13**
of the audit engagement to be revised and whether there is a need to remind the
entity of the existing terms of the audit engagement. (Ref: Para. A28)

## Acceptance of a Change in the Terms of the Audit Engagement

The auditor shall not agree to a change in the terms of the audit engagement where   **14**
there is no reasonable justification for doing so. (Ref: Para. A29-A31)

If, prior to completing the audit engagement, the auditor is requested to change the   **15**
audit engagement to an engagement that conveys a lower level of assurance, the
auditor shall determine whether there is reasonable justification for doing so. (Ref:
Para. A32-A33)

If the terms of the audit engagement are changed, the auditor and management shall   **16**
agree on and record the new terms of the engagement in an engagement letter or
other suitable form of written agreement.

If the auditor is unable to agree to a change of the terms of the audit engagement and   **17**
is not permitted by management to continue the original audit engagement, the
auditor shall:

(a) Withdraw from the audit engagement where possible under applicable law or
 regulation; and

(b)  Determine whether there is any obligation, either contractual or otherwise, to report the circumstances to other parties, such as those charged with governance, owners or regulators. (Ref: Para. A33-1)

## Additional Considerations in Engagement Acceptance

### *Financial Reporting Standards Supplemented by Law or Regulation*

**18**  If financial reporting standards established by an authorized or recognized standards setting organization are supplemented by law or regulation, the auditor shall determine whether there are any conflicts between the financial reporting standards and the additional requirements. If such conflicts exist, the auditor shall discuss with management the nature of the additional requirements and shall agree whether:

(a)  The additional requirements can be met through additional disclosures in the financial statements; or

(b)  The description of the applicable financial reporting framework in the financial statements can be amended accordingly.

If neither of the above actions is possible, the auditor shall determine whether it will be necessary to modify the auditor's opinion in accordance with ISA (UK and Ireland) 705.[3] (Ref: Para. A34)

### *Financial Reporting Framework Prescribed by Law or Regulation—Other Matters Affecting Acceptance*

**19**  If the auditor has determined that the financial reporting framework prescribed by law or regulation would be unacceptable but for the fact that it is prescribed by law or regulation, the auditor shall accept the audit engagement only if the following conditions are present: (Ref: Para. A35)

(a)  Management agrees to provide additional disclosures in the financial statements required to avoid the financial statements being misleading; and

(b)  It is recognized in the terms of the audit engagement that:

(i)  The auditor's report on the financial statements will incorporate an Emphasis of Matter paragraph, drawing users' attention to the additional disclosures, in accordance with ISA (UK and Ireland) 706;[4] and

(ii)  Unless the auditor is required by law or regulation to express the auditor's opinion on the financial statements by using the phrases "present fairly, in all material respects," or "give a true and fair view" in accordance with the applicable financial reporting framework, the auditor's opinion on the financial statements will not include such phrases.

**20**  If the conditions outlined in paragraph 19 are not present and the auditor is required by law or regulation to undertake the audit engagement, the auditor shall:

(a)  Evaluate the effect of the misleading nature of the financial statements on the auditor's report; and

(b)  Include appropriate reference to this matter in the terms of the audit engagement.

[3] *ISA (UK and Ireland) 705, "Modifications to the Opinion in the Independent Auditor's Report."*

[4] *ISA (UK and Ireland) 706, "Emphasis of Matter Paragraphs and Other Matter Paragraphs in the Independent Auditor's Report."*

**Auditor's Report Prescribed by Law or Regulation**

In some cases, law or regulation of the relevant jurisdiction prescribes the layout or **21** wording of the auditor's report in a form or in terms that are significantly different from the requirements of ISAs (UK and Ireland). In these circumstances, the auditor shall evaluate:

(a) Whether users might misunderstand the assurance obtained from the audit of the financial statements and, if so,
(b) Whether additional explanation in the auditor's report can mitigate possible misunderstanding.[5]

If the auditor concludes that additional explanation in the auditor's report cannot mitigate possible misunderstanding, the auditor shall not accept the audit engagement, unless required by law or regulation to do so. An audit conducted in accordance with such law or regulation does not comply with ISAs (UK and Ireland). Accordingly, the auditor shall not include any reference within the auditor's report to the audit having been conducted in accordance with ISAs (UK and Ireland).[6] (Ref: Para. A36-A37)

\*\*\*

# Application and Other Explanatory Material

## Scope of this ISA (UK and Ireland) (Ref: Para. 1)

Assurance engagements, which include audit engagements, may only be accepted **A1** when the practitioner considers that relevant ethical requirements such as independence and professional competence will be satisfied, and when the engagement exhibits certain characteristics.[7] The auditor's responsibilities in respect of ethical requirements in the context of the acceptance of an audit engagement and in so far as they are within the control of the auditor are dealt with in ISA (UK and Ireland) 220.[8] This ISA (UK and Ireland) deals with those matters (or preconditions) that are within the control of the entity and upon which it is necessary for the auditor and the entity's management to agree.

---

[5] *ISA (UK and Ireland) 706.*

[6] *See also ISA 700, "Forming an Opinion and Reporting on Financial Statements," paragraph 43.*
*The APB has not promulgated ISA 700 as issued by the IAASB for application in the UK and Ireland. In the UK and Ireland the applicable auditing standard is ISA (UK and Ireland) 700, "The Auditor's Report on Financial Statements." Paragraph 5 of ISA (UK and Ireland) 700 explains that compliance with that ISA (UK and Ireland) does not preclude the auditor from being able to assert compliance with ISAs in the circumstances contemplated by paragraph 43 of ISA 700.*

[7] *"International Framework for Assurance Engagements," paragraph 17.*
*The "International Framework for Assurance Engagements" has not been promulgated by the APB for application in the UK and Ireland.*

[8] *ISA (UK and Ireland) 220, paragraphs 9-11.*

## Preconditions for an Audit

*The Financial Reporting Framework* (Ref: Para. 6(a))

A2    A condition for acceptance of an assurance engagement is that the criteria referred to in the definition of an assurance engagement are suitable and available to intended users.[9] Criteria are the benchmarks used to evaluate or measure the subject matter including, where relevant, benchmarks for presentation and disclosure. Suitable criteria enable reasonably consistent evaluation or measurement of a subject matter within the context of professional judgment. For purposes of the ISAs (UK and Ireland), the applicable financial reporting framework provides the criteria the auditor uses to audit the financial statements, including where relevant their fair presentation.

A3    Without an acceptable financial reporting framework, management does not have an appropriate basis for the preparation of the financial statements and the auditor does not have suitable criteria for auditing the financial statements. In many cases the auditor may presume that the applicable financial reporting framework is acceptable, as described in paragraphs A8-A9.

*Determining the Acceptability of the Financial Reporting Framework*

A4    Factors that are relevant to the auditor's determination of the acceptability of the financial reporting framework to be applied in the preparation of the financial statements include:

- The nature of the entity (for example, whether it is a business enterprise, a public sector entity or a not for profit organization);
- The purpose of the financial statements (for example, whether they are prepared to meet the common financial information needs of a wide range of users or the financial information needs of specific users);
- The nature of the financial statements (for example, whether the financial statements are a complete set of financial statements or a single financial statement); and
- Whether law or regulation prescribes the applicable financial reporting framework.

A5    Many users of financial statements are not in a position to demand financial statements tailored to meet their specific information needs. While all the information needs of specific users cannot be met, there are financial information needs that are common to a wide range of users. Financial statements prepared in accordance with a financial reporting framework designed to meet the common financial information needs of a wide range of users are referred to as general purpose financial statements.

A6    In some cases, the financial statements will be prepared in accordance with a financial reporting framework designed to meet the financial information needs of specific users. Such financial statements are referred to as special purpose financial statements. The financial information needs of the intended users will determine the

---

[9] *"International Framework for Assurance Engagements," paragraph 17(b)(ii).*
*The "International Framework for Assurance Engagements" has not been promulgated by the APB for application in the UK and Ireland.*

applicable financial reporting framework in these circumstances. ISA 800 discusses the acceptability of financial reporting frameworks designed to meet the financial information needs of specific users.[10]

Deficiencies in the applicable financial reporting framework that indicate that the **A7** framework is not acceptable may be encountered after the audit engagement has been accepted. When use of that framework is prescribed by law or regulation, the requirements of paragraphs 19-20 apply. When use of that framework is not pre-scribed by law or regulation, management may decide to adopt another framework that is acceptable. When management does so, as required by paragraph 16, new terms of the audit engagement are agreed to reflect the change in the framework as the previously agreed terms will no longer be accurate.

*General purpose frameworks*

At present, there is no objective and authoritative basis that has been generally **A8** recognized globally for judging the acceptability of general purpose frameworks. In the absence of such a basis, financial reporting standards established by organiza-tions that are authorized or recognized to promulgate standards to be used by certain types of entities are presumed to be acceptable for general purpose financial state-ments prepared by such entities, provided the organizations follow an established and transparent process involving deliberation and consideration of the views of a wide range of stakeholders. Examples of such financial reporting standards include:

- International Financial Reporting Standards (IFRSs) promulgated by the International Accounting Standards Board;
- International Public Sector Accounting Standards (IPSASs) promulgated by the International Public Sector Accounting Standards Board; and
- Accounting principles promulgated by an authorized or recognized standards setting organization in a particular jurisdiction, provided the organization fol-lows an established and transparent process involving deliberation and consideration of the views of a wide range of stakeholders.

These financial reporting standards are often identified as the applicable financial reporting framework in law or regulation governing the preparation of general purpose financial statements.

*Financial reporting frameworks prescribed by law or regulation*

In accordance with paragraph 6(a), the auditor is required to determine whether the **A9** financial reporting framework, to be applied in the preparation of the financial statements, is acceptable. In some jurisdictions, law or regulation may prescribe the financial reporting framework to be used in the preparation of general purpose financial statements for certain types of entities. In the absence of indications to the contrary, such a financial reporting framework is presumed to be acceptable for general purpose financial statements prepared by such entities. In the event that the framework is not considered to be acceptable, paragraphs 19-20 apply.

---

[10] *ISA 800, "Special Considerations—Audits of Financial Statements Prepared in Accordance with Special Purpose Frameworks," paragraph 8.*
*ISA 800 has not been promulgated by the APB for application in the UK and Ireland.*

*Jurisdictions that do not have standards setting organizations or prescribed financial reporting frameworks*

A10    When an entity is registered or operating in a jurisdiction that does not have an authorized or recognized standards setting organization, or where use of the financial reporting framework is not prescribed by law or regulation, management identifies a financial reporting framework to be applied in the preparation of the financial statements. Appendix 2 contains guidance on determining the acceptability of financial reporting frameworks in such circumstances.

**Agreement of the Responsibilities of Management** (Ref: Para. 6(b))

A11    An audit in accordance with ISAs is conducted on the premise that management has acknowledged and understands that it has the responsibilities set out in paragraph 6(b).[11] In certain jurisdictions, such responsibilities may be specified in law or regulation. In others, there may be little or no legal or regulatory definition of such responsibilities. ISAs (UK and Ireland) do not override law or regulation in such matters. However, the concept of an independent audit requires that the auditor's role does not involve taking responsibility for the preparation of the financial statements or for the entity's related internal control, and that the auditor has a reasonable expectation of obtaining the information necessary for the audit in so far as management is able to provide or procure it. Accordingly, the premise is fundamental to the conduct of an independent audit. To avoid misunderstanding, agreement is reached with management that it acknowledges and understands that it has such responsibilities as part of agreeing and recording the terms of the audit engagement in paragraphs 9-12.

A12    The way in which the responsibilities for financial reporting are divided between management and those charged with governance will vary according to the resources and structure of the entity and any relevant law or regulation, and the respective roles of management and those charged with governance within the entity. In most cases, management is responsible for execution while those charged with governance have oversight of management. In some cases, those charged with governance will have, or will assume, responsibility for approving the financial statements or monitoring the entity's internal control related to financial reporting. In larger or public entities, a subgroup of those charged with governance, such as an audit committee, may be charged with certain oversight responsibilities.

A13    ISA (UK and Ireland) 580 requires the auditor to request management to provide written representations that it has fulfilled certain of its responsibilities.[12] It may therefore be appropriate to make management aware that receipt of such written representations will be expected, together with written representations required by other ISAs (UK and Ireland) and, where necessary, written representations to support other audit evidence relevant to the financial statements or one or more specific assertions in the financial statements.

A14    Where management will not acknowledge its responsibilities, or agree to provide the written representations, the auditor will be unable to obtain sufficient appropriate audit evidence.[13] In such circumstances, it would not be appropriate for the auditor to accept the audit engagement, unless law or regulation requires the auditor to do

---

[11] *ISA (UK and Ireland) 200, paragraph A2.*

[12] *ISA (UK and Ireland) 580, "Written Representations," paragraphs 10-11.*

[13] *ISA (UK and Ireland) 580, paragraph A26.*

so. In cases where the auditor is required to accept the audit engagement, the auditor may need to explain to management the importance of these matters, and the implications for the auditor's report.

*Preparation of the Financial Statements (Ref: Para 6(b)(i))*

Most financial reporting frameworks include requirements relating to the presenta-   **A15**
tion of the financial statements; for such frameworks, *preparation* of the financial statements in accordance with the financial reporting framework includes *presentation*. In the case of a fair presentation framework the importance of the reporting objective of fair presentation is such that the premise agreed with management includes specific reference to fair presentation, or to the responsibility to ensure that the financial statements will "give a true and fair view" in accordance with the financial reporting framework.

*Internal Control (Ref: Para. 6(b)(ii))*

Management maintains such internal control as it determines is necessary to enable   **A16**
the preparation of financial statements that are free from material misstatement, whether due to fraud or error. Internal control, no matter how effective, can provide an entity with only reasonable assurance about achieving the entity's financial reporting objectives due to the inherent limitations of internal control.[14]

An independent audit conducted in accordance with the ISAs (UK and Ireland) does   **A17**
not act as a substitute for the maintenance of internal control necessary for the preparation of financial statements by management. Accordingly, the auditor is required to obtain the agreement of management that it acknowledges and under-stands its responsibility for internal control. However, the agreement required by paragraph 6(b)(ii) does not imply that the auditor will find that internal control maintained by management has achieved its purpose or will be free of deficiencies.

It is for management to determine what internal control is necessary to enable the   **A18**
preparation of the financial statements. The term "internal control" encompasses a wide range of activities within components that may be described as the control environment; the entity's risk assessment process; the information system, including the related business processes relevant to financial reporting, and communication; control activities; and monitoring of controls. This division, however, does not necessarily reflect how a particular entity may design, implement and maintain its internal control, or how it may classify any particular component.[15] An entity's internal control (in particular, its accounting books and records, or accounting systems) will reflect the needs of management, the complexity of the business, the nature of the risks to which the entity is subject, and relevant laws or regulation.

In some jurisdictions, law or regulation may refer to the responsibility of manage-   **A19**
ment for the adequacy of accounting books and records, or accounting systems. In some cases, general practice may assume a distinction between accounting books and records or accounting systems on the one hand, and internal control or controls on the other. As accounting books and records, or accounting systems, are an integral part of internal control as referred to in paragraph A18, no specific reference is made to them in paragraph 6(b)(ii) for the description of the responsibility of management.

---

[14] *ISA (UK and Ireland) 315, "Identifying and Assessing the Risks of Material Misstatement through Understanding the Entity and Its Environment," paragraph A46.*

[15] *ISA (UK and Ireland) 315, paragraph A51 and Appendix 1.*

To avoid misunderstanding, it may be appropriate for the auditor to explain to management the scope of this responsibility.

*Considerations Relevant to Smaller Entities (Ref: Para. 6(b))*

A20    One of the purposes of agreeing the terms of the audit engagement is to avoid misunderstanding about the respective responsibilities of management and the auditor. For example, when a third party has assisted with the preparation of the financial statements, it may be useful to remind management that the preparation of the financial statements in accordance with the applicable financial reporting framework remains its responsibility.

## Agreement on Audit Engagement Terms

### *Agreeing the Terms of the Audit Engagement* (Ref: Para. 9)

A21    The roles of management and those charged with governance in agreeing the terms of the audit engagement for the entity depend on the governance structure of the entity and relevant law or regulation.

### *Audit Engagement Letter or Other Form of Written Agreement*[16] (Ref: Para. 10-11)

A22    It is in the interests of both the entity and the auditor that the auditor sends an audit engagement letter before the commencement of the audit to help avoid mis-understandings with respect to the audit. In some countries, however, the objective and scope of an audit and the responsibilities of management and of the auditor may be sufficiently established by law, that is, they prescribe the matters described in paragraph 10. Although in these circumstances paragraph 11 permits the auditor to include in the engagement letter only reference to the fact that relevant law or regulation applies and that management acknowledges and understands its responsibilities as set out in paragraph 6(b), the auditor may nevertheless consider it appropriate to include the matters described in paragraph 10 in an engagement letter for the information of management.

*Form and Content of the Audit Engagement Letter*

A23    The form and content of the audit engagement letter may vary for each entity. Information included in the audit engagement letter on the auditor's responsibilities may be based on ISA (UK and Ireland) 200.[17] Paragraphs 6(b) and 12 of this ISA (UK and Ireland) deal with the description of the responsibilities of management. In addition to including the matters required by paragraph 10, an audit engagement letter may make reference to, for example:

- Elaboration of the scope of the audit, including reference to applicable legislation, regulations, ISAs (UK and Ireland), and ethical and other pronouncements of professional bodies to which the auditor adheres.
- The form of any other communication of results of the audit engagement.
- The fact that because of the inherent limitations of an audit, together with the inherent limitations of internal control, there is an unavoidable risk that some

---

[16] *In the paragraphs that follow, any reference to an audit engagement letter is to be taken as a reference to an audit engagement letter or other suitable form of written agreement.*

[17] *ISA (UK and Ireland) 200, paragraphs 3-9.*

material misstatements may not be detected, even though the audit is properly planned and performed in accordance with ISAs (UK and Ireland).
- Arrangements regarding the planning and performance of the audit, including the composition of the audit team.
- The expectation that management will provide written representations (see also paragraph A13).
- The agreement of management to make available to the auditor draft financial statements and any accompanying other information in time to allow the auditor to complete the audit in accordance with the proposed timetable.
- The agreement of management to inform the auditor of facts that may affect the financial statements, of which management may become aware during the period from the date of the auditor's report to the date the financial statements are issued.
- The basis on which fees are computed and any billing arrangements.
- A request for management to acknowledge receipt of the audit engagement letter and to agree to the terms of the engagement outlined therein.

When relevant, the following points could also be made in the audit engagement letter:

**A24**

- Arrangements concerning the involvement of other auditors and experts in some aspects of the audit.
- Arrangements concerning the involvement of internal auditors and other staff of the entity.
- Arrangements to be made with the predecessor auditor, if any, in the case of an initial audit.
- Any restriction of the auditor's liability when such possibility exists.
- A reference to any further agreements between the auditor and the entity.
- Any obligations to provide audit working papers to other parties.

An example of an audit engagement letter is set out in Appendix 1[17a].

*Audits of Components*

When the auditor of a parent entity is also the auditor of a component, the factors that may influence the decision whether to send a separate audit engagement letter to the component include the following:

**A25**

- Who appoints the component auditor;
- Whether a separate auditor's report is to be issued on the component;
- Legal requirements in relation to audit appointments;
- Degree of ownership by parent; and
- Degree of independence of the component management from the parent entity.

*Responsibilities of Management Prescribed by Law or Regulation (Ref: Para. 11-12)*

If, in the circumstances described in paragraphs A22 and A27, the auditor concludes that it is not necessary to record certain terms of the audit engagement in an audit engagement letter, the auditor is still required by paragraph 11 to seek the written agreement from management that it acknowledges and understands that it has the responsibilities set out in paragraph 6(b). However, in accordance with paragraph 12, such written agreement may use the wording of the law or regulation if such law or regulation establishes responsibilities for management that are equivalent in effect to those described in paragraph 6(b). The accounting profession, audit standards

**A26**

---

[17a] *The example letter in the Appendix has not been tailored for the UK and Ireland.*

setter, or audit regulator in a jurisdiction may have provided guidance as to whether the description in law or regulation is equivalent.

*Considerations specific to public sector entities*

A27    Law or regulation governing the operations of public sector audits generally mandate the appointment of a public sector auditor and commonly set out the public sector auditor's responsibilities and powers, including the power to access an entity's records and other information. When law or regulation prescribes in sufficient detail the terms of the audit engagement, the public sector auditor may nonetheless consider that there are benefits in issuing a fuller audit engagement letter than permitted by paragraph 11.

## Recurring Audits (Ref: Para. 13)

A28    The auditor may decide not to send a new audit engagement letter or other written agreement each period. However, the following factors may make it appropriate to revise the terms of the audit engagement or to remind the entity of existing terms:

- Any indication that the entity misunderstands the objective and scope of the audit.
- Any revised or special terms of the audit engagement.
- A recent change of senior management.
- A significant change in ownership.
- A significant change in nature or size of the entity's business.
- A change in legal or regulatory requirements.
- A change in the financial reporting framework adopted in the preparation of the financial statements.
- A change in other reporting requirements.

## Acceptance of a Change in the Terms of the Audit Engagement

*Request to Change the Terms of the Audit Engagement* (Ref: Para. 14)

A29    A request from the entity for the auditor to change the terms of the audit engagement may result from a change in circumstances affecting the need for the service, a misunderstanding as to the nature of an audit as originally requested or a restriction on the scope of the audit engagement, whether imposed by management or caused by other circumstances. The auditor, as required by paragraph 14, considers the justification given for the request, particularly the implications of a restriction on the scope of the audit engagement.

A30    A change in circumstances that affects the entity's requirements or a misunderstanding concerning the nature of the service originally requested may be considered a reasonable basis for requesting a change in the audit engagement.

A31    In contrast, a change may not be considered reasonable if it appears that the change relates to information that is incorrect, incomplete or otherwise unsatisfactory. An example might be where the auditor is unable to obtain sufficient appropriate audit evidence regarding receivables and the entity asks for the audit engagement to be changed to a review engagement to avoid a qualified opinion or a disclaimer of opinion.

*Request to Change to a Review or a Related Service (Ref: Para. 15)*

Before agreeing to change an audit engagement to a review or a related service, an auditor who was engaged to perform an audit in accordance with ISAs (UK and Ireland) may need to assess, in addition to the matters referred to in paragraphs A29-A31 above, any legal or contractual implications of the change. **A32**

If the auditor concludes that there is reasonable justification to change the audit engagement to a review or a related service, the audit work performed to the date of change may be relevant to the changed engagement; however, the work required to be performed and the report to be issued would be those appropriate to the revised engagement. In order to avoid confusing the reader, the report on the related service would not include reference to: **A33**

(a) The original audit engagement; or
(b) Any procedures that may have been performed in the original audit engagement, except where the audit engagement is changed to an engagement to undertake agreed-upon procedures and thus reference to the procedures performed is a normal part of the report.

*Statement by Auditor on Ceasing to Hold Office (Ref: Para. 17)*

The auditor of a limited company in the UK who ceases to hold office as auditor is required to comply with the requirements of sections 519 and 521 of the Companies Act 2006 regarding the statement to be made by the auditor in relation to ceasing to hold office. For the Republic of Ireland, equivalent requirements are contained in section 185 of the Companies Act 1990. In addition, in the UK the auditor may need to notify the appropriate audit authority in accordance with section 522 of the Companies Act 2006. **A33-1**

## Additional Considerations in Engagement Acceptance

*Financial Reporting Standards Supplemented by Law or Regulation* (Ref: Para. 18)

In some jurisdictions, law or regulation may supplement the financial reporting standards established by an authorized or recognized standards setting organization with additional requirements relating to the preparation of financial statements. In those jurisdictions, the applicable financial reporting framework for the purposes of applying the ISAs (UK and Ireland) encompasses both the identified financial reporting framework and such additional requirements provided they do not conflict with the identified financial reporting framework. This may, for example, be the case when law or regulation prescribes disclosures in addition to those required by the financial reporting standards or when they narrow the range of acceptable choices that can be made within the financial reporting standards.[18] **A34**

---

[18] *ISA 700, paragraph 15, includes a requirement regarding the evaluation of whether the financial statements adequately refer to or describe the applicable financial reporting framework.*
*The APB has not promulgated ISA 700 as issued by the IAASB for application in the UK and Ireland. In the UK and Ireland the applicable auditing standard is ISA (UK and Ireland) 700, "The Auditor's Report on Financial Statements." Paragraph 9(a) of ISA (UK and Ireland) 700 includes a requirement regarding evaluation of whether the financial statements adequately refer to or describe the relevant financial reporting framework.*

**Financial Reporting Framework Prescribed by Law or Regulation—Other Matters Affecting Acceptance** (Ref: Para. 19)

A35   Law or regulation may prescribe that the wording of the auditor's opinion use the phrases "present fairly, in all material respects" or "give a true and fair view" in a case where the auditor concludes that the applicable financial reporting framework prescribed by law or regulation would otherwise have been unacceptable. In this case, the terms of the prescribed wording of the auditor's report are significantly different from the requirements of ISAs (UK and Ireland) (see paragraph 21).

**Auditor's Report Prescribed by Law or Regulation** (Ref: Para. 21)

A36   ISAs (UK and Ireland) require that the auditor shall not represent compliance with ISAs (UK and Ireland) unless the auditor has complied with all of the ISAs (UK and Ireland) relevant to the audit.[19] When law or regulation prescribes the layout or wording of the auditor's report in a form or in terms that are significantly different from the requirements of ISAs (UK and Ireland) and the auditor concludes that additional explanation in the auditor's report cannot mitigate possible misunderstanding, the auditor may consider including a statement in the auditor's report that the audit is not conducted in accordance with ISAs (UK and Ireland). The auditor is, however, encouraged to apply ISAs (UK and Ireland), including the ISAs (UK and Ireland) that address the auditor's report, to the extent practicable, notwithstanding that the auditor is not permitted to refer to the audit being conducted in accordance with ISAs (UK and Ireland).

*Considerations Specific to Public Sector Entities*

A37   In the public sector, specific requirements may exist within the legislation governing the audit mandate; for example, the auditor may be required to report directly to a minister, the legislature or the public if the entity attempts to limit the scope of the audit.

[19] *ISA (UK and Ireland) 200, paragraph 20.*

# Appendix 1 (Ref: Paras. A23-24)

The example letter in this Appendix has not been tailored for the UK and Ireland.

## Example of an Audit Engagement Letter

The following is an example of an audit engagement letter for an audit of general purpose financial statements prepared in accordance with International Financial Reporting Standards. This letter is not authoritative but is intended only to be a guide that may be used in conjunction with the considerations outlined in this ISA. It will need to be varied according to individual requirements and circumstances. It is drafted to refer to the audit of financial statements for a single reporting period and would require adaptation if intended or expected to apply to recurring audits (see paragraph 13 of this ISA). It may be appropriate to seek legal advice that any proposed letter is suitable.

\*\*\*

To the appropriate representative of management or those charged with governance of ABC Company:[20]

*[The objective and scope of the audit]*

You[21] have requested that we audit the financial statements of ABC Company, which comprise the balance sheet as at December 31, 20X1, and the income statement, statement of changes in equity and cash flow statement for the year then ended, and a summary of significant accounting policies and other explanatory information. We are pleased to confirm our acceptance and our understanding of this audit engagement by means of this letter. Our audit will be conducted with the objective of our expressing an opinion on the financial statements.

*[The responsibilities of the auditor]*

We will conduct our audit in accordance with International Standards on Auditing (ISAs). Those standards require that we comply with ethical requirements and plan and perform the audit to obtain reasonable assurance about whether the financial statements are free from material misstatement. An audit involves performing procedures to obtain audit evidence about the amounts and disclosures in the financial statements. The procedures selected depend on the auditor's judgment, including the assessment of the risks of material misstatement of the financial statements, whether due to fraud or error. An audit also includes evaluating the appropriateness of accounting policies used and the reasonableness of accounting estimates made by management, as well as evaluating the overall presentation of the financial statements.

Because of the inherent limitations of an audit, together with the inherent limitations of internal control, there is an unavoidable risk that some material misstatements may not be detected, even though the audit is properly planned and performed in accordance with ISAs.

---

[20] *The addressees and references in the letter would be those that are appropriate in the circumstances of the engagement, including the relevant jurisdiction. It is important to refer to the appropriate persons – see paragraph A21*

[21] *Throughout this letter, references to "you," "we," "us," "management," "those charged with governance" and "auditor" would be used or amended as appropriate in the circumstances.*

In making our risk assessments, we consider internal control relevant to the entity's preparation of the financial statements in order to design audit procedures that are appropriate in the circumstances, but not for the purpose of expressing an opinion on the effectiveness of the entity's internal control. However, we will communicate to you in writing concerning any significant deficiencies in internal control relevant to the audit of the financial statements that we have identified during the audit.

[*The responsibilities of management and identification of the applicable financial reporting framework (for purposes of this example it is assumed that the auditor has not determined that the law or regulation prescribes those responsibilities in appropriate terms; the descriptions in paragraph 6(b) of this ISA are therefore used).*]

Our audit will be conducted on the basis that [management and, where appropriate, those charged with governance][22] acknowledge and understand that they have responsibility:

(a)   For the preparation and fair presentation of the financial statements in accordance with International Financial Reporting Standards;[23]

(b)   For such internal control as [management] determines is necessary to enable the preparation of financial statements that are free from material misstatement, whether due to fraud or error; and

(c)   To provide us with:
  (i)   Access to all information of which [management] is aware that is relevant to the preparation of the financial statements such as records, documentation and other matters;
  (ii)   Additional information that we may request from [management] for the purpose of the audit; and
  (iii)   Unrestricted access to persons within the entity from whom we determine it necessary to obtain audit evidence.

As part of our audit process, we will request from [management and, where appropriate, those charged with governance], written confirmation concerning representations made to us in connection with the audit.

We look forward to full cooperation from your staff during our audit.

[*Other relevant information*]

[*Insert other information, such as fee arrangements, billings and other specific terms, as appropriate.*]

**[Reporting]**

[*Insert appropriate reference to the expected form and content of the auditor's report.*]

The form and content of our report may need to be amended in the light of our audit findings.

Please sign and return the attached copy of this letter to indicate your acknowledgement of, and agreement with, the arrangements for our audit of the financial statements including our respective responsibilities.

---

[22] *Use terminology as appropriate in the circumstances.*

[23] *Or, if appropriate, "For the preparation of financial statements that give a true and fair view in accordance with International Financial Reporting Standards."*

XYZ & Co.

Acknowledged and agreed on behalf of ABC Company by

(signed)

.......................

Name and Title

Date

**Appendix 2** (Ref: Para. A10)

## Determining the Acceptability of General Purpose Frameworks

### Jurisdictions that Do Not Have Authorized or Recognized Standards Setting Organizations or Financial Reporting Frameworks Prescribed by Law or Regulation

1    As explained in paragraph A10 of this ISA (UK and Ireland), when an entity is registered or operating in a jurisdiction that does not have an authorized or recognized standards setting organization, or where use of the financial reporting framework is not prescribed by law or regulation, management identifies an applicable financial reporting framework. Practice in such jurisdictions is often to use the financial reporting standards established by one of the organizations described in paragraph A8 of this ISA (UK and Ireland).

2    Alternatively, there may be established accounting conventions in a particular jurisdiction that are generally recognized as the financial reporting framework for general purpose financial statements prepared by certain specified entities operating in that jurisdiction. When such a financial reporting framework is adopted, the auditor is required by paragraph 6(a) of this ISA (UK and Ireland) to determine whether the accounting conventions collectively can be considered to constitute an acceptable financial reporting framework for general purpose financial statements. When the accounting conventions are widely used in a particular jurisdiction, the accounting profession in that jurisdiction may have considered the acceptability of the financial reporting framework on behalf of the auditors. Alternatively, the auditor may make this determination by considering whether the accounting conventions exhibit attributes normally exhibited by acceptable financial reporting frameworks (see paragraph 3 below), or by comparing the accounting conventions to the requirements of an existing financial reporting framework considered to be acceptable (see paragraph 4 below).

3    Acceptable financial reporting frameworks normally exhibit the following attributes that result in information provided in financial statements that is useful to the intended users:

(a)   Relevance, in that the information provided in the financial statements is relevant to the nature of the entity and the purpose of the financial statements. For example, in the case of a business enterprise that prepares general purpose financial statements, relevance is assessed in terms of the information necessary to meet the common financial information needs of a wide range of users in making economic decisions. These needs are ordinarily met by presenting the financial position, financial performance and cash flows of the business enterprise.

(b)   Completeness, in that transactions and events, account balances and disclosures that could affect conclusions based on the financial statements are not omitted.

(c)   Reliability, in that the information provided in the financial statements:
 (i)   Where applicable, reflects the economic substance of events and transactions and not merely their legal form; and
 (ii)  Results in reasonably consistent evaluation, measurement, presentation and disclosure, when used in similar circumstances.

(d)   Neutrality, in that it contributes to information in the financial statements that is free from bias.

(e)   Understandability, in that the information in the financial statements is clear and comprehensive and not subject to significantly different interpretation.

The auditor may decide to compare the accounting conventions to the requirements   **4**
of an existing financial reporting framework considered to be acceptable. For
example, the auditor may compare the accounting conventions to IFRSs. For an
audit of a small entity, the auditor may decide to compare the accounting conventions to a financial reporting framework specifically developed for such entities by an
authorized or recognized standards setting organization. When the auditor makes
such a comparison and differences are identified, the decision as to whether the
accounting conventions adopted in the preparation and presentation of the financial
statements constitute an acceptable financial reporting framework includes considering the reasons for the differences and whether application of the accounting
conventions, or the description of the financial reporting framework in the financial
statements, could result in financial statements that are misleading.

A conglomeration of accounting conventions devised to suit individual preferences is   **5**
not an acceptable financial reporting framework for general purpose financial
statements. Similarly, a compliance framework will not be an acceptable financial
reporting framework, unless it is generally accepted in the particular jurisdictions by
preparers and users.

# Addendum

*This addendum provides a summary of APB's rationale for retaining or excluding in the proposed clarified ISA (UK and Ireland) the supplementary requirements in the existing ISA (UK and Ireland). It also sets out the supplementary guidance material in the existing ISA (UK and Ireland) that APB considers is not necessary to retain in light of the improvements in the underlying Clarity ISAs issued by the IAASB as part of the Clarity Project. It is provided for information and does not form part of the proposed clarified ISA (UK and Ireland).*

*The Consultation Paper published with the exposure drafts explains the general approach used by the APB for determining whether current supplementary material should be proposed to be retained.*

## Analysis of proposed treatment of current APB supplementary material in current ISA (UK and Ireland) 210

It should be noted that whilst the underlying ISA has technically only been "redrafted" as part of the IAASB Clarity Project, substantive changes have been made as a result of conforming changes introduced by the revision of other ISAs.

## Requirements

| APB supplementary requirements (*Italic text is from IAASB for context*) | Is it covered in substance in the Clarity ISA? | Should it be retained? |
|---|---|---|
| 2-1.   The terms of the engagement should be recorded in writing. | ✓ The ISA requires the terms of engagement to be recorded in an engagement letter or other suitable form of written agreement. (para 10) | ✗ |
| 5-1.   In the UK and Ireland, the auditor should ensure that the engagement letter documents and confirms the auditor's acceptance of the appointment, and includes a summary of the responsibilities of those charged with governance and of the auditor, the scope of the engagement and the form of any reports. | ✓ This content is required by the ISA (para 10)  There is not an explicit requirement to document the auditor's acceptance but the requirement is to record the agreed terms, which seems sufficient. | ✗ |

## Guidance

The following guidance in current ISA (UK and Ireland) 210 has not been carried forward to the proposed clarified standard.

| Current paragraph reference (*Italic text is from IAASB for context*) |
|---|
| 1-1. – 1-4. [Description of management and those charged with governance.] |
| 1-5.   For the purpose of this ISA (UK and Ireland) 'client' means the addressees of the auditor's report or, when as often will be the case it is not practical to agree such terms with the addressees, the entity itself through those charged with governance. |
| 5-2.   Appendix 2 sets out illustrative wording to describe the responsibilities of the directors and the auditor and the scope of the audit, for a limited (non-listed) company client for an audit conducted in accordance with ISAs (UK and Ireland). |
| 7.   *The auditor may also wish to include in the letter:*<br>• *Request for the client to confirm the terms of the engagement by acknowledging receipt of the engagement letter.*[2]<br>• *Any confidentiality of other letters or reports to be issued and, where appropriate, the conditions, if any, on which permission might be given to those charged with governance to make those reports available to others.*<br><br>[2] Acceptance by the client of the terms of the engagement is normally evidenced by signature by a person at an appropriate level within the entity, for example the finance director or equivalent. |
| 9.   *When the auditor of a parent entity is also the auditor of its subsidiary, branch or division (component), the factors that influence the decision whether to send a separate engagement letter to the component include:*<br>• Whether the terms for each component are the same.<br>• Regulatory requirements. |
| 9-1.   If the auditor sends one letter relating to the group as a whole, it identifies the components for which the auditor is appointed as auditor. Those charged with governance of the parent entity are requested to forward the letter to those charged with governance of the components concerned. Each board is requested to confirm that the terms of the engagement letter are accepted. |
| Appendix 2 – Example letter for UK and Ireland non-listed company – see below |

# ISA (UK and Ireland) 210 – Appendix 2

**Illustrative wording to describe the responsibilities of the directors and the auditor and the scope of the audit, for a limited (non-listed) company client for an audit conducted in accordance with ISAs (UK and Ireland)**

The illustrative wording set out below is not necessarily comprehensive or appropriate to be used in relation to every non-listed company, and it must be tailored to specific circumstances – for example, to the special reporting requirements of regulated entities *(note 1)*, or of small companies to which certain exemptions are given.

The wording reflects legal and professional responsibilities as at 15 December 2004. The wording should be amended as necessary to take account of changes in the responsibilities of the directors and the auditor after that date, for example as a result of changes in company legislation.

The auditor includes other wording as appropriate to address the matters set out in paragraphs 6 to 9-1 of this ISA (UK and Ireland).

### Responsibilities of directors and auditors

As directors of xxxxxx, you are responsible for ensuring that the company maintains proper accounting records and for preparing financial statements which give a true and fair view and have been prepared in accordance with the Companies Act 1985 *(or other relevant legislation – note 2)*. You are also responsible for making available to us, as and when required, all the company's accounting records and all other relevant records and related information, including minutes of all management and shareholders' meetings. We are entitled to require from the company's officers such other information and explanations as we think necessary for the performance of our duties as auditors.

We have a statutory responsibility to report to the members whether in our opinion the financial statements give a true and fair view and whether they have been properly prepared in accordance with the Companies Act 1985 *(or other relevant legislation)*. In arriving at our opinion, we are required to consider the following matters, and to report on any in respect of which we are not satisfied *(note 3)*:

(a)   Whether proper accounting records have been kept by the company *(note 4)* and proper returns adequate for our audit have been received from branches not visited by us;

(b)   Whether the company's *(note 4)* balance sheet and profit and loss account are in agreement with the accounting records and returns;

(c)   Whether we have obtained all the information and explanations which we consider necessary for the purposes of our audit; and

(d)   Whether the information given in the directors' report is consistent with the financial statements.

In addition, there are certain other matters which, according to the circumstances, may need to be dealt with in our report. For example, where the financial statements do not give details of directors' remuneration or of their transactions with the company, the Companies Act 1985 requires us to disclose such matters in our report.

We have a professional responsibility to report if the financial statements do not comply in any material respect with applicable accounting standards, unless in our opinion the non-compliance is justified in the circumstances. In determining whether or not the departure is justified we consider:

(a) Whether the departure is required in order for the financial statements to give a true and fair view; and

(b) Whether adequate disclosure has been made concerning the departure.

Our professional responsibilities also include:

- Including in our report a description of the directors' responsibilities for the financial statements where the financial statements or accompanying information do not include such a description; and
- Considering whether other information in documents containing audited financial statements is consistent with those financial statements.

*(note 5)*

### Scope of audit

Our audit will be conducted in accordance with the International Standards on Auditing (UK and Ireland) issued by the Auditing Practices Board, and will include such tests of transactions and of the existence, ownership and valuation of assets and liabilities as we consider necessary. We shall obtain an understanding of the accounting and internal control systems in order to assess their adequacy as a basis for the preparation of the financial statements and to establish whether proper accounting records have been maintained by the company. We shall expect to obtain such appropriate evidence as we consider sufficient to enable us to draw reasonable conclusions therefrom.

The nature and extent of our procedures will vary according to our assessment of the company's accounting system and, where we wish to place reliance on it, the internal control system, and may cover any aspect of the business's operations that we consider appropriate. Our audit is not designed to identify all significant weaknesses in the company's systems but, if such weaknesses come to our notice during the course of our audit which we think should be brought to your attention, we shall report them to you. Any such report may not be provided to third parties without our prior written consent. Such consent will be granted only on the basis that such reports are not prepared with the interests of anyone other than the company in mind and that we accept no duty or responsibility to any other party as concerns the reports.

As part of our normal audit procedures, we may request you to provide written confirmation of certain oral representations which we have received from you during the course of the audit on matters having a material effect on the financial statements. In connection with representations and the supply of information to us generally, we draw your attention to section 389A of the Companies Act 1985 *(note 6)* under which it is an offence for an officer of the company to mislead the auditors.

In order to assist us with the examination of your financial statements, we shall request sight of all documents or statements, including the chairman's statement, operating and financial review and the directors' report, which are due to be issued with the financial statements. We are also entitled to attend all general meetings of the company and to receive notice of all such meetings.

The responsibility for safeguarding the assets of the company and for the prevention and detection of fraud, error and non-compliance with law or regulations rests with yourselves. However, we shall endeavour to plan our audit so that we have a reasonable expectation of detecting material misstatements in the financial statements or accounting records (including those resulting from fraud, error or non-compliance with law or regulations), but our examination should not be relied upon to disclose all such material misstatements or frauds, errors or instances of non-compliance as may exist.

(*Where appropriate – note 7*) We shall not be treated as having notice, for the purposes of our audit responsibilities, of information provided to members of our firm other than those engaged on the audit (for example information provided in connection with accounting, taxation and other services).

Once we have issued our report we have no further direct responsibility in relation to the financial statements for that financial year. However, we expect that you will inform us of any material event occurring between the date of our report and that of the Annual General Meeting which may affect the financial statements.

### Notes

1    *Additional guidance is provided in APB Practice Notes.*
2    *Relevant legislation for the Republic of Ireland is the Companies Acts 1963 to 2003 and for Northern Ireland is the Companies (Northern Ireland) Order 1986.*
3    *In the Republic of Ireland, auditors are required to report additionally on matters (a) to (d) as identified in the section 'Responsibilities of directors and auditors' of the example engagement letter, and on whether there existed at the balance sheet date a financial situation which, under section 40(1) of the Companies (Amendment) Act 1983, would require the convening of an extraordinary general meeting of the company. Hence this sentence would read:*
     *'... we are required to consider the following matters and to report on:'*
4    *The reference to 'company' does not need to be altered in the case of groups as section 237 of the Companies Act 1985 refers only to the company being audited and not to any parent company or subsidiary or associated undertaking.*
5    *In the Republic of Ireland, auditors have the following additional legal responsibilities which are set out in the engagement letter:*
     ***Company law***
     *To report whether, in their opinion, proper books of account have been kept by the entity.*
     *Where suspected indictable offences under the Companies Acts come to the attention of auditors, while carrying out their audit examination, they are obliged to report these to the Director of Corporate Enforcement. This reporting obligation imposed by Section 194, Companies Act, 1990, as amended by Section 74, Company Law Enforcement Act, 2001, applies regardless of the apparent materiality of the suspected offence, or whether the suspected offence has already been reported to the relevant authorities.*
     ***Criminal law***
     *Where, in the course of conducting professional work, it comes to the attention of certain "relevant persons" (as defined), that information or documents indicate that an offence may have been committed under Section 59 Criminal Justice (Theft and Fraud Offences) Act 2001, auditors have a reporting obligation to the Garda Siochana. This applies regardless of the apparent materiality of the suspected offence, or whether the suspected offence has already been reported to the relevant authorities.*
     ***Taxation***
     *Auditors must report material relevant offences, as defined in Section 1079 of the Taxes Consolidation Act 1997, to the directors of the company in writing, requesting them to rectify the matter or notify an appropriate officer of the*

*Revenue Commissioners of the offence within 6 months. In the event that the auditors request is not complied with, the auditor must cease to act as auditor to the company or to assist the company in any taxation matter. The auditor must also send a copy of the auditor's notice of resignation to an appropriate officer of the Revenue Commissioners within 14 days*

**6** *Relevant references for the Republic of Ireland are sections 193(3), 196 and 197 of the Companies Act 1990. The relevant reference for Northern Ireland is Article 397A of the Companies (Northern Ireland) Order 1986.*

**7** *When accounting, taxation or other services are undertaken on behalf of an audit client, information may be provided to members of the audit firm other than those engaged on the audit. In such cases, it may be appropriate for the audit engagement letter to include this or a similar paragraph to indicate that the auditors are not to be treated as having notice, for the purposes of their audit responsibilities, of such information, to make it clear that a company would not be absolved from informing the auditors directly of a material matter.*

# Proposed Clarified International Standard on Auditing (UK and Ireland) 220

# Quality control for an audit of financial statements

*(Effective for audits of financial statements for periods ending on or after 15 December 2010)*

## Contents

International Standard on Auditing (UK and Ireland) (ISA (UK and Ireland)) 220, "Quality Control for an Audit of Financial Statements" should be read in conjunction with ISA (UK and Ireland) 200, "Overall Objectives of the Independent Auditor and the Conduct of an Audit in Accordance with International Standards on Auditing (UK and Ireland)."

# Introduction

## Scope of this ISA (UK and Ireland)

This International Standard on Auditing (UK and Ireland) (ISA (UK and Ireland)) deals with the specific responsibilities of the auditor regarding quality control procedures for an audit of financial statements. It also addresses, where applicable, the responsibilities of the engagement quality control reviewer. This ISA (UK and Ireland) is to be read in conjunction with relevant ethical requirements.

**1**

## System of Quality Control and Role of Engagement Teams

Quality control systems, policies and procedures are the responsibility of the audit firm. Under ISQC (UK and Ireland) 1, the firm has an obligation to establish and maintain a system of quality control to provide it with reasonable assurance that:

**2**

(a)  The firm and its personnel comply with professional standards and applicable legal and regulatory requirements; and
(b)  The reports issued by the firm or engagement partners are appropriate in the circumstances.[1]

This ISA (UK and Ireland) is premised on the basis that the firm is subject to ISQC (UK and Ireland) 1 or to national requirements that are at least as demanding. (Ref: Para. A1)

Within the context of the firm's system of quality control, engagement teams have a responsibility to implement quality control procedures that are applicable to the audit engagement and provide the firm with relevant information to enable the functioning of that part of the firm's system of quality control relating to independence.

**3**

Engagement teams are entitled to rely on the firm's system of quality control, unless information provided by the firm or other parties suggests otherwise. (Ref: Para. A2)

**4**

## Effective Date

This ISA (UK and Ireland) is effective for audits of financial statements for periods ending on or after 15 December 2010.

**5**

# Objective

The objective of the auditor is to implement quality control procedures at the engagement level that provide the auditor with reasonable assurance that:

**6**

(a)  The audit complies with professional standards and applicable legal and regulatory requirements; and
(b)  The auditor's report issued is appropriate in the circumstances.

---

[1] *ISQC (UK and Ireland) 1, "Quality Control for Firms that Perform Audits and Reviews of Financial Statements, and Other Assurance and Related Services Engagements," paragraph 11.*

# Definitions

7    For purposes of the ISAs (UK and Ireland), the following terms have the meanings
attributed below:

(a) Engagement partner[2] – The partner or other person in the firm who is
responsible for the audit engagement and its performance, and for the auditor's
report that is issued on behalf of the firm, and who, where required, has the
appropriate authority from a professional, legal or regulatory body.

(b) Engagement quality control review – A process designed to provide an objective
evaluation, on or before the date of the auditor's report, of the significant
judgments the engagement team made and the conclusions it reached in formulating the auditor's report. The engagement quality control review process is
only for audits of financial statements of listed entities and those other audit
engagements, if any, for which the firm has determined an engagement quality
control review is required.

(c) Engagement quality control reviewer – A partner, other person in the firm,
suitably qualified external person, or a team made up of such individuals, none
of whom is part of the engagement team, with sufficient and appropriate
experience and authority to objectively evaluate the significant judgments the
engagement team made and the conclusions it reached in formulating the
auditor's report.

(d) Engagement team – All partners and staff performing the engagement, and any
individuals engaged by the firm or a network firm who perform audit procedures
on the engagement. This excludes an auditor's external expert engaged by the
firm or a network firm.[3]

(e) Firm – A sole practitioner, partnership, corporation or other entity of professional accountants.

(f) Inspection – In relation to completed audit engagements, procedures designed to
provide evidence of compliance by engagement teams with the firm's quality
control policies and procedures.

(g) Listed entity – An entity whose shares, stock or debt are quoted or listed on a
recognized stock exchange, or are marketed under the regulations of a recognized stock exchange or other equivalent body.

(h) Monitoring – A process comprising an ongoing consideration and evaluation of
the firm's system of quality control, including a periodic inspection of a selection
of completed engagements, designed to provide the firm with reasonable
assurance that its system of quality control is operating effectively.

(i) Network firm – A firm or entity that belongs to a network.

(j) Network – A larger structure:
    (i) That is aimed at cooperation, and
    (ii) That is clearly aimed at profit or cost-sharing or shares common ownership,
    control or management, common quality control policies and procedures,
    common business strategy, the use of a common brand name, or a sig-
    nificant part of professional resources.

(k) Partner – Any individual with authority to bind the firm with respect to the
performance of a professional services engagement.

(l) Personnel – Partners and staff.

(m) Professional standards – International Standards on Auditing (UK and Ireland)
(ISAs (UK and Ireland)) and relevant ethical requirements.

---

[2] *"Engagement partner," "partner," and "firm" should be read as referring to their public sector equivalents
where relevant.*

[3] *ISA (UK and Ireland) 620, "Using the Work of an Auditor's Expert," paragraph 6(a), defines the term
"auditor's expert."*

(n) Relevant ethical requirements – Ethical requirements to which the engagement team and engagement quality control reviewer are subject, which ordinarily comprise Parts A and B of the International Federation of Accountants' *Code of Ethics for Professional Accountants* (IFAC Code) related to an audit of financial statements together with national requirements that are more restrictive.

> Auditors in the UK and Ireland are subject to ethical requirements from two sources: the Ethical Standards for Auditors established by APB concerning the integrity, objectivity and independence of the auditor, and the ethical pronouncements established by the auditor's relevant professional body. The APB is not aware of any significant instances where the relevant parts of the IFAC Code of Ethics are more restrictive than the Ethical Standards for Auditors.

(o) Staff – Professionals, other than partners, including any experts the firm employs.
(p) Suitably qualified external person – An individual outside the firm with the competence and capabilities to act as an engagement partner, for example a partner of another firm, or an employee (with appropriate experience) of either a professional accountancy body whose members may perform audits of historical financial information or of an organization that provides relevant quality control services.

# Requirements

## Leadership Responsibilities for Quality on Audits

The engagement partner shall take responsibility for the overall quality on each audit engagement to which that partner is assigned. (Ref: Para. A3)  **8**

## Relevant Ethical Requirements

Throughout the audit engagement, the engagement partner shall remain alert, through observation and making inquiries as necessary, for evidence of non-compliance with relevant ethical requirements by members of the engagement team. (Ref: Para. A4-A5)  **9**

If matters come to the engagement partner's attention through the firm's system of quality control or otherwise that indicate that members of the engagement team have not complied with relevant ethical requirements, the engagement partner, in consultation with others in the firm, shall determine the appropriate action. (Ref: Para. A5)  **10**

### Independence

The engagement partner shall form a conclusion on compliance with independence requirements that apply to the audit engagement. In doing so, the engagement partner shall:  **11**

(a) Obtain relevant information from the firm and, where applicable, network firms, to identify and evaluate circumstances and relationships that create threats to independence;

(b)  Evaluate information on identified breaches, if any, of the firm's independence policies and procedures to determine whether they create a threat to independence for the audit engagement; and

(c)  Take appropriate action to eliminate such threats or reduce them to an acceptable level by applying safeguards, or, if considered appropriate, to withdraw from the audit engagement, where withdrawal is possible under applicable law or regulation. The engagement partner shall promptly report to the firm any inability to resolve the matter for appropriate action. (Ref: Para. A5-A7)

## Acceptance and Continuance of Client Relationships and Audit Engagements

12    The engagement partner shall be satisfied that appropriate procedures regarding the acceptance and continuance of client relationships and audit engagements have been followed, and shall determine that conclusions reached in this regard are appropriate. (Ref: Para. A8-A9)

13    If the engagement partner obtains information that would have caused the firm to decline the audit engagement had that information been available earlier, the engagement partner shall communicate that information promptly to the firm, so that the firm and the engagement partner can take the necessary action. (Ref: Para. A9)

## Assignment of Engagement Teams

14    The engagement partner shall be satisfied that the engagement team, and any auditor's experts who are not part of the engagement team, collectively have the appropriate competence and capabilities to:

(a)  Perform the audit engagement in accordance with professional standards and applicable legal and regulatory requirements; and

(b)  Enable an auditor's report that is appropriate in the circumstances to be issued. (Ref: Para. A10-A12)

## Engagement Performance

### *Direction, Supervision and Performance*

15    The engagement partner shall take responsibility for:

(a)  The direction, supervision and performance of the audit engagement in compliance with professional standards and applicable legal and regulatory requirements; and (Ref: Para. A13-A15, A20)

(b)  The auditor's report being appropriate in the circumstances.

### *Reviews*

16    The engagement partner shall take responsibility for reviews being performed in accordance with the firm's review policies and procedures. (Ref: Para. A16-A17, A20)

17    On or before the date of the auditor's report, the engagement partner shall, through a review of the audit documentation and discussion with the engagement team, be satisfied that sufficient appropriate audit evidence has been obtained to support the conclusions reached and for the auditor's report to be issued. (Ref: Para. A18-A20)

## Consultation

The engagement partner shall: **18**

(a)  Take responsibility for the engagement team undertaking appropriate consultation on difficult or contentious matters;
(b)  Be satisfied that members of the engagement team have undertaken appropriate consultation during the course of the engagement, both within the engagement team and between the engagement team and others at the appropriate level within or outside the firm;
(c)  Be satisfied that the nature and scope of, and conclusions resulting from, such consultations are agreed with the party consulted; and
(d)  Determine that conclusions resulting from such consultations have been implemented. (Ref: Para. A21-A22)

## Engagement Quality Control Review

For audits of financial statements of listed entities, and those other audit engage- **19** ments, if any, for which the firm has determined that an engagement quality control review is required, the engagement partner shall:

(a)  Determine that an engagement quality control reviewer has been appointed;
(b)  Discuss significant matters arising during the audit engagement, including those identified during the engagement quality control review, with the engagement quality control reviewer; and
(c)  Not date the auditor's report until the completion of the engagement quality control review. (Ref: Para. A23-A25)

The engagement quality control reviewer shall perform an objective evaluation of the **20** significant judgments made by the engagement team, and the conclusions reached in formulating the auditor's report. This evaluation shall involve:

(a)  Discussion of significant matters with the engagement partner;
(b)  Review of the financial statements and the proposed auditor's report;
(c)  Review of selected audit documentation relating to the significant judgments the engagement team made and the conclusions it reached; and
(d)  Evaluation of the conclusions reached in formulating the auditor's report and consideration of whether the proposed auditor's report is appropriate. (Ref: Para. A26-A27, A29-A31)

For audits of financial statements of listed entities, the engagement quality control **21** reviewer, on performing an engagement quality control review, shall also consider the following:

(a)  The engagement team's evaluation of the firm's independence in relation to the audit engagement;
(b)  Whether appropriate consultation has taken place on matters involving differences of opinion or other difficult or contentious matters, and the conclusions arising from those consultations; and
(c)  Whether audit documentation selected for review reflects the work performed in relation to the significant judgments and supports the conclusions reached. (Ref: Para. A28-A31)

## Differences of Opinion

If differences of opinion arise within the engagement team, with those consulted or, **22** where applicable, between the engagement partner and the engagement quality control reviewer, the engagement team shall follow the firm's policies and procedures for dealing with and resolving differences of opinion.

## Monitoring

23   An effective system of quality control includes a monitoring process designed to provide the firm with reasonable assurance that its policies and procedures relating to the system of quality control are relevant, adequate, and operating effectively. The engagement partner shall consider the results of the firm's monitoring process as evidenced in the latest information circulated by the firm and, if applicable, other network firms and whether deficiencies noted in that information may affect the audit engagement. (Ref: Para A32-A34)

## Documentation

24   The auditor shall include in the audit documentation:[4];

(a)   Issues identified with respect to compliance with relevant ethical requirements and how they were resolved.

(b)   Conclusions on compliance with independence requirements that apply to the audit engagement, and any relevant discussions with the firm that support these conclusions.

(c)   Conclusions reached regarding the acceptance and continuance of client relationships and audit engagements.

(d)   The nature and scope of, and conclusions resulting from, consultations undertaken during the course of the audit engagement. (Ref: Para. A35)

25   The engagement quality control reviewer shall document, for the audit engagement reviewed, that:

(a)   The procedures required by the firm's policies on engagement quality control review have been performed;

(b)   The engagement quality control review has been completed on or before the date of the auditor's report; and

(c)   The reviewer is not aware of any unresolved matters that would cause the reviewer to believe that the significant judgments the engagement team made and the conclusions they reached were not appropriate.

***

# Application and Other Explanatory Material

## System of Quality Control and Role of Engagement Teams (Ref: Para. 2)

A1   ISQC (UK and Ireland) 1, or national requirements that are at least as demanding, deals with the firm's responsibilities to establish and maintain its system of quality control for audit engagements. The system of quality control includes policies and procedures that address each of the following elements:

- Leadership responsibilities for quality within the firm;
- Relevant ethical requirements;
- Acceptance and continuance of client relationships and specific engagements;
- Human resources;

---

[4] *ISA (UK and Ireland) 230, "Audit Documentation," paragraphs 8-11, and paragraph A6.*

- Engagement performance; and
- Monitoring.

National requirements that deal with the firm's responsibilities to establish and maintain a system of quality control are at least as demanding as ISQC (UK and Ireland) 1 when they address all the elements referred to in this paragraph and impose obligations on the firm that achieve the aims of the requirements set out in ISQC (UK and Ireland) 1.

*Reliance on the Firm's System of Quality Control* (Ref: Para. 4)

Unless information provided by the firm or other parties suggest otherwise, the engagement team may rely on the firm's system of quality control in relation to, for example: **A2**

- Competence of personnel through their recruitment and formal training.
- Independence through the accumulation and communication of relevant independence information.
- Maintenance of client relationships through acceptance and continuance systems.
- Adherence to applicable legal and regulatory requirements through the monitoring process.

**Leadership Responsibilities for Quality on Audits** (Ref: Para. 8)

The actions of the engagement partner and appropriate messages to the other members of the engagement team, in taking responsibility for the overall quality on each audit engagement, emphasize: **A3**

(a) The importance to audit quality of:
   (i) Performing work that complies with professional standards and applicable legal and regulatory requirements;
   (ii) Complying with the firm's quality control policies and procedures as applicable;
   (iii) Issuing auditor's reports that are appropriate in the circumstances; and
   (iv) The engagement team's ability to raise concerns without fear of reprisals; and
(b) The fact that quality is essential in performing audit engagements.

**Relevant Ethical Requirements**

*Compliance with Relevant Ethical Requirements* (Ref: Para. 9)

The IFAC Code[4a] establishes the fundamental principles of professional ethics, which include: **A4**

(a) Integrity;
(b) Objectivity;
(c) Professional competence and due care;
(d) Confidentiality; and

---

[4a] *Auditors in the UK and Ireland are subject to ethical requirements from two sources: the Ethical Standards established by APB concerning the integrity, objectivity and independence of the auditor, and the ethical pronouncements established by the auditor's relevant professional body. The APB is not aware of any significant instances where the relevant parts of the IFAC Code of Ethics are more restrictive than the Ethical Standards.*

(e)   Professional behavior.

*Definition of "Firm," "Network" and "Network Firm" (Ref: Para. 9-11)*

A5   The definitions of "firm," "network" or "network firm" in relevant ethical require-ments may differ from those set out in this ISA (UK and Ireland). For example, the IFAC Code[4a] defines the "firm" as:

(a)   A sole practitioner, partnership or corporation of professional accountants;

(b)   An entity that controls such parties through ownership, management or other means; and

(c)   An entity controlled by such parties through ownership, management or other means.

The IFAC Code also provides guidance in relation to the terms "network" and "network firm."

In complying with the requirements in paragraphs 9-11, the definitions used in the relevant ethical requirements apply in so far as is necessary to interpret those ethical requirements.

*Threats to Independence* (Ref: Para. 11(c))

A6   The engagement partner may identify a threat to independence regarding the audit engagement that safeguards may not be able to eliminate or reduce to an acceptable level. In that case, as required by paragraph 11(c), the engagement partner reports to the relevant person(s) within the firm to determine appropriate action, which may include eliminating the activity or interest that creates the threat, or withdrawing from the audit engagement, where withdrawal is possible under applicable law or regulation.

*Considerations Specific to Public Sector Entities*

A7   Statutory measures may provide safeguards for the independence of public sector auditors. However, public sector auditors or audit firms carrying out public sector audits on behalf of the statutory auditor may, depending on the terms of the man-date in a particular jurisdiction, need to adapt their approach in order to promote compliance with the spirit of paragraph 11. This may include, where the public sector auditor's mandate does not permit withdrawal from the engagement, disclosure through a public report, of circumstances that have arisen that would, if they were in the private sector, lead the auditor to withdraw.

**Acceptance and Continuance of Client Relationships and Audit Engagements** (Ref: Para. 12)

A8   ISQC (UK and Ireland) 1 requires the firm to obtain information considered necessary in the circumstances before accepting an engagement with a new client, when deciding whether to continue an existing engagement, and when considering acceptance of a new engagement with an existing client.[5] Information such as the following assists the engagement partner in determining whether the conclusions reached regarding the acceptance and continuance of client relationships and audit engagements are appropriate:

---

[5] *ISQC (UK and Ireland) 1, paragraph 27(a).*

- The integrity of the principal owners, key management and those charged with governance of the entity;
- Whether the engagement team is competent to perform the audit engagement and has the necessary capabilities, including time and resources;
- Whether the firm and the engagement team can comply with relevant ethical requirements; and
- Significant matters that have arisen during the current or previous audit engagement, and their implications for continuing the relationship.

***Considerations Specific to Public Sector Entities*** (Ref: Para. 12-13)

In the public sector, auditors may be appointed in accordance with statutory pro-   **A9**
cedures. Accordingly, certain of the requirements and considerations regarding the
acceptance and continuance of client relationships and audit engagements as set out
in paragraphs 12, 13 and A8 may not be relevant. Nonetheless, information gathered
as a result of the process described may be valuable to public sector auditors in
performing risk assessments and in carrying out reporting responsibilities.

## Assignment of Engagement Teams (Ref: Para. 14)

An engagement team includes a person using expertise in a specialized area of   **A10**
accounting or auditing, whether engaged or employed by the firm, if any, who
performs audit procedures on the engagement. However, a person with such
expertise is not a member of the engagement team if that person's involvement with
the engagement is only consultation. Consultations are addressed in paragraph 18,
and paragraph A21-A22.

When considering the appropriate competence and capabilities expected of the   **A11**
engagement team as a whole, the engagement partner may take into consideration
such matters as the team's:

- Understanding of, and practical experience with, audit engagements of a similar nature and complexity through appropriate training and participation.
- Understanding of professional standards and legal and regulatory requirements.
- Technical expertise, including expertise with relevant information technology and specialized areas of accounting or auditing.
- Knowledge of relevant industries in which the client operates.
- Ability to apply professional judgment.
- Understanding of the firm's quality control policies and procedures.

***Considerations Specific to Public Sector Entities***

In the public sector, additional appropriate competence may include skills that are   **A12**
necessary to discharge the terms of the audit mandate in a particular jurisdiction.
Such competence may include an understanding of the applicable reporting
arrangements, including reporting to the legislature or other governing body or in
the public interest. The wider scope of a public sector audit may include, for example,
some aspects of performance auditing or a comprehensive assessment of compliance
with law, regulation or other authority and preventing and detecting fraud and
corruption.

## Engagement Performance

### *Direction, Supervision and Performance* (Ref: Para. 15(a))

A13   Direction of the engagement team involves informing the members of the engagement team of matters such as:

- Their responsibilities, including the need to comply with relevant ethical requirements, and to plan and perform an audit with professional skepticism as required by ISA (UK and Ireland) 200.[6]
- Responsibilities of respective partners where more than one partner is involved in the conduct of an audit engagement.
- The objectives of the work to be performed.
- The nature of the entity's business.
- Risk-related issues.
- Problems that may arise.
- The detailed approach to the performance of the engagement.

Discussion among members of the engagement team allows less experienced team members to raise questions with more experienced team members so that appropriate communication can occur within the engagement team.

A14   Appropriate teamwork and training assist less experienced members of the engagement team to clearly understand the objectives of the assigned work.

A15   Supervision includes matters such as:

- Tracking the progress of the audit engagement.
- Considering the competence and capabilities of individual members of the engagement team, including whether they have sufficient time to carry out their work, whether they understand their instructions, and whether the work is being carried out in accordance with the planned approach to the audit engagement.
- Addressing significant matters arising during the audit engagement, considering their significance and modifying the planned approach appropriately.
- Identifying matters for consultation or consideration by more experienced engagement team members during the audit engagement.

### *Reviews*

### *Review Responsibilities (Ref: Para. 16)*

A16   Under ISQC (UK and Ireland) 1, the firm's review responsibility policies and procedures are determined on the basis that work of less experienced team members is reviewed by more experienced team members.[7]

A17   A review consists of consideration whether, for example:

- The work has been performed in accordance with professional standards and applicable legal and regulatory requirements;
- Significant matters have been raised for further consideration;

[6] *ISA (UK and Ireland) 200, "Overall Objectives of the Independent Auditor and the Conduct of an Audit in Accordance with International Standards on Auditing (UK and Ireland)," paragraph 15.*

[7] *ISQC (UK and Ireland) 1, paragraph 33.*

- Appropriate consultations have taken place and the resulting conclusions have been documented and implemented;
- There is a need to revise the nature, timing and extent of work performed;
- The work performed supports the conclusions reached and is appropriately documented;
- The evidence obtained is sufficient and appropriate to support the auditor's report; and
- The objectives of the engagement procedures have been achieved.

*The Engagement Partner's Review of Work Performed (Ref: Para. 17)*

Timely reviews of the following by the engagement partner at appropriate stages during the engagement allow significant matters to be resolved on a timely basis to the engagement partner's satisfaction on or before the date of the auditor's report:   **A18**

- Critical areas of judgment, especially those relating to difficult or contentious matters identified during the course of the engagement;
- Significant risks; and
- Other areas the engagement partner considers important.

The engagement partner need not review all audit documentation, but may do so. However, as required by ISA (UK and Ireland) 230, the partner documents the extent and timing of the reviews.[8]

An engagement partner taking over an audit during the engagement may apply the review procedures as described in paragraphs A18 to review the work performed to the date of a change in order to assume the responsibilities of an engagement partner.   **A19**

**Considerations Relevant Where a Member of the Engagement Team with Expertise in a Specialized Area of Accounting or Auditing Is Used** (Ref: Para. 15-17)

Where a member of the engagement team with expertise in a specialized area of accounting or auditing is used, direction, supervision and review of that engagement team member's work may include matters such as:   **A20**

- Agreeing with that member the nature, scope and objectives of that member's work; and the respective roles of, and the nature, timing and extent of communication between that member and other members of the engagement team.
- Evaluating the adequacy of that member's work including the relevance and reasonableness of that member's findings or conclusions and their consistency with other audit evidence.

**Consultation** (Ref: Para. 18)

Effective consultation on significant technical, ethical, and other matters within the firm or, where applicable, outside the firm can be achieved when those consulted:   **A21**

- Are given all the relevant facts that will enable them to provide informed advice; and
- Have appropriate knowledge, seniority and experience.

It may be appropriate for the engagement team to consult outside the firm, for example, where the firm lacks appropriate internal resources. They may take   **A22**

---

[8] *ISA (UK and Ireland) 230, "Audit Documentation," paragraph 9(c).*

advantage of advisory services provided by other firms, professional and regulatory bodies, or commercial organizations that provide relevant quality control services.

### Engagement Quality Control Review

*Completion of the Engagement Quality Control Review before Dating of the Auditor's Report (Ref: Para. 19(c))*

A23   ISA (UK and Ireland) 700 requires the auditor's report to be dated no earlier than the date on which the auditor has obtained sufficient appropriate evidence on which to base the auditor's opinion on the financial statements.[9] In cases of an audit of financial statements of listed entities or when an engagement meets the criteria for an engagement quality control review, such a review assists the auditor in determining whether sufficient appropriate evidence has been obtained.

A24   Conducting the engagement quality control review in a timely manner at appropriate stages during the engagement allows significant matters to be promptly resolved to the engagement quality control reviewer's satisfaction on or before the date of the auditor's report.

A25   Completion of the engagement quality control review means the completion by the engagement quality control reviewer of the requirements in paragraphs 20-21, and where applicable, compliance with paragraph 22. Documentation of the engagement quality control review may be completed after the date of the auditor's report as part of the assembly of the final audit file. ISA (UK and Ireland) 230 establishes requirements and provides guidance in this regard.[10]

*Nature, Extent and Timing of Engagement Quality Control Review (Ref: Para. 20)*

A26   Remaining alert for changes in circumstances allows the engagement partner to identify situations in which an engagement quality control review is necessary, even though at the start of the engagement, such a review was not required.

A27   The extent of the engagement quality control review may depend, among other things, on the complexity of the audit engagement, whether the entity is a listed entity, and the risk that the auditor's report might not be appropriate in the circumstances. The performance of an engagement quality control review does not reduce the responsibilities of the engagement partner for the audit engagement and its performance.

*Engagement Quality Control Review of Listed Entities (Ref: Para. 21)*

A28   Other matters relevant to evaluating the significant judgments made by the engagement team that may be considered in an engagement quality control review of a listed entity include:

---

[9] ISA 700, "Forming an Opinion and Reporting on Financial Statements," paragraph 41.
*The APB has not promulgated ISA 700 as issued by the IAASB for application in the UK and Ireland. In the UK and Ireland the applicable auditing standard is ISA (UK and Ireland) 700, "The Auditor's Report on Financial Statements." Paragraphs 23 and 24 of ISA (UK and Ireland) 700 establish requirements regarding dating of the auditor's report.*

[10] ISA (UK and Ireland) 230, paragraphs 14-16.

- Significant risks identified during the engagement in accordance with ISA (UK and Ireland) 315,[11] and the responses to those risks in accordance with ISA (UK and Ireland) 330,[12] including the engagement team's assessment of, and response to, the risk of fraud in accordance with ISA (UK and Ireland) 240.[13]
- Judgments made, particularly with respect to materiality and significant risks.
- The significance and disposition of corrected and uncorrected misstatements identified during the audit.
- The matters to be communicated to management and those charged with governance and, where applicable, other parties such as regulatory bodies.

These other matters, depending on the circumstances, may also be applicable for engagement quality control reviews for audits of financial statements of other entities.

*Considerations Specific to Smaller Entities (Ref: Para. 20-21)*

In addition to the audits of financial statements of listed entities, an engagement quality control review is required for audit engagements that meet the criteria established by the firm that subjects engagements to an engagement quality control review. In some cases, none of the firm's audit engagements may meet the criteria that would subject them to such a review.  **A29**

*Considerations Specific to Public Sector Entities (Ref: Para. 20-21)*

In the public sector, a statutorily appointed auditor (for example, an Auditor General, or other suitably qualified person appointed on behalf of the Auditor General), may act in a role equivalent to that of engagement partner with overall responsibility for public sector audits. In such circumstances, where applicable, the selection of the engagement quality control reviewer includes consideration of the need for independence from the audited entity and the ability of the engagement quality control reviewer to provide an objective evaluation.  **A30**

Listed entities as referred to in paragraphs 21 and A28 are not common in the public sector. However, there may be other public sector entities that are significant due to size, complexity or public interest aspects, and which consequently have a wide range of stakeholders. Examples include state owned corporations and public utilities. Ongoing transformations within the public sector may also give rise to new types of significant entities. There are no fixed objective criteria on which the determination of significance is based. Nonetheless, public sector auditors evaluate which entities may be of sufficient significance to warrant performance of an engagement quality control review.  **A31**

---

[11] *ISA (UK and Ireland) 315, "Identifying and Assessing the Risks of Material Misstatement through Understanding the Entity and Its Environment."*

[12] *ISA (UK and Ireland) 330, "The Auditor's Responses to Assessed Risks."*

[13] *ISA (UK and Ireland) 240, "The Auditor's Responsibilities Relating to Fraud in an Audit of Financial Statements."*

**Monitoring** (Ref: Para. 23)

**A32**   ISQC (UK and Ireland) 1 requires the firm to establish a monitoring process designed to provide it with reasonable assurance that the policies and procedures relating to the system of quality control is relevant, adequate and operating effectively.[14]

**A33**   In considering deficiencies that may affect the audit engagement, the engagement partner may have regard to measures the firm took to rectify the situation that the engagement partner considers are sufficient in the context of that audit.

**A34**   A deficiency in the firm's system of quality control does not necessarily indicate that a particular audit engagement was not performed in accordance with professional standards and applicable legal and regulatory requirements, or that the auditor's report was not appropriate.

## Documentation

***Documentation of Consultations*** (Ref: Para. 24(d))

**A35**   Documentation of consultations with other professionals that involve difficult or contentious matters that is sufficiently complete and detailed contributes to an understanding of:

- The issue on which consultation was sought; and
- The results of the consultation, including any decisions taken, the basis for those decisions and how they were implemented.

---

[14] *ISQC (UK and Ireland) 1, paragraph 48.*

# Addendum

*This addendum provides a summary of APB's rationale for retaining or excluding in the proposed clarified ISA (UK and Ireland) the supplementary requirements in the existing ISA (UK and Ireland). It also sets out the supplementary guidance material in the existing ISA (UK and Ireland) that APB considers is not necessary to retain in light of the improvements in the underlying Clarity ISAs issued by the IAASB as part of the Clarity Project. It is provided for information and does not form part of the proposed clarified ISA (UK and Ireland).*

*The Consultation Paper published with the exposure drafts explains the general approach used by the APB for determining whether current supplementary material should be proposed to be retained.*

## Analysis of proposed treatment of current APB supplementary material in current ISA (UK and Ireland) 220

## Requirements

There are no supplementary requirements in the current ISA (UK and Ireland) 220

## Guidance

The following guidance in current ISA (UK and Ireland) 220 has not been carried forward to the proposed clarified standard.

| Current paragraph reference (*Italic text is from IAASB for context*) |
| --- |
| 5-1. – 5-4. [Description of management and those charged with governance.] |

# Proposed Clarified International Standard on Auditing (UK and Ireland) 230
## Audit documentation

*(Effective for audits of financial statements for periods ending on or after 15 December 2010)*

## Contents

International Standard on Auditing (UK and Ireland) (ISA (UK and Ireland)) 230, "Audit Documentation" should be read in conjunction with ISA (UK and Ireland) 200, "Overall Objectives of the Independent Auditor and the Conduct of an Audit in Accordance with International Standards on Auditing (UK and Ireland)."

# Introduction

## Scope of this ISA (UK and Ireland)

This International Standard on Auditing (UK and Ireland) (ISA (UK and Ireland)) **1**
deals with the auditor's responsibility to prepare audit documentation for an audit of
financial statements. The Appendix lists other ISAs (UK and Ireland) that contain
specific documentation requirements and guidance. The specific documentation
requirements of other ISAs (UK and Ireland) do not limit the application of this ISA
(UK and Ireland). Law or regulation may establish additional documentation
requirements.

## Nature and Purposes of Audit Documentation

Audit documentation that meets the requirements of this ISA (UK and Ireland) and **2**
the specific documentation requirements of other relevant ISAs (UK and Ireland)
provides:

(a) Evidence of the auditor's basis for a conclusion about the achievement of the
    overall objectives of the auditor;[1] and
(b) Evidence that the audit was planned and performed in accordance with ISAs
    (UK and Ireland) and applicable legal and regulatory requirements.

Audit documentation serves a number of additional purposes, including the **3**
following:

- Assisting the engagement team to plan and perform the audit.
- Assisting members of the engagement team responsible for supervision to direct
  and supervise the audit work, and to discharge their review responsibilities in
  accordance with ISA (UK and Ireland) 220.[2]
- Enabling the engagement team to be accountable for its work.
- Retaining a record of matters of continuing significance to future audits.
- Enabling the conduct of quality control reviews and inspections in accordance
  with ISQC (UK and Ireland) 1[3] or national requirements that are at least as
  demanding.[4]
- Enabling the conduct of external inspections in accordance with applicable
  legal, regulatory or other requirements.

## Effective Date

This ISA (UK and Ireland) is effective for audits of financial statements for periods **4**
ending on or after 15 December 2010.

---

[1] *ISA (UK and Ireland) 200, "Overall Objectives of the Independent Auditor and the Conduct of an Audit in
Accordance with International Standards on Auditing (UK and Ireland)," paragraph 11.*

[2] *ISA (UK and Ireland) 220, "Quality Control for an Audit of Financial Statements," paragraphs 14-17.*

[3] *ISQC (UK and Ireland) 1, "Quality Control for Firms that Perform Audits and Reviews of Financial
Statements, and Other Assurance and Related Services Engagements," paragraphs 32-33, 35-38, and 48].*

[4] *See ISA (UK and Ireland) 220, paragraph 2.*

# Objective

5   The objective of the auditor is to prepare documentation that provides:

(a)  A sufficient and appropriate record of the basis for the auditor's report; and

(b)  Evidence that the audit was planned and performed in accordance with ISAs (UK and Ireland) and applicable legal and regulatory requirements.

# Definitions

6   For purposes of the ISAs (UK and Ireland), the following terms have the meanings attributed below:

(a)  Audit documentation – The record of audit procedures performed, relevant audit evidence obtained, and conclusions the auditor reached (terms such as "working papers" or "workpapers" are also sometimes used).

(b)  Audit file – One or more folders or other storage media, in physical or electronic form, containing the records that comprise the audit documentation for a specific engagement.

(c)  Experienced auditor – An individual (whether internal or external to the firm) who has practical audit experience, and a reasonable understanding of:

(i)   Audit processes;

(ii)  ISAs and applicable legal and regulatory requirements;

(iii) The business environment in which the entity operates; and

(iv)  Auditing and financial reporting issues relevant to the entity's industry.

# Requirements

## Timely Preparation of Audit Documentation

7   The auditor shall prepare audit documentation on a timely basis. (Ref: Para. A1)

## Documentation of the Audit Procedures Performed and Audit Evidence Obtained

### *Form, Content and Extent of Audit Documentation*

8   The auditor shall prepare audit documentation that is sufficient to enable an experienced auditor, having no previous connection with the audit, to understand: (Ref: Para. A2-A5, A16-A17)

(a)  The nature, timing and extent of the audit procedures performed to comply with the ISAs (UK and Ireland) and applicable legal and regulatory requirements; (Ref: Para. A6-A7)

(b)  The results of the audit procedures performed, and the audit evidence obtained; and

(c)  Significant matters arising during the audit, the conclusions reached thereon, and significant professional judgments made in reaching those conclusions. (Ref: Para. A8-A11)

9   In documenting the nature, timing and extent of audit procedures performed, the auditor shall record:

(a)  The identifying characteristics of the specific items or matters tested; (Ref: Para. A12)

(b)  Who performed the audit work and the date such work was completed; and
(c)  Who reviewed the audit work performed and the date and extent of such review. (Ref: Para. A13)

The auditor shall document discussions of significant matters with management, those charged with governance, and others, including the nature of the significant matters discussed and when and with whom the discussions took place. (Ref: Para. A14)    **10**

If the auditor identified information that is inconsistent with the auditor's final conclusion regarding a significant matter, the auditor shall document how the auditor addressed the inconsistency. (Ref: Para. A15)    **11**

### Departure from a Relevant Requirement

If, in exceptional circumstances, the auditor judges it necessary to depart from a relevant requirement in an ISA (UK and Ireland), the auditor shall document how the alternative audit procedures performed achieve the aim of that requirement, and the reasons for the departure. (Ref: Para. A18-A19)    **12**

### Matters Arising after the Date of the Auditor's Report

If, in exceptional circumstances, the auditor performs new or additional audit procedures or draws new conclusions after the date of the auditor's report, the auditor shall document: (Ref: Para. A20)    **13**

(a)  The circumstances encountered;
(b)  The new or additional audit procedures performed, audit evidence obtained, and conclusions reached, and their effect on the auditor's report; and
(c)  When and by whom the resulting changes to audit documentation were made and reviewed.

## Assembly of the Final Audit File

The auditor shall assemble the audit documentation in an audit file and complete the administrative process of assembling the final audit file on a timely basis after the date of the auditor's report. (Ref: Para. A21-A22)    **14**

After the assembly of the final audit file has been completed, the auditor shall not delete or discard audit documentation of any nature before the end of its retention period. (Ref: Para. A23)    **15**

In circumstances other than those envisaged in paragraph 13 where the auditor finds it necessary to modify existing audit documentation or add new audit documentation after the assembly of the final audit file has been completed, the auditor shall, regardless of the nature of the modifications or additions, document: (Ref: Para. A24)    **16**

(a)  The specific reasons for making them; and
(b)  When and by whom they were made and reviewed.

*** *** ***

# Application and Other Explanatory Material

## Timely Preparation of Audit Documentation (Ref: Para. 7)

**A1**   Preparing sufficient and appropriate audit documentation on a timely basis helps to enhance the quality of the audit and facilitates the effective review and evaluation of the audit evidence obtained and conclusions reached before the auditor's report is finalized. Documentation prepared after the audit work has been performed is likely to be less accurate than documentation prepared at the time such work is performed.

## Documentation of the Audit Procedures Performed and Audit Evidence Obtained

### *Form, Content and Extent of Audit Documentation* (Ref: Para. 8)

**A2**   The form, content and extent of audit documentation depend on factors such as:

- The size and complexity of the entity.
- The nature of the audit procedures to be performed.
- The identified risks of material misstatement.
- The significance of the audit evidence obtained.
- The nature and extent of exceptions identified.
- The need to document a conclusion or the basis for a conclusion not readily determinable from the documentation of the work performed or audit evidence obtained.
- The audit methodology and tools used.

**A3**   Audit documentation may be recorded on paper or on electronic or other media. Examples of audit documentation include:

- Audit programs.
- Analyses.
- Issues memoranda.
- Summaries of significant matters.
- Letters of confirmation and representation.
- Checklists.
- Correspondence (including e-mail) concerning significant matters.

The auditor may include abstracts or copies of the entity's records (for example, significant and specific contracts and agreements) as part of audit documentation. Audit documentation, however, is not a substitute for the entity's accounting records.

**A4**   The auditor need not include in audit documentation superseded drafts of working papers and financial statements, notes that reflect incomplete or preliminary thinking, previous copies of documents corrected for typographical or other errors, and duplicates of documents.

**A5**   Oral explanations by the auditor, on their own, do not represent adequate support for the work the auditor performed or conclusions the auditor reached, but may be used to explain or clarify information contained in the audit documentation.

*Documentation of Compliance with ISAs (Ref: Para. 8(a))*

In principle, compliance with the requirements of this ISA (UK and Ireland) will **A6**
result in the audit documentation being sufficient and appropriate in the circumstances. Other ISAs (UK and Ireland) contain specific documentation requirements
that are intended to clarify the application of this ISA (UK and Ireland) in the
particular circumstances of those other ISAs (UK and Ireland). The specific documentation requirements of other ISAs do not limit the application of this ISA (UK
and Ireland). Furthermore, the absence of a documentation requirement in any
particular ISA (UK and Ireland) is not intended to suggest that there is no documentation that will be prepared as a result of complying with that ISA (UK and
Ireland).

Audit documentation provides evidence that the audit complies with the ISAs (UK **A7**
and Ireland). However, it is neither necessary nor practicable for the auditor to
document every matter considered, or professional judgment made, in an audit.
Further, it is unnecessary for the auditor to document separately (as in a checklist,
for example) compliance with matters for which compliance is demonstrated by
documents included within the audit file. For example:

- The existence of an adequately documented audit plan demonstrates that the
  auditor has planned the audit.
- The existence of a signed engagement letter in the audit file demonstrates that
  the auditor has agreed the terms of the audit engagement with management or,
  where appropriate, those charged with governance.
- An auditor's report containing an appropriately qualified opinion on the
  financial statements demonstrates that the auditor has complied with the
  requirement to express a qualified opinion under the circumstances specified in
  the ISAs (UK and Ireland).
- In relation to requirements that apply generally throughout the audit, there may
  be a number of ways in which compliance with them may be demonstrated
  within the audit file:
  - For example, there may be no single way in which the auditor's profes-
    sional skepticism is documented. But the audit documentation may
    nevertheless provide evidence of the auditor's exercise of professional
    skepticism in accordance with the ISAs (UK and Ireland). Such evidence
    may include specific procedures performed to corroborate management's
    responses to the auditor's inquiries.
  - Similarly, that the engagement partner has taken responsibility for the
    direction, supervision and performance of the audit in compliance with the
    ISAs (UK and Ireland) may be evidenced in a number of ways within the
    audit documentation. This may include documentation of the engagement
    partner's timely involvement in aspects of the audit, such as participation in
    the team discussions required by ISA (UK and Ireland) 315.[5]

*Documentation of Significant Matters and Related Significant Professional Judgments
(Ref: Para. 8(c))*

Judging the significance of a matter requires an objective analysis of the facts and **A8**
circumstances. Examples of significant matters include:

---

[5] *ISA (UK and Ireland) 315, "Identifying and Assessing the Risks of Material Misstatement through Understanding the Entity and Its Environment," paragraph 10.*

- Matters that give rise to significant risks (as defined in ISA (UK and Ireland) 315[6]).
- Results of audit procedures indicating (a) that the financial statements could be materially misstated, or (b) a need to revise the auditor's previous assessment of the risks of material misstatement and the auditor's responses to those risks.
- Circumstances that cause the auditor significant difficulty in applying necessary audit procedures.
- Findings that could result in a modification to the audit opinion or the inclusion of an Emphasis of Matter paragraph in the auditor's report.

**A9**  An important factor in determining the form, content and extent of audit documentation of significant matters is the extent of professional judgment exercised in performing the work and evaluating the results. Documentation of the professional judgments made, where significant, serves to explain the auditor's conclusions and to reinforce the quality of the judgment. Such matters are of particular interest to those responsible for reviewing audit documentation, including those carrying out subsequent audits when reviewing matters of continuing significance (for example, when performing a retrospective review of accounting estimates).

**A10**  Some examples of circumstances in which, in accordance with paragraph 8, it is appropriate to prepare audit documentation relating to the use of professional judgment include, where the matters and judgments are significant:

- The rationale for the auditor's conclusion when a requirement provides that the auditor "shall consider" certain information or factors, and that consideration is significant in the context of the particular engagement.
- The basis for the auditor's conclusion on the reasonableness of areas of subjective judgments (for example, the reasonableness of significant accounting estimates).
- The basis for the auditor's conclusions about the authenticity of a document when further investigation (such as making appropriate use of an expert or of confirmation procedures) is undertaken in response to conditions identified during the audit that caused the auditor to believe that the document may not be authentic.

**A11**  The auditor may consider it helpful to prepare and retain as part of the audit documentation a summary (sometimes known as a completion memorandum) that describes the significant matters identified during the audit and how they were addressed, or that includes cross-references to other relevant supporting audit documentation that provides such information. Such a summary may facilitate effective and efficient reviews and inspections of the audit documentation, particularly for large and complex audits. Further, the preparation of such a summary may assist the auditor's consideration of the significant matters. It may also help the auditor to consider whether, in light of the audit procedures performed and conclusions reached, there is any individual relevant ISA (UK and Ireland) objective that the auditor cannot achieve that would prevent the auditor from achieving the overall objectives of the auditor.

***Identification of Specific Items or Matters Tested, and of the Preparer and Reviewer*** (Ref: Para. 9)

**A12**  Recording the identifying characteristics serves a number of purposes. For example, it enables the engagement team to be accountable for its work and facilitates the

[6] *ISA (UK and Ireland) 315, paragraph 4(e).*

investigation of exceptions or inconsistencies. Identifying characteristics will vary with the nature of the audit procedure and the item or matter tested. For example:

- For a detailed test of entity-generated purchase orders, the auditor may identify the documents selected for testing by their dates and unique purchase order numbers.
- For a procedure requiring selection or review of all items over a specific amount from a given population, the auditor may record the scope of the procedure and identify the population (for example, all journal entries over a specified amount from the journal register).
- For a procedure requiring systematic sampling from a population of documents, the auditor may identify the documents selected by recording their source, the starting point and the sampling interval (for example, a systematic sample of shipping reports selected from the shipping log for the period from April 1 to September 30, starting with report number 12345 and selecting every 125th report).
- For a procedure requiring inquiries of specific entity personnel, the auditor may record the dates of the inquiries and the names and job designations of the entity personnel.
- For an observation procedure, the auditor may record the process or matter being observed, the relevant individuals, their respective responsibilities, and where and when the observation was carried out.

ISA (UK and Ireland) 220 requires the auditor to review the audit work performed through review of the audit documentation.[7] The requirement to document who reviewed the audit work performed does not imply a need for each specific working paper to include evidence of review. The requirement, however, means documenting what audit work was reviewed, who reviewed such work, and when it was reviewed. **A13**

*Documentation of Discussions of Significant Matters with Management, Those Charged with Governance, and Others (Ref: Para. 10)*

The documentation is not limited to records prepared by the auditor but may include other appropriate records such as minutes of meetings prepared by the entity's personnel and agreed by the auditor. Others with whom the auditor may discuss significant matters may include other personnel within the entity, and external parties, such as persons providing professional advice to the entity. **A14**

*Documentation of How Inconsistencies have been Addressed (Ref: Para. 11)*

The requirement to document how the auditor addressed inconsistencies in information does not imply that the auditor needs to retain documentation that is incorrect or superseded. **A15**

*Considerations Specific to Smaller Entities (Ref. Para. 8)*

The audit documentation for the audit of a smaller entity is generally less extensive than that for the audit of a larger entity. Further, in the case of an audit where the engagement partner performs all the audit work, the documentation will not include matters that might have to be documented solely to inform or instruct members of an engagement team, or to provide evidence of review by other members of the team (for example, there will be no matters to document relating to team discussions or supervision). Nevertheless, the engagement partner complies with the overriding **A16**

[7] *ISA (UK and Ireland) 220, paragraph 17].*

requirement in paragraph 8 to prepare audit documentation that can be understood by an experienced auditor, as the audit documentation may be subject to review by external parties for regulatory or other purposes.

A17    When preparing audit documentation, the auditor of a smaller entity may also find it helpful and efficient to record various aspects of the audit together in a single document, with cross-references to supporting working papers as appropriate. Examples of matters that may be documented together in the audit of a smaller entity include the understanding of the entity and its internal control, the overall audit strategy and audit plan, materiality determined in accordance with ISA (UK and Ireland) 320,[8] assessed risks, significant matters noted during the audit, and conclusions reached.

### Departure from a Relevant Requirement (Ref: Para. 12)

A18    The requirements of the ISAs (UK and Ireland) are designed to enable the auditor to achieve the objectives specified in the ISAs (UK and Ireland), and thereby the overall objectives of the auditor. Accordingly, other than in exceptional circumstances, the ISAs (UK and Ireland) call for compliance with each requirement that is relevant in the circumstances of the audit.

A19    The documentation requirement applies only to requirements that are relevant in the circumstances. A requirement is not relevant[9] only in the cases where:

(a)    The entire ISA (UK and Ireland) is not relevant (for example, if an entity does not have an internal audit function, nothing in ISA (UK and Ireland) 610[10] is relevant); or

(b)    The requirement is conditional and the condition does not exist (for example, the requirement to modify the auditor's opinion where there is an inability to obtain sufficient appropriate audit evidence, and there is no such inability).

### Matters Arising after the Date of the Auditor's Report (Ref: Para. 13)

A20    Examples of exceptional circumstances include facts which become known to the auditor after the date of the auditor's report but which existed at that date and which, if known at that date, might have caused the financial statements to be amended or the auditor to modify the opinion in the auditor's report.[11] The resulting changes to the audit documentation are reviewed in accordance with the review responsibilities set out in ISA (UK and Ireland) 220,[12] with the engagement partner taking final responsibility for the changes.

---

[8] *ISA (UK and Ireland) 320, "Materiality in Planning and Performing an Audit."*

[9] *ISA (UK and Ireland) 200, paragraph 22.*

[10] *ISA (UK and Ireland) 610, "Using the Work of Internal Auditors."*

[11] *ISA (UK and Ireland) 560, "Subsequent Events," paragraph 14.*

[12] *ISA (UK and Ireland) 220, paragraph 16.*

**Assembly of the Final Audit File** (Ref: Para. 14-16)

ISQC (UK and Ireland) 1 (or national requirements that are at least as demanding) requires firms to establish policies and procedures for the timely completion of the assembly of audit files.[13] An appropriate time limit within which to complete the assembly of the final audit file is ordinarily not more than 60 days after the date of the auditor's report.[14]    **A21**

The completion of the assembly of the final audit file after the date of the auditor's report is an administrative process that does not involve the performance of new audit procedures or the drawing of new conclusions. Changes may, however, be made to the audit documentation during the final assembly process if they are administrative in nature. Examples of such changes include:    **A22**

- Deleting or discarding superseded documentation.
- Sorting, collating and cross-referencing working papers.
- Signing off on completion checklists relating to the file assembly process.
- Documenting audit evidence that the auditor has obtained, discussed and agreed with the relevant members of the engagement team before the date of the auditor's report.

ISQC (UK and Ireland) 1 (or national requirements that are at least as demanding) requires firms to establish policies and procedures for the retention of engagement documentation.[15] The retention period for audit engagements ordinarily is no shorter than five years from the date of the auditor's report, or, if later, the date of the group auditor's report.[16]    **A23**

An example of a circumstance in which the auditor may find it necessary to modify existing audit documentation or add new audit documentation after file assembly has been completed is the need to clarify existing audit documentation arising from comments received during monitoring inspections performed by internal or external parties.    **A24**

---

[13] *ISQC (UK and Ireland) 1, paragraph 45.*

[14] *ISQC (UK and Ireland) 1, paragraph A54.*

[15] *ISQC (UK and Ireland) 1, paragraph 47.*

[16] *ISQC (UK and Ireland) 1, paragraph A61.*
*In the UK and Republic of Ireland the auditor has regard to specific requirements of the Audit Regulations.*
*Audit Regulation 3.08b states that "A Registered Auditor must keep all audit working papers which auditing standards require for a period of at least six years. The period starts with the end of the accounting period to which the papers relate."*
*Audit Regulation 7.06 states that "In carrying out its responsibilities under regulation 7.03, the Registration Committee, any sub-committee, the secretariat, or a monitoring unit may, to the extent necessary for the review of a firm's audit work or how it is complying or intends to comply with these regulations, require a Registered Auditor or an applicant for registration to provide any information, held in whatsoever form (including electronic), about the firm or its clients and to allow access to the firm's systems and personnel."*
*The Audit Regulations referred to above were originally published in December 1995 and updated in June 2005 (Audit News 40).*

**Appendix** (Ref: Para. 1)

## Specific Audit Documentation Requirements in Other ISAs

This appendix identifies paragraphs in other ISAs (UK and Ireland) in effect for audits of financial statements for periods ending on or after 15 December 2010 that contain specific documentation requirements. The list is not a substitute for considering the requirements and related application and other explanatory material in ISAs.

- ISA (UK and Ireland) 210, "Agreeing the Terms of Audit Engagements" – paragraphs 10-12
- ISA (UK and Ireland) 220, "Quality Control for an Audit of Financial Statements" – paragraphs 24-25
- ISA (UK and Ireland) 240, "The Auditor's Responsibilities Relating to Fraud in an Audit of Financial Statements" – paragraphs 44-47
- ISA (UK and Ireland) 250, Section A "Consideration of Laws and Regulations in an Audit of Financial Statements" – paragraph 29
- ISA (UK and Ireland) 260, "Communication with Those Charged with Governance" – paragraph 23
- ISA (UK and Ireland) 300, "Planning an Audit of Financial Statements" – paragraph 12
- ISA (UK and Ireland) 315, "Identifying and Assessing the Risks of Material Misstatement Through Understanding the Entity and Its Environment" – paragraph 32
- ISA (UK and Ireland) 320, "Materiality in Planning and Performing an Audit" – paragraph 14
- ISA (UK and Ireland) 330, "The Auditor's Responses to Assessed Risks" – paragraphs 28-30
- ISA (UK and Ireland) 450, "Evaluation of Misstatements Identified During the Audit" – paragraph 15
- ISA (UK and Ireland) 540, "Auditing Accounting Estimates, Including Fair Value Accounting Estimates, and Related Disclosures" – paragraph 23
- ISA (UK and Ireland) 550, "Related Parties" – paragraph 28
- ISA (UK and Ireland) 570, "Going Concern," – paragraph 17-1

- ISA (UK and Ireland) 600, "Special Considerations—Audits of Group Financial Statements (Including the Work of Component Auditors)" – paragraph 50
- ISA (UK and Ireland) 610, "Using the Work of Internal Auditors" – paragraph 13

- ISA (UK and Ireland) 720, Section B "The Auditor's Statutory Reporting Responsibility in Relation to Directors' reports" – paragraph 12

# Addendum

*This addendum provides a summary of APB's rationale for retaining or excluding in the proposed clarified ISA (UK and Ireland) the supplementary requirements in the existing ISA (UK and Ireland). It also sets out the supplementary guidance material in the existing ISA (UK and Ireland) that APB considers is not necessary to retain in light of the improvements in the underlying Clarity ISAs issued by the IAASB as part of the Clarity Project. It is provided for information and does not form part of the proposed clarified ISA (UK and Ireland).*

*The Consultation Paper published with the exposure drafts explains the general approach used by the APB for determining whether current supplementary material should be proposed to be retained.*

## Analysis of proposed treatment of current APB supplementary material in current ISA (UK and Ireland) 230

## Requirements

There are no supplementary requirements in the current ISA (UK and Ireland) 230.

## Guidance

The following guidance in current ISA (UK and Ireland) 230 has not been carried forward to the proposed clarified standard.

| Current paragraph reference (*Italic text is from IAASB for context*) |
| --- |
| 22.    *... For example, in a continuing engagement, nothing in ISA (UK and Ireland) 510, "Initial Engagements—Opening Balances* and Continuing Engagements–Opening Balances," related to initial engagements *is relevant.* ... |
| *Appendix* |
| *The following lists the main paragraphs that contain specific documentation requirements and guidance in other ISAs (UK and Ireland):* |
| •   ISA (UK and Ireland) 250, Section A "Consideration of Laws and Regulations"–Paragraph 28; Section B "The Auditor's Right and Duty to Report to Regulators in the Financial Sector"-Paragraph 46; |
| •   ISA (UK and Ireland) 402, "Audit Considerations in Relation to Entities using Service Organizations" – Paragraphs 5-3 and 9-13. |

# Proposed Clarified International Standard on Auditing (UK and Ireland) 240

## The auditor's responsibilities relating to fraud in an audit of financial statements

*(Effective for audits of financial statements for periods ending on or after 15 December 2010)*

## Contents

International Standard on Auditing (UK and Ireland) (ISA (UK and Ireland)) 240, "The Auditor's Responsibilities Relating to Fraud in an Audit of Financial Statements" should be read in conjunction with ISA (UK and Ireland) 200, "Overall Objectives of the Independent Auditor and the Conduct of an Audit in Accordance with International Standards on Auditing (UK and Ireland)."

# Introduction

## Scope of this ISA (UK and Ireland)

1   This International Standard on Auditing (UK and Ireland) (ISA (UK and Ireland)) deals with the auditor's responsibilities relating to fraud in an audit of financial statements. Specifically, it expands on how ISA (UK and Ireland) 315[1] and ISA (UK and Ireland) 330[2] are to be applied in relation to risks of material misstatement due to fraud.

## Characteristics of Fraud

2   Misstatements in the financial statements can arise from either fraud or error. The distinguishing factor between fraud and error is whether the underlying action that results in the misstatement of the financial statements is intentional or unintentional.

3   Although fraud is a broad legal concept, for the purposes of the ISAs (UK and Ireland), the auditor is concerned with fraud that causes a material misstatement in the financial statements. Two types of intentional misstatements are relevant to the auditor – misstatements resulting from fraudulent financial reporting and misstatements resulting from misappropriation of assets. Although the auditor may suspect or, in rare cases, identify the occurrence of fraud, the auditor does not make legal determinations of whether fraud has actually occurred. (Ref: Para. A1-A6)

### *Responsibility for the Prevention and Detection of Fraud*

4   The primary responsibility for the prevention and detection of fraud rests with both those charged with governance of the entity and management. It is important that management, with the oversight of those charged with governance, place a strong emphasis on fraud prevention, which may reduce opportunities for fraud to take place, and fraud deterrence, which could persuade individuals not to commit fraud because of the likelihood of detection and punishment. This involves a commitment to creating a culture of honesty and ethical behavior which can be reinforced by an active oversight by those charged with governance. Oversight by those charged with governance includes considering the potential for override of controls or other inappropriate influence over the financial reporting process, such as efforts by management to manage earnings in order to influence the perceptions of analysts as to the entity's performance and profitability

### *Responsibilities of the Auditor*

5   An auditor conducting an audit in accordance with ISAs (UK and Ireland) is responsible for obtaining reasonable assurance that the financial statements taken as a whole are free from material misstatement, whether caused by fraud or error. Owing to the inherent limitations of an audit, there is an unavoidable risk that some material misstatements of the financial statements may not be detected, even though

---

[1] ISA (UK and Ireland) 315, "Identifying and Assessing the Risks of Material Misstatement through Understanding the Entity and Its Environment."

[2] ISA (UK and Ireland) 330, "The Auditor's Responses to Assessed Risks."

the audit is properly planned and performed in accordance with the ISAs (UK and Ireland).[3]

As described in ISA (UK and Ireland) 200,[4] the potential effects of inherent lim-   6
itations are particularly significant in the case of misstatement resulting from fraud.
The risk of not detecting a material misstatement resulting from fraud is higher than
the risk of not detecting one resulting from error. This is because fraud may involve
sophisticated and carefully organized schemes designed to conceal it, such as forgery,
deliberate failure to record transactions, or intentional misrepresentations being
made to the auditor. Such attempts at concealment may be even more difficult to
detect when accompanied by collusion. Collusion may cause the auditor to believe
that audit evidence is persuasive when it is, in fact, false. The auditor's ability to
detect a fraud depends on factors such as the skillfulness of the perpetrator, the
frequency and extent of manipulation, the degree of collusion involved, the relative
size of individual amounts manipulated, and the seniority of those individuals
involved. While the auditor may be able to identify potential opportunities for fraud
to be perpetrated, it is difficult for the auditor to determine whether misstatements in
judgment areas such as accounting estimates are caused by fraud or error.

Furthermore, the risk of the auditor not detecting a material misstatement resulting   7
from management fraud is greater than for employee fraud, because management is
frequently in a position to directly or indirectly manipulate accounting records,
present fraudulent financial information or override control procedures designed to
prevent similar frauds by other employees.

When obtaining reasonable assurance, the auditor is responsible for maintaining   8
professional skepticism throughout the audit, considering the potential for management override of controls and recognizing the fact that audit procedures that are
effective for detecting error may not be effective in detecting fraud. The requirements
in this ISA (UK and Ireland) are designed to assist the auditor in identifying and
assessing the risks of material misstatement due to fraud and in designing procedures
to detect such misstatement.

## Effective Date

This ISA (UK and Ireland) is effective for audits of financial statements for periods   9
ending on or after 15 December 2010.

## Objectives

The objectives of the auditor are:   10

(a) To identify and assess the risks of material misstatement of the financial
    statements due to fraud;
(b) To obtain sufficient appropriate audit evidence regarding the assessed risks of
    material misstatement due to fraud, through designing and implementing
    appropriate responses; and
(c) To respond appropriately to fraud or suspected fraud identified during the
    audit.

---

[3] *ISA (UK and Ireland) 200, "Overall Objectives of the Independent Auditor and the Conduct of an Audit in Accordance with International Standards on Auditing (UK and Ireland)," paragraph A51.*

[4] *ISA (UK and Ireland) 200, paragraph A51.*

# Definitions

11   For purposes of the ISAs (UK and Ireland), the following terms have the meanings attributed below:

(a)   Fraud – An intentional act by one or more individuals among management, those charged with governance, employees, or third parties, involving the use of deception to obtain an unjust or illegal advantage.

(b)   Fraud risk factors – Events or conditions that indicate an incentive or pressure to commit fraud or provide an opportunity to commit fraud.

# Requirements

## Professional Skepticism

12   In accordance with ISA (UK and Ireland) 200,[5] the auditor shall maintain professional skepticism throughout the audit, recognizing the possibility that a material misstatement due to fraud could exist, notwithstanding the auditor's past experience of the honesty and integrity of the entity's management and those charged with governance. (Ref: Para. A7- A8)

13   Unless the auditor has reason to believe the contrary, the auditor may accept records and documents as genuine. If conditions identified during the audit cause the auditor to believe that a document may not be authentic or that terms in a document have been modified but not disclosed to the auditor, the auditor shall investigate further. (Ref: Para. A9)

14   Where responses to inquiries of management or those charged with governance are inconsistent, the auditor shall investigate the inconsistencies.

## Discussion among the Engagement Team

15   ISA (UK and Ireland) 315 requires a discussion among the engagement team members and a determination by the engagement partner of which matters are to be communicated to those team members not involved in the discussion.[6] This discussion shall place particular emphasis on how and where the entity's financial statements may be susceptible to material misstatement due to fraud, including how fraud might occur. The discussion shall occur setting aside beliefs that the engagement team members may have that management and those charged with governance are honest and have integrity. (Ref: Para. A10-A11)

## Risk Assessment Procedures and Related Activities

16   When performing risk assessment procedures and related activities to obtain an understanding of the entity and its environment, including the entity's internal control, required by ISA (UK and Ireland) 315,[7] the auditor shall perform the procedures in paragraphs 17-24 to obtain information for use in identifying the risks of material misstatement due to fraud.

---

[5] *ISA (UK and Ireland) 200, paragraph 15.*

[6] *ISA (UK and Ireland) 315, paragraph 10.*

[7] *ISA (UK and Ireland) 315, paragraphs 5-24.*

*Management and Others within the Entity*

The auditor shall make inquiries of management regarding:  **17**

(a) Management's assessment of the risk that the financial statements may be materially misstated due to fraud, including the nature, extent and frequency of such assessments; (Ref: Para. A12-A13)
(b) Management's process for identifying and responding to the risks of fraud in the entity, including any specific risks of fraud that management has identified or that have been brought to its attention, or classes of transactions, account balances, or disclosures for which a risk of fraud is likely to exist; (Ref: Para. A14)
(c) Management's communication, if any, to those charged with governance regarding its processes for identifying and responding to the risks of fraud in the entity; and
(d) Management's communication, if any, to employees regarding its views on business practices and ethical behavior.

The auditor shall make inquiries of management, and others within the entity as  **18**
appropriate, to determine whether they have knowledge of any actual, suspected or alleged fraud affecting the entity. (Ref: Para. A15-A17)

For those entities that have an internal audit function, the auditor shall make  **19**
inquiries of internal audit to determine whether it has knowledge of any actual, suspected or alleged fraud affecting the entity, and to obtain its views about the risks of fraud. (Ref: Para. A18)

*Those Charged with Governance*

Unless all of those charged with governance are involved in managing the entity[8], the  **20**
auditor shall obtain an understanding of how those charged with governance exercise oversight of management's processes for identifying and responding to the risks of fraud in the entity and the internal control that management has established to mitigate these risks. (Ref: Para. A19-A21)

Unless all of those charged with governance are involved in managing the entity, the  **21**
auditor shall make inquiries of those charged with governance to determine whether they have knowledge of any actual, suspected or alleged fraud affecting the entity. These inquiries are made in part to corroborate the responses to the inquiries of management.

*Unusual or Unexpected Relationships Identified*

The auditor shall evaluate whether unusual or unexpected relationships that have  **22**
been identified in performing analytical procedures, including those related to revenue accounts, may indicate risks of material misstatement due to fraud.

*Other Information*

The auditor shall consider whether other information obtained by the auditor  **23**
indicates risks of material misstatement due to fraud. (Ref: Para. A22)

---

[8] *ISA (UK and Ireland) 260, "Communication with Those Charged with Governance," paragraph 13.*

*Evaluation of Fraud Risk Factors*

24   The auditor shall evaluate whether the information obtained from the other risk assessment procedures and related activities performed indicates that one or more fraud risk factors are present. While fraud risk factors may not necessarily indicate the existence of fraud, they have often been present in circumstances where frauds have occurred and therefore may indicate risks of material misstatement due to fraud. (Ref: Para. A23-A27)

## Identification and Assessment of the Risks of Material Misstatement Due to Fraud

25   In accordance with ISA (UK and Ireland) 315, the auditor shall identify and assess the risks of material misstatement due to fraud at the financial statement level, and at the assertion level for classes of transactions, account balances and disclosures.[9]

26   When identifying and assessing the risks of material misstatement due to fraud, the auditor shall, based on a presumption that there are risks of fraud in revenue recognition, evaluate which types of revenue, revenue transactions or assertions give rise to such risks. Paragraph 47 specifies the documentation required where the auditor concludes that the presumption is not applicable in the circumstances of the engagement and, accordingly, has not identified revenue recognition as a risk of material misstatement due to fraud. (Ref: Para. A28-A30)

27   The auditor shall treat those assessed risks of material misstatement due to fraud as significant risks and accordingly, to the extent not already done so, the auditor shall obtain an understanding of the entity's related controls, including control activities, relevant to such risks. (Ref: Para. A31-A32)

## Responses to the Assessed Risks of Material Misstatement Due to Fraud

*Overall Responses*

28   In accordance with ISA (UK and Ireland) 330, the auditor shall determine overall responses to address the assessed risks of material misstatement due to fraud at the financial statement level.[10] (Ref: Para. A33)

29   In determining overall responses to address the assessed risks of material misstatement due to fraud at the financial statement level, the auditor shall:

(a) Assign and supervise personnel taking account of the knowledge, skill and ability of the individuals to be given significant engagement responsibilities and the auditor's assessment of the risks of material misstatement due to fraud for the engagement; (Ref: Para. A34-A35)

(b) Evaluate whether the selection and application of accounting policies by the entity, particularly those related to subjective measurements and complex transactions, may be indicative of fraudulent financial reporting resulting from management's effort to manage earnings; and

(c) Incorporate an element of unpredictability in the selection of the nature, timing and extent of audit procedures. (Ref: Para. A36)

[9] *ISA (UK and Ireland) 315, paragraph 25.*

[10] *ISA (UK and Ireland) 330, paragraph 5.*

### Audit Procedures Responsive to Assessed Risks of Material Misstatement Due to Fraud at the Assertion Level

In accordance with ISA (UK and Ireland) 330, the auditor shall design and perform further audit procedures whose nature, timing and extent are responsive to the assessed risks of material misstatement due to fraud at the assertion level.[11] (Ref: Para. A37-A40) **30**

### Audit Procedures Responsive to Risks Related to Management Override of Controls

Management[11a] is in a unique position to perpetrate fraud because of management's ability to manipulate accounting records and prepare fraudulent financial statements by overriding controls that otherwise appear to be operating effectively. Although the level of risk of management override of controls will vary from entity to entity, the risk is nevertheless present in all entities. Due to the unpredictable way in which such override could occur, it is a risk of material misstatement due to fraud and thus a significant risk. **31**

Irrespective of the auditor's assessment of the risks of management override of controls, the auditor shall design and perform audit procedures to: **32**

(a) Test the appropriateness of journal entries recorded in the general ledger and other adjustments made in the preparation of the financial statements. In designing and performing audit procedures for such tests, the auditor shall:
   (i) Make inquiries of individuals involved in the financial reporting process about inappropriate or unusual activity relating to the processing of journal entries and other adjustments;
   (ii) Select journal entries and other adjustments made at the end of a reporting period; and
   (iii) Consider the need to test journal entries and other adjustments throughout the period. (Ref: Para. A41-A44)
(b) Review accounting estimates for biases and evaluate whether the circumstances producing the bias, if any, represent a risk of material misstatement due to fraud. In performing this review, the auditor shall:
   (i) Evaluate whether the judgments and decisions made by management in making the accounting estimates included in the financial statements, even if they are individually reasonable, indicate a possible bias on the part of the entity's management that may represent a risk of material misstatement due to fraud. If so, the auditor shall reevaluate the accounting estimates taken as a whole; and
   (ii) Perform a retrospective review of management judgments and assumptions related to significant accounting estimates reflected in the financial statements of the prior year. (Ref: Para. A45-A47)
(c) For significant transactions that are outside the normal course of business for the entity, or that otherwise appear to be unusual given the auditor's understanding of the entity and its environment and other information obtained during the audit, the auditor shall evaluate whether the business rationale (or the lack thereof) of the transactions suggests that they may have been entered into to engage in fraudulent financial reporting or to conceal misappropriation of assets. (Ref: Para. A48)

---

[11] *ISA (UK and Ireland) 330, paragraph 6.*

[11a] *In the UK and Ireland those charged with governance are responsible for the preparation of the financial statements.*

**33**   The auditor shall determine whether, in order to respond to the identified risks of management override of controls, the auditor needs to perform other audit procedures in addition to those specifically referred to above (i.e., where there are specific additional risks of management override that are not covered as part of the procedures performed to address the requirements in paragraph 32).

## Evaluation of Audit Evidence (Ref: Para. A49)

**34**   The auditor shall evaluate whether analytical procedures that are performed near the end of the audit, when forming an overall conclusion as to whether the financial statements are consistent with the auditor's understanding of the entity, indicate a previously unrecognized risk of material misstatement due to fraud. (Ref: Para. A50)

**35**   If the auditor identifies a misstatement, the auditor shall evaluate whether such a misstatement is indicative of fraud. If there is such an indication, the auditor shall evaluate the implications of the misstatement in relation to other aspects of the audit, particularly the reliability of management representations, recognizing that an instance of fraud is unlikely to be an isolated occurrence. (Ref: Para. A51)

**36**   If the auditor identifies a misstatement, whether material or not, and the auditor has reason to believe that it is or may be the result of fraud and that management (in particular, senior management) is involved, the auditor shall reevaluate the assessment of the risks of material misstatement due to fraud and its resulting impact on the nature, timing and extent of audit procedures to respond to the assessed risks. The auditor shall also consider whether circumstances or conditions indicate possible collusion involving employees, management or third parties when reconsidering the reliability of evidence previously obtained. (Ref: Para. A52)

**37**   If the auditor confirms that, or is unable to conclude whether, the financial statements are materially misstated as a result of fraud the auditor shall evaluate the implications for the audit. (Ref: Para. A53)

## Auditor Unable to Continue the Engagement

**38**   If, as a result of a misstatement resulting from fraud or suspected fraud, the auditor encounters exceptional circumstances that bring into question the auditor's ability to continue performing the audit, the auditor shall:

   (a)  Determine the professional and legal responsibilities applicable in the circumstances, including whether there is a requirement for the auditor to report to the person or persons who made the audit appointment or, in some cases, to regulatory authorities;

   (b)  Consider whether it is appropriate to withdraw from the engagement, where withdrawal is possible under applicable law or regulation; and

   (c)  If the auditor withdraws:

      (i)   Discuss with the appropriate level of management and those charged with governance the auditor's withdrawal from the engagement and the reasons for the withdrawal; and

      (ii)  Determine whether there is a professional or legal requirement to report to the person or persons who made the audit appointment or, in some cases, to regulatory authorities, the auditor's withdrawal from the engagement and the reasons for the withdrawal. (Ref: Para. A54-A57)

## Written Representations

The auditor shall obtain written representations from management and, where **39** appropriate, those charged with governance that:

(a) They acknowledge their responsibility for the design, implementation and maintenance of internal control to prevent and detect fraud;

(b) They have disclosed to the auditor the results of management's assessment of the risk that the financial statements may be materially misstated as a result of fraud;

(c) They have disclosed to the auditor their knowledge of fraud or suspected fraud affecting the entity involving:
    (i) Management;
    (ii) Employees who have significant roles in internal control; or
    (iii) Others where the fraud could have a material effect on the financial statements; and

(d) They have disclosed to the auditor their knowledge of any allegations of fraud, or suspected fraud, affecting the entity's financial statements communicated by employees, former employees, analysts, regulators or others. (Ref: Para. A58-A59)

## Communications to Management and with Those Charged with Governance

If the auditor has identified a fraud or has obtained information that indicates that a **40** fraud may exist, the auditor shall communicate these matters on a timely basis to the appropriate level of management in order to inform those with primary responsibility for the prevention and detection of fraud of matters relevant to their responsibilities. (Ref: Para. A60)

Unless all of those charged with governance are involved in managing the entity, if **41** the auditor has identified or suspects fraud involving:

(a) management;

(b) employees who have significant roles in internal control; or

(c) others where the fraud results in a material misstatement in the financial statements,

the auditor shall communicate these matters to those charged with governance on a timely basis. If the auditor suspects fraud involving management, the auditor shall communicate these suspicions to those charged with governance and discuss with them the nature, timing and extent of audit procedures necessary to complete the audit. (Ref: Para. A61-A63)

The auditor shall communicate with those charged with governance any other **42** matters related to fraud that are, in the auditor's judgment, relevant to their responsibilities. (Ref: Para. A64)

## Communications to Regulatory and Enforcement Authorities

If the auditor has identified or suspects a fraud, the auditor shall determine whether **43** there is a responsibility to report the occurrence or suspicion to a party outside the entity. Although the auditor's professional duty to maintain the confidentiality of client information may preclude such reporting, the auditor's legal responsibilities may override the duty of confidentiality in some circumstances. (Ref: Para. A65-A67)

**Documentation**

**44**   The auditor shall include the following in the audit documentation[12] of the auditor's understanding of the entity and its environment and the assessment of the risks of material misstatement required by ISA (UK and Ireland) 315:[13]

    (a)   The significant decisions reached during the discussion among the engagement team regarding the susceptibility of the entity's financial statements to material misstatement due to fraud; and

    (b)   The identified and assessed risks of material misstatement due to fraud at the financial statement level and at the assertion level.

**45**   The auditor shall include the following in the audit documentation of the auditor's responses to the assessed risks of material misstatement required by ISA (UK and Ireland) 330:[14]

    (a)   The overall responses to the assessed risks of material misstatement due to fraud at the financial statement level and the nature, timing and extent of audit procedures, and the linkage of those procedures with the assessed risks of material misstatement due to fraud at the assertion level; and

    (b)   The results of the audit procedures, including those designed to address the risk of management override of controls.

**46**   The auditor shall include in the audit documentation communications about fraud made to management, those charged with governance, regulators and others.

**47**   If the auditor has concluded that the presumption that there is a risk of material misstatement due to fraud related to revenue recognition is not applicable in the circumstances of the engagement, the auditor shall include in the audit documentation the reasons for that conclusion.

***

# Application and Other Explanatory Material

## Characteristics of Fraud (Ref: Para. 3)

**A1**   Fraud, whether fraudulent financial reporting or misappropriation of assets, involves incentive or pressure to commit fraud, a perceived opportunity to do so and some rationalization of the act. For example:

- Incentive or pressure to commit fraudulent financial reporting may exist when management is under pressure, from sources outside or inside the entity, to achieve an expected (and perhaps unrealistic) earnings target or financial outcome – particularly since the consequences to management for failing to meet financial goals can be significant. Similarly, individuals may have an incentive to misappropriate assets, for example, because the individuals are living beyond their means.

- A perceived opportunity to commit fraud may exist when an individual believes internal control can be overridden, for example, because the individual is in a position of trust or has knowledge of specific deficiencies in internal control.

---

[12] *ISA (UK and Ireland) 230, "Audit Documentation," paragraphs 8-11, and paragraph A6.*

[13] *ISA (UK and Ireland) 315, paragraph 32.*

[14] *ISA (UK and Ireland) 330, paragraph 28.*

- Individuals may be able to rationalize committing a fraudulent act. Some individuals possess an attitude, character or set of ethical values that allow them knowingly and intentionally to commit a dishonest act. However, even otherwise honest individuals can commit fraud in an environment that imposes sufficient pressure on them.

Fraudulent financial reporting involves intentional misstatements including omissions of amounts or disclosures in financial statements to deceive financial statement users. It can be caused by the efforts of management to manage earnings in order to deceive financial statement users by influencing their perceptions as to the entity's performance and profitability. Such earnings management may start out with small actions or inappropriate adjustment of assumptions and changes in judgments by management. Pressures and incentives may lead these actions to increase to the extent that they result in fraudulent financial reporting. Such a situation could occur when, due to pressures to meet market expectations or a desire to maximize compensation based on performance, management intentionally takes positions that lead to fraudulent financial reporting by materially misstating the financial statements. In some entities, management may be motivated to reduce earnings by a material amount to minimize tax or to inflate earnings to secure bank financing.   **A2**

Fraudulent financial reporting may be accomplished by the following:   **A3**

- Manipulation, falsification (including forgery), or alteration of accounting records or supporting documentation from which the financial statements are prepared.
- Misrepresentation in, or intentional omission from, the financial statements of events, transactions or other significant information.
- Intentional misapplication of accounting principles relating to amounts, classification, manner of presentation, or disclosure.

Fraudulent financial reporting often involves management override of controls that otherwise may appear to be operating effectively. Fraud can be committed by management overriding controls using such techniques as:   **A4**

- Recording fictitious journal entries, particularly close to the end of an accounting period, to manipulate operating results or achieve other objectives.
- Inappropriately adjusting assumptions and changing judgments used to estimate account balances.
- Omitting, advancing or delaying recognition in the financial statements of events and transactions that have occurred during the reporting period.
- Concealing, or not disclosing, facts that could affect the amounts recorded in the financial statements.
- Engaging in complex transactions that are structured to misrepresent the financial position or financial performance of the entity.
- Altering records and terms related to significant and unusual transactions.

Misappropriation of assets involves the theft of an entity's assets and is often perpetrated by employees in relatively small and immaterial amounts. However, it can also involve management who are usually more able to disguise or conceal misappropriations in ways that are difficult to detect. Misappropriation of assets can be accomplished in a variety of ways including:   **A5**

- Embezzling receipts (for example, misappropriating collections on accounts receivable or diverting receipts in respect of written-off accounts to personal bank accounts).

- Stealing physical assets or intellectual property (for example, stealing inventory for personal use or for sale, stealing scrap for resale, colluding with a competitor by disclosing technological data in return for payment).
- Causing an entity to pay for goods and services not received (for example, payments to fictitious vendors, kickbacks paid by vendors to the entity's purchasing agents in return for inflating prices, payments to fictitious employees).
- Using an entity's assets for personal use (for example, using the entity's assets as collateral for a personal loan or a loan to a related party).

A5    Misappropriation of assets is often accompanied by false or misleading records or documents in order to conceal the fact that the assets are missing or have been pledged without proper authorization.

### *Considerations Specific to Public Sector Entities*

A6    The public sector auditor's responsibilities relating to fraud may be a result of law, regulation or other authority applicable to public sector entities or separately covered by the auditor's mandate. Consequently, the public sector auditor's responsibilities may not be limited to consideration of risks of material misstatement of the financial statements, but may also include a broader responsibility to consider risks of fraud.

## Professional Skepticism (Ref: Para. 12-14)

A7    Maintaining professional skepticism requires an ongoing questioning of whether the information and audit evidence obtained suggests that a material misstatement due to fraud may exist. It includes considering the reliability of the information to be used as audit evidence and the controls over its preparation and maintenance where relevant. Due to the characteristics of fraud, the auditor's attitude of professional skepticism is particularly important when considering the risks of material misstatement due to fraud.

A8    Although the auditor cannot be expected to disregard past experience of the honesty and integrity of the entity's management and those charged with governance, the auditor's professional skepticism is particularly important in considering the risks of material misstatement due to fraud because there may have been changes in circumstances.

A9    An audit performed in accordance with ISAs (UK and Ireland) rarely involves the authentication of documents, nor is the auditor trained as or expected to be an expert in such authentication.[15] However, when the auditor identifies conditions that cause the auditor to believe that a document may not be authentic or that terms in a document have been modified but not disclosed to the auditor, possible procedures to investigate further may include:

- Confirming directly with the third party.
- Using the work of an expert to assess the document's authenticity.

## Discussion among the Engagement Team (Ref: Para. 15)

A10    Discussing the susceptibility of the entity's financial statements to material misstatement due to fraud with the engagement team:

---

[15] *ISA (UK and Ireland) 200, paragraph A47.*

- Provides an opportunity for more experienced engagement team members to share their insights about how and where the financial statements may be susceptible to material misstatement due to fraud.
- Enables the auditor to consider an appropriate response to such susceptibility and to determine which members of the engagement team will conduct certain audit procedures.
- Permits the auditor to determine how the results of audit procedures will be shared among the engagement team and how to deal with any allegations of fraud that may come to the auditor's attention.

The discussion may include such matters as:                                          **A11**

- An exchange of ideas among engagement team members about how and where they believe the entity's financial statements may be susceptible to material misstatement due to fraud, how management could perpetrate and conceal fraudulent financial reporting, and how assets of the entity could be misappropriated.
- A consideration of circumstances that might be indicative of earnings management and the practices that might be followed by management to manage earnings that could lead to fraudulent financial reporting.
- A consideration of the known external and internal factors affecting the entity that may create an incentive or pressure for management or others to commit fraud, provide the opportunity for fraud to be perpetrated, and indicate a culture or environment that enables management or others to rationalize committing fraud.
- A consideration of management's involvement in overseeing employees with access to cash or other assets susceptible to misappropriation.
- A consideration of any unusual or unexplained changes in behavior or lifestyle of management or employees which have come to the attention of the engagement team.
- An emphasis on the importance of maintaining a proper state of mind throughout the audit regarding the potential for material misstatement due to fraud.
- A consideration of the types of circumstances that, if encountered, might indicate the possibility of fraud.
- A consideration of how an element of unpredictability will be incorporated into the nature, timing and extent of the audit procedures to be performed.
- A consideration of the audit procedures that might be selected to respond to the susceptibility of the entity's financial statement to material misstatement due to fraud and whether certain types of audit procedures are more effective than others.
- A consideration of any allegations of fraud that have come to the auditor's attention.
- A consideration of the risk of management override of controls.

## Risk Assessment Procedures and Related Activities

### *Inquiries of Management*

Management's Assessment of the Risk of Material Misstatement Due to Fraud (Ref: Para. 17(a))

Management[11a] accepts responsibility for the entity's internal control and for the       **A12**
preparation of the entity's financial statements. Accordingly, it is appropriate for the
auditor to make inquiries of management regarding management's own assessment

of the risk of fraud and the controls in place to prevent and detect it. The nature, extent and frequency of management's assessment of such risk and controls may vary from entity to entity. In some entities, management may make detailed assessments on an annual basis or as part of continuous monitoring. In other entities, management's assessment may be less structured and less frequent. The nature, extent and frequency of management's assessment are relevant to the auditor's understanding of the entity's control environment. For example, the fact that management has not made an assessment of the risk of fraud may in some circumstances be indicative of the lack of importance that management places on internal control.

*Considerations specific to smaller entities*

A13   In some entities, particularly smaller entities, the focus of management's assessment may be on the risks of employee fraud or misappropriation of assets.

*Management's Process for Identifying and Responding to the Risks of Fraud (Ref: Para. 17(b))*

A14   In the case of entities with multiple locations management's processes may include different levels of monitoring of operating locations, or business segments. Management may also have identified particular operating locations or business segments for which a risk of fraud may be more likely to exist.

**Inquiry of Management and Others within the Entity** (Ref: Para. 18)

A15   The auditor's inquiries of management may provide useful information concerning the risks of material misstatements in the financial statements resulting from employee fraud. However, such inquiries are unlikely to provide useful information regarding the risks of material misstatement in the financial statements resulting from management fraud. Making inquiries of others within the entity may provide individuals with an opportunity to convey information to the auditor that may not otherwise be communicated.

A16   Examples of others within the entity to whom the auditor may direct inquiries about the existence or suspicion of fraud include:

- Operating personnel not directly involved in the financial reporting process.
- Employees with different levels of authority.
- Employees involved in initiating, processing or recording complex or unusual transactions and those who supervise or monitor such employees.
- In-house legal counsel.
- Chief ethics officer or equivalent person.
- The person or persons charged with dealing with allegations of fraud.

A17   Management is often in the best position to perpetrate fraud. Accordingly, when evaluating management's responses to inquiries with an attitude of professional skepticism, the auditor may judge it necessary to corroborate responses to inquiries with other information.

**Inquiry of Internal Audit** (Ref: Para. 19)

ISA (UK and Ireland) 315 and ISA (UK and Ireland) 610 establish requirements and provide guidance in audits of those entities that have an internal audit function.[16] In carrying out the requirements of those ISAs (UK and Ireland) in the context of fraud, the auditor may inquire about specific internal audit activities including, for example:   **A18**

- The procedures performed, if any, by the internal auditors during the year to detect fraud.
- Whether management has satisfactorily responded to any findings resulting from those procedures.

**Obtaining an Understanding of Oversight Exercised by Those Charged with Governance** (Ref: Para. 20)

Those charged with governance of an entity oversee the entity's systems for monitoring risk, financial control and compliance with the law. In many countries, corporate governance practices are well developed and those charged with governance play an active role in oversight of the entity's assessment of the risks of fraud and of the relevant internal control. Since the responsibilities of those charged with governance and management may vary by entity and by country, it is important that the auditor understands their respective responsibilities to enable the auditor to obtain an understanding of the oversight exercised by the appropriate individuals.[17]   **A19**

An understanding of the oversight exercised by those charged with governance may provide insights regarding the susceptibility of the entity to management fraud, the adequacy of internal control over risks of fraud, and the competency and integrity of management. The auditor may obtain this understanding in a number of ways, such as by attending meetings where such discussions take place, reading the minutes from such meetings or making inquiries of those charged with governance.   **A20**

**Considerations Specific to Smaller Entities**

In some cases, all of those charged with governance are involved in managing the entity. This may be the case in a small entity where a single owner manages the entity and no one else has a governance role. In these cases, there is ordinarily no action on the part of the auditor because there is no oversight separate from management.   **A21**

**Consideration of Other Information** (Ref: Para. 23)

In addition to information obtained from applying analytical procedures, other information obtained about the entity and its environment may be helpful in identifying the risks of material misstatement due to fraud. The discussion among team members may provide information that is helpful in identifying such risks. In addition, information obtained from the auditor's client acceptance and retention processes, and experience gained on other engagements performed for the entity, for example engagements to review interim financial information, may be relevant in the identification of the risks of material misstatement due to fraud.   **A22**

[16] *ISA (UK and Ireland) 315, paragraph 23, and ISA 610, "Using the Work of Internal Auditors."*

[17] *ISA (UK and Ireland) 260, "Communication with Those Charged with Governance," paragraphs A1-A8, discuss with whom the auditor communicates when the entity's governance structure is not well defined.*

**Evaluation of Fraud Risk Factors** (Ref: Para. 24)

A23    The fact that fraud is usually concealed can make it very difficult to detect. Never-theless, the auditor may identify events or conditions that indicate an incentive or pressure to commit fraud or provide an opportunity to commit fraud (fraud risk factors). For example:

- The need to meet expectations of third parties to obtain additional equity financing may create pressure to commit fraud;
- The granting of significant bonuses if unrealistic profit targets are met may create an incentive to commit fraud; and
- A control environment that is not effective may create an opportunity to commit fraud.

A24    Fraud risk factors cannot easily be ranked in order of importance. The significance of fraud risk factors varies widely. Some of these factors will be present in entities where the specific conditions do not present risks of material misstatement. Accordingly, the determination of whether a fraud risk factor is present and whether it is to be considered in assessing the risks of material misstatement of the financial statements due to fraud requires the exercise of professional judgment.

A25    Examples of fraud risk factors related to fraudulent financial reporting and mis-appropriation of assets are presented in Appendix 1. These illustrative risk factors are classified based on the three conditions that are generally present when fraud exists:

- An incentive or pressure to commit fraud;
- A perceived opportunity to commit fraud; and
- An ability to rationalize the fraudulent action.

Risk factors reflective of an attitude that permits rationalization of the fraudulent action may not be susceptible to observation by the auditor. Nevertheless, the auditor may become aware of the existence of such information. Although the fraud risk factors described in Appendix 1 cover a broad range of situations that may be faced by auditors, they are only examples and other risk factors may exist.

A26    The size, complexity, and ownership characteristics of the entity have a significant influence on the consideration of relevant fraud risk factors. For example, in the case of a large entity, there may be factors that generally constrain improper conduct by management, such as:

- Effective oversight by those charged with governance.
- An effective internal audit function.
- The existence and enforcement of a written code of conduct.

Furthermore, fraud risk factors considered at a business segment operating level may provide different insights when compared with those obtained when considered at an entity-wide level.

*Considerations Specific to Smaller Entities*

A27    In the case of a small entity, some or all of these considerations may be inapplicable or less relevant. For example, a smaller entity may not have a written code of conduct but, instead, may have developed a culture that emphasizes the importance of integrity and ethical behavior through oral communication and by management example. Domination of management by a single individual in a small entity does not generally, in and of itself, indicate a failure by management to display and communicate an appropriate attitude regarding internal control and the financial reporting process. In some entities, the need for management authorization can compensate for otherwise deficient controls and reduce the risk of employee fraud. However, domination of management by a single individual can be a potential deficiency in internal control since there is an opportunity for management override of controls.

## Identification and Assessment of the Risks of Material Misstatement Due to Fraud

### *Risks of Fraud in Revenue Recognition* (Ref: Para. 26)

Material misstatement due to fraudulent financial reporting relating to revenue recognition often results from an overstatement of revenues through, for example, premature revenue recognition or recording fictitious revenues. It may result also from an understatement of revenues through, for example, improperly shifting revenues to a later period.

A28

The risks of fraud in revenue recognition may be greater in some entities than others. For example, there may be pressures or incentives on management to commit fraudulent financial reporting through inappropriate revenue recognition in the case of listed entities when, for example, performance is measured in terms of year-over-year revenue growth or profit. Similarly, for example, there may be greater risks of fraud in revenue recognition in the case of entities that generate a substantial portion of revenues through cash sales.

A29

The presumption that there are risks of fraud in revenue recognition may be rebutted. For example, the auditor may conclude that there is no risk of material misstatement due to fraud relating to revenue recognition in the case where a there is a single type of simple revenue transaction, for example, leasehold revenue from a single unit rental property.

A30

### *Identifying and Assessing the Risks of Material Misstatement Due to Fraud and Understanding the Entity's Related Controls* (Ref: Para. 27)

Management may make judgments on the nature and extent of the controls it chooses to implement, and the nature and extent of the risks it chooses to assume.[18] In determining which controls to implement to prevent and detect fraud, management considers the risks that the financial statements may be materially misstated as a result of fraud. As part of this consideration, management may conclude that it is not cost effective to implement and maintain a particular control in relation to the reduction in the risks of material misstatement due to fraud to be achieved.

A31

It is therefore important for the auditor to obtain an understanding of the controls that management has designed, implemented and maintained to prevent and detect fraud. In doing so, the auditor may learn, for example, that management has consciously chosen to accept the risks associated with a lack of segregation of duties. Information from obtaining this understanding may also be useful in identifying fraud risks factors that may affect the auditor's assessment of the risks that the financial statements may contain material misstatement due to fraud.

A32

---

[18] *ISA (UK and Ireland) 315, paragraph A48.*

## Responses to the Assessed Risks of Material Misstatement Due to Fraud

*Overall Responses* (Ref: Para. 28)

A33   Determining overall responses to address the assessed risks of material misstatement due to fraud generally includes the consideration of how the overall conduct of the audit can reflect increased professional skepticism, for example, through:

- Increased sensitivity in the selection of the nature and extent of documentation to be examined in support of material transactions.
- Increased recognition of the need to corroborate management explanations or representations concerning material matters.

It also involves more general considerations apart from the specific procedures otherwise planned; these considerations include the matters listed in paragraph 29, which are discussed below.

*Assignment and Supervision of Personnel* (Ref: Para. 29(a))

A34   The auditor may respond to identified risks of material misstatement due to fraud by, for example, assigning additional individuals with specialized skill and knowledge, such as forensic and IT experts, or by assigning more experienced individuals to the engagement.

A35   The extent of supervision reflects the auditor's assessment of risks of material misstatement due to fraud and the competencies of the engagement team members performing the work.

*Unpredictability in the Selection of Audit Procedures* (Ref: Para. 29(c))

A36   Incorporating an element of unpredictability in the selection of the nature, timing and extent of audit procedures to be performed is important as individuals within the entity who are familiar with the audit procedures normally performed on engagements may be more able to conceal fraudulent financial reporting. This can be achieved by, for example:

- Performing substantive procedures on selected account balances and assertions not otherwise tested due to their materiality or risk.
- Adjusting the timing of audit procedures from that otherwise expected.
- Using different sampling methods.
- Performing audit procedures at different locations or at locations on an unannounced basis.

*Audit Procedures Responsive to Assessed Risks of Material Misstatement Due to Fraud at the Assertion Level* (Ref: Para. 30)

A37   The auditor's responses to address the assessed risks of material misstatement due to fraud at the assertion level may include changing the nature, timing, and extent of audit procedures in the following ways:

- The nature of audit procedures to be performed may need to be changed to obtain audit evidence that is more reliable and relevant or to obtain additional corroborative information. This may affect both the type of audit procedures to be performed and their combination. For example:
  - Physical observation or inspection of certain assets may become more important or the auditor may choose to use computer-assisted audit

techniques to gather more evidence about data contained in significant accounts or electronic transaction files.

- The auditor may design procedures to obtain additional corroborative information. For example, if the auditor identifies that management is under pressure to meet earnings expectations, there may be a related risk that management is inflating sales by entering into sales agreements that include terms that preclude revenue recognition or by invoicing sales before delivery. In these circumstances, the auditor may, for example, design external confirmations not only to confirm outstanding amounts, but also to confirm the details of the sales agreements, including date, any rights of return and delivery terms. In addition, the auditor might find it effective to supplement such external confirmations with inquiries of non-financial personnel in the entity regarding any changes in sales agreements and delivery terms.
- The timing of substantive procedures may need to be modified. The auditor may conclude that performing substantive testing at or near the period end better addresses an assessed risk of material misstatement due to fraud. The auditor may conclude that, given the assessed risks of intentional misstatement or manipulation, audit procedures to extend audit conclusions from an interim date to the period end would not be effective. In contrast, because an intentional misstatement – for example, a misstatement involving improper revenue recognition – may have been initiated in an interim period, the auditor may elect to apply substantive procedures to transactions occurring earlier in or throughout the reporting period.
- The extent of the procedures applied reflects the assessment of the risks of material misstatement due to fraud. For example, increasing sample sizes or performing analytical procedures at a more detailed level may be appropriate. Also, computer-assisted audit techniques may enable more extensive testing of electronic transactions and account files. Such techniques can be used to select sample transactions from key electronic files, to sort transactions with specific characteristics, or to test an entire population instead of a sample.

If the auditor identifies a risk of material misstatement due to fraud that affects inventory quantities, examining the entity's inventory records may help to identify locations or items that require specific attention during or after the physical inventory count. Such a review may lead to a decision to observe inventory counts at certain locations on an unannounced basis or to conduct inventory counts at all locations on the same date. **A38**

The auditor may identify a risk of material misstatement due to fraud affecting a number of accounts and assertions. These may include asset valuation, estimates relating to specific transactions (such as acquisitions, restructurings, or disposals of a segment of the business), and other significant accrued liabilities (such as pension and other post-employment benefit obligations, or environmental remediation liabilities). The risk may also relate to significant changes in assumptions relating to recurring estimates. Information gathered through obtaining an understanding of the entity and its environment may assist the auditor in evaluating the reasonableness of such management estimates and underlying judgments and assumptions. A retrospective review of similar management judgments and assumptions applied in prior periods may also provide insight about the reasonableness of judgments and assumptions supporting management estimates. **A39**

Examples of possible audit procedures to address the assessed risks of material misstatement due to fraud, including those that illustrate the incorporation of an element of unpredictability, are presented in Appendix 2. The appendix includes examples of responses to the auditor's assessment of the risks of material **A40** misstatement resulting from both fraudulent financial reporting, including fraudulent financial reporting resulting from revenue recognition, and misappropriation of assets.

### Audit Procedures Responsive to Risks Related to Management Override of Controls

*Journal Entries and Other Adjustments (Ref: Para. 32(a))*

**A41**   Material misstatement of financial statements due to fraud often involve the manipulation of the financial reporting process by recording inappropriate or unauthorized journal entries. This may occur throughout the year or at period end, or by management making adjustments to amounts reported in the financial statements that are not reflected in journal entries, such as through consolidating adjustments and reclassifications.

**A42**   Further, the auditor's consideration of the risks of material misstatement associated with inappropriate override of controls over journal entries is important since automated processes and controls may reduce the risk of inadvertent error but do not overcome the risk that individuals may inappropriately override such automated processes, for example, by changing the amounts being automatically passed to the general ledger or to the financial reporting system. Furthermore, where IT is used to transfer information automatically, there may be little or no visible evidence of such intervention in the information systems.

**A43**   When identifying and selecting journal entries and other adjustments for testing and determining the appropriate method of examining the underlying support for the items selected, the following matters are of relevance:

- *The assessment of the risks of material misstatement due to fraud* – the presence of fraud risk factors and other information obtained during the auditor's assessment of the risks of material misstatement due to fraud may assist the auditor to identify specific classes of journal entries and other adjustments for testing.
- *Controls that have been implemented over journal entries and other adjustments* – effective controls over the preparation and posting of journal entries and other adjustments may reduce the extent of substantive testing necessary, provided that the auditor has tested the operating effectiveness of the controls.
- *The entity's financial reporting process and the nature of evidence that can be obtained* – for many entities routine processing of transactions involves a combination of manual and automated steps and procedures. Similarly, the processing of journal entries and other adjustments may involve both manual and automated procedures and controls. Where information technology is used in the financial reporting process, journal entries and other adjustments may exist only in electronic form.
- *The characteristics of fraudulent journal entries or other adjustments* – inappropriate journal entries or other adjustments often have unique identifying characteristics. Such characteristics may include entries (a) made to unrelated, unusual, or seldom-used accounts, (b) made by individuals who typically do not make journal entries, (c) recorded at the end of the period or as post-closing entries that have little or no explanation or description, (d) made either before or during the preparation of the financial statements that do not have account numbers, or (e) containing round numbers or consistent ending numbers.
- *The nature and complexity of the accounts* – inappropriate journal entries or adjustments may be applied to accounts that (a) contain transactions that are complex or unusual in nature, (b) contain significant estimates and period-end

adjustments, (c) have been prone to misstatements in the past, (d) have not been reconciled on a timely basis or contain unreconciled differences, (e) contain inter-company transactions, or (f) are otherwise associated with an identified risk of material misstatement due to fraud. In audits of entities that have several locations or components, consideration is given to the need to select journal entries from multiple locations.

- *Journal entries or other adjustments processed outside the normal course of business* – non standard journal entries may not be subject to the same level of internal control as those journal entries used on a recurring basis to record transactions such as monthly sales, purchases and cash disbursements.

The auditor uses professional judgment in determining the nature, timing and extent **A44** of testing of journal entries and other adjustments. However, because fraudulent journal entries and other adjustments are often made at the end of a reporting period, paragraph 32(a)(ii) requires the auditor to select the journal entries and other adjustments made at that time. Further, because material misstatements in financial statements due to fraud can occur throughout the period and may involve extensive efforts to conceal how the fraud is accomplished, paragraph 32(a)(iii) requires the auditor to consider whether there is also a need to test journal entries and other adjustments throughout the period.

### *Accounting Estimates* (Ref: Para. 32(b))

The preparation of the financial statements requires management[11a] to make a **A45** number of judgments or assumptions that affect significant accounting estimates and for monitoring the reasonableness of such estimates on an ongoing basis. Fraudulent financial reporting is often accomplished through intentional misstatement of accounting estimates. This may be achieved by, for example, understating or over-stating all provisions or reserves in the same fashion so as to be designed either to smooth earnings over two or more accounting periods, or to achieve a designated earnings level in order to deceive financial statement users by influencing their per-ceptions as to the entity's performance and profitability.

The purpose of performing a retrospective review of management judgments and **A46** assumptions related to significant accounting estimates reflected in the financial statements of the prior year is to determine whether there is an indication of a possible bias on the part of management. It is not intended to call into question the auditor's professional judgments made in the prior year that were based on infor-mation available at the time.

A retrospective review is also required by ISA (UK and Ireland) 540.[19] That review is **A47** conducted as a risk assessment procedure to obtain information regarding the effectiveness of management's prior period estimation process, audit evidence about the outcome, or where applicable, the subsequent re-estimation of prior period accounting estimates that is pertinent to making current period accounting estimates, and audit evidence of matters, such as estimation uncertainty, that may be required to be disclosed in the financial statements. As a practical matter, the auditor's review of management judgments and assumptions for biases that could represent a risk of material misstatement due to fraud in accordance with this ISA (UK and Ireland) may be carried out in conjunction with the review required by ISA (UK and Ireland) 540.

---

[19] *ISA (UK and Ireland) 540, "Auditing Accounting Estimates, Including Fair Value Accounting Estimates, and Related Disclosures," paragraph 9.*

***Business Rationale for Significant Transactions*** (Ref: Para. 32(c))

**A48**     Indicators that may suggest that significant transactions that are outside the normal course of business for the entity, or that otherwise appear to be unusual, may have been entered into to engage in fraudulent financial reporting or to conceal misappropriation of assets include:

- The form of such transactions appears overly complex (for example, the transaction involves multiple entities within a consolidated group or multiple unrelated third parties).
- Management has not discussed the nature of and accounting for such transactions with those charged with governance of the entity, and there is inadequate documentation.
- Management is placing more emphasis on the need for a particular accounting treatment than on the underlying economics of the transaction.
- Transactions that involve non-consolidated related parties, including special purpose entities, have not been properly reviewed or approved by those charged with governance of the entity.
- The transactions involve previously unidentified related parties or parties that do not have the substance or the financial strength to support the transaction without assistance from the entity under audit.

## Evaluation of Audit Evidence (Ref: Para. 34-37)

**A49**     ISA (UK and Ireland) 330 requires the auditor, based on the audit procedures performed and the audit evidence obtained, to evaluate whether the assessments of the risks of material misstatement at the assertion level remain appropriate.[20] This evaluation is primarily a qualitative matter based on the auditor's judgment. Such an evaluation may provide further insight about the risks of material misstatement due to fraud and whether there is a need to perform additional or different audit procedures. Appendix 3 contains examples of circumstances that may indicate the possibility of fraud.

***Analytical Procedures Performed Near the End of the Audit in Forming and Overall Conclusion*** (Ref: Para. 34)

**A50**     Determining which particular trends and relationships may indicate a risk of material misstatement due to fraud requires professional judgment. Unusual relationships involving year-end revenue and income are particularly relevant. These might include, for example: uncharacteristically large amounts of income being reported in the last few weeks of the reporting period or unusual transactions; or income that is inconsistent with trends in cash flow from operations.

***Consideration of Identified Misstatements*** (Ref: Para. 35-37)

**A51**     Since fraud involves incentive or pressure to commit fraud, a perceived opportunity to do so or some rationalization of the act, an instance of fraud is unlikely to be an isolated occurrence. Accordingly, misstatements, such as numerous misstatements at a specific location even though the cumulative effect is not material, may be indicative of a risk of material misstatement due to fraud.

**A52**     The implications of identified fraud depend on the circumstances. For example, an otherwise insignificant fraud may be significant if it involves senior management. In

---

[20] *ISA (UK and Ireland) 330, paragraph 25.*

such circumstances, the reliability of evidence previously obtained may be called into question, since there may be doubts about the completeness and truthfulness of representations made and about the genuineness of accounting records and documentation. There may also be a possibility of collusion involving employees, management or third parties.

ISA (UK and Ireland) 450[21] and ISA (UK and Ireland) 700[22] establish requirements and provide guidance on the evaluation and disposition of misstatements and the effect on the auditor's opinion in the auditor's report.    **A53**

## Auditor Unable to Continue the Engagement (Ref: Para. 38)

Examples of exceptional circumstances that may arise and that may bring into question the auditor's ability to continue performing the audit include:    **A54**

- The entity does not take the appropriate action regarding fraud that the auditor considers necessary in the circumstances, even where the fraud is not material to the financial statements;
- The auditor's consideration of the risks of material misstatement due to fraud and the results of audit tests indicate a significant risk of material and pervasive fraud; or
- The auditor has significant concern about the competence or integrity of management or those charged with governance.

Because of the variety of the circumstances that may arise, it is not possible to describe definitively when withdrawal from an engagement is appropriate. Factors that affect the auditor's conclusion include the implications of the involvement of a member of management or of those charged with governance (which may affect the reliability of management representations) and the effects on the auditor of a continuing association with the entity.    **A55**

The auditor has professional and legal responsibilities in such circumstances and these responsibilities may vary by country. In some countries, for example, the auditor may be entitled to, or required to, make a statement or report to the person or persons who made the audit appointment or, in some cases, to regulatory authorities. Given the exceptional nature of the circumstances and the need to consider the legal requirements, the auditor may consider it appropriate to seek legal advice when deciding whether to withdraw from an engagement and in determining an appropriate course of action, including the possibility of reporting to shareholders, regulators or others.[23]    **A56**

---

[21] *ISA (UK and Ireland) 450, "Evaluation of Misstatements Identified during the Audit.".*

[22] *ISA 700, "Forming an Opinion and Reporting on Financial Statements."*
*The APB has not promulgated ISA 700 as issued by the IAASB for application in the UK and Ireland. In the UK and Ireland the applicable auditing standard is ISA (UK and Ireland) 700, "The Auditor's Report on Financial Statements." Paragraph 8 of ISA (UK and Ireland) 700 requires evaluation of whether uncorrected misstatements are material, individually or in aggregate.*

[23] *The IFAC Code of Ethics for Professional Accountants* provides guidance on communications with an auditor replacing the existing auditor
In the UK and Ireland the relevant ethical guidance on proposed communications with a successor auditor is provided by the ethical pronouncements relating to the work of auditors issued by the auditor's relevant professional body.

### Considerations Specific to Public Sector Entities

A57   In many cases in the public sector, the option of withdrawing from the engagement may not be available to the auditor due to the nature of the mandate or public interest considerations.

## Written Representations (Ref: Para. 39)

A58   ISA (UK and Ireland) 580[24] establishes requirements and provides guidance on obtaining appropriate representations from management and, where appropriate, those charged with governance in the audit. In addition to acknowledging that they have fulfilled their responsibility for the preparation of the financial statements[11a], it is important that, irrespective of the size of the entity, management and, where appropriate, those charged with governance acknowledge their responsibility for internal control designed, implemented and maintained to prevent and detect fraud.

A59   Because of the nature of fraud and the difficulties encountered by auditors in detecting material misstatements in the financial statements resulting from fraud, it is important that the auditor obtain a written representation from management and, where appropriate, those charged with governance confirming that they have disclosed to the auditor:

(a)   The results of management's assessment of the risk that the financial statements may be materially misstated as a result of fraud; and

(b)   Their knowledge of actual, suspected or alleged fraud affecting the entity.

## Communications to Management and with Those Charged with Governance

### Communication to Management (Ref: Para. 40)

A60   When the auditor has obtained evidence that fraud exists or may exist, it is important that the matter be brought to the attention of the appropriate level of management as soon as practicable. This is so even if the matter might be considered inconsequential (for example, a minor defalcation by an employee at a low level in the entity's organization). The determination of which level of management is the appropriate one is a matter of professional judgment and is affected by such factors as the likelihood of collusion and the nature and magnitude of the suspected fraud. Ordinarily, the appropriate level of management is at least one level above the persons who appear to be involved with the suspected fraud.

### Communication with Those Charged with Governance (Ref: Para. 41)

A61   The auditor's communication with those charged with governance may be made orally or in writing. ISA (UK and Ireland) 260 identifies factors the auditor considers in determining whether to communicate orally or in writing.[25] Due to the nature and sensitivity of fraud involving senior management, or fraud that results in a material misstatement in the financial statements, the auditor reports such matters on a timely basis and may consider it necessary to also report such matters in writing.

---

[24] *ISA (UK and Ireland) 580, "Written Representations."*

[25] *ISA (UK and Ireland) 260, paragraph A38.*

In some cases, the auditor may consider it appropriate to communicate with those **A62** charged with governance when the auditor becomes aware of fraud involving employees other than management that does not result in a material misstatement. Similarly, those charged with governance may wish to be informed of such circumstances. The communication process is assisted if the auditor and those charged with governance agree at an early stage in the audit about the nature and extent of the auditor's communications in this regard.

In the exceptional circumstances where the auditor has doubts about the integrity or **A63** honesty of management or those charged with governance, the auditor may consider it appropriate to obtain legal advice to assist in determining the appropriate course of action.

### *Other Matters Related to Fraud* (Ref: Para. 42)

Other matters related to fraud to be discussed with those charged with governance of **A64** the entity may include, for example:

- Concerns about the nature, extent and frequency of management's assessments of the controls in place to prevent and detect fraud and of the risk that the financial statements may be misstated.
- A failure by management to appropriately address identified significant deficiencies in internal control, or to appropriately respond to an identified fraud.
- The auditor's evaluation of the entity's control environment, including questions regarding the competence and integrity of management.
- Actions by management that may be indicative of fraudulent financial reporting, such as management's selection and application of accounting policies that may be indicative of management's effort to manage earnings in order to deceive financial statement users by influencing their perceptions as to the entity's performance and profitability.
- Concerns about the adequacy and completeness of the authorization of transactions that appear to be outside the normal course of business.

### Communications to Regulatory and Enforcement Authorities (Ref: Para. 43)

The auditor's professional duty to maintain the confidentiality of client information **A65** may preclude reporting fraud to a party outside the client entity. However, the auditor's legal responsibilities vary by country[25a] and, in certain circumstances, the duty of confidentiality may be overridden by statute, the law or courts of law. In some countries, the auditor of a financial institution has a statutory duty to report the occurrence of fraud to supervisory authorities. Also, in some countries the auditor has a duty to report misstatements to authorities in those cases where management and those charged with governance fail to take corrective action.

The auditor may consider it appropriate to obtain legal advice to determine the **A66** appropriate course of action in the circumstances, the purpose of which is to ascertain the steps necessary in considering the public interest aspects of identified fraud.

---

[25a] *In the UK and Ireland, anti-money laundering legislation imposes a duty on auditors to report suspected money laundering activity. Suspicions relating to fraud are likely to be required to be reported under this legislation (see paragraph A11-1 in ISA (UK and Ireland) 250 Section A, "Consideration of laws and regulations").*

**Considerations Specific to Public Sector Entities**

**A67**   In the public sector, requirements for reporting fraud, whether or not discovered
through the audit process, may be subject to specific provisions of the audit mandate
or related law, regulation or other authority.

# Appendix 1 (Ref: Para. A25)

# Examples of Fraud Risk Factors

The fraud risk factors identified in this Appendix are examples of such factors that may be faced by auditors in a broad range of situations. Separately presented are examples relating to the two types of fraud relevant to the auditor's consideration – that is, fraudulent financial reporting and misappropriation of assets. For each of these types of fraud, the risk factors are further classified based on the three conditions generally present when material misstatements due to fraud occur: (a) incentives/pressures, (b) opportunities, and (c) attitudes/rationalizations. Although the risk factors cover a broad range of situations, they are only examples and, accordingly, the auditor may identify additional or different risk factors. Not all of these examples are relevant in all circumstances, and some may be of greater or lesser significance in entities of different size or with different ownership characteristics or circumstances. Also, the order of the examples of risk factors provided is not intended to reflect their relative importance or frequency of occurrence.

## Risk Factors Relating to Misstatements Arising from Fraudulent Financial Reporting

The following are examples of risk factors relating to misstatements arising from fraudulent financial reporting.

### *Incentives/Pressures*

Financial stability or profitability is threatened by economic, industry, or entity operating conditions, such as (or as indicated by):

- High degree of competition or market saturation, accompanied by declining margins.
- High vulnerability to rapid changes, such as changes in technology, product obsolescence, or interest rates.
- Significant declines in customer demand and increasing business failures in either the industry or overall economy.
- Operating losses making the threat of bankruptcy, foreclosure, or hostile takeover imminent.
- Recurring negative cash flows from operations or an inability to generate cash flows from operations while reporting earnings and earnings growth.
- Rapid growth or unusual profitability especially compared to that of other companies in the same industry.
- New accounting, statutory, or regulatory requirements.

Excessive pressure exists for management to meet the requirements or expectations of third parties due to the following:

- Profitability or trend level expectations of investment analysts, institutional investors, significant creditors, or other external parties (particularly expectations that are unduly aggressive or unrealistic), including expectations created by management in, for example, overly optimistic press releases or annual report messages.
- Need to obtain additional debt or equity financing to stay competitive – including financing of major research and development or capital expenditures.
- Marginal ability to meet exchange listing requirements or debt repayment or other debt covenant requirements.

- Perceived or real adverse effects of reporting poor financial results on significant pending transactions, such as business combinations or contract awards.

Information available indicates that the personal financial situation of management or those charged with governance is threatened by the entity's financial performance arising from the following:

- Significant financial interests in the entity.
- Significant portions of their compensation (for example, bonuses, stock options, and earn-out arrangements) being contingent upon achieving aggressive targets for stock price, operating results, financial position, or cash flow.[26]
- Personal guarantees of debts of the entity.

There is excessive pressure on management or operating personnel to meet financial targets established by those charged with governance, including sales or profitability incentive goals.

## *Opportunities*

The nature of the industry or the entity's operations provides opportunities to engage in fraudulent financial reporting that can arise from the following:

- Significant related-party transactions not in the ordinary course of business or with related entities not audited or audited by another firm.
- A strong financial presence or ability to dominate a certain industry sector that allows the entity to dictate terms or conditions to suppliers or customers that may result in inappropriate or non-arm's-length transactions.
- Assets, liabilities, revenues, or expenses based on significant estimates that involve subjective judgments or uncertainties that are difficult to corroborate.
- Significant, unusual, or highly complex transactions, especially those close to period end that pose difficult "substance over form" questions.
- Significant operations located or conducted across international borders in jurisdictions where differing business environments and cultures exist.
- Use of business intermediaries for which there appears to be no clear business justification.
- Significant bank accounts or subsidiary or branch operations in tax-haven jurisdictions for which there appears to be no clear business justification.

The monitoring of management is not effective as a result of the following:

- Domination of management by a single person or small group (in a non owner-managed business) without compensating controls.
- Oversight by those charged with governance over the financial reporting process and internal control is not effective.

There is a complex or unstable organizational structure, as evidenced by the following:

- Difficulty in determining the organization or individuals that have controlling interest in the entity.
- Overly complex organizational structure involving unusual legal entities or managerial lines of authority.

---

[26] *Management incentive plans may be contingent upon achieving targets relating only to certain accounts or selected activities of the entity, even though the related accounts or activities may not be material to the entity as a whole.*

- High turnover of senior management, legal counsel, or those charged with governance.

Internal control components are deficient as a result of the following:

- Inadequate monitoring of controls, including automated controls and controls over interim financial reporting (where external reporting is required).
- High turnover rates or employment of accounting, internal audit, or information technology staff that are not effective.
- Accounting and information systems that are not effective, including situations involving significant deficiencies in internal control.

### *Attitudes/Rationalizations*

- Communication, implementation, support, or enforcement of the entity's values or ethical standards by management, or the communication of inappropriate values or ethical standards, that are not effective.
- Nonfinancial management's excessive participation in or preoccupation with the selection of accounting policies or the determination of significant estimates.
- Known history of violations of securities laws or other laws and regulations, or claims against the entity, its senior management, or those charged with governance alleging fraud or violations of laws and regulations.
- Excessive interest by management in maintaining or increasing the entity's stock price or earnings trend.
- The practice by management of committing to analysts, creditors, and other third parties to achieve aggressive or unrealistic forecasts.
- Management failing to remedy known significant deficiencies in internal control on a timely basis.
- An interest by management in employing inappropriate means to minimize reported earnings for tax-motivated reasons.
- Low morale among senior management.
- The owner-manager makes no distinction between personal and business transactions.
- Dispute between shareholders in a closely held entity.
- Recurring attempts by management to justify marginal or inappropriate accounting on the basis of materiality.
- The relationship between management and the current or predecessor auditor is strained, as exhibited by the following:
  - Frequent disputes with the current or predecessor auditor on accounting, auditing, or reporting matters.
  - Unreasonable demands on the auditor, such as unrealistic time constraints regarding the completion of the audit or the issuance of the auditor's report.
  - Restrictions on the auditor that inappropriately limit access to people or information or the ability to communicate effectively with those charged with governance.
  - Domineering management behavior in dealing with the auditor, especially involving attempts to influence the scope of the auditor's work or the selection or continuance of personnel assigned to or consulted on the audit engagement.

## Risk Factors Arising from Misstatements Arising from Misappropriation of Assets

Risk factors that relate to misstatements arising from misappropriation of assets are also classified according to the three conditions generally present when fraud exists: incentives/pressures, opportunities, and attitudes/rationalization. Some of the risk factors related to misstatements arising from fraudulent financial reporting also may be present when misstatements arising from misappropriation of assets occur. For example, ineffective monitoring of management and other deficiencies in internal control may be present when misstatements due to either fraudulent financial reporting or misappropriation of assets exist. The following are examples of risk factors related to misstatements arising from misappropriation of assets.

### *Incentives/Pressures*

Personal financial obligations may create pressure on management or employees with access to cash or other assets susceptible to theft to misappropriate those assets.

Adverse relationships between the entity and employees with access to cash or other assets susceptible to theft may motivate those employees to misappropriate those assets. For example, adverse relationships may be created by the following:

- Known or anticipated future employee layoffs.
- Recent or anticipated changes to employee compensation or benefit plans.
- Promotions, compensation, or other rewards inconsistent with expectations.

### *Opportunities*

Certain characteristics or circumstances may increase the susceptibility of assets to misappropriation. For example, opportunities to misappropriate assets increase when there are the following:

- Large amounts of cash on hand or processed.
- Inventory items that are small in size, of high value, or in high demand.
- Easily convertible assets, such as bearer bonds, diamonds, or computer chips.
- Fixed assets which are small in size, marketable, or lacking observable identification of ownership.

Inadequate internal control over assets may increase the susceptibility of misappropriation of those assets. For example, misappropriation of assets may occur because there is the following:

- Inadequate segregation of duties or independent checks.
- Inadequate oversight of senior management expenditures, such as travel and other re-imbursements.
- Inadequate management oversight of employees responsible for assets, for example, inadequate supervision or monitoring of remote locations.
- Inadequate job applicant screening of employees with access to assets.
- Inadequate record keeping with respect to assets.
- Inadequate system of authorization and approval of transactions (for example, in purchasing).
- Inadequate physical safeguards over cash, investments, inventory, or fixed assets.
- Lack of complete and timely reconciliations of assets.
- Lack of timely and appropriate documentation of transactions, for example, credits for merchandise returns.

- Lack of mandatory vacations for employees performing key control functions.
- Inadequate management understanding of information technology, which enables information technology employees to perpetrate a misappropriation.
- Inadequate access controls over automated records, including controls over and review of computer systems event logs.

*Attitudes/Rationalizations*

- Disregard for the need for monitoring or reducing risks related to misappropriations of assets.
- Disregard for internal control over misappropriation of assets by overriding existing controls or by failing to take appropriate remedial action on known deficiencies in internal control.
- Behavior indicating displeasure or dissatisfaction with the entity or its treatment of the employee.
- Changes in behavior or lifestyle that may indicate assets have been misappropriated.
- Tolerance of petty theft.

**Appendix 2** (Ref: Para. A40)

## Examples of Possible Audit Procedures to Address the Assessed Risks of Material Misstatement Due to Fraud

The following are examples of possible audit procedures to address the assessed risks of material misstatement due to fraud resulting from both fraudulent financial reporting and misappropriation of assets. Although these procedures cover a broad range of situations, they are only examples and, accordingly they may not be the most appropriate nor necessary in each circumstance. Also the order of the procedures provided is not intended to reflect their relative importance.

### Consideration at the Assertion Level

Specific responses to the auditor's assessment of the risks of material misstatement due to fraud will vary depending upon the types or combinations of fraud risk factors or conditions identified, and the classes of transactions, account balances, disclosures and assertions they may affect.

The following are specific examples of responses:

- Visiting locations or performing certain tests on a surprise or unannounced basis. For example, observing inventory at locations where auditor attendance has not been previously announced or counting cash at a particular date on a surprise basis.
- Requesting that inventories be counted at the end of the reporting period or on a date closer to period end to minimize the risk of manipulation of balances in the period between the date of completion of the count and the end of the reporting period.
- Altering the audit approach in the current year. For example, contacting major customers and suppliers orally in addition to sending written confirmation, sending confirmation requests to a specific party within an organization, or seeking more or different information.
- Performing a detailed review of the entity's quarter-end or year-end adjusting entries and investigating any that appear unusual as to nature or amount.
- For significant and unusual transactions, particularly those occurring at or near year-end, investigating the possibility of related parties and the sources of financial resources supporting the transactions.
- Performing substantive analytical procedures using disaggregated data. For example, comparing sales and cost of sales by location, line of business or month to expectations developed by the auditor.
- Conducting interviews of personnel involved in areas where a risk of material misstatement due to fraud has been identified, to obtain their insights about the risk and whether, or how, controls address the risk.
- When other independent auditors are auditing the financial statements of one or more subsidiaries, divisions or branches, discussing with them the extent of work necessary to be performed to address the assessed risk of material misstatement due to fraud resulting from transactions and activities among these components.
- If the work of an expert becomes particularly significant with respect to a financial statement item for which the assessed risk of misstatement due to fraud is high, performing additional procedures relating to some or all of the expert's assumptions, methods or findings to determine that the findings are not unreasonable, or engaging another expert for that purpose.
- Performing audit procedures to analyze selected opening balance sheet accounts of previously audited financial statements to assess how certain issues involving

accounting estimates and judgments, for example, an allowance for sales returns, were resolved with the benefit of hindsight.

- Performing procedures on account or other reconciliations prepared by the entity, including considering reconciliations performed at interim periods.
- Performing computer-assisted techniques, such as data mining to test for anomalies in a population.
- Testing the integrity of computer-produced records and transactions.
- Seeking additional audit evidence from sources outside of the entity being audited.

## Specific Responses—Misstatement Resulting from Fraudulent Financial Reporting

Examples of responses to the auditor's assessment of the risks of material misstatement due to fraudulent financial reporting are as follows:

### *Revenue Recognition*

- Performing substantive analytical procedures relating to revenue using disaggregated data, for example, comparing revenue reported by month and by product line or business segment during the current reporting period with comparable prior periods. Computer-assisted audit techniques may be useful in identifying unusual or unexpected revenue relationships or transactions.
- Confirming with customers certain relevant contract terms and the absence of side agreements, because the appropriate accounting often is influenced by such terms or agreements and basis for rebates or the period to which they relate are often poorly documented. For example, acceptance criteria, delivery and payment terms, the absence of future or continuing vendor obligations, the right to return the product, guaranteed resale amounts, and cancellation or refund provisions often are relevant in such circumstances.
- Inquiring of the entity's sales and marketing personnel or in-house legal counsel regarding sales or shipments near the end of the period and their knowledge of any unusual terms or conditions associated with these transactions.
- Being physically present at one or more locations at period end to observe goods being shipped or being readied for shipment (or returns awaiting processing) and performing other appropriate sales and inventory cutoff procedures.
- For those situations for which revenue transactions are electronically initiated, processed, and recorded, testing controls to determine whether they provide assurance that recorded revenue transactions occurred and are properly recorded.

### *Inventory Quantities*

- Examining the entity's inventory records to identify locations or items that require specific attention during or after the physical inventory count.
- Observing inventory counts at certain locations on an unannounced basis or conducting inventory counts at all locations on the same date.
- Conducting inventory counts at or near the end of the reporting period to minimize the risk of inappropriate manipulation during the period between the count and the end of the reporting period.
- Performing additional procedures during the observation of the count, for example, more rigorously examining the contents of boxed items, the manner in which the goods are stacked (for example, hollow squares) or labeled, and the quality (that is, purity, grade, or concentration) of liquid substances such as

perfumes or specialty chemicals. Using the work of an expert may be helpful in this regard.
- Comparing the quantities for the current period with prior periods by class or category of inventory, location or other criteria, or comparison of quantities counted with perpetual records.
- Using computer-assisted audit techniques to further test the compilation of the physical inventory counts – for example, sorting by tag number to test tag controls or by item serial number to test the possibility of item omission or duplication.

### Management Estimates

- Using an expert to develop an independent estimate for comparison to management's estimate.
- Extending inquiries to individuals outside of management and the accounting department to corroborate management's ability and intent to carry out plans that are relevant to developing the estimate.

## Specific Responses—Misstatements Due to Misappropriation of Assets

Differing circumstances would necessarily dictate different responses. Ordinarily, the audit response to an assessed risk of material misstatement due to fraud relating to misappropriation of assets will be directed toward certain account balances and classes of transactions. Although some of the audit responses noted in the two categories above may apply in such circumstances, the scope of the work is to be linked to the specific information about the misappropriation risk that has been identified.

Examples of responses to the auditor's assessment of the risk of material misstatements due to misappropriation of assets are as follows:

- Counting cash or securities at or near year-end.
- Confirming directly with customers the account activity (including credit memo and sales return activity as well as dates payments were made) for the period under audit.
- Analyzing recoveries of written-off accounts.
- Analyzing inventory shortages by location or product type.
- Comparing key inventory ratios to industry norm.
- Reviewing supporting documentation for reductions to the perpetual inventory records.
- Performing a computerized match of the vendor list with a list of employees to identify matches of addresses or phone numbers.
- Performing a computerized search of payroll records to identify duplicate addresses, employee identification or taxing authority numbers or bank accounts
- Reviewing personnel files for those that contain little or no evidence of activity, for example, lack of performance evaluations.
- Analyzing sales discounts and returns for unusual patterns or trends.
- Confirming specific terms of contracts with third parties.
- Obtaining evidence that contracts are being carried out in accordance with their terms.
- Reviewing the propriety of large and unusual expenses.
- Reviewing the authorization and carrying value of senior management and related party loans.
- Reviewing the level and propriety of expense reports submitted by senior management.

# Appendix 3 (Ref: Para. A49)
# Examples of Circumstances that Indicate the Possibility of Fraud

The following are examples of circumstances that may indicate the possibility that the financial statements may contain a material misstatement resulting from fraud.

Discrepancies in the accounting records, including:

- Transactions that are not recorded in a complete or timely manner or are improperly recorded as to amount, accounting period, classification, or entity policy.
- Unsupported or unauthorized balances or transactions.
- Last-minute adjustments that significantly affect financial results.
- Evidence of employees' access to systems and records inconsistent with that necessary to perform their authorized duties.
- Tips or complaints to the auditor about alleged fraud.

Conflicting or missing evidence, including:

- Missing documents.
- Documents that appear to have been altered.
- Unavailability of other than photocopied or electronically transmitted documents when documents in original form are expected to exist.
- Significant unexplained items on reconciliations.
- Unusual balance sheet changes, or changes in trends or important financial statement ratios or relationships – for example, receivables growing faster than revenues.
- Inconsistent, vague, or implausible responses from management or employees arising from inquiries or analytical procedures.
- Unusual discrepancies between the entity's records and confirmation replies.
- Large numbers of credit entries and other adjustments made to accounts receivable records.
- Unexplained or inadequately explained differences between the accounts receivable sub-ledger and the control account, or between the customer statements and the accounts receivable sub-ledger.
- Missing or non-existent cancelled checks in circumstances where cancelled checks are ordinarily returned to the entity with the bank statement.
- Missing inventory or physical assets of significant magnitude.
- Unavailable or missing electronic evidence, inconsistent with the entity's record retention practices or policies.
- Fewer responses to confirmations than anticipated or a greater number of responses than anticipated.
- Inability to produce evidence of key systems development and program change testing and implementation activities for current-year system changes and deployments.

Problematic or unusual relationships between the auditor and management, including:

- Denial of access to records, facilities, certain employees, customers, vendors, or others from whom audit evidence might be sought.
- Undue time pressures imposed by management to resolve complex or contentious issues.
- Complaints by management about the conduct of the audit or management intimidation of engagement team members, particularly in connection with the

auditor's critical assessment of audit evidence or in the resolution of potential disagreements with management.

- Unusual delays by the entity in providing requested information.
- Unwillingness to facilitate auditor access to key electronic files for testing through the use of computer-assisted audit techniques.
- Denial of access to key IT operations staff and facilities, including security, operations, and systems development personnel.
- An unwillingness to add or revise disclosures in the financial statements to make them more complete and understandable.
- An unwillingness to address identified deficiencies in internal control on a timely basis.

*Other*

- Unwillingness by management to permit the auditor to meet privately with those charged with governance.
- Accounting policies that appear to be at variance with industry norms.
- Frequent changes in accounting estimates that do not appear to result from changed circumstances.
- Tolerance of violations of the entity's code of conduct.

# Addendum

*This addendum provides a summary of APB's rationale for retaining or excluding in the proposed clarified ISA (UK and Ireland) the supplementary requirements in the existing ISA (UK and Ireland). It also sets out the supplementary guidance material in the existing ISA (UK and Ireland) that APB considers is not necessary to retain in light of the improvements in the underlying Clarity ISAs issued by the IAASB as part of the Clarity Project. It is provided for information and does not form part of the proposed clarified ISA (UK and Ireland).*

*The Consultation Paper published with the exposure drafts explains the general approach used by the APB for determining whether current supplementary material should be proposed to be retained.*

## Analysis of proposed treatment of current APB supplementary material in current ISA (UK and Ireland) 240

### Requirements

There are no supplementary requirements in the current ISA (UK and Ireland) 240.

### Guidance

The following guidance in current ISA (UK and Ireland) 240 has not been carried forward to the proposed clarified standard.

| Current paragraph reference (*Italic text is from IAASB for context*) |
|---|
| 1-1. – 1-4. [Description of management and those charged with governance.] |
| 2.  *This standard* <br> • *Requires the auditor to:* <br>   • *Obtain written representations from management[1a] relating to fraud; and* |
| [1a] In the UK and Ireland, the auditor obtains written representations from those charged with governance. |
| 90.  ***The auditor should obtain written representations from management[1a] that:...*** <br> *(c)  **It has disclosed to the auditor its knowledge of fraud or suspected fraud affecting the entity involving:*** <br> *(i)  **Management[2a];...*** |
| [2a] In the UK and Ireland, and those charged with governance. |

# Proposed Clarified International Standard on Auditing (UK and Ireland) 250

# Section A – consideration of laws and regulations in an audit of financial statements

*(Effective for audits of financial statements for periods ending on or after 15 December 2010)*

## Contents

International Standard on Auditing (UK and Ireland) (ISA (UK and Ireland)) 250, "Consideration of Laws and Regulations in an Audit of Financial Statements" should be read in conjunction with ISA (UK and Ireland) 200, "Overall Objectives of the Independent Auditor and the Conduct of an Audit in Accordance with International Standards on Auditing (UK and Ireland)."

# Introduction

## Scope of this ISA (UK and Ireland)

This International Standard on Auditing (UK and Ireland) (ISA (UK and Ireland)) 1
deals with the auditor's responsibility to consider laws and regulations in an audit of
financial statements. This ISA (UK and Ireland) does not apply to other assurance
engagements in which the auditor is specifically engaged to test and report separately
on compliance with specific laws or regulations.

Guidance on the auditor's responsibility to report direct to regulators in the financial 1-1
sector is provided in Section B of this ISA (UK and Ireland).

## Effect of Laws and Regulations

The effect on financial statements of laws and regulations varies considerably. Those 2
laws and regulations to which an entity is subject constitute the legal and regulatory
framework. The provisions of some laws or regulations have a direct effect on the
financial statements in that they determine the reported amounts and disclosures in
an entity's financial statements. Other laws or regulations are to be complied with by
management or set the provisions under which the entity is allowed to conduct its
business but do not have a direct effect on an entity's financial statements. Some
entities operate in heavily regulated industries (such as banks and chemical companies). Others are subject only to the many laws and regulations that relate
generally to the operating aspects of the business (such as those related to occupa-
tional safety and health, and equal employment opportunity). Non-compliance with
laws and regulations may result in fines, litigation or other consequences for the
entity that may have a material effect on the financial statements.

## Responsibility for Compliance with Laws and Regulations (Ref: Para. A1-A6)

It is the responsibility of management, with the oversight of those charged with 3
governance, to ensure that the entity's operations are conducted in accordance with
the provisions of laws and regulations, including compliance with the provisions of
laws and regulations that determine the reported amounts and disclosures in an
entity's financial statements.[1a]

### *Responsibility of the Auditor*

The requirements in this ISA (UK and Ireland) are designed to assist the auditor in 4
identifying material misstatement of the financial statements due to non-compliance
with laws and regulations. However, the auditor is not responsible for preventing
non-compliance and cannot be expected to detect non-compliance with all laws and
regulations.

The auditor is responsible for obtaining reasonable assurance that the financial 5
statements, taken as a whole, are free from material misstatement, whether caused by
fraud or error.[1] In conducting an audit of financial statements, the auditor takes into

---

[1a] *In the UK and Ireland those charged with governance are responsible for the preparation of the financial
statements.*

[1] *ISA (UK and Ireland) 200, "Overall Objectives of the Independent Auditor and the Conduct of an Audit in
Accordance with International Standards on Auditing," paragraph 5.*

account the applicable legal and regulatory framework. Owing to the inherent limitations of an audit, there is an unavoidable risk that some material misstatements in the financial statements may not be detected, even though the audit is properly planned and performed in accordance with the ISAs (UK and Ireland).[2] In the context of laws and regulations, the potential effects of inherent limitations on the auditor's ability to detect material misstatements are greater for such reasons as the following:

- There are many laws and regulations, relating principally to the operating aspects of an entity, that typically do not affect the financial statements and are not captured by the entity's information systems relevant to financial reporting.
- Non-compliance may involve conduct designed to conceal it, such as collusion, forgery, deliberate failure to record transactions, management override of controls or intentional misrepresentations being made to the auditor.
- Whether an act constitutes non-compliance is ultimately a matter for legal determination by a court of law.

Ordinarily, the further removed non-compliance is from the events and transactions reflected in the financial statements, the less likely the auditor is to become aware of it or to recognize the non-compliance.

6    This ISA (UK and Ireland) distinguishes the auditor's responsibilities in relation to compliance with two different categories of laws and regulations as follows:

(a)  The provisions of those laws and regulations generally recognized to have a direct effect on the determination of material amounts and disclosures in the financial statements such as tax and pension laws and regulations (see paragraph 13); and

(b)  Other laws and regulations that do not have a direct effect on the determination of the amounts and disclosures in the financial statements, but compliance with which may be fundamental to the operating aspects of the business, to an entity's ability to continue its business, or to avoid material penalties (for example, compliance with the terms of an operating license, compliance with regulatory solvency requirements, or compliance with environmental regulations); non-compliance with such laws and regulations may therefore have a material effect on the financial statements (see paragraph 14).

7    In this ISA (UK and Ireland), differing requirements are specified for each of the above categories of laws and regulations. For the category referred to in paragraph 6(a), the auditor's responsibility is to obtain sufficient appropriate audit evidence regarding compliance with the provisions of those laws and regulations. For the category referred to in paragraph 6(b), the auditor's responsibility is limited to undertaking specified audit procedures to help identify non-compliance with those laws and regulations that may have a material effect on the financial statements.

8    The auditor is required by this ISA (UK and Ireland) to remain alert to the possibility that other audit procedures applied for the purpose of forming an opinion on financial statements may bring instances of identified or suspected non-compliance to the auditor's attention. Maintaining professional skepticism throughout the audit, as required by ISA (UK and Ireland) 200,[3] is important in this context, given the extent of laws and regulations that affect the entity.

---

[2] *ISA (UK and Ireland) 200, paragraph A51.*

[3] *ISA (UK and Ireland) 200, paragraph 15.*

**Effective Date**

This ISA (UK and Ireland) is effective for audits of financial statements for periods   **9**
ending on or after 15 December 2010.

# Objectives

The objectives of the auditor are:   **10**

(a)  To obtain sufficient appropriate audit evidence regarding compliance with the
provisions of those laws and regulations generally recognized to have a direct
effect on the determination of material amounts and disclosures in the financial
statements;

(b)  To perform specified audit procedures to help identify instances of non-compliance with other laws and regulations that may have a material effect on the
financial statements; and

(c)  To respond appropriately to non-compliance or suspected non-compliance with
laws and regulations identified during the audit.

# Definition

For the purposes of this ISA (UK and Ireland), the following term has the meaning   **11**
attributed below:

Non-compliance – Acts of omission or commission by the entity, either intentional
or unintentional, which are contrary to the prevailing laws or regulations. Such acts
include transactions entered into by, or in the name of, the entity, or on its behalf, by
those charged with governance, management or employees. Non-compliance does
not include personal misconduct (unrelated to the business activities of the entity) by
those charged with governance, management or employees of the entity.

This ISA (UK and Ireland) also refers to 'money laundering' and 'tipping off'.   **11-1**

'Money laundering' is defined in legislation[3a] and in general terms involves an act
which conceals, disguises, converts, transfers, removes, uses, acquires or possesses
property resulting from criminal conduct.

---

[3a] *In the UK, the Money Laundering Regulations 2007 and the requirements of the Proceeds of Crime Act 2002
(POCA) bring auditors within the regulated sector, requiring them to report suspected money laundering
activity and adopt rigorous client identification procedures and appropriate anti-money laundering procedures.
In Ireland, the Criminal Justice Act 1994 (Section 32) Regulations 2003 designate accountants, auditors, and
tax advisors and others for the purposes of the anti-money laundering provisions of the Criminal Justice Act,
1994, as amended.*

'Tipping off' involves a disclosure that is likely to prejudice any investigation into suspected money laundering or could otherwise alert a money launderer[3b].

# Requirements

## The Auditor's Consideration of Compliance with Laws and Regulations

12   As part of obtaining an understanding of the entity and its environment in accordance with ISA (UK and Ireland) 315,[4] the auditor shall obtain a general understanding of:

(a)   The legal and regulatory framework applicable to the entity and the industry or sector in which the entity operates; and

(b)   How the entity is complying with that framework. (Ref: Para. A7)

13   The auditor shall obtain sufficient appropriate audit evidence regarding compliance with the provisions of those laws and regulations generally recognized to have a direct effect on the determination of material amounts and disclosures in the financial statements. (Ref: Para. A8)

14   The auditor shall perform the following audit procedures to help identify instances of non-compliance with other laws and regulations that may have a material effect on the financial statements:

(a)   Inquiring of management and, where appropriate, those charged with governance, as to whether the entity is in compliance with such laws and regulations; and

(b)   Inspecting correspondence, if any, with the relevant licensing or regulatory authorities. (Ref: Para. A9-A10)

15   During the audit, the auditor shall remain alert to the possibility that other audit procedures applied may bring instances of non-compliance or suspected non-compliance with laws and regulations to the auditor's attention. (Ref: Para. A11)

15-1   In the UK and Ireland, when carrying out procedures for the purpose of forming an opinion on the financial statements, the auditor shall be alert for those

---

[3b] *In the UK, 'tipping off' is an offence under POCA section 333A. It arises when an individual discloses:*

*(a)   that a report (internal or external) has already been made where the disclosure by the individual is likely to prejudice an investigation which might be conducted following the internal or external report that has been made; or*

*(b)   that an investigation is being contemplated or is being carried out into allegations that a money laundering offence has been committed and the disclosure by the individual is likely to prejudice that investigation.*

*Whilst 'tipping off' requires a person to have knowledge or suspicion that a report has been or will be made, a further offence of prejudicing an investigation is included in POCA section 342. Under this provision, it is an offence to make any disclosure which may prejudice an investigation of which a person has knowledge or suspicion, or to falsify, conceal, destroy or otherwise dispose of, or cause or permit the falsification, concealment, destruction or disposal of, documents relevant to such an investigation.*

*The disclosure offences under sections 333A and 342 are not committed if the person disclosing does not know or suspect that it is likely to prejudice an investigation.*

*In Ireland Section 58 of the Criminal Justice Act, 1994, as amended, establishes the offence of "prejudicing an investigation". This relates both to when a person, knowing or suspecting that an investigation is taking place, makes any disclosure likely to prejudice the investigation or when a person, knowing that a report has been made, makes any disclosure likely to prejudice any investigation arising from the report."*

[4] *ISA (UK and Ireland) 315, "Identifying and Assessing the Risks of Material Misstatement through Understanding the Entity and Its Environment," paragraph 11.*

instances of possible or actual non-compliance with laws and regulations that might incur obligations for partners and staff in audit firms to report money laundering offences. (Ref: Para. A11-1)

The auditor shall request management and, where appropriate, those charged with governance to provide written representations that all known instances of non-compliance or suspected non-compliance with laws and regulations whose effects should be considered when preparing financial statements have been disclosed to the auditor. (Ref: Para. A12) | **16**

In the absence of identified or suspected non-compliance, the auditor is not required to perform audit procedures regarding the entity's compliance with laws and regulations, other than those set out in paragraphs 12-16. | **17**

## Audit Procedures When Non-Compliance Is Identified or Suspected

If the auditor becomes aware of information concerning an instance of non-compliance or suspected non-compliance with laws and regulations, the auditor shall obtain: (Ref: Para. A13) | **18**

(a)  An understanding of the nature of the act and the circumstances in which it has occurred; and
(b)  Further information to evaluate the possible effect on the financial statements. (Ref: Para. A14)

If the auditor suspects there may be non-compliance, the auditor shall[4a] discuss the matter with management and, where appropriate, those charged with governance. If management or, as appropriate, those charged with governance do not provide sufficient information that supports that the entity is in compliance with laws and regulations and, in the auditor's judgment, the effect of the suspected non-compliance may be material to the financial statements, the auditor shall consider the need to obtain legal advice. (Ref: Para. A15-A16) | **19**

If sufficient information about suspected non-compliance cannot be obtained, the auditor shall evaluate the effect of the lack of sufficient appropriate audit evidence on the auditor's opinion. | **20**

The auditor shall evaluate the implications of non-compliance in relation to other aspects of the audit, including the auditor's risk assessment and the reliability of written representations, and take appropriate action. (Ref: Para. A17 – A18-1) | **21**

## Reporting of Identified or Suspected Non-Compliance

### *Reporting Non-Compliance to Those Charged with Governance*

Unless all of those charged with governance are involved in management of the entity, and therefore are aware of matters involving identified or suspected non-compliance already communicated by the auditor,[5] the auditor shall[4a] communicate with those charged with governance matters involving non-compliance with laws and | **22**

---

[4a] *Subject to compliance with legislation relating to 'tipping off'.*

[5] *ISA (UK and Ireland) 260, "Communication with Those Charged with Governance," paragraph 13.*

regulations that come to the auditor's attention during the course of the audit, other than when the matters are clearly inconsequential.

23   If, in the auditor's judgment, the non-compliance referred to in paragraph 22 is believed to be intentional and material, the auditor shall[4a] communicate the matter to those charged with governance as soon as practicable. (Ref: Para. A18-2)

24   If the auditor suspects that management or those charged with governance are involved in non-compliance, the auditor shall[4a] communicate the matter to the next higher level of authority at the entity, if it exists, such as an audit committee or supervisory board. Where no higher authority exists, or if the auditor believes that the communication may not be acted upon or is unsure as to the person to whom to report, the auditor shall consider the need to obtain legal advice. (Ref: Para. A18-3)

### Reporting Non-Compliance in the Auditor's Report on the Financial Statements

25   If the auditor concludes that the non-compliance has a material effect on the financial statements, and has not been adequately reflected in the financial statements, the auditor shall,[4a] in accordance with ISA (UK and Ireland) 705, express a qualified opinion or an adverse opinion on the financial statements. [6]

26   If the auditor is precluded by management or those charged with governance from obtaining sufficient appropriate audit evidence to evaluate whether non-compliance that may be material to the financial statements has, or is likely to have, occurred, the auditor shall[4a] express a qualified opinion or disclaim an opinion on the financial statements on the basis of a limitation on the scope of the audit in accordance with ISA (UK and Ireland) 705.

27   If the auditor is unable to determine whether non-compliance has occurred because of limitations imposed by the circumstances rather than by management or those charged with governance, the auditor shall evaluate the effect on the auditor's opinion in accordance with ISA (UK and Ireland) 705. (Ref: Para. A18-4)

### Reporting Non-Compliance to Regulatory and Enforcement Authorities

28   If the auditor has identified or suspects non-compliance with laws and regulations, the auditor shall determine whether the auditor has a responsibility to report the identified or suspected non-compliance to parties outside the entity. (Ref: Para. A19-A20)

28-1   If the auditor becomes aware of a suspected or actual non-compliance with law and regulations which gives rise to a statutory duty to report, the auditor shall make a report to the appropriate authority as soon as practicable. (Ref: Para. A19-1 – A19-11)

[6] *ISA (UK and Ireland) 705, "Modifications to the Opinion in the Independent Auditor's Report," paragraphs 7-8.*

## Documentation

The auditor shall include in the audit documentation identified or suspected non-compliance with laws and regulations and the results of discussion with management and, where applicable, those charged with governance and other parties outside the entity.[7] (Ref: Para. A21)

29

*\*\*\**

## Application and Other Explanatory Material

### Responsibility for Compliance with Laws and Regulations (Ref: Para. 3-8)

It is the responsibility of management, with the oversight of those charged with governance, to ensure that the entity's operations are conducted in accordance with laws and regulations. Laws and regulations may affect an entity's financial statements in different ways: for example, most directly, they may affect specific disclosures required of the entity in the financial statements or they may prescribe the applicable financial reporting framework. They may also establish certain legal rights and obligations of the entity, some of which will be recognized in the entity's financial statements. In addition, laws and regulations may impose penalties in cases of non-compliance.

A1

The following are examples of the types of policies and procedures an entity may implement to assist in the prevention and detection of non-compliance with laws and regulations:

A2

- Monitoring legal requirements and ensuring that operating procedures are designed to meet these requirements.
- Instituting and operating appropriate systems of internal control.
- Developing, publicizing and following a code of conduct.
- Ensuring employees are properly trained and understand the code of conduct.
- Monitoring compliance with the code of conduct and acting appropriately to discipline employees who fail to comply with it.
- Engaging legal advisors to assist in monitoring legal requirements.
- Maintaining a register of significant laws and regulations with which the entity has to comply within its particular industry and a record of complaints.

In larger entities, these policies and procedures may be supplemented by assigning appropriate responsibilities to the following:

- An internal audit function.
- An audit committee.
- A compliance function.

In the UK and Ireland, in certain sectors or activities (for example financial services), there are detailed laws and regulations that specifically require directors to have systems to ensure compliance. These laws and regulations could, if breached, have a material effect on the financial statements. In addition, the

A2-1

---

[7] *ISA (UK and Ireland) 230, "Audit Documentation," paragraphs 8-11, and paragraph A6.*

directors are required to report certain instances of non-compliance to the proper authorities on a timely basis.

A2-2    In the UK and Ireland, it is the directors' responsibility to prepare financial statements that give a true and fair view of the state of affairs of a company or group and of its profit or loss for the financial year. Accordingly it is necessary, where possible non-compliance with law or regulations has occurred which may result in a material misstatement in the financial statements, for them to ensure that the matter is appropriately reflected and/or disclosed in the financial statements.

A2-3    In the UK and Ireland directors and officers of companies have responsibility to provide information required by the auditor, to which they have a legal right of access[7a]. Such legislation also provides that it is a criminal offence to give to the auditor information or explanations which are misleading, false or deceptive.

### Responsibility of the Auditor

A3    Non-compliance by the entity with laws and regulations may result in a material misstatement of the financial statements. Detection of non-compliance, regardless of materiality, may affect other aspects of the audit including, for example, the auditor's consideration of the integrity of management or employees.

A4    Whether an act constitutes non-compliance with laws and regulations is a matter for legal determination, which is ordinarily beyond the auditor's professional competence to determine. Nevertheless, the auditor's training, experience and understanding of the entity and its industry or sector may provide a basis to recognize that some acts, coming to the auditor's attention, may constitute non-compliance with laws and regulations.

A5    In accordance with specific statutory requirements, the auditor may be specifically required to report, as part of the audit of the financial statements, on whether the entity complies with certain provisions of laws or regulations. In these circumstances, ISA (UK and Ireland) 700[8] or ISA 800[9] deal with how these audit responsibilities are addressed in the auditor's report. Furthermore, where there are specific statutory reporting requirements, it may be necessary for the audit plan to include appropriate tests for compliance with these provisions of the laws and regulations.

### Considerations Specific to Public Sector Entities

A6    In the public sector, there may be additional audit responsibilities with respect to the consideration of laws and regulations which may relate to the audit of financial statements or may extend to other aspects of the entity's operations.

---

[7a] *In the UK under Section 499 of the Companies Act 2006 or Sections 193(3) and 197 of the Companies Act 1990 in Ireland.*

[8] *ISA (UK and Ireland) 700, "Forming an Opinion and Reporting on Financial Statements," paragraph 38. The APB has not promulgated ISA 700 as issued by the IAASB for application in the UK and Ireland. In the UK and Ireland the applicable auditing standard is ISA (UK and Ireland) 700, "The Auditor's Report on Financial Statements." Paragraph 21 of ISA (UK and Ireland) 700 is the equivalent to paragraph 38 of ISA 700.*

[9] *ISA 800 "Special Considerations—Audits of Financial Statements Prepared in Accordance with Special Purpose Frameworks," paragraph 11.*
*ISA 800 has not been promulgated by the APB for application in the UK and Ireland.*

## The Auditor's Consideration of Compliance with Laws and Regulations

### *Obtaining an Understanding of the Legal and Regulatory Framework* (Ref: Para. 12)

To obtain a general understanding of the legal and regulatory framework, and how the entity complies with that framework, the auditor may, for example:   **A7**

- Use the auditor's existing understanding of the entity's industry, regulatory and other external factors;
- Update the understanding of those laws and regulations that directly determine the reported amounts and disclosures in the financial statements;
- Inquire of management as to other laws or regulations that may be expected to have a fundamental effect on the operations of the entity;
- Inquire of management concerning the entity's policies and procedures regarding compliance with laws and regulations; and
- Inquire of management regarding the policies or procedures adopted for identifying, evaluating and accounting for litigation claims.

### *Laws and Regulations Generally Recognized to Have a Direct Effect on the Determination of Material Amounts and Disclosures in the Financial Statements* (Ref: Para. 13)

Certain laws and regulations are well-established, known to the entity and within the   **A8**
entity's industry or sector, and relevant to the entity's financial statements (as described in paragraph 6(a)). They could include those that relate to, for example:

- The form and content of financial statements[9a];
- Industry-specific financial reporting issues;
- Accounting for transactions under government contracts; or
- The accrual or recognition of expenses for income tax or pension costs.

In the UK and Ireland, these laws and regulations include:

- Those which determine the circumstances under which a company is prohibited from making a distribution except out of profits available for the purpose[9b],
- Those laws which require auditors expressly to report non-compliance, such as the requirements relating to the maintenance of adequate accounting records[9c] or the disclosure of particulars of directors' remuneration in a company's financial statements[9d].

Some provisions in those laws and regulations may be directly relevant to specific assertions in the financial statements (for example, the completeness of income tax provisions), while others may be directly relevant to the financial statements as a

[9a] *In the UK under The Small Companies and Groups (Accounts and Directors' Report) Regulations 2008 (SI 2008-409) and The Large and Medium-sized Companies and Groups (Accounts and Reports) Regulations 2008 (SI 2008-410) or The Companies (Amendment) Act, 1986 in Ireland.*

[9b] *In the UK under Section 830 of the Companies Act 2006 or Section 45 of the Companies (Amendment) Act, 1983 in Ireland.*

[9c] *In the UK under Section 498 of the Companies Act 2006 and, in Ireland, under Section 193 and 194 of the Companies Act, 1990.*

[9d] *In the UK under Section 497 of the Companies Act 2006. There is no equivalent in Ireland.*

whole (for example, the required statements constituting a complete set of financial statements). The aim of the requirement in paragraph 13 is for the auditor to obtain sufficient appropriate audit evidence regarding the determination of amounts and disclosures in the financial statements in compliance with the relevant provisions of those laws and regulations.

Non-compliance with other provisions of such laws and regulations and other laws and regulations may result in fines, litigation or other consequences for the entity, the costs of which may need to be provided for in the financial statements, but are not considered to have a direct effect on the financial statements as described in paragraph 6(a).

**A8-1**   In the UK and Ireland, the auditor's responsibility to express an opinion on an entity's financial statements does not extend to determining whether the entity has complied in every respect with applicable tax legislation. The auditor needs to obtain sufficient appropriate evidence to give reasonable assurance that the amounts included in the financial statements in respect of taxation are not materially misstated. This will usually include making appropriate enquiries of those advising the entity on taxation matters (whether within the audit firm or elsewhere). If the auditor becomes aware that the entity has failed to comply with the requirements of tax legislation, the auditor considers whether to report the matter to parties outside the entity.

***Procedures to Identify Instances of Non-Compliance – Other Laws and Regulations***
(Ref: Para. 14)

**A9**   Certain other laws and regulations may need particular attention by the auditor because they have a fundamental effect on the operations of the entity (as described in paragraph 6(b)). Non-compliance with laws and regulations that have a fundamental effect on the operations of the entity may cause the entity to cease operations, or call into question the entity's continuance as a going concern. For example, non-compliance with the requirements of the entity's license or other entitlement to perform its operations could have such an impact (for example, for a bank, non-compliance with capital or investment requirements)[9c]. There are also many laws and regulations relating principally to the operating aspects of the entity that typically do not affect the financial statements and are not captured by the entity's information systems relevant to financial reporting.

**A10**   As the financial reporting consequences of other laws and regulations can vary depending on the entity's operations, the audit procedures required by paragraph 14 are directed to bringing to the auditor's attention instances of non-compliance with laws and regulations that may have a material effect on the financial statements.

**A10-1**   When determining the type of procedures necessary in a particular instance the auditor takes account of the particular entity concerned and the complexity of the regulations with which it is required to comply. In general, a small company which does not operate in a regulated area will require few specific procedures compared with a large multinational corporation carrying on complex, regulated business.

---

[9c] *Such requirements exist in the UK under the Financial Services and Markets Act 2000 and in Ireland under the Investment Intermediaries Act 1995, the Central Bank Acts 1942 to 1989 and the Credit Union Act, 1997.*

**Non-Compliance Brought to the Auditor's Attention by Other Audit Procedures** (Ref: Para. 15)

Audit procedures applied to form an opinion on the financial statements may bring instances of non-compliance or suspected non-compliance with laws and regulations to the auditor's attention. For example, such audit procedures may include:

A11

- Reading minutes;
- Inquiring of the entity's management and in-house legal counsel or external legal counsel concerning litigation, claims and assessments; and
- Performing substantive tests of details of classes of transactions, account balances or disclosures.

**Money Laundering Offences** (Ref: Para. 15-1)

Anti-money laundering legislation in the UK and Ireland imposes a duty on the auditor to report suspected money laundering activity. There are similar laws and regulations relating to financing terrorist offences[9f]. The detailed legislation in both countries differs but the impact on the auditor can broadly be summarised as follows:

A11-1

- Partners and staff in audit firms are required to report suspicions that conduct which would constitute a criminal offence, if it occurred in the UK, which gives rise to direct or indirect benefit has been committed, regardless of whether such conduct has been committed by a client or by a third party.
- Partners and staff in audit firms need to be alert to the dangers of 'tipping-off', as this will constitute a criminal offence under the anti-money laundering legislation.

For the UK further detail is set out in Practice Note 12: Money Laundering – Guidance for auditors on UK legislation.

**Written Representations** (Ref: Para. 16)

Because the effect on financial statements of laws and regulations can vary considerably, written representations provide necessary audit evidence about management's knowledge of identified or suspected non-compliance with laws and regulations, whose effects may have a material effect on the financial statements. However, written representations do not provide sufficient appropriate audit evidence on their own and, accordingly, do not affect the nature and extent of other audit evidence that is to be obtained by the auditor.[10]

A12

---

[9f] *In the UK, the Terrorism Act 2000 contains reporting requirements for the laundering of terrorist funds which include any funds that are likely to be used for the financing of terrorism.*
*In Ireland, the Criminal Justice Act 1994 (as amended) requires reporting suspicions of terrorist financing to the appropriate authorities.*

[10] *ISA (UK and Ireland) 580, "Written Representations," paragraph 4.*

## Audit Procedures When Non-Compliance Is Identified or Suspected

*Indications of Non-Compliance with Laws and Regulations* (Ref: Para. 18)

A13 If the auditor becomes aware of the existence of, or information about, the following matters, it may be an indication of non-compliance with laws and regulations:

- Investigations by regulatory organizations and government departments or payment of fines or penalties.
- Payments for unspecified services or loans to consultants, related parties, employees or government employees.
- Sales commissions or agent's fees that appear excessive in relation to those ordinarily paid by the entity or in its industry or to the services actually received.
- Purchasing at prices significantly above or below market price.
- Unusual payments in cash, purchases in the form of cashiers' cheques payable to bearer or transfers to numbered bank accounts.
- Unusual transactions with companies registered in tax havens.
- Payments for goods or services made other than to the country from which the goods or services originated.
- Payments without proper exchange control documentation.
- Existence of an information system which fails, whether by design or by accident, to provide an adequate audit trail or sufficient evidence.
- Unauthorized transactions or improperly recorded transactions.
- Adverse media comment.

*Matters Relevant to the Auditor's Evaluation* (Ref: Para. 18(b))

A14 Matters relevant to the auditor's evaluation[10a] of the possible effect on the financial statements include:

- The potential financial consequences of non-compliance with laws and regulations on the financial statements including, for example, the imposition of fines, penalties, damages, threat of expropriation of assets[10b], enforced discontinuation of operations, and litigation.
- Whether the potential financial consequences require disclosure.
- Whether the potential financial consequences are so serious as to call into question the fair presentation of the financial statements, or otherwise make the financial statements misleading.

*Audit Procedures* (Ref: Para. 19)

A15 The auditor may discuss the findings with those charged with governance where they may be able to provide additional audit evidence. For example, the auditor may confirm that those charged with governance have the same understanding of the facts and circumstances relevant to transactions or events that have led to the possibility of non-compliance with laws and regulations.

---

[10a] *ISA (UK and Ireland) 620, "Using the Work of an Auditor's Expert" applies if the auditor judges it necessary to obtain appropriate expert advice in connection with the evaluation of the possible effect of legal matters the financial statements.*

[10b] *The Proceeds of Crime Act 2002 ("POCA") provides procedures to enable the authorities to confiscate in criminal proceedings or bring an action for civil recovery of assets which represent the benefits of criminal conduct.*
*In Ireland, the Criminal Assets Bureau, an agency responsible for the confiscation of assets, was established by the Criminal Assets Bureau Act 1996.*

If management or, as appropriate, those charged with governance do not provide sufficient information to the auditor that the entity is in fact in compliance with laws and regulations, the auditor may consider it appropriate to consult with the entity's in-house legal counsel or external legal counsel about the application of the laws and regulations to the circumstances, including the possibility of fraud, and the possible effects on the financial statements. If it is not considered appropriate to consult with the entity's legal counsel or if the auditor is not satisfied with the legal counsel's opinion, the auditor may consider it appropriate to consult the auditor's own legal counsel as to whether a contravention of a law or regulation is involved, the possible legal consequences, including the possibility of fraud, and what further action, if any, the auditor would take.

**A16**

### *Evaluating the Implications of Non-Compliance* (Ref: Para. 21)

As required by paragraph 21, the auditor evaluates the implications of non-compliance in relation to other aspects of the audit, including the auditor's risk assessment and the reliability of written representations. The implications of particular instances of non-compliance identified by the auditor will depend on the relationship of the perpetration and concealment, if any, of the act to specific control activities and the level of management or employees involved, especially implications arising from the involvement of the highest authority within the entity.

**A17**

In exceptional cases, the auditor may consider whether withdrawal from the engagement, where withdrawal is possible under applicable law or regulation, is necessary when management or those charged with governance do not take the remedial action that the auditor considers appropriate in the circumstances, even when the non-compliance is not material to the financial statements. When deciding whether withdrawal from the engagement is necessary, the auditor may consider seeking legal advice. If withdrawal from the engagement is not possible, the auditor may consider alternative actions, including describing the non-compliance in an Other Matter(s) paragraph in the auditor's report.[11]

**A18**

Resignation by the auditor is a step of last resort. It is normally preferable for the auditor to remain in office to fulfil the auditor's statutory duties, particularly where minority interests are involved. However, there are circumstances where there may be no alternative to resignation, for example where the directors of a company refuse to issue its financial statements or the auditor wishes to inform the shareholders or creditors of the company of the auditor's concerns and there is no immediate occasion to do so.

**A18-1**

---

[11] *ISA (UK and Ireland) 706, "Emphasis of Matter Paragraphs and Other Matter Paragraphs in the Independent Auditor's Report," paragraph 8.*
*In the UK and Ireland, if the auditor concludes that the view given by the financial statements could be affected by a level of uncertainty concerning the consequences of a suspected or actual non-compliance which, in the auditor's opinion, is significant, the auditor, subject to a consideration of 'tipping off', includes an explanatory paragraph referring to the matter in the auditor's report.*

### Reporting of Identified or Suspected Non-Compliance

*Reporting Non-Compliance to Those Charged with Governance* (Ref: Para. 23)

A18-2   If a non-compliance is intentional but not material the auditor considers whether the nature and circumstances make it appropriate to communicate to those charged with governance as soon as practicable.

*Suspicion that Management or Those Charged with Governance are Involved in Non-Compliance* (Ref: Para. 24)

A18-3   In the case of suspected Money Laundering it may be appropriate to report the matter direct to the appropriate authority.

*Reporting Non-Compliance in the Auditor's Report on the Financial Statements* (Ref: Para. 27)

A18-4   In the UK and Ireland, when considering whether the financial statements reflect the possible consequences of any suspected or actual non-compliance, the auditor has regard to the requirements of applicable accounting standards (e.g. FRS 12 "Provisions, contingent liabilities and contingent assets"/IAS 37, "Provisions, contingent liabilities and contingent assets"). Suspected or actual non-compliance with laws or regulations may require disclosure in the financial statements because, although the immediate financial effect on the entity may not be material[11a], there could be future material consequences such as fines or litigation. For example, an illegal payment may not itself be material but may result in criminal proceedings against the entity or loss of business which could have a material effect on the true and fair view given by the financial statements.

*Reporting Non-Compliance to Regulatory and Enforcement Authorities* (Ref: Para. 28 – 28-1)

A19   The auditor's professional duty to maintain the confidentiality of client information may preclude reporting identified or suspected non-compliance with laws and regulations to a party outside the entity. However, the auditor's legal responsibilities vary by jurisdiction and, in certain circumstances, the duty of confidentiality may be overridden by statute, the law or courts of law. In some jurisdictions, the auditor of a financial institution has a statutory duty to report the occurrence, or suspected occurrence, of non-compliance with laws and regulations to supervisory authorities. Also, in some jurisdictions, the auditor has a duty to report misstatements to authorities in those cases where management and, where applicable, those charged with governance fail to take corrective action. The auditor may consider it appropriate to obtain legal advice to determine the appropriate course of action.

---

[11a] *As discussed in ISA (UK and Ireland) 320, "Materiality in Planning and Performing an Audit," judgments about materiality are made in light of surrounding circumstances and are affected by the size or nature of a matter or a combination of both.*

Legislation in the UK and Ireland establishes specific responsibilities for the auditor to report suspicions regarding certain criminal offences. In addition, the auditor of entities subject to statutory regulation[11b], has separate responsibilities to report certain information direct to the relevant regulator. Standards and guidance on these responsibilities is given in Section B of this ISA (UK and Ireland) and relevant APB Practice Notes.

**A19-1**

The procedures and guidance in Section B of this ISA (UK and Ireland) can be adapted to circumstances in which the auditor of other types of entity becomes aware of a suspected instance of non-compliance with laws or regulations which the auditor is under a statutory duty to report.

**A19-2**

Where the auditor becomes aware of a suspected or actual instance of non-compliance with law or regulations which does not give rise to a statutory duty to report to an appropriate authority the auditor considers whether the matter may be one that ought to be reported to a proper authority in the public interest and, where this is the case, except in the circumstances covered in paragraph A19-5 below, discusses the matter with those charged with governance, including any audit committee[11c].

**A19-3**

If, having considered any views expressed on behalf of the entity and in the light of any legal advice obtained, the auditor concludes that the matter ought to be reported to an appropriate authority in the public interest, the auditor notifies those charged with governance in writing of the view and, if the entity does not voluntarily do so itself or is unable to provide evidence that the matter has been reported, the auditor reports it.

**A19-4**

The auditor reports a matter direct to a proper authority in the public interest and without discussing the matter with the entity if the auditor concludes that the suspected or actual instance of non-compliance has caused the auditor no longer to have confidence in the integrity of the those charged with governance.

**A19-5**

Examples of circumstances which may cause the auditor no longer to have confidence in the integrity of those charged with governance include situations:

**A19-6**

- Where the auditor suspects or has evidence of the involvement or intended involvement of those charged with governance in possible non-compliance with law or regulations which could have a material effect on the financial statements; or
- Where the auditor is aware that those charged with governance are aware of such non-compliance and, contrary to regulatory requirements or the public interest, have not reported it to a proper authority within a reasonable period. In such a case, if the auditor determines that continued holding of office is untenable or the auditor is removed from office by the client, the auditor will be mindful of the auditor's reporting duties[11d].

---

[11b] *Auditors of financial service entities, pension schemes and, in the UK, charities have a statutory responsibility, subject to compliance with legislation relating to 'tipping off', to report matters that are likely to be of material significance to the regulator.*

[11c] *In rare circumstances, according to common law, disclosure might also be justified in the public interest where there is no instance of non-compliance with law or regulations, e.g. where the public is being misled or their financial interests are being damaged; where a miscarriage of justice has occurred; where the health and safety of members of the public or the environment is being endangered – although such events may well constitute breaches of law or regulation.*

[11d] *In the UK, under Part 16 of the Companies Act 2006.*

**A19-7**    Determination of where the balance of public interest lies requires careful consideration. An auditor whose suspicions have been aroused uses professional judgment to determine whether the auditor's misgivings justify the auditor in carrying the matter further or are too insubstantial to deserve reporting. The auditor is protected from the risk of liability for breach of confidence or defamation provided that:

- In the case of breach of confidence, disclosure is made in the public interest, and such disclosure is made to an appropriate body or person[11e], and there is no malice motivating the disclosure; and
- In the case of defamation disclosure is made in the auditor's capacity as auditor of the entity concerned, and there is no malice motivating the disclosure.

In addition, the auditor is protected from such risks where the auditor is expressly permitted or required by legislation to disclose information[11f].

**A19-8**    'Public interest' is a concept that is not capable of general definition. Each situation must be considered individually. Matters to be taken into account when considering whether disclosure is justified in the public interest may include:

- The extent to which the suspected or actual non-compliance with law or regulations is likely to affect members of the public;
- Whether those charged with governance have rectified the matter or are taking, or are likely to take, effective corrective action;
- The extent to which non-disclosure is likely to enable the suspected or actual non-compliance with law or regulations to recur with impunity;
- The gravity of the matter;
- Whether there is a general ethos within the entity of disregarding law or regulations; and
- The weight of evidence and the degree of the auditor's suspicion that there has been an instance of non-compliance with law or regulations.

**A19-9**    An auditor who can demonstrate having acted reasonably and in good faith in informing an authority of a breach of law or regulations which the auditor thinks has been committed would not be held by the court to be in breach of duty to the client even if, an investigation or prosecution having occurred, it were found that there had been no offence.

---

[11e] *In the UK, proper authorities could include the Serious Fraud Office, the Crown Prosecution Service, police forces, the Financial Services Authority the Panel on Takeovers and Mergers, the Society of Lloyd's, local authorities, the Charity Commissioners for England and Wales, the Scottish Office For Scottish Charities, the Inland Revenue, HM Customs and Excise, the Department of Trade and Industry and the Health and Safety Executive.*
*In Ireland, comparable bodies could include the Garda Bureau of Fraud Investigation, the Revenue Commissioners, the Irish Stock Exchange, the Irish Financial Services Regulatory Authority, the Pensions Board, the Director of Corporate Enforcement, the Health and Safety Authority, The Charities Regulatory Authority and the Department of Enterprise Trade and Employment.*

[11f] *In the UK, the Employments Rights Act 1996 would give similar protection to an individual member of the audit engagement team who made an appropriate report in the public interest. However, ordinarily a member of the engagement team who believed there was a reportable matter would follow the audit firm's policies and procedures to address such matters. ISA (UK and Ireland) 220, "Quality Control for an Audit of Financial Statements," paragraph 18(a), requires that the engagement partner shall take responsibility for the engagement team undertaking appropriate consultation on difficult or contentious matters. If differences of opinion arise within the engagement team, ISA (UK and Ireland) 220, paragraph 22, requires that the engagement team shall follow the firm's policies and procedures for dealing with and resolving differences of opinion.*

The auditor needs to remember that the auditor's decision as to whether to report, and if so to whom, may be called into question at a future date, for example on the basis of:

- What the auditor knew at the time;
- What the auditor ought to have known in the course of the audit;
- What the auditor ought to have concluded; and
- What the auditor ought to have done.

**A19-10**

The auditor may also wish to consider the possible consequences if financial loss is occasioned by non-compliance with law or regulations which the auditor suspects (or ought to suspect) has occurred but decided not to report.

The auditor may need to take legal advice before making a decision on whether the matter needs to be reported to a proper authority in the public interest.

**A19-11**

*Considerations Specific to Public Sector Entities*

A public sector auditor may be obliged to report on instances of non-compliance to the legislature or other governing body or to report them in the auditor's report.

**A20**

## Documentation (Ref: Para. 29)

The auditor's documentation of findings regarding identified or suspected non-compliance with laws and regulations may include, for example:

- Copies of records or documents.
- Minutes of discussions held with management, those charged with governance or parties outside the entity.

**A21**

# Addendum

*This addendum provides a summary of APB's rationale for retaining or excluding in the proposed clarified ISA (UK and Ireland) the supplementary requirements in the existing ISA (UK and Ireland). It also sets out the supplementary guidance material in the existing ISA (UK and Ireland) that APB considers is not necessary to retain in light of the improvements in the underlying Clarity ISAs issued by the IAASB as part of the Clarity Project. It is provided for information and does not form part of the proposed clarified ISA (UK and Ireland).*

*The Consultation Paper published with the exposure drafts explains the general approach used by the APB for determining whether current supplementary material should be proposed to be retained.*

## Analysis of proposed treatment of current APB supplementary material in current ISA (UK and Ireland) 250 Section A

### Requirements

| APB supplementary requirements (*Italic text is from IAASB for context*) | Is it covered in substance in the Clarity ISA? | Should it be retained? |
|---|---|---|
| 15. *In order to plan the audit, the auditor should obtain a general understanding of the legal and regulatory framework applicable to the entity and the industry and how the entity is complying with that framework.* | | |
| 15-1. **In the UK and Ireland, the auditor should obtain a general understanding of the procedures followed by the entity to ensure compliance with that framework.** | ✓ This issue is addressed in the Application Material (A7) which indicates that to obtain a general understanding the auditor may, inter alia, "inquire of management concerning the entity's policies and procedures regarding compliance with laws and regulations." | ✗ |

| APB supplementary requirements (*Italic text is from IAASB for context*) | Is it covered in substance in the Clarity ISA? | Should it be retained? |
|---|---|---|
| 18. *After obtaining the general understanding, the auditor should perform further audit procedures to help identify instances of noncompliance with those laws and regulations where noncompliance should be considered when preparing financial statements, specifically:*<br><br>**(c) Enquiring of those charged with governance as to whether they are on notice of any such possible instances of non-compliance with law or regulations.** | ✓ The auditor is required to inquire of management <u>and, where appropriate, those charged with governance</u>. (14(a))<br><br>The auditor is also required to ask management <u>and, where appropriate, those charged with governance</u> for a written representation that all known instances of non-compliance or suspected non-compliance with laws and regulations whose effects should be considered when preparing financial statements have been disclosed to the auditor. (16) | ✗ |

| APB supplementary requirements (*Italic text is from IAASB for context*) | Is it covered in substance in the Clarity ISA? | Should it be retained? |
|---|---|---|
| 18-1. **In the UK and Ireland, the auditor's procedures should be designed to help identify possible or actual instances of non-compliance with those laws and regulations which provide a legal framework within which the entity conducts its business and which are central to the entity's ability to conduct its business and hence to its financial statements.** | ✗ Under the ISA, the auditor is required to perform <u>specified</u> audit procedures (inquiry of management and inspection of correspondence with authorities) to help identify instances of non-compliance with other laws and regulations that may have a material effect on the financial statements (14); remain alert (15), and obtain representations (16). There is explicit guidance that "In the absence of identified or suspected non-compliance, the auditor is <u>not</u> required to perform audit procedures regarding the entity's compliance with laws and regulations, other than those set out in paragraphs 12-16." (17) | ✗ But guidance has been added that laws and regulations that may have a material effect on the financial statements are likely to be those which are central to the entity's ability to conduct its business. <br><br>**A9-1** |
| 22-1. **In the UK and Ireland, when carrying out procedures for the purpose of forming an opinion on the financial statements, the auditor should be alert for those instances of possible or actual noncompliance with laws and regulations that might incur obligations for partners and staff in audit firms to report money laundering offences.** | ✗ | ✓ (Regulatory) **15-1** |
| 23-1. **Where applicable, the written representations should include the actual or contingent consequences which may arise from the non-compliance.** | ✗ Not important for audit quality. | ✗ |

| APB supplementary requirements (*Italic text is from IAASB for context*) | Is it covered in substance in the Clarity ISA? | Should it be retained? |
|---|---|---|
| 28-1. **Any discussion of findings with those charged with governance and with management should be subject to compliance with legislation relating to 'tipping off' and any requirement to report the findings direct to a third party.** | ✗ | ✓ (Regulatory) But converted to a footnote (4a) to para 19. |
| *Reporting to management*<br>33-1. **In the UK and Ireland the auditor should communicate the finding where the non-compliance is material or is believed to be intentional. The non-compliance does not have to be both material and intentional.** | ✗ These are conditions for communicating "as soon as practicable". In the ISA the condition is "intentional and material". (23) | ✗ But guidance has been added indicating that if a non-compliance is intentional but not material the auditor considers whether the nature and circumstances make it appropriate to communicate to those charged with governance as soon as practicable. **A18-2** |
| 38-1. **If the auditor becomes aware of a suspected or actual non-compliance with law and regulations which gives rise to a statutory duty to report, the auditor should, subject to compliance with legislation relating to "tipping off", make a report to the appropriate authority without undue delay.** | ✗ There is requirement to determine whether the auditor has a responsibility to report the identified or suspected non-compliance to parties outside the entity. (28, A19) However, the actual requirement to report is implicit rather than explicit and the "timing" and consideration of "tipping off" legislation are not covered. | ✓ **28-1** (Regulatory) |

## Guidance

The following guidance in current ISA (UK and Ireland) 250 Section A has not been carried forward to the draft clarity version.

| **Current paragraph reference (*Italic text is from IAASB for context*)** |
| --- |
| 1-1. – 1-4. [Description of management and those charged with governance.] |
| 2     *... Detection of noncompliance, regardless of materiality, requires consideration of the implications for the integrity of management[1] or employees and the possible effect on other aspects of the audit* <br><br> [1]   In the UK and Ireland, the auditor also considers the implications for the integrity of those charged with governance. |
| 3.     *The term "noncompliance" as used in this ISA (UK and Ireland) refers to acts of omission or commission by the entity being audited, either intentional or unintentional, which are contrary to the prevailing laws or regulations. Such acts, include transactions entered into by, or in the name of, the entity or on its behalf by its management[2] or employees. ...* <br><br> [2]   In the UK and Ireland, such acts include transactions entered into by, or in the name of, the entity or on its behalf by those charged with governance. |
| 5.     *Laws and regulations vary considerably in their relation to the financial statements. Some laws or regulations determine the form or content of an entity's financial statements or the amounts to be recorded or disclosures to be made in financial statements. Other laws or regulations are to be complied with by management[3] or set the provisions under which the entity is allowed to conduct its business. ...* <br><br> [3]   In the UK and Ireland, there are also laws or regulations that are to be complied with by those charged with governance. |
| 9     *It is management's responsibility to ensure that the entity's operations are conducted in accordance with laws and regulations[4]. The responsibility for the prevention and detection of noncompliance rests with management[4].* <br><br> [4]   In the UK and Ireland, this responsibility rests with those charged with governance. |
| 10     *The following policies and procedures, among others, may assist management[5] in discharging its responsibilities for the prevention and detection of noncompliance: ...* <br><br>    •   A legal department. <br>    •   A compliance function <br><br> [5]   In the UK and Ireland, the policies and procedures may also assist those charged with governance in discharging their responsibilities for the prevention and detection of noncompliance. |

**Current paragraph reference (*Italic text is from IAASB for context*)**

12. *An audit is subject to the unavoidable risk that some material misstatements of the financial statements will not be detected, even though the audit is properly planned and performed in accordance with ISAs (UK and Ireland). This risk is higher with regard to material misstatements resulting from noncompliance with laws and regulations due to factors such as the following:*
    - *Noncompliance may involve conduct designed to conceal it, such as collusion, forgery, deliberate failure to record transactions, senior management[7] override of controls or intentional misrepresentations being made to the auditor.*

[7] In the UK and Ireland, an additional factor is override of controls by those charged with governance.

14. *In accordance with specific statutory requirements, the auditor may be specifically required to report as part of the audit of the financial statements whether the entity complies with certain provisions of laws or regulations[8]. In these circumstances, the auditor would plan to test for compliance with these provisions of the laws and regulations.*

[8] In Ireland, the Companies (Auditing and Accounting) Act 2003 contains provisions that will require, when commenced, directors of "large" companies to make statements regarding compliance with the Companies Acts, tax laws and any other elements that provide a legal framework within which the company operates and that may materially affect the company's financial statements. Auditors of such companies will be required to review the statements to determine whether they are fair and reasonable having regard to information obtained by the auditor in the course of the audit or other work undertaken for the company. The auditors' review requirements are not addressed in this ISA (UK and Ireland)).

17. *To obtain the general understanding of laws and regulations, the auditor would ordinarily:*
    - *Inquire of management[10] concerning the entity's policies and procedures regarding compliance with laws and regulations;*
    - *Inquire of management[10] as to the laws or regulations that may be expected to have a fundamental effect on the operations of the entity;*
    - *Discuss with management[11] the policies or procedures adopted for identifying, evaluating and accounting for litigation claims and assessments; and*

[10] In the UK and Ireland, the auditor makes inquiries of such matters with those charged with governance.
[11] In the UK and Ireland, the auditor discusses such matters with those charged with governance.

22. ***The auditor should be alert to the fact that audit procedures applied for the purpose of forming an opinion on the financial statements may bring instances of possible noncompliance with laws and regulations to the auditor's attention.*** *For example, such audit procedures include reading minutes; inquiring of the entity's management[10] and legal counsel concerning litigation, claims and assessments; and performing substantive tests of details of classes of transactions, account balances, or disclosures.*

| Current paragraph reference (*Italic text is from IAASB for context*) |
|---|

[Being alert to possible reportable money laundering offences]

22-2. There may be a wide range of laws and regulations falling into this category, many of which fall outside the expertise of individuals trained in financial auditing. There can therefore be no assurance that the auditor appointed to report on an entity's statements will detect all material breaches of such laws and regulations. However, when the auditor suspects the existence of breaches which could be material, the auditor needs to consider whether and how the matter ought to be reported, as set out later in this ISA (UK and Ireland).

23.   *The auditor should obtain written representations that management[22] has disclosed to the auditor all known actual or possible noncompliance with laws and regulations whose effects should be considered when preparing financial statements.*

[22]   In the UK and Ireland the auditor obtains this written representation from those charged with governance.

28   *When the auditor believes there may be noncompliance, the auditor should document the findings and discuss them with management[21]. Documentation of findings would include copies of records and documents and making minutes of conversations, if appropriate.*

29.   *If management[25] does not provide satisfactory information that it is in fact in compliance, the auditor would consult with the entity's lawyer about the application of the laws and regulations to the circumstances and the possible effects on the financial statements. ...*

[25]   In the UK and Ireland, the auditor obtains such information from those charged with governance.

31.   *The auditor should consider the implications of noncompliance in relation to other aspects of the audit, particularly the reliability of management[26] representations. ...*

[26]   In the UK and Ireland, the auditor also considers the reliability of representations from those charged with governance.

33-2. Any communication with those charged with governance, or action by the auditor to obtain evidence that they are appropriately informed is subject to compliance with legislation relating to 'tipping off'.

34   *If the auditor suspects that members of senior management, including members of the board of directors[27], are involved in noncompliance, the auditor should report the matter to the next higher level of authority at the entity, if it exists, such as an audit committee or a supervisory board. ...*

[27]   In the UK and Ireland, the auditor also reports such matters if those charged with governance are suspected of being involved in non compliance.

| Current paragraph reference (*Italic text is from IAASB for context*) |
|---|
| 37-2. In the UK and Ireland, in determining whether disclosures concerning the matter are adequate, or whether an explanatory paragraph needs to be included in the auditor's report, the auditor bases the decision primarily on the adequacy of the overall view given by the financial statements. Steps taken to regularize the position (for example, where there has been an unauthorized material transaction for which authority has subsequently been obtained), or the possible consequences of qualification, are not, on their own, grounds on which the auditor may refrain from expressing a qualified opinion or from including an explanatory paragraph reflecting a significant uncertainty. |
| 37-3. In the UK and Ireland, when determining whether a suspected or actual instance of non-compliance with laws or regulations requires disclosure in the financial statements, the auditor has regard to whether shareholders require the information to enable them to assess the performance of the company and any potential implications for its future operations or standing. Where a suspected or actual instance of non-compliance needs to be reflected in the financial statements, a true and fair view will require that sufficient particulars are provided to enable users of the financial statements to appreciate the significance of the information disclosed. This would usually require the full potential consequences to be disclosed and, in some cases, it may be necessary for this purpose that the financial statements indicate that non-compliance with laws or regulations is or may be involved |
| 39. *The auditor may conclude that withdrawal from the engagement is necessary when the entity does not take the remedial action that the auditor considers necessary in the circumstances, even when the noncompliance is not material to the financial statements. Factors that would affect the auditor's conclusion include the implications of the involvement of the highest authority within the entity which may affect the reliability of management[26] representations, and the effects on the auditor of continuing association with the entity. In reaching such a conclusion, the auditor would ordinarily seek legal advice.* |
| 40 **As stated in the Code of Ethics for Professional Accountants[30] issued by the International Federation of Accountants, on receipt of an inquiry from the proposed auditor, the existing auditor should advise whether there are any professional reasons why the proposed auditor should not accept the appointment. ...** |
| [30] In the UK and Ireland the relevant ethical pronouncements with which the auditor complies are the APB's Ethical Standards and the ethical pronouncements relating to the work of auditors issued by the auditor's relevant professional body – see the Statement "The Auditing practices Board – Scope and Authority of Pronouncements. |
| 40-2. In the UK, the Money Laundering Regulations 2003 came into force on 1 March 2004. In Ireland, the Criminal Justice Act 1994 (Section 32) Regulations 2003 are effective from 15 September 2003. |

**Current paragraph reference (*Italic text is from IAASB for context*)**

Appendix

*Examples of the type of information that may come to the auditor's attention that may indicate that noncompliance with laws or regulations has occurred are listed below: ...*

- Complex corporate structures including offshore companies where ownership cannot be identified.
- Tax evasion such as the under declaring of income and over claiming of expenses.
- Transactions undertaken by the entity that have no apparent purpose or that make no obvious economic sense.
- Where those charged with governance of the entity refuse to provide necessary information and explanations to support transactions and other dealings of the company.

# Proposed Clarified International Standard on Auditing (UK and Ireland) 250

## Section B – The auditor's right and duty to report to regulators in the financial sector

*(Effective for audits of financial statements for periods ending on or after 15 December 2010)*

## Contents

International Standard on Auditing (UK and Ireland) (ISA (UK and Ireland)) 250, "Consideration of Laws and Regulations in an Audit of Financial Statements" should be read in conjunction with ISA (UK and Ireland) 200, "Overall Objectives of the Independent Auditor and the Conduct of an Audit in Accordance with International Standards on Auditing (UK and Ireland)."

# Introduction

## Scope of this Section

1    This Section of ISA (UK and Ireland) 250 deals with the circumstances in which the auditor of a financial institution subject to statutory regulation (a 'regulated entity') is required to report direct to a regulator information which comes to the auditor's attention in the course of the work undertaken in the auditor's capacity as auditor of the regulated entity. This may include work undertaken to express an opinion on the entity's financial statements, other financial information or on other matters specified by legislation or by a regulator.

## The Auditor's Responsibilities (Ref: Para. A1-A8)

2    The auditor of a regulated entity generally has special reporting responsibilities in addition to the responsibility to report on financial statements. These special reporting responsibilities take two forms:

(a) *A responsibility to provide a report on matters specified in legislation or by a regulator*. This form of report is often made on an annual or other routine basis and does not derive from another set of reporting responsibilities. The auditor is required to carry out appropriate procedures sufficient to form an opinion on the matters concerned. These procedures may be in addition to those carried out to form an opinion on the financial statements; and

(b) *A statutory duty to report certain information, relevant to the regulators' functions, that come to the auditor's attention in the course of the audit work*. The auditor has no responsibility to carry out procedures to search out the information relevant to the regulator. This form of report is derivative in nature, arising only in the context of another set of reporting responsibilities, and is initiated by the auditor on discovery of a reportable matter.

3    This section of this ISA (UK and Ireland) deals with both forms of direct reports. Guidance on the auditor's responsibility to provide special reports on a routine basis on other matters specified in legislation or by a regulator is given in the Practice Notes dealing with regulated business, for example banks, building societies, investment businesses and insurers.

4    The statutory duty to report to a regulator applies to information which comes to the attention of the auditor in the auditor's capacity as auditor. In determining whether information is obtained in that capacity, two criteria in particular need to be considered: first, whether the person who obtained the information also undertook the audit work; and if so, whether it was obtained in the course of or as a result of undertaking the audit work. Appendix 2 to this section of this ISA (UK and Ireland) sets out guidance on the application of these criteria.

5    The auditor may have a statutory right to bring information to the attention of the regulator in particular circumstances which lie outside those giving rise to a statutory duty to initiate a direct report. Where this is so, the auditor may use that right to make a direct report relevant to the regulator on a specific matter which comes to the auditor's attention when the auditor concludes that doing so is necessary to protect the interests of those for whose benefit the regulator is required to act.

The requirements and explanatory material in this section of this ISA (UK and Ireland) complement but do not replace the legal and regulatory requirements applicable to each regulated entity. Where the application of those legal and regulatory requirements, taking into account any published interpretations, is insufficiently clear for the auditor to determine whether a particular circumstance results in a legal duty to make a report to a regulator, or a right to make such a report, it may be appropriate to take legal advice.

**6**

## Effective Date

This Section of ISA (UK and Ireland) 250 is effective for audits of financial statements for periods ending on or after 15 December 2010.

**7**

# Objective

The objective of the auditor of a regulated entity is to bring information of which the auditor has become aware in the ordinary course of performing work undertaken to fulfil the auditor's audit responsibilities to the attention of the appropriate regulator as soon as practicable when:

**8**

(a) The auditor concludes that it is relevant to the regulator's functions having regard to such matters as may be specified in statute or any related regulations; and

(b) In the auditor's opinion there is reasonable cause to believe it is or may be of material significance to the regulator.

# Definitions

For purposes of this Section of this ISA (UK and Ireland), the following terms have the meanings attributed below:

**9**

(a) **The Act(s)**: means those Acts that give rise to a duty to report to a regulator. For example:
In the United Kingdom, this includes the Financial Services and Markets Act 2000 and regulations made under that Act, and any future legislation including provisions relating to the duties of auditors similar to those contained in that statute.
In the Republic of Ireland, this includes the Central Bank Acts 1942 to 1989, the Building Societies Act 1989, The Central Bank and Financial Services Authority of Ireland Act, 2003, the Trustees Savings Bank Act 1989, the Insurance Act 1989, the European Communities (Undertakings for Collective Investment in Transferable Securities) Regulations 1989, the Unit Trusts Act 1990 and, in the case of investment companies, the Companies Act 1990 and any future legislation including provisions relating to the duties of auditors similar to those contained in those Acts, together with other regulations made under them.

(b) **Audit**: for the purpose of this Section of this ISA (UK and Ireland), the term *audit* refers both to an engagement to report on the financial statements of a regulated entity and to an engagement to provide a report on other matters specified by statute or by a regulator undertaken in the capacity of auditor.

(c) **Auditor**: the term 'auditor' should be interpreted in accordance with the requirements of the Acts. Guidance on its interpretation is contained in

Practice Notes relating to each area of the financial sector to which the duty applies.

(d) **Material significance**: the term 'material significance' requires interpretation in the context of the specific legislation applicable to the regulated entity. A matter or group of matters is normally of material significance to a regulator's functions when, due either to its nature or its potential financial impact, it is likely of itself to require investigation by the regulator. Further guidance on the interpretation of the term in the context of specific legislation is contained in Practice Notes dealing with the rights and duties of auditors of regulated entities to report direct to regulators.

(e) **Regulated entity**: an individual, company or other type of entity authorised to carry on business in the financial sector which is subject to statutory regulation.

(f) **Regulator**: such persons as are empowered by the Act to regulate business in the financial sector. The term includes the Financial Services Authority (FSA), Irish Financial Services Regulatory Authority (IFSRA) and such other bodies as may be so empowered in future legislation.

(g) **'Tipping off'** involves a disclosure that is likely to prejudice any investigation into suspected money laundering which might arise from a report being made to a regulatory authority[1]. Money laundering involves an act which conceals, disguises, converts, transfers, removes, uses, acquires or possesses property which constitutes or represents a benefit from criminal conduct.

# Requirements

## Conduct of the Audit

### Planning

10    When obtaining an understanding of the business for the purpose of the audit, the auditor of a regulated entity shall obtain an understanding of its current activities, the scope of its authorisation and the effectiveness of its control environment. (Ref: Para. A9-A16)

### Supervision and Control

11    The auditor shall ensure that all staff involved in the audit of a regulated entity have an understanding of:

(a) The provisions of applicable legislation;
(b) The regulator's rules and any guidance issued by the regulator; and
(c) Any specific requirements which apply to the particular regulated entity,

appropriate to their role in the audit and sufficient (in the context of that role) to enable them to identify situations which may give reasonable cause to believe that a matter should be reported to the regulator. (Ref: Para. A17-A23)

---

[1] *More detail is provided in the definition contained in Section A of ISA (UK and Ireland) 250.*

### Identifying Matters Requiring a Report Direct to Regulators

Where an apparent breach of statutory or regulatory requirements comes to the auditor's attention, the auditor shall:

    **12**

(a) Obtain such evidence as is available to assess its implications for the auditor's reporting responsibilities;

(b) Determine whether, in the auditor's opinion, there is reasonable cause to believe that the breach is of material significance to the regulator; and

(c) Consider whether the apparent breach is criminal conduct that gives rise to criminal property and, as such, should be reported to the specified authorities. (Ref: Para. A24-A30)

## Reporting (Ref: Para. A31-A46)

### The Auditor's Statutory Duty to Report Direct to Regulators

When the auditor concludes, after appropriate discussion and investigations, that a matter which has come to the auditor's attention gives rise to a statutory duty to make a report the auditor shall[2] bring the matter to the attention of the regulator as soon as practicable in a form and manner which will facilitate appropriate action by the regulator. When the initial report is made orally, the auditor shall make a contemporaneous written record of the oral report and shall confirm the matter in writing to the regulator. (Ref: Para. A31-A35)

    **13**

When the matter giving rise to a statutory duty to make a report direct to a regulator casts doubt on the integrity of those charged with governance or their competence to conduct the business of the regulated entity, the auditor shall[2] make the report to the regulator as soon as practicable and without informing those charged with governance in advance. (Ref: Para. A35)

    **14**

### The Auditor's Right to Report Direct to Regulators

When a matter comes to the auditor's attention which the auditor concludes does not give rise to a statutory duty to report but nevertheless may be relevant to the regulator's exercise of its functions, the auditor shall[2]:

    **15**

(a) Consider whether the matter should be brought to the attention of the regulator under the terms of the appropriate legal provisions enabling the auditor to report direct to the regulator; and, if so

(b) Advise those charged with governance that in the auditor's opinion the matter should be drawn to the regulators' attention.

Where the auditor is unable to obtain, within a reasonable period, adequate evidence that those charged with governance have properly informed the regulator of the matter, the auditor shall[2] make a report direct to the regulator as soon as practicable. (Ref: Para. A36-A37)

### Contents of a Report Initiated by the Auditor

When making or confirming in writing a report direct to a regulator, the auditor shall:

    **16**

---

[2] *Subject to compliance with legislation relating to 'tipping off'.*

(a)  State the name of the regulated entity concerned;
(b)  State the statutory power under which the report is made;
(c)  State that the report has been prepared in accordance with ISA (UK and Ireland) 250, Section B 'The auditor's Right and Duty to Report to Regulators in the Financial Sector';
(d)  Describe the context in which the report is given;
(e)  Describe the matter giving rise to the report;
(f)  Request the regulator to confirm that the report has been received; and
(g)  State the name of the auditor, the date of the written report and, where appropriate, the date on which an oral report was made to the regulator and the name and title of the individual to whom the oral report was made. (Ref: Para. A38-A39)

### Relationship With Other Reporting Responsibilities

17    When issuing a report expressing an opinion on a regulated entity's financial statements or on other matters specified by legislation or a regulator, the auditor:

(a)  Shall consider whether there are consequential reporting issues affecting the auditor's opinion which arise from any report previously made direct to the regulator in the course of the auditor's appointment; and
(b)  Shall assess whether any matters encountered in the course of the audit indicate a need for a further direct report. (Ref: Para. A40-A43)

\*\*\*

# Application and Other Explanatory Material

## The Auditor's Responsibilities (Ref: Para. 2-6)

A1    Before accepting appointment, the auditor follows the procedures identified in the APB's Ethical Standards and the ethical pronouncements and Audit Regulations issued by the auditor's relevant professional body.

A2    In the case of regulated entities, the auditor would in particular obtain an understanding of the appropriate statutory and regulatory requirements and a preliminary knowledge of the management and operations of the entity, so as to enable the auditor to determine whether a level of knowledge of the business adequate to perform the audit can be obtained. The procedures carried out by the auditor in seeking to obtain this preliminary understanding may include discussion with the previous auditor and, in some circumstances, with the regulator.

A3    On ceasing to hold office, the auditor may be required by statute or by regulation to make specific reports concerning the circumstances relating to that event, and would also follow the procedures identified in the ethical guidance issued by the relevant professional body.

A4    In addition, the auditor of a regulated entity would assess whether it is appropriate to bring any matters of which the auditor is then aware to the notice of the regulator. Under legislation in the UK, this may be done either before or after ceasing to hold office, as the auditor's statutory right to disclose to a regulator information obtained in the course of the auditor's appointment is not affected by the auditor's removal, resignation or otherwise ceasing to hold office.

The duty to make a report direct to a regulator does not impose upon the auditor a duty to carry out specific work: it arises solely in the context of work carried out to fulfil other reporting responsibilities. Accordingly, no auditing procedures in addition to those carried out in the normal course of auditing the financial statements, or for the purpose of making any other specified report, are necessary for the fulfilment of the auditor's responsibilities. **A5**

It will, however, be necessary for the auditor to take additional time in carrying out a financial statement audit or other engagement to assess whether matters which come to the auditor's attention should be included in a direct report and, where appropriate, to prepare and submit the report. These additional planning and follow-up procedures do not constitute an extension of the scope of the financial statement audit or of other work undertaken to provide a specified report relating to a regulated entity. They are necessary solely in order to understand and clarify the reporting responsibility and, where appropriate, to make a report. **A6**

The circumstances in which the auditor is required by statute to make a report direct to a regulator include matters which are not considered as part of the audit of financial statements or of work undertaken to discharge other routine responsibilities. For example, the duty to report would apply to information of which the auditor became aware in the course of the auditor's work which is relevant to the FSA's criteria for approved persons, although the auditor is not otherwise required to express an opinion on such matters. However, the legislation imposing a duty to make reports direct to regulators does not require the auditor to change the scope of the audit work, nor does it place on the auditor an obligation to conduct the audit work in such a way that there is reasonable certainty that the auditor will discover all matters which regulators might consider as being of material significance. Therefore, whilst the auditor of a regulated entity is required to be alert to matters which may require a report, the auditor is not expected to be aware of all circumstances which, had the auditor known of them, would have led the auditor to make such a report. It is only when the auditor becomes aware of such a matter during the conduct of the normal audit work that the auditor has an obligation to determine whether a report to the regulator is required by statute or appropriate for other reasons. **A7**

Similarly, the auditor is not responsible for reporting on a regulated entity's overall compliance with rules with which it is required to comply nor is the auditor required to conduct the audit work in such a way that there is reasonable certainty that the auditor will discover breaches. Nevertheless, breaches of rules with which a regulated entity is required to comply may have implications for the financial statements and, accordingly, the auditor of a regulated entity needs to consider whether any actual or contingent liabilities may have arisen from breaches of regulatory requirements. Breaches of a regulator's requirements may also have consequences for other matters on which the auditor of a regulated entity is required to express an opinion and, if such breaches represent criminal conduct, could give rise to the need to report to specified authorities. **A8**

### Conduct of the Audit

*Planning* (Ref: Para. 10)

A9   ISAs (UK and Ireland) require the auditor to obtain an understanding of the entity and its environment[3].

A10   In the context of a regulated entity, the auditor's understanding of its business needs to extend to the applicable statutory provisions, the rules of the regulator concerned and any guidance issued by the regulator on the interpretation of those rules, together with other guidance issued by the APB.

A11   The auditor is also required to identify and assess the risks of material misstatements to provide a basis for designing and performing further audit procedures[4]. In making such an assessment the auditor takes into account the control environment, including the entity's higher level procedures for complying with the requirements of its regulator. Such a review gives an indication of the extent to which the general atmosphere and controls in the regulated entity are conducive to compliance, for example through consideration of *inter alia*:

- The adequacy of procedures and training to inform staff of the requirements of relevant legislation and the rules or other regulations of the regulator;
- The adequacy of procedures for authorisation of transactions;
- Procedures for internal review of the entity's compliance with regulatory or other requirements;
- The authority of, and any resources available to, the compliance officer/Money Laundering Reporting Officer ('MLRO'); and
- Procedures to ensure that possible breaches of requirements are investigated by an appropriate person and are brought to the attention of senior management.

A12   In some areas of the financial sector, conducting business outside the scope of the entity's authorisation is a serious regulatory breach, and therefore of material significance to the regulator. In addition, it may result in fines, suspension or loss of authorisation.

A13   Where the auditor's review of the reporting entity's activities indicates that published guidance by the regulator may not be sufficiently precise to enable the auditor to identify circumstances in which it is necessary to initiate a report, the auditor would consider whether it is necessary to discuss the matters specified in legislation with the appropriate regulator with a view to reaching agreement on its interpretation.

A14   Similarly, where a group includes two or more companies separately regulated by different regulators, there may be a need to clarify the regulators' requirements in any overlapping areas of activity. However, the statutory duty to make a report as presently defined arises only in respect of the legal entity subject to regulation. Therefore the auditor of an unregulated company in a group that includes one or

---

[3] *ISA (UK and Ireland) 315, "Identifying and Assessing the Risks of Material Misstatement through Understanding the Entity and Its Environment," paragraph 11.*

[4] *ISA (UK and Ireland) 315, paragraph 25.*

more other companies which are authorised by regulators would not have a duty to report matters to the regulators of those companies.

When a regulated entity is subject to provisions of two or more regulators, the auditor needs to take account of the separate reporting requirements in planning and conducting the audit work. Arrangements may exist for one regulatory body to rely on financial monitoring being carried out by another body (the 'lead regulator') and where this is the case, routine reports by the regulated entity's auditor may be made to the lead regulator alone.  **A15**

However, the auditor's statutory duty to report cannot be discharged by reliance on the lead regulator informing others. Therefore, where the auditor concludes that a matter is of material significance to one regulator, the auditor needs to assess the need for separate reports informing each regulator of matters which the auditor concludes are or may be of material significance to it.  **A16**

### *Supervision and Control* (Ref: Para. 11)

ISAs (UK and Ireland) require the engagement partner to take responsibility for the direction, supervision and performance of the audit engagement in compliance with professional standards and applicable legal and regulatory requirements[5]. Consequently, in planning and conducting the audit of a regulated entity the auditor needs to ensure that staff are alert to the possibility that a report to its regulator may be required.  **A17**

Auditing firms also need to establish adequate procedures to ensure that any matters which are discovered in the course of or as a result of audit work and may give rise to a duty to report are brought to the attention of the partner responsible for the audit on a timely basis.  **A18**

The right and duty to report to a regulator applies to information of which the auditor becomes aware in the auditor's capacity as such. They do not extend automatically to any information obtained by an accounting firm regardless of its source. Consequently partners and staff undertaking work in another capacity are not required to have detailed knowledge of the regulator's requirements (unless necessary for that other work) nor to bring information to the attention of the partner responsible for the audit on a routine basis.  **A19**

However, as discussed further in Appendix 2, firms need to establish lines of communications, commensurate with their size and complexity, sufficient to ensure that non-audit work undertaken for a regulated entity which is likely to have an effect on the audit is brought to the attention of the partner responsible for the audit, who will need to determine whether the results of non-audit work undertaken for a regulated entity ought to be assessed as part of the audit process.  **A20**

### *Reliance on Other Auditors*

An auditor with responsibilities for reporting on financial statements including financial information of one or more components audited by other auditors is required to obtain sufficient appropriate audit evidence that the work of the other  **A21**

---

[5] *ISA (UK and Ireland) 220, "Quality Control for an Audit of Financial Statements," paragraph 15.*

auditors is adequate for the purposes of the audit. The same principle applies to reliance on another auditor in a different type of engagement. The auditor of a regulated entity who relies on work undertaken by other auditors needs to establish reporting arrangements such that the other auditors bring to the attention of the auditor of the regulated entity matters arising from their work which may give rise to a duty to report to a regulator.

A22     The nature of the reporting arrangements will depend on the nature of the work undertaken by the other auditors. For example, the statutory duty to make a report relates to the legal entity subject to regulation rather than to the entire group to which that entity may belong. Consequently, the auditor of a holding company authorised by one regulator would not be expected to have knowledge of all matters which come to the attention of a subsidiary's auditor. The auditor of the regulated entity would, however, have a duty to report, where appropriate, matters which arise from the audit of the regulated entity's own financial statements and of the consolidated group figures.

A23     Where the audit of a regulated entity is undertaken by joint auditors, knowledge obtained by one auditing firm is likely to be deemed to be known by the other. Care will therefore be needed in agreeing and implementing arrangements to exchange information relating to matters which may give rise to a duty to report to a regulator.

### Identifying Matters Requiring a Report Direct to Regulators (Ref: Para. 12)

A24     The precise matters which give rise to a statutory duty on auditors to make a report to a regulator derive from the relevant Acts. Broadly, such matters fall into three general categories:

(a)  The financial position of the regulated entity;
(b)  Its compliance with requirements for the management of its business; and
(c)  The status of those charged with governance as fit and proper persons.

Further detailed guidance on the interpretation of these matters in the context of specific legislation applicable to each type of regulated entity is contained in Practice Notes dealing with the rights and duties of auditors of regulated entities to report direct to regulators.

A25     In assessing the effect of an apparent breach, the auditor takes into account the quantity and type of evidence concerning such a matter which may reasonably be expected to be available. If the auditor concludes that the auditor has been prevented from obtaining all such evidence concerning a matter which may give rise to a duty to report, the auditor would normally make a report direct to the regulator as soon as practicable.

A26     An apparent breach of statutory or regulatory requirements may not of itself give rise to a statutory duty to make a report to a regulator. There will normally be a need for some further investigation and discussion of the circumstances surrounding the apparent breach with the directors in order to obtain sufficient information to determine whether it points to a matter which is or may be of material significance to the regulator. For example, a minor breach which has been corrected by the regulated entity and reported (if appropriate) to the regulator, and which from the evidence available to the auditor appears to be an isolated occurrence, would not normally give the auditor reasonable cause to believe that it is or may be of material significance to the regulator. However a minor breach that results in a criminal offence that gave rise to the criminal property would be reportable to the specified authorities under the anti-money laundering legislation.

When determining whether a breach of statutory or regulatory requirements gives rise to a statutory duty to make a report direct to a regulator, the auditor considers factors such as:  **A27**

- Whether the breach, though minor, is indicative of a general lack of compliance with the regulator's requirements or otherwise casts doubt on the status of those charged with governance as fit and proper persons;
- Whether a breach which occurred before the auditor's visit to the regulated entity was reported by the entity itself and has since been corrected, such that, at the date of the auditor's discovery, no breach exists;
- Whether the circumstances giving rise to a breach which occurred before the auditors visit to the regulated entity continue to exist, or those charged with governance have not taken corrective action, or the breach has re-occurred; and
- Whether the circumstances suggest that an immediate report to the regulator is necessary in order to protect the interests of depositors, investors, policyholders, clients of the entity or others in whose interests the regulator is required to act.

The auditor would normally seek evidence to assess the implications of a suspected breach before reporting a matter to the regulator. However, the auditor's responsibility to make a report does not require the auditor to determine the full implications of a matter before reporting: the auditor is required to exercise professional judgment as to whether or not there is reasonable cause to believe that a matter is or may be of material significance to the regulator. In forming that judgment, the auditor undertakes appropriate investigations to determine the circumstances but does not require the degree of evidence which would be a normal part of forming an opinion on financial statements. Such investigations would normally include:  **A28**

- Enquiry of appropriate level of staff;
- Review of correspondence and documents relating to the transaction or event concerned; and
- Discussion with those charged with governance, or other senior management where appropriate.

In the case of a life company, it would also be appropriate to consult with the appointed actuary, who also has various statutory duties under insurance companies legislation.

The potential gravity of some apparent breaches may be such that an immediate report to the regulator is essential in order to enable the regulator to take appropriate action: in particular, prompt reporting of a loss of client assets may be necessary to avoid further loss to investors or others in whose interests the  **A29** regulator is required to act. The auditor is therefore required to balance the need for further investigation of the matter with the need for prompt reporting.

A30   On completion of the auditor's investigations, the auditor needs to ensure that the facts and the basis for the auditor's decision (whether to report or not) is adequately documented such that the reasons for that decision may be clearly demonstrated should the need to do so arise in future.

## Reporting

### *The Auditor's Statutory Duty to Report Direct to Regulators* (Ref: Para. 13-14)

A31   Except in the circumstances referred to in paragraph 14 the auditor seeks to reach agreement with those charged with governance on the circumstances giving rise to a report direct to the regulator. However, where a statutory duty to report arises, the auditor is required to make such a report regardless of:

(a)   Whether the matter has been referred to the regulator by other parties (including the company, whether by those charged with governance or otherwise); and

(b)   Any duty owed to other parties, including the those charged with governance of the regulated entity and its shareholders (or equivalent persons).

A32   Except in the circumstances set out in paragraph 14, the auditor sends a copy of the auditor's written report to those charged with governance and (where appropriate) audit committee of the regulated entity.

A33   In normal circumstances, the auditor would wish to communicate with the regulator with the knowledge and agreement of those charged with governance of the regulated entity. However, in some circumstances immediate notification of the discovery of a matter giving reasonable grounds to believe that a reportable matter exists will be necessary – for example, a phone call to alert the regulator followed by a meeting to discuss the circumstances.

A34   Speed of reporting is essential where the circumstances cause the auditor no longer to have confidence in the integrity of those charged with governance. In such circumstances, there may be a serious and immediate threat to the interests of depositors or other persons for whose protection the regulator is required to act; for example where the auditor believes that a fraud or other irregularity may have been committed by, or with the knowledge of, those charged with governance, or have evidence of the intention of those charged with governance to commit or condone a suspected fraud or other irregularity.

A35   In circumstances where the auditor no longer has confidence in the integrity of those charged with governance, it is not appropriate to provide those charged with governance with copies of the auditor's report. Since such circumstances will be exceptional and extreme, the auditor may wish to seek legal advice as to the auditor's responsibilities and the appropriate course of action.

## The Auditor's Right to Report Direct to Regulators (Ref: Para. 15)

The auditor may become aware of matters which the auditor concludes are relevant to the exercise of the regulator's functions even though they fall outside the statutory definition of matters which must be reported to a regulator. In such circumstances, the Acts provide the auditor with protection for making disclosure of the matter to the appropriate regulator.

**A36**

Where the auditor considers that a matter which does not give rise to a statutory duty to report is nevertheless, in the auditor's professional judgment, such that it should be brought to the attention of the regulator, it is normally appropriate for the auditor to request those charged with governance of the regulated entity in writing to draw it to the attention of the regulator.

**A37**

## Contents of a Report Initiated by the Auditor (Ref: Para. 16)

Such a report is a by-product of other work undertaken by the auditor. As a result it is not possible for the auditor or the regulator to conclude that all matters relevant to the regulator were encountered in the course of the auditor's work. The auditor's report therefore sets out the context in which the information reported was identified and indicates the extent to which the matter has been investigated and discussed with those charged with governance.

**A38**

Matters to which the auditor may wish to refer when describing the context in which a report is made direct to a regulator include:

**A39**

- The nature of the appointment from which the report derives. For example, it may be appropriate to distinguish between a report made in the course of an audit of financial statements and one which arises in the course of a more limited engagement, such as an appointment to report on specified matters by the FSA or IFSRA;
- The applicable legislative requirements and interpretations of those requirements which have informed the auditor's judgment;
- The extent to which the auditor has investigated the circumstances giving rise to the matter reported;
- Whether the matter reported has been discussed with those charged with governance;
- Whether steps to rectify the matter have been taken.

## Relationship With Other Reporting Responsibilities (Ref: Para. 17)

The circumstances which give rise to a report direct to a regulator may involve an uncertainty or other matter which requires disclosure in the financial statements. The auditor will therefore need to consider whether the disclosures made in the financial statements are adequate for the purposes of giving a true and fair view of the regulated entity's state of affairs and profit or loss. Where the auditor considers it necessary to draw users' attention to a matter presented or disclosed in the financial statements that, in the auditor's judgment, is of such importance that it is fundamental to users' understanding of the financial statements, the auditor is required to include an emphasis of matter paragraph in the auditor's report[6].

**A40**

[6] *ISA (UK and Ireland) 706 "Emphasis of Matter Paragraphs and Other Matter Paragraphs in the Independent Auditor's Report," paragraph 6.*

**A41**  Similarly, circumstances giving rise to a report direct to a regulator may also require reflection in the auditor's reports on other matters required by legislation or another regulator.

**A42**  In fulfilling the responsibility to report direct to a regulator, it is important that the auditor not only assess the significance of individual transactions or events but also consider whether a combination of such items over the course of the work undertaken for the auditor's primary reporting responsibilities may give the auditor reasonable grounds to believe that they constitute a matter of material significance to the regulator, and so give rise to a statutory duty to make a report.

**A43**  As there is no requirement for the auditor to extend the scope of the audit work to search for matters which may give rise to a statutory duty to report, such an assessment of the cumulative effect of evidence obtained in the course of an audit would be made when reviewing the evidence in support of the opinions to be expressed in the reports the auditor has been appointed to make. Where such a review leads to the conclusion that the cumulative effect of matters noted in the course of the audit is of material significance to the regulator, it will be appropriate for a report to be made as set out in paragraph 16 above. However, reports indicating a 'nil return' are not appropriate.

### Communication of Information by the Regulator

**A44**  The Acts provide that, in certain exceptional circumstances, regulators may pass confidential information to another party. The precise circumstances in which regulators may disclose information varies, but in general they may do so if considered necessary to fulfil their own obligations under the appropriate Act, or, in some cases, to enable the auditor to fulfil the auditor's duties either to the regulated entity or, in other cases, to the regulator. Confidential information remains confidential in the hands of the recipient.

**A45**  In so far as the law permits, regulators have confirmed that they will consider taking the initiative in bringing a matter to the attention of the auditor of a regulated entity in circumstances where:

(a)  They believe the matter is of such importance that the auditor's knowledge of it could significantly affect the form of the auditor's report on the entity's financial statements or other matters on which the auditor is required to report, or the way in which the auditor discharges the auditor's reporting responsibilities; and

(b)  The disclosure is for the purpose of enabling or assisting the regulator to discharge its functions under the Acts.

**A46**  The auditor needs to be aware that there may be circumstances in which the regulators are unable to disclose such information. Where the auditor of a regulated entity is not informed by the regulator of any matter, therefore, the auditor cannot assume that there are no matters known to the regulator which could affect the auditor's judgment as to whether information is of material significance. However, in the absence of disclosure by the regulator, the auditor can only form a judgment in the light of evidence to which the auditor has access.

# Appendix 1

# The Regulatory Framework

In both the UK and Ireland, legislation exists in the principal areas of financial services to protect the interests of investors, depositors in banks and other users of financial services. Regulated entities operating in the financial sector are required to comply with legal and regulatory requirements concerning the way their business is conducted. Compliance with those rules is monitored in four principal ways:

1

- Internal monitoring by those charged with governance of the regulated entity;
- Submission of regular returns by the regulated entity to the regulator;
- Monitoring and, in some cases, inspection of the entity by the regulator;
- Reports[2] by the reporting entity's auditor on its financial statements and other specified matters required by legislation or by the regulator.

## Responsibility for Ensuring Compliance

Ensuring compliance with the requirements with which a regulated entity is required to comply in carrying out its business is the responsibility of those charged with governance of a regulated entity. It requires adequate organisation and systems of controls. The regulatory framework provides that adequate procedures for compliance must be established and maintained. Those charged with governance of a regulated entity are also normally required to undertake regular reviews of compliance and to inform the regulator of any breach of the rules and regulations applicable to its regulated business. In addition, regulators may undertake compliance visits.

2

The auditor of a regulated entity normally has responsibilities for reporting[2] on particular aspects of its compliance with the regulator's requirements. However, the auditor has no direct responsibility for expressing an opinion on an entity's overall compliance with the requirements for the conduct of its business, nor does an audit provide any assurance that breaches of requirements which are not the subject of regular auditors' reports will be detected.

3

## The Role of Auditors

Those charged with governance of regulated entities have primary responsibility for ensuring that all appropriate information is made available to regulators. Normal reporting procedures (including auditor's reports on records, systems and returns, and regular meetings with those charged with governance and/or management and auditors) supplemented by any inspection visits considered necessary by the regulators should provide the regulators with all the information they need to carry out their responsibilities under the relevant Act.

4

## Routine Reporting by Auditors

Regulators' requirements for reports by auditors vary. In general terms, however, such reports may include opinions on:

5

- The regulated entity's annual financial statements;

- The regulated entity's compliance with requirements for financial resources; and
- The adequacy of the regulated entity's system of controls over its transactions and in particular over its clients' money and other property.

6    As a result of performing the work necessary to discharge their routine reporting responsibilities, or those arising from an appointment to provide a special report required by the regulator, the auditor of a regulated entity may become aware of matters which the auditor considers need to be brought to the regulator's attention sooner than would be achieved by routine reports by the entity or its auditor.

7    The auditor of a regulated entity normally has a right to communicate in good faith[2] information the auditor considers is relevant to the regulators' functions.

## The Auditor's Statutory Duty to Report to the Regulator

8    In addition, the auditor is required by law to report[2] direct to a regulator when the auditor concludes that there is reasonable cause to believe that a matter is or may be of material significance to the regulator. The precise matters which result in a statutory duty to make such a report vary, depending upon the specific requirements of relevant legislation and the regulator's rules. In general, however, a duty to report to a regulator arises when the auditor becomes aware that:

- The regulated entity is in serious breach of:
  - Requirements to maintain adequate financial resources; or
  - Requirements for those charged with governance to conduct its business in a sound and prudent manner (including the maintenance of systems of control over transactions and over any clients' assets held by the business); or
- There are circumstances which give reason to doubt the status of those charged with governance or senior management as fit and proper persons.

## Confidentiality

9    Confidentiality is an implied term of the auditor's contracts with client entities. However[2] in the circumstances leading to a right or duty to report, the auditor is entitled to communicate to regulators in good faith information or opinions relating to the business or affairs of the entity or any associated body without contravening the duty of confidence owed to the entity and, in the case of a bank, building society and friendly society, its associated bodies.

10    The statutory provisions permitting the auditor to communicate information to regulators relate to information obtained in the auditor's capacity as auditor of the regulated entity concerned. Auditors and regulators therefore should be aware that confidential information obtained in other capacities may not normally be disclosed to another party.

# Appendix 2

# The Application of the Statutory Duty to Report to Regulators

## Introduction

The statutory duty to report to a regulator[2] applies to information which comes to the attention of the auditor in the auditor's capacity as auditor. However, neither the term 'auditor' nor the phrase "in the capacity of auditor" are defined in the legislation, nor has the court determined how these expressions should be construed.   **1**

As a result, it is not always clearly apparent when an accounting firm should regard itself as having a duty to report to a regulator. For example, information about a regulated entity may be obtained when partners or staff of the firm which is appointed as its auditor carry out work for another client entity; or when the firm undertakes other work for the regulated entity. Auditors, regulated entities and regulators need to be clear as to when the normal duty of confidentiality will be overridden by the auditor's statutory duty to report to the regulator.   **2**

In order to clarify whether or not an accounting firm should regard itself as bound by the duty, the APB has developed, in conjunction with HM Treasury, the IFSRA and the regulators, guidance on the interpretation of the key conditions for the existence of that duty, namely that the firm is to be regarded as auditor of a regulated entity and that information is obtained in the capacity of auditor.   **3**

Guidance on the interpretation of the term 'auditor' in the context of each Act is contained in the separate Practice Notes dealing with each area affected by the legislation.   **4**

This appendix sets out guidance on the interpretation of the phrase "in the capacity of auditor". The Board nevertheless continues to hold the view that the meaning of the phrase should be clarified in legislation in the longer term.   **5**

## In the Capacity of Auditor

In determining whether information is obtained in the capacity of auditor, two criteria in particular should be considered:   **6**

(a) Whether the person who obtained the information also undertook the audit work; and if so
(b) Whether it was obtained in the course of or as a result of undertaking the audit work.

It is then necessary to apply these criteria to information about a regulated entity which may become known from a number of sources, and by a number of different individuals within an accounting firm. Within a large firm, for example, information may come to the attention of the partner responsible for the audit of a regulated entity, a partner in another office who undertakes a different type of work, or members of the firm's staff at any level. In the case of a sole practitioner who is the auditor of a regulated entity, information about a regulated entity may also be obtained by the practitioner in the course of work other than its audit.   **7**

## Non-Audit Work Carried out in Relation to a Regulated Entity

8    Where partners or staff involved in the audit of a regulated entity carry out work other than its audit (non-audit work) information about the regulated entity will be known to them as individuals. In circumstances which suggest that a matter would otherwise give rise to a statutory duty to report[2] if obtained in the capacity of auditor, it will be prudent for them to make enquiries in the course of their audit work in order to establish whether this is the case from information obtained in that capacity.

9    However where non-audit work is carried out by other partners or staff, neither of the criteria set out in paragraph 6 is met in respect of information which becomes known to them. Nevertheless the firm should take proper account of such information when it could affect the audit so that it is treated in a responsible manner, particularly since in partnership law the knowledge obtained by one partner in the course of the partnership business may be imputed to the entire partnership. In doing so, two types of work may be distinguished: first, work which could affect the firm's work as auditor and, secondly, work which is undertaken purely in an advisory capacity.

10   A firm appointed as auditor of a regulated entity needs to have in place appropriate procedures to ensure that the partner responsible for the audit function is made aware of any other relationship which exists between any department of the firm and the regulated entity when that relationship could affect the firm's work as auditor. Common examples of such work include accounting work, particularly for smaller entities, and provision of tax services to the regulated entity.

11   *Prima facie*, information obtained in the course of non-audit work is not covered by either the right or the duty to report to a regulator. However, the firm appointed as auditor needs to consider whether the results of other work undertaken for a regulated entity need to be assessed as part of the audit process. In principle, this is no different to seeking to review a report prepared by outside consultants on, say, the entity's accounting systems so as to ensure that the auditor makes a proper assessment of the risks of misstatement in the financial statements and of the work needed to form an opinion. Consequently, the partner responsible for the audit needs to make appropriate enquiries in the process of planning and completing the audit (see paragraph 17 above). Such enquiries would be directed to those aspects of the non-audit work which might reasonably be expected to be relevant to the audit. When, as a result of such enquiries, those involved in the audit become aware of issues which may be of material significance to a regulator such issues should be considered, and if appropriate reported[2] following the requirements set out in this Section of this ISA (UK and Ireland).

12   Work which is undertaken in an advisory capacity, for example to assist the directors of a regulated entity to determine effective and efficient methods of discharging their duties, would not normally affect the work undertaken for the audit. Nevertheless, in rare instances, the partner responsible for such advisory work may conclude that steps considered necessary in order to comply with the regulator's requirements have not been taken by the directors or that the directors intend in some respect not to comply with the regulator's requirements. Such circumstances would require consideration in the course of work undertaken for the audit, both to consider the effect on the auditor's routine reports and to determine whether the possible non-compliance is or is likely to be of material significance to the regulator.

## Work Relating to a Separate Entity

Information obtained in the course of work relating to another entity audited by the same firm (or the same practitioner) is confidential to that other entity. The auditor is not required, and has no right, to report to a regulator confidential information which arises from work undertaken by the same auditing firm for another client. However, as a matter of sound practice, individuals involved in the audit of a regulated entity who become aware (in a capacity other than that of auditor of a regulated entity) of a matter which could otherwise give rise to a statutory duty to report would normally make enquiries in the course of their audit of the regulated entity to establish whether the information concerned is substantiated.
    **13**

In carrying out the audit work, the auditor is required to have due regard to whether disclosure of non-compliance with laws and regulations to a proper authority is appropriate in the public interest. standards and guidance on this general professional obligation is set out in Section A of this ISA (UK and Ireland).
    **14**

## Conclusion

The phrase "in his capacity as auditor" limits information subject to the duty to report to matters of which the auditor becomes aware in the auditor's capacity as such. Consequently, it is unlikely that a partnership can be said to be acting in its capacity as auditor of a particular regulated entity whenever any apparently unrelated material comes to the attention of a partner or member of staff not engaged in that audit, particularly if that material is confidential to another client.
    **15**

The statutory duty to report to a regulator[2] therefore does not extend automatically to any information obtained by an accounting firm regardless of its source. Accounting firms undertaking audits of regulated entities need, however, to establish lines of communication, commensurate with their size and organisational structure, sufficient to ensure that non-audit work undertaken for a regulated entity which is likely to have an effect on the audit is brought to the attention of the partner responsible for the audit and to establish procedures for the partner responsible for the audit to make appropriate enquiries of those conducting such other work as part of the process of planning and completing the audit.
    **16**

# Appendix 3

## Action by the Auditor on Discovery of a Breach of a Regulator's Requirements

1   This appendix sets out in the form of a flowchart the steps involved in assessing whether a report to a regulator is required when a breach of the regulator's requirements comes to the attention of the auditor.

2   The flowchart is intended to provide guidance to readers in understanding this Section of this ISA (UK and Ireland). It does not form part of the auditing standards contained in the ISA (UK and Ireland).

**Action by the Auditor on Discovery of a Breach of a Regulator's Requirement**

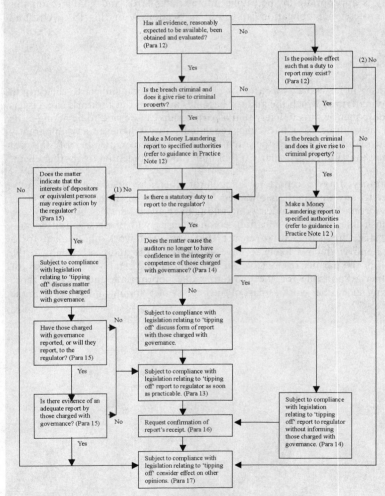

(1) This route would be only followed when a distinct right to report to the regulator exists. Otherwise, where no duty to report exists, the auditor would next consider the effect on other opinions.

(2) Where the auditor considers that a distinct right to report to the regulator exists, the auditor would next consider the question marked (1).

# Addendum

*This addendum is provided for information and does not form part of proposed clarified ISA (UK and Ireland) 250 Section B.*

*ISA (UK and Ireland) 250 Section B is, in effect, a complete supplementary standard addressing legal and regulatory requirements. The proposed clarified standard has been reformatted to match the Clarity format (i.e. stating an objective and having separate sections for requirements and application material). However, present tense guidance in the current standard has not been eliminated. APB believes it more appropriate to address any present tense guidance at such a time as the standard needs to be revised for other reasons such as a change in related regulatory requirements.*

# Proposed Clarified International Standard on Auditing (UK and Ireland) 260

## Communication with those charged with governance

*(Effective for audits of financial statements for periods ending on or after 15 December 2010)*

## Contents

International Standard on Auditing (UK and Ireland) (ISA (UK and Ireland)) 260, "Communication with Those Charged with Governance" should be read in conjunction with ISA (UK and Ireland) 200, "Overall Objectives of the Independent Auditor and the Conduct of an Audit in Accordance with International Standards on Auditing (UK and Ireland)."

# Introduction

## Scope of this ISA (UK and Ireland)

This International Standard on Auditing (UK and Ireland) (ISA (UK and Ireland)) deals with the auditor's responsibility to communicate with those charged with governance in an audit of financial statements. Although this ISA (UK and Ireland) applies irrespective of an entity's governance structure or size, particular considerations apply where all of those charged with governance are involved in managing an entity, and for listed entities. This ISA (UK and Ireland) does not establish requirements regarding the auditor's communication with an entity's management or owners unless they are also charged with a governance role.   **1**

This ISA (UK and Ireland) is written in the context of an audit of financial statements, but may also be applicable, adapted as necessary in the circumstances, to audits of other historical financial information when those charged with governance have a responsibility to oversee the preparation of the other historical financial information.   **2**

Recognizing the importance of effective two-way communication in an audit of financial statements, this ISA (UK and Ireland) provides an overarching framework for the auditor's communication with those charged with governance, and identifies some specific matters to be communicated with them. Additional matters to be communicated, which complement the requirements of this ISA (UK and Ireland), are identified in other ISAs (UK and Ireland) (see Appendix 1). In addition, ISA (UK and Ireland) 265[1] establishes specific requirements regarding the communication of significant deficiencies in internal control the auditor has identified during the audit to those charged with governance. Further matters, not required by this or other ISAs (UK and Ireland), may be required to be communicated by law or regulation, by agreement with the entity, or by additional requirements applicable to the engagement, for example, the standards of a national professional accountancy body. Nothing in this ISA (UK and Ireland) precludes the auditor from communicating any other matters to those charged with governance. (Ref: Para. A24-A27)   **3**

## The Role of Communication

This ISA (UK and Ireland) focuses primarily on communications from the auditor to those charged with governance. Nevertheless, effective two-way communication is important in assisting:   **4**

(a) The auditor and those charged with governance in understanding matters related to the audit in context, and in developing a constructive working relationship. This relationship is developed while maintaining the auditor's independence and objectivity;

(b) The auditor in obtaining from those charged with governance information relevant to the audit[1a]. For example, those charged with governance may assist the auditor in understanding the entity and its environment, in identifying appropriate sources of audit evidence, and in providing information about specific transactions or events; and

---

[1] *ISA (UK and Ireland) 265, "Communicating Deficiencies in Internal Control to Those Charged with Governance and Management."*

[1a] *Sections 499 and 500 of the Companies Act 2006 set legal requirements in relation to the auditor's right to obtain information. For the Republic of Ireland, relevant requirements are set out in Sections 193(3) and 196, Companies Act 1990.*

(c)  Those charged with governance in fulfilling their responsibility to oversee the financial reporting process, thereby reducing the risks of material misstatement of the financial statements.

5    Although the auditor is responsible for communicating matters required by this ISA (UK and Ireland), management also has a responsibility to communicate matters of governance interest to those charged with governance. Communication by the auditor does not relieve management of this responsibility. Similarly, communication by management with those charged with governance of matters that the auditor is required to communicate does not relieve the auditor of the responsibility to also communicate them. Communication of these matters by management may, however, affect the form or timing of the auditor's communication with those charged with governance.

6    Clear communication of specific matters required to be communicated by ISAs (UK and Ireland) is an integral part of every audit. ISAs (UK and Ireland) do not, however, require the auditor to perform procedures specifically to identify any other matters to communicate with those charged with governance.

7    Law or regulation may restrict the auditor's communication of certain matters with those charged with governance. For example, laws or regulations may specifically prohibit a communication, or other action, that might prejudice an investigation by an appropriate authority into an actual, or suspected, illegal act. In some circumstances, potential conflicts between the auditor's obligations of confidentiality and obligations to communicate may be complex. In such cases, the auditor may consider obtaining legal advice.

## Effective Date

8    This ISA (UK and Ireland) is effective for audits of financial statements for periods ending on or after 15 December 2010.

# Objectives

9    The objectives of the auditor are:

(a)  To communicate clearly with those charged with governance the responsibilities of the auditor in relation to the financial statement audit, and an overview of the planned scope and timing of the audit;

(b)  To obtain from those charged with governance information relevant to the audit;

(c)  To provide those charged with governance with timely observations arising from the audit that are significant and relevant to their responsibility to oversee the financial reporting process; and

(d)  To promote effective two-way communication between the auditor and those charged with governance.

# Definitions

10   For purposes of the ISAs (UK and Ireland), the following terms have the meanings attributed below:

(a)  Those charged with governance – The person(s) or organization(s) (e.g., a corporate trustee) with responsibility for overseeing the strategic direction of the entity and obligations related to the accountability of the entity. This includes overseeing the financial reporting process. For some entities in some jurisdictions, those charged with governance may include management personnel, for example, executive members of a governance board of a private or public sector entity, or an owner-manager. For discussion of the diversity of governance structures, see paragraphs A1-A8.

> In the UK and Ireland, those charged with governance include the directors (executive and non-executive) of a company or other body, the members of an audit committee where one exists, the partners, proprietors, committee of management or trustees of other forms of entity, or equivalent persons responsible for directing the entity's affairs and preparing its financial statements.

(b)  Management – The person(s) with executive responsibility for the conduct of the entity's operations. For some entities in some jurisdictions, management includes some or all of those charged with governance, for example, executive members of a governance board, or an owner-manager.

> In the UK and Ireland, depending on the nature and circumstances of the entity, management may include some or all of those charged with governance (e.g. executive directors). Management will not normally include non-executive directors.

# Requirements

## Those Charged with Governance

The auditor shall determine the appropriate person(s) within the entity's governance structure with whom to communicate. (Ref: Para. A1-A4)  **11**

### Communication with a Subgroup of Those Charged with Governance

If the auditor communicates with a subgroup of those charged with governance, for example, an audit committee, or an individual, the auditor shall determine whether the auditor also needs to communicate with the governing body. (Ref: Para. A5-A7)  **12**

### When All of Those Charged with Governance Are Involved in Managing the Entity

In some cases, all of those charged with governance are involved in managing the entity, for example, a small business where a single owner manages the entity and no one else has a governance role. In these cases, if matters required by this ISA (UK and Ireland) are communicated with person(s) with management responsibilities, and those person(s) also have governance responsibilities, the matters need not be communicated again with those same person(s) in their governance role. These matters are noted in paragraph 16(c). The auditor shall nonetheless be satisfied that communication with person(s) with management responsibilities adequately informs all of those with whom the auditor would otherwise communicate in their governance capacity. (Ref: Para. A8)  **13**

## Matters to Be Communicated

### The Auditor's Responsibilities in Relation to the Financial Statement Audit

**14** The auditor shall communicate with those charged with governance the responsibilities of the auditor in relation to the financial statement audit, including that:

(a) The auditor is responsible for forming and expressing an opinion on the financial statements that have been prepared by management[1b] with the oversight of those charged with governance; and

(b) The audit of the financial statements does not relieve management or those charged with governance of their responsibilities. (Ref: Para. A9-A10)

### Planned Scope and Timing of the Audit

**15** The auditor shall communicate with those charged with governance an overview of the planned scope and timing of the audit. (Ref: Para. A11-A15)

### Significant Findings from the Audit

**16** The auditor shall communicate with those charged with governance: (Ref: Para. A16)

(a) The auditor's views about significant qualitative aspects of the entity's accounting practices, including accounting policies, accounting estimates and financial statement disclosures. When applicable, the auditor shall explain to those charged with governance why the auditor considers a significant accounting practice, that is acceptable under the applicable financial reporting framework, not to be most appropriate to the particular circumstances of the entity; (Ref: Para. A17)

(b) Significant difficulties, if any, encountered during the audit; (Ref: Para. A18)

(c) Unless all of those charged with governance are involved in managing the entity:
(i) Significant matters, if any, arising from the audit that were discussed, or subject to correspondence with management; and (Ref: Para. A19)
(ii) Written representations the auditor is requesting; and

(d) Other matters, if any, arising from the audit that, in the auditor's professional judgment, are significant to the oversight of the financial reporting process. (Ref: Para. A20)

### Auditor Independence

**17** In the case of listed entities, the auditor shall communicate with those charged with governance: (Ref: Para. A21-A23)

(a) A statement that the engagement team and others in the firm as appropriate, the firm and, when applicable, network firms have complied with relevant ethical requirements regarding independence[1c]; and

(b)

---

[1b] *In the UK and Ireland those charged with governance are responsible for the preparation of the financial statements.*

[1c] *In the UK and Ireland, auditors are subject to ethical requirements from two sources: the APB's Ethical Standards for Auditors (ESs), including ES 1 (Revised), "Integrity, Objectivity and Independence," and the ethical pronouncements established by the auditor's relevant professional body. In the case of listed companies, ES 1 (Revised) specifies information to be communicated to those charged with governance (see Para A21-1 in this ISA (UK and Ireland)).*

(i)   All relationships and other matters between the firm, network firms, and the entity that, in the auditor's professional judgment, may reasonably be thought to bear on independence. This shall include total fees charged during the period covered by the financial statements for audit and non-audit services provided by the firm and network firms to the entity and components controlled by the entity. These fees shall be allocated to categories that are appropriate to assist those charged with governance in assessing the effect of services on the independence of the auditor; and

(ii)  The related safeguards that have been applied to eliminate identified threats to independence or reduce them to an acceptable level.

# The Communication Process

## Establishing the Communication Process

The auditor shall communicate with those charged with governance the form, timing and expected general content of communications. (Ref: Para. A28-A36)   **18**

### Forms of Communication

The auditor shall communicate in writing with those charged with governance regarding significant findings from the audit if, in the auditor's professional judgment, oral communication would not be adequate. Written communications need not include all matters that arose during the course of the audit. (Ref: Para. A37-A39)   **19**

The auditor shall communicate in writing with those charged with governance regarding auditor independence when required by paragraph 17.   **20**

### Timing of Communications

The auditor shall communicate with those charged with governance on a timely basis. (Ref: Para. A40-A41)   **21**

### Adequacy of the Communication Process

The auditor shall evaluate whether the two-way communication between the auditor and those charged with governance has been adequate for the purpose of the audit. If it has not, the auditor shall evaluate the effect, if any, on the auditor's assessment of the risks of material misstatement and ability to obtain sufficient appropriate audit evidence, and shall take appropriate action. (Ref: Para. A42-A44)   **22**

# Documentation

Where matters required by this ISA (UK and Ireland) to be communicated are communicated orally, the auditor shall include them in the audit documentation, and when and to whom they were communicated. Where matters have been communicated in writing, the auditor shall retain a copy of the communication as part of the audit documentation.[2] (Ref: Para. A45)   **23**

\*\*\*

---

[2] *ISA (UK and Ireland) 230, "Audit Documentation," paragraphs 8-11, and paragraph A6.*

# Application and Other Explanatory Material

## Those Charged with Governance (Ref: Para. 11)

A1   Governance structures vary by jurisdiction and by entity, reflecting influences such as different cultural and legal backgrounds, and size and ownership characteristics. For example:

- In some jurisdictions a supervisory (wholly or mainly non-executive) board exists that is legally separate from an executive (management) board (a "two-tier board" structure). In other jurisdictions, both the supervisory and executive functions are the legal responsibility of a single, or unitary, board (a "one-tier board" structure).
- In some entities, those charged with governance hold positions that are an integral part of the entity's legal structure, for example, company directors. In others, for example, some government entities, a body that is not part of the entity is charged with governance.
- In some cases, some or all of those charged with governance are involved in managing the entity. In others, those charged with governance and management comprise different persons.
- In some cases, those charged with governance are responsible for approving[3] the entity's financial statements (in other cases management has this responsibility).

A2   In most entities, governance is the collective responsibility of a governing body, such as a board of directors, a supervisory board, partners, proprietors, a committee of management, a council of governors, trustees, or equivalent persons. In some smaller entities, however, one person may be charged with governance, for example, the owner-manager where there are no other owners, or a sole trustee. When governance is a collective responsibility, a subgroup such as an audit committee or even an individual, may be charged with specific tasks to assist the governing body in meeting its responsibilities. Alternatively, a subgroup or individual may have specific, legally identified responsibilities that differ from those of the governing body.

A3   Such diversity means that it is not possible for this ISA (UK and Ireland) to specify for all audits the person(s) with whom the auditor is to communicate particular matters. Also, in some cases the appropriate person(s) with whom to communicate may not be clearly identifiable from the applicable legal framework or other engagement circumstances, for example, entities where the governance structure is not formally defined, such as some family-owned entities, some not-for-profit organizations, and some government entities. In such cases, the auditor may need to discuss and agree with the engaging party the relevant person(s) with whom to communicate. In deciding with whom to communicate, the auditor's understanding of an entity's governance structure and processes obtained in accordance with ISA (UK and Ireland) 315[4] is relevant. The appropriate person(s) with whom to communicate may vary depending on the matter to be communicated.

---

[3] *As described at paragraph A40 of ISA 700, "Forming an Opinion and Reporting on Financial Statements," having responsibility for approving in this context means having the authority to conclude that all the statements that comprise the financial statements, including the related notes, have been prepared.*
*In the UK and Ireland, those charged with governance are responsible for the approval of the financial statements.*
*The APB has not promulgated ISA 700 as issued by the IAASB for application in the UK and Ireland. In the UK and Ireland the applicable auditing standard is ISA (UK and Ireland) 700, "The Auditor's Report on Financial Statements."*

[4] *ISA (UK and Ireland) 315, "Identifying and Assessing the Risks of Material Misstatement through Understanding the Entity and Its Environment."*

ISA (UK and Ireland) 600 includes specific matters to be communicated by group    **A4**
auditors with those charged with governance[5] When the entity is a component of a
group, the appropriate person(s) with whom the component auditor communicates
depends on the engagement circumstances and the matter to be communicated. In
some cases, a number of components may be conducting the same businesses within
the same system of internal control and using the same accounting practices. Where
those charged with governance of those components are the same (e.g., common
board of directors), duplication may be avoided by dealing with these components
concurrently for the purpose of communication.

> In the UK and Ireland there are statutory obligations on corporate subsidiary    **A4-1**
> undertakings, and their auditors and other parties, to provide the auditor of a
> corporate parent undertaking with such information and explanations as that
> auditor may reasonably require for the purposes of the audit[5a]. Where there is no
> such statutory obligation (e.g. for non corporate entities), permission may be
> needed by the auditors of the subsidiary undertakings, from those charged with
> governance of the subsidiary undertakings, to disclose the contents of any com-
> munication to them to the auditor of the parent undertaking and also for the
> auditor of the parent undertaking to pass those disclosures onto those charged
> with governance of the parent undertaking. The auditor of the parent under-
> taking seeks to ensure that appropriate arrangements are made at the planning
> stage for these disclosures. Normally, such arrangements for groups are recorded
> in the instructions to the auditors of subsidiary undertakings and relevant
> engagement letters.

*Communication with a Subgroup of Those Charged with Governance* (Ref: Para. 12)

When considering communicating with a subgroup of those charged with govern-    **A5**
ance, the auditor may take into account such matters as:

- The respective responsibilities of the subgroup and the governing body.
- The nature of the matter to be communicated.
- Relevant legal or regulatory requirements.
- Whether the subgroup has the authority to take action in relation to the
  information communicated, and can provide further information and expla-
  nations the auditor may need.

When deciding whether there is also a need to communicate information, in full or in    **A6**
summary form, with the governing body, the auditor may be influenced by the
auditor's assessment of how effectively and appropriately the subgroup communicates relevant information with the governing body. The auditor may make explicit

---

[5] *ISA (UK and Ireland) 600, "Special Considerations—Audits of Group Financial Statements (Including the Work of Component Auditors)," paragraphs 46-49.*

[5a] *In the UK, Section 499 of the Companies Act 2006 specifies that the auditor of a company may require any subsidiary undertaking of the company which is a body corporate incorporated in the UK, and any officer, employee or auditor of any such subsidiary undertaking or any person holding or accountable for any books, accounts or vouchers of any such subsidiary undertaking, to provide him with such information or explanations as he thinks necessary for the performance of his duties as auditor. If a parent company has a subsidiary undertaking that is not a body corporate incorporated in the UK, Section 500 of the Companies Act 2006 specifies that the auditor of the parent company may require it to take all such steps as are reasonably open to it to obtain from the subsidiary undertaking, any officer, employee or auditor of the undertaking, or any person holding or accountable for any of the undertaking's books, accounts or vouchers, such information and expla- nations as he may reasonably require for the purposes of his duties as auditor. Similar obligations regarding companies incorporated in the Republic of Ireland are set out in Section 196, Companies Act 1990.*

in agreeing the terms of engagement that, unless prohibited by law or regulation, the auditor retains the right to communicate directly with the governing body.

**A7**   Audit committees (or similar subgroups with different names) exist in many jurisdictions. Although their specific authority and functions may differ, communication with the audit committee, where one exists, has become a key element in the auditor's communication with those charged with governance. Good governance principles suggest that:

- The auditor will be invited to regularly attend meetings of the audit committee.
- The chair of the audit committee and, when relevant, the other members of the audit committee, will liaise with the auditor periodically.
- The audit committee will meet the auditor without management present at least annually.

### When All of Those Charged with Governance Are Involved in Managing the Entity (Ref: Para.13)

**A8**   In some cases, all of those charged with governance are involved in managing the entity, and the application of communication requirements is modified to recognize this position. In such cases, communication with person(s) with management responsibilities may not adequately inform all of those with whom the auditor would otherwise communicate in their governance capacity. For example, in a company where all directors are involved in managing the entity, some of those directors (e.g., one responsible for marketing) may be unaware of significant matters discussed with another director (e.g., one responsible for the preparation of the financial statements).

## Matters to Be Communicated

### The Auditor's Responsibilities in Relation to the Financial Statement Audit (Ref: Para. 14)

**A9**   The auditor's responsibilities in relation to the financial statement audit are often included in the engagement letter or other suitable form of written agreement that records the agreed terms of the engagement. Providing those charged with governance with a copy of that engagement letter or other suitable form of written agreement may be an appropriate way to communicate with them regarding such matters as:

- The auditor's responsibility for performing the audit in accordance with ISAs (UK and Ireland), which is directed towards the expression of an opinion on the financial statements. The matters that ISAs (UK and Ireland) require to be communicated, therefore, include significant matters arising from the audit of the financial statements that are relevant to those charged with governance in overseeing the financial reporting process.
- The fact that ISAs (UK and Ireland) do not require the auditor to design procedures for the purpose of identifying supplementary matters to communicate with those charged with governance.
- When applicable, the auditor's responsibility for communicating particular matters required by law or regulation, by agreement with the entity or by additional requirements applicable to the engagement, for example, the standards of a national professional accountancy body.

The provision of copies of the audit engagement letter to those charged with governance facilitates the review and agreement of the audit engagement letter by the Audit Committee, as recommended by the Combined Code Guidance on Audit Committees. As part of their review, the guidance further recommends the audit committee to consider whether the audit engagement letter has been updated to reflect changes in circumstances since the previous year.

A9-1

Law or regulation, an agreement with the entity or additional requirements applicable to the engagement may provide for broader communication with those charged with governance. For example, (a) an agreement with the entity may provide for particular matters to be communicated when they arise from services provided by a firm or network firm other than the financial statement audit; or (b) the mandate of a public sector auditor may provide for matters to be communicated that come to the auditor's attention as a result of other work, such as performance audits.

A10

## Planned Scope and Timing of the Audit (Ref: Para. 15)

Communication regarding the planned scope and timing of the audit may:

A11

(a) Assist those charged with governance to understand better the consequences of the auditor's work, to discuss issues of risk and the concept of materiality with the auditor, and to identify any areas in which they may request the auditor to undertake additional procedures[5b]; and

(b) Assist the auditor to understand better the entity and its environment.

The communication of the planned scope of the audit includes, where relevant, any limitations on the work the auditor proposes to undertake (e.g. if limitations are imposed by management)[5c].

A11-1

Care is required when communicating with those charged with governance about the planned scope and timing of the audit so as not to compromise the effectiveness of the audit, particularly where some or all of those charged with governance are involved in managing the entity. For example, communicating the nature and timing of detailed audit procedures may reduce the effectiveness of those procedures by making them too predictable.

A12

Matters communicated may include:

A13

• How the auditor proposes to address the significant risks of material misstatement, whether due to fraud or error.
• The auditor's approach to internal control relevant to the audit.
• The application of the concept of materiality in the context of an audit.[6]

---

[5b] *The Combined Code on Corporate Governance, and the FRC Guidance on Audit Committees contain, inter alia, recommendations about the audit committee's relationship with the auditor.*

[5c] *ISA (UK and Ireland) 210, "Agreeing the Terms of Audit Engagements," paragraph 7 requires that if management or those charged with governance impose a limitation on the scope of the auditor's work in the terms of a proposed audit engagement such that the auditor believes the limitation will result in the auditor disclaiming an opinion on the financial statements, the auditor shall not accept such a limited engagement as an audit engagement, unless required by law or regulation to do so.*

[6] *ISA (UK and Ireland) 320, "Materiality in Planning and Performing an Audit."*

A13-1    The nature and detail of the planning information communicated will reflect the size and nature of the entity and the manner in which those charged with governance operate.

A13-2    In any particular year, the auditor may decide that there are no significant changes in the planned scope and timing of the audit that have been communicated previously and judge that it is unnecessary to remind those charged with governance of all or part of that information. In these circumstances, the auditor need only make those charged with governance aware that the auditor has no new matters to communicate concerning the planned scope and timing of the audit. Matters that are included in the audit engagement letter need not be repeated.

A14    Other planning matters that it may be appropriate to discuss with those charged with governance include:

- Where the entity has an internal audit function, the extent to which the auditor will use the work of internal audit, and how the external and internal auditors can best work together in a constructive and complementary manner.
- The views of those charged with governance of:
  - The appropriate person(s) in the entity's governance structure with whom to communicate.
  - The allocation of responsibilities between those charged with governance and management.
  - The entity's objectives and strategies, and the related business risks that may result in material misstatements.
  - Matters those charged with governance consider warrant particular attention during the audit, and any areas where they request additional procedures to be undertaken.
  - Significant communications with regulators.
  - Other matters those charged with governance consider may influence the audit of the financial statements.
- The attitudes, awareness, and actions of those charged with governance concerning (a) the entity's internal control and its importance in the entity, including how those charged with governance oversee the effectiveness of internal control, and (b) the detection or possibility of fraud.
- The actions of those charged with governance in response to developments in accounting standards, corporate governance practices, exchange listing rules, and related matters.
- The responses of those charged with governance to previous communications with the auditor.

A15    While communication with those charged with governance may assist the auditor to plan the scope and timing of the audit, it does not change the auditor's sole responsibility to establish the overall audit strategy and the audit plan, including the nature, timing and extent of procedures necessary to obtain sufficient appropriate audit evidence.

***Significant Findings from the Audit*** (Ref: Para. 16)

A16    The communication of findings from the audit may include requesting further information from those charged with governance in order to complete the audit evidence obtained. For example, the auditor may confirm that those charged with governance have the same understanding of the facts and circumstances relevant to specific transactions or events.

*Significant Qualitative Aspects of Accounting Practices (Ref: Para. 16(a))*

Financial reporting frameworks ordinarily allow for the entity to make accounting **A17** estimates, and judgments about accounting policies and financial statement disclosures. Open and constructive communication about significant qualitative aspects of the entity's accounting practices may include comment on the acceptability of significant accounting practices. Appendix 2 identifies matters that may be included in this communication.

*Significant Difficulties Encountered during the Audit (Ref: Para. 16(b))*

Significant difficulties encountered during the audit may include such matters as: **A18**

- Significant delays in management providing required information.
- An unnecessarily brief time within which to complete the audit.
- Extensive unexpected effort required to obtain sufficient appropriate audit evidence.
- The unavailability of expected information.
- Restrictions imposed on the auditor by management.
- Management's unwillingness to make or extend its assessment of the entity's ability to continue as a going concern when requested.

In some circumstances, such difficulties may constitute a scope limitation that leads to a modification of the auditor's opinion.[7]

*Significant Matters Discussed, or Subject to Correspondence with Management (Ref: Para. 16(c)(i))*

Significant matters discussed, or subject to correspondence with management may **A19** include such matters as:

- Business conditions affecting the entity, and business plans and strategies that may affect the risks of material misstatement.
- Concerns about management's consultations with other accountants on accounting or auditing matters.
- Discussions or correspondence in connection with the initial or recurring appointment of the auditor regarding accounting practices, the application of auditing standards, or fees for audit or other services.

*Other Significant Matters Relevant to the Financial Reporting Process (Ref: Para. 16(d))*

Other significant matters arising from the audit that are directly relevant to those **A20** charged with governance in overseeing the financial reporting process may include such matters as material misstatements of fact or material inconsistencies in information accompanying the audited financial statements that have been corrected.

---

[7] *ISA (UK and Ireland) 705, "Modifications to the Opinion in the Independent Auditor's Report."*

***Auditor Independence*** (Ref: Para. 17)

**A21**    The auditor is required to comply with relevant ethical requirements, including those pertaining to independence, relating to financial statement audit engagements.[8]

**A21-1**    In the UK and Ireland, auditors are subject to ethical requirements from two sources: the APB's Ethical Standards for Auditors (ESs), including ES 1 (Revised), "Integrity, Objectivity and Independence," and the ethical pronouncements established by the auditor's relevant professional body. In the case of listed companies ES 1 (Revised) requires that:

"The audit engagement partner shall ensure that those charged with the governance of the audit client are appropriately informed on a timely basis of all significant facts and matters that bear upon the auditor's objectivity and independence." and

"In the case of listed companies, the audit engagement partner shall ensure that the audit committee is provided with:
(a) a written disclosure of relationships that bear on the auditor's objectivity and independence, any safeguards that are in place and details of non-audit services provided to the audited entity and the fees charged in relation thereto;
(b) written confirmation that the auditor is independent;
(c) details of any inconsistencies between APB Ethical Standards and the company's policy for the supply of non-audit services by the audit firm and any apparent breach of that policy.
(d) an opportunity to discuss auditor independence issues."

**A22**    The relationships and other matters, and safeguards to be communicated, vary with the circumstances of the engagement, but generally address:

(a) Threats to independence, which may be categorized as: self-interest threats, self-review threats, advocacy threats, familiarity threats, and intimidation threats; and

(b) Safeguards created by the profession, legislation or regulation, safeguards within the entity, and safeguards within the firm's own systems and procedures.

The communication required by paragraph 17(a) may include an inadvertent violation of relevant ethical requirements as they relate to auditor independence, and any remedial action taken or proposed.

**A23**    The communication requirements relating to auditor independence that apply in the case of listed entities may also be relevant in the case of some other entities, particularly those that may be of significant public interest because, as a result of their business, their size or their corporate status, they have a wide range of stakeholders. Examples of entities that are not listed entities, but where communication of auditor independence may be appropriate, include public sector entities, credit institutions, insurance companies, and retirement benefit funds. On the other hand, there may be situations where communications regarding independence may not be relevant, for example, where all of those charged with governance have been informed of relevant facts through their management activities. This is particularly likely where the entity is owner-managed, and the auditor's firm and network firms have little involvement with the entity beyond a financial statement audit.

---

[8] *ISA (UK and Ireland) 200, "Overall Objectives of the Independent Auditor and the Conduct of an Audit in Accordance with International Standards on Auditing," paragraph 14.*

*Supplementary Matters* (Ref: Para. 3)

The oversight of management by those charged with governance includes ensuring   **A24**
that the entity designs, implements and maintains appropriate internal control with
regard to reliability of financial reporting, effectiveness and efficiency of operations
and compliance with applicable laws and regulations.

The auditor may become aware of supplementary matters that do not necessarily   **A25**
relate to the oversight of the financial reporting process but which are, nevertheless,
likely to be significant to the responsibilities of those charged with governance in
overseeing the strategic direction of the entity or the entity's obligations related to
accountability. Such matters may include, for example, significant issues regarding
governance structures or processes, and significant decisions or actions by senior
management that lack appropriate authorization.

In determining whether to communicate supplementary matters with those charged   **A26**
with governance, the auditor may discuss matters of this kind of which the auditor
has become aware with the appropriate level of management, unless it is inappropriate to do so in the circumstances.

If a supplementary matter is communicated, it may be appropriate for the auditor to   **A27**
make those charged with governance aware that:

(a)  Identification and communication of such matters is incidental to the purpose of
    the audit, which is to form an opinion on the financial statements;
(b)  No procedures were carried out with respect to the matter other than any that
    were necessary to form an opinion on the financial statements; and
(c)  No procedures were carried out to determine whether other such matters exist.

## The Communication Process

*Establishing the Communication Process* (Ref: Para. 18)

Clear communication of the auditor's responsibilities, the planned scope and timing   **A28**
of the audit, and the expected general content of communications helps establish the
basis for effective two-way communication.

Matters that may also contribute to effective two-way communication include dis-   **A29**
cussion of:

- The purpose of communications. When the purpose is clear, the auditor and
  those charged with governance are better placed to have a mutual understanding
  of relevant issues and the expected actions arising from the communication
  process.
- The form in which communications will be made.
- The person(s) in the audit team and amongst those charged with governance
  who will communicate regarding particular matters.
- The auditor's expectation that communication will be two-way, and that those
  charged with governance will communicate with the auditor matters they consider relevant to the audit, for example, strategic decisions that may significantly
  affect the nature, timing and extent of audit procedures, the suspicion or the
  detection of fraud, and concerns with the integrity or competence of senior
  management.
- The process for taking action and reporting back on matters communicated by
  the auditor.

- The process for taking action and reporting back on matters communicated by those charged with governance.

A30   The communication process will vary with the circumstances, including the size and governance structure of the entity, how those charged with governance operate, and the auditor's view of the significance of matters to be communicated. Difficulty in establishing effective two-way communication may indicate that the communication between the auditor and those charged with governance is not adequate for the purpose of the audit (see paragraph A48).

*Considerations Specific to Smaller Entities*

A31   In the case of audits of smaller entities, the auditor may communicate in a less structured manner with those charged with governance than in the case of listed or larger entities.

*Communication with Management*

A32   Many matters may be discussed with management in the ordinary course of an audit, including matters required by this ISA (UK and Ireland) to be communicated with those charged with governance. Such discussions recognize management's executive responsibility for the conduct of the entity's operations and, in particular, management's responsibility for the preparation of the financial statements.

A33   Before communicating matters with those charged with governance, the auditor may discuss them with management, unless that is inappropriate. For example, it may not be appropriate to discuss questions of management's competence or integrity with management. In addition to recognizing management's executive responsibility, these initial discussions may clarify facts and issues, and give management an opportunity to provide further information and explanations. Similarly, when the entity has an internal audit function, the auditor may discuss matters with the internal auditor before communicating with those charged with governance.

*Communication with Third Parties*

A34   Those charged with governance may wish to provide third parties, for example, bankers or certain regulatory authorities, with copies of a written communication from the auditor. In some cases, disclosure to third parties may be illegal or otherwise inappropriate. When a written communication prepared for those charged with governance is provided to third parties, it may be important in the circumstances that the third parties be informed that the communication was not prepared with them in mind, for example, by stating in written communications with those charged with governance:

(a)  That the communication has been prepared for the sole use of those charged with governance and, where applicable, the group management and the group auditor, and should not be relied upon by third parties;

(b)  That no responsibility is assumed by the auditor to third parties; and

(c)  Any restrictions on disclosure or distribution to third parties.

A35   In some jurisdictions the auditor may be required by law or regulation to, for example:

- Notify a regulatory or enforcement body of certain matters communicated with those charged with governance. For example, in some countries the auditor has a duty to report misstatements to authorities where management and those charged with governance fail to take corrective action;

- Submit copies of certain reports prepared for those charged with governance to relevant regulatory or funding bodies, or other bodies such as a central authority in the case of some public sector entities; or
- Make reports prepared for those charged with governance publicly available.

Unless required by law or regulation to provide a third party with a copy of the auditor's written communications with those charged with governance, the auditor may need the prior consent of those charged with governance before doing so.   **A36**

### *Forms of Communication* (Ref: Para. 19-20)

Effective communication may involve structured presentations and written reports as well as less structured communications, including discussions. The auditor may communicate matters other than those identified in paragraphs 19 and 20 either orally or in writing. Written communications may include an engagement letter that is provided to those charged with governance.   **A37**

The auditor discusses issues clearly and unequivocally with those charged with governance so that the implications of those issues are likely to be fully comprehended by them.   **A37-1**

In addition to the significance of a particular matter, the form of communication (e.g., whether to communicate orally or in writing, the extent of detail or summarization in the communication, and whether to communicate in a structured or unstructured manner) may be affected by such factors as:   **A38**

- Whether the matter has been satisfactorily resolved.
- Whether management has previously communicated the matter.
- The size, operating structure, control environment, and legal structure of the entity.
- In the case of an audit of special purpose financial statements, whether the auditor also audits the entity's general purpose financial statements.
- Legal requirements. In some jurisdictions, a written communication with those charged with governance is required in a prescribed form by local law.
- The expectations of those charged with governance, including arrangements made for periodic meetings or communications with the auditor.
- The amount of ongoing contact and dialogue the auditor has with those charged with governance.
- Whether there have been significant changes in the membership of a governing body.

The judgment of whether to communicate significant matters orally or in writing may also be affected by the evaluation, required by paragraph 22, of whether the two-way communication between the auditor and those charged with governance has been adequate for the purpose of the audit. The auditor may judge also that for effective communication a written communication is issued even if its content is limited to explaining that there is nothing the auditor wishes to draw to the attention of those charged with governance. To avoid doubt where there are no matters the auditor wishes to communicate in writing, the auditor may communicate that fact in writing to those charged with governance.   **A38-1**

**A39**    When a significant matter is discussed with an individual member of those charged with governance, for example, the chair of an audit committee, it may be appropriate for the auditor to summarize the matter in later communications so that all of those charged with governance have full and balanced information.

*Timing of Communications* (Ref: Para. 21)

**A40**    The appropriate timing for communications will vary with the circumstances of the engagement. Relevant circumstances include the significance and nature of the matter, and the action expected to be taken by those charged with governance. For example:

- Communications regarding planning matters may often be made early in the audit engagement and, for an initial engagement, may be made as part of agreeing the terms of the engagement.
- It may be appropriate to communicate a significant difficulty encountered during the audit as soon as practicable if those charged with governance are able to assist the auditor to overcome the difficulty, or if it is likely to lead to a modified opinion. Similarly, the auditor may communicate orally to those charged with governance as soon as practicable significant deficiencies in internal control that the auditor has identified, prior to communicating these in writing as required by ISA (UK and Ireland) 265.[9] Communications regarding independence may be appropriate whenever significant judgments are made about threats to independence and related safeguards, for example, when accepting an engagement to provide non-audit services, and at a concluding discussion. A concluding discussion may also be an appropriate time to communicate findings from the audit, including the auditor's views about the qualitative aspects of the entity's accounting practices.
- When auditing both general purpose and special purpose financial statements, it may be appropriate to coordinate the timing of communications.

**A41**    Other factors that may be relevant to the timing of communications include:

- The size, operating structure, control environment, and legal structure of the entity being audited.
- Any legal obligation to communicate certain matters within a specified timeframe.
- The expectations of those charged with governance, including arrangements made for periodic meetings or communications with the auditor.
- The time at which the auditor identifies certain matters, for example, the auditor may not identify a particular matter (e.g., noncompliance with a law) in time for preventive action to be taken, but communication of the matter may enable remedial action to be taken.

**A41-1**    In certain circumstances the auditor may identify matters that need to be communicated to those charged with governance without delay. Findings from the audit that are relevant to the financial statements, including the auditor's views about the qualitative aspects of the entity's accounting and financial reporting, are communicated to those charged with governance before they approve the financial statements.

---

[9] ISA (UK and Ireland) 265, "Communicating Deficiencies in Internal Control to Those Charged with Governance and Management," paragraphs 9 and A14.

**Adequacy of the Communication Process** (Ref: Para. 22)

The auditor need not design specific procedures to support the evaluation of the two-way communication between the auditor and those charged with governance; rather, that evaluation may be based on observations resulting from audit procedures performed for other purposes. Such observations may include: **A42**

- The appropriateness and timeliness of actions taken by those charged with governance in response to matters raised by the auditor. Where significant matters raised in previous communications have not been dealt with effectively, it may be appropriate for the auditor to inquire as to why appropriate action has not been taken, and to consider raising the point again. This avoids the risk of giving an impression that the auditor is satisfied that the matter has been adequately addressed or is no longer significant.
- The apparent openness of those charged with governance in their communications with the auditor.
- The willingness and capacity of those charged with governance to meet with the auditor without management present.
- The apparent ability of those charged with governance to fully comprehend matters raised by the auditor, for example, the extent to which those charged with governance probe issues, and question recommendations made to them.
- Difficulty in establishing with those charged with governance a mutual understanding of the form, timing and expected general content of communications.
- Where all or some of those charged with governance are involved in managing the entity, their apparent awareness of how matters discussed with the auditor affect their broader governance responsibilities, as well as their management responsibilities.
- Whether the two-way communication between the auditor and those charged with governance meets applicable legal and regulatory requirements.

As noted in paragraph 4, effective two-way communication assists both the auditor and those charged with governance. Further, ISA (UK and Ireland) 315 identifies participation by those charged with governance, including their interaction with internal audit, if any, and external auditors, as an element of the entity's control environment.[10] Inadequate two-way communication may indicate an unsatisfactory control environment and influence the auditor's assessment of the risks of material misstatements. There is also a risk that the auditor may not have obtained sufficient appropriate audit evidence to form an opinion on the financial statements. **A43**

If the two-way communication between the auditor and those charged with governance is not adequate and the situation cannot be resolved, the auditor may take such actions as: **A44**

- Modifying the auditor's opinion on the basis of a scope limitation.
- Obtaining legal advice about the consequences of different courses of action.
- Communicating with third parties (e.g., a regulator), or a higher authority in the governance structure that is outside the entity, such as the owners of a business (e.g., shareholders in a general meeting), or the responsible government minister or parliament in the public sector.
- Withdrawing from the engagement, where withdrawal is possible under applicable law or regulation.

---

[10] *ISA (UK and Ireland) 315, paragraph A70.*

## Documentation (Ref: Para. 23)

**A45**   Documentation of oral communication may include a copy of minutes prepared by the entity retained as part of the audit documentation where those minutes are an appropriate record of the communication.

# Appendix 1 (Ref: Para. 3)

## Specific Requirements in ISQC (UK and Ireland) 1 and Other ISAs (UK and Ireland) that Refer to Communications with Those Charged With Governance

This appendix identifies paragraphs in ISQC (UK and Ireland) 1[11] and other ISAs (UK and Ireland) in effect for audits of financial statements for periods ending on or after 15 December 2010 that require communication of specific matters with those charged with governance. The list is not a substitute for considering the requirements and related application and other explanatory material in ISAs (UK and Ireland).

- ISQC (UK and Ireland) 1, "Quality Control for Firms that Perform Audits and Reviews of Financial Statements, and Other Assurance and Related Services Engagements" – paragraph 30(a)
- ISA (UK and Ireland) 240, "The Auditor's Responsibilities Relating to Fraud in an Audit of Financial Statements" – paragraphs 21, 38(c)(i) and 40-42
- ISA (UK and Ireland) 250, "Consideration of Laws and Regulations in an Audit of Financial Statements" – paragraphs 14, 19 and 22-24]
- ISA (UK and Ireland) 265, "Communicating Deficiencies in Internal Control to Those Charged with Governance and Management" – paragraph 9
- ISA (UK and Ireland) 450, "Evaluation of Misstatements Identified during the Audit" – paragraphs 12-13
- ISA (UK and Ireland) 505, "External Confirmations" – paragraph 9
- ISA (UK and Ireland) 510, "Initial Audit Engagements—Opening Balances" – paragraph 7
- ISA (UK and Ireland) 550, "Related Parties" – paragraph 27
- ISA (UK and Ireland) 560, "Subsequent Events" – paragraphs 7(b)-(c), 9, 10(a), 13(b), 14(a) and 17
- ISA (UK and Ireland) 570, "Going Concern" – paragraph 23
- ISA (UK and Ireland) 600, "Special ConsiderationsAudits of Group Financial Statements (Including the Work of Component Auditors)" – paragraph 49
- ISA (UK and Ireland) 705, "Modifications to the Opinion in the Independent Auditor's Report" – paragraphs 12, 14, 19(a) and 28
- ISA (UK and Ireland) 706, "Emphasis of Matter Paragraphs and Other Matter Paragraphs in the Independent Auditor's Report" – paragraph 9
- ISA (UK and Ireland) 710, "Comparative Information—Corresponding Figures and Comparative Financial Statements" – paragraph 18
- ISA (UK and Ireland) 720, "The Auditor's Responsibilities Relating to Other Information in Documents Containing Audited Financial Statements" – paragraphs 10. 13 and 16

---

[11] *ISQC (UK and Ireland) 1, "Quality Control for Firms that Perform Audits and Reviews of Financial Statements, and Other Assurance and Related Services Engagements."*

## Appendix 2 (Ref: Para. 16(a), A17)

## Qualitative Aspects of Accounting Practices

The communication required by paragraph 16(a), and discussed in paragraph A17, may include such matters as:

### Accounting Policies

- The appropriateness of the accounting policies to the particular circumstances of the entity, having regard to the need to balance the cost of providing information with the likely benefit to users of the entity's financial statements. Where acceptable alternative accounting policies exist, the communication may include identification of the financial statement items that are affected by the choice of significant accounting policies as well as information on accounting policies used by similar entities.
- The initial selection of, and changes in significant accounting policies, including the application of new accounting pronouncements. The communication may include: the effect of the timing and method of adoption of a change in accounting policy on the current and future earnings of the entity; and the timing of a change in accounting policies in relation to expected new accounting pronouncements.
- The effect of significant accounting policies in controversial or emerging areas (or those unique to an industry, particularly when there is a lack of authoritative guidance or consensus).
- The effect of the timing of transactions in relation to the period in which they are recorded.

### Accounting Estimates

- For items for which estimates are significant, issues discussed in ISA (UK and Ireland) 540,[12] including, for example:
  - Management's identification of accounting estimates.
  - Management's process for making accounting estimates.
  - Risks of material misstatement.
  - Indicators of possible management bias.
  - Disclosure of estimation uncertainty in the financial statements.

### Financial Statement Disclosures

- The issues involved, and related judgments made, in formulating particularly sensitive financial statement disclosures (e.g., disclosures related to revenue recognition, remuneration, going concern, subsequent events, and contingency issues).
- The overall neutrality, consistency and clarity of the disclosures in the financial statements.

---

[12] *ISA (UK and Ireland) 540, "Auditing Accounting Estimates, Including Fair Value Accounting Estimates, and Related Disclosures."*

## Related Matters

- The potential effect on the financial statements of significant risks, exposures and uncertainties, such as pending litigation, that are disclosed in the financial statements.
- The extent to which the financial statements are affected by unusual transactions, including non-recurring amounts recognized during the period, and the extent to which such transactions are separately disclosed in the financial statements.
- The factors affecting asset and liability carrying values, including the entity's bases for determining useful lives assigned to tangible and intangible assets. The communication may explain how factors affecting carrying values were selected and how alternative selections would have affected the financial statements.
- The selective correction of misstatements, for example, correcting misstatements with the effect of increasing reported earnings, but not those that have the effect of decreasing reported earnings.

# Addendum

*This addendum provides a summary of APB's rationale for retaining or excluding in the proposed clarified ISA (UK and Ireland) the supplementary requirements in the existing ISA (UK and Ireland). It also sets out the supplementary guidance material in the existing ISA (UK and Ireland) that APB considers is not necessary to retain in light of the improvements in the underlying Clarity ISAs issued by the IAASB as part of the Clarity Project. It is provided for information and does not form part of the proposed clarified ISA (UK and Ireland).*

*The Consultation Paper published with the exposure drafts explains the general approach used by the APB for determining whether current supplementary material should be proposed to be retained.*

**Analysis of proposed treatment of current APB supplementary material in current ISA (UK and Ireland) 260**

It should be noted that ISA 260 has been revised as well as clarified. The APB's current ISA (UK and Ireland) 260 was very influential on the revision.

## Requirements

| APB supplementary requirements (*Italic text is from IAASB for context*) | Is it covered in substance in the Clarity ISA? | Should it be retained? |
|---|---|---|
| 8-2. **The auditor should ensure that those charged with governance are provided with a copy of the audit engagement letter on a timely basis.** | – There is a requirement to communicate with those charged with governance the responsibilities of the auditor in relation to the financial statement audit (14). Reference to this often being included in the engagement letter is made in the Application Material (A9). Also, ISA 210.9 includes a requirement for the auditor to agree the terms of the audit engagement with management or those charged with governance as appropriate. And 210.10 requires the agreed terms to be included in an engagement letter or other suitable form of written agreement. | ✗ |

| APB supplementary requirements (*Italic text is from IAASB for context*) | Is it covered in substance in the Clarity ISA? | Should it be retained? |
|---|---|---|
| **Planning Information**<br>**11-7. The auditor should communicate to those charged with governance an outline of the nature and scope, including, where relevant, any limitations thereon, of the work the auditor proposes to undertake and the form of the reports the auditor expects to make.** | ✓ Re scope and timing. (15)<br><br>Form of report is covered in ISA 210.<br><br>✗ Re "nature" and "limitations" on scope. ISA 210.7 requires that if a limitation is to be imposed that will result in a disclaimer of opinion, the engagement should not be accepted (unless required to do so by law). However, it does not address limitations that may not result in a disclaimer.<br><br>Details of the auditor's approach are a "may" in the Application Material of ISA 260. (A13) | ✗<br><br>✗<br>But guidance has been added indicating that the communication of the planned scope of the audit includes, where relevant, any limitations on the work. **A11-1** |
| **11-12. The auditor should communicate the following findings from the audit to those charged with governance:**<br>**(a) The auditor's views about the qualitative aspects of the entity's accounting practices and financial reporting;** | ✓ 16(a) | ✗ |
| **(b) The final draft of the representation letter, that the auditor is requesting management and those charged with governance to sign. The communication should specifically refer to any matters where management is reluctant to make the representations requested by the auditor;** | ✓ First sentence. (16(c)(ii)).<br><br>– Last sentence is not in the ISA. However, there is a requirement to communicate significant matters discussed with or subject to correspondence with management. (16(c)(i)) | ✗<br><br>✗ |
| **(c) Uncorrected misstatements;** | ✓ In ISA 450 (12) | ✗ |

| APB supplementary requirements (*Italic text is from IAASB for context*) | Is it covered in substance in the Clarity ISA? | Should it be retained? |
|---|---|---|
| (d) **Expected modifications to the auditor's report;** | ✓ In ISA 705 (28) | ✗ |
| (e) **Material weaknesses in internal control identified during the audit;** | ✓ In ISA 265. (control deficiencies) | ✗ |
| (f) **Matters specifically required by other ISAs (UK and Ireland) to be communicated to those charged with governance; and** | ✗ However, the appendix summarising these is included and referred to in the introduction in the ISA. | ✗ |
| (g) **Any other audit matters of governance interest.** | ✓ 16(d) | ✗ |
| 11-19. **The auditor should seek to obtain a written representation from those charged with governance that explains their reasons for not correcting misstatements brought to their attention by the auditor.** | ✗ ISA 450 includes a requirement for a written representation whether effects of uncorrected misstatements are immaterial (14). The Application Material indicates that in some circumstances management/TCWG may wish to give reasons why they believe a matter is not a misstatement (A24). | ✓ (Audit Quality)<br><br>**In ISA 450 – para 14-1**<br><br>Mandating a reason to be given focuses the attention of management and those charged with governance. |
| 13-1. **The auditor should plan with those charged with governance the form and timing of communications to them.** | ✓ 18 | ✗ |

| APB supplementary requirements (*Italic text is from IAASB for context*) | Is it covered in substance in the Clarity ISA? | Should it be retained? |
|---|---|---|
| 16-1. **In the UK and Ireland, the auditor should communicate in writing with those charged with governance regarding the significant findings from the audit.** | – ISA is softer, requiring written communication if, in the auditor's judgment, oral communication would not be adequate. (19) | ✗<br><br>However, guidance has been added to indicate that the judgment of whether to communicate significant matters orally or in writing may also be affected by the evaluation, required by paragraph 22, of whether the two-way communication between the auditor and those charged with governance has been adequate for the purpose of the audit. **A38-1** |
| 17-2. **The auditor should consider whether the two-way communication between the auditor and those charged with governance has been adequate for an effective audit and, if it has not, should take appropriate action.** | ✓ 22 | ✗ |

## Guidance

The following guidance in current ISA (UK and Ireland) 260 has not been carried forward to the proposed clarified standard.

| Current paragraph reference (*Italic text is from IAASB for context*) |
|---|
| 2-1. For the purposes of this ISA (UK and Ireland) the term "communicate" is used in the sense of an active two-way communication (dialogue) between the auditor and those charged with governance. Effective communication is unlikely to be achieved when the auditor communicates with those charged with governance solely by means of formal written reports. |
| 4-1. The principal purposes of communications with those charged with governance are to:<br>(a) Reach a mutual understanding of the scope of the audit and the respective responsibilities of the auditor and those charged with governance;<br>(b) Share information to assist both the auditor and those charged with governance fulfill their respective responsibilities; and<br>(c) Provide to those charged with governance constructive observations arising from the audit process. |
| 4-2. Although the requirements of this ISA (UK and Ireland) focus on the auditor's communications to those charged with governance, it is important that there is effective two-way communication (see paragraphs 2-1 and 2-2). The auditor reasonably expects those charged with governance to give the auditor such information and explanations as the auditor requires for the purposes of the audit. |
| 4-3. The extent, form and frequency of communications with those charged with governance will vary, reflecting the size and nature of the entity and the manner in which those charged with governance operate, as well as the auditor's views as to the importance of the audit matters of governance interest relating to the audit. In particular, communications with those charged with governance of listed companies might be more formal than communications with those charged with governance of smaller entities, or of subsidiary undertakings. |
| 7-1. In most UK and Irish entities a board or equivalent governing body comprises individuals who are collectively charged with governance, including financial reporting. In some smaller entities a single individual may be charged with governance. In other cases, committees of a board or individual members of it may be charged with specific tasks in order to assist a board to meet its governance responsibilities (e.g. there may be an audit committee, a remuneration committee or a nomination committee). |
| 7-2. When considering communicating with a committee the auditor considers whether the committee is in a position to provide the information and explanations the auditor needs for the purpose of the audit, whether the committee has the authority to act on the auditor's findings and whether there may be a need to repeat the communication to the board or governing body. Irrespective of what may be agreed, the auditor may judge it necessary to communicate directly with the board or governing body when a matter is sufficiently important. |
| 7-3. The establishment of audit committees by the boards of listed companies, many public sector bodies and some other organizations has meant that communication with the audit committee, where one exists, has become a |

| | **Current paragraph reference (*Italic text is from IAASB for context*)** |
|---|---|
| | key element in the auditor's communication with those charged with governance. It is to be expected that the engagement partner will be invited regularly to attend meetings of the audit committee and that the audit committee chairman, and to a lesser extent the other members of the audit committee, will wish to liaise on a continuing basis with the engagement partner. |
| 7-4 | The audit committee ordinarily will, at least annually, meet the auditor, without management, to discuss matters relating to the audit committee's remit and issues arising from the audit. |
| 7-5. | As part of obtaining an understanding of the control environment, the auditor obtains an understanding of how the audit committee operates, including the particular remit given to the committee by the entity's board and its role in relation to governance matters such as reviewing the identification, evaluation and management of business risks. An entity's board and its auditor bear in mind that communication to audit committees forms only part of the auditor's overall obligation to communicate effectively with those charged with governance. |
| 8-1. | In order to ensure that effective two-way communication is established, the expectations both of the auditor and those charged with governance regarding the form, level of detail and timing of communications are established at an early stage in the audit process. The manner in which these expectations are established will vary, reflecting the size and nature of the entity and the manner in which those charged with governance operate. |
| 9-1. | ISA (UK and Ireland) 210, "Terms of Audit Engagements," requires that the auditor and the client should agree on the terms of the engagement. "Client" means the addressees of the of the auditor's report or, when as often will be the case it is not practical to agree such terms with the addressees, the entity itself through those charged with governance. |
| *Groups* | |
| 10-1. | Where a parent undertaking is preparing group financial statements, the auditor of the parent undertaking communicates to those charged with governance of the parent undertaking such matters brought to the attention of those charged with governance of its subsidiary undertakings, by the auditors of the subsidiary undertakings, as they judge to be of significance in the context of the group (e.g. weaknesses in systems of internal control that have resulted, or could result, in material errors in the group financial statements). |
| 10-3. | The auditor of the parent undertaking considers the manner in which the group is managed and the wishes of those charged with governance of the parent undertaking when deciding with whom the auditor should communicate in the group about particular matters. In recognition of the responsibilities of those charged with governance of subsidiary undertakings, the auditors of those subsidiary undertakings communicate audit matters of governance interest to those charged with governance of the subsidiary undertakings. |
| **Audit Matters of Governance Interest to be Communicated** | |
| 11 | *The auditor should consider audit matters of governance interest that arise from the audit of the financial statements and communicate them with those charged with governance. Ordinarily such matters include the following:* |

| **Current paragraph reference (*Italic text is from IAASB for context*)** |
|---|
| • Relationships that may bear on the firm's independence and the integrity and objectivity of the audit engagement partner and audit staff.<br>See paragraphs 11-2 – 11-6 below.<br>• *The general approach and overall scope of the audit, including any expected limitations thereon, or any additional requirements.*<br>See paragraphs 11-7 – 11-11 below.<br>• *The selection of, or changes in, significant accounting policies and practices that have, or could have, a material effect on the entity's financial statements.*<br>See paragraph 11-13 – 11-14 below.<br>• *Audit adjustments, whether or not recorded by the entity that have, or could have, a material effect on the entity's financial statements.*<br>See paragraphs 11-16 – 11-20 below<br>• *Expected modifications to the auditor's report.*<br>See paragraph 11-21 below.<br>• *Other matters warranting attention by those charged with governance, such as material weaknesses in internal control, questions regarding management integrity, and fraud involving management.*<br>See paragraph 11-22 – 11-23 below. |
| 11.a. ***The auditor should inform those charged with governance of those uncorrected misstatements aggregated[4] by the auditor during the audit that were determined by management to be immaterial, both individually and in the aggregate, to the financial statements taken as a whole.***<br><br>[4] In the UK and Ireland, the term "aggregated" used in this particular context is taken to mean "identified". |
| 11.b. *The uncorrected misstatements communicated to those charged with governance need not include the misstatements below a designated amount[5].*<br><br>[5] In the UK and Ireland, the auditor communicates all uncorrected misstatements other than those that the auditor believes are clearly trivial (see paragraph 11-16). |
| 11-1. Additional standards and guidance, for auditors in the UK and Ireland, relating to the communication of uncorrected misstatements are set out in paragraphs 11-16 to 11-20 below. |
| **Integrity, Objectivity and Independence**<br>11-3. The audit committee where one exists, is usually responsible for oversight of the relationship between the auditor and the entity and of the conduct of the audit process. It therefore has a particular interest in being informed about the auditor's ability to express an objective opinion on the financial statements. Where there is no audit committee, this role is taken by the board of directors. |
| 11-4. The aim of these communications is to ensure full and fair disclosure by the auditor to those charged with governance of the audit client on matters in which they have an interest. These will generally include the key elements of the audit engagement partner's consideration of objectivity and independence such as: |

**Current paragraph reference (*Italic text is from IAASB for context*)**

- The principal threats, if any to objectivity and independence identified by the auditor, including consideration of all relationships between the audit client, its affiliates and directors and the audit firm.
- Any safeguards adopted and the reasons why they are considered to be effective.
- Any independent partner review.
- The overall assessment of threats and safeguards.
- Information about the general policies and processes within the audit firm for maintaining objectivity and independence.

11-5. In the case of listed companies, the auditor, as a minimum:

    (a) Discloses in writing:

        (i) Details of all relationships between the auditor and the client, its directors and senior management and its affiliates, including all services provided by the audit firm and its network to the client, its directors and senior management and its affiliates, that the auditor considers may reasonably be thought to bear on the auditor's objectivity and independence;

        (ii) The related safeguards that are in place; and

        (iii) The total amount of fees that the auditor and the auditor's network firms have charged to the client and its affiliates for the provision of services during the reporting period, analyzed into appropriate categories, for example, statutory audit services, further audit services, tax advisory services and other non-audit services. For each category, the amounts of any future services which have been contracted or where a written proposal has been submitted, are separately disclosed;

    (b) Confirms in writing that the auditor complies with APB Ethical Standards and that, in the auditor's professional judgment, the auditor is independent and the auditor's objectivity is not compromised, or otherwise declare that the auditor has concerns that the auditor's objectivity and independence may be compromised (including instances where the group audit engagement partner does not consider the other auditors to be objective); and explaining the actions which necessarily follow from this; and

    (c) Seeks to discuss these matters with the audit committee.

11-6. The most appropriate time for such communications [about independence] is usually at the conclusion of the audit. However, communications between the auditor and those charged with governance of the audit client will also be needed at the planning stage and whenever significant judgments are made about threats to objectivity and the appropriateness of safeguards put in place, for example, when accepting an engagement to provide non audit services.

11-9. The auditor communicates in outline the principal ways in which the auditor proposes to address the risks of material misstatement, with particular reference to areas of higher risk. As part of the two-way communication process the auditor seeks to gain an understanding of the attitude of those charged with governance to the business risks of the entity. When describing the planned approach to addressing the risk of material misstatement, the auditor does not describe the plan in such detail that the "surprise" element of the audit is lost. Other matters that might be communicated in outline include:

- The concept of materiality and its application to the audit approach.

| Current paragraph reference (*Italic text is from IAASB for context*) |
|---|

- The auditor's approach to the assessment of, and reliance on, internal controls.
- The extent, if any, to which reliance will be placed on the work of internal audit and on the way in which the external and internal auditors can best work together on a constructive and complementary basis.
- Where relevant, the work to be undertaken by any other firms of auditors (including related firms) and how the principal auditor intends to obtain assurance as to the adequacy of the other auditors' procedures in so far as it relates to the principal auditor's role.

11-11. Other matters that the auditor may, for the purpose of the audit, find beneficial to discuss with those charged with governance include:

- The views of those charged with governance of the nature and extent of significant internal and external operational, financial, compliance and other risks facing the entity which might affect the financial statements, including the likelihood of those risks materializing and how they are managed.
- The control environment within the entity, including the attitude of management to controls, and whether those charged with governance have a process for keeping under review the effectiveness of the system of internal control and, where a review of the effectiveness of internal control has been carried out, the results of that review.
- Actions those charged with governance plan to take in response to matters such as developments in law, accounting standards, corporate governance reporting, Listing Rules, and other developments relevant to the entity's financial statements and annual report.

*Qualitative Aspects of Accounting Practices and Financial Reporting*

11-13. The accounting requirements of company law, accounting standards and interpretations issued by the relevant accounting standard setters, permit a degree of choice in some areas as to the specific accounting policies and practices that may be adopted by an entity. Additionally, there are matters for which those charged with governance have to make accounting estimates and judgments.

11-14. In the course of the audit of the financial statements, the auditor considers the qualitative aspects of the financial reporting process, including items that have a significant impact on the relevance, reliability, comparability, understandability and materiality of the information provided by the financial statements. The auditor discusses in an open and frank manner with those charged with governance the auditor's views on the quality and acceptability of the entity's accounting practices and financial reporting. Such discussions may include:

- The appropriateness of the accounting policies to the particular circumstances of the entity, judged against the objectives of relevance, reliability, comparability and understandability but having regard also to the need to balance the different objectives and the need to balance the cost of providing information with the likely benefit to users of the entity's financial statements.

The auditor explains to those charged with governance why the auditor considers any accounting policy not to be appropriate, and requests those charged with governance to make appropriate changes. If those charged with governance decline to make the changes on the grounds that the effect is not material, the auditor informs them that the auditor will consider qualifying the auditor's report when the effect

| **Current paragraph reference (*Italic text is from IAASB for context*)** |
|---|

of not using an appropriate policy can reasonably be expected to influence the economic decisions of users of the financial statements.
- The timing of transactions and the period in which they are recorded.
- The appropriateness of accounting estimates and judgments, for example in relation to provisions, including the consistency of assumptions and degree of prudence reflected in the recorded amounts.
- The potential effect on the financial statements of any material risks and exposures, such as pending litigation, that are required to be disclosed in the financial statements.
- Material uncertainties related to events and conditions that may cast significant doubt on the entity's ability to continue as a going concern.
- The extent to which the financial statements are affected by any unusual transactions including non-recurring profits and losses recognized during the period and the extent to which such transactions are separately disclosed in the financial statements.
- Apparent misstatements in the other information in the document containing the audited financial statements or material inconsistencies between it and the audited financial statements.
- The overall balance and clarity of the information contained in the annual report.
- Disagreements about matters that, individually or in aggregate, could be significant to the entity's financial statements or the auditor's report. These communications include consideration of whether the matters have, or have not, been resolved and the significance of the matters.

*Management Representation Letter*

11-15. The auditor reviews the content of management's representation letter with those charged with governance. The auditor explains the significance of representations that have been requested relating to non-standard issues.

*Uncorrected Misstatements*

11-16. The auditor communicates all uncorrected misstatements, other than those that the auditor believes are clearly trivial[6], to the entity's management and requests that management correct them. When communicating misstatements, the auditor distinguishes between misstatements that are errors of fact and misstatements that arise from differences in judgment and explain why the latter are considered misstatements. When such misstatements identified by the auditor are not corrected by management the auditor communicates the misstatements to those charged with governance, in accordance with the requirement set out in paragraph 11a, and requests them to make the corrections. Where those charged with governance refuse to make some or all of the corrections, the auditor discusses with them the reasons for, and appropriateness of, not making those corrections, having regard to qualitative as well as quantitative considerations, and considers the implications for their audit report of the effect of misstatements that remain uncorrected.

[6] This is not another expression for 'immaterial'. Matters which are 'clearly trivial' will be of an wholly different (smaller) order of magnitude than the materiality thresholds used in the audit, and will be matters that are clearly inconsequential, whether taken individually or in aggregate and whether judged by any quantitative and/or qualitative criteria. Further, whenever there is any uncertainty about whether one or more items are 'clearly trivial' (in accordance with this definition), the presumption should be that the matter is not 'clearly trivial'.

| **Current paragraph reference (*Italic text is from IAASB for context*)** |
|:---|
| 11-17. If management have corrected material misstatements, the auditor considers whether those corrections of which the auditor is aware should be communicated to those charged with governance so as to assist them to fulfill their governance responsibilities, including reviewing the effectiveness of the system of internal control. |
| 11-18. Paragraph 5a.(b) of ISA (UK and Ireland) 580, "Management Representations," requires the auditor to obtain written representations from management that it believes the effects of those uncorrected misstatements identified by the auditor during the audit are immaterial, both individually and in the aggregate, to the financial statements taken as a whole. A summary of such misstatements is required to be included in or attached to the written representations. |
| 11-20. If those charged with governance refuse to make some or all of the corrections the auditor has requested, a representation is obtained to reduce the possibility of misunderstandings concerning their reasons for not making the corrections. A summary of the uncorrected misstatements[7] is included in, or attached to, the representation letter. Obtaining the representation does not relieve the auditor of the need to form an independent opinion as to the materiality of uncorrected misstatements. |
| [7] The summary need not include any misstatements that the auditors believe are 'clearly trivial' (see footnote 6). |
| *Expected Modifications to the Auditor's Report*<br>11-21. The auditor discusses expected modifications to the auditor's report on the financial statements with those charged with governance to ensure that:<br>(a) Those charged with governance are aware of the proposed modification and the reasons for it before the report is finalized;<br>(b) There are no disputed facts in respect of the matter(s) giving rise to the proposed modification (or that matters of disagreement are confirmed as such); and<br>(c) Those charged with governance have an opportunity, where appropriate, to provide the auditor with further information and explanations in respect of the matter(s) giving rise to the proposed modification. |
| *Material Weaknesses in Internal Control*<br>11-22. A material weakness in internal control is a deficiency in design or operation which could adversely affect the entity's ability to record, process, summarize and report financial and other relevant data so as to result in a material misstatement in the financial statements. The auditor normally does not need to communicate information concerning a material weakness of which those charged with governance are aware and in respect of which, in the view of the auditor, appropriate corrective action has been taken, unless the weakness is symptomatic of broader weaknesses in the overall control environment and there is a risk that other material weaknesses may occur. Material weaknesses of which the auditor is aware are communicated where they have been corrected by management without the knowledge of those charged with governance. |
| 11-23. The auditor explains to those charged with governance that the auditor has not provided a comprehensive statement of all weaknesses which may exist in internal control or of all improvements which may be made, but has |

| Current paragraph reference (*Italic text is from IAASB for context*) |
|---|

addressed only those matters which have come to the auditor's attention as a result of the audit procedures performed.

### Forms of Communications

15.  *The auditor's communications with those charged with governance may be made orally or in writing. The auditor's decision whether to communicate orally or in writing is affected by factors such as:*
  - Statutory and regulatory requirements.

15-1.  As stated in paragraph 10-3, in relation to the audit of groups, the auditor of the parent undertaking considers the manner in which the group is managed and the wishes of those charged with governance of the parent undertaking when deciding with whom the auditor should communicate in the group about particular matters. These considerations include whether it is necessary and appropriate to communicate in writing with those charged with governance of subsidiary undertakings.

17-1.  The auditor incorporates in the communication of audit matters of governance interest to those charged with governance comments made by management, where those comments will aid the understanding of those charged with governance, and any actions management have indicated that they will take

17-3.  Paragraph 69 of ISA 315 "Understanding the Entity and Its Environment and Assessing the Risks of Material Misstatement", identifies participation by those charged with governance, including their interaction with internal and external auditors, as an element the auditor considers when evaluating the design of the entity's control environment. Inadequate two-way communication may indicate an unsatisfactory control environment, which will influence the auditor's assessment of the risks of material misstatements. Examples of evidence about the adequacy of the two-way communication process may include:
  - The appropriateness and timeliness of actions taken by those charged with governance in response to the recommendations made by the auditor. (See also paragraph 19-1 regarding significant matters raised in previous communications.)
  - The apparent openness of those charged with governance in their communications with the auditor.
  - The willingness and capacity of those charged with governance to meet with the auditor without management present.
  - The apparent ability of those charged with governance to fully comprehend the recommendations made by the auditor. For example, the extent to which those charged with governance probe issues and question recommendations made to them.

17-4.  If the two-way communication between the auditor and those charged with governance is inadequate, there is a risk that the auditor may not obtain all the audit evidence required to form an opinion on the financial statements. In such a situation, the auditor considers taking actions such as:
  - Obtaining legal advice about the consequences of different courses of action.
  - Communicating with third parties (e.g. an appropriate regulator), or higher authority in the governance structure that is outside the entity (such as the owners of a small business).

If the auditor concludes that the two way communication is unlikely to become adequate for the purposes of the audit, the auditor considers withdrawing from the engagement.

| Current paragraph reference (*Italic text is from IAASB for context*) |
|---|
| 19-1. The auditor considers the actions taken by those charged with governance in response to previous communications. Where significant matters raised in previous communications to those charged with governance have not been dealt with effectively, the auditor enquires as to why appropriate action has not been taken. If the auditor considers that a matter raised previously has not been adequately addressed, consideration is given to repeating the point in a current communication; otherwise there is a risk that the auditor may give an impression that the auditor is satisfied that the matter has been adequately addressed or is no longer significant. |
| 20-1. Occasionally those charged with governance may wish to provide third parties, for example bankers or certain regulatory authorities, with copies of a written communication from the auditor. It is appropriate to ensure that third parties who see the communication understand that it was not prepared with third parties in mind. Furthermore, where the written communications contain open and frank discussion of aspects of the entity's accounting and financial reporting practices, it may not be appropriate for such communications to be disclosed to third parties. Thus the auditor normally states in the communication to those charged with governance that:<br>(a) The report has been prepared for the sole use of the entity and, where appropriate, any parent undertaking and its auditor;<br>(b) It must not be disclosed to a third party, or quoted or referred to, without the written consent of the auditor; and<br>(c) No responsibility is assumed by the auditor to any other person. |
| 20-2. In the public or regulated sectors, the auditor may have a duty to submit a report to those charged with governance annually, and also to submit copies of the report to relevant regulatory or funding bodies. In the public sector, there may also be a requirement or expectation that reports will be made public and in such circumstances some or all of the restrictions set out in the preceding paragraph may not be appropriate. |
| 20-3. Any communication with those charged with governance is confidential information. Thus, when the auditor communicates in writing with those charged with governance, the auditor requires the prior consent of those charged with governance if the auditor is to provide a copy of the communication to a third party. |
| Appendix – Sets out requirements in other ISAs that refer to communications with those charged with governance and with management. (Not reproduced here.) |

# Proposed Clarified International Standard on Auditing (UK and Ireland) 265

## Communicating deficiencies in internal control to those charged with governance and management

*(Effective for audits of financial statements for periods ending on or after 15 December 2010)*

## Contents

International Standard on Auditing (UK and Ireland) (ISA (UK and Ireland)) 265, "Communicating Deficiencies in Internal Control to Those Charged with Governance and Management" should be read in conjunction with ISA (UK and Ireland) 200, "Overall Objectives of the Independent Auditor and the Conduct of an Audit in Accordance with International Standards on Auditing (UK and Ireland)."

# Introduction

## Scope of this ISA (UK and Ireland)

1   This International Standard on Auditing (UK and Ireland) (ISA (UK and Ireland)) deals with the auditor's responsibility to communicate appropriately to those charged with governance and management deficiencies in internal control[1] that the auditor has identified in an audit of financial statements. This ISA (UK and Ireland) does not impose additional responsibilities on the auditor regarding obtaining an understanding of internal control and designing and performing tests of controls over and above the requirements of ISA (UK and Ireland) 315 and ISA (UK and Ireland) 330.[2] ISA (UK and Ireland) 260[3] establishes further requirements and provides guidance regarding the auditor's responsibility to communicate with those charged with governance in relation to the audit.

2   The auditor is required to obtain an understanding of internal control relevant to the audit when identifying and assessing the risks of material misstatement.[4] In making those risk assessments, the auditor considers internal control in order to design audit procedures that are appropriate in the circumstances, but not for the purpose of expressing an opinion on the effectiveness of internal control. The auditor may identify deficiencies in internal control not only during this risk assessment process but also at any other stage of the audit. This ISA (UK and Ireland) specifies which identified deficiencies the auditor is required to communicate to those charged with governance and management.

3   Nothing in this ISA (UK and Ireland) precludes the auditor from communicating to those charged with governance and management other internal control matters that the auditor has identified during the audit.

## Effective Date

4   This ISA (UK and Ireland) is effective for audits of financial statements for periods ending on or after 15 December 2010.

# Objective

5   The objective of the auditor is to communicate appropriately to those charged with governance and management deficiencies in internal control that the auditor has identified during the audit and that, in the auditor's professional judgment, are of sufficient importance to merit their respective attentions.

---

[1] *ISA (UK and Ireland) 315, "Identifying and Assessing the Risks of Material Misstatement through Understanding the Entity and Its Environment," paragraphs 4 and 12.*

[2] *ISA (UK and Ireland) 330, "The Auditor's Responses to Assessed Risks."*

[3] *ISA (UK and Ireland) 260, "Communication with Those Charged with Governance."*

[4] *ISA (UK and Ireland) 315, paragraph 12. Paragraphs A60-A65 provide guidance on controls relevant to the audit.*

# Definitions

For purposes of the ISAs (UK and Ireland), the following terms have the meanings attributed below:    **6**

(a) Deficiency in internal control – This exists when:
  (i)  A control is designed, implemented or operated in such a way that it is unable to prevent, or detect and correct, misstatements in the financial statements on a timely basis; or
  (ii) A control necessary to prevent, or detect and correct, misstatements in the financial statements on a timely basis is missing.
(b) Significant deficiency in internal control – A deficiency or combination of deficiencies in internal control that, in the auditor's professional judgment, is of sufficient importance to merit the attention of those charged with governance. (Ref: Para. A5)

# Requirements

The auditor shall determine whether, on the basis of the audit work performed, the auditor has identified one or more deficiencies in internal control. (Ref: Para. A1-A4)    **7**

If the auditor has identified one or more deficiencies in internal control, the auditor shall determine, on the basis of the audit work performed, whether, individually or in combination, they constitute significant deficiencies. (Ref: Para. A5-A11)    **8**

The auditor shall communicate in writing significant deficiencies in internal control identified during the audit to those charged with governance on a timely basis. (Ref: Para. A12-A18, A27)    **9**

The auditor shall also communicate to management at an appropriate level of responsibility on a timely basis: (Ref: Para. A19, A27)    **10**

(a) In writing, significant deficiencies in internal control that the auditor has communicated or intends to communicate to those charged with governance, unless it would be inappropriate to communicate directly to management in the circumstances; and (Ref: Para. A14, A20-A21)
(b) Other deficiencies in internal control identified during the audit that have not been communicated to management by other parties and that, in the auditor's professional judgment, are of sufficient importance to merit management's attention. (Ref: Para. A22-A26)

The auditor shall include in the written communication of significant deficiencies in internal control:    **11**

(a) A description of the deficiencies and an explanation of their potential effects; and (Ref: Para. A28)
(b) Sufficient information to enable those charged with governance and management to understand the context of the communication. In particular, the auditor shall explain that: (Ref: Para. A29-A30)
  (i)  The purpose of the audit was for the auditor to express an opinion on the financial statements;
  (ii) The audit included consideration of internal control relevant to the preparation of the financial statements in order to design audit procedures that are appropriate in the circumstances, but not for the purpose of expressing an opinion on the effectiveness of internal control; and

(iii) The matters being reported are limited to those deficiencies that the auditor has identified during the audit and that the auditor has concluded are of sufficient importance to merit being reported to those charged with governance.

\*\*\*

# Application and Other Explanatory Material

## Determination of Whether Deficiencies in Internal Control Have Been Identified (Ref: Para. 7)

A1   In determining whether the auditor has identified one or more deficiencies in internal control, the auditor may discuss the relevant facts and circumstances of the auditor's findings with the appropriate level of management. This discussion provides an opportunity for the auditor to alert management on a timely basis to the existence of deficiencies of which management may not have been previously aware. The level of management with whom it is appropriate to discuss the findings is one that is familiar with the internal control area concerned and that has the authority to take remedial action on any identified deficiencies in internal control. In some circumstances, it may not be appropriate for the auditor to discuss the auditor's findings directly with management, for example, if the findings appear to call management's integrity or competence into question (see paragraph A20).

A2   In discussing the facts and circumstances of the auditor's findings with management, the auditor may obtain other relevant information for further consideration, such as:

- Management's understanding of the actual or suspected causes of the deficiencies.
- Exceptions arising from the deficiencies that management may have noted, for example, misstatements that were not prevented by the relevant information technology (IT) controls.
- A preliminary indication from management of its response to the findings.

### Considerations Specific to Smaller Entities

A3   While the concepts underlying control activities in smaller entities are likely to be similar to those in larger entities, the formality with which they operate will vary. Further, smaller entities may find that certain types of control activities are not necessary because of controls applied by management. For example, management's sole authority for granting credit to customers and approving significant purchases can provide effective control over important account balances and transactions, lessening or removing the need for more detailed control activities.

A4   Also, smaller entities often have fewer employees which may limit the extent to which segregation of duties is practicable. However, in a small owner-managed entity, the owner-manager may be able to exercise more effective oversight than in a larger entity. This higher level of management oversight needs to be balanced against the greater potential for management override of controls.

## Significant Deficiencies in Internal Control (Ref: Para. 6(b), 8)

A5   The significance of a deficiency or a combination of deficiencies in internal control depends not only on whether a misstatement has actually occurred, but also on the likelihood that a misstatement could occur and the potential magnitude of the misstatement. Significant deficiencies may therefore exist even though the auditor has not identified misstatements during the audit.

Examples of matters that the auditor may consider in determining whether a deficiency or combination of deficiencies in internal control constitutes a significant deficiency include:   **A6**

- The likelihood of the deficiencies leading to material misstatements in the financial statements in the future.
- The susceptibility to loss or fraud of the related asset or liability.
- The subjectivity and complexity of determining estimated amounts, such as fair value accounting estimates.
- The financial statement amounts exposed to the deficiencies.
- The volume of activity that has occurred or could occur in the account balance or class of transactions exposed to the deficiency or deficiencies.
- The importance of the controls to the financial reporting process; for example:
  - General monitoring controls (such as oversight of management).
  - Controls over the prevention and detection of fraud.
  - Controls over the selection and application of significant accounting policies.
  - Controls over significant transactions with related parties.
  - Controls over significant transactions outside the entity's normal course of business.
  - Controls over the period-end financial reporting process (such as controls over non-recurring journal entries).
- The cause and frequency of the exceptions detected as a result of the deficiencies in the controls.
- The interaction of the deficiency with other deficiencies in internal control.

Indicators of significant deficiencies in internal control include, for example:   **A7**

- Evidence of ineffective aspects of the control environment, such as:
  - Indications that significant transactions in which management is financially interested are not being appropriately scrutinized by those charged with governance.
  - Identification of management fraud, whether or not material, that was not prevented by the entity's internal control.
  - Management's failure to implement appropriate remedial action on significant deficiencies previously communicated.
- Absence of a risk assessment process within the entity where such a process would ordinarily be expected to have been established.
- Evidence of an ineffective entity risk assessment process, such as management's failure to identify a risk of material misstatement that the auditor would expect the entity's risk assessment process to have identified.
- Evidence of an ineffective response to identified significant risks (e.g., absence of controls over such a risk).
- Misstatements detected by the auditor's procedures that were not prevented, or detected and corrected, by the entity's internal control.
- Restatement of previously issued financial statements to reflect the correction of a material misstatement due to error or fraud.
- Evidence of management's inability to oversee the preparation of the financial statements.

**A8**    Controls may be designed to operate individually or in combination to effectively prevent, or detect and correct, misstatements.[5] For example, controls over accounts receivable may consist of both automated and manual controls designed to operate together to prevent, or detect and correct, misstatements in the account balance. A deficiency in internal control on its own may not be sufficiently important to constitute a significant deficiency. However, a combination of deficiencies affecting the same account balance or disclosure, relevant assertion, or component of internal control may increase the risks of misstatement to such an extent as to give rise to a significant deficiency.

**A9**    Law or regulation in some jurisdictions may establish a requirement (particularly for audits of listed entities) for the auditor to communicate to those charged with governance or to other relevant parties (such as regulators) one or more specific types of deficiency in internal control that the auditor has identified during the audit. Where law or regulation has established specific terms and definitions for these types of deficiency and requires the auditor to use these terms and definitions for the purpose of the communication, the auditor uses such terms and definitions when communicating in accordance with the legal or regulatory requirement.

**A10**    Where the jurisdiction has established specific terms for the types of deficiency in internal control to be communicated but has not defined such terms, it may be necessary for the auditor to use judgment to determine the matters to be communicated further to the legal or regulatory requirement. In doing so, the auditor may consider it appropriate to have regard to the requirements and guidance in this ISA (UK and Ireland). For example, if the purpose of the legal or regulatory requirement is to bring to the attention of those charged with governance certain internal control matters of which they should be aware, it may be appropriate to regard such matters as being generally equivalent to the significant deficiencies required by this ISA (UK and Ireland) to be communicated to those charged with governance.

**A11**    The requirements of this ISA (UK and Ireland) remain applicable notwithstanding that law or regulation may require the auditor to use specific terms or definitions.

## Communication of Deficiencies in Internal Control

*Communication of Significant Deficiencies in Internal Control to Those Charged with Governance* (Ref: Para. 9)

**A12**    Communicating significant deficiencies in writing to those charged with governance reflects the importance of these matters, and assists those charged with governance in fulfilling their oversight responsibilities. ISA (UK and Ireland) 260 establishes relevant considerations regarding communication with those charged with governance when all of them are involved in managing the entity.[6]

**A12-1**    In the UK and Ireland, timely communication of significant deficiencies in writing to directors of listed entities can assist them apply the revised "Turnbull Guidance"[6a] on the requirements of the Combined Code relating to internal control and reporting to shareholders thereon.

---

[5] *ISA (UK and Ireland) 315, paragraph A66.*

[6] *ISA (UK and Ireland) 260, paragraph 13.*

[6a] *"Internal Control – Revised Guidance for Directors on the Combined Code" issued by the Financial Reporting Council, October 2005.*

In determining when to issue the written communication, the auditor may consider **A13** whether receipt of such communication would be an important factor in enabling those charged with governance to discharge their oversight responsibilities. In addition, for listed entities in certain jurisdictions, those charged with governance may need to receive the auditor's written communication before the date of approval of the financial statements in order to discharge specific responsibilities in relation to internal control for regulatory or other purposes. For other entities, the auditor may issue the written communication at a later date. Nevertheless, in the latter case, as the auditor's written communication of significant deficiencies forms part of the final audit file, the written communication is subject to the overriding requirement[7] for the auditor to complete the assembly of the final audit file on a timely basis. ISA (UK and Ireland) 230 states that an appropriate time limit within which to complete the assembly of the final audit file is ordinarily not more than 60 days after the date of the auditor's report.[8]

Regardless of the timing of the written communication of significant deficiencies, the **A14** auditor may communicate these orally in the first instance to management and, when appropriate, to those charged with governance to assist them in taking timely remedial action to minimize the risks of material misstatement. Doing so, however, does not relieve the auditor of the responsibility to communicate the significant deficiencies in writing, as this ISA (UK and Ireland) requires.

The level of detail at which to communicate significant deficiencies is a matter of the **A15** auditor's professional judgment in the circumstances. Factors that the auditor may consider in determining an appropriate level of detail for the communication include, for example:

- The nature of the entity. For instance, the communication required for a public interest entity may be different from that for a non-public interest entity.
- The size and complexity of the entity. For instance, the communication required for a complex entity may be different from that for an entity operating a simple business.
- The nature of significant deficiencies that the auditor has identified.
- The entity's governance composition. For instance, more detail may be needed if those charged with governance include members who do not have significant experience in the entity's industry or in the affected areas.
- Legal or regulatory requirements regarding the communication of specific types of deficiency in internal control.

Management and those charged with governance may already be aware of significant **A16** deficiencies that the auditor has identified during the audit and may have chosen not to remedy them because of cost or other considerations. The responsibility for evaluating the costs and benefits of implementing remedial action rests with management and those charged with governance. Accordingly, the requirement in paragraph 9 applies regardless of cost or other considerations that management and those charged with governance may consider relevant in determining whether to remedy such deficiencies.

The fact that the auditor communicated a significant deficiency to those charged with **A17** governance and management in a previous audit does not eliminate the need for the auditor to repeat the communication if remedial action has not yet been taken. If a previously communicated significant deficiency remains, the current year's

---

[7] ISA (UK and Ireland) 230, "Audit Documentation," paragraph 14.

[8] ISA (UK and Ireland) 230, paragraph A21.

communication may repeat the description from the previous communication, or simply reference the previous communication. The auditor may ask management or, where appropriate, those charged with governance, why the significant deficiency has not yet been remedied. A failure to act, in the absence of a rational explanation, may in itself represent a significant deficiency.

*Considerations Specific to Smaller Entities*

**A18**  In the case of audits of smaller entities, the auditor may communicate in a less structured manner with those charged with governance than in the case of larger entities.

**Communication of Deficiencies in Internal Control to Management** (Ref: Para. 10)

**A19**  Ordinarily, the appropriate level of management is the one that has responsibility and authority to evaluate the deficiencies in internal control and to take the necessary remedial action. For significant deficiencies, the appropriate level is likely to be the chief executive officer or chief financial officer (or equivalent) as these matters are also required to be communicated to those charged with governance. For other deficiencies in internal control, the appropriate level may be operational management with more direct involvement in the control areas affected and with the authority to take appropriate remedial action.

*Communication of Significant Deficiencies in Internal Control to Management (Ref: Para. 10(a))*

**A20**  Certain identified significant deficiencies in internal control may call into question the integrity or competence of management. For example, there may be evidence of fraud or intentional non-compliance with laws and regulations by management, or management may exhibit an inability to oversee the preparation of adequate financial statements that may raise doubt about management's competence. Accordingly, it may not be appropriate to communicate such deficiencies directly to management.

**A21**  ISA (UK and Ireland) 250 establishes requirements and provides guidance on the reporting of identified or suspected non-compliance with laws and regulations, including when those charged with governance are themselves involved in such non-compliance.[9] ISA (UK and Ireland) 240 establishes requirements and provides guidance regarding communication to those charged with governance when the auditor has identified fraud or suspected fraud involving management.[10]

*Communication of Other Deficiencies in Internal Control to Management (Ref: Para. 10(b))*

**A22**  During the audit, the auditor may identify other deficiencies in internal control that are not significant deficiencies but that may be of sufficient importance to merit management's attention. The determination as to which other deficiencies in internal control merit management's attention is a matter of professional judgment in the

[9] *ISA (UK and Ireland) 250, "Consideration of Laws and Regulations in an Audit of Financial Statements," paragraphs 22-28.*

[10] *ISA (UK and Ireland) 240, "The Auditor's Responsibilities Relating to Fraud in an Audit of Financial Statements," paragraph 41.*

circumstances, taking into account the likelihood and potential magnitude of misstatements that may arise in the financial statements as a result of those deficiencies.

The communication of other deficiencies in internal control that merit management's **A23** attention need not be in writing but may be oral. Where the auditor has discussed the facts and circumstances of the auditor's findings with management, the auditor may consider an oral communication of the other deficiencies to have been made to management at the time of these discussions. Accordingly, a formal communication need not be made subsequently.

If the auditor has communicated deficiencies in internal control other than significant **A24** deficiencies to management in a prior period and management has chosen not to remedy them for cost or other reasons, the auditor need not repeat the communication in the current period. The auditor is also not required to repeat information about such deficiencies if it has been previously communicated to management by other parties, such as internal auditors or regulators. It may, however, be appropriate for the auditor to re-communicate these other deficiencies if there has been a change of management, or if new information has come to the auditor's attention that alters the prior understanding of the auditor and management regarding the deficiencies. Nevertheless, the failure of management to remedy other deficiencies in internal control that were previously communicated may become a significant deficiency requiring communication with those charged with governance. Whether this is the case depends on the auditor's judgment in the circumstances.

In some circumstances, those charged with governance may wish to be made aware **A25** of the details of other deficiencies in internal control the auditor has communicated to management, or be briefly informed of the nature of the other deficiencies. Alternatively, the auditor may consider it appropriate to inform those charged with governance of the communication of the other deficiencies to management. In either case, the auditor may report orally or in writing to those charged with governance as appropriate.

ISA (UK and Ireland) 260 establishes relevant considerations regarding communi- **A26** cation with those charged with governance when all of them are involved in managing the entity.[11]

### *Considerations Specific to Public Sector Entities* (Ref: Para. 9-10)

Public sector auditors may have additional responsibilities to communicate defi- **A27** ciencies in internal control that the auditor has identified during the audit, in ways, at a level of detail and to parties not envisaged in this ISA (UK and Ireland). For example, significant deficiencies may have to be communicated to the legislature or other governing body. Law, regulation or other authority may also mandate that public sector auditors report deficiencies in internal control, irrespective of the significance of the potential effects of those deficiencies. Further, legislation may require public sector auditors to report on broader internal control-related matters than the deficiencies in internal control required to be communicated by this ISA (UK and Ireland), for example, controls related to compliance with legislative authorities, regulations, or provisions of contracts or grant agreements.

---

[11] *ISA (UK and Ireland) 260, paragraph 9.*

**Content of Written Communication of Significant Deficiencies in Internal Control** (Ref: Para. 11)

A28   In explaining the potential effects of the significant deficiencies, the auditor need not quantify those effects. The significant deficiencies may be grouped together for reporting purposes where it is appropriate to do so. The auditor may also include in the written communication suggestions for remedial action on the deficiencies, management's actual or proposed responses, and a statement as to whether or not the auditor has undertaken any steps to verify whether management's responses have been implemented.

A29   The auditor may consider it appropriate to include the following information as additional context for the communication:

- An indication that if the auditor had performed more extensive procedures on internal control, the auditor might have identified more deficiencies to be reported, or concluded that some of the reported deficiencies need not, in fact, have been reported.
- An indication that such communication has been provided for the purposes of those charged with governance, and that it may not be suitable for other purposes.

A30   Law or regulation may require the auditor or management to furnish a copy of the auditor's written communication on significant deficiencies to appropriate regulatory authorities. Where this is the case, the auditor's written communication may identify such regulatory authorities.

# Addendum

*This addendum is provided for information and does not form part of the proposed clarified ISA (UK and Ireland) 265.*

*Proposed ISA (UK and Ireland) 265 represents a new standard. It will supersede the requirement and related guidance currently in ISA (UK and Ireland) 260 relating to communication of material weaknesses in internal control identified during the audit. The APB is not proposing to add any supplementary requirements but is proposing a small amount of supplementary guidance to emphasise that, in the UK and Ireland, timely communication of significant deficiencies in writing to directors of listed entities can assist them apply the revised "Turnbull Guidance" on the requirements of the Combined Code relating to internal control and reporting to shareholders thereon (see paragraph A12-1).*

# Proposed Clarified International Standard on Auditing (UK and Ireland) 300

# Planning an audit of financial statements

*(Effective for audits of financial statements for periods ending on or after 15 December 2010)*

## Contents

---

International Standard on Auditing (UK and Ireland) (ISA (UK and Ireland)) 300, "Planning an Audit of Financial Statements" should be read in conjunction with ISA (UK and Ireland) 200, "Overall Objectives of the Independent Auditor and the Conduct of an Audit in Accordance with International Standards on Auditing (UK and Ireland)."

# Introduction

## Scope of this ISA (UK and Ireland)

This International Standard on Auditing (UK and Ireland) (ISA (UK and Ireland)) 1
deals with the auditor's responsibility to plan an audit of financial statements. This
ISA (UK and Ireland) is written in the context of recurring audits. Additional
considerations in an initial audit engagement are separately identified.

## The Role and Timing of Planning

Planning an audit involves establishing the overall audit strategy for the engagement 2
and developing an audit plan. Adequate planning benefits the audit of financial
statements in several ways, including the following: (Ref: Para. A1-A3)

- Helping the auditor to devote appropriate attention to important areas of the
audit.
- Helping the auditor identify and resolve potential problems on a timely basis.
- Helping the auditor properly organize and manage the audit engagement so that
it is performed in an effective and efficient manner.
- Assisting in the selection of engagement team members with appropriate levels
of capabilities and competence to respond to anticipated risks, and the proper
assignment of work to them.
- Facilitating the direction and supervision of engagement team members and the
review of their work.
- Assisting, where applicable, in coordination of work done by auditors of
components and experts.

## Effective Date

This ISA (UK and Ireland) is effective for audits of financial statements for periods 3
ending on or after 15 December 2010.

# Objective

The objective of the auditor is to plan the audit so that it will be performed in an 4
effective manner.

# Requirements

## Involvement of Key Engagement Team Members

The engagement partner and other key members of the engagement team shall be 5
involved in planning the audit, including planning and participating in the discussion
among engagement team members. (Ref: Para. A4)

## Preliminary Engagement Activities

The auditor shall undertake the following activities at the beginning of the current 6
audit engagement:

(a)  Performing procedures required by ISA (UK and Ireland) 220 regarding the continuance of the client relationship and the specific audit engagement;[1]

(b)  Evaluating compliance with relevant ethical requirements, including independence, in accordance with ISA (UK and Ireland) 220;[2] and

(c)  Establishing an understanding of the terms of the engagement, as required by ISA (UK and Ireland) 210.[3] (Ref: Para. A5-A7)

## Planning Activities

7    The auditor shall establish an overall audit strategy that sets the scope, timing and direction of the audit, and that guides the development of the audit plan.

8    In establishing the overall audit strategy, the auditor shall:

(a)  Identify the characteristics of the engagement that define its scope;

(b)  Ascertain the reporting objectives of the engagement to plan the timing of the audit and the nature of the communications required;

(c)  Consider the factors that, in the auditor's professional judgment, are significant in directing the engagement team's efforts;

(d)  Consider the results of preliminary engagement activities and, where applicable, whether knowledge gained on other engagements performed by the engagement partner for the entity is relevant; and

(e)  Ascertain the nature, timing and extent of resources necessary to perform the engagement. (Ref: Para. A8-A11)

9    The auditor shall develop an audit plan that shall include a description of:

(a)  The nature, timing and extent of planned risk assessment procedures, as determined under ISA (UK and Ireland) 315.[4]

(b)  The nature, timing and extent of planned further audit procedures at the assertion level, as determined under ISA (UK and Ireland) 330.[5]

(c)  Other planned audit procedures that are required to be carried out so that the engagement complies with ISAs (UK and Ireland). (Ref: Para. A12)

10    The auditor shall update and change the overall audit strategy and the audit plan as necessary during the course of the audit. (Ref: Para. A13)

11    The auditor shall plan the nature, timing and extent of direction and supervision of engagement team members and the review of their work. (Ref: Para. A14-A15)

## Documentation

12    The auditor shall include in the audit documentation:[6]

(a)  The overall audit strategy;

[1] *ISA (UK and Ireland) 220, "Quality Control for an Audit of Financial Statements," paragraphs 12-13.*

[2] *ISA (UK and Ireland) 220, paragraphs 9-11.*

[3] *ISA (UK and Ireland) 210, "Agreeing the Terms of Audit Engagements," paragraphs 9-13.*

[4] *ISA (UK and Ireland) 315, "Identifying and Assessing the Risks of Material Misstatement through Understanding the Entity and Its Environment."*

[5] *ISA (UK and Ireland) 330, "The Auditor's Responses to Assessed Risks."*

[6] *ISA (UK and Ireland) 230, "Audit Documentation," paragraphs 8-11, and paragraph A6.*

(b)  The audit plan; and
(c)  Any significant changes made during the audit engagement to the overall audit strategy or the audit plan, and the reasons for such changes. (Ref: Para. A16-A19)

## Additional Considerations in Initial Audit Engagements

The auditor shall undertake the following activities prior to starting an initial audit:  **13**

(a)  Performing procedures required by ISA (UK and Ireland) 220 regarding the acceptance of the client relationship and the specific audit engagement;[7] and
(b)  Communicating with the predecessor auditor, where there has been a change of auditors, in compliance with relevant ethical requirements. (Ref: Para. A20)

***

# Application and Other Explanatory Material

## The Role and Timing of Planning (Ref: Para. 2)

The nature and extent of planning activities will vary according to the size and  **A1** complexity of the entity, the key engagement team members' previous experience with the entity, and changes in circumstances that occur during the audit engagement.

Planning is not a discrete phase of an audit, but rather a continual and iterative  **A2** process that often begins shortly after (or in connection with) the completion of the previous audit and continues until the completion of the current audit engagement. Planning, however, includes consideration of the timing of certain activities and audit procedures that need to be completed prior to the performance of further audit procedures. For example, planning includes the need to consider, prior to the auditor's identification and assessment of the risks of material misstatement, such matters as:

●  The analytical procedures to be applied as risk assessment procedures.
●  Obtaining a general understanding of the legal and regulatory framework applicable to the entity and how the entity is complying with that framework.
●  The determination of materiality.
●  The involvement of experts.
●  The performance of other risk assessment procedures.

The auditor may decide to discuss elements of planning with the entity's manage-  **A3** ment to facilitate the conduct and management of the audit engagement (for example, to coordinate some of the planned audit procedures with the work of the entity's personnel). Although these discussions often occur, the overall audit strategy and the audit plan remain the auditor's responsibility. When discussing matters included in the overall audit strategy or audit plan, care is required in order not to compromise the effectiveness of the audit. For example, discussing the nature and timing of detailed audit procedures with management may compromise the effectiveness of the audit by making the audit procedures too predictable.

---

[7] *ISA (UK and Ireland) 220, paragraphs 12-13.*

## Involvement of Key Engagement Team Members (Ref: Para. 5)

A4   The involvement of the engagement partner and other key members of the engagement team in planning the audit draws on their experience and insight, thereby enhancing the effectiveness and efficiency of the planning process.[8]

## Preliminary Engagement Activities (Ref: Para. 6)

A5   Performing the preliminary engagement activities specified in paragraph 5 at the beginning of the current audit engagement assists the auditor in identifying and evaluating events or circumstances that may adversely affect the auditor's ability to plan and perform the audit engagement.

A6   Performing these preliminary engagement activities enables the auditor to plan an audit engagement for which, for example:

- The auditor maintains the necessary independence and ability to perform the engagement.
- There are no issues with management[8a] integrity that may affect the auditor's willingness to continue the engagement.
- There is no misunderstanding with the client as to the terms of the engagement.

A7   The auditor's consideration of client continuance and relevant ethical requirements, including independence, occurs throughout the audit engagement as conditions and changes in circumstances occur. Performing initial procedures on both client continuance and evaluation of relevant ethical requirements (including independence) at the beginning of the current audit engagement means that they are completed prior to the performance of other significant activities for the current audit engagement. For continuing audit engagements, such initial procedures often occur shortly after (or in connection with) the completion of the previous audit.

## Planning Activities

### *The Overall Audit Strategy* (Ref: Para. 7-8)

A8   The process of establishing the overall audit strategy assists the auditor to determine, subject to the completion of the auditor's risk assessment procedures, such matters as:

- The resources to deploy for specific audit areas, such as the use of appropriately experienced team members for high risk areas or the involvement of experts on complex matters;
- The amount of resources to allocate to specific audit areas, such as the number of team members assigned to observe the inventory count at material locations, the extent of review of other auditors' work in the case of group audits, or the audit budget in hours to allocate to high risk areas;
- When these resources are to be deployed, such as whether at an interim audit stage or at key cut-off dates; and

---

[8] *ISA (UK and Ireland) 315, paragraph 10, establishes requirements and provides guidance on the engagement team's discussion of the susceptibility of the entity to material misstatements of the financial statements. ISA (UK and Ireland) 240, "The Auditor's Responsibilities Relating to Fraud in an Audit of Financial Statements," paragraph 15, provides guidance on the emphasis given during this discussion to the susceptibility of the entity's financial statements to material misstatement due to fraud.*

[8a] *In the UK and Ireland, the auditor is also concerned to establish that there are no issues with the integrity of those charged with governance that may affect the auditor's willingness to continue the engagement.*

- How such resources are managed, directed and supervised, such as when team briefing and debriefing meetings are expected to be held, how engagement partner and manager reviews are expected to take place (for example, on-site or off-site), and whether to complete engagement quality control reviews.

The Appendix lists examples of considerations in establishing the overall audit strategy. **A9**

Once the overall audit strategy has been established, an audit plan can be developed to address the various matters identified in the overall audit strategy, taking into account the need to achieve the audit objectives through the efficient use of the auditor's resources. The establishment of the overall audit strategy and the detailed audit plan are not necessarily discrete or sequential processes, but are closely inter-related since changes in one may result in consequential changes to the other. **A10**

*Considerations Specific to Smaller Entities*

In audits of small entities, the entire audit may be conducted by a very small audit team. Many audits of small entities involve the engagement partner (who may be a sole practitioner) working with one engagement team member (or without any engagement team members). With a smaller team, co-ordination of, and communication between, team members are easier. Establishing the overall audit strategy for the audit of a small entity need not be a complex or time-consuming exercise; it varies according to the size of the entity, the complexity of the audit, and the size of the engagement team. For example, a brief memorandum prepared at the completion of the previous audit, based on a review of the working papers and highlighting issues identified in the audit just completed, updated in the current period based on discussions with the owner-manager, can serve as the documented audit strategy for the current audit engagement if it covers the matters noted in paragraph 8. **A11**

*The Audit Plan* (Ref: Para. 9)

The audit plan is more detailed than the overall audit strategy in that it includes the nature, timing and extent of audit procedures to be performed by engagement team members. Planning for these audit procedures takes place over the course of the audit as the audit plan for the engagement develops. For example, planning of the auditor's risk assessment procedures occurs early in the audit process. However, planning the nature, timing and extent of specific further audit procedures depends on the outcome of those risk assessment procedures. In addition, the auditor may begin the execution of further audit procedures for some classes of transactions, account balances and disclosures before planning all remaining further audit procedures. **A12**

*Changes to Planning Decisions during the Course of the Audit* (Ref: Para. 10)

As a result of unexpected events, changes in conditions, or the audit evidence obtained from the results of audit procedures, the auditor may need to modify the overall audit strategy and audit plan and thereby the resulting planned nature, timing and extent of further audit procedures, based on the revised consideration of assessed risks. This may be the case when information comes to the auditor's attention that differs significantly from the information available when the auditor planned the audit procedures. For example, audit evidence obtained through the performance of substantive procedures may contradict the audit evidence obtained through tests of controls. **A13**

**Direction, Supervision and Review** (Ref: Para. 11)

A14   The nature, timing and extent of the direction and supervision of engagement team members and review of their work vary depending on many factors, including:

  • The size and complexity of the entity.
  • The area of the audit.
  • The assessed risks of material misstatement (for example, an increase in the assessed risk of material misstatement for a given area of the audit ordinarily requires a corresponding increase in the extent and timeliness of direction and supervision of engagement team members, and a more detailed review of their work).
  • The capabilities and competence of the individual team members performing the audit work.

ISA (UK and Ireland) 220 contains further guidance on the direction, supervision and review of audit work.[9]

*Considerations Specific to Smaller Entities*

A15   If an audit is carried out entirely by the engagement partner, questions of direction and supervision of engagement team members and review of their work do not arise. In such cases, the engagement partner, having personally conducted all aspects of the work, will be aware of all material issues. Forming an objective view on the appropriateness of the judgments made in the course of the audit can present practical problems when the same individual also performs the entire audit. If particularly complex or unusual issues are involved, and the audit is performed by a sole practitioner, it may be desirable to consult with other suitably-experienced auditors or the auditor's professional body.

**Documentation** (Ref: Para. 12)

A16   The documentation of the overall audit strategy is a record of the key decisions considered necessary to properly plan the audit and to communicate significant matters to the engagement team. For example, the auditor may summarize the overall audit strategy in the form of a memorandum that contains key decisions regarding the overall scope, timing and conduct of the audit.

A17   The documentation of the audit plan is a record of the planned nature, timing and extent of risk assessment procedures and further audit procedures at the assertion level in response to the assessed risks. It also serves as a record of the proper planning of the audit procedures that can be reviewed and approved prior to their performance. The auditor may use standard audit programs or audit completion checklists, tailored as needed to reflect the particular engagement circumstances.

A18   A record of the significant changes to the overall audit strategy and the audit plan, and resulting changes to the planned nature, timing and extent of audit procedures, explains why the significant changes were made, and the overall strategy and audit plan finally adopted for the audit. It also reflects the appropriate response to the significant changes occurring during the audit.

[9] *ISA (UK and Ireland) 220, paragraphs 15-17.*

*Considerations Specific to Smaller Entities*

As discussed in paragraph A11, a suitable, brief memorandum may serve as the documented strategy for the audit of a smaller entity. For the audit plan, standard audit programs or checklists (see paragraph A17) drawn up on the assumption of few relevant control activities, as is likely to be the case in a smaller entity, may be used provided that they are tailored to the circumstances of the engagement, including the auditor's risk assessments.

**A19**

## Additional Considerations in Initial Audit Engagements (Ref: Para. 13)

The purpose and objective of planning the audit are the same whether the audit is an initial or recurring engagement. However, for an initial audit, the auditor may need to expand the planning activities because the auditor does not ordinarily have the previous experience with the entity that is considered when planning recurring engagements. For an initial audit engagement, additional matters the auditor may consider in establishing the overall audit strategy and audit plan include the following:

**A20**

- Unless prohibited by law or regulation, arrangements to be made with the predecessor auditor, for example, to review the predecessor auditor's working papers.
- Any major issues (including the application of accounting principles or of auditing and reporting standards) discussed with management in connection with the initial selection as auditor, the communication of these matters to those charged with governance and how these matters affect the overall audit strategy and audit plan.
- The audit procedures necessary to obtain sufficient appropriate audit evidence regarding opening balances.[10]
- Other procedures required by the firm's system of quality control for initial audit engagements (for example, the firm's system of quality control may require the involvement of another partner or senior individual to review the overall audit strategy prior to commencing significant audit procedures or to review reports prior to their issuance).

[10] *ISA (UK and Ireland) 510, "Initial Audit Engagements—Opening Balances."*

**Appendix** (Ref: Para. 7-8, A8-A11)

# Considerations in Establishing the Overall Audit Strategy

This appendix provides examples of matters the auditor may consider in establishing the overall audit strategy. Many of these matters will also influence the auditor's detailed audit plan. The examples provided cover a broad range of matters applicable to many engagements. While some of the matters referred to below may be required by other ISAs (UK and Ireland), not all matters are relevant to every audit engagement and the list is not necessarily complete.

## Characteristics of the Engagement

- The financial reporting framework on which the financial information to be audited has been prepared, including any need for reconciliations to another financial reporting framework.
- Industry-specific reporting requirements such as reports mandated by industry regulators.
- The expected audit coverage, including the number and locations of components to be included.
- The nature of the control relationships between a parent and its components that determine how the group is to be consolidated.
- The extent to which components are audited by other auditors.
- The nature of the business segments to be audited, including the need for specialized knowledge.
- The reporting currency to be used, including any need for currency translation for the financial information audited.
- The need for a statutory audit of standalone financial statements in addition to an audit for consolidation purposes.
- The availability of the work of internal auditors and the extent of the auditor's potential reliance on such work.
- The entity's use of service organizations and how the auditor may obtain evidence concerning the design or operation of controls performed by them.
- The expected use of audit evidence obtained in previous audits, for example, audit evidence related to risk assessment procedures and tests of controls.
- The effect of information technology on the audit procedures, including the availability of data and the expected use of computer-assisted audit techniques.
- The coordination of the expected coverage and timing of the audit work with any reviews of interim financial information and the effect on the audit of the information obtained during such reviews.
- The availability of client personnel and data.

## Reporting Objectives, Timing of the Audit, and Nature of Communications

- The entity's timetable for reporting, such as at interim and final stages.
- The organization of meetings with management and those charged with governance to discuss the nature, timing and extent of the audit work.
- The discussion with management and those charged with governance regarding the expected type and timing of reports to be issued and other communications, both written and oral, including the auditor's report, management letters and communications to those charged with governance.
- The discussion with management regarding the expected communications on the status of audit work throughout the engagement.

- Communication with auditors of components regarding the expected types and timing of reports to be issued and other communications in connection with the audit of components.
- The expected nature and timing of communications among engagement team members, including the nature and timing of team meetings and timing of the review of work performed.
- Whether there are any other expected communications with third parties, including any statutory or contractual reporting responsibilities arising from the audit.

## Significant Factors, Preliminary Engagement Activities, and Knowledge Gained on Other Engagements

- The determination of materiality in accordance with ISA (UK and Ireland) 320[11] and, where applicable:
  - The determination of materiality for components and communication thereof to component auditors in accordance with ISA (UK and Ireland) 600.[12]
  - The preliminary identification of significant components and material classes of transactions, account balances and disclosures.
- Preliminary identification of areas where there may be a higher risk of material misstatement.
- The impact of the assessed risk of material misstatement at the overall financial statement level on direction, supervision and review.
- The manner in which the auditor emphasizes to engagement team members the need to maintain a questioning mind and to exercise professional skepticism in gathering and evaluating audit evidence.
- Results of previous audits that involved evaluating the operating effectiveness of internal control, including the nature of identified deficiencies and action taken to address them.
- The discussion of matters that may affect the audit with firm personnel responsible for performing other services to the entity.
- Evidence of management's[12a] commitment to the design, implementation and maintenance of sound internal control, including evidence of appropriate documentation of such internal control.
- Volume of transactions, which may determine whether it is more efficient for the auditor to rely on internal control.
- Importance attached to internal control throughout the entity to the successful operation of the business.
- Significant business developments affecting the entity, including changes in information technology and business processes, changes in key management, and acquisitions, mergers and divestments.
- Significant industry developments such as changes in industry regulations and new reporting requirements.
- Significant changes in the financial reporting framework, such as changes in accounting standards.
- Other significant relevant developments, such as changes in the legal environment affecting the entity.

[11] *ISA (UK and Ireland) 320, "Materiality in Planning and Performing an Audit."*

[12] *ISA (UK and Ireland) 600, "Special Considerations—Audits of Group Financial Statements (Including the Work of Component Auditors), paragraphs 21-23 and 40(c).*

[12a] *In the UK and Ireland, the auditor also considers evidence of the commitment of those charged with governance to the design and operation of sound internal control.*

## Nature, Timing and Extent of Resources

- The selection of the engagement team (including, where necessary, the engagement quality control reviewer) and the assignment of audit work to the team members, including the assignment of appropriately experienced team members to areas where there may be higher risks of material misstatement.
- Engagement budgeting, including considering the appropriate amount of time to set aside for areas where there may be higher risks of material misstatement.

# Addendum

*This addendum provides a summary of APB's rationale for retaining or excluding in the proposed clarified ISA (UK and Ireland) the supplementary requirements in the existing ISA (UK and Ireland). It also sets out the supplementary guidance material in the existing ISA (UK and Ireland) that APB considers is not necessary to retain in light of the improvements in the underlying Clarity ISAs issued by the IAASB as part of the Clarity Project. It is provided for information and does not form part of the proposed clarified ISA (UK and Ireland).*

*The Consultation Paper published with the exposure drafts explains the general approach used by the APB for determining whether current supplementary material should be proposed to be retained.*

### Analysis of proposed treatment of current APB supplementary material in current ISA (UK and Ireland) 300

<u>Requirements</u>

There are no supplementary requirements in the current ISA (UK and Ireland) 300.

<u>Guidance</u>

The following guidance in current ISA (UK and Ireland) 300 has not been carried forward to the proposed clarified standard.

| Current paragraph reference (*Italic text is from IAASB for context*) |
| --- |
| 1-1. – 1-4. [Description of management and those charged with governance.] |
| 27   ...*Discussions with those charged with governance ordinarily include the overall audit strategy and timing of the audit, including any limitations thereon, or any additional requirements[3]. ...* |
| [3] ISA (UK and Ireland) 260, "Communication of Audit Matters With Those Charged With Governance," requires the auditor to communicate to those charged with governance an outline of the nature and scope, including, where relevant, any limitations thereon, of the work the auditor proposes to undertake. Examples are given of planning information that might be communicated. |

# Proposed Clarified International Standard on Auditing (UK and Ireland) 315

## Identifying and assessing the risks of material misstatement through understanding the entity and its environment

*(Effective for audits of financial statements for periods ending on or after 15 December 2010)*

## Contents

International Standard on Auditing (UK and Ireland) (ISA (UK and Ireland)) 315, "Identifying and Assessing the Risks of Material Misstatement through Understanding the Entity and Its Environment" should be read in conjunction with ISA (UK and Ireland) 200, "Overall Objectives of the Independent Auditor and the Conduct of an Audit in Accordance with International Standards on Auditing (UK and Ireland)."

# Introduction

## Scope of this ISA (UK and Ireland)

This International Standard on Auditing (UK and Ireland) (ISA (UK and Ireland))   **1**
deals with the auditor's responsibility to identify and assess the risks of material
misstatement in the financial statements, through understanding the entity and its
environment, including the entity's internal control.

## Effective Date

2. This ISA (UK and Ireland) is effective for audits of financial statements for periods ending on
or after 15 December 2010.

# Objective

The objective of the auditor is to identify and assess the risks of material misstate-   **3**
ment, whether due to fraud or error, at the financial statement and assertion levels,
through understanding the entity and its environment, including the entity's internal
control, thereby providing a basis for designing and implementing responses to the
assessed risks of material misstatement.

## Definitions

For purposes of the ISAs (UK and Ireland), the following terms have the meanings   **4**
attributed below:

(a) Assertions – Representations by management[1a], explicit or otherwise, that are
    embodied in the financial statements, as used by the auditor to consider the
    different types of potential misstatements that may occur.
(b) Business risk – A risk resulting from significant conditions, events, circum-
    stances, actions or inactions that could adversely affect an entity's ability to
    achieve its objectives and execute its strategies, or from the setting of inap-
    propriate objectives and strategies.
(c) Internal control – The process designed, implemented and maintained by those
    charged with governance, management and other personnel to provide rea-
    sonable assurance about the achievement of an entity's objectives with regard to
    reliability of financial reporting, effectiveness and efficiency of operations, and
    compliance with applicable laws and regulations. The term "controls" refers to
    any aspects of one or more of the components of internal control.
(d) Risk assessment procedures – The audit procedures performed to obtain an
    understanding of the entity and its environment, including the entity's internal
    control, to identify and assess the risks of material misstatement, whether due to
    fraud or error, at the financial statement and assertion levels.
(e) Significant risk – An identified and assessed risk of material misstatement that,
    in the auditor's judgment, requires special audit consideration.

---

[1a] *In the UK and Ireland, those charged with governance are responsible for preparing the financial statements.*

# Requirements

## Risk Assessment Procedures and Related Activities

5    The auditor shall perform risk assessment procedures to provide a basis for the identification and assessment of risks of material misstatement at the financial statement and assertion levels. Risk assessment procedures by themselves, however, do not provide sufficient appropriate audit evidence on which to base the audit opinion. (Ref: Para. A1-A5)

6    The risk assessment procedures shall include the following:

   (a) Inquiries of management, and of others within the entity who in the auditor's judgment may have information that is likely to assist in identifying risks of material misstatement due to fraud or error. (Ref: Para. A6)
   (b) Analytical procedures. (Ref: Para. A7-A10)
   (c) Observation and inspection. (Ref: Para. A11)

7    The auditor shall consider whether information obtained from the auditor's client acceptance or continuance process is relevant to identifying risks of material misstatement.

8    If the engagement partner has performed other engagements for the entity, the engagement partner shall consider whether information obtained is relevant to identifying risks of material misstatement.

9    Where the auditor intends to use information obtained from the auditor's previous experience with the entity and from audit procedures performed in previous audits, the auditor shall determine whether changes have occurred since the previous audit that may affect its relevance to the current audit. (Ref: Para. A12-A13)

10    The engagement partner and other key engagement team members shall discuss the susceptibility of the entity's financial statements to material misstatement, and the application of the applicable financial reporting framework to the entity's facts and circumstances. The engagement partner shall determine which matters are to be communicated to engagement team members not involved in the discussion. (Ref: Para. A14-A16)

## The Required Understanding of the Entity and Its Environment, Including the Entity's Internal Control

### *The Entity and Its Environment*

11    The auditor shall obtain an understanding of the following:

   (a) Relevant industry, regulatory, and other external factors including the applicable financial reporting framework. (Ref: Para. A17-A22)
   (b) The nature of the entity, including:
      (i) its operations;
      (ii) its ownership and governance structures;
      (iii) the types of investments that the entity is making and plans to make, including investments in special-purpose entities; and
      (iv) the way that the entity is structured and how it is financed
      to enable the auditor to understand the classes of transactions, account balances, and disclosures to be expected in the financial statements. (Ref: Para. A23-A27)

(c) The entity's selection and application of accounting policies, including the reasons for changes thereto. The auditor shall evaluate whether the entity's accounting policies are appropriate for its business and consistent with the applicable financial reporting framework and accounting policies used in the relevant industry. (Ref: Para. A28)

(d) The entity's objectives and strategies, and those related business risks that may result in risks of material misstatement. (Ref: Para. A29-A35)

(e) The measurement and review of the entity's financial performance. (Ref: Para. A36-A41)

### The Entity's Internal Control

The auditor shall obtain an understanding of internal control relevant to the audit. **12** Although most controls relevant to the audit are likely to relate to financial reporting, not all controls that relate to financial reporting are relevant to the audit. It is a matter of the auditor's professional judgment whether a control, individually or in combination with others, is relevant to the audit. (Ref: Para. A42-A65)

### Nature and Extent of the Understanding of Relevant Controls

When obtaining an understanding of controls that are relevant to the audit, the **13** auditor shall evaluate the design of those controls and determine whether they have been implemented, by performing procedures in addition to inquiry of the entity's personnel. (Ref: Para. A66-A68)

### Components of Internal Control

### Control environment

The auditor shall obtain an understanding of the control environment. As part of **14** obtaining this understanding, the auditor shall evaluate whether:

(a) Management, with the oversight of those charged with governance, has created and maintained a culture of honesty and ethical behavior; and

(b) The strengths in the control environment elements collectively provide an appropriate foundation for the other components of internal control, and whether those other components are not undermined by deficiencies in the control environment. (Ref: Para. A69-A78)

### The entity's risk assessment process

The auditor shall obtain an understanding of whether the entity has a process for: **15**

(a) Identifying business risks relevant to financial reporting objectives;
(b) Estimating the significance of the risks;
(c) Assessing the likelihood of their occurrence; and
(d) Deciding about actions to address those risks. (Ref: Para. A79)

If the entity has established such a process (referred to hereafter as the "entity's risk **16** assessment process"), the auditor shall obtain an understanding of it, and the results thereof. If the auditor identifies risks of material misstatement that management failed to identify, the auditor shall evaluate whether there was an underlying risk of a kind that the auditor expects would have been identified by the entity's risk assessment process. If there is such a risk, the auditor shall obtain an understanding of why that process failed to identify it, and evaluate whether the process is appropriate to its circumstances or determine if there is a significant deficiency in internal control with regard to the entity's risk assessment process.

**17**   If the entity has not established such a process or has an ad hoc process, the auditor shall discuss with management whether business risks relevant to financial reporting objectives have been identified and how they have been addressed. The auditor shall evaluate whether the absence of a documented risk assessment process is appropriate in the circumstances, or determine whether it represents a significant deficiency in internal control. (Ref: Para. A80)

The information system, including the related business processes, relevant to financial reporting, and communication

**18**   The auditor shall obtain an understanding of the information system, including the related business processes, relevant to financial reporting, including the following areas:

   (a)   The classes of transactions in the entity's operations that are significant to the financial statements;

   (b)   The procedures, within both information technology (IT) and manual systems, by which those transactions are initiated, recorded, processed, corrected as necessary, transferred to the general ledger and reported in the financial statements;

   (c)   The related accounting records, supporting information and specific accounts in the financial statements that are used to initiate, record, process and report transactions; this includes the correction of incorrect information and how information is transferred to the general ledger. The records may be in either manual or electronic form;

   (d)   How the information system captures events and conditions, other than transactions, that are significant to the financial statements;

   (e)   The financial reporting process used to prepare the entity's financial statements, including significant accounting estimates and disclosures; and

   (f)   Controls surrounding journal entries, including non-standard journal entries used to record non-recurring, unusual transactions or adjustments. (Ref: Para. A81-A85)

**19**   The auditor shall obtain an understanding of how the entity communicates financial reporting roles and responsibilities and significant matters relating to financial reporting, including:

   (a)   Communications between management and those charged with governance; and

   (b)   External communications, such as those with regulatory authorities. (Ref: Para. A86-A87)

*Control activities relevant to the audit*

**20**   The auditor shall obtain an understanding of control activities relevant to the audit, being those the auditor judges it necessary to understand in order to assess the risks of material misstatement at the assertion level and design further audit procedures responsive to assessed risks. An audit does not require an understanding of all the control activities related to each significant class of transactions, account balance, and disclosure in the financial statements or to every assertion relevant to them. (Ref: Para. A88-A94)

In understanding the entity's control activities, the auditor shall obtain an under-   **21**
standing of how the entity has responded to risks arising from IT. (Ref: Para. A95-
A97)

*Monitoring of controls*

The auditor shall obtain an understanding of the major activities that the entity uses   **22**
to monitor internal control over financial reporting, including those related to those
control activities relevant to the audit, and how the entity initiates remedial actions
to deficiencies in its controls. (Ref: Para. A98-A100)

If the entity has an internal audit function,[1] the auditor shall obtain an under-   **23**
standing of the following in order to determine whether the internal audit function is
likely to be relevant to the audit:

(a)   The nature of the internal audit function's responsibilities and how the internal
      audit function fits in the entity's organizational structure; and
(b)   The activities performed, or to be performed, by the internal audit function.
      (Ref: Para. A101-A103)

The auditor shall obtain an understanding of the sources of the information used in   **24**
the entity's monitoring activities, and the basis upon which management considers
the information to be sufficiently reliable for the purpose. (Ref: Para. A104)

## Identifying and Assessing the Risks of Material Misstatement

The auditor shall identify and assess the risks of material misstatement at:   **25**

(a)   the financial statement level; and (Ref: Para. A105-A108)
(b)   the assertion level for classes of transactions, account balances, and disclosures
      (Ref: Para. A109-A113)

to provide a basis for designing and performing further audit procedures.

For this purpose, the auditor shall:   **26**

(a)   Identify risks throughout the process of obtaining an understanding of the
      entity and its environment, including relevant controls that relate to the risks,
      and by considering the classes of transactions, account balances, and disclosures
      in the financial statements; (Ref: Para. A114-A115)
(b)   Assess the identified risks, and evaluate whether they relate more pervasively to
      the financial statements as a whole and potentially affect many assertions;
(c)   Relate the identified risks to what can go wrong at the assertion level, taking
      account of relevant controls that the auditor intends to test; and (Ref: Para.
      A116-A118)
(d)   Consider the likelihood of misstatement, including the possibility of multiple
      misstatements, and whether the potential misstatement is of a magnitude that
      could result in a material misstatement.

---

[1] *The term "internal audit function" is defined in ISA (UK and Ireland) 610, "Using the Work of Internal
Auditors," paragraph 7(a), as: "An appraisal activity established or provided as a service to the entity. Its
functions include, amongst other things, examining, evaluating and monitoring the adequacy and effectiveness of
internal control."*

### Risks That Require Special Audit Consideration

27    As part of the risk assessment as described in paragraph 25, the auditor shall determine whether any of the risks identified are, in the auditor's judgment, a significant risk. In exercising this judgment, the auditor shall exclude the effects of identified controls related to the risk.

28    In exercising judgment as to which risks are significant risks, the auditor shall consider at least the following:

(a)    Whether the risk is a risk of fraud;

(b)    Whether the risk is related to recent significant economic, accounting or other developments and, therefore, requires specific attention;

(c)    The complexity of transactions;

(d)    Whether the risk involves significant transactions with related parties;

(e)    The degree of subjectivity in the measurement of financial information related to the risk, especially those measurements involving a wide range of measurement uncertainty; and

(f)    Whether the risk involves significant transactions that are outside the normal course of business for the entity, or that otherwise appear to be unusual. (Ref: Para. A119-A123)

29    If the auditor has determined that a significant risk exists, the auditor shall obtain an understanding of the entity's controls, including control activities, relevant to that risk. (Ref: Para. A124-A126)

### Risks for Which Substantive Procedures Alone Do Not Provide Sufficient Appropriate Audit Evidence

30    In respect of some risks, the auditor may judge that it is not possible or practicable to obtain sufficient appropriate audit evidence only from substantive procedures. Such risks may relate to the inaccurate or incomplete recording of routine and significant classes of transactions or account balances, the characteristics of which often permit highly automated processing with little or no manual intervention. In such cases, the entity's controls over such risks are relevant to the audit and the auditor shall obtain an understanding of them. (Ref: Para. A127-A129)

### Revision of Risk Assessment

31    The auditor's assessment of the risks of material misstatement at the assertion level may change during the course of the audit as additional audit evidence is obtained. In circumstances where the auditor obtains audit evidence from performing further audit procedures, or if new information is obtained, either of which is inconsistent with the audit evidence on which the auditor originally based the assessment, the auditor shall revise the assessment and modify the further planned audit procedures accordingly. (Ref: Para. A130)

## Documentation

32    The auditor shall include in the audit documentation:[2]

(a)    The discussion among the engagement team where required by paragraph 10, and the significant decisions reached;

---

[2] *ISA (UK and Ireland) 230, "Audit Documentation," paragraphs 8-11, and paragraph A6.*

(b) Key elements of the understanding obtained regarding each of the aspects of the entity and its environment specified in paragraph 11 and of each of the internal control components specified in paragraphs 14-24; the sources of information from which the understanding was obtained; and the risk assessment procedures performed;

(c) The identified and assessed risks of material misstatement at the financial statement level and at the assertion level as required by paragraph 25; and

(d) The risks identified, and related controls about which the auditor has obtained an understanding, as a result of the requirements in paragraphs 27-30. (Ref: Para. A131-A134)

\*\*\*

# Application and Other Explanatory Material

## Risk Assessment Procedures and Related Activities (Ref: Para. 5)

Obtaining an understanding of the entity and its environment, including the entity's **A1** internal control (referred to hereafter as an "understanding of the entity"), is a continuous, dynamic process of gathering, updating and analyzing information throughout the audit. The understanding establishes a frame of reference within which the auditor plans the audit and exercises professional judgment throughout the audit, for example, when:

- Assessing risks of material misstatement of the financial statements;
- Determining materiality in accordance with ISA (UK and Ireland) 320;[3]
- Considering the appropriateness of the selection and application of accounting policies, and the adequacy of financial statement disclosures;
- Identifying areas where special audit consideration may be necessary, for example, related party transactions, the appropriateness of management's use of the going concern assumption, or considering the business purpose of transactions;
- Developing expectations for use when performing analytical procedures;
- Responding to the assessed risks of material misstatement, including designing and performing further audit procedures to obtain sufficient appropriate audit evidence; and
- Evaluating the sufficiency and appropriateness of audit evidence obtained, such as the appropriateness of assumptions and of management's[3a] oral and written representations.

Information obtained by performing risk assessment procedures and related activ- **A2** ities may be used by the auditor as audit evidence to support assessments of the risks of material misstatement. In addition, the auditor may obtain audit evidence about classes of transactions, account balances, or disclosures and related assertions and about the operating effectiveness of controls, even though such procedures were not specifically planned as substantive procedures or as tests of controls. The auditor also may choose to perform substantive procedures or tests of controls concurrently with risk assessment procedures because it is efficient to do so.

---

[3] *ISA (UK and Ireland) 320, "Materiality in Planning and Performing an Audit."*

[3a] *In the UK and Ireland, as explained in paragraph A2-1 of ISA (UK and Ireland) 580, "Written Representations," it is appropriate for written representations that are critical to obtaining sufficient appropriate audit evidence to be provided by those charged with governance, rather than other levels of the entity's management.*

**A3**   The auditor uses professional judgment to determine the extent of the understanding required. The auditor's primary consideration is whether the understanding that has been obtained is sufficient to meet the objective stated in this ISA (UK and Ireland). The depth of the overall understanding that is required by the auditor is less than that possessed by management in managing the entity.

**A4**   The risks to be assessed include both those due to error and those due to fraud, and both are covered by this ISA (UK and Ireland). However, the significance of fraud is such that further requirements and guidance are included in ISA (UK and Ireland) 240 in relation to risk assessment procedures and related activities to obtain information that is used to identify the risks of material misstatement due to fraud.[4]

**A5**   Although the auditor is required to perform all the risk assessment procedures described in paragraph 6 in the course of obtaining the required understanding of the entity (see paragraphs 11-24), the auditor is not required to perform all of them for each aspect of that understanding. Other procedures may be performed where the information to be obtained therefrom may be helpful in identifying risks of material misstatement. Examples of such procedures include:

- Reviewing information obtained from external sources such as trade and economic journals; reports by analysts, banks, or rating agencies; or regulatory or financial publications.
- Making inquiries of the entity's external legal counsel or of valuation experts that the entity has used.

*Inquiries of Management and Others within the Entity* (Ref: Para. 6(a))

**A6**   Much of the information obtained by the auditor's inquiries is obtained from management and those responsible for financial reporting. However, the auditor may also obtain information, or a different perspective in identifying risks of material misstatement, through inquiries of others within the entity and other employees with different levels of authority. For example:

- Inquiries directed towards those charged with governance may help the auditor understand the environment in which the financial statements are prepared.
- Inquiries directed toward internal audit personnel may provide information about internal audit procedures performed during the year relating to the design and effectiveness of the entity's internal control and whether management has satisfactorily responded to findings from those procedures.
- Inquiries of employees involved in initiating, processing or recording complex or unusual transactions may help the auditor to evaluate the appropriateness of the selection and application of certain accounting policies.
- Inquiries directed toward in-house legal counsel may provide information about such matters as litigation, compliance with laws and regulations, knowledge of fraud or suspected fraud affecting the entity, warranties, post-sales obligations, arrangements (such as joint ventures) with business partners and the meaning of contract terms.
- Inquiries directed towards marketing or sales personnel may provide information about changes in the entity's marketing strategies, sales trends, or contractual arrangements with its customers.

---

[4] *ISA (UK and Ireland) 240, "The Auditor's Responsibilities Relating to Fraud in an Audit of Financial Statements," paragraphs 12-24.*

### Analytical Procedures (Ref: Para. 6(b))

Analytical procedures performed as risk assessment procedures may identify aspects **A7** of the entity of which the auditor was unaware and may assist in assessing the risks of material misstatement in order to provide a basis for designing and implementing responses to the assessed risks. Analytical procedures performed as risk assessment procedures may include both financial and non-financial information, for example, the relationship between sales and square footage of selling space or volume of goods sold.

Analytical procedures may help identify the existence of unusual transactions or **A8** events, and amounts, ratios, and trends that might indicate matters that have audit implications. Unusual or unexpected relationships that are identified may assist the auditor in identifying risks of material misstatement, especially risks of material misstatement due to fraud.

However, when such analytical procedures use data aggregated at a high level (which **A9** may be the situation with analytical procedures performed as risk assessment procedures), the results of those analytical procedures only provide a broad initial indication about whether a material misstatement may exist. Accordingly, in such cases, consideration of other information that has been gathered when identifying the risks of material misstatement together with the results of such analytical procedures may assist the auditor in understanding and evaluating the results of the analytical procedures.

#### Considerations Specific to Smaller Entities

Some smaller entities may not have interim or monthly financial information that **A10** can be used for purposes of analytical procedures. In these circumstances, although the auditor may be able to perform limited analytical procedures for purposes of planning the audit or obtain some information through inquiry, the auditor may need to plan to perform analytical procedures to identify and assess the risks of material misstatement when an early draft of the entity's financial statements is available.

### Observation and Inspection (Ref: Para. 6(c))

Observation and inspection may support inquiries of management and others, and **A11** may also provide information about the entity and its environment. Examples of such audit procedures include observation or inspection of the following:

* The entity's operations.
* Documents (such as business plans and strategies), records, and internal control manuals.
* Reports prepared by management (such as quarterly management reports and interim financial statements) and those charged with governance (such as minutes of board of directors' meetings).
* The entity's premises and plant facilities.

### Information Obtained in Prior Periods (Ref: Para. 9)

The auditor's previous experience with the entity and audit procedures performed in **A12** previous audits may provide the auditor with information about such matters as:

* Past misstatements and whether they were corrected on a timely basis.

- The nature of the entity and its environment, and the entity's internal control (including deficiencies in internal control).
- Significant changes that the entity or its operations may have undergone since the prior financial period, which may assist the auditor in gaining a sufficient understanding of the entity to identify and assess risks of material misstatement.

**A13**  The auditor is required to determine whether information obtained in prior periods remains relevant, if the auditor intends to use that information for the purposes of the current audit. This is because changes in the control environment, for example, may affect the relevance of information obtained in the prior year. To determine whether changes have occurred that may affect the relevance of such information, the auditor may make inquiries and perform other appropriate audit procedures, such as walk-throughs of relevant systems.

### *Discussion among the Engagement Team* (Ref: Para. 10)

**A14**  The discussion among the engagement team about the susceptibility of the entity's financial statements to material misstatement:

- Provides an opportunity for more experienced engagement team members, including the engagement partner, to share their insights based on their knowledge of the entity.
- Allows the engagement team members to exchange information about the business risks to which the entity is subject and about how and where the financial statements might be susceptible to material misstatement due to fraud or error.
- Assists the engagement team members to gain a better understanding of the potential for material misstatement of the financial statements in the specific areas assigned to them, and to understand how the results of the audit procedures that they perform may affect other aspects of the audit including the decisions about the nature, timing, and extent of further audit procedures.
- Provides a basis upon which engagement team members communicate and share new information obtained throughout the audit that may affect the assessment of risks of material misstatement or the audit procedures performed to address these risks.

ISA (UK and Ireland) 240 provides further requirements and guidance in relation to the discussion among the engagement team about the risks of fraud.[5]

**A15**  It is not always necessary or practical for the discussion to include all members in a single discussion (as, for example, in a multi-location audit), nor is it necessary for all of the members of the engagement team to be informed of all of the decisions reached in the discussion. The engagement partner may discuss matters with key members of the engagement team including, if considered appropriate, specialists and those responsible for the audits of components, while delegating discussion with others, taking account of the extent of communication considered necessary throughout the engagement team. A communications plan, agreed by the engagement partner, may be useful.

### *Considerations Specific to Smaller Entities*

**A16**  Many small audits are carried out entirely by the engagement partner (who may be a sole practitioner). In such situations, it is the engagement partner who, having

---

[5] *ISA (UK and Ireland) 240, paragraph 15.*

personally conducted the planning of the audit, would be responsible for considering the susceptibility of the entity's financial statements to material misstatement due to fraud or error.

## The Required Understanding of the Entity and Its Environment, Including the Entity's Internal Control

### The Entity and Its Environment

*Industry, Regulatory and Other External Factors* (Ref: Para. 11(a))

*Industry Factors*

Relevant industry factors include industry conditions such as the competitive environment, supplier and customer relationships, and technological developments. Examples of matters the auditor may consider include:

**A17**

- The market and competition, including demand, capacity, and price competition.
- Cyclical or seasonal activity.
- Product technology relating to the entity's products.
- Energy supply and cost.

The industry in which the entity operates may give rise to specific risks of material misstatement arising from the nature of the business or the degree of regulation. For example, long-term contracts may involve significant estimates of revenues and expenses that give rise to risks of material misstatement. In such cases, it is important that the engagement team include members with sufficient relevant knowledge and experience.[6]

**A18**

*Regulatory Factors*

Relevant regulatory factors include the regulatory environment. The regulatory environment encompasses, among other matters, the applicable financial reporting framework and the legal and political environment. Examples of matters the auditor may consider include:

**A19**

- Accounting principles and industry specific practices.
- Regulatory framework for a regulated industry.
- Legislation and regulation that significantly affect the entity's operations, including direct supervisory activities.
- Taxation (corporate and other).
- Government policies currently affecting the conduct of the entity's business, such as monetary, including foreign exchange controls, fiscal, financial incentives (for example, government aid programs), and tariffs or trade restrictions policies.
- Environmental requirements affecting the industry and the entity's business.

---

[6] *ISA (UK and Ireland) 220, "Quality Control for an Audit of Financial Statements," paragraph 14.*

A20   ISA (UK and Ireland) 250 includes some specific requirements related to the legal and regulatory framework applicable to the entity and the industry or sector in which the entity operates.[7]

*Considerations specific to public sector entities*

A21   For the audits of public sector entities, law, regulation other authority may affect the entity's operations. Such elements are essential to consider when obtaining an understanding of the entity and its environment.

*Other External Factors*

A22   Examples of other external factors affecting the entity that the auditor may consider include the general economic conditions, interest rates and availability of financing, and inflation or currency revaluation.

**Nature of the Entity** (Ref: Para. 11(b))

A23   An understanding of the nature of an entity enables the auditor to understand such matters as:

- Whether the entity has a complex structure, for example with subsidiaries or other components in multiple locations. Complex structures often introduce issues that may give rise to risks of material misstatement. Such issues may include whether goodwill, joint ventures, investments, or special-purpose entities are accounted for appropriately.
- The ownership, and relations between owners and other people or entities. This understanding assists in determining whether related party transactions have been identified and accounted for appropriately. ISA (UK and Ireland) 550[8] establishes requirements and provides guidance on the auditor's considerations relevant to related parties.

A24   Examples of matters that the auditor may consider when obtaining an understanding of the nature of the entity include:

- Business operations – such as:
  - Nature of revenue sources, products or services, and markets, including involvement in electronic commerce such as Internet sales and marketing activities.
  - Conduct of operations (for example, stages and methods of production, or activities exposed to environmental risks).
  - Alliances, joint ventures, and outsourcing activities.
  - Geographic dispersion and industry segmentation.
  - Location of production facilities, warehouses, and offices, and location and quantities of inventories.
  - Key customers and important suppliers of goods and services, employment arrangements (including the existence of union contracts, pension and other post employment benefits, stock option or incentive bonus arrangements, and government regulation related to employment matters).
  - Research and development activities and expenditures.

[7] *ISA (UK and Ireland) 250, "Consideration of Laws and Regulations in an Audit of Financial Statements," paragraph 12.*

[8] *ISA (UK and Ireland) 550, "Related Parties."*

- Transactions with related parties.
- Investments and investment activities – such as:
  - Planned or recently executed acquisitions or divestitures.
  - Investments and dispositions of securities and loans.
  - Capital investment activities.
  - Investments in non-consolidated entities, including partnerships, joint ventures and special-purpose entities.
- Financing and financing activities – such as:
  - Major subsidiaries and associated entities, including consolidated and non-consolidated structures.
  - Debt structure and related terms, including off-balance-sheet financing arrangements and leasing arrangements.
  - Beneficial owners (local, foreign, business reputation and experience) and related parties.
  - Use of derivative financial instruments.
- Financial reporting – such as:
  - Accounting principles and industry specific practices, including industry-specific significant categories (for example, loans and investments for banks, or research and development for pharmaceuticals).
  - Revenue recognition practices.
  - Accounting for fair values.
  - Foreign currency assets, liabilities and transactions.
  - Accounting for unusual or complex transactions including those in controversial or emerging areas (for example, accounting for stock-based compensation).

Significant changes in the entity from prior periods may give rise to, or change, risks of material misstatement.  **A25**

*Nature of Special Purpose Entities*

A special-purpose entity (sometimes referred to as a special purpose vehicle) is an entity that is generally established for a narrow and well-defined purpose, such as to effect a lease or a securitization of financial assets, or to carry out research and development activities. It may take the form of a corporation, trust, partnership or unincorporated entity. The entity on behalf of which the special-purpose entity has been created may often transfer assets to the latter (e.g., as part of a derecognition transaction involving financial assets), obtain the right to use the latter's assets, or perform services for the latter, while other parties may provide the funding to the latter. As ISA (UK and Ireland) 550 indicates, in some circumstances, a special-purpose entity may be a related party of the entity.[9]  **A26**

Financial reporting frameworks often specify detailed conditions that are deemed to amount to control, or circumstances under which the special-purpose entity should be considered for consolidation. The interpretation of the requirements of such frameworks often demands a detailed knowledge of the relevant agreements involving the special-purpose entity.  **A27**

**The Entity's Selection and Application of Accounting Policies** (Ref: Para. 11(c))

An understanding of the entity's selection and application of accounting policies may encompass such matters as:  **A28**

---

[9] ISA (UK and Ireland) 550, "Related Parties," paragraph A7.

- The methods the entity uses to account for significant and unusual transactions.
- The effect of significant accounting policies in controversial or emerging areas for which there is a lack of authoritative guidance or consensus.
- Changes in the entity's accounting policies.
- Financial reporting standards and laws and regulations that are new to the entity and when and how the entity will adopt such requirements.

**Objectives and Strategies and Related Business Risks** (Ref. Para. 11(d))

A29 The entity conducts its business in the context of industry, regulatory and other internal and external factors. To respond to these factors, the entity's management or those charged with governance define objectives, which are the overall plans for the entity. Strategies are the approaches by which management intends to achieve its objectives. The entity's objectives and strategies may change over time.

A30 Business risk is broader than the risk of material misstatement of the financial statements, though it includes the latter. Business risk may arise from change or complexity. A failure to recognize the need for change may also give rise to business risk. Business risk may arise, for example, from:

- The development of new products or services that may fail;
- A market which, even if successfully developed, is inadequate to support a product or service; or
- Flaws in a product or service that may result in liabilities and reputational risk.

A31 An understanding of the business risks facing the entity increases the likelihood of identifying risks of material misstatement, since most business risks will eventually have financial consequences and, therefore, an effect on the financial statements. However, the auditor does not have a responsibility to identify or assess all business risks because not all business risks give rise to risks of material misstatement.

A32 Examples of matters that the auditor may consider when obtaining an understanding of the entity's objectives, strategies and related business risks that may result in a risk of material misstatement of the financial statements include:

- Industry developments (a potential related business risk might be, for example, that the entity does not have the personnel or expertise to deal with the changes in the industry).
- New products and services (a potential related business risk might be, for example, that there is increased product liability).
- Expansion of the business (a potential related business risk might be, for example, that the demand has not been accurately estimated).
- New accounting requirements (a potential related business risk might be, for example, incomplete or improper implementation, or increased costs).
- Regulatory requirements (a potential related business risk might be, for example, that there is increased legal exposure).
- Current and prospective financing requirements (a potential related business risk might be, for example, the loss of financing due to the entity's inability to meet requirements).
- Use of IT (a potential related business risk might be, for example, that systems and processes are incompatible).
- The effects of implementing a strategy, particularly any effects that will lead to new accounting requirements (a potential related business risk might be, for example, incomplete or improper implementation).

A business risk may have an immediate consequence for the risk of material mis-statement for classes of transactions, account balances, and disclosures at the assertion level or the financial statement level. For example, the business risk arising from a contracting customer base may increase the risk of material misstatement associated with the valuation of receivables. However, the same risk, particularly in combination with a contracting economy, may also have a longer-term consequence, which the auditor considers when assessing the appropriateness of the going concern assumption. Whether a business risk may result in a risk of material misstatement is, therefore, considered in light of the entity's circumstances. Examples of conditions and events that may indicate risks of material misstatement are indicated in Appendix 2.

**A33**

Usually, management identifies business risks and develops approaches to address them. Such a risk assessment process is part of internal control and is discussed in paragraph 15 and paragraphs A79-A80.

**A34**

*Considerations Specific to Public Sector Entities*

For the audits of public sector entities, "management objectives" may be influenced by concerns regarding public accountability and may include objectives which have their source in law, regulation or other authority.

**A35**

**Measurement and Review of the Entity's Financial Performance** (Ref: Para.11(e))

Management and others will measure and review those things they regard as important. Performance measures, whether external or internal, create pressures on the entity. These pressures, in turn, may motivate management to take action to improve the business performance or to misstate the financial statements. Accordingly, an understanding of the entity's performance measures assists the auditor in considering whether pressures to achieve performance targets may result in management actions that increase the risks of material misstatement, including those due to fraud. See ISA (UK and Ireland) 240 for requirements and guidance in relation to the risks of fraud.

**A36**

The measurement and review of financial performance is not the same as the monitoring of controls (discussed as a component of internal control in paragraphs A98-A104), though their purposes may overlap:

**A37**

- The measurement and review of performance is directed at whether business performance is meeting the objectives set by management (or third parties).
- Monitoring of controls is specifically concerned with the effective operation of internal control.
- In some cases, however, performance indicators also provide information that enables management to identify deficiencies in internal control.

Examples of internally-generated information used by management for measuring and reviewing financial performance, and which the auditor may consider, include:

**A38**

- Key performance indicators (financial and non-financial) and key ratios, trends and operating statistics.
- Period-on-period financial performance analyses.
- Budgets, forecasts, variance analyses, segment information and divisional, departmental or other level performance reports.
- Employee performance measures and incentive compensation policies.
- Comparisons of an entity's performance with that of competitors.

**A39**   External parties may also measure and review the entity's financial performance. For example, external information such as analysts' reports and credit rating agency reports may represent useful information for the auditor. Such reports can often be obtained from the entity being audited.

**A40**   Internal measures may highlight unexpected results or trends requiring management to determine their cause and take corrective action (including, in some cases, the detection and correction of misstatements on a timely basis). Performance measures may also indicate to the auditor that risks of misstatement of related financial statement information do exist. For example, performance measures may indicate that the entity has unusually rapid growth or profitability when compared to that of other entities in the same industry. Such information, particularly if combined with other factors such as performance-based bonus or incentive remuneration, may indicate the potential risk of management bias in the preparation of the financial statements.

*Considerations Specific to Smaller Entities*

**A41**   Smaller entities often do not have processes to measure and review financial performance. Inquiry of management may reveal that it relies on certain key indicators for evaluating financial performance and taking appropriate action. If such inquiry indicates an absence of performance measurement or review, there may be an increased risk of misstatements not being detected and corrected.

## The Entity's Internal Control

**A42**   An understanding of internal control assists the auditor in identifying types of potential misstatements and factors that affect the risks of material misstatement, and in designing the nature, timing, and extent of further audit procedures.

**A43**   The following application material on internal control is presented in four sections, as follows:

- General Nature and Characteristics of Internal Control.
- Controls Relevant to the Audit.
- Nature and Extent of the Understanding of Relevant Controls.
- Components of Internal Control.

***General Nature and Characteristics of Internal Control*** (Ref: Para. 12)

*Purpose of Internal Control*

**A44**   Internal control is designed, implemented and maintained to address identified business risks that threaten the achievement of any of the entity's objectives that concern:

- The reliability of the entity's financial reporting;
- The effectiveness and efficiency of its operations; and
- Its compliance with applicable laws and regulations.

The way in which internal control is designed, implemented and maintained varies with an entity's size and complexity.

*Considerations specific to smaller entities*

Smaller entities may use less structured means and simpler processes and procedures to achieve their objectives.  **A45**

*Limitations of Internal Control*

Internal control, no matter how effective, can provide an entity with only reasonable assurance about achieving the entity's financial reporting objectives. The likelihood of their achievement is affected by the inherent limitations of internal control. These include the realities that human judgment in decision-making can be faulty and that breakdowns in internal control can occur because of human error. For example, there may be an error in the design of, or in the change to, a control. Equally, the operation of a control may not be effective, such as where information produced for the purposes of internal control (for example, an exception report) is not effectively used because the individual responsible for reviewing the information does not understand its purpose or fails to take appropriate action.  **A46**

Additionally, controls can be circumvented by the collusion of two or more people or inappropriate management override of internal control. For example, management may enter into side agreements with customers that alter the terms and conditions of the entity's standard sales contracts, which may result in improper revenue recognition. Also, edit checks in a software program that are designed to identify and report transactions that exceed specified credit limits may be overridden or disabled.  **A47**

Further, in designing and implementing controls, management may make judgments on the nature and extent of the controls it chooses to implement, and the nature and extent of the risks it chooses to assume.  **A48**

*Considerations specific to smaller entities*

Smaller entities often have fewer employees which may limit the extent to which segregation of duties is practicable. However, in a small owner-managed entity, the owner-manager may be able to exercise more effective oversight than in a larger entity. This oversight may compensate for the generally more limited opportunities for segregation of duties.  **A49**

On the other hand, the owner-manager may be more able to override controls because the system of internal control is less structured. This is taken into account by the auditor when identifying the risks of material misstatement due to fraud.  **A50**

*Division of Internal Control into Components*

The division of internal control into the following five components, for purposes of the ISAs (UK and Ireland), provides a useful framework for auditors to consider how different aspects of an entity's internal control may affect the audit:  **A51**

(a)  The control environment;
(b)  The entity's risk assessment process;
(c)  The information system, including the related business processes, relevant to financial reporting, and communication;
(d)  Control activities; and
(e)  Monitoring of controls.

The division does not necessarily reflect how an entity designs, implements and maintains internal control, or how it may classify any particular component. Auditors may use different terminology or frameworks to describe the various aspects of internal control, and their effect on the audit than those used in this ISA (UK and Ireland), provided all the components described in this ISA (UK and Ireland) are addressed.

A52 Application material relating to the five components of internal control as they relate to a financial statement audit is set out in paragraphs A69-A104 below. Appendix 1 provides further explanation of these components of internal control.

*Characteristics of Manual and Automated Elements of Internal Control Relevant to the Auditor's Risk Assessment*

A53 An entity's system of internal control contains manual elements and often contains automated elements. The characteristics of manual or automated elements are relevant to the auditor's risk assessment and further audit procedures based thereon.

A54 The use of manual or automated elements in internal control also affects the manner in which transactions are initiated, recorded, processed, and reported:

- Controls in a manual system may include such procedures as approvals and reviews of transactions, and reconciliations and follow-up of reconciling items. Alternatively, an entity may use automated procedures to initiate, record, process, and report transactions, in which case records in electronic format replace paper documents.
- Controls in IT systems consist of a combination of automated controls (for example, controls embedded in computer programs) and manual controls. Further, manual controls may be independent of IT, may use information produced by IT, or may be limited to monitoring the effective functioning of IT and of automated controls, and to handling exceptions. When IT is used to initiate, record, process or report transactions, or other financial data for inclusion in financial statements, the systems and programs may include controls related to the corresponding assertions for material accounts or may be critical to the effective functioning of manual controls that depend on IT.

An entity's mix of manual and automated elements in internal control varies with the nature and complexity of the entity's use of IT.

A55 Generally, IT benefits an entity's internal control by enabling an entity to:

- Consistently apply predefined business rules and perform complex calculations in processing large volumes of transactions or data;
- Enhance the timeliness, availability, and accuracy of information;
- Facilitate the additional analysis of information;
- Enhance the ability to monitor the performance of the entity's activities and its policies and procedures;
- Reduce the risk that controls will be circumvented; and
- Enhance the ability to achieve effective segregation of duties by implementing security controls in applications, databases, and operating systems.

A56 IT also poses specific risks to an entity's internal control, including, for example:

- Reliance on systems or programs that are inaccurately processing data, processing inaccurate data, or both.
- Unauthorized access to data that may result in destruction of data or improper changes to data, including the recording of unauthorized or non-existent

transactions, or inaccurate recording of transactions. Particular risks may arise where multiple users access a common database.

- The possibility of IT personnel gaining access privileges beyond those necessary to perform their assigned duties thereby breaking down segregation of duties.
- Unauthorized changes to data in master files.
- Unauthorized changes to systems or programs.
- Failure to make necessary changes to systems or programs.
- Inappropriate manual intervention.
- Potential loss of data or inability to access data as required.

Manual elements in internal control may be more suitable where judgment and discretion are required such as for the following circumstances:  **A57**

- Large, unusual or non-recurring transactions.
- Circumstances where errors are difficult to define, anticipate or predict.
- In changing circumstances that require a control response outside the scope of an existing automated control.
- In monitoring the effectiveness of automated controls.

Manual elements in internal control may be less reliable than automated elements because they can be more easily bypassed, ignored, or overridden and they are also more prone to simple errors and mistakes. Consistency of application of a manual control element cannot therefore be assumed. Manual control elements may be less suitable for the following circumstances:  **A58**

- High volume or recurring transactions, or in situations where errors that can be anticipated or predicted can be prevented, or detected and corrected, by control parameters that are automated.
- Control activities where the specific ways to perform the control can be adequately designed and automated.

The extent and nature of the risks to internal control vary depending on the nature and characteristics of the entity's information system. The entity responds to the risks arising from the use of IT or from use of manual elements in internal control by establishing effective controls in light of the characteristics of the entity's information system.  **A59**

### Controls Relevant to the Audit

There is a direct relationship between an entity's objectives and the controls it implements to provide reasonable assurance about their achievement. The entity's objectives, and therefore controls, relate to financial reporting, operations and compliance; however, not all of these objectives and controls are relevant to the auditor's risk assessment.  **A60**

Factors relevant to the auditor's judgment about whether a control, individually or in combination with others, is relevant to the audit may include such matters as the following:  **A61**

- Materiality.
- The significance of the related risk.
- The size of the entity.
- The nature of the entity's business, including its organization and ownership characteristics.
- The diversity and complexity of the entity's operations.
- Applicable legal and regulatory requirements.
- The circumstances and the applicable component of internal control.

- The nature and complexity of the systems that are part of the entity's internal control, including the use of service organizations.
- Whether, and how, a specific control, individually or in combination with others, prevents, or detects and corrects, material misstatement.

A62   Controls over the completeness and accuracy of information produced by the entity may be relevant to the audit if the auditor intends to make use of the information in designing and performing further procedures. Controls relating to operations and compliance objectives may also be relevant to an audit if they relate to data the auditor evaluates or uses in applying audit procedures.

A63   Internal control over safeguarding of assets against unauthorized acquisition, use, or disposition may include controls relating to both financial reporting and operations objectives. The auditor's consideration of such controls is generally limited to those relevant to the reliability of financial reporting.

A64   An entity generally has controls relating to objectives that are not relevant to an audit and therefore need not be considered. For example, an entity may rely on a sophisticated system of automated controls to provide efficient and effective operations (such as an airline's system of automated controls to maintain flight schedules), but these controls ordinarily would not be relevant to the audit. Further, although internal control applies to the entire entity or to any of its operating units or business processes, an understanding of internal control relating to each of the entity's operating units and business processes may not be relevant to the audit.

*Considerations Specific to Public Sector Entities*

A65   Public sector auditors often have additional responsibilities with respect to internal control, for example to report on compliance with an established code of practice. Public sector auditors can also have responsibilities to report on compliance with law, regulation or other authority. As a result, their review of internal control may be broader and more detailed.

**Nature and Extent of the Understanding of Relevant Controls** (Ref: Para. 13)

A66   Evaluating the design of a control involves considering whether the control, individually or in combination with other controls, is capable of effectively preventing, or detecting and correcting, material misstatements. Implementation of a control means that the control exists and that the entity is using it. There is little point in assessing the implementation of a control that is not effective, and so the design of a control is considered first. An improperly designed control may represent a significant deficiency in internal control.

A67   Risk assessment procedures to obtain audit evidence about the design and implementation of relevant controls may include:

- Inquiring of entity personnel.
- Observing the application of specific controls.
- Inspecting documents and reports.
- Tracing transactions through the information system relevant to financial reporting.

Inquiry alone, however, is not sufficient for such purposes.

Obtaining an understanding of an entity's controls is not sufficient to test their operating effectiveness, unless there is some automation that provides for the consistent operation of the controls. For example, obtaining audit evidence about the implementation of a manual control at a point in time does not provide audit evidence about the operating effectiveness of the control at other times during the period under audit. However, because of the inherent consistency of IT processing (see paragraph A55), performing audit procedures to determine whether an automated control has been implemented may serve as a test of that control's operating effectiveness, depending on the auditor's assessment and testing of controls such as those over program changes. Tests of the operating effectiveness of controls are further described in ISA (UK and Ireland) 330.[10]  **A68**

*Components of Internal Control—Control Environment* (Ref: Para. 14)

The control environment includes the governance and management functions and the attitudes, awareness, and actions of those charged with governance and management concerning the entity's internal control and its importance in the entity. The control environment sets the tone of an organization, influencing the control consciousness of its people.  **A69**

Elements of the control environment that may be relevant when obtaining an understanding of the control environment include the following:  **A70**

(a) *Communication and enforcement of integrity and ethical values* – These are essential elements that influence the effectiveness of the design, administration and monitoring of controls.

(b) *Commitment to competence* – Matters such as management's consideration of the competence levels for particular jobs and how those levels translate into requisite skills and knowledge.

(c) *Participation by those charged with governance* – Attributes of those charged with governance such as:
   • Their independence from management.
   • Their experience and stature.
   • The extent of their involvement and the information they receive, and the scrutiny of activities.
   • The appropriateness of their actions, including the degree to which difficult questions are raised and pursued with management, and their interaction with internal and external auditors.

(d) *Management's philosophy and operating style* – Characteristics such as management's:
   • Approach to taking and managing business risks.
   • Attitudes and actions toward financial reporting.
   • Attitudes toward information processing and accounting functions and personnel.

(e) *Organizational structure* – The framework within which an entity's activities for achieving its objectives are planned, executed, controlled, and reviewed.

(f) *Assignment of authority and responsibility* – Matters such as how authority and responsibility for operating activities are assigned and how reporting relationships and authorization hierarchies are established.

(g) *Human resource policies and practices* – Policies and practices that relate to, for example, recruitment, orientation, training, evaluation, counselling, promotion, compensation, and remedial actions.

---

[10] *ISA (UK and Ireland) 330, "The Auditor's Responses to Assessed Risks."*

*Audit Evidence for Elements of the Control Environment*

**A71**    Relevant audit evidence may be obtained through a combination of inquiries and other risk assessment procedures such as corroborating inquiries through observation or inspection of documents. For example, through inquiries of management and employees, the auditor may obtain an understanding of how management communicates to employees its views on business practices and ethical behavior. The auditor may then determine whether relevant controls have been implemented by considering, for example, whether management has a written code of conduct and whether it acts in a manner that supports the code.

*Effect of the Control Environment on the Assessment of the Risks of Material Misstatement*

**A72**    Some elements of an entity's control environment have a pervasive effect on assessing the risks of material misstatement. For example, an entity's control consciousness is influenced significantly by those charged with governance, because one of their roles is to counterbalance pressures on management in relation to financial reporting that may arise from market demands or remuneration schemes. The effectiveness of the design of the control environment in relation to participation by those charged with governance is therefore influenced by such matters as:

- Their independence from management and their ability to evaluate the actions of management.
- Whether they understand the entity's business transactions.
- The extent to which they evaluate whether the financial statements are prepared in accordance with the applicable financial reporting framework.

**A73**    An active and independent board of directors may influence the philosophy and operating style of senior management. However, other elements may be more limited in their effect. For example, although human resource policies and practices directed toward hiring competent financial, accounting, and IT personnel may reduce the risk of errors in processing financial information, they may not mitigate a strong bias by top management to overstate earnings.

**A74**    The existence of a satisfactory control environment can be a positive factor when the auditor assesses the risks of material misstatement. However, although it may help reduce the risk of fraud, a satisfactory control environment is not an absolute deterrent to fraud. Conversely, deficiencies in the control environment may undermine the effectiveness of controls, in particular in relation to fraud. For example, management's failure to commit sufficient resources to address IT security risks may adversely affect internal control by allowing improper changes to be made to computer programs or to data, or unauthorized transactions to be processed. As explained in ISA (UK and Ireland) 330, the control environment also influences the nature, timing, and extent of the auditor's further procedures.[11]

**A75**    The control environment in itself does not prevent, or detect and correct, a material misstatement. It may, however, influence the auditor's evaluation of the effectiveness of other controls (for example, the monitoring of controls and the operation of specific control activities) and thereby, the auditor's assessment of the risks of material misstatement.

---

[11] *ISA (UK and Ireland) 330, paragraphs A2-A3.*

*Considerations Specific to Smaller Entities*

The control environment within small entities is likely to differ from larger entities. **A76**
For example, those charged with governance in small entities may not include an
independent or outside member, and the role of governance may be undertaken
directly by the owner-manager where there are no other owners. The nature of the
control environment may also influence the significance of other controls, or their
absence. For example, the active involvement of an owner-manager may mitigate
certain of the risks arising from a lack of segregation of duties in a small business; it
may, however, increase other risks, for example, the risk of override of controls.

In addition, audit evidence for elements of the control environment in smaller entities **A77**
may not be available in documentary form, in particular where communication
between management and other personnel may be informal, yet effective. For
example, small entities might not have a written code of conduct but, instead,
develop a culture that emphasizes the importance of integrity and ethical behavior
through oral communication and by management example.

Consequently, the attitudes, awareness and actions of management or the owner- **A78**
manager are of particular importance to the auditor's understanding of a smaller
entity's control environment.

**Components of Internal Control—The Entity's Risk Assessment Process** (Ref: Para.
15)

The entity's risk assessment process forms the basis for how management determines **A79**
the risks to be managed. If that process is appropriate to the circumstances, including
the nature, size and complexity of the entity, it assists the auditor in identifying risks
of material misstatement. Whether the entity's risk assessment process is appropriate
to the circumstances is a matter of judgment.

*Considerations Specific to Smaller Entities (Ref: Para. 17)*

There is unlikely to be an established risk assessment process in a small entity. In **A80**
such cases, it is likely that management will identify risks through direct personal
involvement in the business. Irrespective of the circumstances, however, inquiry
about identified risks and how they are addressed by management is still necessary.

**Components of Internal Control—The Information System, Including the Related
Business Processes, Relevant to Financial Reporting, and Communication**

*The Information System, Including Related Business Processes, Relevant to Financial
Reporting (Ref: Para. 18).*

The information system relevant to financial reporting objectives, which includes the **A81**
accounting system, consists of the procedures and records designed and established
to:

- Initiate, record, process, and report entity transactions (as well as events and
  conditions) and to maintain accountability for the related assets, liabilities, and
  equity;
- Resolve incorrect processing of transactions, for example, automated suspense
  files and procedures followed to clear suspense items out on a timely basis;
- Process and account for system overrides or bypasses to controls;

- Transfer information from transaction processing systems to the general ledger;
- Capture information relevant to financial reporting for events and conditions other than transactions, such as the depreciation and amortization of assets and changes in the recoverability of accounts receivables; and
- Ensure information required to be disclosed by the applicable financial reporting framework is accumulated, recorded, processed, summarized and appropriately reported in the financial statements.

*Journal Entries*

**A82**    An entity's information system typically includes the use of standard journal entries that are required on a recurring basis to record transactions. Examples might be journal entries to record sales, purchases, and cash disbursements in the general ledger, or to record accounting estimates that are periodically made by management, such as changes in the estimate of uncollectible accounts receivable.

**A83**    An entity's financial reporting process also includes the use of non-standard journal entries to record non-recurring, unusual transactions or adjustments. Examples of such entries include consolidating adjustments and entries for a business combination or disposal or non-recurring estimates such as the impairment of an asset. In manual general ledger systems, non-standard journal entries may be identified through inspection of ledgers, journals, and supporting documentation. When automated procedures are used to maintain the general ledger and prepare financial statements, such entries may exist only in electronic form and may therefore be more easily identified through the use of computer-assisted audit techniques.

*Related Business Processes*

**A84**    An entity's business processes are the activities designed to:

- Develop, purchase, produce, sell and distribute an entity's products and services;
- Ensure compliance with laws and regulations; and
- Record information, including accounting and financial reporting information.

Business processes result in the transactions that are recorded, processed and reported by the information system. Obtaining an understanding of the entity's business processes, which include how transactions are originated, assists the auditor obtain an understanding of the entity's information system relevant to financial reporting in a manner that is appropriate to the entity's circumstances.

*Considerations specific to smaller entities*

**A85**    Information systems and related business processes relevant to financial reporting in small entities are likely to be less sophisticated than in larger entities, but their role is just as significant. Small entities with active management involvement may not need extensive descriptions of accounting procedures, sophisticated accounting records, or written policies. Understanding the entity's systems and processes may therefore be easier in an audit of smaller entities, and may be more dependent on inquiry than on review of documentation. The need to obtain an understanding, however, remains important.

*Communication (Ref: Para. 19)*

Communication by the entity of the financial reporting roles and responsibilities and of significant matters relating to financial reporting involves providing an understanding of individual roles and responsibilities pertaining to internal control over financial reporting. It includes such matters as the extent to which personnel understand how their activities in the financial reporting information system relate to the work of others and the means of reporting exceptions to an appropriate higher level within the entity. Communication may take such forms as policy manuals and financial reporting manuals. Open communication channels help ensure that exceptions are reported and acted on. **A86**

*Considerations specific to smaller entities*

Communication may be less structured and easier to achieve in a small entity than in a larger entity due to fewer levels of responsibility and management's greater visibility and availability. **A87**

**Components of Internal Control—Control Activities** (Ref: Para. 20)

Control activities are the policies and procedures that help ensure that management directives are carried out. Control activities, whether within IT or manual systems, have various objectives and are applied at various organizational and functional levels. Examples of specific control activities include those relating to the following: **A88**

- Authorization.
- Performance reviews.
- Information processing.
- Physical controls.
- Segregation of duties.

Control activities that are relevant to the audit are: **A89**

- Those that are required to be treated as such, being control activities that relate to significant risks and those that relate to risks for which substantive procedures alone do not provide sufficient appropriate audit evidence, as required by paragraphs 29 and 30, respectively; or
- Those that are considered to be relevant in the judgment of the auditor.

The auditor's judgment about whether a control activity is relevant to the audit is influenced by the risk that the auditor has identified that may give rise to a material misstatement and whether the auditor thinks it is likely to be appropriate to test the operating effectiveness of the control in determining the extent of substantive testing. **A90**

The auditor's emphasis may be on identifying and obtaining an understanding of control activities that address the areas where the auditor considers that risks of material misstatement are likely to be higher. When multiple control activities each achieve the same objective, it is unnecessary to obtain an understanding of each of the control activities related to such objective. **A91**

The auditor's knowledge about the presence or absence of control activities obtained from the understanding of the other components of internal control assists the auditor in determining whether it is necessary to devote additional attention to obtaining an understanding of control activities. **A92**

*Considerations Specific to Smaller Entities*

**A93**    The concepts underlying control activities in small entities are likely to be similar to those in larger entities, but the formality with which they operate may vary. Further, small entities may find that certain types of control activities are not relevant because of controls applied by management. For example, management's sole authority for granting credit to customers and approving significant purchases can provide strong control over important account balances and transactions, lessening or removing the need for more detailed control activities.

**A94**    Control activities relevant to the audit of a smaller entity are likely to relate to the main transaction cycles such as revenues, purchases and employment expenses.

*Risks Arising from IT* (Ref: Para. 21)

**A95**    The use of IT affects the way that control activities are implemented. From the auditor's perspective, controls over IT systems are effective when they maintain the integrity of information and the security of the data such systems process, and include effective general IT-controls and application controls.

**A96**    General IT-controls are policies and procedures that relate to many applications and support the effective functioning of application controls. They apply to mainframe, miniframe, and end-user environments. General IT-controls that maintain the integrity of information and security of data commonly include controls over the following:

- Data center and network operations.
- System software acquisition, change and maintenance.
- Program change.
- Access security.
- Application system acquisition, development, and maintenance.

They are generally implemented to deal with the risks referred to in paragraph A56 above.

**A97**    Application controls are manual or automated procedures that typically operate at a business process level and apply to the processing of transactions by individual applications. Application controls can be preventive or detective in nature and are designed to ensure the integrity of the accounting records. Accordingly, application controls relate to procedures used to initiate, record, process and report transactions or other financial data. These controls help ensure that transactions occurred, are authorized, and are completely and accurately recorded and processed. Examples include edit checks of input data, and numerical sequence checks with manual follow-up of exception reports or correction at the point of data entry.

**Components of Internal Control—Monitoring of Controls** (Ref: Para. 22)

**A98**    Monitoring of controls is a process to assess the effectiveness of internal control performance over time. It involves assessing the effectiveness of controls on a timely basis and taking necessary remedial actions. Management accomplishes monitoring of controls through ongoing activities, separate evaluations, or a combination of the two. Ongoing monitoring activities are often built into the normal recurring activities of an entity and include regular management and supervisory activities.

Management's monitoring activities may include using information from commu- **A99** nications from external parties such as customer complaints and regulator comments that may indicate problems or highlight areas in need of improvement.

### Considerations Specific to Smaller Entities

Management's monitoring of control is often accomplished by management's or the **A100** owner-manager's close involvement in operations. This involvement often will identify significant variances from expectations and inaccuracies in financial data leading to remedial action to the control.

### Internal Audit Functions (Ref: Para. 23)

The entity's internal audit function is likely to be relevant to the audit if the nature of **A101** the internal audit function's responsibilities and activities are related to the entity's financial reporting, and the auditor expects to use the work of the internal auditors to modify the nature or timing, or reduce the extent, of audit procedures to be performed. If the auditor determines that the internal audit function is likely to be relevant to the audit, ISA (UK and Ireland) 610 applies.

The objectives of an internal audit function, and therefore the nature of its **A102** responsibilities and its status within the organization, vary widely and depend on the size and structure of the entity and the requirements of management and, where applicable, those charged with governance. The responsibilities of an internal audit function may include, for example, monitoring of internal control, risk management, and review of compliance with laws and regulations. On the other hand, the responsibilities of the internal audit function may be limited to the review of the economy, efficiency and effectiveness of operations, for example, and accordingly, may not relate to the entity's financial reporting.

If the nature of the internal audit function's responsibilities are related to the entity's **A103** financial reporting, the external auditor's consideration of the activities performed, or to be performed by, the internal audit function may include review of the internal audit function's audit plan for the period, if any, and discussion of that plan with the internal auditors.

### Sources of Information (Ref: Para. 24)

Much of the information used in monitoring may be produced by the entity's **A104** information system. If management assumes that data used for monitoring are accurate without having a basis for that assumption, errors that may exist in the information could potentially lead management to incorrect conclusions from its monitoring activities. Accordingly, an understanding of:

- the sources of the information related to the entity's monitoring activities; and
- the basis upon which management considers the information to be sufficiently reliable for the purpose

is required as part of the auditor's understanding of the entity's monitoring activities as a component of internal control.

## Identifying and Assessing the Risks of Material Misstatement

*Assessment of Risks of Material Misstatement at the Financial Statement Level* (Ref: Para. 25 (a))

A105   Risks of material misstatement at the financial statement level refer to risks that relate pervasively to the financial statements as a whole and potentially affect many assertions. Risks of this nature are not necessarily risks identifiable with specific assertions at the class of transactions, account balance, or disclosure level. Rather, they represent circumstances that may increase the risks of material misstatement at the assertion level, for example, through management override of internal control. Financial statement level risks may be especially relevant to the auditor's consideration of the risks of material misstatement arising from fraud.

A106   Risks at the financial statement level may derive in particular from a deficient control environment (although these risks may also relate to other factors, such as declining economic conditions). For example, deficiencies such as management's lack of competence may have a more pervasive effect on the financial statements and may require an overall response by the auditor.

A107   The auditor's understanding of internal control may raise doubts about the auditability of an entity's financial statements. For example:

- Concerns about the integrity of the entity's management may be so serious as to cause the auditor to conclude that the risk of management misrepresentation in the financial statements is such that an audit cannot be conducted.
- Concerns about the condition and reliability of an entity's records may cause the auditor to conclude that it is unlikely that sufficient appropriate audit evidence will be available to support an unmodified opinion on the financial statements.

A108   ISA (UK and Ireland) 705[12] establishes requirements and provides guidance in determining whether there is a need for the auditor to express a qualified opinion or disclaim an opinion or, as may be required in some cases, to withdraw from the engagement where withdrawal is possible under applicable law or regulation.

*Assessment of Risks of Material Misstatement at the Assertion Level* (Ref: Para. 25(b))

A109   Risks of material misstatement at the assertion level for classes of transactions, account balances, and disclosures need to be considered because such consideration directly assists in determining the nature, timing, and extent of further audit procedures at the assertion level necessary to obtain sufficient appropriate audit evidence. In identifying and assessing risks of material misstatement at the assertion level, the auditor may conclude that the identified risks relate more pervasively to the financial statements as a whole and potentially affect many assertions.

*The Use of Assertions*

A110   In representing that the financial statements are in accordance with the applicable financial reporting framework, management[1a] implicitly or explicitly makes assertions regarding the recognition, measurement, presentation and disclosure of the various elements of financial statements and related disclosures.

---

[12] ISA (UK and Ireland) 705, "Modifications to the Opinion in the Independent Auditor's Report."

Assertions used by the auditor to consider the different types of potential mis-statements that may occur fall into the following three categories and may take the following forms:

    **A111**

(a) Assertions about classes of transactions and events for the period under audit:
  (i) Occurrence—transactions and events that have been recorded have occurred and pertain to the entity.
  (ii) Completeness—all transactions and events that should have been recorded have been recorded.
  (iii) Accuracy—amounts and other data relating to recorded transactions and events have been recorded appropriately.
  (iv) Cutoff—transactions and events have been recorded in the correct accounting period.
  (v) Classification—transactions and events have been recorded in the proper accounts.
(b) Assertions about account balances at the period end:
  (i) Existence—assets, liabilities, and equity interests exist.
  (ii) Rights and obligations—the entity holds or controls the rights to assets, and liabilities are the obligations of the entity.
  (iii) Completeness—all assets, liabilities and equity interests that should have been recorded have been recorded.
  (iv) Valuation and allocation—assets, liabilities, and equity interests are included in the financial statements at appropriate amounts and any resulting valuation or allocation adjustments are appropriately recorded.
(c) Assertions about presentation and disclosure:
  (i) Occurrence and rights and obligations—disclosed events, transactions, and other matters have occurred and pertain to the entity.
  (ii) Completeness—all disclosures that should have been included in the financial statements have been included.
  (iii) Classification and understandability—financial information is appropriately presented and described, and disclosures are clearly expressed.
  (iv) Accuracy and valuation—financial and other information are disclosed fairly and at appropriate amounts.

The auditor may use the assertions as described above or may express them differently provided all aspects described above have been covered. For example, the auditor may choose to combine the assertions about transactions and events with the assertions about account balances.

    **A112**

*Considerations specific to public sector entities*

When making assertions about the financial statements of public sector entities, in addition to those assertions set out in paragraph A111, management[1a] may often assert that transactions and events have been carried out in accordance with law, regulation or other authority. Such assertions may fall within the scope of the financial statement audit.

    **A113**

**Process of Identifying Risks of Material Misstatement** (Ref: Para. 26(a))

Information gathered by performing risk assessment procedures, including the audit evidence obtained in evaluating the design of controls and determining whether they have been implemented, is used as audit evidence to support the risk assessment. The risk assessment determines the nature, timing, and extent of further audit procedures to be performed.

    **A114**

**A115**    Appendix 2 provides examples of conditions and events that may indicate the existence of risks of material misstatement.

### *Relating Controls to Assertions* (Ref: Para. 26(c))

**A116**    In making risk assessments, the auditor may identify the controls that are likely to prevent, or detect and correct, material misstatement in specific assertions. Generally, it is useful to obtain an understanding of controls and relate them to assertions in the context of processes and systems in which they exist because individual control activities often do not in themselves address a risk. Often, only multiple control activities, together with other components of internal control, will be sufficient to address a risk.

**A117**    Conversely, some control activities may have a specific effect on an individual assertion embodied in a particular class of transactions or account balance. For example, the control activities that an entity established to ensure that its personnel are properly counting and recording the annual physical inventory relate directly to the existence and completeness assertions for the inventory account balance.

**A118**    Controls can be either directly or indirectly related to an assertion. The more indirect the relationship, the less effective that control may be in preventing, or detecting and correcting, misstatements in that assertion. For example, a sales manager's review of a summary of sales activity for specific stores by region ordinarily is only indirectly related to the completeness assertion for sales revenue. Accordingly, it may be less effective in reducing risk for that assertion than controls more directly related to that assertion, such as matching shipping documents with billing documents.

### *Significant Risks*

#### *Identifying Significant Risks (Ref: Para. 28)*

**A119**    Significant risks often relate to significant non-routine transactions or judgmental matters. Non-routine transactions are transactions that are unusual, due to either size or nature, and that therefore occur infrequently. Judgmental matters may include the development of accounting estimates for which there is significant measurement uncertainty. Routine, non-complex transactions that are subject to systematic processing are less likely to give rise to significant risks.

**A120**    Risks of material misstatement may be greater for significant non-routine transactions arising from matters such as the following:

- Greater management intervention to specify the accounting treatment.
- Greater manual intervention for data collection and processing.
- Complex calculations or accounting principles.
- The nature of non-routine transactions, which may make it difficult for the entity to implement effective controls over the risks.

**A121**    Risks of material misstatement may be greater for significant judgmental matters that require the development of accounting estimates, arising from matters such as the following:

- Accounting principles for accounting estimates or revenue recognition may be subject to differing interpretation.
- Required judgment may be subjective or complex, or require assumptions about the effects of future events, for example, judgment about fair value.

ISA (UK and Ireland) 330 describes the consequences for further audit procedures of identifying a risk as significant.[13]  **A122**

*Significant risks relating to the risks of material misstatement due to fraud*

ISA (UK and Ireland) 240 provides further requirements and guidance in relation to the identification and assessment of the risks of material misstatement due to fraud.[14]  **A123**

*Understanding Controls Related to Significant Risks (Ref: Para. 29)*

Although risks relating to significant non-routine or judgmental matters are often less likely to be subject to routine controls, management may have other responses intended to deal with such risks. Accordingly, the auditor's understanding of whether the entity has designed and implemented controls for significant risks arising from non-routine or judgmental matters includes whether and how management responds to the risks. Such responses might include:  **A124**

- Control activities such as a review of assumptions by senior management or experts.
- Documented processes for estimations.
- Approval by those charged with governance.

For example, where there are one-off events such as the receipt of notice of a significant lawsuit, consideration of the entity's response may include such matters as whether it has been referred to appropriate experts (such as internal or external legal counsel), whether an assessment has been made of the potential effect, and how it is proposed that the circumstances are to be disclosed in the financial statements.  **A125**

In some cases, management may not have appropriately responded to significant risks of material misstatement by implementing controls over these significant risks. Failure by management to implement such controls is an indicator of a significant deficiency in internal control.[15]  **A126**

*Risks for Which Substantive Procedures Alone Do Not Provide Sufficient Appropriate Audit Evidence (Ref: Para. 30)*

Risks of material misstatement may relate directly to the recording of routine classes of transactions or account balances, and the preparation of reliable financial statements. Such risks may include risks of inaccurate or incomplete processing for routine and significant classes of transactions such as an entity's revenue, purchases, and cash receipts or cash payments.  **A127**

Where such routine business transactions are subject to highly automated processing with little or no manual intervention, it may not be possible to perform only substantive procedures in relation to the risk. For example, the auditor may consider this to be the case in circumstances where a significant amount of an entity's information is initiated, recorded, processed, or reported only in electronic form such as in an integrated system. In such cases:  **A128**

---

[13] *ISA (UK and Ireland) 330, paragraphs 15 and 21.*

[14] *ISA (UK and Ireland) 240, paragraphs 25-27.*

[15] *ISA (UK and Ireland) 265, "Communicating Deficiencies in Internal Control to Those Charged with Governance and Management," paragraph A7.*

- Audit evidence may be available only in electronic form, and its sufficiency and appropriateness usually depend on the effectiveness of controls over its accuracy and completeness.
- The potential for improper initiation or alteration of information to occur and not be detected may be greater if appropriate controls are not operating effectively.

**A129**   The consequences for further audit procedures of identifying such risks are described in ISA (UK and Ireland) 330.[16]

*Revision of Risk Assessment* (Ref: Para. 31)

**A130**   During the audit, information may come to the auditor's attention that differs significantly from the information on which the risk assessment was based. For example, the risk assessment may be based on an expectation that certain controls are operating effectively. In performing tests of those controls, the auditor may obtain audit evidence that they were not operating effectively at relevant times during the audit. Similarly, in performing substantive procedures the auditor may detect misstatements in amounts or frequency greater than is consistent with the auditor's risk assessments. In such circumstances, the risk assessment may not appropriately reflect the true circumstances of the entity and the further planned audit procedures may not be effective in detecting material misstatements. See ISA (UK and Ireland) 330 for further guidance.

**Documentation** (Ref: Para. 32)

**A131**   The manner in which the requirements of paragraph 32 are documented is for the auditor to determine using professional judgment. For example, in audits of small entities the documentation may be incorporated in the auditor's documentation of the overall strategy and audit plan.[17] Similarly, for example, the results of the risk assessment may be documented separately, or may be documented as part of the auditor's documentation of further procedures.[18] The form and extent of the documentation is influenced by the nature, size and complexity of the entity and its internal control, availability of information from the entity and the audit methodology and technology used in the course of the audit.

**A132**   For entities that have uncomplicated businesses and processes relevant to financial reporting, the documentation may be simple in form and relatively brief. It is not necessary to document the entirety of the auditor's understanding of the entity and matters related to it. Key elements of understanding documented by the auditor include those on which the auditor based the assessment of the risks of material misstatement.

**A133**   The extent of documentation may also reflect the experience and capabilities of the members of the audit engagement team. Provided the requirements of ISA (UK and Ireland) 230 are always met, an audit undertaken by an engagement team comprising less experienced individuals may require more detailed documentation to assist them to obtain an appropriate understanding of the entity than one that includes experienced individuals.

[16] *ISA (UK and Ireland) 330, paragraph 8.*

[17] *ISA (UK and Ireland) 300, "Planning an Audit of Financial Statements," paragraphs 7 and 9.*

[18] *ISA (UK and Ireland) 330, paragraph 28.*

For recurring audits, certain documentation may be carried forward, updated as   **A134**
necessary to reflect changes in the entity's business or processes.

# Appendix 1

(Ref: Paras. 4(c), 14-24, A69-A104)

## Internal Control Components

1    This appendix further explains the components of internal control, as set out in paragraphs 4(c), 14-24 and A69-A104, as they relate to a financial statement audit.

### Control Environment

2    The control environment encompasses the following elements:

(a) *Communication and enforcement of integrity and ethical values.* The effectiveness of controls cannot rise above the integrity and ethical values of the people who create, administer, and monitor them. Integrity and ethical behavior are the product of the entity's ethical and behavioral standards, how they are communicated, and how they are reinforced in practice. The enforcement of integrity and ethical values includes, for example, management actions to eliminate or mitigate incentives or temptations that might prompt personnel to engage in dishonest, illegal, or unethical acts. The communication of entity policies on integrity and ethical values may include the communication of behavioral standards to personnel through policy statements and codes of conduct and by example.

(b) *Commitment to competence.* Competence is the knowledge and skills necessary to accomplish tasks that define the individual's job.

(c) *Participation by those charged with governance.* An entity's control consciousness is influenced significantly by those charged with governance. The importance of the responsibilities of those charged with governance is recognized in codes of practice and other laws and regulations or guidance produced for the benefit of those charged with governance. Other responsibilities of those charged with governance include oversight of the design and effective operation of whistle blower procedures and the process for reviewing the effectiveness of the entity's internal control.

(d) *Management's philosophy and operating style.* Management's philosophy and operating style encompass a broad range of characteristics. For example, management's attitudes and actions toward financial reporting may manifest themselves through conservative or aggressive selection from available alternative accounting principles, or conscientiousness and conservatism with which accounting estimates are developed.

(e) *Organizational structure.* Establishing a relevant organizational structure includes considering key areas of authority and responsibility and appropriate lines of reporting. The appropriateness of an entity's organizational structure depends, in part, on its size and the nature of its activities.

(f) *Assignment of authority and responsibility.* The assignment of authority and responsibility may include policies relating to appropriate business practices, knowledge and experience of key personnel, and resources provided for carrying out duties. In addition, it may include policies and communications directed at ensuring that all personnel understand the entity's objectives, know how their individual actions interrelate and contribute to those objectives, and recognize how and for what they will be held accountable.

(g) *Human resource policies and practices.* Human resource policies and practices often demonstrate important matters in relation to the control consciousness of an entity. For example, standards for recruiting the most qualified individuals – with emphasis on educational background, prior work experience, past accomplishments, and evidence of integrity and ethical behavior – demonstrate an entity's commitment to competent and trustworthy people. Training policies that communicate prospective roles and responsibilities and include practices such as training schools and seminars illustrate expected levels of performance and behavior. Promotions driven by periodic performance appraisals demonstrate the entity's commitment to the advancement of qualified personnel to higher levels of responsibility.

## Entity's Risk Assessment Process

For financial reporting purposes, the entity's risk assessment process includes how **3** management identifies business risks relevant to the preparation of financial statements in accordance with the entity's applicable financial reporting framework, estimates their significance, assesses the likelihood of their occurrence, and decides upon actions to respond to and manage them and the results thereof. For example, the entity's risk assessment process may address how the entity considers the possibility of unrecorded transactions or identifies and analyzes significant estimates recorded in the financial statements.

Risks relevant to reliable financial reporting include external and internal events, **4** transactions or circumstances that may occur and adversely affect an entity's ability to initiate, record, process, and report financial data consistent with the assertions of management[1a] in the financial statements. Management may initiate plans, programs, or actions to address specific risks or it may decide to accept a risk because of cost or other considerations. Risks can arise or change due to circumstances such as the following:

- *Changes in operating environment.* Changes in the regulatory or operating environment can result in changes in competitive pressures and significantly different risks.
- *New personnel.* New personnel may have a different focus on or understanding of internal control.
- *New or revamped information systems.* Significant and rapid changes in information systems can change the risk relating to internal control.
- *Rapid growth.* Significant and rapid expansion of operations can strain controls and increase the risk of a breakdown in controls.
- *New technology.* Incorporating new technologies into production processes or information systems may change the risk associated with internal control.
- *New business models, products, or activities.* Entering into business areas or transactions with which an entity has little experience may introduce new risks associated with internal control.
- *Corporate restructurings.* Restructurings may be accompanied by staff reductions and changes in supervision and segregation of duties that may change the risk associated with internal control.
- *Expanded foreign operations.* The expansion or acquisition of foreign operations carries new and often unique risks that may affect internal control, for example, additional or changed risks from foreign currency transactions.
- *New accounting pronouncements.* Adoption of new accounting principles or changing accounting principles may affect risks in preparing financial statements.

## Information System, Including the Related Business Processes, Relevant to Financial Reporting, and Communication

An information system consists of infrastructure (physical and hardware components), software, people, procedures, and data. Many information systems make **5** extensive use of information technology (IT).

6   The information system relevant to financial reporting objectives, which includes the financial reporting system, encompasses methods and records that:

- Identify and record all valid transactions.
- Describe on a timely basis the transactions in sufficient detail to permit proper classification of transactions for financial reporting.
- Measure the value of transactions in a manner that permits recording their proper monetary value in the financial statements.
- Determine the time period in which transactions occurred to permit recording of transactions in the proper accounting period.
- Present properly the transactions and related disclosures in the financial statements.

7   The quality of system-generated information affects management's ability to make appropriate decisions in managing and controlling the entity's activities and to prepare reliable financial reports.

8   Communication, which involves providing an understanding of individual roles and responsibilities pertaining to internal control over financial reporting, may take such forms as policy manuals, accounting and financial reporting manuals, and memoranda. Communication also can be made electronically, orally, and through the actions of management.

**Control Activities**

9   Generally, control activities that may be relevant to an audit may be categorized as policies and procedures that pertain to the following:

- *Performance reviews.* These control activities include reviews and analyses of actual performance versus budgets, forecasts, and prior period performance; relating different sets of data – operating or financial – to one another, together with analyses of the relationships and investigative and corrective actions; comparing internal data with external sources of information; and review of functional or activity performance.
- *Information processing.* The two broad groupings of information systems control activities are application controls, which apply to the processing of individual applications, and general IT-controls, which are policies and procedures that relate to many applications and support the effective functioning of application controls by helping to ensure the continued proper operation of information systems. Examples of application controls include checking the arithmetical accuracy of records, maintaining and reviewing accounts and trial balances, automated controls such as edit checks of input data and numerical sequence checks, and manual follow-up of exception reports. Examples of general IT-controls are program change controls, controls that restrict access to programs or data, controls over the implementation of new releases of packaged software applications, and controls over system software that restrict access to or monitor the use of system utilities that could change financial data or records without leaving an audit trail.
- *Physical controls.* Controls that encompass:
  - The physical security of assets, including adequate safeguards such as secured facilities over access to assets and records.
  - The authorization for access to computer programs and data files.
  - The periodic counting and comparison with amounts shown on control records (for example, comparing the results of cash, security and inventory counts with accounting records).

- The extent to which physical controls intended to prevent theft of assets are relevant to the reliability of financial statement preparation, and therefore the audit, depends on circumstances such as when assets are highly susceptible to misappropriation.
- *Segregation of duties*. Assigning different people the responsibilities of authorizing transactions, recording transactions, and maintaining custody of assets. Segregation of duties is intended to reduce the opportunities to allow any person to be in a position to both perpetrate and conceal errors or fraud in the normal course of the person's duties.

Certain control activities may depend on the existence of appropriate higher level policies established by management or those charged with governance. For example, authorization controls may be delegated under established guidelines, such as investment criteria set by those charged with governance; alternatively, non-routine transactions such as major acquisitions or divestments may require specific high level approval, including in some cases that of shareholders. **10**

## Monitoring of Controls

An important management responsibility is to establish and maintain internal control on an ongoing basis. Management's monitoring of controls includes considering whether they are operating as intended and that they are modified as appropriate for changes in conditions. Monitoring of controls may include activities such as management's review of whether bank reconciliations are being prepared on a timely basis, internal auditors' evaluation of sales personnel's compliance with the entity's policies on terms of sales contracts, and a legal department's oversight of compliance with the entity's ethical or business practice policies. Monitoring is done also to ensure that controls continue to operate effectively over time. For example, if the timeliness and accuracy of bank reconciliations are not monitored, personnel are likely to stop preparing them. **11**

Internal auditors or personnel performing similar functions may contribute to the monitoring of an entity's controls through separate evaluations. Ordinarily, they regularly provide information about the functioning of internal control, focusing considerable attention on evaluating the effectiveness of internal control, and communicate information about strengths and deficiencies in internal control and recommendations for improving internal control. **12**

Monitoring activities may include using information from communications from external parties that may indicate problems or highlight areas in need of improvement. Customers implicitly corroborate billing data by paying their invoices or complaining about their charges. In addition, regulators may communicate with the entity concerning matters that affect the functioning of internal control, for example, communications concerning examinations by bank regulatory agencies. Also, management may consider communications relating to internal control from external auditors in performing monitoring activities. **13**

## Appendix 2
(Ref: Para. A33, A115)

# Conditions and Events That May Indicate Risks of Material Misstatement

The following are examples of conditions and events that may indicate the existence of risks of material misstatement. The examples provided cover a broad range of conditions and events; however, not all conditions and events are relevant to every audit engagement and the list of examples is not necessarily complete.

- Operations in regions that are economically unstable, for example, countries with significant currency devaluation or highly inflationary economies.
- Operations exposed to volatile markets, for example, futures trading.
- Operations that are subject to a high degree of complex regulation.
- Going concern and liquidity issues including loss of significant customers.
- Constraints on the availability of capital and credit.
- Changes in the industry in which the entity operates.
- Changes in the supply chain.
- Developing or offering new products or services, or moving into new lines of business.
- Expanding into new locations.
- Changes in the entity such as large acquisitions or reorganizations or other unusual events.
- Entities or business segments likely to be sold.
- The existence of complex alliances and joint ventures.
- Use of off-balance-sheet finance, special-purpose entities, and other complex financing arrangements.
- Significant transactions with related parties.
- Lack of personnel with appropriate accounting and financial reporting skills.
- Changes in key personnel including departure of key executives.
- Deficiencies in internal control, especially those not addressed by management.
- Inconsistencies between the entity's IT strategy and its business strategies.
- Changes in the IT environment.
- Installation of significant new IT systems related to financial reporting.
- Inquiries into the entity's operations or financial results by regulatory or government bodies.
- Past misstatements, history of errors or a significant amount of adjustments at period end.
- Significant amount of non-routine or non-systematic transactions including intercompany transactions and large revenue transactions at period end.
- Transactions that are recorded based on management's intent, for example, debt refinancing, assets to be sold and classification of marketable securities.
- Application of new accounting pronouncements.
- Accounting measurements that involve complex processes.
- Events or transactions that involve significant measurement uncertainty, including accounting estimates.
- Pending litigation and contingent liabilities, for example, sales warranties, financial guarantees and environmental remediation.

# Addendum

*This addendum provides a summary of APB's rationale for retaining or excluding in the proposed clarified ISA (UK and Ireland) the supplementary requirements in the existing ISA (UK and Ireland). It also sets out the supplementary guidance material in the existing ISA (UK and Ireland) that APB considers is not necessary to retain in light of the improvements in the underlying Clarity ISAs issued by the IAASB as part of the Clarity Project. It is provided for information and does not form part of the proposed clarified ISA (UK and Ireland).*

*The Consultation Paper published with the exposure drafts explains the general approach used by the APB for determining whether current supplementary material should be proposed to be retained.*

## Analysis of proposed treatment of current APB supplementary material in current ISA (UK and Ireland) 315

### Requirements

There are no supplementary requirements in the current ISA (UK and Ireland) 315.

### Guidance

The following guidance in current ISA (UK and Ireland) 315 has not been carried forward to the proposed clarified standard.

| Current paragraph reference (*Italic text is from IAASB for context*) |
|---|
| 1-1. – 1-4. [Description of management and those charged with governance.] |
| 24     *Legislative and regulatory requirements often determine the applicable financial reporting framework to be used by management[2a] in preparing the entity's financial statements. ... The auditor considers whether local regulations specify certain financial reporting requirements for the industry in which the entity operates, since the financial statements may be materially misstated in the context of the applicable financial reporting framework if management[2a] fails to prepare the financial statements in accordance with such regulations.* |
| [2a] In the UK and Ireland, those charged with governance are responsible for preparing the financial statements. |

# Proposed Clarified International Standard on Auditing (UK and Ireland) 320

# Materiality in planning and performing an audit

*(Effective for audits of financial statements for periods ending on or after 15 December 2010)*

## Contents

International Standard on Auditing (UK and Ireland) (ISA (UK and Ireland)) 320, "Materiality in Planning and Performing an Audit" should be read in the context of ISA (UK and Ireland) 200, "Overall Objectives of the Independent Auditor and the Conduct of an Audit in Accordance with International Standards on Auditing (UK and Ireland)."

# Introduction

## Scope of this ISA (UK and Ireland)

This International Standard on Auditing (UK and Ireland) (ISA (UK and Ireland)) deals with the auditor's responsibility to apply the concept of materiality in planning and performing an audit of financial statements. ISA (UK and Ireland) 450[1] explains how materiality is applied in evaluating the effect of identified misstatements on the audit and of uncorrected misstatements, if any, on the financial statements. **1**

## Materiality in the Context of an Audit

Financial reporting frameworks often discuss the concept of materiality in the context of the preparation and presentation of financial statements. Although financial reporting frameworks may discuss materiality in different terms, they generally explain that: **2**

- Misstatements, including omissions, are considered to be material if they, individually or in the aggregate, could reasonably be expected to influence the economic decisions of users taken on the basis of the financial statements;
- Judgments about materiality are made in light of surrounding circumstances, and are affected by the size or nature of a misstatement, or a combination of both; and
- Judgments about matters that are material to users of the financial statements are based on a consideration of the common financial information needs of users as a group.[2] The possible effect of misstatements on specific individual users, whose needs may vary widely, is not considered.

Such a discussion, if present in the applicable financial reporting framework, provides a frame of reference to the auditor in determining materiality for the audit. If the applicable financial reporting framework does not include a discussion of the concept of materiality, the characteristics referred to in paragraph 2 provide the auditor with such a frame of reference. **3**

The auditor's determination of materiality is a matter of professional judgment, and is affected by the auditor's perception of the financial information needs of users of the financial statements. In this context, it is reasonable for the auditor to assume that users: **4**

(a) Have a reasonable knowledge of business and economic activities and accounting and a willingness to study the information in the financial statements with reasonable diligence;
(b) Understand that financial statements are prepared, presented and audited to levels of materiality;
(c) Recognize the uncertainties inherent in the measurement of amounts based on the use of estimates, judgment and the consideration of future events; and
(d) Make reasonable economic decisions on the basis of the information in the financial statements.

[1] *ISA (UK and Ireland) 450, "Evaluation of Misstatements Identified during the Audit."*

[2] *For example, the "Framework for the Preparation and Presentation of Financial Statements," adopted by the International Accounting Standards Board in April 2001, indicates that, for a profit-oriented entity, as investors are providers of risk capital to the enterprise, the provision of financial statements that meet their needs will also meet most of the needs of other users that financial statements can satisfy.*
*The "Framework for the Preparation and Presentation of Financial Statements," has not been promulgated by the APB for application in the UK and Ireland.*

5    The concept of materiality is applied by the auditor both in planning and performing the audit, and in evaluating the effect of identified misstatements on the audit and of uncorrected misstatements, if any, on the financial statements and in forming the opinion in the auditor's report. (Ref: Para. A1)

6    In planning the audit, the auditor makes judgments about the size of misstatements that will be considered material. These judgments provide a basis for:

(a)   Determining the nature, timing and extent of risk assessment procedures;
(b)   Identifying and assessing the risks of material misstatement; and
(c)   Determining the nature, timing and extent of further audit procedures.

The materiality determined when planning the audit does not necessarily establish an amount below which uncorrected misstatements, individually or in the aggregate, will always be evaluated as immaterial. The circumstances related to some mis-statements may cause the auditor to evaluate them as material even if they are below materiality. Although it is not practicable to design audit procedures to detect misstatements that could be material solely because of their nature, the auditor considers not only the size but also the nature of uncorrected misstatements, and the particular circumstances of their occurrence, when evaluating their effect on the financial statements.[3]

## Effective Date

7    This ISA (UK and Ireland) is effective for audits of financial statements for periods ending on or after 15 December 2010.

## Objective

8    The objective of the auditor is to apply the concept of materiality appropriately in planning and performing the audit.

## Definition

9    For purposes of the ISAs (UK and Ireland), performance materiality means the amount or amounts set by the auditor at less than materiality for the financial statements as a whole to reduce to an appropriately low level the probability that the aggregate of uncorrected and undetected misstatements exceeds materiality for the financial statements as a whole. If applicable, performance materiality also refers to the amount or amounts set by the auditor at less than the materiality level or levels for particular classes of transactions, account balances or disclosures.

## Requirements

### Determining Materiality and Performance Materiality When Planning the Audit

10   When establishing the overall audit strategy, the auditor shall determine materiality for the financial statements as a whole. If, in the specific circumstances of the entity, there is one or more particular classes of transactions, account balances or

---

[3] *ISA (UK and Ireland) 450, paragraph A16.*

disclosures for which misstatements of lesser amounts than materiality for the financial statements as a whole could reasonably be expected to influence the economic decisions of users taken on the basis of the financial statements, the auditor shall also determine the materiality level or levels to be applied to those particular classes of transactions, account balances or disclosures. (Ref: Para. A2-A11)

The auditor shall determine performance materiality for purposes of assessing the risks of material misstatement and determining the nature, timing and extent of further audit procedures. (Ref: Para. A12)    **11**

## Revision as the Audit Progresses

The auditor shall revise materiality for the financial statements as a whole (and, if applicable, the materiality level or levels for particular classes of transactions, account balances or disclosures) in the event of becoming aware of information during the audit that would have caused the auditor to have determined a different amount (or amounts) initially. (Ref: Para. A13)    **12**

If the auditor concludes that a lower materiality for the financial statements as a whole (and, if applicable, materiality level or levels for particular classes of transactions, account balances or disclosures) than that initially determined is appropriate, the auditor shall determine whether it is necessary to revise performance materiality, and whether the nature, timing and extent of the further audit procedures remain appropriate.    **13**

## Documentation

The auditor shall include in the audit documentation the following amounts and the factors considered in their determination:[4]    **14**

(a)  Materiality for the financial statements as a whole (see paragraph 10);
(b)  If applicable, the materiality level or levels for particular classes of transactions, account balances or disclosures (see paragraph 10);
(c)  Performance materiality (see paragraph 11); and
(d)  Any revision of (a)-(c) as the audit progressed (see paragraphs 12-13).

\*\*\*

# Application and Other Explanatory Material

## Materiality and Audit Risk (Ref: Para. 5)

In conducting an audit of financial statements, the overall objectives of the auditor are to obtain reasonable assurance about whether the financial statements as a whole are free from material misstatement, whether due to fraud or error, thereby enabling the auditor to express an opinion on whether the financial statements are prepared, in all material respects, in accordance with an applicable financial reporting framework; and to report on the financial statements, and communicate as required by the ISAs (UK and Ireland), in accordance with the auditor's findings.[5] The auditor obtains reasonable assurance by obtaining sufficient appropriate audit evidence to    **A1**

---

[4] *ISA (UK and Ireland) 230, "Audit Documentation," paragraphs 8-11, and paragraph A6.*

[5] *ISA (UK and Ireland) 200, "Overall Objectives of the Independent Auditor and the Conduct of an Audit in Accordance with International Standards on Auditing (UK and Ireland)," paragraph 11.*

reduce audit risk to an acceptably low level.[6] Audit risk is the risk that the auditor expresses an inappropriate audit opinion when the financial statements are materially misstated. Audit risk is a function of the risks of material misstatement and detection risk.[7] Materiality and audit risk are considered throughout the audit, in particular, when:

(a) Identifying and assessing the risks of material misstatement;[3]
(b) Determining the nature, timing and extent of further audit procedures;[9] and
(c) Evaluating the effect of uncorrected misstatements, if any, on the financial statements[10] and in forming the opinion in the auditor's report.[11]

## Determining Materiality and Performance Materiality When Planning the Audit

### Considerations Specific to Public Sector Entities (Ref: Para. 10)

A2 In the case of a public sector entity, legislators and regulators are often the primary users of its financial statements. Furthermore, the financial statements may be used to make decisions other than economic decisions. The determination of materiality for the financial statements as a whole (and, if applicable, materiality level or levels for particular classes of transactions, account balances or disclosures) in an audit of the financial statements of a public sector entity is therefore influenced by law, regulation or other authority, and by the financial information needs of legislators and the public in relation to public sector programs.

### Use of Benchmarks in Determining Materiality for the Financial Statements as a Whole (Ref: Para. 10)

A3 Determining materiality involves the exercise of professional judgment. A percentage is often applied to a chosen benchmark as a starting point in determining materiality for the financial statements as a whole. Factors that may affect the identification of an appropriate benchmark include the following:

- The elements of the financial statements (for example, assets, liabilities, equity, revenue, expenses);
- Whether there are items on which the attention of the users of the particular entity's financial statements tends to be focused (for example, for the purpose of evaluating financial performance users may tend to focus on profit, revenue or net assets);

[6] *ISA (UK and Ireland) 200, paragraph 17.*

[7] *ISA (UK and Ireland) 200, paragraph 13(c).*

[8] *ISA (UK and Ireland) 315, "Identifying and Assessing the Risks of Material Misstatements through Understanding the Entity and Its Environment."*

[9] *ISA (UK and Ireland) 330, "The Auditor's Responses to Assessed Risks."*

[10] *ISA (UK and Ireland) 450.*

[11] *ISA 700, "Forming an Opinion and Reporting on Financial Statements."*
*The APB has not promulgated ISA 700 as issued by the IAASB for application in the UK and Ireland. In the UK and Ireland the applicable auditing standard is ISA (UK and Ireland) 700, "The Auditor's Report on Financial Statements." Paragraph 8 of ISA (UK and Ireland) 700 requires evaluation of whether uncorrected misstatements are material, individually or in aggregate.*

- The nature of the entity, where the entity is in its life cycle, and the industry and economic environment in which the entity operates;
- The entity's ownership structure and the way it is financed (for example, if an entity is financed solely by debt rather than equity, users may put more emphasis on assets, and claims on them, than on the entity's earnings); and
- The relative volatility of the benchmark.

Examples of benchmarks that may be appropriate, depending on the circumstances of the entity, include categories of reported income such as profit before tax, total revenue, gross profit and total expenses, total equity or net asset value. Profit before tax from continuing operations is often used for profit-oriented entities. When profit before tax from continuing operations is volatile, other benchmarks may be more appropriate, such as gross profit or total revenues.   **A4**

In relation to the chosen benchmark, relevant financial data ordinarily includes prior periods' financial results and financial positions, the period-to-date financial results and financial position, and budgets or forecasts for the current period, adjusted for significant changes in the circumstances of the entity (for example, a significant business acquisition) and relevant changes of conditions in the industry or economic environment in which the entity operates. For example, when, as a starting point, materiality for the financial statements as a whole is determined for a particular entity based on a percentage of profit before tax from continuing operations, circumstances that give rise to an exceptional decrease or increase in such profit may lead the auditor to conclude that materiality for the financial statements as a whole is more appropriately determined using a normalized profit before tax from continuing operations figure based on past results.   **A5**

Materiality relates to the financial statements on which the auditor is reporting. Where the financial statements are prepared for a financial reporting period of more or less than twelve months, such as may be the case for a new entity or a change in the financial reporting period, materiality relates to the financial statements prepared for that financial reporting period.   **A6**

Determining a percentage to be applied to a chosen benchmark involves the exercise of professional judgment. There is a relationship between the percentage and the chosen benchmark, such that a percentage applied to profit before tax from continuing operations will normally be higher than a percentage applied to total revenue. For example, the auditor may consider five percent of profit before tax from continuing operations to be appropriate for a profit-oriented entity in a manufacturing industry, while the auditor may consider one percent of total revenue or total expenses to be appropriate for a not-for-profit entity. Higher or lower percentages, however, may be deemed appropriate in the circumstances.   **A7**

*Considerations Specific to Small Entities*

When an entity's profit before tax from continuing operations is consistently nominal, as might be the case for an owner-managed business where the owner takes much of the profit before tax in the form of remuneration, a benchmark such as profit before remuneration and tax may be more relevant.   **A8**

*Considerations Specific to Public Sector Entities*

In an audit of a public sector entity, total cost or net cost (expenses less revenues or expenditure less receipts) may be appropriate benchmarks for program activities.   **A9**

Where a public sector entity has custody of public assets, assets may be an appropriate benchmark.

### *Materiality Level or Levels for Particular Classes of Transactions, Account Balances or Disclosures* (Ref: Para. 10)

A10 Factors that may indicate the existence of one or more particular classes of transactions, account balances or disclosures for which misstatements of lesser amounts than materiality for the financial statements as a whole could reasonably be expected to influence the economic decisions of users taken on the basis of the financial statements include the following:

- Whether law, regulation or the applicable financial reporting framework affect users' expectations regarding the measurement or disclosure of certain items (for example, related party transactions, and the remuneration of management and those charged with governance).
- The key disclosures in relation to the industry in which the entity operates (for example, research and development costs for a pharmaceutical company).
- Whether attention is focused on a particular aspect of the entity's business that is separately disclosed in the financial statements (for example, a newly acquired business).

A11 In considering whether, in the specific circumstances of the entity, such classes of transactions, account balances or disclosures exist, the auditor may find it useful to obtain an understanding of the views and expectations of those charged with governance and management.

### *Performance Materiality* (Ref: Para. 11)

A12 Planning the audit solely to detect individually material misstatements overlooks the fact that the aggregate of individually immaterial misstatements may cause the financial statements to be materially misstated, and leaves no margin for possible undetected misstatements. Performance materiality (which, as defined, is one or more amounts) is set to reduce to an appropriately low level the probability that the aggregate of uncorrected and undetected misstatements in the financial statements exceeds materiality for the financial statements as a whole. Similarly, performance materiality relating to a materiality level determined for a particular class of transactions, account balance or disclosure is set to reduce to an appropriately low level the probability that the aggregate of uncorrected and undetected misstatements in that particular class of transactions, account balance or disclosure exceeds the materiality level for that particular class of transactions, account balance or disclosure. The determination of performance materiality is not a simple mechanical calculation and involves the exercise of professional judgment. It is affected by the auditor's understanding of the entity, updated during the performance of the risk assessment procedures; and the nature and extent of misstatements identified in previous audits and thereby the auditor's expectations in relation to misstatements in the current period.

### Revision as the Audit Progresses (Ref: Para. 12)

A13 Materiality for the financial statements as a whole (and, if applicable, the materiality level or levels for particular classes of transactions, account balances or disclosures) may need to be revised as a result of a change in circumstances that occurred during the audit (for example, a decision to dispose of a major part of the entity's business), new information, or a change in the auditor's understanding of the entity and its operations as a result of performing further audit procedures. For example, if during the audit it appears as though actual financial results are likely to be substantially different from the anticipated period end financial results that were used initially to determine materiality for the financial statements as a whole, the auditor revises that materiality.

# Addendum

*This addendum provides a summary of APB's rationale for retaining or excluding in the proposed clarified ISA (UK and Ireland) the supplementary requirements in the existing ISA (UK and Ireland). It also sets out the supplementary guidance material in the existing ISA (UK and Ireland) that APB considers is not necessary to retain in light of the improvements in the underlying Clarity ISAs issued by the IAASB as part of the Clarity Project. It is provided for information and does not form part of the proposed clarified ISA (UK and Ireland).*

*The Consultation Paper published with the exposure drafts explains the general approach used by the APB for determining whether current supplementary material should be proposed to be retained.*

## Analysis of proposed treatment of current APB supplementary material in current ISA (UK and Ireland) 320

### Requirements

There are no supplementary requirements in the current ISA (UK and Ireland) 320.

### Guidance

The following guidance in current ISA (UK and Ireland) 320 has not been carried forward to the proposed clarified standard.

| Current paragraph reference (*Italic text is from IAASB for context*) |
|---|
| 1-1. – 1-4. [Description of management and those charged with governance.] |
| 7-1. For example, in the UK and Ireland, the expected degree of accuracy of certain statutory disclosures, such as directors' emoluments, may make normal materiality considerations irrelevant |
| 9-1. If the auditor identifies factors which result in the revision of the preliminary materiality assessment, the auditor considers the implications for the audit approach and may modify the nature, timing and extent of planned audit procedures. |
| 12-1. In the UK and Ireland the auditor ordinarily evaluates whether the financial statements give a true and fair view. |

# Proposed Clarified International Standard on Auditing (UK and Ireland) 330
# The auditor's responses to assessed risks

*(Effective for audits of financial statements for periods ending on or after 15 December 2010)*

## Contents

---

International Standard on Auditing (UK and Ireland) (ISA (UK and Ireland))
330, "The Auditor's Responses to Assessed Risks" should be read in conjunction
with ISA (UK and Ireland) 200, "Overall Objectives of the Independent Auditor
and the Conduct of an Audit in Accordance with International Standards on
Auditing (UK and Ireland)."

# Introduction

## Scope of this ISA (UK and Ireland)

1    This International Standard on Auditing (UK and Ireland) (ISA (UK and Ireland)) deals with the auditor's responsibility to design and implement responses to the risks of material misstatement identified and assessed by the auditor in accordance with ISA (UK and Ireland) 315[1] in an audit of financial statements.

## Effective Date

2    This ISA (UK and Ireland) is effective for audits of financial statements for periods ending on or after 15 December 2010.

# Objective

3    The objective of the auditor is to obtain sufficient appropriate audit evidence regarding the assessed risks of material misstatement, through designing and implementing appropriate responses to those risks.

# Definitions

4    For purposes of the ISAs (UK and Ireland), the following terms have the meanings attributed below:

(a)  Substantive procedure – An audit procedure designed to detect material misstatements at the assertion level. Substantive procedures comprise:
    (i)   Tests of details (of classes of transactions, account balances, and disclosures); and
    (ii)  Substantive analytical procedures.

(b)  Test of controls – An audit procedure designed to evaluate the operating effectiveness of controls in preventing, or detecting and correcting, material misstatements at the assertion level.

# Requirements

## Overall Responses

5    The auditor shall design and implement overall responses to address the assessed risks of material misstatement at the financial statement level. (Ref: Para. A1-A3)

## Audit Procedures Responsive to the Assessed Risks of Material Misstatement at the Assertion Level

6    The auditor shall design and perform further audit procedures whose nature, timing, and extent are based on and are responsive to the assessed risks of material misstatement at the assertion level. (Ref: Para. A4-A8)

7    In designing the further audit procedures to be performed, the auditor shall:

[1] ISA (UK and Ireland) 315, "Identifying and Assessing the Risks of Material Misstatement through Understanding the Entity and Its Environment."

(a) Consider the reasons for the assessment given to the risk of material misstatement at the assertion level for each class of transactions, account balance, and disclosure, including:
   (i) The likelihood of material misstatement due to the particular characteristics of the relevant class of transactions, account balance, or disclosure (i.e., the inherent risk); and
   (ii) Whether the risk assessment takes account of relevant controls (i.e., the control risk), thereby requiring the auditor to obtain audit evidence to determine whether the controls are operating effectively (i.e., the auditor intends to rely on the operating effectiveness of controls in determining the nature, timing and extent of substantive procedures); and (Ref: Para. A9-A18)
(b) Obtain more persuasive audit evidence the higher the auditor's assessment of risk. (Ref: Para. A19)

## Tests of Controls

The auditor shall design and perform tests of controls to obtain sufficient appropriate audit evidence as to the operating effectiveness of relevant controls if:  **8**

(a) The auditor's assessment of risks of material misstatement at the assertion level includes an expectation that the controls are operating effectively (i.e., the auditor intends to rely on the operating effectiveness of controls in determining the nature, timing and extent of substantive procedures); or
(b) Substantive procedures alone cannot provide sufficient appropriate audit evidence at the assertion level. (Ref: Para. A20-A24)

In designing and performing tests of controls, the auditor shall obtain more persuasive audit evidence the greater the reliance the auditor places on the effectiveness of a control. (Ref: Para. A25)  **9**

## Nature and Extent of Tests of Controls

In designing and performing tests of controls, the auditor shall:  **10**

(a) Perform other audit procedures in combination with inquiry to obtain audit evidence about the operating effectiveness of the controls, including:
   (i) How the controls were applied at relevant times during the period under audit.
   (ii) The consistency with which they were applied.
   (iii) By whom or by what means they were applied. (Ref: Para. A26-29)
(b) Determine whether the controls to be tested depend upon other controls (indirect controls) and, if so, whether it is necessary to obtain audit evidence supporting the effective operation of those indirect controls. (Ref: Para. A30-31)

## Timing of Tests of Controls

The auditor shall test controls for the particular time, or throughout the period, for which the auditor intends to rely on those controls, subject to paragraphs 12 and 15 below, in order to provide an appropriate basis for the auditor's intended reliance. (Ref: Para. A32)  **11**

*Using audit evidence obtained during an interim period*

**12**  If the auditor obtains audit evidence about the operating effectiveness of controls during an interim period, the auditor shall:

(a)  Obtain audit evidence about significant changes to those controls subsequent to the interim period; and
(b)  Determine the additional audit evidence to be obtained for the remaining period. (Ref: Para. A33-A34)

*Using audit evidence obtained in previous audits*

**13**  In determining whether it is appropriate to use audit evidence about the operating effectiveness of controls obtained in previous audits, and, if so, the length of the time period that may elapse before retesting a control, the auditor shall consider the following:

(a)  The effectiveness of other elements of internal control, including the control environment, the entity's monitoring of controls, and the entity's risk assessment process;
(b)  The risks arising from the characteristics of the control, including whether it is manual or automated;
(c)  The effectiveness of general IT-controls;
(d)  The effectiveness of the control and its application by the entity, including the nature and extent of deviations in the application of the control noted in previous audits, and whether there have been personnel changes that significantly affect the application of the control;
(e)  Whether the lack of a change in a particular control poses a risk due to changing circumstances; and
(f)  The risks of material misstatement and the extent of reliance on the control. (Ref: Para. A35)

**14**  If the auditor plans to use audit evidence from a previous audit about the operating effectiveness of specific controls, the auditor shall establish the continuing relevance of that evidence by obtaining audit evidence about whether significant changes in those controls have occurred subsequent to the previous audit. The auditor shall obtain this evidence by performing inquiry combined with observation or inspection, to confirm the understanding of those specific controls, and:

(a)  If there have been changes that affect the continuing relevance of the audit evidence from the previous audit, the auditor shall test the controls in the current audit. (Ref: Para. A36)
(b)  If there have not been such changes, the auditor shall test the controls at least once in every third audit, and shall test some controls each audit to avoid the possibility of testing all the controls on which the auditor intends to rely in a single audit period with no testing of controls in the subsequent two audit periods. (Ref: Para. A37-39)

*Controls over significant risks*

**15**  If the auditor plans to rely on controls over a risk the auditor has determined to be a significant risk, the auditor shall test those controls in the current period.

*Evaluating the Operating Effectiveness of Controls*

When evaluating the operating effectiveness of relevant controls, the auditor shall **16** evaluate whether misstatements that have been detected by substantive procedures indicate that controls are not operating effectively. The absence of misstatements detected by substantive procedures, however, does not provide audit evidence that controls related to the assertion being tested are effective. (Ref: Para. A40)

If deviations from controls upon which the auditor intends to rely are detected, the **17** auditor shall make specific inquiries to understand these matters and their potential consequences, and shall determine whether:

(a) The tests of controls that have been performed provide an appropriate basis for reliance on the controls;
(b) Additional tests of controls are necessary; or
(c) The potential risks of misstatement need to be addressed using substantive procedures. (Ref: Para. A41)

**Substantive Procedures**

Irrespective of the assessed risks of material misstatement, the auditor shall design **18** and perform substantive procedures for each material class of transactions, account balance, and disclosure. (Ref: Para. A42-A47)

The auditor shall consider whether external confirmation procedures are to be per- **19** formed as substantive audit procedures. (Ref: Para. A48-A51)

*Substantive Procedures Related to the Financial Statement Closing Process*

The auditor's substantive procedures shall include the following audit procedures **20** related to the financial statement closing process:

(a) Agreeing or reconciling the financial statements with the underlying accounting records; and
(b) Examining material journal entries and other adjustments made during the course of preparing the financial statements. (Ref: Para. A52)

*Substantive Procedures Responsive to Significant Risks*

If the auditor has determined that an assessed risk of material misstatement at the **21** assertion level is a significant risk, the auditor shall perform substantive procedures that are specifically responsive to that risk. When the approach to a significant risk consists only of substantive procedures, those procedures shall include tests of details. (Ref: Para. A53)

*Timing of Substantive Procedures*

If substantive procedures are performed at an interim date, the auditor shall cover **22** the remaining period by performing:

(a) substantive procedures, combined with tests of controls for the intervening period; or
(b) if the auditor determines that it is sufficient, further substantive procedures only

that provide a reasonable basis for extending the audit conclusions from the interim date to the period end. (Ref: Para. A55-A57)

23    If misstatements that the auditor did not expect when assessing the risks of material misstatement are detected at an interim date, the auditor shall evaluate whether the related assessment of risk and the planned nature, timing, or extent of substantive procedures covering the remaining period need to be modified. (Ref: Para. A58)

## Adequacy of Presentation and Disclosure

24    The auditor shall perform audit procedures to evaluate whether the overall pre-sentation of the financial statements, including the related disclosures, is in accordance with the applicable financial reporting framework. (Ref: Para. A59)

## Evaluating the Sufficiency and Appropriateness of Audit Evidence

25    Based on the audit procedures performed and the audit evidence obtained, the auditor shall evaluate before the conclusion of the audit whether the assessments of the risks of material misstatement at the assertion level remain appropriate. (Ref: Para. A60-A61)

26    The auditor shall conclude whether sufficient appropriate audit evidence has been obtained. In forming an opinion, the auditor shall consider all relevant audit evi-dence, regardless of whether it appears to corroborate or to contradict the assertions in the financial statements. (Ref: Para. A62)

27    If the auditor has not obtained sufficient appropriate audit evidence as to a material financial statement assertion, the auditor shall attempt to obtain further audit evi-dence. If the auditor is unable to obtain sufficient appropriate audit evidence, the auditor shall express a qualified opinion or disclaim an opinion on the financial statements.

## Documentation

28    The auditor shall include in the audit documentation:[2]

(a) The overall responses to address the assessed risks of material misstatement at the financial statement level, and the nature, timing, and extent of the further audit procedures performed;

(b) The linkage of those procedures with the assessed risks at the assertion level; and

(c) The results of the audit procedures, including the conclusions where these are not otherwise clear. (Ref: Para. A63)

29    If the auditor plans to use audit evidence about the operating effectiveness of con-trols obtained in previous audits, the auditor shall include in the audit documentation the conclusions reached about relying on such controls that were tested in a previous audit.

30    The auditors' documentation shall demonstrate that the financial statements agree or reconcile with the underlying accounting records.

\*\*\*

---

[2] *ISA (UK and Ireland) 230, "Audit Documentation," paragraphs 8-11, and paragraph A6.*

# Application and Other Explanatory Material

## Overall Responses (Ref: Para. 5)

Overall responses to address the assessed risks of material misstatement at the financial statement level may include:  **A1**

- Emphasizing to the audit team the need to maintain professional skepticism.
- Assigning more experienced staff or those with special skills or using experts.
- Providing more supervision.
- Incorporating additional elements of unpredictability in the selection of further audit procedures to be performed.
- Making general changes to the nature, timing, or extent of audit procedures, for example: performing substantive procedures at the period end instead of at an interim date; or modifying the nature of audit procedures to obtain more persuasive audit evidence.

The assessment of the risks of material misstatement at the financial statement level, and thereby the auditor's overall responses, is affected by the auditor's understanding of the control environment. An effective control environment may allow the auditor to have more confidence in internal control and the reliability of audit evidence generated internally within the entity and thus, for example, allow the auditor to conduct some audit procedures at an interim date rather than at the period end. Deficiencies in the control environment, however, have the opposite effect; for example, the auditor may respond to an ineffective control environment by:  **A2**

- Conducting more audit procedures as of the period end rather than at an interim date.
- Obtaining more extensive audit evidence from substantive procedures.
- Increasing the number of locations to be included in the audit scope.

Such considerations, therefore, have a significant bearing on the auditor's general approach, for example, an emphasis on substantive procedures (substantive approach), or an approach that uses tests of controls as well as substantive procedures (combined approach).  **A3**

## Audit Procedures Responsive to the Assessed Risks of Material Misstatement at the Assertion Level

### *The Nature, Timing, and Extent of Further Audit Procedures* (Ref: Para. 6)

The auditor's assessment of the identified risks at the assertion level provides a basis for considering the appropriate audit approach for designing and performing further audit procedures. For example, the auditor may determine that:  **A4**

(a) Only by performing tests of controls may the auditor achieve an effective response to the assessed risk of material misstatement for a particular assertion;

(b) Performing only substantive procedures is appropriate for particular assertions and, therefore, the auditor excludes the effect of controls from the relevant risk assessment. This may be because the auditor's risk assessment procedures have not identified any effective controls relevant to the assertion, or because testing controls would be inefficient and therefore the auditor does not intend to rely on the operating effectiveness of controls in determining the nature, timing and extent of substantive procedures; or

(c)   A combined approach using both tests of controls and substantive procedures is an effective approach.

However, as required by paragraph 18, irrespective of the approach selected, the auditor designs and performs substantive procedures for each material class of transactions, account balance, and disclosure.

**A5**   The nature of an audit procedure refers to its purpose (i.e., test of controls or substantive procedure) and its type (i.e., inspection, observation, inquiry, confirmation, recalculation, reperformance, or analytical procedure). The nature of the audit procedures is of most importance in responding to the assessed risks.

**A6**   Timing of an audit procedure refers to when it is performed, or the period or date to which the audit evidence applies.

**A7**   Extent of an audit procedure refers to the quantity to be performed, for example, a sample size or the number of observations of a control activity.

**A8**   Designing and performing further audit procedures whose nature, timing, and extent are based on and are responsive to the assessed risks of material misstatement at the assertion level provides a clear linkage between the auditors' further audit procedures and the risk assessment.

*Responding to the Assessed Risks at the Assertion Level (Ref: Para. 7(a))*

*Nature*

**A9**   The auditor's assessed risks may affect both the types of audit procedures to be performed and their combination. For example, when an assessed risk is high, the auditor may confirm the completeness of the terms of a contract with the counterparty, in addition to inspecting the document. Further, certain audit procedures may be more appropriate for some assertions than others. For example, in relation to revenue, tests of controls may be most responsive to the assessed risk of misstatement of the completeness assertion, whereas substantive procedures may be most responsive to the assessed risk of misstatement of the occurrence assertion.

**A10**   The reasons for the assessment given to a risk are relevant in determining the nature of audit procedures. For example, if an assessed risk is lower because of the particular characteristics of a class of transactions without consideration of the related controls, then the auditor may determine that substantive analytical procedures alone provide sufficient appropriate audit evidence. On the other hand, if the assessed risk is lower because of internal controls, and the auditor intends to base the substantive procedures on that low assessment, then the auditor performs tests of those controls, as required by paragraph 8(a). This may be the case, for example, for a class of transactions of reasonably uniform, non-complex characteristics that are routinely processed and controlled by the entity's information system.

*Timing*

**A11**   The auditor may perform tests of controls or substantive procedures at an interim date or at the period end. The higher the risk of material misstatement, the more likely it is that the auditor may decide it is more effective to perform substantive procedures nearer to, or at, the period end rather than at an earlier date, or to perform audit procedures unannounced or at unpredictable times (for example, performing audit procedures at selected locations on an unannounced basis). This is particularly relevant when considering the response to the risks of fraud. For example, the auditor may conclude that, when the risks of intentional misstatement or manipulation have been identified, audit procedures to extend audit conclusions from interim date to the period end would not be effective.

On the other hand, performing audit procedures before the period end may assist the auditor in identifying significant matters at an early stage of the audit, and consequently resolving them with the assistance of management or developing an effective audit approach to address such matters. **A12**

In addition, certain audit procedures can be performed only at or after the period end, for example: **A13**

- Agreeing the financial statements to the accounting records;
- Examining adjustments made during the course of preparing the financial statements; and
- Procedures to respond to a risk that, at the period end, the entity may have entered into improper sales contracts, or transactions may not have been finalized.

Further relevant factors that influence the auditor's consideration of when to perform audit procedures include the following: **A14**

- The control environment.
- When relevant information is available (for example, electronic files may subsequently be overwritten, or procedures to be observed may occur only at certain times).
- The nature of the risk (for example, if there is a risk of inflated revenues to meet earnings expectations by subsequent creation of false sales agreements, the auditor may wish to examine contracts available on the date of the period end).
- The period or date to which the audit evidence relates.

*Extent*

The extent of an audit procedure judged necessary is determined after considering the materiality, the assessed risk, and the degree of assurance the auditor plans to obtain. When a single purpose is met by a combination of procedures, the extent of each procedure is considered separately. In general, the extent of audit procedures increases as the risk of material misstatement increases. For example, in response to the assessed risk of material misstatement due to fraud, increasing sample sizes or performing substantive analytical procedures at a more detailed level may be appropriate. However, increasing the extent of an audit procedure is effective only if the audit procedure itself is relevant to the specific risk. **A15**

The use of computer-assisted audit techniques (CAATs) may enable more extensive testing of electronic transactions and account files, which may be useful when the auditor decides to modify the extent of testing, for example, in responding to the risks of material misstatement due to fraud. Such techniques can be used to select sample transactions from key electronic files, to sort transactions with specific characteristics, or to test an entire population instead of a sample. **A16**

*Considerations specific to public sector entities*

**A17** For the audits of public sector entities, the audit mandate and any other special auditing requirements may affect the auditor's consideration of the nature, timing and extent of further audit procedures.

*Considerations specific to smaller entities*

**A18** In the case of very small entities, there may not be many control activities that could be identified by the auditor, or the extent to which their existence or operation have been documented by the entity may be limited. In such cases, it may be more efficient for the auditor to perform further audit procedures that are primarily substantive procedures. In some rare cases, however, the absence of control activities or of other components of control may make it impossible to obtain sufficient appropriate audit evidence.

*Higher Assessments of Risk (Ref: Para 7(b))*

**A19** When obtaining more persuasive audit evidence because of a higher assessment of risk, the auditor may increase the quantity of the evidence, or obtain evidence that is more relevant or reliable, for example, by placing more emphasis on obtaining third party evidence or by obtaining corroborating evidence from a number of independent sources.

**Tests of Controls**

*Designing and Performing Tests of Controls (Ref: Para. 8)*

**A20** Tests of controls are performed only on those controls that the auditor has determined are suitably designed to prevent, or detect and correct, a material misstatement in an assertion. If substantially different controls were used at different times during the period under audit, each is considered separately.

**A21** Testing the operating effectiveness of controls is different from obtaining an understanding of and evaluating the design and implementation of controls. However, the same types of audit procedures are used. The auditor may, therefore, decide it is efficient to test the operating effectiveness of controls at the same time as evaluating their design and determining that they have been implemented.

**A22** Further, although some risk assessment procedures may not have been specifically designed as tests of controls, they may nevertheless provide audit evidence about the operating effectiveness of the controls and, consequently, serve as tests of controls. For example, the auditor's risk assessment procedures may have included:

- Inquiring about management's use of budgets.
- Observing management's comparison of monthly budgeted and actual expenses.
- Inspecting reports pertaining to the investigation of variances between budgeted and actual amounts.

These audit procedures provide knowledge about the design of the entity's budgeting policies and whether they have been implemented, but may also provide audit evidence about the effectiveness of the operation of budgeting policies in preventing or detecting material misstatements in the classification of expenses.

In addition, the auditor may design a test of controls to be performed concurrently **A23**
with a test of details on the same transaction. Although the purpose of a test of
controls is different from the purpose of a test of details, both may be accomplished
concurrently by performing a test of controls and a test of details on the same
transaction, also known as a dual-purpose test. For example, the auditor may design,
and evaluate the results of, a test to examine an invoice to determine whether it has
been approved and to provide substantive audit evidence of a transaction. A dual-
purpose test is designed and evaluated by considering each purpose of the test
separately.

In some cases, the auditor may find it impossible to design effective substantive **A24**
procedures that by themselves provide sufficient appropriate audit evidence at the
assertion level.[3] This may occur when an entity conducts its business using IT and no
documentation of transactions is produced or maintained, other than through the IT
system. In such cases, paragraph 8(b) requires the auditor to perform tests of relevant
controls.

*Audit Evidence and Intended Reliance (Ref: Para. 9)*

A higher level of assurance may be sought about the operating effectiveness of **A25**
controls when the approach adopted consists primarily of tests of controls, in particular where it is not possible or practicable to obtain sufficient appropriate audit
evidence only from substantive procedures.

*Nature and Extent of Tests of Controls*

*Other audit procedures in combination with inquiry (Ref: Para. 10(a))*

Inquiry alone is not sufficient to test the operating effectiveness of controls. **A26**
Accordingly, other audit procedures are performed in combination with inquiry. In
this regard, inquiry combined with inspection or reperformance may provide more
assurance than inquiry and observation, since an observation is pertinent only at the
point in time at which it is made.

The nature of the particular control influences the type of procedure required to **A27**
obtain audit evidence about whether the control was operating effectively. For
example, if operating effectiveness is evidenced by documentation, the auditor may
decide to inspect it to obtain audit evidence about operating effectiveness. For other
controls, however, documentation may not be available or relevant. For example,
documentation of operation may not exist for some factors in the control environment, such as assignment of authority and responsibility, or for some types of
control activities, such as control activities performed by a computer. In such circumstances, audit evidence about operating effectiveness may be obtained through
inquiry in combination with other audit procedures such as observation or the use of
CAATs.

*Extent of tests of controls*

When more persuasive audit evidence is needed regarding the effectiveness of a **A28**
control, it may be appropriate to increase the extent of testing of the control. As well
as the degree of reliance on controls, matters the auditor may consider in determining the extent of tests of controls include the following:

[3] *ISA (UK and Ireland) 315, paragraph 30.*

- The frequency of the performance of the control by the entity during the period.
- The length of time during the audit period that the auditor is relying on the operating effectiveness of the control.
- The expected rate of deviation from a control.
- The relevance and reliability of the audit evidence to be obtained regarding the operating effectiveness of the control at the assertion level.
- The extent to which audit evidence is obtained from tests of other controls related to the assertion.

ISA (UK and Ireland) 530[4] contains further guidance on the extent of testing.

A29    Because of the inherent consistency of IT processing, it may not be necessary to increase the extent of testing of an automated control. An automated control can be expected to function consistently unless the program (including the tables, files, or other permanent data used by the program) is changed. Once the auditor determines that an automated control is functioning as intended (which could be done at the time the control is initially implemented or at some other date), the auditor may consider performing tests to determine that the control continues to function effectively. Such tests might include determining that:

- Changes to the program are not made without being subject to the appropriate program change controls;
- The authorized version of the program is used for processing transactions; and
- Other relevant general controls are effective.

Such tests also might include determining that changes to the programs have not been made, as may be the case when the entity uses packaged software applications without modifying or maintaining them. For example, the auditor may inspect the record of the administration of IT security to obtain audit evidence that unauthorized access has not occurred during the period.

*Testing of indirect controls (Ref: Para. 10(b))*

A30    In some circumstances, it may be necessary to obtain audit evidence supporting the effective operation of indirect controls. For example, when the auditor decides to test the effectiveness of a user review of exception reports detailing sales in excess of authorized credit limits, the user review and related follow up is the control that is directly of relevance to the auditor. Controls over the accuracy of the information in the reports (for example, the general IT-controls) are described as "indirect" controls.

A31    Because of the inherent consistency of IT processing, audit evidence about the implementation of an automated application control, when considered in combination with audit evidence about the operating effectiveness of the entity's general controls (in particular, change controls), may also provide substantial audit evidence about its operating effectiveness.

*Timing of Tests of Controls*

*Intended period of reliance (Ref: Para. 11)*

A32    Audit evidence pertaining only to a point in time may be sufficient for the auditor's purpose, for example, when testing controls over the entity's physical inventory

---

[4] *ISA (UK and Ireland) 530, "Audit Sampling."*

counting at the period end. If, on the other hand, the auditor intends to rely on a control over a period, tests that are capable of providing audit evidence that the control operated effectively at relevant times during that period are appropriate. Such tests may include tests of the entity's monitoring of controls.

*Using audit evidence obtained during an interim period (Ref: Para. 12)*

Relevant factors in determining what additional audit evidence to obtain about controls that were operating during the period remaining after an interim period, include:   **A33**

- The significance of the assessed risks of material misstatement at the assertion level.
- The specific controls that were tested during the interim period, and significant changes to them since they were tested, including changes in the information system, processes, and personnel.
- The degree to which audit evidence about the operating effectiveness of those controls was obtained.
- The length of the remaining period.
- The extent to which the auditor intends to reduce further substantive procedures based on the reliance of controls.
- The control environment.

Additional audit evidence may be obtained, for example, by extending tests of controls over the remaining period or testing the entity's monitoring of controls.   **A34**

*Using audit evidence obtained in previous audits (Ref: Para. 13)*

In certain circumstances, audit evidence obtained from previous audits may provide audit evidence where the auditor performs audit procedures to establish its continuing relevance. For example, in performing a previous audit, the auditor may have determined that an automated control was functioning as intended. The auditor may obtain audit evidence to determine whether changes to the automated control have been made that affect its continued effective functioning through, for example, inquiries of management and the inspection of logs to indicate what controls have been changed. Consideration of audit evidence about these changes may support either increasing or decreasing the expected audit evidence to be obtained in the current period about the operating effectiveness of the controls.   **A35**

*Controls that have changed from previous audits (Ref: Para. 14(a))*

Changes may affect the relevance of the audit evidence obtained in previous audits such that there may no longer be a basis for continued reliance. For example, changes in a system that enable an entity to receive a new report from the system probably do not affect the relevance of audit evidence from a previous audit; however, a change that causes data to be accumulated or calculated differently does affect it.   **A36**

*Controls that have not changed from previous audits (Ref: Para. 14(b))*

The auditor's decision on whether to rely on audit evidence obtained in previous audits for controls that:   **A37**

(a) have not changed since they were last tested; and
(b) are not controls that mitigate a significant risk

is a matter of professional judgment. In addition, the length of time between retesting such controls is also a matter of professional judgment, but is required by paragraph 14 (b) to be at least once in every third year.

**A38**    In general, the higher the risk of material misstatement, or the greater the reliance on controls, the shorter the time period elapsed, if any, is likely to be. Factors that may decrease the period for retesting a control, or result in not relying on audit evidence obtained in previous audits at all, include the following:

- A deficient control environment.
- Deficient monitoring of controls.
- A significant manual element to the relevant controls.
- Personnel changes that significantly affect the application of the control.
- Changing circumstances that indicate the need for changes in the control.
- Deficient general IT-controls.

**A39**    When there are a number of controls for which the auditor intends to rely on audit evidence obtained in previous audits, testing some of those controls in each audit provides corroborating information about the continuing effectiveness of the control environment. This contributes to the auditor's decision about whether it is appropriate to rely on audit evidence obtained in previous audits.

*Evaluating the Operating Effectiveness of Controls (Ref: Para. 16-17)*

**A40**    A material misstatement detected by the auditor's procedures is a strong indicator of the existence of a significant deficiency in internal control.

**A41**    The concept of effectiveness of the operation of controls recognizes that some deviations in the way controls are applied by the entity may occur. Deviations from prescribed controls may be caused by such factors as changes in key personnel, significant seasonal fluctuations in volume of transactions and human error. The detected rate of deviation, in particular in comparison with the expected rate, may indicate that the control cannot be relied on to reduce risk at the assertion level to that assessed by the auditor.

**Substantive Procedures** (Ref: Para. 18)

**A42**    Paragraph 18 requires the auditor to design and perform substantive procedures for each material class of transactions, account balance, and disclosure, irrespective of the assessed risks of material misstatement. This requirement reflects the facts that: (a) the auditor's assessment of risk is judgmental and so may not identify all risks of material misstatement; and (b) there are inherent limitations to internal control, including management override.

*Nature and Extent of Substantive Procedures*

**A43**    Depending on the circumstances, the auditor may determine that:

- Performing only substantive analytical procedures will be sufficient to reduce audit risk to an acceptably low level. For example, where the auditor's assessment of risk is supported by audit evidence from tests of controls.
- Only tests of details are appropriate.
- A combination of substantive analytical procedures and tests of details are most responsive to the assessed risks.

Substantive analytical procedures are generally more applicable to large volumes of **A44** transactions that tend to be predictable over time. ISA (UK and Ireland) 520[5] establishes requirements and provides guidance on the application of analytical procedures during an audit.

The nature of the risk and assertion is relevant to the design of tests of details. For **A45** example, tests of details related to the existence or occurrence assertion may involve selecting from items contained in a financial statement amount and obtaining the relevant audit evidence. On the other hand, tests of details related to the completeness assertion may involve selecting from items that are expected to be included in the relevant financial statement amount and investigating whether they are included.

Because the assessment of the risk of material misstatement takes account of internal **A46** control, the extent of substantive procedures may need to be increased when the results from tests of controls are unsatisfactory. However, increasing the extent of an audit procedure is appropriate only if the audit procedure itself is relevant to the specific risk.

In designing tests of details, the extent of testing is ordinarily thought of in terms of **A47** the sample size. However, other matters are also relevant, including whether it is more effective to use other selective means of testing. See ISA (UK and Ireland) 500.[6]

*Considering Whether External Confirmation Procedures Are to Be Performed (Ref: Para. 19)*

External confirmation procedures frequently are relevant when addressing assertions **A48** associated with account balances and their elements, but need not be restricted to these items. For example, the auditor may request external confirmation of the terms of agreements, contracts, or transactions between an entity and other parties. External confirmation procedures also may be performed to obtain audit evidence about the absence of certain conditions. For example, a request may specifically seek confirmation that no "side agreement" exists that may be relevant to an entity's revenue cut-off assertion. Other situations where external confirmation procedures may provide relevant audit evidence in responding to assessed risks of material misstatement include:

- Bank balances and other information relevant to banking relationships.
- Accounts receivable balances and terms.
- Inventories held by third parties at bonded warehouses for processing or on consignment.
- Property title deeds held by lawyers or financiers for safe custody or as security.
- Investments held for safekeeping by third parties, or purchased from stockbrokers but not delivered at the balance sheet date.
- Amounts due to lenders, including relevant terms of repayment and restrictive covenants.
- Accounts payable balances and terms.

Although external confirmations may provide relevant audit evidence relating to **A49** certain assertions, there are some assertions for which external confirmations provide less relevant audit evidence. For example, external confirmations provide less relevant audit evidence relating to the recoverability of accounts receivable balances, than they do of their existence.

[5] *ISA (UK and Ireland) 520, "Analytical Procedures."*

[6] *ISA (UK and Ireland) 500, "Audit Evidence," paragraph 10.*

**A50**   The auditor may determine that external confirmation procedures performed for one purpose provide an opportunity to obtain audit evidence about other matters. For example, confirmation requests for bank balances often include requests for information relevant to other financial statement assertions. Such considerations may influence the auditor's decision about whether to perform external confirmation procedures.

**A51**   Factors that may assist the auditor in determining whether external confirmation procedures are to be performed as substantive audit procedures include:

- The confirming party's knowledge of the subject matter – responses may be more reliable if provided by a person at the confirming party who has the requisite knowledge about the information being confirmed.
- The ability or willingness of the intended confirming party to respond – for example, the confirming party:
  - May not accept responsibility for responding to a confirmation request;
  - May consider responding too costly or time consuming;
  - May have concerns about the potential legal liability resulting from responding;
  - May account for transactions in different currencies; or
  - May operate in an environment where responding to confirmation requests is not a significant aspect of day-to-day operations.

In such situations, confirming parties may not respond, may respond in a casual manner or may attempt to restrict the reliance placed on the response.

- The objectivity of the intended confirming party – if the confirming party is a related party of the entity, responses to confirmation requests may be less reliable.

*Substantive Procedures Related to the Financial Statement Closing Process (Ref: Para. 20(b))*

**A52**   The nature, and also the extent, of the auditor's examination of journal entries and other adjustments depends on the nature and complexity of the entity's financial reporting process and the related risks of material misstatement.

*Substantive Procedures Responsive to Significant Risks (Ref: Para. 21)*

**A53**   Paragraph 21 of this ISA (UK and Ireland) requires the auditor to perform substantive procedures that are specifically responsive to risks the auditor has determined to be significant risks. Audit evidence in the form of external confirmations received directly by the auditor from appropriate confirming parties may assist the auditor in obtaining audit evidence with the high level of reliability that the auditor requires to respond to significant risks of material misstatement, whether due to fraud or error. For example, if the auditor identifies that management is under pressure to meet earnings expectations, there may be a risk that management is inflating sales by improperly recognizing revenue related to sales agreements with terms that preclude revenue recognition or by invoicing sales before shipment. In these circumstances, the auditor may, for example, design external confirmation procedures not only to confirm outstanding amounts, but also to confirm the details of the sales agreements, including date, any rights of return and delivery terms. In addition, the auditor may find it effective to supplement such external confirmation procedures with inquiries of non-financial personnel in the entity regarding any changes in sales agreements and delivery terms.

*Timing of Substantive Procedures (Ref: Para. 22-23)*

In most cases, audit evidence from a previous audit's substantive procedures pro-   **A54**
vides little or no audit evidence for the current period. There are, however,
exceptions, for example, a legal opinion obtained in a previous audit related to the
structure of a securitization to which no changes have occurred, may be relevant in
the current period. In such cases, it may be appropriate to use audit evidence from a
previous audit's substantive procedures if that evidence and the related subject
matter have not fundamentally changed, and audit procedures have been performed
during the current period to establish its continuing relevance.

*Using audit evidence obtained during an interim period (Ref: Para. 22)*

In some circumstances, the auditor may determine that it is effective to perform   **A55**
substantive procedures at an interim date, and to compare and reconcile information
concerning the balance at the period end with the comparable information at the
interim date to:

(a)  Identify amounts that appear unusual;
(b)  Investigate any such amounts; and
(c)  Perform substantive analytical procedures or tests of details to test the inter-
     vening period.

Performing substantive procedures at an interim date without undertaking addi-   **A56**
tional procedures at a later date increases the risk that the auditor will not detect
misstatements that may exist at the period end. This risk increases as the remaining
period is lengthened. Factors such as the following may influence whether to perform
substantive procedures at an interim date:

• The control environment and other relevant controls.
• The availability at a later date of information necessary for the auditor's
  procedures.
• The purpose of the substantive procedure.
• The assessed risk of material misstatement.
• The nature of the class of transactions or account balance and related
  assertions.
• The ability of the auditor to perform appropriate substantive procedures or
  substantive procedures combined with tests of controls to cover the remaining
  period in order to reduce the risk that misstatements that may exist at the period
  end will not be detected.

Factors such as the following may influence whether to perform substantive analy-   **A57**
tical procedures with respect to the period between the interim date and the period
end:

• Whether the period end balances of the particular classes of transactions or
  account balances are reasonably predictable with respect to amount, relative
  significance, and composition.
• Whether the entity's procedures for analyzing and adjusting such classes of
  transactions or account balances at interim dates and for establishing proper
  accounting cutoffs are appropriate.
• Whether the information system relevant to financial reporting will provide
  information concerning the balances at the period end and the transactions in
  the remaining period that is sufficient to permit investigation of:
     (a)  Significant unusual transactions or entries (including those at or near the
          period end);

(b)  Other causes of significant fluctuations, or expected fluctuations that did not occur; and

(c)  Changes in the composition of the classes of transactions or account balances.

*Misstatements detected at an interim date (Ref: Para. 23)*

**A58**   When the auditor concludes that the planned nature, timing, or extent of substantive procedures covering the remaining period need to be modified as a result of unexpected misstatements detected at an interim date, such modification may include extending or repeating the procedures performed at the interim date at the period end.

## Adequacy of Presentation and Disclosure (Ref: Para. 24)

**A59**   Evaluating the overall presentation of the financial statements, including the related disclosures, relates to whether the individual financial statements are presented in a manner that reflects the appropriate classification and description of financial information, and the form, arrangement, and content of the financial statements and their appended notes. This includes, for example, the terminology used, the amount of detail given, the classification of items in the statements, and the bases of amounts set forth.

## Evaluating the Sufficiency and Appropriateness of Audit Evidence (Ref: Para. 25-27)

**A60**   An audit of financial statements is a cumulative and iterative process. As the auditor performs planned audit procedures, the audit evidence obtained may cause the auditor to modify the nature, timing, or extent of other planned audit procedures. Information may come to the auditor's attention that differs significantly from the information on which the risk assessment was based. For example,

- The extent of misstatements that the auditor detects by performing substantive procedures may alter the auditor's judgment about the risk assessments and may indicate a significant deficiency in internal control.
- The auditor may become aware of discrepancies in accounting records, or conflicting or missing evidence.
- Analytical procedures performed at the overall review stage of the audit may indicate a previously unrecognized risk of material misstatement.

In such circumstances, the auditor may need to reevaluate the planned audit procedures, based on the revised consideration of assessed risks for all or some of the classes of transactions, account balances, or disclosures and related assertions. ISA (UK and Ireland) 315 contains further guidance on revising the auditor's risk assessment.[7]

**A61**   The auditor cannot assume that an instance of fraud or error is an isolated occurrence. Therefore, the consideration of how the detection of a misstatement affects the assessed risks of material misstatement is important in determining whether the assessment remains appropriate.

**A62**   The auditor's judgment as to what constitutes sufficient appropriate audit evidence is influenced by such factors as the following:

[7] *ISA (UK and Ireland) 315, paragraph 31.*

- Significance of the potential misstatement in the assertion and the likelihood of its having a material effect, individually or aggregated with other potential misstatements, on the financial statements.
- Effectiveness of management's responses and controls to address the risks.
- Experience gained during previous audits with respect to similar potential misstatements.
- Results of audit procedures performed, including whether such audit procedures identified specific instances of fraud or error.
- Source and reliability of the available information.
- Persuasiveness of the audit evidence.
- Understanding of the entity and its environment, including the entity's internal control.

**Documentation** (Ref: Para. 28)

The form and extent of audit documentation is a matter of professional judgment, and is influenced by the nature, size and complexity of the entity and its internal control, availability of information from the entity and the audit methodology and technology used in the audit.

A63

# Addendum

*This addendum provides a summary of APB's rationale for retaining or excluding in the proposed clarified ISA (UK and Ireland) the supplementary requirements in the existing ISA (UK and Ireland). It also sets out the supplementary guidance material in the existing ISA (UK and Ireland) that APB considers is not necessary to retain in light of the improvements in the underlying Clarity ISAs issued by the IAASB as part of the Clarity Project. It is provided for information and does not form part of the proposed clarified ISA (UK and Ireland).*

*The Consultation Paper published with the exposure drafts explains the general approach used by the APB for determining whether current supplementary material should be proposed to be retained.*

## Analysis of proposed treatment of current APB supplementary material in current ISA (UK and Ireland) 330

### Requirements

There are no supplementary requirements in the current ISA (UK and Ireland) 330.

### Guidance

The following guidance in current ISA (UK and Ireland) 330 has not been carried forward to the proposed clarified standard.

| Current paragraph reference (*Italic text is from IAASB for context*) |
| --- |
| 1-1. – 1-4. [Description of management and those charged with governance] |

# Proposed Clarified International Standard on Auditing (UK and Ireland) 402

# Audit considerations relating to an entity using a service organization

*(Effective for audits of financial statements for periods ending on or after 15 December 2010)*

# Contents

---

International Standard on Auditing (UK and Ireland) (ISA (UK and Ireland)) 402, "Audit Considerations Relating to an Entity Using a Service Organization" should be read in conjunction with ISA (UK and Ireland) 200, "Overall Objectives of the Independent Auditor and the Conduct of an Audit in Accordance with International Standards on Auditing (UK and Ireland)."

# Introduction

## Scope of this ISA (UK and Ireland)

1   This International Standard on Auditing (UK and Ireland) (ISA (UK and Ireland)) deals with the user auditor's responsibility to obtain sufficient appropriate audit evidence when a user entity uses the services of one or more service organizations. Specifically, it expands on how the user auditor applies ISA (UK and Ireland) 315[1] and ISA (UK and Ireland) 330[2] in obtaining an understanding of the user entity, including internal control relevant to the audit, sufficient to identify and assess the risks of material misstatement and in designing and performing further audit procedures responsive to those risks.

2   Many entities outsource aspects of their business to organizations that provide services ranging from performing a specific task under the direction of an entity to replacing an entity's entire business units or functions, such as the tax compliance function. Many of the services provided by such organizations are integral to the entity's business operations; however, not all those services are relevant to the audit.

3   Services provided by a service organization are relevant to the audit of a user entity's financial statements when those services, and the controls over them, are part of the user entity's information system, including related business processes, relevant to financial reporting. Although most controls at the service organization are likely to relate to financial reporting, there may be other controls that may also be relevant to the audit, such as controls over the safeguarding of assets. A service organization's services are part of a user entity's information system, including related business processes, relevant to financial reporting if these services affect any of the following:

   (a)   The classes of transactions in the user entity's operations that are significant to the user entity's financial statements;
   (b)   The procedures, within both information technology (IT) and manual systems, by which the user entity's transactions are initiated, recorded, processed, corrected as necessary, transferred to the general ledger and reported in the financial statements;
   (c)   The related accounting records, either in electronic or manual form, supporting information and specific accounts in the user entity's financial statements that are used to initiate, record, process and report the user entity's transactions; this includes the correction of incorrect information and how information is transferred to the general ledger;
   (d)   How the user entity's information system captures events and conditions, other than transactions, that are significant to the financial statements;
   (e)   The financial reporting process used to prepare the user entity's financial statements, including significant accounting estimates and disclosures; and
   (f)   Controls surrounding journal entries, including non-standard journal entries used to record non-recurring, unusual transactions or adjustments.

4   The nature and extent of work to be performed by the user auditor regarding the services provided by a service organization depend on the nature and significance of those services to the user entity and the relevance of those services to the audit.

---

[1] ISA (UK and Ireland) 315, "Identifying and Assessing the Risks of Material Misstatement through Understanding the Entity and Its Environment."

[2] ISA (UK and Ireland) 330, "The Auditor's Responses to Assessed Risks."

This ISA (UK and Ireland) does not apply to services provided by financial insti-   5
tutions that are limited to processing, for an entity's account held at the financial
institution, transactions that are specifically authorized by the entity, such as the
processing of checking account transactions by a bank or the processing of securities
transactions by a broker. In addition, this ISA (UK and Ireland) does not apply to
the audit of transactions arising from proprietary financial interests in other entities,
such as partnerships, corporations and joint ventures, when proprietary interests are
accounted for and reported to interest holders.

## Effective Date

This ISA (UK and Ireland) is effective for audits of financial statements for periods   6
ending on or after 15 December 2010.

## Objectives

The objectives of the user auditor, when the user entity uses the services of a service   7
organization, are:

(a)  To obtain an understanding of the nature and significance of the services pro-
     vided by the service organization and their effect on the user entity's internal
     control relevant to the audit, sufficient to identify and assess the risks of material
     misstatement; and
(b)  To design and perform audit procedures responsive to those risks.

## Definitions

For purposes of the ISAs (UK and Ireland), the following terms have the meanings   8
attributed below:

(a)  Complementary user entity controls – Controls that the service organization
     assumes, in the design of its service, will be implemented by user entities, and
     which, if necessary to achieve control objectives, are identified in the description
     of its system.
(b)  Report on the description and design of controls at a service organization
     (referred to in this ISA (UK and Ireland) as a type 1 report) – A report that
     comprises:
     (i)   A description, prepared by management of the service organization, of the
           service organization's system, control objectives and related controls that
           have been designed and implemented as at a specified date; and
     (ii)  A report by the service auditor with the objective of conveying reasonable
           assurance that includes the service auditor's opinion on the description of
           the service organization's system, control objectives and related controls
           and the suitability of the design of the controls to achieve the specified
           control objectives.
(c)  Report on the description, design, and operating effectiveness of controls at a
     service organization (referred to in this ISA (UK and Ireland) as a type 2 report)
     – A report that comprises:
     (i)   A description, prepared by management of the service organization, of the
           service organization's system, control objectives and related controls, their
           design and implementation as at a specified date or throughout a specified
           period and, in some cases, their operating effectiveness throughout a spe-
           cified period; and

    (ii)  A report by the service auditor with the objective of conveying reasonable assurance that includes:

        a.  The service auditor's opinion on the description of the service organization's system, control objectives and related controls, the suitability of the design of the controls to achieve the specified control objectives, and the operating effectiveness of the controls; and

        b.  A description of the service auditor's tests of the controls and the results thereof.

(d)  Service auditor – An auditor who, at the request of the service organization, provides an assurance report on the controls of a service organization.

(e)  Service organization – A third-party organization (or segment of a third-party organization) that provides services to user entities that are part of those entities' information systems relevant to financial reporting.

(f)  Service organization's system – The policies and procedures designed, implemented and maintained by the service organization to provide user entities with the services covered by the service auditor's report.

(g)  Subservice organization – A service organization used by another service organization to perform some of the services provided to user entities that are part of those user entities' information systems relevant to financial reporting.

(h)  User auditor – An auditor who audits and reports on the financial statements of a user entity.

(i)  User entity – An entity that uses a service organization and whose financial statements are being audited.

# Requirements

## Obtaining an Understanding of the Services Provided by a Service Organization, Including Internal Control

**9**    When obtaining an understanding of the user entity in accordance with ISA (UK and Ireland) 315,[3] the user auditor shall obtain an understanding of how a user entity uses the services of a service organization in the user entity's operations, including: (Ref: Para. A1-A2)

(a)  The nature of the services provided by the service organization and the significance of those services to the user entity, including the effect thereof on the user entity's internal control; (Ref: Para. A3-A5)

(b)  The nature and materiality of the transactions processed or accounts or financial reporting processes affected by the service organization; (Ref: Para. A6)

(c)  The degree of interaction between the activities of the service organization and those of the user entity; and (Ref: Para. A7)

(d)  The nature of the relationship between the user entity and the service organization, including the relevant contractual terms for the activities undertaken by the service organization. (Ref: Para. A8-A11)

(e)  Whether, if the service organisation maintains all or part of a user entity's accounting records, the arrangements affect the user auditor's reporting responsibilities in relation to accounting records arising from law or regulation. (Ref: Para. A11-1 – A11-6)

---

[3] *ISA (UK and Ireland) 315, paragraph 11.*

When obtaining an understanding of internal control relevant to the audit in **10** accordance with ISA (UK and Ireland) 315,[4] the user auditor shall evaluate the design and implementation of relevant controls at the user entity that relate to the services provided by the service organization, including those that are applied to the transactions processed by the service organization. (Ref: Para. A12-A14)

The user auditor shall determine whether a sufficient understanding of the nature **11** and significance of the services provided by the service organization and their effect on the user entity's internal control relevant to the audit has been obtained to provide a basis for the identification and assessment of risks of material misstatement.

If the user auditor is unable to obtain a sufficient understanding from the user entity, **12** the user auditor shall obtain that understanding from one or more of the following procedures: (Ref: Para. A15-A20)

(a) Obtaining a type 1 or type 2 report, if available;
(b) Contacting the service organization, through the user entity, to obtain specific information;
(c) Visiting the service organization and performing procedures that will provide the necessary information about the relevant controls at the service organization; or
(d) Using another auditor to perform procedures that will provide the necessary information about the relevant controls at the service organization.

### *Using a Type 1 or Type 2 Report to Support the User Auditor's Understanding of the Service Organization*

In determining the sufficiency and appropriateness of the audit evidence provided by **13** a type 1 or type 2 report, the user auditor shall be satisfied as to: (Ref: Para. A21)

(a) The service auditor's professional competence and independence from the service organization; and
(b) The adequacy of the standards under which the type 1 or type 2 report was issued.

If the user auditor plans to use a type 1 or type 2 report as audit evidence to support **14** the user auditor's understanding about the design and implementation of controls at the service organization, the user auditor shall: (Ref: Para. A22-A23)

(a) Evaluate whether the description and design of controls at the service organization is at a date or for a period that is appropriate for the user auditor's purposes;
(b) Evaluate the sufficiency and appropriateness of the evidence provided by the report for the understanding of the user entity's internal control relevant to the audit; and
(c) Determine whether complementary user entity controls identified by the service organization are relevant to the user entity and, if so, obtain an understanding of whether the user entity has designed and implemented such controls.

### Responding to the Assessed Risks of Material Misstatement

In responding to assessed risks in accordance with ISA (UK and Ireland) 330, the **15** user auditor shall: (Ref: Para. A24-A28)

---

[4] *ISA (UK and Ireland) 315, paragraph 12.*

(a) Determine whether sufficient appropriate audit evidence concerning the relevant financial statement assertions is available from records held at the user entity; and, if not,

(b) Perform further audit procedures to obtain sufficient appropriate audit evidence or use another auditor to perform those procedures at the service organization on the user auditor's behalf.

### *Tests of Controls*

**16** When the user auditor's risk assessment includes an expectation that controls at the service organization are operating effectively, the user auditor shall obtain audit evidence about the operating effectiveness of those controls from one or more of the following procedures: (Ref: Para. A29-A30)

(a) Obtaining a type 2 report, if available;

(b) Performing appropriate tests of controls at the service organization; or

(c) Using another auditor to perform tests of controls at the service organization on behalf of the user auditor.

### *Using a Type 2 Report as Audit Evidence that Controls at the Service Organization Are Operating Effectively*

**17** If, in accordance with paragraph 16(a), the user auditor plans to use a type 2 report as audit evidence that controls at the service organization are operating effectively, the user auditor shall determine whether the service auditor's report provides sufficient appropriate audit evidence about the effectiveness of the controls to support the user auditor's risk assessment by: (Ref: Para. A31-A39)

(a) Evaluating whether the description, design and operating effectiveness of controls at the service organization is at a date or for a period that is appropriate for the user auditor's purposes;

(b) Determining whether complementary user entity controls identified by the service organization are relevant to the user entity and, if so, obtaining an understanding of whether the user entity has designed and implemented such controls and, if so, testing their operating effectiveness;

(c) Evaluating the adequacy of the time period covered by the tests of controls and the time elapsed since the performance of the tests of controls; and

(d) Evaluating whether the tests of controls performed by the service auditor and the results thereof, as described in the service auditor's report, are relevant to the assertions in the user entity's financial statements and provide sufficient appropriate audit evidence to support the user auditor's risk assessment.

### Type 1 and Type 2 Reports that Exclude the Services of a Subservice Organization

**18** If the user auditor plans to use a type 1 or a type 2 report that excludes the services provided by a subservice organization and those services are relevant to the audit of the user entity's financial statements, the user auditor shall apply the requirements of this ISA (UK and Ireland) with respect to the services provided by the subservice organization. (Ref: Para. A40)

**Fraud, Non-Compliance with Laws and Regulations and Uncorrected Misstatements in Relation to Activities at the Service Organization**

The user auditor shall inquire of management of the user entity whether the service **19** organization has reported to the user entity, or whether the user entity is otherwise aware of, any fraud, non-compliance with laws and regulations or uncorrected misstatements affecting the financial statements of the user entity. The user auditor shall evaluate how such matters affect the nature, timing and extent of the user auditor's further audit procedures, including the effect on the user auditor's conclusions and user auditor's report. (Ref: Para. A41)

**Reporting by the User Auditor**

The user auditor shall modify the opinion in the user auditor's report in accordance **20** with ISA (UK and Ireland) 705[5] if the user auditor is unable to obtain sufficient appropriate audit evidence regarding the services provided by the service organization relevant to the audit of the user entity's financial statements. (Ref: Para. A42)

The user auditor shall not refer to the work of a service auditor in the user auditor's **21** report containing an unmodified opinion unless required by law or regulation to do so. If such reference is required by law or regulation, the user auditor's report shall indicate that the reference does not diminish the user auditor's responsibility for the audit opinion. (Ref: Para. A43)

If reference to the work of a service auditor is relevant to an understanding of a **22** modification to the user auditor's opinion, the user auditor's report shall indicate that such reference does not diminish the user auditor's responsibility for that opinion. (Ref: Para. A44)

\*\*\*

# Application and Other Explanatory Material

**Obtaining an Understanding of the Services Provided by a Service Organization, Including Internal Control**

*Sources of Information* (Ref: Para. 9)

Information on the nature of the services provided by a service organization may be **A1** available from a wide variety of sources, such as:

- User manuals.
- System overviews.
- Technical manuals.
- The contract or service level agreement between the user entity and the service organization.
- Reports by service organizations, internal auditors or regulatory authorities on controls at the service organization.
- Reports by the service auditor, including management letters, if available.

Knowledge obtained through the user auditor's experience with the service organi- **A2** zation, for example through experience with other audit engagements, may also be helpful in obtaining an understanding of the nature of the services provided by the

---

[5] *ISA (UK and Ireland) 705, "Modifications to the Opinion in the Independent Auditor's Report," paragraph 6.*

service organization. This may be particularly helpful if the services and controls at the service organization over those services are highly standardized.

*Nature of the Services Provided by the Service Organization* (Ref: Para. 9(a))

A3   A user entity may use a service organization such as one that processes transactions and maintains related accountability, or records transactions and processes related data. Service organizations that provide such services include, for example, bank trust departments that invest and service assets for employee benefit plans or for others; mortgage bankers that service mortgages for others; and application service providers that provide packaged software applications and a technology environment that enables customers to process financial and operational transactions.

A4   Examples of service organization services that are relevant to the audit include:
- Maintenance of the user entity's accounting records.
- Management of assets.
- Initiating, recording or processing transactions as agent of the user entity.

*Compliance with Law and Regulations*

A4-1   An auditor appointed to report on a user entity's financial statements may have additional reporting responsibilities, which could be affected by the entity's use of a service organisation (for example, reporting on compliance with the requirement of company law concerning maintenance of adequate accounting records; or the expression of an opinion on reports by the entity to its regulator).

A4-2   The user auditor considers whether the activities undertaken by the service organisation are in an area in which the user entity is required to comply with requirements of law and regulations. In such circumstances, non-compliance may have a significant effect on the financial statements. The user auditor therefore determines whether the law and regulations concerned are to be regarded as relevant to the audit[5a] in order to meet the requirements of ISA (UK and Ireland) 250 "Consideration of Laws and Regulations in an Audit of Financial Statements" and undertake procedures to assess the risk of a misstatement arising from non-compliance as set out in that ISA (UK and Ireland).

A4-3   When a service organisation undertakes maintenance of accounting records, factors of particular importance to the user auditor's assessment of risk include the following:
- The knowledge and expertise of service organisation staff in matters relevant to the user entity's business.
- The practicability of control by the user entity's management, and the nature of controls actually implemented. Some types of business facilitate the use of analytical control techniques subsequent to completion of transactions (for example payroll processing); others need detailed processing controls operated on a concurrent basis (for example, distribution centres which hold stock belonging to the entity and arrange deliveries for the entity). (See paragraph A12)

[5a] *Laws and regulations are relevant to the audit when they either relate directly to the preparation of the financial statements of the entity, or are fundamental to the operating aspects of its business (ISA (UK and Ireland) 250 Section A, "Consideration of Laws and Regulations in an Audit of Financial Statements," paragraph 6).*

- The use of quality assurance processes by the service organisation (e.g. its internal audit function).

*Considerations Specific to Smaller Entities*

Smaller entities may use external bookkeeping services ranging from the processing  A5
of certain transactions (e.g., payment of payroll taxes) and maintenance of their
accounting records to the preparation of their financial statements. The use of such a
service organization for the preparation of its financial statements does not relieve
management of the smaller entity and, where appropriate, those charged with governance of their responsibilities for the financial statements.[6]

**Nature and Materiality of Transactions Processed by the Service Organization** (Ref:
Para. 9(b))

A service organization may establish policies and procedures that affect the user  A6
entity's internal control. These policies and procedures are at least in part physically
and operationally separate from the user entity. The significance of the controls of
the service organization to those of the user entity depends on the nature of the
services provided by the service organization, including the nature and materiality of
the transactions it processes for the user entity. In certain situations, the transactions
processed and the accounts affected by the service organization may not appear to be
material to the user entity's financial statements, but the nature of the transactions
processed may be significant and the user auditor may determine that an understanding of those controls is necessary in the circumstances.

**The Degree of Interaction between the Activities of the Service Organization and the
User Entity** (Ref: Para. 9(c))

The significance of the controls of the service organization to those of the user entity  A7
also depends on the degree of interaction between its activities and those of the user
entity. The degree of interaction refers to the extent to which a user entity is able to
and elects to implement effective controls over the processing performed by the
service organization. For example, a high degree of interaction exists between the
activities of the user entity and those at the service organization when the user entity
authorizes transactions and the service organization processes and does the
accounting for those transactions. In these circumstances, it may be practicable for
the user entity to implement effective controls over those transactions. On the other
hand, when the service organization initiates or initially records, processes, and does
the accounting for the user entity's transactions, there is a lower degree of interaction
between the two organizations. In these circumstances, the user entity may be unable
to, or may elect not to, implement effective controls over these transactions at the
user entity and may rely on controls at the service organization.

**Nature of the Relationship between the User Entity and the Service Organization** (Ref:
Para. 9(d))

The contract or service level agreement between the user entity and the service  A8
organization may provide for matters such as:

---

[6] *ISA (UK and Ireland) 200, "Overall Objectives of the Independent Auditor and the Conduct of an Audit in
Accordance with International Standards on Auditing," paragraphs 4 and A2-A3.*

- The information to be provided to the user entity and responsibilities for initiating transactions relating to the activities undertaken by the service organization;
- The application of requirements of regulatory bodies concerning the form of records to be maintained, or access to them;
- The indemnification, if any, to be provided to the user entity in the event of a performance failure;
- Whether the service organization will provide a report on its controls and, if so, whether such report would be a type 1 or type 2 report;
- Whether the user auditor has rights of access to the accounting records of the user entity maintained by the service organization and other information necessary for the conduct of the audit; and
- Whether the agreement allows for direct communication between the user auditor and the service auditor.

**A8-1**    Other matters which the auditor may consider include:

- The way that accounting records relating to relevant activities are maintained.
- Whether the entity has rights of access to accounting records prepared by the service organisation concerning the activities undertaken, and relevant underlying information held by it, and the conditions in which such access may be sought.
- The nature of relevant performance standards.
- The way in which the entity monitors performance of relevant activities and the extent to which its monitoring process relies on controls operated by the service organization.

**A8-2**    Agreement by a service organisation to provide an indemnity does not provide information directly relevant to the user auditor's assessment of the risk of material misstatements relating to financial statement assertions. However, such agreements may help to inform the user auditor's judgment concerning the effect of performance failure on the user entity's financial statements: this may be relevant in instances of performance failure, when the existence of an indemnity may help to ensure that the user entity's status as a going concern is not threatened. Where the user auditor wishes to rely on the operation of the indemnity for this purpose, the resources available to the service organisation also need to be considered.

**A8-3**    The financial standing of a service organisation is relevant to the audit insofar as the user auditor considers it necessary to rely on the operation of an indemnity from the service organisation in assessing the entity's status as a going concern (see paragraph A8-2). However, a service organisation whose cash and/or capital resources are low in relation to the nature of services provided or the volume of its customers may be susceptible to pressures resulting in errors or deliberate misstatements in reporting to the entity, or fraud. If the user auditor considers that this factor may be relevant to the assessment of risk, the user auditor also takes into account the existence of binding arrangements to provide resources to the service organisations from a holding company or other group company, and the financial strength of the group as a whole.

**A9**    *There is a direct relationship between the service organization and the user entity and between the service organization and the service auditor. These relationships do not necessarily create a direct relationship between the user auditor and the service* auditor. When there is no direct relationship between the user auditor and the service auditor, communications between the user auditor and the service auditor are usually conducted through the user entity and the service organization. A direct relationship may also be created between a user auditor and a service auditor, taking into account the relevant ethical and confidentiality considerations. A user auditor, for example, may use a service auditor to perform procedures on the user auditor's behalf, such as:

(a) Tests of controls at the service organization; or

(b) Substantive procedures on the user entity's financial statement transactions and balances maintained by a service organization.

### Considerations Specific to Public Sector Entities

Public sector auditors generally have broad rights of access established by legislation. However, there may be situations where such rights of access are not available, for example when the service organization is located in a different jurisdiction. In such cases, a public sector auditor may need to obtain an understanding of the legislation applicable in the different jurisdiction to determine whether appropriate access rights can be obtained. A public sector auditor may also obtain or ask the user entity to incorporate rights of access in any contractual arrangements between the user entity and the service organization.  **A10**

Public sector auditors may also use another auditor to perform tests of controls or substantive procedures in relation to compliance with law, regulation or other authority.  **A11**

### Accounting Records (Ref: Para. 9(e))

Use of a service organisation does not diminish the ultimate responsibility of those charged with governance of a user entity for conducting its business in a manner which meets their legal responsibilities, including those of safeguarding the user entity's assets, maintaining adequate accounting records and preparing financial statements which provide information about its economic activities and financial position. Practical issues, including the way in which accounting records will be kept and the manner in which those charged with governance assess the quality of the service, need to be addressed.  **A11-1**

For each relevant activity involving maintenance of material elements of the entity's accounting records by a service organisation, the user auditor obtains and documents an understanding as to the way that the accounting records are maintained, including the way in which those charged with governance ensure that its accounting records meet any relevant legal obligations. Such obligations may arise under statute, regulation (for example, specific requirements apply to authorised investment businesses) or under the terms of the entity's governing document (for example, the trust deed establishing a charity may require it to maintain particular records).  **A11-2**

Key obligations of entities incorporated under company law include:  **A11-3**

(a) To maintain accounting records which are sufficient to:

> (i)   Disclose with reasonable accuracy, at any time, the financial position of the company at that time, and
>
> (ii)  Enable the directors to ensure that the company's financial statements meet statutory requirements;
>
> (b)  To guard against falsification; and
>
> (c)  To provide its directors, officers and auditor with access to its accounting records at any time[6a].

**A11-4**   When a user entity incorporated under company law arranges for a service organisation to maintain its accounting records, the contractual arrangements can only be regarded as appropriate if they establish the company's legal ownership of the records and provide for access to them at any time by those charged with governance of the company and by its auditor.

**A11-5**   An auditor of entities incorporated under company law has statutory reporting obligations relating to compliance with requirements for companies to maintain adequate accounting records. Where such an entity outsources the preparation of its accounting records to a service organisation, issues relating to whether the arrangements with the service organisation are such as to permit the user entity to meet its statutory obligations may require careful consideration, by both those charged with governance and the user auditor. Where there is doubt, the user auditor may wish to encourage the those charged with governance to take legal advice before issuing the auditor's report on its financial statements.

**A11-6**   A particular issue arises in relation to companies incorporated in the United Kingdom. The wording of UK company law appears to be prescriptive and to require the company itself to keep accounting records. Consequently, whether a company 'keeps' records (as opposed to 'causes records to be kept') will depend upon the particular terms of the outsourcing arrangements and, in particular, the extent to which the company retains ownership of, has access to, or holds copies of, those records[6b].

***Understanding the Controls Relating to Services Provided by the Service Organization***
(Ref: Para. 10)

**A12**   The user entity may establish controls over the service organization's services that may be tested by the user auditor and that may enable the user auditor to conclude that the user entity's controls are operating effectively for some or all of the related assertions, regardless of the controls in place at the service organization. If a user entity, for example, uses a service organization to process its payroll transactions, the user entity may establish controls over the submission and receipt of payroll information that could prevent or detect material misstatements. These controls may include:

- Comparing the data submitted to the service organization with reports of information received from the service organization after the data has been processed.
- Recomputing a sample of the payroll amounts for clerical accuracy and reviewing the total amount of the payroll for reasonableness.

[6a] *In the UK, Companies Act 2006, sections 386, 388, 499 and 1138 and in Ireland, Companies Act 1963, section 378 and Companies Act 1990, sections 193 and 202.*

[6b] *In Ireland, company law requires that companies shall cause records to be kept in accordance with its requirements.*

In this situation, the user auditor may perform tests of the user entity's controls over   **A13**
payroll processing that would provide a basis for the user auditor to conclude that
the user entity's controls are operating effectively for the assertions related to payroll
transactions.

As noted in ISA (UK and Ireland) 315,[7] in respect of some risks, the user auditor   **A14**
may judge that it is not possible or practicable to obtain sufficient appropriate audit
evidence only from substantive procedures. Such risks may relate to the inaccurate or
incomplete recording of routine and significant classes of transactions and account
balances, the characteristics of which often permit highly automated processing with
little or no manual intervention. Such automated processing characteristics may be
particularly present when the user entity uses service organizations. In such cases, the
user entity's controls over such risks are relevant to the audit and the user auditor is
required to obtain an understanding of, and to evaluate, such controls in accordance
with paragraphs 9 and 10 of this ISA (UK and Ireland).

***Further Procedures When a Sufficient Understanding Cannot Be Obtained from the
User Entity*** (Ref: Para. 12)

The user auditor's decision as to which procedure, individually or in combination, in   **A15**
paragraph 12 to undertake, in order to obtain the information necessary to provide a
basis for the identification and assessment of the risks of material misstatement in
relation to the user entity's use of the service organization, may be influenced by such
matters as:

- The size of both the user entity and the service organization;
- The complexity of the transactions at the user entity and the complexity of the
  services provided by the service organization;
- The location of the service organization (for example, the user auditor may
  decide to use another auditor to perform procedures at the service organization
  on the user auditor's behalf if the service organization is in a remote location);
- Whether the procedure(s) is expected to effectively provide the user auditor with
  sufficient appropriate audit evidence; and
- The nature of the relationship between the user entity and the service
  organization.

A service organization may engage a service auditor to report on the description and   **A16**
design of its controls (type 1 report) or on the description and design of its controls
and their operating effectiveness (type 2 report). Type 1 or type 2 reports may be
issued under [proposed] International Standard on Assurance Engagements (ISAE)
3402[8] or under standards established by an authorized or recognized standards
setting organization (which may identify them by different names, such as Type A or
Type B reports).

The availability of a type 1 or type 2 report will generally depend on whether the   **A17**
contract between a service organization and a user entity includes the provision of
such a report by the service organization. A service organization may also elect, for
practical reasons, to make a type 1 or type 2 report available to the user entities.
However, in some cases, a type 1 or type 2 report may not be available to user
entities.

---

[7] *ISA (UK and Ireland) 315, paragraph 30.*

[8] *[Proposed] ISAE 3402, "Assurance Reports on Controls at a Third-Party Service Organization."*

**A18**    In some circumstances, a user entity may outsource one or more significant business units or functions, such as its entire tax planning and compliance functions, or finance and accounting or the controllership function to one or more service organizations. As a report on controls at the service organization may not be available in these circumstances, visiting the service organization may be the most effective procedure for the user auditor to gain an understanding of controls at the service organization, as there is likely to be direct interaction of management of the user entity with management at the service organization.

**A19**    Another auditor may be used to perform procedures that will provide the necessary information about the relevant controls at the service organization. If a type 1 or type 2 report has been issued, the user auditor may use the service auditor to perform these procedures as the service auditor has an existing relationship with the service organization. The user auditor using the work of another auditor may find the guidance in ISA (UK and Ireland) 600[9] useful as it relates to understanding another auditor (including that auditor's independence and professional competence), involvement in the work of another auditor in planning the nature, extent and timing of such work, and in evaluating the sufficiency and appropriateness of the audit evidence obtained.

**A20**    A user entity may use a service organization that in turn uses a subservice organization to provide some of the services provided to a user entity that are part of the user entity's information system relevant to financial reporting. The subservice organization may be a separate entity from the service organization or may be related to the service organization. A user auditor may need to consider controls at the subservice organization. In situations where one or more subservice organizations are used, the interaction between the activities of the user entity and those of the service organization is expanded to include the interaction between the user entity, the service organization and the subservice organizations. The degree of this interaction, as well as the nature and materiality of the transactions processed by the service organization and the subservice organizations are the most important factors for the user auditor to consider in determining the significance of the service organization's and subservice organization's controls to the user entity's controls.

*Using a Type 1 or Type 2 Report to Support the User Auditor's Understanding of the Service Organization* (Ref: Para. 13-14)

**A21**    The user auditor may make inquiries about the service auditor to the service auditor's professional organization or other practitioners and inquire whether the service auditor is subject to regulatory oversight. The service auditor may be practicing in a jurisdiction where different standards are followed in respect of reports on controls at a service organization, and the user auditor may obtain information about the standards used by the service auditor from the standard setting organization.

**A22**    A type 1 or type 2 report, along with information about the user entity, may assist the user auditor in obtaining an understanding of:

(a)    The aspects of controls at the service organization that may affect the processing of the user entity's transactions, including the use of subservice organizations;

(b)    The flow of significant transactions through the service organization to determine the points in the transaction flow where material misstatements in the user entity's financial statements could occur;

---

[9] *ISA (UK and Ireland) 600, paragraph 2, states: "An auditor may find this ISA (UK and Ireland), adapted as necessary in the circumstances, useful when that auditor involves other auditors in the audit of financial statements that are not group financial statements ..." See also paragraph 19 of ISA (UK and Ireland) 600.*

(c) The control objectives at the service organization that are relevant to the user entity's financial statement assertions; and

(d) Whether controls at the service organization are suitably designed and implemented to prevent or detect processing errors that could result in material misstatements in the user entity's financial statements.

A type 1 or type 2 report may assist the user auditor in obtaining a sufficient understanding to identify and assess the risks of material misstatement. A type 1 report, however, does not provide any evidence of the operating effectiveness of the relevant controls.

A type 1 or type 2 report that is as of a date or for a period that is outside of the reporting period of a user entity may assist the user auditor in obtaining a preliminary understanding of the controls implemented at the service organization if the report is supplemented by additional current information from other sources. If the service organization's description of controls is as of a date or for a period that precedes the beginning of the period under audit, the user auditor may perform procedures to update the information in a type 1 or type 2 report, such as:

    **A23**

- Discussing the changes at the service organization with user entity personnel who would be in a position to know of such changes;
- Reviewing current documentation and correspondence issued by the service organization; or
- Discussing the changes with service organization personnel.

## Responding to the Assessed Risks of Material Misstatement (Ref: Para. 15)

Whether the use of a service organization increases a user entity's risk of material misstatement depends on the nature of the services provided and the controls over these services; in some cases, the use of a service organization may decrease a user entity's risk of material misstatement, particularly if the user entity itself does not possess the expertise necessary to undertake particular activities, such as initiating, processing, and recording transactions, or does not have adequate resources (e.g., an IT system).

    **A24**

When the service organization maintains material elements of the accounting records of the user entity, direct access to those records may be necessary in order for the user auditor to obtain sufficient appropriate audit evidence relating to the operations of controls over those records or to substantiate transactions and balances recorded in them, or both. Such access may involve either physical inspection of records at the service organization's premises or interrogation of records maintained electronically from the user entity or another location, or both. Where direct access is achieved electronically, the user auditor may thereby obtain evidence as to the adequacy of controls operated by the service organization over the completeness and integrity of the user entity's data for which the service organization is responsible.

    **A25**

In determining the nature and extent of audit evidence to be obtained in relation to balances representing assets held or transactions undertaken by a service organization on behalf of the user entity, the following procedures may be considered by the user auditor:

    **A26**

(a) Inspecting records and documents held by the user entity: the reliability of this source of evidence is determined by the nature and extent of the accounting records and supporting documentation retained by the user entity. In some cases, the user entity may not maintain independent detailed records or documentation of specific transactions undertaken on its behalf.

(b) Inspecting records and documents held by the service organization: the user auditor's access to the records of the service organization may be established as part of the contractual arrangements between the user entity and the service organization. The user auditor may also use another auditor, on its behalf, to gain access to the user entity's records maintained by the service organization.

(c) Obtaining confirmations of balances and transactions from the service organization: where the user entity maintains independent records of balances and transactions, confirmation from the service organization corroborating the user entity's records may constitute reliable audit evidence concerning the existence of the transactions and assets concerned. For example, when multiple service organizations are used, such as an investment manager and a custodian, and these service organizations maintain independent records, the user auditor may confirm balances with these organizations in order to compare this information with the independent records of the user entity.

> If the user entity does not maintain independent records, information obtained in confirmations from the service organization is merely a statement of what is reflected in the records maintained by the service organization. Therefore, such confirmations do not, taken alone, constitute reliable audit evidence. In these circumstances, the user auditor may consider whether an alternative source of independent evidence can be identified.

(d) Performing analytical procedures on the records maintained by the user entity or on the reports received from the service organization: the effectiveness of analytical procedures is likely to vary by assertion and will be affected by the extent and detail of information available.

A27 Another auditor may perform procedures that are substantive in nature for the benefit of user auditors. Such an engagement may involve the performance, by another auditor, of procedures agreed upon by the user entity and its user auditor and by the service organization and its service auditor. The findings resulting from the procedures performed by another auditor are reviewed by the user auditor to determine whether they constitute sufficient appropriate audit evidence. In addition, there may be requirements imposed by governmental authorities or through contractual arrangements whereby a service auditor performs designated procedures that are substantive in nature. The results of the application of the required procedures to balances and transactions processed by the service organization may be used by user auditors as part of the evidence necessary to support their audit opinions. In these circumstances, it may be useful for the user auditor and the service auditor to agree, prior to the performance of the procedures, to the audit documentation or access to audit documentation that will be provided to the user auditor.

A28 In certain circumstances, in particular when a user entity outsources some or all of its finance function to a service organization, the user auditor may face a situation where a significant portion of the audit evidence resides at the service organization. Substantive procedures may need to be performed at the service organization by the user auditor or another auditor on its behalf. A service auditor may provide a type 2 report and, in addition, may perform substantive procedures on behalf of the user auditor. The involvement of another auditor does not alter the user auditor's responsibility to obtain sufficient appropriate audit evidence to afford a reasonable basis to support the user auditor's opinion. Accordingly, the user auditor's consideration of whether sufficient appropriate audit evidence has been obtained and whether the user auditor needs to perform further substantive procedures includes the user auditor's involvement with, or evidence of, the direction, supervision and performance of the substantive procedures performed by another auditor.

*Tests of Controls* (Ref: Para. 16)

The user auditor is required by ISA (UK and Ireland) 330[10] to design and perform **A29** tests of controls to obtain sufficient appropriate audit evidence as to the operating effectiveness of relevant controls in certain circumstances. In the context of a service organization, this requirement applies when:

(a) The user auditor's assessment of risks of material misstatement includes an expectation that the controls at the service organization are operating effectively (i.e., the user auditor intends to rely on the operating effectiveness of controls at the service organization in determining the nature, timing and extent of substantive procedures); or

(b) Substantive procedures alone, or in combination with tests of the operating effectiveness of controls at the user entity, cannot provide sufficient appropriate audit evidence at the assertion level.

If a type 2 report is not available, a user auditor may contact the service organiza- **A30** tion, through the user entity, to request that a service auditor be engaged to provide a type 2 report that includes tests of the operating effectiveness of the relevant controls or the user auditor may use another auditor to perform procedures at the service organization that test the operating effectiveness of those controls. A user auditor may also visit the service organization and perform tests of relevant controls if the service organization agrees to it. The user auditor's risk assessments are based on the combined evidence provided by the work of another auditor and the user auditor's own procedures.

### *Using a Type 2 Report as Audit Evidence that Controls at the Service Organization Are Operating Effectively* (Ref: Para. 17)

A type 2 report may be intended to satisfy the needs of several different user audi- **A31** tors; therefore tests of controls and results described in the service auditor's report may not be relevant to assertions that are significant in the user entity's financial statements. The relevant tests of controls and results are evaluated to determine that the service auditor's report provides sufficient appropriate audit evidence about the effectiveness of the controls to support the user auditor's risk assessment. In doing so, the user auditor may consider the following factors:

(a) The time period covered by the tests of controls and the time elapsed since the performance of the tests of controls;

(b) The scope of the service auditor's work and the services and processes covered, the controls tested and tests that were performed, and the way in which tested controls relate to the user entity's controls; and

(c) The results of those tests of controls and the service auditor's opinion on the operating effectiveness of the controls.

For certain assertions, the shorter the period covered by a specific test and the longer **A32** the time elapsed since the performance of the test, the less audit evidence the test may provide. In comparing the period covered by the type 2 report to the user entity's financial reporting period, the user auditor may conclude that the type 2 report offers less audit evidence if there is little overlap between the period covered by the type 2 report and the period for which the user auditor intends to rely on the report. When this is the case, a type 2 report covering a preceding or subsequent period may provide additional audit evidence. In other cases, the user auditor may determine it is necessary to perform, or use another auditor to perform, tests of controls at the

---

[10] *ISA (UK and Ireland) 330, paragraph 8.*

service organization in order to obtain sufficient appropriate audit evidence about the operating effectiveness of those controls.

A33    It may also be necessary for the user auditor to obtain additional evidence about significant changes to the relevant controls at the service organization outside of the period covered by the type 2 report or determine additional audit procedures to be performed. Relevant factors in determining what additional audit evidence to obtain about controls at the service organization that were operating outside of the period covered by the service auditor's report may include:

- The significance of the assessed risks of material misstatement at the assertion level;
- The specific controls that were tested during the interim period, and significant changes to them since they were tested, including changes in the information system, processes, and personnel;
- The degree to which audit evidence about the operating effectiveness of those controls was obtained;
- The length of the remaining period;
- The extent to which the user auditor intends to reduce further substantive procedures based on the reliance on controls; and
- The effectiveness of the control environment and monitoring of controls at the user entity.

A34    Additional audit evidence may be obtained, for example, by extending tests of controls over the remaining period or testing the user entity's monitoring of controls.

A35    If the service auditor's testing period is completely outside the user entity's financial reporting period, the user auditor will be unable to rely on such tests for the user auditor to conclude that the user entity's controls are operating effectively because they do not provide current audit period evidence of the effectiveness of the controls, unless other procedures are performed.

A36    In certain circumstances, a service provided by the service organization may be designed with the assumption that certain controls will be implemented by the user entity. For example, the service may be designed with the assumption that the user entity will have controls in place for authorizing transactions before they are sent to the service organization for processing. In such a situation, the service organization's description of controls may include a description of those complementary user entity controls. The user auditor considers whether those complementary user entity controls are relevant to the service provided to the user entity.

A37    If the user auditor believes that the service auditor's report may not provide sufficient appropriate audit evidence, for example, if a service auditor's report does not contain a description of the service auditor's tests of controls and results thereon, the user auditor may supplement the understanding of the service auditor's procedures and conclusions by contacting the service organization, through the user entity, to request a discussion with the service auditor about the scope and results of the service auditor's work. Also, if the user auditor believes it is necessary, the user auditor may contact the service organization, through the user entity, to request that the service auditor perform procedures at the service organization. Alternatively, the user auditor, or another auditor at the request of the user auditor, may perform such procedures.

A38    The service auditor's type 2 report identifies results of tests, including exceptions and other information that could affect the user auditor's conclusions. Exceptions noted by the service auditor or a modified opinion in the service auditor's type 2 report do not automatically mean that the service auditor's type 2 report will not be useful for the audit of the user entity's financial statements in assessing the risks of material misstatement. Rather, the exceptions and the matter giving rise to a modified opinion in the service auditor's type 2 report are considered in the user auditor's assessment of the testing of controls performed by the service auditor. In considering the exceptions and matters giving rise to a modified opinion, the user auditor may discuss such matters with the service auditor. Such communication is dependent upon the user entity contacting the service organization, and obtaining the service organization's approval for the communication to take place.

*Communication of deficiencies in internal control identified during the audit*

The user auditor is required to communicate in writing significant deficiencies   **A39**
identified during the audit to both management and those charged with governance on a timely basis.[11] The user auditor is also required to communicate to management at an appropriate level of responsibility on a timely basis other deficiencies in internal control identified during the audit that, in the user auditor's professional judgment, are of sufficient importance to merit management's attention.[12] Matters that the user auditor may identify during the audit and may communicate to management and those charged with governance of the user entity include:

(a) Any monitoring of controls that could be implemented by the user entity, including those identified as a result of obtaining a type 1 or type 2 report;
(b) Instances where complementary user entity controls are noted in the type 1 or type 2 report and are not implemented at the user entity; and
(c) Controls that may be needed at the service organization that do not appear to have been implemented or that are not specifically covered by a type 2 report.

## Type 1 and Type 2 Reports that Exclude the Services of a Subservice Organization (Ref: Para. 18)

If a service organization uses a subservice organization, the service auditor's report   **A40**
may either include or exclude the subservice organization's relevant control objectives and related controls in the service organization's description of its system and in the scope of the service auditor's engagement. These two methods of reporting are known as the inclusive method and the carve-out method, respectively. If the type 1 or type 2 report excludes the controls at a subservice organization, and the services provided by the subservice organization are relevant to the audit of the user entity's financial statements, the user auditor is required to apply the requirements of this ISA (UK and Ireland) in respect of the subservice organization. The nature and extent of work to be performed by the user auditor regarding the services provided by a subservice organization depend on the nature and significance of those services to the user entity and the relevance of those services to the audit. The application of the requirement in paragraph 9 assists the user auditor in determining the effect of the subservice organization and the nature and extent of work to be performed.

---

[11] *ISA (UK and Ireland) 265, "Communicating Deficiencies in Internal Control to Those Charged with Governance and Management," paragraphs 9-10.*

[12] *ISA (UK and Ireland) 265, paragraph 10.*

**Fraud, Non-Compliance with Laws and Regulations and Uncorrected Misstatements in Relation to Activities at the Service Organization** (Ref: Para. 19)

A41    A service organization may be required under the terms of the contract with user entities to disclose to affected user entities any fraud, non-compliance with laws and regulations or uncorrected misstatements attributable to the service organization's management or employees. As required by paragraph 19, the user auditor makes inquiries of the user entity management regarding whether the service organization has reported any such matters and evaluates whether any matters reported by the service organization affect the nature, timing and extent of the user auditor's further audit procedures. In certain circumstances, the user auditor may require additional information to perform this evaluation, and may request the user entity to contact the service organization to obtain the necessary information.

**Reporting by the User Auditor** (Ref: Para. 20)

A42    When a user auditor is unable to obtain sufficient appropriate audit evidence regarding the services provided by the service organization relevant to the audit of the user entity's financial statements, a limitation on the scope of the audit exists. This may be the case when:

- The user auditor is unable to obtain a sufficient understanding of the services provided by the service organization and does not have a basis for the identification and assessment of the risks of material misstatement;
- A user auditor's risk assessment includes an expectation that controls at the service organization are operating effectively and the user auditor is unable to obtain sufficient appropriate audit evidence about the operating effectiveness of these controls; or
- Sufficient appropriate audit evidence is only available from records held at the service organization, and the user auditor is unable to obtain direct access to these records.

Whether the user auditor expresses a qualified opinion or disclaims an opinion depends on the user auditor's conclusion as to whether the possible effects on the financial statements are material or pervasive.

*Reference to the Work of a Service Auditor* (Ref: Para. 21-22)

A43    In some cases, law or regulation may require a reference to the work of a service auditor in the user auditor's report, for example, for the purposes of transparency in the public sector. In such circumstances, the user auditor may need the consent of the service auditor before making such a reference.

A44    The fact that a user entity uses a service organization does not alter the user auditor's responsibility under ISAs (UK and Ireland) to obtain sufficient appropriate audit evidence to afford a reasonable basis to support the user auditor's opinion. Therefore, the user auditor does not make reference to the service auditor's report as a basis, in part, for the user auditor's opinion on the user entity's financial statements. However, when the user auditor expresses a modified opinion because of a modified opinion in a service auditor's report, the user auditor is not precluded from referring to the service auditor's report if such reference assists in explaining the reason for the user auditor's modified opinion. In such circumstances, the user auditor may need the consent of the service auditor before making such a reference.

# Addendum

*This addendum provides a summary of APB's rationale for retaining or excluding in the proposed clarified ISA (UK and Ireland) the supplementary requirements in the existing ISA (UK and Ireland). It also sets out the supplementary guidance material in the existing ISA (UK and Ireland) that APB considers is not necessary to retain in light of the improvements in the underlying Clarity ISAs issued by the IAASB as part of the Clarity Project. It is provided for information and does not form part of the proposed clarified ISA (UK and Ireland).*

*The Consultation Paper published with the exposure drafts explains the general approach used by the APB for determining whether current supplementary material should be proposed to be retained.*

## Analysis of proposed treatment of current APB supplementary material in current ISA (UK and Ireland) 402

It should be noted that ISA 402 has been revised as well as clarified.

## Requirements

| APB supplementary requirements (*Italic text is from IAASB for context*) | Is it covered in substance in the Clarity ISA? | Should it be retained? |
|---|---|---|
| 5-3. The auditor should obtain and document an understanding of the contractual terms which apply to relevant activities undertaken by the service organization and the way that the entity monitors those activities so as to ensure that it meets its fiduciary and other legal responsibilities. | ✓ 9(d)<br><br>✗ No explicit reference to monitoring those activities so as to ensure the entity meets its fiduciary and other legal responsibilities. However, there is a requirement, in paragraph 10, to understand user entity controls. | ✗<br><br>✗ |
| 9-1. The auditor should determine the effect of relevant activities on their assessment of risk and the client's control environment. | ✓ 9 – 11 | ✗ |
| 9-12. If a service organisation maintains all or part of an entity's accounting records, the auditor should assess whether the arrangements affect the auditor's reporting responsibilities in relation to accounting records arising from law or regulation. | ✗ | ✓ (Regulatory) 9(e) |

| APB supplementary requirements (*Italic text is from IAASB for context*) | Is it covered in substance in the Clarity ISA? | Should it be retained? |
|---|---|---|
| 9-18. Based on the auditor's understanding of the aspects of the entity's accounting system and control environment relating to relevant activities, the auditor should:<br>(a) Assess whether sufficient appropriate audit evidence concerning the relevant financial statement assertions is available from records held at the entity; and if not, | ✓ 15(a) | ✗ |
| (b) Determine effective procedures to obtain evidence necessary for the audit, either by direct access to records kept by service organisations or through information obtained from the service organisations or their auditor. | ✓ 15(b), 16 | ✗ |
| 13-1. The auditor should consider whether the report issued by the service organization auditor is sufficient for its intended use. | ✓ 14, 17 | ✗ |
| Reporting<br>18-1. If an auditor concludes that evidence from records held by a service organization is necessary in order to form an opinion on the client's financial statements and the auditor is unable to obtain such evidence, the auditor should include a description of the factors leading to the lack of evidence in the basis of opinion section of their report and qualify their opinion or issue a disclaimer of opinion on the financial statements. | ✗ However, the guidance indicates this condition is a limitation in scope (A42). Such a form of opinion and explanation will be driven by the requirements of ISA 705. | ✗ |

## Guidance

The following guidance in current ISA (UK and Ireland) 402 has not been carried forward to the proposed clarified standard.

| Current paragraph reference (*Italic text is from IAASB for context*) |
|---|
| 1-1. – 1-4. [Description of management and those charged with governance.] |
| **Definitions**<br>3-3.  Service organisation: the term 'service organisation' is used in this ISA (UK and Ireland) to refer to any entity that provides services to another. Service organisations undertake a wide variety of activities, including:<br>• Information processing.<br>• Maintenance of accounting records.<br>• Facilities management.<br>• Maintenance of safe custody of assets, such as investments.<br>• Initiation or execution of transactions on behalf of the other entity.<br>Service organisations may undertake activities on a dedicated basis for one entity, or on a shared basis, either for members of a single group of entities or for unrelated customers. |
| 3-4.  *Relevant activities*: this term is used to refer to activities undertaken by a service organisation that are relevant to the audit. Relevant activities are those that:<br>(a) Relate directly to:<br> (i) The preparation of the entity's financial statements, including the maintenance of material elements of its accounting records which form the basis for those financial statements; and<br> (ii) The reporting of material assets, liabilities and transactions which are required to be included or disclosed in the financial statements (excluding the charge for provision of the service concerned); or<br>(b) Are subject to law and regulations that are central to the entity's ability to conduct its business.[1]<br><br>[1] ISA (UK and Ireland) 250, paragraph 18-1. |
| 5-1.  Examples of service organisation activities that are relevant to the audit include:<br>• Maintenance of the entity's accounting records.<br>• Other finance functions (such as the computation of tax liabilities, or debtor management and credit risk analysis) which involve establishing the carrying value of items in the financial statements.<br>• Management of assets.<br>• Undertaking or making arrangements for transactions as agent of the entity. |
| 5-2.  Other types of services, for example facilities management, may involve activities which do not fall within the definition of relevant activities. |
| 6-1.  Access to information held by the service organisation is not always necessary in order to obtain sufficient appropriate audit evidence: sufficient evidence may, depending on the nature of activities undertaken by the service organisation, be available at the client itself. If the auditor concludes that access to information or records held by the service organisation is necessary for the purposes of the audit, and the contract terms do not provide for such access, the auditor requests those charged with governance to make appropriate arrangements to obtain it. |

| **Current paragraph reference (*Italic text is from IAASB for context*)** |
|---|
| 6-2    The auditor evaluates the efficiency and effectiveness of visiting the service organisation or using evidence provided by the service organisation's auditor, by;<br><br>(a)    Requesting the service organisation auditor or the entity's internal audit function to perform specified procedures: where information necessary to form an opinion on the entity's financial statements is not available without access to the service organisation's underlying records, its auditor may conclude that the most effective manner to obtain that information is to request the service organisation's auditor or the entity's internal audit function (where the function is established on a suitable basis[2]) to do so. The feasibility of this approach will depend on whether the contractual arrangements with the service organisation entitle the entity to obtain supplementary information when considered necessary;<br><br>(b)    Reviewing information from the service organisation and its auditor concerning the design and operation of its controls systems: those charged with governance may use such information as part of their arrangements for monitoring the activities undertaken by a service organisation. Where this is the case, those charged with governance of the entity periodically obtain reports from the service organisation, its auditor, or both, confirming that controls have operated as agreed. Such reports may provide information on the operation of controls at the service organisation relevant to the auditor's judgment as to the extent to which controls reduce the necessity to obtain evidence from substantive procedures.<br><br>[2] The auditor determines whether this is the case by applying the criteria set out in ISA (UK and Ireland) 610 'Considering the work of internal auditing'. |
| 6-3.    Where the contractual terms do not provide for access to information held by the service organisation which the auditor considers necessary in order to report on the entity's financial statements, the auditor discusses with the those charged with governance at the entity the way in which such information may be obtained and, unless it is made available, qualify the auditor's opinion on the entity's financial statements. If, following discussions with those charged with governance, the auditor concludes that necessary changes in arrangements agreed between the entity and service organisation will not be made in the future, the auditor considers withdrawing from the engagement. |
| 9-2.    The auditor assesses risk in relation to financial statement assertions. An entity's decision to commission a service organisation to undertake activities which are relevant to the audit (as defined in paragraph 3-4) affects risk in relation to financial statement assertions about material account balances and classes of transactions arising from those activities. The auditor's assessment of risk will be affected inter alia by:<br><br>• *The nature of the services provided*: the complexity of activities undertaken by the service organisation may affect the auditor's assessment of risk. For example, outsourcing the treasury function involves a considerably greater degree of risk than straightforward custody of investments.<br><br>• *The degree to which authority is delegated to the* service *organisations*: the provision of accounting services consisting of maintenance of accounting records limited to recording completed transactions carries a relatively low risk of error compared with accounting services which involve initiating transactions (for example, VAT payments). In some cases, the entity may delegate wide powers of decision-making to the |

| **Current paragraph reference (*Italic text is from IAASB for context*)** |
|---|
| service provider, as is the case where an investment manager is given discretionary powers in relation to an entity's investment portfolio. <br>• *The arrangements for ensuring quality of the service provided*: such arrangements may vary considerably, depending upon the nature of the service and the degree of delegation involved. In general, the greater degree of delegation, the more likely it is that the entity's management will rely on controls operated by the service organisation over the completeness and integrity of information and records of the entity. <br>• *Whether the activities involve assets which are susceptible to loss or misappropriation.* <br>• *The reputation for integrity of those responsible for direction and management of the service organisation*: the extent to which a service organisation has a proven record for ensuring quality both of service and of information may provide indicative factors relating to the likely reliability of information it provides to the entity. The auditor therefore considers the extent and frequency of errors in and adjustments to information provided by the service organisation. |
| 9-3. Some outsourced activities are the subject of regulation, notably investment management. However, the existence of regulation does not eliminate the need for the auditor to obtain independent evidence because controls required by regulators, and inspection work undertaken by them in service organisations, may not be relevant to or sufficiently focussed on aspects of importance to the entity. Furthermore, reports from the service organisation's auditor required by its regulator are not ordinarily available to an entity or its auditor. |
| 9-5. The arrangements made by those charged with governance to monitor the way in which activities are undertaken by a service organisation may include a number of factors relevant to the auditor's assessment of risk. These include: <br>• The extent and nature of controls operated by the entity's personnel. <br>• Undertakings by the service organisation for the operation of internal controls, and whether such controls are adequately specified, having regard to the size and complexity of the activities undertaken by the service organization. <br>• Actual experience of adjustments to, or errors and omissions in, reports received from the service organization. <br>• The way in which the entity determines whether the service organisation complies with its contractual undertakings, in particular the way in which it monitors compliance with applicable law and regulations. <br>• Whether the service organisation provides information on the design and operation of systems of controls, possibly accompanied by reports from its external auditor. |
| 9-7. Examples of ways in which different activities undertaken by service organisations can affect the risk of misstatement are given in the Appendix to this ISA (UK and Ireland).. |
| **Designing Audit Procedures** <br>9-8. Following the assessment of risk, the auditor determines the nature, timing and extent of tests of control and substantive procedures required to provide sufficient appropriate audit evidence as to whether the financial statements are free of material misstatement. |
| 9-9. Assessing the sufficiency and appropriateness of audit evidence as a basis for reporting on financial statements requires the auditor to exercise judgment |

| **Current paragraph reference (*Italic text is from IAASB for context*)** |
|---|
| concerning both the quantity of evidence required and its quality. This judgment is affected by the degree of risk of material misstatements in the financial statements, the quality of the entity's accounting and internal control systems and the reliability of information available. |
| 9-10.  The reliability of information for use as audit evidence is determined by a number of factors, including its source. In general terms, evidence supporting an item in an entity's financial statements is more reliable when it is obtained from an independent source; similarly, documentary evidence is normally regarded as more reliable than oral representations. |
| 9-11.  The use of service organisations to undertake particular activities introduces an additional element in the auditor's judgment as to whether evidence can be regarded as coming from an independent source. Whilst the service organisation is a third party, the nature of the activities undertaken or the arrangements for their management may mean that information it provides concerning transactions initiated, processed or recorded on behalf of the entity cannot be regarded as independent for audit purposes. Hence the auditor needs to assess carefully the nature and source of information available in order to establish the most effective way to obtain evidence competent to support an independent opinion on its financial statements. |
| 9-19.  In general, the most cost effective audit approach is likely to be based on information obtained from the entity, together with confirmations from the service organisation, where these provide independent evidence. However, such an approach may not always be feasible, particularly in instances where the service organisation can initiate transactions or payments on the entity's behalf without prior agreement or approval. |
| 9-20.  When the service organisation maintains material elements of the accounting records of the entity, the auditor may require direct access to those records in order to obtain sufficient appropriate audit evidence relating to the operation of controls over those records or to substantiate transactions and balances recorded in them, or both. Such access may involve either physical inspection of records at the service organisation's premises or interrogation of records maintained electronically from the entity or another location, or both. Where direct access is achieved electronically, the auditor may also need to consider obtaining evidence as to the adequacy of controls operated by the service organisation over the completeness and integrity of the entity's data for which it is responsible. |
| 9-21.  In determining the extent and nature of audit evidence to be obtained in relation to balances representing assets held or transactions undertaken by service organisations undertaking relevant activities, the auditor evaluates the efficiency and effectiveness of the following procedures: <br> (a)  Inspecting records and documents held by the entity: the effectiveness of this source of evidence is determined by the nature and extent of the accounting records and supporting documentation retained by the entity. In some cases the entity may not maintain detailed records or documentation initiating transactions, nor will it receive documentation confirming specific transactions undertaken on its behalf; <br> (b)  Establishing the effectiveness of controls: entities may monitor performance of activities undertaken by a service organisation in a variety of ways. Where a entity has established direct controls over such activities, its auditor may, if the auditor proposes to place reliance on their operation, undertake tests of those controls. Alternatively, the arrangements for monitoring the activity concerned may include |

| Current paragraph reference (*Italic text is from IAASB for context*) |
|---|

obtaining an undertaking from the service organisation that its control systems will provide assurance as to the reliability of financial information;

(c) Obtaining representations to confirm balances and transactions from the service organisation: where the entity maintains independent records of balances and transactions and a service organisation executes transactions only at the specific authorisation of the entity or acts as a simple custodian of assets, confirmation from the service provider corroborating those records usually constitutes reliable audit evidence concerning the existence of the transactions and assets concerned. If the entity does not maintain independent records, information obtained in representations from the service provider is merely a statement of what is reflected in the records maintained by the service organisation. Hence such representations do not, taken alone, constitute reliable audit evidence. In these circumstances, the auditor considers whether there is a separation of functions for the services provided such that an alternative source of independent evidence can be identified. For example:

- When one service organisation initiates transactions and another independent organisation holds related documents of title or other records (for example an investment manager initiates trades and another entity acts as custodian), the auditor may confirm year end balances with the latter, apply other substantive procedures to transactions reported by the first service organisation and review the reconciliation of differences between the records of the two organizations.
- If one organisation both initiates transactions on behalf of the entity and also holds related documents of title, all the information available to the auditor is based on that organisation's information. In such circumstances, the auditor is unable to obtain reliable audit evidence to corroborate representations from the service organisation unless effective separation of functions exists, for example where there are separate departments to provide the investment management and custodian services, which operate independently and whose records are independently generated and maintained.

(d) Performing analytical review procedures on the records maintained by the entity or on the returns received from the service organisation: the effectiveness of analytical procedures is likely to vary by assertion and will be affected by the extent and detail of information available;

(e) Inspecting records and documents held by the service organisation: the auditor's access to the records of the service organisation is likely to be established as part of the contractual arrangements between the entity and the service organisation.

13-2. In assessing the relevance of reports from the auditor of the service organisation or from the client's internal audit function regarding the operation of its accounting and internal control systems, the auditor considers whether the report:

(a) Addresses controls and procedures concerning financial statement assertions that are relevant to the auditor's examination;

(b) Provides an adequate level of information concerning relevant aspects of the systems' design, implementation and operation over a specified period, including:

| Current paragraph reference (*Italic text is from IAASB for context*) |
|---|
|       (i)  The way in which the service organization monitors the completeness and integrity of data relating to reports to its customers; and<br>     (ii)  Whether the service organization auditor's testing of operational effectiveness of controls was undertaken in relation to all customers (or all customers of a specified type, that includes the entity) and addressed transactions and balances that could be expected to be representative of the population as a whole; and<br>  (c)  Covers the period during which the entity auditor intends to rely on an assessment of control risk at the service organization. |
| 15-1.  If the service organization auditor's Type B reports do not fully cover the period during which the auditor intends to rely on internal control at the service organization, the auditor determines whether additional auditing procedures or a change in audit strategy are necessary. In making this determination, the length of the period not covered by the report is considered. |
| 15-2.  Additional auditing procedures which may be carried out with respect to a period not covered by such test include:<br>    •  Review of stewardship reports or any other correspondence from the service organization to the client relating to the intervening period.<br>    •  Consideration of any previous or subsequent reports issued by the service organization's auditor.<br>    •  Consideration of the reputation of the service organization as a provider of reliable information (in order to form a judgment about the risk of error in the 'stub period').<br>    •  A request for assurance from the service organization, or possibly its auditor, that there were no significant changes in the intervening period to the stated control objectives or control procedures designed to achieve those objectives that are relevant to the audit. |
| 18-2.  The auditor is unlikely to be able to obtain sufficient appropriate evidence to express an unqualified opinion if all of the following three conditions exist:<br>  (a)  The client does not maintain adequate records of, or controls over, the activities undertaken by the service organisation or cause such records to be maintained independently of the service organisation;<br>  (b)  The service organization has not made available a report from its auditor concerning the operation of aspects of its systems of controls which the auditor considers sufficient for the purposes of their audit; and<br>  (c)  The auditor is unable to carry out such tests as the auditor considers appropriate at the service organization itself, nor has it been possible for those tests to be undertaken by the service organization's auditor.<br>In such circumstances, the auditor issues a disclaimer of opinion when the possible effect of the resulting limitation on the scope of their work is so material or pervasive that the auditor is unable to express an opinion. When the effect of the limitation is not so material or pervasive, the auditor indicates that the auditor's opinion is qualified as to the possible adjustments to the financial statements that might have been determined to be necessary had the limitation not existed. |
| Appendix – Examples of factors relating to activities undertaken by service organizations which may increase the risk of material misstatements – see below |

## ISA (UK and Ireland) 402 – Appendix

## Examples of Factors Relating to Activities Undertaken by Service Organizations Which May Increase the Risk of Material Misstatements

### 1 Outsourced Accounting Functions

| Degree of risk | Characteristics | Examples |
|---|---|---|
| High | <ul><li>Complex transactions</li><li>Those undertaking accounting work need extensive business or specialist knowledge</li><li>Delegated authority to initiate and execute transactions</li><li>Effective controls only possible on 'real time' basis</li><li>Reversal of outsourcing costly/difficult</li><li>High cost of performance failure (e.g. misleading management reports leading to poor decision making)</li><li>High proportion of finance functions outsourced</li></ul> | <ul><li>Maintenance of both accounting records and preparation of budgets and control reports</li><li>Accounting records of retail business</li></ul> |
| Medium | <ul><li>Some business knowledge needed but parameters for necessary judgements can be identified and agreed in advance</li><li>Transactions can be initiated but execution requires approval from entity</li><li>Execution of transactions on instruction from entity</li><li>Analytical techniques insufficient for adequate degree of control</li><li>Discrete functions outsourced.</li></ul> | <ul><li>Outsourcing of accounting records by a supplier of raw materials</li><li>Credit control</li><li>Leasing arrangements</li></ul> |

| Degree of risk | Characteristics | Examples |
|---|---|---|
| Low | • Little requirement for judgment in processing transactions<br>• Non-complex transactions<br>• Little business knowledge required<br>• Analytical control techniques effective<br>• Effects of failure can be contained.<br>• Easy to rearrange/ find alternate service organisations<br>• Low proportion of discrete functions outsourced | • Processing salary payments<br>• Preparation of invoices<br>• Data entry |

## 2  Outsourced Investment Custody and Management

| Degree of risk | Characteristics | Examples |
|---|---|---|
| High | • Transactions can be initiated on a discretionary basis<br>• Entity does not maintain and cannot generate independent records of assets and interest, dividends or other income<br>• Complex financial instruments<br>• Custody and investment management undertaken by two separate entities but records are not independently generated, or one combined report is provided to the entity | • Discretionary trading, same custodian |
| Medium | • Combination of custody and execution of transactions/ collection of income but entity maintains or can generate (for example by reference to Extel) independent records of income<br>• Custody and investment | • Custodian responsible for collection of dividends and reporting of income: entity reviews information<br>• Independent custodian and investment manager |

| Degree of risk | Characteristics | Examples |
|---|---|---|
| | management undertaken by two unrelated entities which maintain independently generated records (i.e. derived from different source data) and report separately direct to the entity | |
| Low | <ul><li>Entity initiates and maintains records of transactions</li><li>Separation of execution and custody functions</li><li>Low frequency of transactions and/or counterparties</li><li>Non-complex financial instruments</li><li>Analytical control techniques effective</li></ul> | <ul><li>Custody of assets only</li><li>Execution of investment transactions pursuant to entity's instructions</li></ul> |

# Proposed Clarified International Standard on Auditing (UK and Ireland) 450

# Evaluation of misstatements identified during the audit

*(Effective for audits of financial statements for periods ending on or after 15 December 2010)*

## Contents

> International Standard on Auditing (UK and Ireland) (ISA (UK and Ireland)) 450, "Evaluation of Misstatements Identified during the Audit" should be read in the context of ISA (UK and Ireland) 200, "Overall Objectives of the Independent Auditor and the Conduct of an Audit in Accordance with International Standards on Auditing (UK and Ireland)."

# Introduction

## Scope of this ISA (UK and Ireland)

This International Standard on Auditing (UK and Ireland) (ISA (UK and Ireland)) **1** deals with the auditor's responsibility to evaluate the effect of identified misstatements on the audit and of uncorrected misstatements, if any, on the financial statements. ISA (UK and Ireland) 700 deals with the auditor's responsibility, in forming an opinion on the financial statements, to conclude whether reasonable assurance has been obtained about whether the financial statements as a whole are free from material misstatement. The auditor's conclusion required by ISA (UK and Ireland) 700 takes into account the auditor's evaluation of uncorrected misstatements, if any, on the financial statements, in accordance with this ISA (UK and Ireland).[1] ISA (UK and Ireland) 320[2] deals with the auditor's responsibility to apply the concept of materiality appropriately in planning and performing an audit of financial statements.

## Effective Date

This ISA (UK and Ireland) is effective for audits of financial statements for periods **2** ending on or after 15 December 2010.

# Objective

The objective of the auditor is to evaluate: **3**

(a) The effect of identified misstatements on the audit; and
(b) The effect of uncorrected misstatements, if any, on the financial statements.

# Definitions

For purposes of the ISAs (UK and Ireland), the following terms have the meanings **4** attributed below:

(a) Misstatement – A difference between the amount, classification, presentation, or disclosure of a reported financial statement item and the amount, classification, presentation, or disclosure that is required for the item to be in accordance with the applicable financial reporting framework. Misstatements can arise from error or fraud. (Ref: Para. A1)
   When the auditor expresses an opinion on whether the financial statements give a true and fair view or are presented fairly, in all material respects, misstatements also include those adjustments of amounts, classifications, presentation, or disclosures that, in the auditor's judgment, are necessary for the financial statements to give a true and fair view or present fairly, in all material respects.
(b) Uncorrected misstatements – Misstatements that the auditor has accumulated during the audit and that have not been corrected.

---

[1] ISA 700, *"Forming an Opinion and Reporting on Financial Statements,"* paragraphs 10-11.
*The APB has not promulgated ISA 700 as issued by the IAASB for application in the UK and Ireland. In the UK and Ireland the applicable auditing standard is ISA (UK and Ireland) 700, "The Auditor's Report on Financial Statements." Paragraph 8 of ISA (UK and Ireland) 700 requires evaluation of whether uncorrected misstatements are material, individually or in aggregate.*

[2] *ISA (UK and Ireland) 320, "Materiality in Planning and Performing an Audit."*

# Requirements

## Accumulation of Identified Misstatements

5   The auditor shall accumulate misstatements identified during the audit, other than those that are clearly trivial. (Ref: Para. A2-A3)

## Consideration of Identified Misstatements as the Audit Progresses

6   The auditor shall determine whether the overall audit strategy and audit plan need to be revised if:

(a)   The nature of identified misstatements and the circumstances of their occurrence indicate that other misstatements may exist that, when aggregated with misstatements accumulated during the audit, could be material; or (Ref: Para. A4)

(b)   The aggregate of misstatements accumulated during the audit approaches materiality determined in accordance with ISA (UK and Ireland) 320. (Ref: Para. A5)

7   If, at the auditor's request, management has examined a class of transactions, account balance or disclosure and corrected misstatements that were detected, the auditor shall perform additional audit procedures to determine whether misstatements remain. (Ref: Para. A6)

## Communication and Correction of Misstatements

8   The auditor shall communicate on a timely basis all misstatements accumulated during the audit with the appropriate level of management, unless prohibited by law or regulation.[3] The auditor shall request management to correct those misstatements. (Ref: Para. A7-A9)

9   If management refuses to correct some or all of the misstatements communicated by the auditor, the auditor shall obtain an understanding of management's reasons for not making the corrections and shall take that understanding into account when evaluating whether the financial statements as a whole are free from material misstatement. (Ref: Para. A10)

## Evaluating the Effect of Uncorrected Misstatements

10   Prior to evaluating the effect of uncorrected misstatements, the auditor shall reassess materiality determined in accordance with ISA (UK and Ireland) 320 to confirm whether it remains appropriate in the context of the entity's actual financial results. (Ref: Para. A11-A12)

11   The auditor shall determine whether uncorrected misstatements are material, individually or in aggregate. In making this determination, the auditor shall consider:

(a)   The size and nature of the misstatements, both in relation to particular classes of transactions, account balances or disclosures and the financial statements as a whole, and the particular circumstances of their occurrence; and (Ref: Para. A13-A17, A19-A20)

---

[3] *ISA (UK and Ireland) 260, "Communication with Those Charged with Governance," paragraph 7.*

(b)  The effect of uncorrected misstatements related to prior periods on the relevant classes of transactions, account balances or disclosures, and the financial statements as a whole. (Ref: Para. A18)

## Communication with Those Charged with Governance

The auditor shall communicate with those charged with governance uncorrected misstatements and the effect that they, individually or in aggregate, may have on the opinion in the auditor's report, unless prohibited by law or regulation.[4] The auditor's communication shall identify material uncorrected misstatements individually. The auditor shall request that uncorrected misstatements be corrected. (Ref: Para. A21-A23)   **12**

The auditor shall also communicate with those charged with governance the effect of uncorrected misstatements related to prior periods on the relevant classes of transactions, account balances or disclosures, and the financial statements as a whole.   **13**

## Written Representation

The auditor shall request a written representation from management and, where appropriate, those charged with governance whether they believe the effects of uncorrected misstatements are immaterial, individually and in aggregate, to the financial statements as a whole. A summary of such items shall be included in or attached to the written representation. (Ref: Para. A24)   **14**

The auditor shall, if applicable, seek to obtain a written representation from those charged with governance that explains their reasons for not correcting misstatements brought to their attention by the auditor.   **14-1**

## Documentation

The auditor shall include in the audit documentation:[5] (Ref: Para. A25)   **15**

(a)  The amount below which misstatements would be regarded as clearly trivial (paragraph 5);
(b)  All misstatements accumulated during the audit and whether they have been corrected (paragraphs 5, 8 and 12); and
(c)  The auditor's conclusion as to whether uncorrected misstatements are material, individually or in aggregate, and the basis for that conclusion (paragraph 11).

*** 

# Application and Other Explanatory Material

## Definition of Misstatement (Ref: Para. 4(a))

Misstatements may result from:   **A1**

(a)  An inaccuracy in gathering or processing data from which the financial statements are prepared;

---

[4] *See footnote 3.*

[5] *ISA (UK and Ireland) 230, "Audit Documentation," paragraphs 8-11, and paragraph A6.*

(b)   An omission of an amount or disclosure;

(c)   An incorrect accounting estimate arising from overlooking, or clear misinterpretation of, facts; and

(d)   Judgments of management concerning accounting estimates that the auditor considers unreasonable or the selection and application of accounting policies that the auditor considers inappropriate.

Examples of misstatements arising from fraud are provided in ISA (UK and Ireland) 240.[6]

### Accumulation of Identified Misstatements (Ref: Para. 5)

A2   The auditor may designate an amount below which misstatements would be clearly trivial and would not need to be accumulated because the auditor expects that the accumulation of such amounts clearly would not have a material effect on the financial statements. "Clearly trivial" is not another expression for "not material." Matters that are clearly trivial will be of a wholly different (smaller) order of magnitude than materiality determined in accordance with ISA (UK and Ireland) 320, and will be matters that are clearly inconsequential, whether taken individually or in aggregate and whether judged by any criteria of size, nature or circumstances. When there is any uncertainty about whether one or more items are clearly trivial, the matter is considered not to be clearly trivial.

A3   To assist the auditor in evaluating the effect of misstatements accumulated during the audit and in communicating misstatements to management and those charged with governance, it may be useful to distinguish between factual misstatements, judgmental misstatements and projected misstatements.

- Factual misstatements are misstatements about which there is no doubt.
- Judgmental misstatements are differences arising from the judgments of management concerning accounting estimates that the auditor considers unreasonable, or the selection or application of accounting policies that the auditor considers inappropriate.
- Projected misstatements are the auditor's best estimate of misstatements in populations, involving the projection of misstatements identified in audit samples to the entire populations from which the samples were drawn. Guidance on the determination of projected misstatements and evaluation of the results is set out in ISA (UK and Ireland) 530.[7]

### Consideration of Identified Misstatements as the Audit Progresses (Ref: Para. 6-7)

A4   A misstatement may not be an isolated occurrence. Evidence that other misstatements may exist include, for example, where the auditor identifies that a misstatement arose from a breakdown in internal control or from inappropriate assumptions or valuation methods that have been widely applied by the entity.

A5   If the aggregate of misstatements accumulated during the audit approaches materiality determined in accordance with ISA (UK and Ireland) 320, there may be a greater than acceptably low level of risk that possible undetected misstatements,

---

[6] *ISA (UK and Ireland) 240, "The Auditor's Responsibilities Relating to Fraud in an Audit of Financial Statements," paragraphs A1-A6.*

[7] *ISA (UK and Ireland) 530, "Audit Sampling," paragraphs 14-15.*

when taken with the aggregate of misstatements accumulated during the audit, could exceed materiality. Undetected misstatements could exist because of the presence of sampling risk and non-sampling risk.[8]

The auditor may request management to examine a class of transactions, account balance or disclosure in order for management to understand the cause of a misstatement identified by the auditor, perform procedures to determine the amount of the actual misstatement in the class of transactions, account balance or disclosure, and to make appropriate adjustments to the financial statements. Such a request may be made, for example, based on the auditor's projection of misstatements identified in an audit sample to the entire population from which it was drawn. **A6**

## Communication and Correction of Misstatements (Ref: Para. 8-9)

Timely communication of misstatements to the appropriate level of management is important as it enables management to evaluate whether the items are misstatements, inform the auditor if it disagrees, and take action as necessary. Ordinarily, the appropriate level of management is the one that has responsibility and authority to evaluate the misstatements and to take the necessary action. **A7**

Law or regulation may restrict the auditor's communication of certain misstatements to management, or others, within the entity. For example, laws or regulations may specifically prohibit a communication, or other action, that might prejudice an investigation by an appropriate authority into an actual, or suspected, illegal act. In some circumstances, potential conflicts between the auditor's obligations of confidentiality and obligations to communicate may be complex. In such cases, the auditor may consider seeking legal advice. **A8**

The correction by management of all misstatements, including those communicated by the auditor, enables management to maintain accurate accounting books and records and reduces the risks of material misstatement of future financial statements because of the cumulative effect of immaterial uncorrected misstatements related to prior periods. **A9**

ISA (UK and Ireland) 700 requires the auditor to evaluate whether the financial statements are prepared and presented, in all material respects, in accordance with the requirements of the applicable financial reporting framework. This evaluation includes consideration of the qualitative aspects of the entity's accounting practices, including indicators of possible bias in management's judgments,[9] which may be affected by the auditor's understanding of management's reasons for not making the corrections. **A10**

## Evaluating the Effect of Uncorrected Misstatements (Ref: Para. 10-11)

The auditor's determination of materiality in accordance with ISA (UK and Ireland) 320 is often based on estimates of the entity's financial results, because the actual financial results may not yet be known. Therefore, prior to the auditor's evaluation **A11**

[8] *ISA (UK and Ireland) 530, paragraphs 5(c)-(d).*

[9] *ISA 700, paragraph 12.*
*The APB has not promulgated ISA 700 as issued by the IAASB for application in the UK and Ireland. In the UK and Ireland the applicable auditing standard is ISA (UK and Ireland) 700, "The Auditor's Report on Financial Statements." Paragraph 8 of ISA (UK and Ireland) 700 includes requirements equivalent to those in paragraph 12 of ISA 700.*

of the effect of uncorrected misstatements, it may be necessary to revise materiality determined in accordance with ISA (UK and Ireland) 320 based on the actual financial results.

**A12**   ISA (UK and Ireland) 320 explains that, as the audit progresses, materiality for the financial statements as a whole (and, if applicable, the materiality level or levels for particular classes of transactions, account balances or disclosures) is revised in the event of the auditor becoming aware of information during the audit that would have caused the auditor to have determined a different amount (or amounts) initially.[10] Thus, any significant revision is likely to have been made before the auditor evaluates the effect of uncorrected misstatements. However, if the auditor's reassessment of materiality determined in accordance with ISA (UK and Ireland) 320 (see paragraph 10 of this ISA (UK and Ireland)) gives rise to a lower amount (or amounts), then performance materiality and the appropriateness of the nature, timing and extent of the further audit procedures are reconsidered so as to obtain sufficient appropriate audit evidence on which to base the audit opinion.

**A13**   Each individual misstatement is considered to evaluate its effect on the relevant classes of transactions, account balances or disclosures, including whether the materiality level for that particular class of transactions, account balance or disclosure, if any, has been exceeded.

**A14**   If an individual misstatement is judged to be material, it is unlikely that it can be offset by other misstatements. For example, if revenue has been materially overstated, the financial statements as a whole will be materially misstated, even if the effect of the misstatement on earnings is completely offset by an equivalent overstatement of expenses. It may be appropriate to offset misstatements within the same account balance or class of transactions; however, the risk that further undetected misstatements may exist is considered before concluding that offsetting even immaterial misstatements is appropriate.[11]

**A15**   Determining whether a classification misstatement is material involves the evaluation of qualitative considerations, such as the effect of the classification misstatement on debt or other contractual covenants, the effect on individual line items or sub-totals, or the effect on key ratios. There may be circumstances where the auditor concludes that a classification misstatement is not material in the context of the financial statements as a whole, even though it may exceed the materiality level or levels applied in evaluating other misstatements. For example, a misclassification between balance sheet line items may not be considered material in the context of the financial statements as a whole when the amount of the misclassification is small in relation to the size of the related balance sheet line items and the misclassification does not affect the income statement or any key ratios.

**A16**   The circumstances related to some misstatements may cause the auditor to evaluate them as material, individually or when considered together with other misstatements accumulated during the audit, even if they are lower than materiality for the financial statements as a whole. Circumstances that may affect the evaluation include the extent to which the misstatement:

- Affects compliance with regulatory requirements;
- Affects compliance with debt covenants or other contractual requirements;

---

[10] ISA (UK and Ireland) 320, paragraph 12.

[11] *The identification of a number of immaterial misstatements within the same account balance or class of transactions may require the auditor to reassess the risk of material misstatement for that account balance or class of transactions.*

- Relates to the incorrect selection or application of an accounting policy that has an immaterial effect on the current period's financial statements but is likely to have a material effect on future periods' financial statements;
- Masks a change in earnings or other trends, especially in the context of general economic and industry conditions;
- Affects ratios used to evaluate the entity's financial position, results of operations or cash flows;
- Affects segment information presented in the financial statements (for example, the significance of the matter to a segment or other portion of the entity's business that has been identified as playing a significant role in the entity's operations or profitability);
- Has the effect of increasing management compensation, for example, by ensuring that the requirements for the award of bonuses or other incentives are satisfied;
- Is significant having regard to the auditor's understanding of known previous communications to users, for example, in relation to forecast earnings;
- Relates to items involving particular parties (for example, whether external parties to the transaction are related to members of the entity's management);
- Is an omission of information not specifically required by the applicable financial reporting framework but which, in the judgment of the auditor, is important to the users' understanding of the financial position, financial performance or cash flows of the entity; or
- Affects other information that will be communicated in documents containing the audited financial statements (for example, information to be included in a "Management Discussion and Analysis" or an "Operating and Financial Review") that may reasonably be expected to influence the economic decisions of the users of the financial statements. ISA (UK and Ireland) 720[12] deals with the auditor's consideration of other information, on which the auditor has no obligation to report, in documents containing audited financial statements.

These circumstances are only examples; not all are likely to be present in all audits nor is the list necessarily complete. The existence of any circumstances such as these does not necessarily lead to a conclusion that the misstatement is material.

ISA (UK and Ireland) 240[13] explains how the implications of a misstatement that is, or may be, the result of fraud ought to be considered in relation to other aspects of the audit, even if the size of the misstatement is not material in relation to the financial statements. **A17**

The cumulative effect of immaterial uncorrected misstatements related to prior periods may have a material effect on the current period's financial statements. There are different acceptable approaches to the auditor's evaluation of such uncorrected misstatements on the current period's financial statements. Using the same evaluation approach provides consistency from period to period. **A18**

### Considerations Specific to Public Sector Entities

In the case of an audit of a public sector entity, the evaluation whether a misstatement is material may also be affected by the auditor's responsibilities established by **A19**

---

[12] ISA (UK and Ireland) 720, "The Auditor's Responsibilities Relating to Other Information in Documents Containing Audited Financial Statements."

[13] ISA (UK and Ireland) 240, paragraph 35.

law, regulation or other authority to report specific matters, including, for example, fraud.

A20   Furthermore, issues such as public interest, accountability, probity and ensuring effective legislative oversight, in particular, may affect the assessment whether an item is material by virtue of its nature. This is particularly so for items that relate to compliance with law, regulation or other authority.

### Communication with Those Charged with Governance (Ref: Para. 12)

A21   If uncorrected misstatements have been communicated with person(s) with management responsibilities, and those person(s) also have governance responsibilities, they need not be communicated again with those same person(s) in their governance role. The auditor nonetheless has to be satisfied that communication with person(s) with management responsibilities adequately informs all of those with whom the auditor would otherwise communicate in their governance capacity.[14]

A22   Where there is a large number of individual immaterial uncorrected misstatements, the auditor may communicate the number and overall monetary effect of the uncorrected misstatements, rather than the details of each individual uncorrected misstatement.

A23   ISA (UK and Ireland) 260 requires the auditor to communicate with those charged with governance the written representations the auditor is requesting (see paragraph 14 of this ISA (UK and Ireland)).[15] The auditor may discuss with those charged with governance the reasons for, and the implications of, a failure to correct misstatements, having regard to the size and nature of the misstatement judged in the surrounding circumstances, and possible implications in relation to future financial statements.

A23-1   If management have corrected material misstatements, communicating those corrections of which the auditor is aware to those charged with governance may assist them to fulfill their governance responsibilities, including reviewing the effectiveness of the system of internal control.

### Written Representation (Ref: Para. 14)

A24   Because the preparation of the financial statements requires management and, where appropriate, those charged with governance to adjust the financial statements to correct material misstatements, the auditor is required to request them to provide a written representation about uncorrected misstatements. In some circumstances, management and, where appropriate, those charged with governance may not believe that certain uncorrected misstatements are misstatements. For that reason, they may want to add to their written representation words such as: "We do not agree that items ... and ... constitute misstatements because [description of reasons]." Obtaining this representation does not, however, relieve the auditor of the need to form a conclusion on the effect of uncorrected misstatements.

[14] *ISA (UK and Ireland) 260, paragraph 13.*

[15] *ISA (UK and Ireland) 260, paragraph 16(c)(ii).*

## Documentation (Ref: Para. 15)

The auditor's documentation of uncorrected misstatements may take into account:  **A25**

(a) The consideration of the aggregate effect of uncorrected misstatements;

(b) The evaluation of whether the materiality level or levels for particular classes of transactions, account balances or disclosures, if any, have been exceeded; and

(c) The evaluation of the effect of uncorrected misstatements on key ratios or trends, and compliance with legal, regulatory and contractual requirements (for example, debt covenants).

# Addendum

*This addendum provides a summary of APB's rationale for retaining or excluding in the proposed clarified ISA (UK and Ireland) the supplementary requirements in the existing ISA (UK and Ireland). It also sets out the supplementary guidance material in the existing ISA (UK and Ireland) that APB considers is not necessary to retain in light of the improvements in the underlying Clarity ISAs issued by the IAASB as part of the Clarity Project. It is provided for information and does not form part of the proposed clarified ISA (UK and Ireland).*

*The Consultation Paper published with the exposure drafts explains the general approach used by the APB for determining whether current supplementary material should be proposed to be retained.*

## Analysis of proposed treatment of current APB supplementary material

ISA (UK and Ireland) 450 is a new standard. It addresses matters currently covered in ISAs (UK and Ireland) 320 and 260.

## Requirements

There are no related supplementary requirements in the current ISA (UK and Ireland) 320.

There are related supplementary requirements in ISA (UK and Ireland) 260 – see the Addendum to proposed Clarified ISA (UK and Ireland) 260. One of these, relating to written representations from those charged with governance, is considered important to include in ISA (UK and Ireland) 450 and has been added as paragraph 14-1.

# Proposed Clarified International Standard on Auditing (UK and Ireland) 500

## Audit evidence

*(Effective for audits of financial statements for periods ending on or after 15 December 2010)*

## Contents

> International Standard on Auditing (UK and Ireland) (ISA (UK and Ireland)) 500, "Audit Evidence" should be read in conjunction with ISA (UK and Ireland) 200, "Overall Objectives of the Independent Auditor and the Conduct of an Audit in Accordance with International Standards on Auditing (UK and Ireland)."

# Introduction

## Scope of this ISA (UK and Ireland)

1   This International Standard on Auditing (UK and Ireland) (ISA (UK and Ireland)) explains what constitutes audit evidence in an audit of financial statements, and deals with the auditor's responsibility to design and perform audit procedures to obtain sufficient appropriate audit evidence to be able to draw reasonable conclusions on which to base the auditor's opinion.

2   This ISA (UK and Ireland) is applicable to all the audit evidence obtained during the course of the audit. Other ISAs (UK and Ireland) deal with specific aspects of the audit (for example, ISA (UK and Ireland) 315[1]), the audit evidence to be obtained in relation to a particular topic (for example, ISA (UK and Ireland) 570[2]), specific procedures to obtain audit evidence (for example, ISA (UK and Ireland) 520[3]), and the evaluation of whether sufficient appropriate audit evidence has been obtained (ISA (UK and Ireland) 200[4] and ISA (UK and Ireland) 330[5]).

## Effective Date

3   This ISA (UK and Ireland) is effective for audits of financial statements for periods ending on or after 15 December 2010.

# Objective

4   The objective of the auditor is to design and perform audit procedures in such a way as to enable the auditor to obtain sufficient appropriate audit evidence to be able to draw reasonable conclusions on which to base the auditor's opinion.

# Definitions

5   For purposes of the ISAs (UK and Ireland), the following terms have the meanings attributed below:

   (a)   Accounting records – The records of initial accounting entries and supporting records, such as checks and records of electronic fund transfers; invoices; contracts; the general and subsidiary ledgers, journal entries and other adjustments to the financial statements that are not reflected in journal entries; and records such as work sheets and spreadsheets supporting cost allocations, computations, reconciliations and disclosures.
   (b)   Appropriateness (of audit evidence) – The measure of the quality of audit evidence; that is, its relevance and its reliability in providing support for the conclusions on which the auditor's opinion is based.

[1] *ISA (UK and Ireland) 315, "Identifying and Assessing the Risks of Material Misstatement through Understanding the Entity and Its Environment."*

[2] *ISA (UK and Ireland) 570, "Going Concern."*

[3] *ISA (UK and Ireland) 520, "Analytical Procedures."*

[4] *ISA (UK and Ireland) 200, "Overall Objectives of the Independent Auditor and the Conduct of an Audit in Accordance with International Standards on Auditing (UK and Ireland)."*

[5] *ISA (UK and Ireland) 330, "The Auditor's Responses to Assessed Risks."*

(c) Audit evidence – Information used by the auditor in arriving at the conclusions on which the auditor's opinion is based. Audit evidence includes both information contained in the accounting records underlying the financial statements and other information.

(d) Management's expert – An individual or organization possessing expertise in a field other than accounting or auditing, whose work in that field is used by the entity to assist the entity in preparing the financial statements.

(e) Sufficiency (of audit evidence) – The measure of the quantity of audit evidence. The quantity of the audit evidence needed is affected by the auditor's assessment of the risks of material misstatement and also by the quality of such audit evidence.

# Requirements

## Sufficient Appropriate Audit Evidence

The auditor shall design and perform audit procedures that are appropriate in the circumstances for the purpose of obtaining sufficient appropriate audit evidence. (Ref: Para. A1-A25)   **6**

## Information to Be Used as Audit Evidence

When designing and performing audit procedures, the auditor shall consider the relevance and reliability of the information to be used as audit evidence. (Ref: Para. A26-A33)   **7**

If information to be used as audit evidence has been prepared using the work of a management's expert, the auditor shall, to the extent necessary, having regard to the significance of that expert's work for the auditor's purposes,: (Ref: Para. A34-A36)   **8**

(a) Evaluate the competence, capabilities and objectivity of that expert; (Ref: Para. A37-A43)

(b) Obtain an understanding of the work of that expert; and (Ref: Para. A44-A47)

(c) Evaluate the appropriateness of that expert's work as audit evidence for the relevant assertion. (Ref: Para. A48)

When using information produced by the entity, the auditor shall evaluate whether the information is sufficiently reliable for the auditor's purposes, including as necessary in the circumstances:   **9**

(a) Obtaining audit evidence about the accuracy and completeness of the information; and (Ref: Para. A49-A50)

(b) Evaluating whether the information is sufficiently precise and detailed for the auditor's purposes. (Ref: Para. A51)

## Selecting Items for Testing to Obtain Audit Evidence

When designing tests of controls and tests of details, the auditor shall determine means of selecting items for testing that are effective in meeting the purpose of the audit procedure. (Ref: Para. A52-A56)   **10**

**Inconsistency in, or Doubts over Reliability of, Audit Evidence**

11   If:

    (a)   audit evidence obtained from one source is inconsistent with that obtained from another; or

    (b)   the auditor has doubts over the reliability of information to be used as audit evidence,

the auditor shall determine what modifications or additions to audit procedures are necessary to resolve the matter, and shall consider the effect of the matter, if any, on other aspects of the audit. (Ref: Para. A57)

***

# Application and Other Explanatory Material

### Sufficient Appropriate Audit Evidence (Ref: Para. 6)

A1   Audit evidence is necessary to support the auditor's opinion and report. It is cumulative in nature and is primarily obtained from audit procedures performed during the course of the audit. It may, however, also include information obtained from other sources such as previous audits (provided the auditor has determined whether changes have occurred since the previous audit that may affect its relevance to the current audit[6]) or a firm's quality control procedures for client acceptance and continuance. In addition to other sources inside and outside the entity, the entity's accounting records are an important source of audit evidence. Also, information that may be used as audit evidence may have been prepared using the work of a management's expert. Audit evidence comprises both information that supports and corroborates management's assertions, and any information that contradicts such assertions. In addition, in some cases the absence of information (for example, management's refusal to provide a requested representation) is used by the auditor, and therefore, also constitutes audit evidence.

A2   Most of the auditor's work in forming the auditor's opinion consists of obtaining and evaluating audit evidence. Audit procedures to obtain audit evidence can include inspection, observation, confirmation, recalculation, reperformance and analytical procedures, often in some combination, in addition to inquiry. Although inquiry may provide important audit evidence, and may even produce evidence of a misstatement, inquiry alone ordinarily does not provide sufficient audit evidence of the absence of a material misstatement at the assertion level, nor of the operating effectiveness of controls.

A3   As explained in ISA (UK and Ireland) 200,[7] reasonable assurance is obtained when the auditor has obtained sufficient appropriate audit evidence to reduce audit risk (i.e., the risk that the auditor expresses an inappropriate opinion when the financial statements are materially misstated) to an acceptably low level.

A4   The sufficiency and appropriateness of audit evidence are interrelated. Sufficiency is the measure of the quantity of audit evidence. The quantity of audit evidence needed is affected by the auditor's assessment of the risks of misstatement (the higher the assessed risks, the more audit evidence is likely to be required) and also by the quality

[6] *ISA (UK and Ireland) 315, paragraph 9.*

[7] *ISA (UK and Ireland) 200, paragraph 5.*

of such audit evidence (the higher the quality, the less may be required). Obtaining more audit evidence, however, may not compensate for its poor quality.

Appropriateness is the measure of the quality of audit evidence; that is, its relevance **A5** and its reliability in providing support for the conclusions on which the auditor's opinion is based. The reliability of evidence is influenced by its source and by its nature, and is dependent on the individual circumstances under which it is obtained.

ISA (UK and Ireland) 330 requires the auditor to conclude whether sufficient **A6** appropriate audit evidence has been obtained.[8] Whether sufficient appropriate audit evidence has been obtained to reduce audit risk to an acceptably low level, and thereby enable the auditor to draw reasonable conclusions on which to base the auditor's opinion, is a matter of professional judgment. ISA (UK and Ireland) 200 contains discussion of such matters as the nature of audit procedures, the timeliness of financial reporting, and the balance between benefit and cost, which are relevant factors when the auditor exercises professional judgment regarding whether sufficient appropriate audit evidence has been obtained.

### Sources of Audit Evidence

Some audit evidence is obtained by performing audit procedures to test the **A7** accounting records, for example, through analysis and review, reperforming procedures followed in the financial reporting process, and reconciling related types and applications of the same information. Through the performance of such audit procedures, the auditor may determine that the accounting records are internally consistent and agree to the financial statements.

More assurance is ordinarily obtained from consistent audit evidence obtained from **A8** different sources or of a different nature than from items of audit evidence considered individually. For example, corroborating information obtained from a source independent of the entity may increase the assurance the auditor obtains from audit evidence that is generated internally, such as evidence existing within the accounting records, minutes of meetings, or a management representation.

Information from sources independent of the entity that the auditor may use as audit **A9** evidence may include confirmations from third parties, analysts' reports, and comparable data about competitors (benchmarking data).

### Audit Procedures for Obtaining Audit Evidence

As required by, and explained further in, ISA (UK and Ireland) 315 and ISA (UK **A10** and Ireland) 330, audit evidence to draw reasonable conclusions on which to base the auditor's opinion is obtained by performing:

(a) Risk assessment procedures; and
(b) Further audit procedures, which comprise:
   (i) Tests of controls, when required by the ISAs (UK and Ireland) or when the auditor has chosen to do so; and
   (ii) Substantive procedures, including tests of details and substantive analytical procedures.

The audit procedures described in paragraphs A14-A25 below may be used as risk **A11** assessment procedures, tests of controls or substantive procedures, depending on the

[8] *ISA (UK and Ireland) 330, paragraph 28.*

context in which they are applied by the auditor. As explained in ISA (UK and Ireland) 330, audit evidence obtained from previous audits may, in certain circumstances, provide appropriate audit evidence where the auditor performs audit procedures to establish its continuing relevance.[9]

A12    The nature and timing of the audit procedures to be used may be affected by the fact that some of the accounting data and other information may be available only in electronic form or only at certain points or periods in time. For example, source documents, such as purchase orders and invoices, may exist only in electronic form when an entity uses electronic commerce, or may be discarded after scanning when an entity uses image processing systems to facilitate storage and reference.

A13    Certain electronic information may not be retrievable after a specified period of time, for example, if files are changed and if backup files do not exist. Accordingly, the auditor may find it necessary as a result of an entity's data retention policies to request retention of some information for the auditor's review or to perform audit procedures at a time when the information is available.

*Inspection*

A14    Inspection involves examining records or documents, whether internal or external, in paper form, electronic form, or other media, or a physical examination of an asset. Inspection of records and documents provides audit evidence of varying degrees of reliability, depending on their nature and source and, in the case of internal records and documents, on the effectiveness of the controls over their production. An example of inspection used as a test of controls is inspection of records for evidence of authorization.

A15    Some documents represent direct audit evidence of the existence of an asset, for example, a document constituting a financial instrument such as a stock or bond. Inspection of such documents may not necessarily provide audit evidence about ownership or value. In addition, inspecting an executed contract may provide audit evidence relevant to the entity's application of accounting policies, such as revenue recognition.

A16    Inspection of tangible assets may provide reliable audit evidence with respect to their existence, but not necessarily about the entity's rights and obligations or the valuation of the assets. Inspection of individual inventory items may accompany the observation of inventory counting.

*Observation*

A17    Observation consists of looking at a process or procedure being performed by others, for example, the auditor's observation of inventory counting by the entity's personnel, or of the performance of control activities. Observation provides audit evidence about the performance of a process or procedure, but is limited to the point in time at which the observation takes place, and by the fact that the act of being observed may affect how the process or procedure is performed. See ISA (UK and Ireland) 501 for further guidance on observation of the counting of inventory.[10]

[9] *ISA (UK and Ireland) 330, paragraph A35.*

[10] *ISA (UK and Ireland) 501, "Audit Evidence—Specific Considerations for Selected Items."*

## External Confirmation

An external confirmation represents audit evidence obtained by the auditor as a direct written response to the auditor from a third party (the confirming party), in paper form, or by electronic or other medium. External confirmation procedures frequently are relevant when addressing assertions associated with certain account balances and their elements. However, external confirmations need not be restricted to account balances only. For example, the auditor may request confirmation of the terms of agreements or transactions an entity has with third parties; the confirmation request may be designed to ask if any modifications have been made to the agreement and, if so, what the relevant details are. External confirmation procedures also are used to obtain audit evidence about the absence of certain conditions, for example, the absence of a "side agreement" that may influence revenue recognition. See ISA (UK and Ireland) 505 for further guidance.[11]

**A18**

## Recalculation

Recalculation consists of checking the mathematical accuracy of documents or records. Recalculation may be performed manually or electronically.

**A19**

## Reperformance

Reperformance involves the auditor's independent execution of procedures or controls that were originally performed as part of the entity's internal control.

**A20**

## Analytical Procedures

Analytical procedures consist of evaluations of financial information made by a study of plausible relationships among both financial and non-financial data. Analytical procedures also encompass the investigation of identified fluctuations and relationships that are inconsistent with other relevant information or deviate significantly from predicted amounts. See ISA (UK and Ireland) 520 for further guidance.

**A21**

## Inquiry

Inquiry consists of seeking information of knowledgeable persons, both financial and non-financial, within the entity or outside the entity. Inquiry is used extensively throughout the audit in addition to other audit procedures. Inquiries may range from formal written inquiries to informal oral inquiries. Evaluating responses to inquiries is an integral part of the inquiry process.

**A22**

Responses to inquiries may provide the auditor with information not previously possessed or with corroborative audit evidence. Alternatively, responses might provide information that differs significantly from other information that the auditor has obtained, for example, information regarding the possibility of management override of controls. In some cases, responses to inquiries provide a basis for the auditor to modify or perform additional audit procedures.

**A23**

Although corroboration of evidence obtained through inquiry is often of particular importance, in the case of inquiries about management intent, the information available to support management's intent may be limited. In these cases,

**A24**

<hr>

[11] *ISA (UK and Ireland) 505, "External Confirmations."*

understanding management's past history of carrying out its stated intentions, management's stated reasons for choosing a particular course of action, and management's ability to pursue a specific course of action may provide relevant information to corroborate the evidence obtained through inquiry.

A25   In respect of some matters, the auditor may consider it necessary to obtain written representations from management and, where appropriate, those charged with governance to confirm responses to oral inquiries. See ISA (UK and Ireland) 580 for further guidance.[12]

## Information to Be Used as Audit Evidence

**Relevance and Reliability** (Ref: Para. 7)

A26   As noted in paragraph A1, while audit evidence is primarily obtained from audit procedures performed during the course of the audit, it may also include information obtained from other sources such as, for example, previous audits, in certain circumstances, and a firm's quality control procedures for client acceptance and continuance. The quality of all audit evidence is affected by the relevance and reliability of the information upon which it is based.

*Relevance*

A27   Relevance deals with the logical connection with, or bearing upon, the purpose of the audit procedure and, where appropriate, the assertion under consideration. The relevance of information to be used as audit evidence may be affected by the direction of testing. For example, if the purpose of an audit procedure is to test for overstatement in the existence or valuation of accounts payable, testing the recorded accounts payable may be a relevant audit procedure. On the other hand, when testing for understatement in the existence or valuation of accounts payable, testing the recorded accounts payable would not be relevant, but testing such information as subsequent disbursements, unpaid invoices, suppliers' statements, and unmatched receiving reports may be relevant.

A28   A given set of audit procedures may provide audit evidence that is relevant to certain assertions, but not others. For example, inspection of documents related to the collection of receivables after the period end may provide audit evidence regarding existence and valuation, but not necessarily cutoff. Similarly, obtaining audit evidence regarding a particular assertion, for example, the existence of inventory, is not a substitute for obtaining audit evidence regarding another assertion, for example, the valuation of that inventory. On the other hand, audit evidence from different sources or of a different nature may often be relevant to the same assertion.

A29   Tests of controls are designed to evaluate the operating effectiveness of controls in preventing, or detecting and correcting, material misstatements at the assertion level. Designing tests of controls to obtain relevant audit evidence includes identifying conditions (characteristics or attributes) that indicate performance of a control, and deviation conditions which indicate departures from adequate performance. The presence or absence of those conditions can then be tested by the auditor.

A30   Substantive procedures are designed to detect material misstatements at the assertion level. They comprise tests of details and substantive analytical procedures. Designing

---

[12] ISA (UK and Ireland) 580, "Written Representations."

substantive procedures includes identifying conditions relevant to the purpose of the test that constitute a misstatement in the relevant assertion.

*Reliability*

The reliability of information to be used as audit evidence, and therefore of the audit evidence itself, is influenced by its source and its nature, and the circumstances under which it is obtained, including the controls over its preparation and maintenance where relevant. Therefore, generalizations about the reliability of various kinds of audit evidence are subject to important exceptions. Even when information to be used as audit evidence is obtained from sources external to the entity, circumstances may exist that could affect its reliability. For example, information obtained from an independent external source may not be reliable if the source is not knowledgeable, or a management's expert may lack objectivity. While recognizing that exceptions may exist, the following generalizations about the reliability of audit evidence may be useful:

   **A31**

- The reliability of audit evidence is increased when it is obtained from independent sources outside the entity.
- The reliability of audit evidence that is generated internally is increased when the related controls, including those over its preparation and maintenance, imposed by the entity are effective.
- Audit evidence obtained directly by the auditor (for example, observation of the application of a control) is more reliable than audit evidence obtained indirectly or by inference (for example, inquiry about the application of a control).
- Audit evidence in documentary form, whether paper, electronic, or other medium, is more reliable than evidence obtained orally (for example, a contemporaneously written record of a meeting is more reliable than a subsequent oral representation of the matters discussed).
- Audit evidence provided by original documents is more reliable than audit evidence provided by photocopies or facsimiles, or documents that have been filmed, digitized or otherwise transformed into electronic form, the reliability of which may depend on the controls over their preparation and maintenance.

ISA (UK and Ireland) 520 provides further guidance regarding the reliability of data used for purposes of designing analytical procedures as substantive procedures.[13]

   **A32**

ISA (UK and Ireland) 240 deals with circumstances where the auditor has reason to believe that a document may not be authentic, or may have been modified without that modification having been disclosed to the auditor.[14]

   **A33**

### Reliability of Information Produced by a Management's Expert (Ref: Para. 8)

The preparation of an entity's financial statements may require expertise in a field other than accounting or auditing, such as actuarial calculations, valuations, or engineering data. The entity may employ or engage experts in these fields to obtain the needed expertise to prepare the financial statements. Failure to do so when such expertise is necessary increases the risks of material misstatement.

   **A34**

---

[13] *ISA (UK and Ireland) 520, paragraphs 5(a).*

[14] *ISA (UK and Ireland) 240, "The Auditor's Responsibilities Relating to Fraud in an Audit of Financial Statements," paragraph 13.*

**A35** When information to be used as audit evidence has been prepared using the work of a management's expert, the requirement in paragraph 8 of this ISA (UK and Ireland) applies. For example, an individual or organization may possess expertise in the application of models to estimate the fair value of securities for which there is no observable market. If the individual or organization applies that expertise in making an estimate which the entity uses in preparing its financial statements, the individual or organization is a management's expert and paragraph 8 applies. If, on the other hand, that individual or organization merely provides price data regarding private transactions not otherwise available to the entity which the entity uses in its own estimation methods, such information, if used as audit evidence, is subject to paragraph 7 of this ISA (UK and Ireland), but is not the use of a management's expert by the entity.

**A36** The nature, timing and extent of audit procedures in relation to the requirement in paragraph 8 of this ISA (UK and Ireland), may be affected by such matters as:

- The nature and complexity of the matter to which the management's expert relates.
- The risks of material misstatement in the matter.
- The availability of alternative sources of audit evidence.
- The nature, scope and objectives of the management's expert's work.
- Whether the management's expert is employed by the entity, or is a party engaged by it to provide relevant services.
- The extent to which management can exercise control or influence over the work of the management's expert.
- Whether the management's expert is subject to technical performance standards or other professional or industry requirements.
- The nature and extent of any controls within the entity over the management's expert's work.
- The auditor's knowledge and experience of the management's expert's field of expertise.
- The auditor's previous experience of the work of that expert.
- The Competence, Capabilities and Objectivity of a Management's Expert (Ref: Para. 8(a))

**A37** Competence relates to the nature and level of expertise of the management's expert. Capability relates the ability of the management's expert to exercise that competence in the circumstances. Factors that influence capability may include, for example, geographic location, and the availability of time and resources. Objectivity relates to the possible effects that bias, conflict of interest or the influence of others may have on the professional or business judgment of the management's expert. The competence, capabilities and objectivity of a management's expert, and any controls within the entity over that expert's work, are important factors in relation to the reliability of any information produced by a management's expert.

**A38** Information regarding the competence, capabilities and objectivity of a management's expert may come from a variety of sources, such as:

- Personal experience with previous work of that expert.
- Discussions with that expert.
- Discussions with others who are familiar with that expert's work.
- Knowledge of that expert's qualifications, membership of a professional body or industry association, license to practice, or other forms of external recognition.
- Published papers or books written by that expert.
- An auditor's expert, if any, who assists the auditor in obtaining sufficient appropriate audit evidence with respect to information produced by the management's expert.

Matters relevant to evaluating the competence, capabilities and objectivity of a management's expert include whether that expert's work is subject to technical performance standards or other professional or industry requirements, for example, ethical standards and other membership requirements of a professional body or industry association, accreditation standards of a licensing body, or requirements imposed by law or regulation.

**A39**

Other matters that may be relevant include:

**A40**

- The relevance of the management's expert's competence to the matter for which that expert's work will be used, including any areas of specialty within that expert's field. For example, a particular actuary may specialize in property and casualty insurance, but have limited expertise regarding pension calculations.
- The management's expert's competence with respect to relevant accounting requirements, for example, knowledge of assumptions and methods, including models where applicable, that are consistent with the applicable financial reporting framework.
- Whether unexpected events, changes in conditions, or the audit evidence obtained from the results of audit procedures indicate that it may be necessary to reconsider the initial evaluation of the competence, capabilities and objectivity of the management's expert as the audit progresses.

A broad range of circumstances may threaten objectivity, for example, self-interest threats, advocacy threats, familiarity threats, self-review threats and intimidation threats. Safeguards may reduce such threats, and may be created either by external structures (for example, the management's expert's profession, legislation or regulation), or by the management's expert's work environment (for example, quality control policies and procedures).

**A41**

Although safeguards cannot eliminate all threats to a management's expert's objectivity, threats such as intimidation threats may be of less significance to an expert engaged by the entity than to an expert employed by the entity, and the effectiveness of safeguards such as quality control policies and procedures may be greater. Because the threat to objectivity created by being an employee of the entity will always be present, an expert employed by the entity cannot ordinarily be regarded as being more likely to be objective than other employees of the entity.

**A42**

When evaluating the objectivity of an expert engaged by the entity, it may be relevant to discuss with management and that expert any interests and relationships that may create threats to the expert's objectivity, and any applicable safeguards, including any professional requirements that apply to the expert; and to evaluate whether the safeguards are adequate. Interests and relationships creating threats may include:

**A43**

- Financial interests.
- Business and personal relationships.
- Provision of other services.

*Obtaining an Understanding of the Work of the Management's Expert (Ref: Para. 8(b))*

An understanding of the work of the management's expert includes an understanding of the relevant field of expertise. An understanding of the relevant field of expertise may be obtained in conjunction with the auditor's determination of

**A44**

whether the auditor has the expertise to evaluate the work of the management's expert, or whether the auditor needs an auditor's expert for this purpose.[15]

A45 Aspects of the management's expert's field relevant to the auditor's understanding may include:

- Whether that expert's field has areas of specialty within it that are relevant to the audit.
- Whether any professional or other standards, and regulatory or legal requirements apply.
- What assumptions and methods are used by the management's expert, and whether they are generally accepted within that expert's field and appropriate for financial reporting purposes.
- The nature of internal and external data or information the auditor's expert uses.

A46 In the case of a management's expert engaged by the entity, there will ordinarily be an engagement letter or other written form of agreement between the entity and that expert. Evaluating that agreement when obtaining an understanding of the work of the management's expert may assist the auditor in determining the appropriateness of the following for the auditor's purposes:

- The nature, scope and objectives of that expert's work;
- The respective roles and responsibilities of management and that expert; and
- The nature, timing and extent of communication between management and that expert, including the form of any report to be provided by that expert.

A47 In the case of a management's expert employed by the entity, it is less likely there will be a written agreement of this kind. Inquiry of the expert and other members of management may be the most appropriate way for the auditor to obtain the necessary understanding.

*Evaluating the Appropriateness of the Management's Expert's Work (Ref: Para. 8(c))*

A48 Considerations when evaluating the appropriateness of the management's expert's work as audit evidence for the relevant assertion may include:

- The relevance and reasonableness of that expert's findings or conclusions, their consistency with other audit evidence, and whether they have been appropriately reflected in the financial statements;
- If that expert's work involves use of significant assumptions and methods, the relevance and reasonableness of those assumptions and methods; and
- If that expert's work involves significant use of source data the relevance, completeness, and accuracy of that source data.

**Information Produced by the Entity and Used for the Auditor's Purposes** (Ref: Para. 9(a)-(b))

A49 In order for the auditor to obtain reliable audit evidence, information produced by the entity that is used for performing audit procedures needs to be sufficiently complete and accurate. For example, the effectiveness of auditing revenue by applying standard prices to records of sales volume is affected by the accuracy of the price information and the completeness and accuracy of the sales volume data.

---

[15] ISA (UK and Ireland) 620, "Using the Work of an Auditor's Expert," paragraph 7.

Similarly, if the auditor intends to test a population (for example, payments) for a certain characteristic (for example, authorization), the results of the test will be less reliable if the population from which items are selected for testing is not complete.

Obtaining audit evidence about the accuracy and completeness of such information **A50** may be performed concurrently with the actual audit procedure applied to the information when obtaining such audit evidence is an integral part of the audit procedure itself. In other situations, the auditor may have obtained audit evidence of the accuracy and completeness of such information by testing controls over the preparation and maintenance of the information. In some situations, however, the auditor may determine that additional audit procedures are needed.

In some cases, the auditor may intend to use information produced by the entity for **A51** other audit purposes. For example, the auditor may intend to make use of the entity's performance measures for the purpose of analytical procedures, or to make use of the entity's information produced for monitoring activities, such as internal auditor's reports. In such cases, the appropriateness of the audit evidence obtained is affected by whether the information is sufficiently precise or detailed for the auditor's purposes. For example, performance measures used by management may not be precise enough to detect material misstatements.

## Selecting Items for Testing to Obtain Audit Evidence (Ref: Para. 10)

An effective test provides appropriate audit evidence to an extent that, taken with **A52** other audit evidence obtained or to be obtained, will be sufficient for the auditor's purposes. In selecting items for testing, the auditor is required by paragraph 7 to determine the relevance and reliability of information to be used as audit evidence; the other aspect of effectiveness (sufficiency) is an important consideration in selecting items to test. The means available to the auditor for selecting items for testing are:

(a)  Selecting all items (100% examination);
(b)  Selecting specific items; and
(c)  Audit sampling.

The application of any one or combination of these means may be appropriate depending on the particular circumstances, for example, the risks of material misstatement related to the assertion being tested, and the practicality and efficiency of the different means.

### Selecting All Items

The auditor may decide that it will be most appropriate to examine the entire **A53** population of items that make up a class of transactions or account balance (or a stratum within that population). 100% examination is unlikely in the case of tests of controls; however, it is more common for tests of details. 100% examination may be appropriate when, for example:

• The population constitutes a small number of large value items;
• There is a significant risk and other means do not provide sufficient appropriate audit evidence; or
• The repetitive nature of a calculation or other process performed automatically by an information system makes a 100% examination cost effective.

### Selecting Specific Items

A54   The auditor may decide to select specific items from a population. In making this decision, factors that may be relevant include the auditor's understanding of the entity, the assessed risks of material misstatement, and the characteristics of the population being tested. The judgmental selection of specific items is subject to non-sampling risk. Specific items selected may include:

- *High value or key items.* The auditor may decide to select specific items within a population because they are of high value, or exhibit some other characteristic, for example, items that are suspicious, unusual, particularly risk-prone or that have a history of error.
- *All items over a certain amount.* The auditor may decide to examine items whose recorded values exceed a certain amount so as to verify a large proportion of the total amount of a class of transactions or account balance.
- *Items to obtain information.* The auditor may examine items to obtain information about matters such as the nature of the entity or the nature of transactions.

A55   While selective examination of specific items from a class of transactions or account balance will often be an efficient means of obtaining audit evidence, it does not constitute audit sampling. The results of audit procedures applied to items selected in this way cannot be projected to the entire population; accordingly, selective examination of specific items does not provide audit evidence concerning the remainder of the population.

### Audit Sampling

A56   Audit sampling is designed to enable conclusions to be drawn about an entire population on the basis of testing a sample drawn from it. Audit sampling is discussed in ISA (UK and Ireland) 530.[16]

## Inconsistency in, or Doubts over Reliability of, Audit Evidence (Ref: Para. 11)

A57   Obtaining audit evidence from different sources or of a different nature may indicate that an individual item of audit evidence is not reliable, such as when audit evidence obtained from one source is inconsistent with that obtained from another. This may be the case when, for example, responses to inquiries of management, internal audit, and others are inconsistent, or when responses to inquiries of those charged with governance made to corroborate the responses to inquiries of management are inconsistent with the response by management. ISA (UK and Ireland) 230 includes a specific documentation requirement if the auditor identified information that is inconsistent with the auditor's final conclusion regarding a significant matter.[17]

---

[16] *ISA (UK and Ireland) 530, "Audit Sampling."*

[17] *ISA (UK and Ireland) 230, "Audit Documentation," paragraph 11.*

# Addendum

*This addendum provides a summary of APB's rationale for retaining or excluding in the proposed clarified ISA (UK and Ireland) the supplementary requirements in the existing ISA (UK and Ireland). It also sets out the supplementary guidance material in the existing ISA (UK and Ireland) that APB considers is not necessary to retain in light of the improvements in the underlying Clarity ISAs issued by the IAASB as part of the Clarity Project. It is provided for information and does not form part of the proposed clarified ISA (UK and Ireland).*

*The Consultation Paper published with the exposure drafts explains the general approach used by the APB for determining whether current supplementary material should be proposed to be retained.*

## Analysis of proposed treatment of current APB supplementary material in current ISA (UK and Ireland) 500

### Requirements

There are no supplementary requirements in the current ISA (UK and Ireland) 500.

### Guidance

The following guidance in current ISA (UK and Ireland) 500 has not been carried forward to the proposed clarified standard.

| Current paragraph reference (*Italic text is from IAASB for context*) |
|---|
| 1-1. – 1-4. [Description of management and those charged with governance] |
| 5. *Management[1a] is responsible for the preparation of the financial statements based upon the accounting records of the entity. ...* <br><br> [1a] In the UK and Ireland, the auditor obtains written representations from those charged with governance. |
| 15. *Management[3] is responsible for the fair presentation of financial statements that reflect the nature and operations of the entity. ...* <br><br> [3] In the UK and Ireland, those charged with governance are responsible for the preparation of the financial statements. |

# Proposed Clarified International Standard on Auditing (UK and Ireland) 501

## Audit evidence—specific considerations for selected items

*(Effective for audits of financial statements for periods ending on or after 15 December 2010)*

## Contents

International Standard on Auditing (UK and Ireland) (ISA (UK and Ireland)) 501, "Audit Evidence—Specific Considerations for Selected Items" should be read in conjunction with ISA (UK and Ireland) 200, "Overall Objectives of the Independent Auditor and the Conduct of an Audit in Accordance with International Standards on Auditing (UK and Ireland)."

# Introduction

## Scope of this ISA (UK and Ireland)

This International Standard on Auditing (UK and Ireland) (ISA (UK and Ireland)) **1**
deals with specific considerations by the auditor in obtaining sufficient appropriate
audit evidence in accordance with ISA (UK and Ireland) 330,[1] ISA (UK and Ireland)
500[2] and other relevant ISAs (UK and Ireland), with respect to certain aspects of
inventory, litigation and claims involving the entity, and segment information in an
audit of financial statements.

## Effective Date

This ISA (UK and Ireland) is effective for audits of financial statements for periods **2**
ending on or after 15 December 2010.

## Objective

The objective of the auditor is to obtain sufficient appropriate audit evidence **3**
regarding the:

(a) Existence and condition of inventory;
(b) Completeness of litigation and claims involving the entity; and
(c) Presentation and disclosure of segment information in accordance with the
applicable financial reporting framework.

# Requirements

## Inventory

If inventory is material to the financial statements, the auditor shall obtain sufficient **4**
appropriate audit evidence regarding the existence and condition of inventory by:

(a) Attendance at physical inventory counting, unless impracticable, to: (Ref: Para.
A1-A3)
(i) Evaluate management's instructions and procedures for recording and
controlling the results of the entity's physical inventory counting; (Ref:
Para. A4)
(ii) Observe the performance of management's count procedures; (Ref: Para.
A5)
(iii) Inspect the inventory; and (Ref: Para. A6)
(iv) Perform test counts; and (Ref: Para. A7-A8)
(b) Performing audit procedures over the entity's final inventory records to determine whether they accurately reflect actual inventory count results.

If physical inventory counting is conducted at a date other than the date of the **5**
financial statements, the auditor shall, in addition to the procedures required by
paragraph 4, perform audit procedures to obtain audit evidence about whether
changes in inventory between the count date and the date of the financial statements
are properly recorded. (Ref: Para. A9-A11)

---

[1] *ISA (UK and Ireland) 330, "The Auditor's Responses to Assessed Risks."*

[2] *ISA (UK and Ireland) 500, "Audit Evidence."*

**6**    If the auditor is unable to attend physical inventory counting due to unforeseen circumstances, the auditor shall make or observe some physical counts on an alternative date, and perform audit procedures on intervening transactions.

**7**    If attendance at physical inventory counting is impracticable, the auditor shall perform alternative audit procedures to obtain sufficient appropriate audit evidence regarding the existence and condition of inventory. If it is not possible to do so, the auditor shall modify the opinion in the auditor's report in accordance with ISA (UK and Ireland) 705.[3] (Ref: Para. A12-A14)

**8**    If inventory under the custody and control of a third party is material to the financial statements, the auditor shall obtain sufficient appropriate audit evidence regarding the existence and condition of that inventory by performing one or both of the following:

  (a)  Request confirmation from the third party as to the quantities and condition of inventory held on behalf of the entity. (Ref: Para. A15)
  (b)  Perform inspection or other audit procedures appropriate in the circumstances. (Ref: Para. A16)

## Litigation and Claims

**9**    The auditor shall design and perform audit procedures in order to identify litigation and claims involving the entity which may give rise to a risk of material misstatement, including: (Ref: Para. A17-A19)

  (a)  Inquiry of management[3a] and, where applicable, others within the entity, including in-house legal counsel;
  (b)  Reviewing minutes of meetings of those charged with governance and correspondence between the entity and its external legal counsel; and
  (c)  Reviewing legal expense accounts. (Ref: Para. A20)

**10**    If the auditor assesses a risk of material misstatement regarding litigation or claims that have been identified, or when audit procedures performed indicate that other material litigation or claims may exist, the auditor shall, in addition to the procedures required by other ISAs (UK and Ireland), seek direct communication with the entity's external legal counsel. The auditor shall do so through a letter of inquiry, prepared by management[3b] and sent by the auditor, requesting the entity's external legal counsel to communicate directly with the auditor. If law, regulation or the respective legal professional body prohibits the entity's external legal counsel from communicating directly with the auditor, the auditor shall perform alternative audit procedures. (Ref: Para. A21-A25)

**11**    If:

  (a)  management[3c] refuses to give the auditor permission to communicate or meet with the entity's external legal counsel, or the entity's external legal counsel refuses to respond appropriately to the letter of inquiry, or is prohibited from responding; and

[3] *ISA (UK and Ireland) 705, "Modifications to the Opinion in the Independent Auditor's Report."*

[3a] *In the UK and Ireland the auditor also makes appropriate inquiry of those charged with governance.*

[3b] *In the UK and Ireland the letter may need to be prepared by those charged with governance.*

[3c] *In the UK and Ireland permission may be denied by those charged with governance.*

(b)  the auditor is unable to obtain sufficient appropriate audit evidence by performing alternative audit procedures,

the auditor shall modify the opinion in the auditor's report in accordance with ISA
(UK and Ireland) 705.

## *Written Representations*

The auditor shall request management and, where appropriate, those charged with **12**
governance to provide written representations that all known actual or possible
litigation and claims whose effects should be considered when preparing the financial
statements have been disclosed to the auditor and accounted for and disclosed in
accordance with the applicable financial reporting framework.

## Segment Information

The auditor shall obtain sufficient appropriate audit evidence regarding the pre- **13**
sentation and disclosure of segment information in accordance with the applicable
financial reporting framework by: (Ref: Para. A26)

(a)  Obtaining an understanding of the methods used by management in determining segment information, and: (Ref: Para. A27)
(i)   Evaluating whether such methods are likely to result in disclosure in
accordance with the applicable financial reporting framework; and
(ii)  Where appropriate, testing the application of such methods; and
(b)  Performing analytical procedures or other audit procedures appropriate in the
circumstances.

\*\*\*

# Application and Other Explanatory Material

## Inventory[3d]

### *Attendance at Physical Inventory Counting* (Ref: Para. 4(a))

Management ordinarily establishes procedures under which inventory is physically **A1**
counted at least once a year to serve as a basis for the preparation of the financial
statements and, if applicable, to ascertain the reliability of the entity's perpetual
inventory system.

Attendance at physical inventory counting involves: **A2**

•   Inspecting the inventory to ascertain its existence and evaluate its condition, and
performing test counts;
•   Observing compliance with management's instructions and the performance of
procedures for recording and controlling the results of the physical inventory
count; and
•   Obtaining audit evidence as to the reliability of management's count procedures.

---

[3d] *For auditors in the UK and Ireland further guidance has been promulgated by the APB in Practice Note 25,
"Attendance at Stocktaking."*

These procedures may serve as test of controls or substantive procedures depending on the auditor's risk assessment, planned approach and the specific procedures carried out.

A3    Matters relevant in planning attendance at physical inventory counting (or in designing and performing audit procedures pursuant to paragraphs 4-8 of this ISA (UK and Ireland)) include, for example:

- The risks of material misstatement related to inventory.
- The nature of the internal control related to inventory.
- Whether adequate procedures are expected to be established and proper instructions issued for physical inventory counting.
- The timing of physical inventory counting.
- Whether the entity maintains a perpetual inventory system.
- The locations at which inventory is held, including the materiality of the inventory and the risks of material misstatement at different locations, in deciding at which locations attendance is appropriate. ISA (UK and Ireland) 600[4] deals with the involvement of other auditors and accordingly may be relevant if such involvement is with regards to attendance of physical inventory counting at a remote location.
- Whether the assistance of an auditor's expert is needed. ISA (UK and Ireland) 620[5] deals with the use of an auditor's expert to assist the auditor to obtain sufficient appropriate audit evidence.

*Evaluate Management's Instructions and Procedures (Ref: Para. 4(a)(i))*

A4    Matters relevant in evaluating management's instructions and procedures for recording and controlling the physical inventory counting include whether they address, for example:

- The application of appropriate control activities, for example, collection of used physical inventory count records, accounting for unused physical inventory count records, and count and re-count procedures.
- The accurate identification of the stage of completion of work in progress, of slow moving, obsolete or damaged items and of inventory owned by a third party, for example, on consignment.
- The procedures used to estimate physical quantities, where applicable, such as may be needed in estimating the physical quantity of a coal pile.
- Control over the movement of inventory between areas and the shipping and receipt of inventory before and after the cutoff date.

*Observe the Performance of Management's Count Procedures (Ref: Para. 4(a)(ii))*

A5    Observing the performance of management's count procedures, for example those relating to control over the movement of inventory before, during and after the count, assists the auditor in obtaining audit evidence that management's instructions and count procedures are adequately designed and implemented. In addition, the auditor may obtain copies of cutoff information, such as details of the movement of inventory, to assist the auditor in performing audit procedures over the accounting for such movements at a later date.

[4] *ISA (UK and Ireland) 600, "Special Considerations—Audits of Group Financial Statements (Including the Work of the Component Auditors)."*

[5] *ISA (UK and Ireland) 620, "Using the Work of an Auditor's Expert."*

*Inspect the Inventory (Ref: Para. 4(a)(iii))*

Inspecting inventory when attending physical inventory counting assists the auditor **A6** in ascertaining the existence of the inventory (though not necessarily its ownership), and in identifying, for example, obsolete, damaged or ageing inventory.

*Perform Test Counts (Ref: Para. 4(a)(iv))*

Performing test counts, for example by tracing items selected from management's **A7** count records to the physical inventory and tracing items selected from the physical inventory to management's count records, provides audit evidence about the completeness and the accuracy of those records.

In addition to recording the auditor's test counts, obtaining copies of management's **A8** completed physical inventory count records assists the auditor in performing subsequent audit procedures to determine whether the entity's final inventory records accurately reflect actual inventory count results.

**Physical Inventory Counting Conducted Other than At the Date of the Financial Statements** (Ref: Para. 5)

For practical reasons, the physical inventory counting may be conducted at a date, or **A9** dates, other than the date of the financial statements. This may be done irrespective of whether management determines inventory quantities by an annual physical inventory counting or maintains a perpetual inventory system. In either case, the effectiveness of the design, implementation and maintenance of controls over changes in inventory determines whether the conduct of physical inventory counting at a date, or dates, other than the date of the financial statements is appropriate for audit purposes. ISA (UK and Ireland) 330 establishes requirements and provides guidance on substantive procedures performed at an interim date.[6]

Where a perpetual inventory system is maintained, management may perform **A10** physical counts or other tests to ascertain the reliability of inventory quantity information included in the entity's perpetual inventory records. In some cases, management or the auditor may identify differences between the perpetual inventory records and actual physical inventory quantities on hand; this may indicate that the controls over changes in inventory are not operating effectively.

Relevant matters for consideration when designing audit procedures to obtain audit **A11** evidence about whether changes in inventory amounts between the count date, or dates, and the final inventory records are properly recorded include:

- Whether the perpetual inventory records are properly adjusted.
- Reliability of the entity's perpetual inventory records.
- Reasons for significant differences between the information obtained during the physical count and the perpetual inventory records.

**Attendance at Physical Inventory Counting Is Impracticable** (Ref: Para. 7)

In some cases, attendance at physical inventory counting may be impracticable. This **A12** may be due to factors such as the nature and location of the inventory, for example, where inventory is held in a location that may pose threats to the safety of the auditor. The matter of general inconvenience to the auditor, however, is not

---

[6] *ISA (UK and Ireland) 330, paragraphs 22-23.*

sufficient to support a decision by the auditor that attendance is impracticable. Further, as explained in ISA (UK and Ireland) 200,[7] the matter of difficulty, time, or cost involved is not in itself a valid basis for the auditor to omit an audit procedure for which there is no alternative or to be satisfied with audit evidence that is less than persuasive.

A13    In some cases where attendance is impracticable, alternative audit procedures, for example inspection of documentation of the subsequent sale of specific inventory items acquired or purchased prior to the physical inventory counting, may provide sufficient appropriate audit evidence about the existence and condition of inventory.

A14    In other cases, however, it may not be possible to obtain sufficient appropriate audit evidence regarding the existence and condition of inventory by performing alternative audit procedures. In such cases, ISA (UK and Ireland) 705 requires the auditor to modify the opinion in the auditor's report as a result of the scope limitation.[8]

### Inventory under the Custody and Control of a Third Party

*Confirmation (Ref: Para. 8(a))*

A15    ISA (UK and Ireland) 505[9] establishes requirements and provides guidance for performing external confirmation procedures.

*Other Audit Procedures (Ref: Para. 8(b))*

A16    Depending on the circumstances, for example where information is obtained that raises doubt about the integrity and objectivity of the third party, the auditor may consider it appropriate to perform other audit procedures instead of, or in addition to, confirmation with the third party. Examples of other audit procedures include:

- Attending, or arranging for another auditor to attend, the third party's physical counting of inventory, if practicable.
- Obtaining another auditor's report, or a service auditor's report, on the adequacy of the third party's internal control for ensuring that inventory is properly counted and adequately safeguarded.
- Inspecting documentation regarding inventory held by third parties, for example, warehouse receipts.
- Requesting confirmation from other parties when inventory has been pledged as collateral.

---

[7] *ISA (UK and Ireland) 200, "Overall Objectives of the Independent Auditor and the Conduct of an Audit in Accordance with International Standards on Auditing (UK and Ireland)," paragraph A48.*

[8] *ISA (UK and Ireland) 705, paragraph 13.*

[9] *ISA (UK and Ireland) 505, "External Confirmations."*

## Litigation and Claims

*Completeness of Litigations and Claims* (Ref: Para. 9)

Litigation and claims involving the entity may have a material effect on the financial statements and thus may be required to be disclosed or accounted for in the financial statements.

**A17**

In addition to the procedures identified in paragraph 9, other relevant procedures include, for example, using information obtained through risk assessment procedures carried out as part of obtaining an understanding of the entity and its environment to assist the auditor to become aware of litigation and claims involving the entity.

**A18**

Audit evidence obtained for purposes of identifying litigation and claims that may give rise to a risk of material misstatement also may provide audit evidence regarding other relevant considerations, such as valuation or measurement, regarding litigation and claims. ISA (UK and Ireland) 540[10] establishes requirements and provides guidance relevant to the auditor's consideration of litigation and claims requiring accounting estimates or related disclosures in the financial statements.

**A19**

*Reviewing Legal Expense Accounts (Ref: Para. 9(c))*

Depending on the circumstances, the auditor may judge it appropriate to examine related source documents, such as invoices for legal expenses, as part of the auditor's review of legal expense accounts.

**A20**

### Communication with the Entity's External Legal Counsel (Ref: Para. 10-11)

Direct communication with the entity's external legal counsel assists the auditor in obtaining sufficient appropriate audit evidence as to whether potentially material litigation and claims are known and management's estimates of the financial implications, including costs, are reasonable.

**A21**

In some cases, the auditor may seek direct communication with the entity's external legal counsel through a letter of general inquiry. For this purpose, a letter of general inquiry requests the entity's external legal counsel to inform the auditor of any litigation and claims that the counsel is aware of, together with an assessment of the outcome of the litigation and claims, and an estimate of the financial implications, including costs involved.

**A22**

If it is considered unlikely that the entity's external legal counsel will respond appropriately to a letter of general inquiry, for example if the professional body to which the external legal counsel belongs prohibits response to such a letter[10a], the auditor may seek direct communication through a letter of specific inquiry. For this purpose, a letter of specific inquiry includes:

**A23**

(a)  A list of litigation and claims;

[10] *ISA (UK and Ireland) 540, "Auditing Accounting Estimates, Including Fair Value Accounting Estimates, and Related Disclosures."*

[10a] *In the UK, the Council of the Law Society has advised solicitors that it is unable to recommend them to comply with non-specific requests for information.*

(b) Where available, management's assessment of the outcome of each of the identified litigation and claims and its estimate of the financial implications, including costs involved; and

(c) A request that the entity's external legal counsel confirm the reasonableness of management's assessments and provide the auditor with further information if the list is considered by the entity's external legal counsel to be incomplete or incorrect.

**A24**   In certain circumstances, the auditor also may judge it necessary to meet with the entity's external legal counsel to discuss the likely outcome of the litigation or claims. This may be the case, for example, where:

- The auditor determines that the matter is a significant risk.
- The matter is complex.
- There is disagreement between management and the entity's external legal counsel.

Ordinarily, such meetings require management's permission[3c] and are held with a representative of management in attendance.

**A25**   In accordance with ISA (UK and Ireland) 700,[11] the auditor is required to date the auditor's report no earlier than the date on which the auditor has obtained sufficient appropriate audit evidence on which to base the auditor's opinion on the financial statements. Audit evidence about the status of litigation and claims up to the date of the auditor's report may be obtained by inquiry of management[3a], including in-house legal counsel, responsible for dealing with the relevant matters. In some instances, the auditor may need to obtain updated information from the entity's external legal counsel.

## Segment Information (Ref: Para. 13)

**A26**   Depending on the applicable financial reporting framework, the entity may be required or permitted to disclose segment information in the financial statements. The auditor's responsibility regarding the presentation and disclosure of segment information is in relation to the financial statements taken as a whole. Accordingly, the auditor is not required to perform audit procedures that would be necessary to express an opinion on the segment information presented on a stand alone basis.

### Understanding of the Methods Used by Management (Ref: Para. 13(a))

**A27**   Depending on the circumstances, example of matters that may be relevant when obtaining an understanding of the methods used by management in determining segment information and whether such methods are likely to result in disclosure in accordance with the applicable financial reporting framework include:

- Sales, transfers and charges between segments, and elimination of inter-segment amounts.
- Comparisons with budgets and other expected results, for example, operating profits as a percentage of sales.

---

[11] *ISA 700, "Forming an Opinion and Reporting on Financial Statements," paragraph 41.*
*The APB has not promulgated ISA 700 as issued by the IAASB for application in the UK and Ireland. In the UK and Ireland the applicable auditing standard is ISA (UK and Ireland) 700, "The Auditor's Report on Financial Statements." Paragraphs 23 and 24 of ISA (UK and Ireland) 700 establish requirements regarding dating of the auditor's report.*

- The allocation of assets and costs among segments.
- Consistency with prior periods, and the adequacy of the disclosures with respect to inconsistencies.

# Addendum

*This addendum provides a summary of APB's rationale for retaining or excluding in the proposed clarified ISA (UK and Ireland) the supplementary requirements in the existing ISA (UK and Ireland). It also sets out the supplementary guidance material in the existing ISA (UK and Ireland) that APB considers is not necessary to retain in light of the improvements in the underlying Clarity ISAs issued by the IAASB as part of the Clarity Project. It is provided for information and does not form part of the proposed clarified ISA (UK and Ireland).*

*The Consultation Paper published with the exposure drafts explains the general approach used by the APB for determining whether current supplementary material should be proposed to be retained.*

## Analysis of proposed treatment of current APB supplementary material in current ISA (UK and Ireland) 501

### Requirements

There are no supplementary requirements in the current ISA (UK and Ireland) 501.

### Guidance

The following guidance in current ISA (UK and Ireland) 501 has not been carried forward to the proposed clarified standard. This includes the significant amount of supplementary guidance on attendance at inventory counts as it is covered in Practice Note 25 which is still in issue.

| Current paragraph reference (*Italic text is from IAASB for context*) |
| --- |
| 1-1. – 1-4. [Description of management and those charged with governance.] |
| **Attendance at inventory counts**<br>4    *Management[1] ordinarily establishes procedures under which inventory is physically counted at least once a year to serve as a basis for the preparation of the financial statements or to ascertain the reliability of the perpetual inventory system.* |
| [1] In the UK and Ireland, those charged with governance are responsible for the preparation and presentation of the financial statements. |
| 4-1.   In accordance with ISA (UK and Ireland) 315, "Understanding the Entity and its Environment and Assessing the Risks of Material misstatement" the auditor uses professional judgment to assess the risks of material misstatement. Risk factors relating to the existence assertion in the context of the audit of inventory include the:<br>• Reliability of accounting and inventory recording systems including, in relation to work in progress, the systems that track location, quantities and stages of completion.<br>• Timing of physical inventory counts relative to the year-end date, and the reliability of records used in any 'roll-forward' of balances.<br>• Location of inventory, including inventory on 'consignment' and inventory held at third-party warehouses.<br>• Physical controls over the inventory, and its susceptibility to theft or deterioration. |

| Current paragraph reference (*Italic text is from IAASB for context*) |
|---|
| • Objectivity, experience and reliability of the inventory counters and of those monitoring their work.<br>• The degree of fluctuation in inventory levels.<br>• Nature of the inventory, for example whether specialist knowledge is needed to identify the quantity, quality and/or identity of inventory items.<br>• Difficulty in carrying out the assessment of quantity, for example whether a significant degree of estimation is involved. |
| 4-2. When planning the audit, the auditor also assesses the risk of material misstatements due to fraud. Based on this risk assessment, the auditor designs audit procedures so as to have a reasonable expectation of detecting material misstatements arising from fraud. Fraudulent activities which can occur in relation to inventory include:<br>• 'False sales' involving the movement of inventory still owned by the entity to a location not normally used for storing inventory.<br>• Movement of inventory between entity sites with physical inventory counts at different dates.<br>• The appearance of inventory and work in progress being misrepresented so that they seem to be of a higher value/greater quantity.<br>• The application of inappropriate estimating techniques.<br>• Inventory count records prepared during physical inventory counts deliberately being incorrectly completed or altered after the event.<br>• Additional (false) inventory count records being added to those prepared during the count. |
| 5-1. The principal sources of evidence relating to the existence of inventory are:<br>(a) Evidence from audit procedures which confirm the reliability of the accounting records upon which the amount in the financial statements is based;<br>(b) Evidence from tests of the operation of internal controls over inventory, including the reliability of inventory counting procedures applied by the entity; and<br>(c) Substantive evidence from the physical inspection tests undertaken by the auditor. |
| 8-1. The effectiveness of the auditor's attendance at a physical inventory count is increased by the use of audit staff who are familiar with the entity's business and where advance planning has been undertaken. Planning procedures include:<br>• Performing analytical procedures, and discussing with management any significant changes in inventory over the year and any problems with inventory that have recently occurred, for example unexpected 'stock-out' reports and negative inventory balances.<br>• Discussing inventory counting arrangements and instructions with management.<br>• Familiarisation with the nature and volume of the inventory, the identification of high value items, the method of accounting for inventory and the conditions giving rise to obsolescence.<br>• Assessing the implications of the locations at which inventory is held for inventory control and recording.<br>• Considering the quantity and nature of work in progress, the quantity of inventory held by third parties, and whether expert valuers or inventory counters will be engaged (further guidance on these issues is set out in paragraphs 8-2 and 8-3 below). |

| Current paragraph reference (*Italic text is from IAASB for context*) |
|---|
| • Reviewing internal control relating to inventory, so as to identify potential areas of difficulty (for example cut-off).<br>• Considering any internal audit involvement, with a view to deciding the reliance which can be placed on it.<br>• Considering the results of previous physical inventory counts made by the entity.<br>• Reviewing the auditor's working papers for the previous year. |
| 8-2.   Prior to attending a physical inventory count, the auditor establishes whether expert help, such as that provided by a quantity surveyor, needs to be obtained by management to substantiate quantities, or to identify the nature and condition of the inventories, where they are very specialised. In cases where the entity engages a third party expert the auditor assesses, in accordance with ISA (UK and Ireland) 620 "Using the Work of an Expert", the objectivity and professional qualifications, experience and resources of the expert engaged to carry out this work, and also the instructions given to the expert. |
| 8-3.   Management may from time to time appoint inventory counters from outside the entity, a practice common for inventory at, for example, farms, petrol stations and public houses. The use of independent inventory counters does not eliminate the need for the auditor to obtain audit evidence as to the existence of inventory. In addition, as well as obtaining satisfaction as to the competence and objectivity of the independent inventory counters, the auditor considers how to obtain evidence as to the procedures followed by them to ensure that the inventory count records have been properly prepared. In this connection, the auditor has regard to the relevant guidance set out in ISA (UK and Ireland) 402, "Auditor's Considerations Relating to Entities Using Service Organizations". |
| 9-1.   The nature of the auditor's procedures during their attendance at a physical inventory count will depend upon the results of the assessment of risks of material misstatements carried out in accordance with ISA (UK and Ireland) 315. In cases where the auditor decides to place reliance on accounting systems and internal controls, the auditor attends a physical inventory count primarily to obtain evidence regarding the design and operating effectiveness of management procedures for confirming inventory quantities. |
| 9-2.   Where entities maintain detailed inventory records and check these by regular test counts the auditor performs audit procedures designed to confirm whether management:<br>(a)  Maintains adequate inventory records that are kept up-to-date;<br>(b)  Has satisfactory procedures for inventory counting and test-counting; and<br>(c)  Investigates and corrects all material differences between the book inventory records and the physical counts.<br>The auditor attends a physical inventory count to gain assurance that the inventory checking as a whole is effective in confirming that accurate inventory records are maintained. If the entity's inventory records are not reliable the auditor may need to request management to perform alternative procedures which may include a full count at the year end. |
| 9-3.   In entities that do not maintain detailed inventory records the quantification of inventory for financial statement purposes is likely to be based on a full physical count of all inventory held at a date close to the company's year end. In such circumstances the auditor will consider the date of the physical |

| Current paragraph reference (*Italic text is from IAASB for context*) |
|---|
| inventory count recognising that the evidence of the existence of inventory provided by the inventory count is greater when the inventory count is carried out at the end of the financial year. Physical inventory counts carried out before or after the year end may also be acceptable for audit purposes provided the auditor is satisfied that the records of inventory movements in the intervening period are reliable |
| 12-1. The auditor examines the way the physical inventory count is organised and evaluates the adequacy of the client's instructions for the physical inventory count. Such instructions, preferably in writing, should cover all phases of the inventory counting procedures, be issued in good time and be discussed with the person responsible for the physical inventory count to check that the procedures are understood and that potential difficulties are anticipated. If the instructions are found to be inadequate, the auditor seeks improvements to them. |
| 13-1. If the manner of carrying out the inventory count or the results of the test-counts are not satisfactory, the auditor immediately draws the matter to the attention of the management supervising the inventory count and may have to request a recount of part, or all of the inventory. |
| 13-2. When carrying out test counts, the auditor gives particular consideration to those inventory items which the auditor believes to have a high value either individually or as a category of inventory. The auditor includes in the audit working papers items for any subsequent testing considered necessary, such as copies of (or extracts from) inventory count records and details of the sequence of those records, and any differences noted between the records and the physical inventory counted. |
| 13-3 The auditor determines whether the procedures for identifying damaged, obsolete and slow moving stock operate properly. The auditor obtains (from observation and by discussion e.g. with storekeepers and inventory counters) information about the inventory condition, age, usage and, in the case of work in progress, its stage of completion. Further, the auditor ascertains that stock held on behalf of third parties is separately identified and accounted for. |
| 14-1. The auditor considers whether management has instituted adequate cut-off procedures, i.e. procedures intended to ensure that movements into, within and out of inventory are properly identified and reflected in the accounting records in the correct period. The auditor's procedures during the inventory count will depend on the manner in which the year end inventory value is to be determined. For example, where inventory is determined by a full count and evaluation at the year end, the auditor tests the arrangements made to identify inventory that corresponds to sales made before the cut-off point and the auditor identifies goods movement documents for reconciliation with financial records of purchases and sales. Alternatively, where the full count and evaluation is at an interim date and year end inventory is determined by updating such valuation by the cost of purchases and sales, the auditor performs appropriate procedures during attendance at the physical inventory count and in addition tests the financial cut-off (involving the matching of costs with revenues) at the year end. |
| 18 *When inventory is under the custody and control of a third party, the auditor would ordinarily obtain direct confirmation from the third party as to the quantities and condition of inventory held on behalf of the entity. Depending on materiality of this inventory the auditor would also consider the following:* |

| Current paragraph reference (*Italic text is from IAASB for context*) |
|---|
| • Testing the owner's procedures for investigating the custodian and evaluating the custodian's performance.<br>• The guidance set out in ISA (UK and Ireland) 402. |
| 18-1. The auditor's working papers include details of the auditor's observations and tests (for example, of physical quantity, cut-off date and controls over inventory count records), the manner in which points that are relevant and material to the inventory being counted or measured have been dealt with by the entity, instances where the entity's procedures have not been satisfactorily carried out and the auditor's conclusions. |
| 18-2. Although the principal reason for attendance at a physical inventory count is usually to obtain evidence to substantiate the existence of the inventory, attendance can also enhance the auditor's understanding of the business by providing an opportunity to observe the production process and/or business locations at first hand and providing evidence regarding the completeness and valuation of inventory and the entity's internal control. Matters that the auditor may wish to observe whilst attending a physical inventory count include:<br>Understanding the business<br>• The production process.<br>• Evidence of significant pollution and environmental damage.<br>• Unused buildings and machinery.<br>Completeness and valuation of inventory<br>• Physical controls.<br>• Obsolete inventory (for example goods beyond their sale date).<br>• Scrap, and goods marked for re-work.<br>• Returned goods.<br>Internal control<br>• Exceptions identified by the production process (for example missing work tickets).<br>• The operation of 'shop-floor' disciplines regarding the inputting of data such as inventory movements into the computer systems. |
| 18-3. Some entities use computer-assisted techniques to perform inventory counts; for example hand held scanners can be used to record inventory items which update computerised records. In some situations there are no stock-sheets, no physical count records, and no paper records available at the time of the count. In these circumstances the auditor considers the IT environment surrounding the inventory count and considers the need for specialist assistance when evaluating the techniques used and the controls surrounding them. Relevant issues involve systems interfaces, and the controls over ensuring that the computerised inventory records are properly updated for the inventory count information.<br>The auditor considers the following aspects of the physical inventory count:<br>(a) How the test counts (and double counts where two people are checking) are recorded;<br>(b) How differences are investigated before the computerised inventory records are updated for the counts; and<br>(c) How the computerised inventory records are updated, and how inventory differences are recorded. |
| **After the Physical Inventory Count**<br>18-4. After the physical inventory count, the matters recorded in the auditor's working papers at the time of the count or measurement, including apparent instances of obsolete or deteriorating inventory, are followed up. For |

| Current paragraph reference (*Italic text is from IAASB for context*) |
|---|
| example, details of the last serial numbers of goods inwards and outwards records and of movements during the inventory count may be used in order to check cut-off. Further, copies of (or extracts from) the inventory count records and details of test counts, and of the sequence of inventory count records may be used to check that the results of the count have been properly reflected in the accounting records of the entity. |
| 18-5. Where appropriate, the auditor considers whether management has instituted procedures to ensure that all inventory movements between the observed inventory count and the period end have been adjusted in the accounting records, and the auditor tests these procedures to the extent considered necessary to address the assessed risk of material misstatement. In addition, the auditor follows up all queries and notifies senior management of serious problems encountered during the physical inventory count. |
| 18-6. In conclusion, the auditor considers whether attendance at the physical inventory count has provided sufficient reliable audit evidence in relation to relevant assertions (principally existence) and, if not, the other procedures that should be performed. |
| **Work in Progress** |
| 18-7. Management may place substantial reliance on internal controls designed to ensure the completeness and accuracy of records of work in progress. In such circumstances there may not be a physical inventory count which can be attended by the auditor. Nevertheless, inspection of the work in progress may assist the auditor in understanding the entity's control systems and processes. It will also assist the auditor in planning further audit procedures, and it may also help on such matters as the determination of the stage of completion of construction or engineering work in progress. For this purpose, the auditor identifies the accounting records that will be used by management to produce the work in progress figure in the year-end accounts and, where unfinished items are uniquely identifiable (for example by reference to work tickets or labels), the auditor physically examine items to obtain evidence that supports the recorded stage of completion. In some cases, for example in connection with building projects, photographic evidence can also be useful evidence as to the state of work in progress at the date of the physical inventory count, particularly if provided by independent third parties or the auditor. |
| **Litigation and claims** |
| 33. *When the auditor assesses a risk of material misstatement regarding litigation or claims that have been identified or when the auditor believes they may exist, the auditor should seek direct communication with the entity's legal counsel.* *Such communication will assist in obtaining sufficient appropriate audit evidence as to whether potentially material litigation and claims are known and management's[1] estimates of the financial implications, including costs, are reliable. ...* |
| 34. *... When it is considered unlikely that the entity's legal counsel will respond to a general inquiry the letter would ordinarily specify the following: ...* Management's[1] assessment of the outcome of the litigation or claim and its estimate of the financial implications, including costs involved. ... |
| **Segment information** |
| 45. *The auditor would discuss with management[1] the methods used in determining segment information, ...* |

# Proposed Clarified International Standard on Auditing (UK and Ireland) 505
# External confirmations

*(Effective for audits of financial statements for periods ending on or after 15 December 2010)*

## Contents

---

International Standard on Auditing (UK and Ireland) (ISA (UK and Ireland)) 505, "External Confirmations" should be read in conjunction with ISA (UK and Ireland) 200, "Overall Objectives of the Independent Auditor and the Conduct of an Audit in Accordance with International Standards on Auditing (UK and Ireland)."

# Introduction

## Scope of this ISA (UK and Ireland)

This International Standard on Auditing (UK and Ireland) (ISA (UK and Ireland)) **1**
deals with the auditor's use of external confirmation procedures to obtain audit
evidence in accordance with the requirements of ISA (UK and Ireland) 330[1] and ISA
(UK and Ireland) 500.[2] It does not address inquiries regarding litigation and claims,
which are dealt with in ISA (UK and Ireland) 501[3].

## External Confirmation Procedures to Obtain Audit Evidence

ISA (UK and Ireland) 500 indicates that the reliability of audit evidence is influenced **2**
by its source and by its nature, and is dependent on the individual circumstances
under which it is obtained.[4] That ISA (UK and Ireland) also includes the following
generalizations applicable to audit evidence:[5]

- Audit evidence is more reliable when it is obtained from independent sources
  outside the entity.
- Audit evidence obtained directly by the auditor is more reliable than audit
  evidence obtained indirectly or by inference.
- Audit evidence is more reliable when it exists in documentary form, whether
  paper, electronic or other medium.

Accordingly, depending on the circumstances of the audit, audit evidence in the form
of external confirmations received directly by the auditor from confirming parties
may be more reliable than evidence generated internally by the entity. This ISA (UK
and Ireland) is intended to assist the auditor in designing and performing external
confirmation procedures to obtain relevant and reliable audit evidence.

Other ISAs (UK and Ireland) recognize the importance of external confirmations as **3**
audit evidence, for example:

- ISA (UK and Ireland) 330 discusses the auditor's responsibility to design and
  implement overall responses to address the assessed risks of material misstatement at the financial statement level, and to design and perform further audit
  procedures whose nature, timing and extent are based on, and are responsive to,
  the assessed risks of material misstatement at the assertion level.[6] In addition,
  ISA (UK and Ireland) 330 requires that, irrespective of the assessed risks of
  material misstatement, the auditor designs and performs substantive procedures
  for each material class of transactions, account balance, and disclosure. The
  auditor is also required to consider whether external confirmation procedures
  are to be performed as substantive audit procedures.[7]

---

[1] *ISA (UK and Ireland) 330, "The Auditor's Responses to Assessed Risks."*

[2] *ISA (UK and Ireland) 500, "Audit Evidence."*

[3] *ISA (UK and Ireland) 501, "Audit Evidence—Specific Considerations for Selected Items."*

[4] *ISA (UK and Ireland) 500, paragraph A5.*

[5] *ISA (UK and Ireland) 500, paragraph A31.*

[6] *ISA (UK and Ireland) 330, paragraphs 5-6.*

[7] *ISA (UK and Ireland) 330, paragraphs 18-19.*

- ISA (UK and Ireland) 330 requires that the auditor obtain more persuasive audit evidence the higher the auditor's assessment of risk.[8] To do this, the auditor may increase the quantity of the evidence or obtain evidence that is more relevant or reliable, or both. For example, the auditor may place more emphasis on obtaining evidence directly from third parties or obtaining corroborating evidence from a number of independent sources. ISA (UK and Ireland) 330 also indicates that external confirmation procedures may assist the auditor in obtaining audit evidence with the high level of reliability that the auditor requires to respond to significant risks of material misstatement, whether due to fraud or error.[9]
- ISA (UK and Ireland) 240 indicates that the auditor may design confirmation requests to obtain additional corroborative information as a response to address the assessed risks of material misstatement due to fraud at the assertion level.[10]
- ISA (UK and Ireland) 500 indicates that corroborating information obtained from a source independent of the entity, such as external confirmations, may increase the assurance the auditor obtains from evidence existing within the accounting records or from representations made by management.[11]

## Effective Date

4   This ISA (UK and Ireland) is effective for audits of financial statements for periods ending on or after 15 December 2010.

## Objective

5   The objective of the auditor, when using external confirmation procedures, is to design and perform such procedures to obtain relevant and reliable audit evidence.

## Definitions

6   For purposes of the ISAs (UK and Ireland), the following terms have the meanings attributed below:

(a) External confirmation – Audit evidence obtained as a direct written response to the auditor from a third party (the confirming party), in paper form, or by electronic or other medium.

(b) Positive confirmation request – A request that the confirming party respond directly to the auditor indicating whether the confirming party agrees or disagrees with the information in the request, or providing the requested information.

(c) Negative confirmation request – A request that the confirming party respond directly to the auditor only if the confirming party disagrees with the information provided in the request.

[8] *ISA (UK and Ireland) 330, paragraph 7(b).*

[9] *ISA (UK and Ireland) 330, paragraph A53.*

[10] *ISA (UK and Ireland) 240, "The Auditor's Responsibilities Relating to Fraud in an Audit of Financial Statements," paragraph A37.*

[11] *ISA (UK and Ireland) 500, paragraph A8.*

(d) Non-response – A failure of the confirming party to respond, or fully respond, to a positive confirmation request, or a confirmation request returned undelivered.
(e) Exception – A response that indicates a difference between information requested to be confirmed, or contained in the entity's records, and information provided by the confirming party.

# Requirements

## External Confirmation Procedures

When using external confirmation procedures, the auditor shall maintain control over external confirmation requests, including:   **7**

(a) Determining the information to be confirmed or requested; (Ref: Para. A1)
(b) Selecting the appropriate confirming party; (Ref: Para. A2)
(c) Designing the confirmation requests, including determining that requests are properly addressed and contain return information for responses to be sent directly to the auditor; and (Ref: Para. A3-A6)
(d) Sending the requests, including follow-up requests when applicable, to the confirming party. (Ref: Para. A7)

### Management's Refusal to Allow the Auditor to Send a Confirmation Request

If management refuses to allow the auditor to send a confirmation request, the auditor shall:   **8**

(a) Inquire as to management's reasons for the refusal, and seek audit evidence as to their validity and reasonableness; (Ref: Para. A8)
(b) Evaluate the implications of management's refusal on the auditor's assessment of the relevant risks of material misstatement, including the risk of fraud, and on the nature, timing and extent of other audit procedures; and (Ref: Para. A9)
(c) Perform alternative audit procedures designed to obtain relevant and reliable audit evidence. (Ref: Para. A10)

If the auditor concludes that management's refusal to allow the auditor to send a confirmation request is unreasonable, or the auditor is unable to obtain relevant and reliable audit evidence from alternative audit procedures, the auditor shall communicate with those charged with governance in accordance with ISA (UK and Ireland) 260.[12] The auditor also shall determine the implications for the audit and the auditor's opinion in accordance with ISA (UK and Ireland) 705.[13]   **9**

## Results of the External Confirmation Procedures

### *Reliability of Responses to Confirmation Requests*

If the auditor identifies factors that give rise to doubts about the reliability of the response to a confirmation request, the auditor shall obtain further audit evidence to resolve those doubts. (Ref: Para. A11-A16)   **10**

---

[12] *ISA (UK and Ireland) 260, "Communication with Those Charged with Governance," paragraph 16.*

[13] *ISA (UK and Ireland) 705, "Modifications to the Opinion in the Independent Auditor's Report."*

11    If the auditor determines that a response to a confirmation request is not reliable, the auditor shall evaluate the implications on the assessment of the relevant risks of material misstatement, including the risk of fraud, and on the related nature, timing and extent of other audit procedures. (Ref: Para. A17)

*Non-Responses*

12    In the case of each non-response, the auditor shall perform alternative audit procedures to obtain relevant and reliable audit evidence. (Ref: Para A18-A19)

***When a Response to a Positive Confirmation Request Is Necessary to Obtain Sufficient Appropriate Audit Evidence***

13    If the auditor has determined that a response to a positive confirmation request is necessary to obtain sufficient appropriate audit evidence, alternative audit procedures will not provide the audit evidence the auditor requires. If the auditor does not obtain such confirmation, the auditor shall determine the implications for the audit and the auditor's opinion in accordance with ISA (UK and Ireland) 705 (Revised and Redrafted). (Ref: Para A20)

*Exceptions*

14    The auditor shall investigate exceptions to determine whether or not they are indicative of misstatements. (Ref: Para. A21-A22)

## Negative Confirmations

15    Negative confirmations provide less persuasive audit evidence than positive confirmations. Accordingly, the auditor shall not use negative confirmation requests as the sole substantive audit procedure to address an assessed risk of material misstatement at the assertion level unless all of the following are present: (Ref: Para. A23)

(a)    The auditor has assessed the risk of material misstatement as low and has obtained sufficient appropriate audit evidence regarding the operating effectiveness of controls relevant to the assertion;

(b)    The population of items subject to negative confirmation procedures comprises a large number of small, homogeneous, account balances, transactions or conditions;

(c)    A very low exception rate is expected; and

(d)    The auditor is not aware of circumstances or conditions that would cause recipients of negative confirmation requests to disregard such requests.

## Evaluating the Evidence Obtained

16    The auditor shall evaluate whether the results of the external confirmation procedures provide relevant and reliable audit evidence, or whether further audit evidence is necessary. (Ref: Para A24-A25)

***

# Application and Other Explanatory Material

## External Confirmation Procedures

### *Determining the Information to Be Confirmed or Requested* (Ref: Para. 7(a))

External confirmation procedures frequently are performed to confirm or request **A1**
information regarding account balances and their elements. They may also be used
to confirm terms of agreements, contracts, or transactions between an entity and
other parties, or to confirm the absence of certain conditions, such as a "side
agreement."

### *Selecting the Appropriate Confirming Party* (Ref: Para. 7(b))

Responses to confirmation requests provide more relevant and reliable audit evi- **A2**
dence when confirmation requests are sent to a confirming party the auditor believes
is knowledgeable about the information to be confirmed. For example, a financial
institution official who is knowledgeable about the transactions or arrangements for
which confirmation is requested may be the most appropriate person at the financial
institution from whom to request confirmation.

### *Designing Confirmation Requests* (Ref: Para. 7(c))

The design of a confirmation request may directly affect the confirmation response **A3**
rate, and the reliability and the nature of the audit evidence obtained from responses.

Factors to consider when designing confirmation requests include: **A4**

- The assertions being addressed.
- Specific identified risks of material misstatement, including fraud risks.
- The layout and presentation of the confirmation request.
- Prior experience on the audit or similar engagements.
- The method of communication (for example, in paper form, or by electronic or other medium).
- Management's authorization or encouragement to the confirming parties to respond to the auditor. Confirming parties may only be willing to respond to a confirmation request containing management's authorization.
- The ability of the intended confirming party to confirm or provide the requested information (for example, individual invoice amount versus total balance).

A positive external confirmation request asks the confirming party to reply to the **A5**
auditor in all cases, either by indicating the confirming party's agreement with the
given information, or by asking the confirming party to provide information. A
response to a positive confirmation request ordinarily is expected to provide reliable
audit evidence. There is a risk, however, that a confirming party may reply to the
confirmation request without verifying that the information is correct. The auditor
may reduce this risk by using positive confirmation requests that do not state the
amount (or other information) on the confirmation request, and ask the confirming
party to fill in the amount or furnish other information. On the other hand, use of
this type of "blank" confirmation request may result in lower response rates because
additional effort is required of the confirming parties.

Determining that requests are properly addressed includes testing the validity of **A6**
some or all of the addresses on confirmation requests before they are sent out.

**Follow-Up on Confirmation Requests** (Ref: Para. 7(d))

A7   The auditor may send an additional confirmation request when a reply to a previous request has not been received within a reasonable time. For example, the auditor may, having re-verified the accuracy of the original address, send an additional or follow-up request.

## Management's Refusal to Allow the Auditor to Send a Confirmation Request

*Reasonableness of Management's Refusal* (Ref: Para. 8(a))

A8   A refusal by management to allow the auditor to send a confirmation request is a limitation on the audit evidence the auditor may wish to obtain. The auditor is therefore required to inquire as to the reasons for the limitation. A common reason advanced is the existence of a legal dispute or ongoing negotiation with the intended confirming party, the resolution of which may be affected by an untimely confirmation request. The auditor is required to seek audit evidence as to the validity and reasonableness of the reasons because of the risk that management may be attempting to deny the auditor access to audit evidence that may reveal fraud or error.

*Implications for the Assessment of Risks of Material Misstatement* (Ref: Para. 8(b))

A9   The auditor may conclude from the evaluation in paragraph 8(b) that it would be appropriate to revise the assessment of the risks of material misstatement at the assertion level and modify planned audit procedures in accordance with ISA (UK and Ireland) 315.[14] For example, if management's request to not confirm is unreasonable, this may indicate a fraud risk factor that requires evaluation in accordance with ISA (UK and Ireland) 240.[15]

*Alternative Audit Procedures* (Ref: Para. 8(c))

A10   The alternative audit procedures performed may be similar to those appropriate for a non-response as set out in paragraphs A18-A19 of this ISA (UK and Ireland). Such procedures also would take account of the results of the auditor's evaluation in paragraph 8(b) of this ISA (UK and Ireland).

## Results of the External Confirmation Procedures

*Reliability of Responses to Confirmation Requests* (Ref: Para. 10)

A11   ISA (UK and Ireland) 500 indicates that even when audit evidence is obtained from sources external to the entity, circumstances may exist that affect its reliability.[16] All responses carry some risk of interception, alteration or fraud. Such risk exists regardless of whether a response is obtained in paper form, or by electronic or other medium. Factors that may indicate doubts about the reliability of a response include that it:

---

[14] *ISA (UK and Ireland) 315, "Identifying and Assessing the Risks of Material Misstatement through Understanding the Entity and Its Environment," paragraph 31.*

[15] *ISA (UK and Ireland) 240, paragraph 24.*

[16] *ISA (UK and Ireland) 500, paragraph A31.*

- Was received by the auditor indirectly; or
- Appeared not to come from the originally intended confirming party.

Responses received electronically, for example by facsimile or electronic mail, involve risks as to reliability because proof of origin and authority of the respondent may be difficult to establish, and alterations may be difficult to detect. A process used by the auditor and the respondent that creates a secure environment for responses received electronically may mitigate these risks. If the auditor is satisfied that such a process is secure and properly controlled, the reliability of the related responses is enhanced. An electronic confirmation process might incorporate various techniques for validating the identity of a sender of information in electronic form, for example, through the use of encryption, electronic digital signatures, and procedures to verify web site authenticity.    **A12**

If a confirming party uses a third party to coordinate and provide responses to confirmation requests, the auditor may perform procedures to address the risks that:    **A13**

(a) The response may not be from the proper source;
(b) A respondent may not be authorized to respond; and
(c) The integrity of the transmission may have been compromised.

The auditor is required by ISA (UK and Ireland) 500 to determine whether to modify or add procedures to resolve doubts over the reliability of information to be used as audit evidence.[17] The auditor may choose to verify the source and contents of a response to a confirmation request by contacting the confirming party. For example, when a confirming party responds by electronic mail, the auditor may telephone the confirming party to determine whether the confirming party did, in fact, send the response. When a response has been returned to the auditor indirectly (for example, because the confirming party incorrectly addressed it to the entity rather than to the auditor), the auditor may request the confirming party to respond in writing directly to the auditor.    **A14**

On its own, an oral response to a confirmation request does not meet the definition of an external confirmation because it is not a direct written response to the auditor. However, upon obtaining an oral response to a confirmation request, the auditor may, depending on the circumstances, request the confirming party to respond in writing directly to the auditor. If no such response is received, in accordance with paragraph 12, the auditor seeks other audit evidence to support the information in the oral response.    **A15**

A response to a confirmation request may contain restrictive language regarding its use. Such restrictions do not necessarily invalidate the reliability of the response as audit evidence.    **A16**

***Unreliable Responses*** (Ref: Para. 11)

When the auditor concludes that a response is unreliable, the auditor may need to revise the assessment of the risks of material misstatement at the assertion level and modify planned audit procedures accordingly, in accordance with ISA (UK and    **A17**

---

[17] *ISA (UK and Ireland) 500, paragraph 11.*

428    *Proposed Clarified ISA (UK and Ireland) 505*

Ireland) 315.[18] For example, an unreliable response may indicate a fraud risk factor that requires evaluation in accordance with ISA (UK and Ireland) 240.[19]

***Non-Responses*** (Ref: Para. 12)

A18    Examples of alternative audit procedures the auditor may perform include:

- For accounts receivable balances – examining specific subsequent cash receipts, shipping documentation, and sales near the period-end.
- For accounts payable balances – examining subsequent cash disbursements or correspondence from third parties, and other records, such as goods received notes.

A19    The nature and extent of alternative audit procedures are affected by the account and assertion in question. A non-response to a confirmation request may indicate a previously unidentified risk of material misstatement. In such situations, the auditor may need to revise the assessed risk of material misstatement at the assertion level, and modify planned audit procedures, in accordance with ISA (UK and Ireland) 315.[20] For example, fewer responses to confirmation requests than anticipated, or a greater number of responses than anticipated, may indicate a previously unidentified fraud risk factor that requires evaluation in accordance with ISA (UK and Ireland) 240.[21]

***When a Response to a Positive Confirmation Request Is Necessary to Obtain Sufficient Appropriate Audit Evidence*** (Ref. Para. 13)

A20    In certain circumstances, the auditor may identify an assessed risk of material misstatement at the assertion level for which a response to a positive confirmation request is necessary to obtain sufficient appropriate audit evidence. Such circumstances may include where:

- The information available to corroborate management's assertion(s) is only available outside the entity.
- Specific fraud risk factors, such as the risk of management override of controls, or the risk of collusion which can involve employee(s) and/or management, prevent the auditor from relying on evidence from the entity.

***Exceptions*** (Ref: Para. 14)

A21    Exceptions noted in responses to confirmation requests may indicate misstatements or potential misstatements in the financial statements. When a misstatement is identified, the auditor is required by ISA (UK and Ireland) 240 to evaluate whether such misstatement is indicative of fraud.[22] Exceptions may provide a guide to the quality of responses from similar confirming parties or for similar accounts. Exceptions also may indicate a deficiency, or deficiencies, in the entity's internal control over financial reporting.

[18] *ISA (UK and Ireland) 315, paragraph 31.*

[19] *ISA (UK and Ireland) 240, paragraph 24.*

[20] *ISA (UK and Ireland) 315, paragraph 31.*

[21] *ISA (UK and Ireland) 240, paragraph 24.*

[22] *ISA (UK and Ireland) 240, paragraph 35.*

Some exceptions do not represent misstatements. For example, the auditor may conclude that differences in responses to confirmation requests are due to timing, measurement, or clerical errors in the external confirmation procedures.

**A22**

## Negative Confirmations (Ref: Para. 15)

The failure to receive a response to a negative confirmation request does not explicitly indicate receipt by the intended confirming party of the confirmation request or verification of the accuracy of the information contained in the request. Accordingly, a failure of a confirming party to respond to a negative confirmation request provides significantly less persuasive audit evidence than does a response to a positive confirmation request. Confirming parties also may be more likely to respond indicating their disagreement with a confirmation request when the information in the request is not in their favor, and less likely to respond otherwise. For example, holders of bank deposit accounts may be more likely to respond if they believe that the balance in their account is understated in the confirmation request, but may be less likely to respond when they believe the balance is overstated. Therefore, sending negative confirmation requests to holders of bank deposit accounts may be a useful procedure in considering whether such balances may be understated, but is unlikely to be effective if the auditor is seeking evidence regarding overstatement.

**A23**

## Evaluating the Evidence Obtained (Ref: Para. 16)

When evaluating the results of individual external confirmation requests, the auditor may categorize such results as follows:

**A24**

(a) A response by the appropriate confirming party indicating agreement with the information provided in the confirmation request, or providing requested information without exception;

(b) A response deemed unreliable;

(c) A non-response; or

(d) A response indicating an exception.

The auditor's evaluation, when taken into account with other audit procedures the auditor may have performed, may assist the auditor in concluding whether sufficient appropriate audit evidence has been obtained or whether further audit evidence is necessary, as required by ISA (UK and Ireland) 330.[23]

**A25**

---

[23] *ISA (UK and Ireland) 330, paragraphs 28-29.*

# Addendum

*This addendum provides a summary of APB's rationale for retaining or excluding in the proposed clarified ISA (UK and Ireland) the supplementary requirements in the existing ISA (UK and Ireland). It also sets out the supplementary guidance material in the existing ISA (UK and Ireland) that APB considers is not necessary to retain in light of the improvements in the underlying Clarity ISAs issued by the IAASB as part of the Clarity Project. It is provided for information and does not form part of the proposed clarified ISA (UK and Ireland).*

*The Consultation Paper published with the exposure drafts explains the general approach used by the APB for determining whether current supplementary material should be proposed to be retained.*

## Analysis of proposed treatment of current APB supplementary material in current ISA (UK and Ireland) 505

### Requirements

There are no supplementary requirements in current ISA (UK and Ireland) 505.

### Guidance

The following guidance in current ISA (UK and Ireland) 505 has not been carried forward to the proposed clarified standard.

| Current paragraph reference (*Italic text is from IAASB for context*) |
| --- |
| 1-1. – 1-4. [Description of management and those charged with governance.] |
| 6.     ...*Factors affecting the reliability of confirmations include the control the auditor exercises over confirmation requests and responses, the characteristics of the respondents, and any restrictions included in the response or imposed by management*[1]. |
| [1] In the UK and Ireland such restrictions might be imposed by those charged with governance. |

# Proposed Clarified International Standard on Auditing (UK and Ireland) 510

## Initial audit engagements—opening balances and continuing engagements – opening balances

*(Effective for audits of financial statements for periods ending on or after 15 December 2010)*

## Contents

International Standard on Auditing (UK and Ireland) (ISA (UK and Ireland)) 510, "Initial Engagements—Opening Balances and Continuing Engagements—Opening Balances" should be read in conjunction with ISA (UK and Ireland) 200, "Overall Objectives of the Independent Auditor and the Conduct of an Audit in Accordance with International Standards on Auditing (UK and Ireland)."

# Introduction

## Scope of this ISA (UK and Ireland)

1   This International Standard on Auditing (UK and Ireland) (ISA (UK and Ireland)) deals with the auditor's responsibilities relating to opening balances in an initial audit engagement. In addition to financial statement amounts, opening balances include matters requiring disclosure that existed at the beginning of the period, such as contingencies and commitments. When the financial statements include comparative financial information, the requirements and guidance in ISA (UK and Ireland) 710[1] also apply. ISA (UK and Ireland) 300[2] includes additional requirements and guidance regarding activities prior to starting an initial audit.

1-1   This ISA (UK and Ireland) also provides requirements and guidance regarding opening balances for a continuing auditor (an auditor who audited and reported on the preceding periods financial statements and continues as auditor for the current period).

## Effective Date

2   This ISA (UK and Ireland) is effective for audits of financial statements for periods ending on or after 15 December 2010.

# Objective

3   In conducting an initial audit engagement, the objective of the auditor with respect to opening balances is to obtain sufficient appropriate audit evidence about whether:

(a)   Opening balances contain misstatements that materially affect the current period's financial statements; and

(b)   Appropriate accounting policies reflected in the opening balances have been consistently applied in the current period's financial statements, or changes thereto are appropriately accounted for and adequately presented and disclosed in accordance with the applicable financial reporting framework.

This objective also applies when conducting a continuing audit engagement.

# Definitions

4   For the purposes of the ISAs (UK and Ireland), the following terms have the meanings attributed below:

(a)   Initial audit engagement – An engagement in which either:
   (i)   The financial statements for the prior period were not audited; or
   (ii)   The financial statements for the prior period were audited by a predecessor auditor.

---

[1] *ISA (UK and Ireland) 710, "Comparative Information*—Corresponding Figures and Comparative Financial Statements."

[2] *ISA 300 (UK and Ireland), "Planning an Audit of Financial Statements."*

(b) Opening balances – Those account balances that exist at the beginning of the period. Opening balances are based upon the closing balances of the prior period and reflect the effects of transactions and events of prior periods and accounting policies applied in the prior period. Opening balances also include matters requiring disclosure that existed at the beginning of the period, such as contingencies and commitments.

(c) Predecessor auditor – The auditor from a different audit firm, who audited the financial statements of an entity in the prior period and who has been replaced by the current auditor.

# Requirements

## Audit Procedures

### Opening Balances

The auditor shall read the most recent financial statements, if any, and the predecessor auditor's report thereon, if any, for information relevant to opening balances, including disclosures. **5**

The auditor shall obtain sufficient appropriate audit evidence about whether the opening balances contain misstatements that materially affect the current period's financial statements by: (Ref: Para. A1–A2) **6**

(a) Determining whether the prior period's closing balances have been correctly brought forward to the current period or, when appropriate, have been restated;

(b) Determining whether the opening balances reflect the application of appropriate accounting policies; and

(c) Performing one or more of the following: (Ref: Para. A3–A7)
   (i) Where the prior year financial statements were audited, reviewing the predecessor auditor's working papers to obtain evidence regarding the opening balances;
   (ii) Evaluating whether audit procedures performed in the current period provide evidence relevant to the opening balances; or
   (iii) Performing specific audit procedures to obtain evidence regarding the opening balances.

If the auditor obtains audit evidence that the opening balances contain misstatements that could materially affect the current period's financial statements, the auditor shall perform such additional audit procedures as are appropriate in the circumstances to determine the effect on the current period's financial statements. If the auditor concludes that such misstatements exist in the current period's financial statements, the auditor shall communicate the misstatements with the appropriate level of management and those charged with governance in accordance with ISA (UK and Ireland) 450.[3] **7**

### Consistency of Accounting Policies

The auditor shall obtain sufficient appropriate audit evidence about whether the accounting policies reflected in the opening balances have been consistently applied in the current period's financial statements, and whether changes in the accounting **8**

[3] *ISA (UK and Ireland) 450, "Evaluation of Misstatements Identified during the Audit," paragraphs 8 and 12.*

policies have been appropriately accounted for and adequately presented and disclosed in accordance with the applicable financial reporting framework.

### Relevant Information in the Predecessor Auditor's Report

9   If the prior period's financial statements were audited by a predecessor auditor and there was a modification to the opinion, the auditor shall evaluate the effect of the matter giving rise to the modification in assessing the risks of material misstatement in the current period's financial statements in accordance with ISA (UK and Ireland) 315.[4]

## Audit Conclusions and Reporting

### Opening Balances

10   If the auditor is unable to obtain sufficient appropriate audit evidence regarding the opening balances, the auditor shall express a qualified opinion or disclaim an opinion on the financial statements, as appropriate, in accordance with ISA (UK and Ireland) 705.[5] (Ref: Para. A8)

11   If the auditor concludes that the opening balances contain a misstatement that materially affects the current period's financial statements, and the effect of the misstatement is not appropriately accounted for or not adequately presented or disclosed, the auditor shall express a qualified opinion or an adverse opinion, as appropriate, in accordance with ISA (UK and Ireland) 705.

### Consistency of Accounting Policies

12   If the auditor concludes that:

(a) the current period's accounting policies are not consistently applied in relation to opening balances in accordance with the applicable financial reporting framework; or

(b) a change in accounting policies is not appropriately accounted for or not adequately presented or disclosed in accordance with the applicable financial reporting framework,

the auditor shall express a qualified opinion or an adverse opinion as appropriate in accordance with ISA (UK and Ireland) 705.

### Modification to the Opinion in the Predecessor Auditor's Report

13   If the predecessor auditor's opinion regarding the prior period's financial statements included a modification to the auditor's opinion that remains relevant and material to the current period's financial statements, the auditor shall modify the auditor's opinion on the current period's financial statements in accordance with ISA (UK and Ireland) 705 and ISA (UK and Ireland) 710. (Ref: Para. A9)

\*\*\*

[4] *ISA (UK and Ireland) 315, "Identifying and Assessing the Risks of Material Misstatement through Understanding the Entity and Its Environment."*

[5] *ISA (UK and Ireland) 705, "Modifications to the Opinion in the Independent Auditor's Report."*

# Application and Other Explanatory Material

## Audit Procedures

*Considerations Specific to Public Sector Entities* (Ref: Para. 6)

In the public sector, there may be legal or regulatory limitations on the information
that the current auditor can obtain from a predecessor auditor. For example, if a
public sector entity that has previously been audited by a statutorily appointed
auditor (e.g., an Auditor General, or other suitably qualified person appointed on
behalf of the Auditor General) is privatized, the amount of access to working papers
or other information that the statutorily appointed auditor can provide a newly-
appointed auditor that is in the private sector may be constrained by privacy or
secrecy laws or regulations. In situations where such communications are constrained, audit evidence may need to be obtained through other means and, if
sufficient appropriate audit evidence cannot be obtained, consideration given to the
effect on the auditor's opinion.

A1

If the statutorily appointed auditor outsources an audit of a public sector entity to a
private sector audit firm, and the statutorily appointed auditor appoints an audit
firm other than the firm that audited the financial statements of the public sector
entity in the prior period, this is not usually regarded as a change in auditors for the
statutorily appointed auditor. Depending on the nature of the outsourcing
arrangement, however, the audit engagement may be considered an initial audit
engagement from the perspective of the private sector auditor in fulfilling their
responsibilities, and therefore this ISA (UK and Ireland) applies.

A2

*Opening Balances* (Ref: Para. 6(c))

The nature and extent of audit procedures necessary to obtain sufficient appropriate
audit evidence regarding opening balances depend on such matters as:

A3

- The accounting policies followed by the entity.
- The nature of the account balances, classes of transactions and disclosures and
  the risks of material misstatement in the current period's financial statements.
- The significance of the opening balances relative to the current period's financial
  statements.
- Whether the prior period's financial statements were audited and, if so, whether
  the predecessor auditor's opinion was modified.

If a continuing auditor issued an unqualified report on the preceding period's
financial statements and the audit of the current period has not revealed any
matters which cast doubt on those financial statements, the procedures regarding
opening balances need not extend beyond ensuring that opening balances have
been appropriately brought forward and that current accounting policies have
been consistently applied.

A3-1

If a continuing auditor issued a modified opinion on the preceding period's
financial statements the auditor considers whether the matter which gave rise to
the qualification has been resolved and properly dealt with in the current period's
financial statements.

A3-2

**A4**   If the prior period's financial statements were audited by a predecessor auditor, the auditor may be able to obtain sufficient appropriate audit evidence regarding the opening balances by reviewing the predecessor auditor's working papers. Whether such a review provides sufficient appropriate audit evidence is influenced by the professional competence and independence of the predecessor auditor.

**A5**   Relevant ethical and professional requirements guide the current auditor's communications with the predecessor auditor.

**A5-1**   In the UK and Ireland the relevant ethical guidance on proposed communications with a predecessor auditor is provided by the ethical pronouncements relating to the work of auditors issued by the auditor's relevant professional body.

**A6**   For current assets and liabilities, some audit evidence about opening balances may be obtained as part of the current period's audit procedures. For example, the collection (payment) of opening accounts receivable (accounts payable) during the current period will provide some audit evidence of their existence, rights and obligations, completeness and valuation at the beginning of the period. In the case of inventories, however, the current period's audit procedures on the closing inventory balance provide little audit evidence regarding inventory on hand at the beginning of the period. Therefore, additional audit procedures may be necessary, and one or more of the following may provide sufficient appropriate audit evidence:

- Observing a current physical inventory count and reconciling it to the opening inventory quantities.
- Performing audit procedures on the valuation of the opening inventory items.
- Performing audit procedures on gross profit and cutoff.

**A7**   For non-current assets and liabilities, such as property plant and equipment, investments and long-term debt, some audit evidence may be obtained by examining the accounting records and other information underlying the opening balances. In certain cases, the auditor may be able to obtain some audit evidence regarding opening balances through confirmation with third parties, for example, for long-term debt and investments. In other cases, the auditor may need to carry out additional audit procedures.

## Audit Conclusions and Reporting

*Opening Balances* (Ref: Para. 10)

**A8**   ISA (UK and Ireland) 705 establishes requirements and provides guidance on circumstances that may result in a modification to the auditor's opinion on the financial statements, the type of opinion appropriate in the circumstances, and the content of the auditor's report when the auditor's opinion is modified. The inability of the auditor to obtain sufficient appropriate audit evidence regarding opening balances may result in one of the following modifications to the opinion in the auditor's report:

(a) A qualified opinion or a disclaimer of opinion, as is appropriate in the circumstances; or

(b) Unless prohibited by law or regulation, an opinion which is qualified or disclaimed, as appropriate, regarding the results of operations, and cash flows, where relevant, and unmodified regarding financial position[5a].

The Appendix includes illustrative auditors' reports.

With respect to companies, illustrative examples of auditor's reports tailored for use with audits conducted in accordance with ISAs (UK and Ireland) are given in the most recent versions of the APB Bulletins, "Auditor's Reports on Financial Statements in the United Kingdom"/"Auditor's Reports on Financial Statements in the Republic of Ireland." Illustrative examples for various other entities are give in other Bulletins and Practice Notes issued by the APB.

*Modification to the Opinion in the Predecessor Auditor's Report* (Ref: Para. 13)

In some situations, a modification to the predecessor auditor's opinion may not be relevant and material to the opinion on the current period's financial statements. This may be the case where, for example, there was a scope limitation in the prior period, but the matter giving rise to the scope limitation has been resolved in the current period.

A9

---

[5a] *This form of opinion is permitted in the UK and Ireland.*

## Appendix (Ref: Para. A8)

# Illustrations of Auditors' Reports with Modified Opinions

These examples have not been tailored for the UK and Ireland. With respect to companies, illustrative examples of auditor's reports tailored for use with audits conducted in accordance with ISAs (UK and Ireland) are given in the most recent versions of the APB Bulletins, "Auditor's Reports on Financial Statements in the United Kingdom"/"Auditor's Reports on Financial Statements in the Republic of Ireland." Illustrative examples for various other entities are give in other Bulletins and Practice Notes issued by the APB.

---

**Illustration 1:**

**Circumstances described in paragraph A8(a) include the following:**

- **The auditor did not observe the counting of the physical inventory at the beginning of the current period and was unable to obtain sufficient appropriate audit evidence regarding the opening balances of inventory.**
- **The possible effects of the inability to obtain sufficient appropriate audit evidence regarding opening balances of inventory are deemed to be material but not pervasive to the entity's financial performance and cash flows.[6]**
- **The financial position at year end is fairly presented.**
- **In this particular jurisdiction, law and regulation prohibit the auditor from giving an opinion which is qualified regarding the financial performance and cash flows and unmodified regarding financial position.**

---

INDEPENDENT AUDITOR'S REPORT

[Appropriate Addressee]

**Report on the Financial Statements[7]**

We have audited the accompanying financial statements of ABC Company, which comprise the balance sheet as at December 31, 20X1, and the income statement, statement of changes in equity and cash flow statement for the year then ended, and a summary of significant accounting policies and other explanatory information.

*Management's[8] Responsibility for the Financial Statements*

Management is responsible for the preparation and fair presentation of these financial statements in accordance with International Financial Reporting Standards,[9] and for such internal control as management determines is necessary to

---

[6] *If the possible effects, in the auditor's judgment, are considered to be material and pervasive to the entity's financial performance and cash flows, the auditor would disclaim an opinion on the financial performance and cash flows.*

[7] *The sub-title "Report on the Financial Statements" is unnecessary in circumstances when the second sub-title "Report on Other Legal and Regulatory Requirements" is not applicable.*

[8] *Or other term that is appropriate in the context of the legal framework in the particular jurisdiction.*

[9] *Where management's responsibility is to prepare financial statements that give a true and fair view, this may read: "Management is responsible for the preparation of financial statements that give a true and fair view in accordance with International Financial Reporting Standards, and for such ..."*

enable the preparation of financial statements that are free from material misstatement, whether due to fraud or error.

### Auditor's Responsibility

Our responsibility is to express an opinion on these financial statements based on our audit. We conducted our audit in accordance with International Standards on Auditing. Those standards require that we comply with ethical requirements and plan and perform the audit to obtain reasonable assurance about whether the financial statements are free from material misstatement.

An audit involves performing procedures to obtain audit evidence about the amounts and disclosures in the financial statements. The procedures selected depend on the auditor's judgment, including the assessment of the risks of material misstatement of the financial statements, whether due to fraud or error. In making those risk assessments, the auditor considers internal control relevant to the entity's preparation and fair presentation[10]; of the financial statements in order to design audit procedures that are appropriate in the circumstances, but not for the purpose of expressing an opinion on the effectiveness of the entity's internal control.[11] An audit also includes evaluating the appropriateness of accounting policies used and the reasonableness of accounting estimates made by management, as well as evaluating the overall presentation of the financial statements.

We believe that the audit evidence we have obtained is sufficient and appropriate to provide a basis for our qualified audit opinion.

### Basis for Qualified Opinion

We were appointed as auditors of the company on June 30, 20X1 and thus did not observe the counting of the physical inventories at the beginning of the year. We were unable to satisfy ourselves by alternative means concerning inventory quantities held at December 31, 20X0. Since opening inventories enter into the determination of the financial performance and cash flows, we were unable to determine whether adjustments might have been necessary in respect of the profit for the year reported in the income statement and the net cash flows from operating activities reported in the cash flow statement.

### Qualified Opinion

In our opinion, except for the possible effects of the matter described in the Basis for Qualified Opinion paragraph, the financial statements present fairly, in all material respects, (or *give a true and fair view of*) the financial position of ABC Company as at

---

[10] *In the case of footnote 9, this may read: "In making those risk assessments, the auditor considers internal control relevant to the entity's preparation of financial statements that give a true and fair view in order to design audit procedures that are appropriate in the circumstances, but not for the purpose of expressing an opinion on the effectiveness of the entity's internal control."*

[11] *In circumstances when the auditor also has responsibility to express an opinion on the effectiveness of internal control in conjunction with the audit of the financial statements, this sentence would be worded as follows: "In making those risk assessments, the auditor considers internal control relevant to the entity's preparation and fair presentation of the financial statements in order to design audit procedures that are appropriate in the circumstances." In the case of footnote 9, this may read: "In making those risk assessments, the auditor considers internal control relevant to the entity's preparation of financial statements that give a true and fair view in order to design audit procedures that are appropriate in the circumstances."*

December 31, 20X1, and (*of*) its financial performance and its cash flows for the year
then ended in accordance with International Financial Reporting Standards.

### Other Matter

The financial statements of ABC Company for the year ended December 31, 20X0
were audited by another auditor who expressed an unmodified opinion on those
statements on March 31, 20X1.

## Report on Other Legal and Regulatory Requirements

[Form and content of this section of the auditor's report will vary depending on the
nature of the auditor's other reporting responsibilities.]

[Auditor's signature]

[Date of the auditor's report]

[Auditor's address]

---

**Illustration 2:**

**Circumstances described in paragraph A8(b) include the following:**

- **The auditor did not observe the counting of the physical inventory at the beginning of the current period and was unable to obtain sufficient appropriate audit evidence regarding the opening balances of inventory.**
- **The possible effects of the inability to obtain sufficient appropriate audit evidence regarding opening balances of inventory are deemed to be material but not pervasive to the entity's financial performance and cash flows.[12]**
- **The financial position at year end is fairly presented.**
- **An opinion that is qualified regarding the financial performance and cash flows and unmodified regarding financial position is considered appropriate in the circumstances.**

---

## INDEPENDENT AUDITOR'S REPORT

[Appropriate Addressee]

### Report on the Financial Statements[13]

We have audited the accompanying financial statements of ABC Company, which comprise the balance sheet as at December 31, 20X1, and the income statement, statement of changes in equity and cash flow statement for the year then ended, and a summary of significant accounting policies and other explanatory information.

### *Management's[14] Responsibility for the Financial Statements*

Management is responsible for the preparation and fair presentation of these financial statements in accordance with International Financial Reporting Standards,[15] and for such internal control as management determines is necessary to enable the preparation of financial statements that are free from material misstatement, whether due to fraud or error

### *Auditor's Responsibility*

Our responsibility is to express an opinion on these financial statements based on our audit. We conducted our audit in accordance with International Standards on Auditing. Those standards require that we comply with ethical requirements and plan and perform the audit to obtain reasonable assurance about whether the financial statements are free from material misstatement.

---

[12] *If the possible effects, in the auditor's judgment, are considered to be material and pervasive to the entity's financial performance and cash flows, the auditor would disclaim the opinion on the financial performance and cash flows.*

[13] *The sub-title "Report on the Financial Statements" is unnecessary in circumstances when the second sub-title "Report on Other Legal and Regulatory Requirements" is not applicable.*

[14] *Or other term that is appropriate in the context of the legal framework in the particular jurisdiction.*

[15] *Where management's responsibility is to prepare financial statements that give a true and fair view, this may read: "Management is responsible for the preparation and presentation of financial statements that give a true and fair view in accordance with International Financial Reporting Standards."*

An audit involves performing procedures to obtain audit evidence about the amounts and disclosures in the financial statements. The procedures selected depend on the auditor's judgment, including the assessment of the risks of material misstatement of the financial statements, whether due to fraud or error. In making those risk assessments, the auditor considers internal control relevant to the entity's preparation and fair presentation[16] of the financial statements in order to design audit procedures that are appropriate in the circumstances, but not for the purpose of expressing an opinion on the effectiveness of the entity's internal control.[17] An audit also includes evaluating the appropriateness of accounting policies used and the reasonableness of accounting estimates made by management, as well as evaluating the overall presentation of the financial statements.

We believe that the audit evidence we have obtained is sufficient and appropriate to provide a basis for our unmodified opinion on the financial position and our qualified audit opinion on the financial performance and cash flows.

### *Basis for Qualified Opinion on the Financial Performance and Cash Flows*

We were appointed as auditors of the company on June 30, 20X1 and thus did not observe the counting of the physical inventories at the beginning of the year. We were unable to satisfy ourselves by alternative means concerning inventory quantities held at December 31, 20X0. Since opening inventories enter into the determination of the financial performance and cash flows, we were unable to determine whether adjustments might have been necessary in respect of the profit for the year reported in the income statement and the net cash flows from operating activities reported in the cash flow statement.

### *Qualified Opinion on the Financial Performance and Cash Flows*

In our opinion, except for the possible effects of the matter described in the Basis for Qualified Opinion paragraph, the Income Statement and Cash Flow Statement present fairly, in all material respects (or *give a true and fair view of*) the financial performance and cash flows of ABC Company for the year ended December 31, 20X1 in accordance with International Financial Reporting Standards.

### *Opinion on the financial position*

In our opinion, the balance sheet presents fairly, in all material respects (or *gives a true and fair view of*) the financial position of ABC Company as at December 31, 20X1 in accordance with International Financial Reporting Standards.

---

[16] *In the case of footnote 15, this may read: "In making those risk assessments, the auditor considers internal control relevant to the entity's preparation of financial statements that give a true and fair view in order to design audit procedures that are appropriate in the circumstances, but not for the purpose of expressing an opinion on the effectiveness of the entity's internal control."*

[17] *In circumstances when the auditor also has responsibility to express an opinion on the effectiveness of internal control in conjunction with the audit of the financial statements, this sentence would be worded as follows: "In making those risk assessments, the auditor considers internal control relevant to the entity's preparation and fair presentation of the financial statements in order to design audit procedures that are appropriate in the circumstances." In the case of footnote 15, this may read: "In making those risk assessments, the auditor considers internal control relevant to the entity's preparation of financial statements that give a true and fair view in order to design audit procedures that are appropriate in the circumstances."*

### Other Matter

The financial statements of ABC Company for the year ended December 31, 20X0 were audited by another auditor who expressed an unmodified opinion on those statements on March 31, 20X1.

### Report on Other Legal and Regulatory Requirements

[Form and content of this section of the auditor's report will vary depending on the nature of the auditor's other reporting responsibilities.]

[Auditor's signature]

[Date of the auditor's report]

[Auditor's address]

# Addendum

*This addendum provides a summary of APB's rationale for retaining or excluding in the proposed clarified ISA (UK and Ireland) the supplementary requirements in the existing ISA (UK and Ireland). It also sets out the supplementary guidance material in the existing ISA (UK and Ireland) that APB considers is not necessary to retain in light of the improvements in the underlying Clarity ISAs issued by the IAASB as part of the Clarity Project. It is provided for information and does not form part of the proposed clarified ISA (UK and Ireland).*

*The Consultation Paper published with the exposure drafts explains the general approach used by the APB for determining whether current supplementary material should be proposed to be retained.*

## Analysis of proposed treatment of current APB supplementary material in current ISA (UK and Ireland) 510

## Requirements

| APB supplementary requirements (*Italic text is from IAASB for context*) | Is it covered in substance in the Clarity ISA? | Should it be retained? |
|---|---|---|
| 2.  For initial audit engagements, the auditor should obtain sufficient appropriate audit evidence that: <br> (a) The opening balances do not contain misstatements that materially affect the current period's financial statements; <br> (b) The prior period's closing balances have been correctly brought forward to the current period or, when appropriate, have been restated; and <br> (c) Appropriate accounting policies are consistently applied or changes in accounting policies have been properly accounted for and adequately presented and disclosed. | | |

| APB supplementary requirements (*Italic text is from IAASB for context*) | Is it covered in substance in the Clarity ISA? | Should it be retained? |
|---|---|---|
| 2-1. The auditor should also obtain sufficient appropriate audit evidence for the matters set out in paragraph 2 for continuing audit engagements (see paragraphs 10-1 and 10-2). | ✗ The ISA only relates to initial engagements. ISA 710.7(b) has some relevant requirements relating the audit of comparatives. However, ISA 710 does not include requirements to determine that opening balances are not misstated and were brought forward correctly. | ✓ (Audit Quality) However, the Requirements no longer refer specifically to initial engagements. Extending the standard to continuing audit engagements can be effected by extending the scope of the standard and its objective. **1-1, and After 3(b)** |

## Guidance

The following guidance in current ISA (UK and Ireland) 510 has not been carried forward to the proposed clarified standard.

| Current paragraph reference (*Italic text is from IAASB for context*) |
|---|
| 1-2. – 1-5. [Definitions of management and those charged with governance.] |
| 12. *If the opening balances contain misstatements which could materially affect the current period's financial statements, the auditor would inform management[2] and, after having obtained management's authorization, the predecessor auditor, if any. ...* |
| [2] In the UK and Ireland the auditor would inform those charged with governance and seek their authorization to inform the predecessor auditor, if any. |

# Proposed Clarified International Standard on Auditing (UK and Ireland) 520
# Analytical procedures

*(Effective for audits of financial statements for periods ending on or after 15 December 2010)*

## Contents

> International Standard on Auditing (UK and Ireland) (ISA (UK and Ireland)) 520, "Analytical Procedures" should be read in conjunction with ISA (UK and Ireland) 200, "Overall Objectives of the Independent Auditor and the Conduct of an Audit in Accordance with International Standards on Auditing (UK and Ireland)."

# Introduction

## Scope of this ISA (UK and Ireland)

This International Standard on Auditing (UK and Ireland) (ISA (UK and Ireland)) 1
deals with the auditor's use of analytical procedures as substantive procedures
("substantive analytical procedures"). It also deals with the auditor's responsibility
to perform analytical procedures near the end of the audit that assist the auditor
when forming an overall conclusion on the financial statements. ISA (UK and Ireland) 315[1] deals with the use of analytical procedures as risk assessment procedures.
ISA (UK and Ireland) 330 includes requirements and guidance regarding the nature,
timing and extent of audit procedures in response to assessed risks; these audit
procedures may include substantive analytical procedures.[2]

## Effective Date

This ISA (UK and Ireland) is effective for audits of financial statements for periods 2
ending on or after 15 December 2010.

# Objectives

The objectives of the auditor are: 3

(a) To obtain relevant and reliable audit evidence when using substantive analytical
procedures; and
(b) To design and perform analytical procedures near the end of the audit that assist
the auditor when forming an overall conclusion as to whether the financial
statements are consistent with the auditor's understanding of the entity.

# Definition

For the purposes of the ISAs (UK and Ireland), the term "analytical procedures" 4
means evaluations of financial information through analysis of plausible relationships among both financial and non-financial data. Analytical procedures also
encompass such investigation as is necessary of identified fluctuations or relationships that are inconsistent with other relevant information or that differ from
expected values by a significant amount. (Ref: Para. A1-A3)

# Requirements

## Substantive Analytical Procedures

When designing and performing substantive analytical procedures, either alone or in 5
combination with tests of details, as substantive procedures in accordance with ISA
(UK and Ireland) 330,[3] the auditor shall: (Ref: Para. A4-A5)

---

[1] *ISA (UK and Ireland) 315, "Identifying and Assessing the Risks of Material Misstatement through Understanding the Entity and Its Environment," paragraphs 6(b).*

[2] *ISA (UK and Ireland) 330, "The Auditor's Reponses to Assessed Risks," paragraphs 6 and 18.*

[3] *ISA (UK and Ireland) 330, paragraph 18.*

(a) Determine the suitability of particular substantive analytical procedures for given assertions, taking account of the assessed risks of material misstatement and tests of details, if any, for these assertions; (Ref: Para. A6-A11)
(b) Evaluate the reliability of data from which the auditor's expectation of recorded amounts or ratios is developed, taking account of source, comparability, and nature and relevance of information available, and controls over preparation; (Ref: Para. A12-A14)
(c) Develop an expectation of recorded amounts or ratios and evaluate whether the expectation is sufficiently precise to identify a misstatement that, individually or when aggregated with other misstatements, may cause the financial statements to be materially misstated; and (Ref: Para. A15)
(d) Determine the amount of any difference of recorded amounts from expected values that is acceptable without further investigation as required by paragraph 7. (Ref: Para. A16)

### Analytical Procedures that Assist When Forming an Overall Conclusion

6   The auditor shall design and perform analytical procedures near the end of the audit that assist the auditor when forming an overall conclusion as to whether the financial statements are consistent with the auditor's understanding of the entity. (Ref: Para. A17-A19)

### Investigating Results of Analytical Procedures

7   If analytical procedures performed in accordance with this ISA (UK and Ireland) identify fluctuations or relationships that are inconsistent with other relevant information or that differ from expected values by a significant amount, the auditor shall investigate such differences by:

(a) Inquiring of management and obtaining appropriate audit evidence relevant to management's responses; and
(b) Performing other audit procedures as necessary in the circumstances. (Ref: Para. A20-A21)

*** 

# Application and Other Explanatory Material

### Definition of Analytical Procedures (Ref: Para. 4)

A1   Analytical procedures include the consideration of comparisons of the entity's financial information with, for example:

- Comparable information for prior periods.
- Anticipated results of the entity, such as budgets or forecasts, or expectations of the auditor, such as an estimation of depreciation.
- Similar industry information, such as a comparison of the entity's ratio of sales to accounts receivable with industry averages or with other entities of comparable size in the same industry.

A2   Analytical procedures also include consideration of relationships, for example:

- Among elements of financial information that would be expected to conform to a predictable pattern based on the entity's experience, such as gross margin percentages.

- Between financial information and relevant non-financial information, such as payroll costs to number of employees.

Various methods may be used to perform analytical procedures. These methods **A3** range from performing simple comparisons to performing complex analyses using advanced statistical techniques. Analytical procedures may be applied to consolidated financial statements, components and individual elements of information.

## Substantive Analytical Procedures (Ref: Para. 5)

The auditor's substantive procedures at the assertion level may be tests of details, **A4** substantive analytical procedures, or a combination of both. The decision about which audit procedures to perform, including whether to use substantive analytical procedures, is based on the auditor's judgment about the expected effectiveness and efficiency of the available audit procedures to reduce audit risk at the assertion level to an acceptably low level.

The auditor may inquire of management as to the availability and reliability of **A5** information needed to apply substantive analytical procedures, and the results of any such analytical procedures performed by the entity. It may be effective to use analytical data prepared by management, provided the auditor is satisfied that such data is properly prepared.

### *Suitability of Particular Analytical Procedures for Given Assertions* (Ref: Para. 5(a))

Substantive analytical procedures are generally more applicable to large volumes of **A6** transactions that tend to be predictable over time. The application of planned analytical procedures is based on the expectation that relationships among data exist and continue in the absence of known conditions to the contrary. However, the suitability of a particular analytical procedure will depend upon the auditor's assessment of how effective it will be in detecting a misstatement that, individually or when aggregated with other misstatements, may cause the financial statements to be materially misstated.

In some cases, even an unsophisticated predictive model may be effective as an **A7** analytical procedure. For example, where an entity has a known number of employees at fixed rates of pay throughout the period, it may be possible for the auditor to use this data to estimate the total payroll costs for the period with a high degree of accuracy, thereby providing audit evidence for a significant item in the financial statements and reducing the need to perform tests of details on the payroll. The use of widely recognized trade ratios (such as profit margins for different types of retail entities) can often be used effectively in substantive analytical procedures to provide evidence to support the reasonableness of recorded amounts.

Different types of analytical procedures provide different levels of assurance. Ana- **A8** lytical procedures involving, for example, the prediction of total rental income on a building divided into apartments, taking the rental rates, the number of apartments and vacancy rates into consideration, can provide persuasive evidence and may eliminate the need for further verification by means of tests of details, provided the elements are appropriately verified. In contrast, calculation and comparison of gross margin percentages as a means of confirming a revenue figure may provide less persuasive evidence, but may provide useful corroboration if used in combination with other audit procedures.

**A9** The determination of the suitability of particular substantive analytical procedures is influenced by the nature of the assertion and the auditor's assessment of the risk of material misstatement. For example, if controls over sales order processing are deficient, the auditor may place more reliance on tests of details rather than on substantive analytical procedures for assertions related to receivables.

**A10** Particular substantive analytical procedures may also be considered suitable when tests of details are performed on the same assertion. For example, when obtaining audit evidence regarding the valuation assertion for accounts receivable balances, the auditor may apply analytical procedures to an aging of customers' accounts in addition to performing tests of details on subsequent cash receipts to determine the collectability of the receivables.

*Considerations Specific to Public Sector Entities*

**A11** The relationships between individual financial statement items traditionally considered in the audit of business entities may not always be relevant in the audit of governments or other non-business public sector entities; for example, in many public sector entities there may be little direct relationship between revenue and expenditure. In addition, because expenditure on the acquisition of assets may not be capitalized, there may be no relationship between expenditures on, for example, inventories and fixed assets and the amount of those assets reported in the financial statements. Also, industry data or statistics for comparative purposes may not be available in the public sector. However, other relationships may be relevant, for example, variations in the cost per kilometer of road construction or the number of vehicles acquired compared with vehicles retired.

***The Reliability of the Data*** (Ref: Para. 5(b))

**A12** The reliability of data is influenced by its source and nature and is dependent on the circumstances under which it is obtained. Accordingly, the following are relevant when determining whether data is reliable for purposes of designing substantive analytical procedures:

(a) Source of the information available. For example, information may be more reliable when it is obtained from independent sources outside the entity;[4]

(b) Comparability of the information available. For example, broad industry data may need to be supplemented to be comparable to that of an entity that produces and sells specialized products;

(c) Nature and relevance of the information available. For example, whether budgets have been established as results to be expected rather than as goals to be achieved; and

(d) Controls over the preparation of the information that are designed to ensure its completeness, accuracy and validity. For example, controls over the preparation, review and maintenance of budgets.

(e) Prior year knowledge and understanding. For example, the knowledge gained during previous audits, together with the auditor's understanding of the effectiveness of the accounting and internal control systems and the types of problems that in prior periods have given rise to accounting adjustments.

[4] *ISA (UK and Ireland) 500, "Audit Evidence," paragraph A31.*

The auditor may consider testing the operating effectiveness of controls, if any, over   **A13**
the entity's preparation of information used by the auditor in performing substantive
analytical procedures in response to assessed risks. When such controls are effective,
the auditor generally has greater confidence in the reliability of the information and,
therefore, in the results of analytical procedures. The operating effectiveness of
controls over non-financial information may often be tested in conjunction with
other tests of controls. For example, in establishing controls over the processing of
sales invoices, an entity may include controls over the recording of unit sales. In these
circumstances, the auditor may test the operating effectiveness of controls over the
recording of unit sales in conjunction with tests of the operating effectiveness of
controls over the processing of sales invoices. Alternatively, the auditor may consider
whether the information was subjected to audit testing. ISA (UK and Ireland) 500
(Redrafted) establishes requirements and provides guidance in determining the audit
procedures to be performed on the information to be used for substantive analytical
procedures.[5]

The matters discussed in paragraphs A12(a)-A12(d) are relevant irrespective of   **A14**
whether the auditor performs substantive analytical procedures on the entity's period
end financial statements, or at an interim date and plans to perform substantive
analytical procedures for the remaining period. ISA (UK and Ireland) 330 establishes
requirements and provides guidance on substantive procedures performed at an
interim date.[6]

### *Evaluation Whether the Expectation Is Sufficiently Precise* (Ref: Para. 5(c))

Matters relevant to the auditor's evaluation of whether the expectation can be   **A15**
developed sufficiently precisely to identify a misstatement that, when aggregated with
other misstatements, may cause the financial statements to be materially misstated,
include:

- The accuracy with which the expected results of substantive analytical procedures can be predicted. For example, the auditor may expect greater consistency
  in comparing gross profit margins from one period to another than in comparing discretionary expenses, such as research or advertising.
- The degree to which information can be disaggregated. For example, substantive analytical procedures may be more effective when applied to financial
  information on individual sections of an operation or to financial statements of
  components of a diversified entity, than when applied to the financial statements
  of the entity as a whole.
- The availability of the information, both financial and non-financial. For
  example, the auditor may consider whether financial information, such as
  budgets or forecasts, and non-financial information, such as the number of units
  produced or sold, is available to design substantive analytical procedures. If the
  information is available, the auditor may also consider the reliability of the
  information as discussed in paragraphs A12-A13 above.

---

[5] *ISA (UK and Ireland) 500, paragraph 10.*

[6] *ISA (UK and Ireland) 330, paragraphs 22-23.*

**Amount of Difference of Recorded Amounts from Expected Values that Is Acceptable** (Ref: Para. 5(d))

A16    The auditor's determination of the amount of difference from the expectation that can be accepted without further investigation is influenced by materiality[7] and the consistency with the desired level of assurance, taking account of the possibility that a misstatement, individually or when aggregated with other misstatements, may cause the financial statements to be materially misstated. ISA (UK and Ireland) 330 requires the auditor to obtain more persuasive audit evidence the higher the auditor's assessment of risk.[8] Accordingly, as the assessed risk increases, the amount of difference considered acceptable without investigation decreases in order to achieve the desired level of persuasive evidence.[9]

## Analytical Procedures that Assist When Forming an Overall Conclusion (Ref: Para. 6)

A17    The conclusions drawn from the results of analytical procedures designed and performed in accordance with paragraph 6 are intended to corroborate conclusions formed during the audit of individual components or elements of the financial statements. This assists the auditor to draw reasonable conclusions on which to base the auditor's opinion.

A17-1    Considerations when carrying out such procedures may include:

(a)  Whether the financial statements adequately reflect the information and explanations previously obtained and conclusions previously reached during the course of the audit;

(b)  Whether the procedures reveal any new factors which may affect the presentation of, or disclosures in, the financial statements;

(c)  Whether analytical procedures applied when completing the audit, such as comparing the information in the financial statements with other pertinent data, produce results which assist in arriving at the overall conclusion as to whether the financial statements as a whole are consistent with the auditor's knowledge of the entity's business;

(d)  Whether the presentation adopted in the financial statements may have been unduly influenced by the desire of those charged with governance to present matters in a favourable or unfavourable light; and

(e)  The potential impact on the financial statements of the aggregate of uncorrected misstatements (including those arising from bias in making accounting estimates) identified during the course of the audit and the preceding period's audit, if any.

A18    The results of such analytical procedures may identify a previously unrecognized risk of material misstatement. In such circumstances, ISA (UK and Ireland) 315 requires the auditor to revise the auditor's assessment of the risks of material misstatement and modify the further planned audit procedures accordingly.[10]

---

[7] *ISA (UK and Ireland) 320, "Materiality in Planning and Performing an Audit," paragraph A13.*

[8] *ISA (UK and Ireland) 330, paragraph 7(b).*

[9] *ISA (UK and Ireland) 330, paragraph A19.*

[10] *ISA (UK and Ireland) 315, paragraph 31.*

The analytical procedures performed in accordance with paragraph 6 may be similar to those that would be used as risk assessment procedures.　**A19**

## Investigating Results of Analytical Procedures (Ref: Para. 7)

Audit evidence relevant to management's responses may be obtained by evaluating those responses taking into account the auditor's understanding of the entity and its environment, and with other audit evidence obtained during the course of the audit.　**A20**

The need to perform other audit procedures may arise when, for example, management is unable to provide an explanation, or the explanation, together with the audit evidence obtained relevant to management's response, is not considered adequate.　**A21**

# Addendum

*This addendum provides a summary of APB's rationale for retaining or excluding in the proposed clarified ISA (UK and Ireland) the supplementary requirements in the existing ISA (UK and Ireland). It also sets out the supplementary guidance material in the existing ISA (UK and Ireland) that APB considers is not necessary to retain in light of the improvements in the underlying Clarity ISAs issued by the IAASB as part of the Clarity Project. It is provided for information and does not form part of the proposed clarified ISA (UK and Ireland).*

*The Consultation Paper published with the exposure drafts explains the general approach used by the APB for determining whether current supplementary material should be proposed to be retained.*

## Analysis of proposed treatment of current APB supplementary material in current ISA (UK and Ireland) 520

## Requirements

There are no supplementary requirements in the current ISA (UK and Ireland) 520.

## Guidance

The following guidance in current ISA (UK and Ireland) 520 has not been carried forward to the proposed clarified standard.

| Current paragraph reference (*Italic text is from IAASB for context*) |
|---|
| 3-1. – 3-4. [Description of management and those charged with governance.] |
| 9-1  Analytical procedures at this stage are usually based on interim financial information, budgets and management accounts. However, for those entities with less formal means of controlling and monitoring performance, it may be possible to extract relevant financial information from the accounting system, VAT returns and bank statements. Discussions with management, focused on identifying significant changes in the business since the prior financial period, may also be useful. |
| 12c.  *The reliability of data is influenced by its source and by its nature and is dependent on the circumstances under which it is obtained. In determining whether data is reliable for purposes of designing substantive analytical procedures, the auditor considers:...* <br> (f)   Whether the information is produced internally. For example, if the information is produced internally, its reliability is enhanced if it is produced independently of the accounting system or there are adequate controls over its preparation. The necessity for evidence on the reliability of such information depends on the results of the other audit procedures and on the importance of the results of analytical procedures as a basis for the auditor's opinion. |
| 12e.  *In assessing whether the expectation can be developed sufficiently precise to identify a material misstatement at the desired level of assurance, the auditor considers factors such as:...* <br> •   The frequency with which a relationship is observed. For example, a pattern repeated monthly as opposed to annually. |

| Current paragraph reference (*Italic text is from IAASB for context*) |
|---|
| *Overall review at the end of the audit*<br>13-1.  These procedures will also involve consideration of whether the assertions contained in the financial statements are consistent with the auditor's understanding of the entity. |

# Proposed Clarified International Standard on Auditing (UK and Ireland) 530
## Audit sampling

*(Effective for audits of financial statements for periods ending on or after 15 December 2010)*

# Contents

International Standard on Auditing (UK and Ireland) (ISA (UK and Ireland)) 530, "Audit Sampling" should be read in conjunction with ISA (UK and Ireland) 200, "Overall Objectives of the Independent Auditor and the Conduct of an Audit in Accordance with International Standards on Auditing (UK and Ireland)."

# Introduction

## Scope of this ISA (UK and Ireland)

This International Standard on Auditing (UK and Ireland) (ISA (UK and Ireland)) applies when the auditor has decided to use audit sampling in performing audit procedures. It deals with the auditor's use of statistical and non-statistical sampling when designing and selecting the audit sample, performing tests of controls and tests of details, and evaluating the results from the sample.   **1**

This ISA (UK and Ireland) complements ISA (UK and Ireland) 500,[1] which deals with the auditor's responsibility to design and perform audit procedures to obtain sufficient appropriate audit evidence to be able to draw reasonable conclusions on which to base the auditor's opinion. ISA (UK and Ireland) 500 provides guidance on the means available to the auditor for selecting items for testing, of which audit sampling is one means.   **2**

## Effective Date

This ISA (UK and Ireland) is effective for audits of financial statements for periods ending on or after 15 December 2010.   **3**

# Objective

The objective of the auditor, when using audit sampling, is to provide a reasonable basis for the auditor to draw conclusions about the population from which the sample is selected.   **4**

# Definitions

For purposes of the ISAs (UK and Ireland), the following terms have the meanings attributed below:   **5**

(a) Audit sampling (sampling) – The application of audit procedures to less than 100% of items within a population of audit relevance such that all sampling units have a chance of selection in order to provide the auditor with a reasonable basis on which to draw conclusions about the entire population.

(b) Population – The entire set of data from which a sample is selected and about which the auditor wishes to draw conclusions.

(c) Sampling risk – The risk that the auditor's conclusion based on a sample may be different from the conclusion if the entire population were subjected to the same audit procedure. Sampling risk can lead to two types of erroneous conclusions:

  (i) In the case of a test of controls, that controls are more effective than they actually are, or in the case of a test of details, that a material misstatement does not exist when in fact it does. The auditor is primarily concerned with this type of erroneous conclusion because it affects audit effectiveness and is more likely to lead to an inappropriate audit opinion.

  (ii) In the case of a test of controls, that controls are less effective than they actually are, or in the case of a test of details, that a material misstatement exists when in fact it does not. This type of erroneous conclusion affects

---

[1] *ISA (UK and Ireland) 500, "Audit Evidence."*

audit efficiency as it would usually lead to additional work to establish that initial conclusions were incorrect.

(d) Non-sampling risk – The risk that the auditor reaches an erroneous conclusion for any reason not related to sampling risk. (Ref: Para A1)

(e) Anomaly – A misstatement or deviation that is demonstrably not representative of misstatements or deviations in a population.

(f) Sampling unit – The individual items constituting a population. (Ref: Para A2)

(g) Statistical sampling – An approach to sampling that has the following characteristics:
  (i) Random selection of the sample items; and
  (ii) The use of probability theory to evaluate sample results, including measurement of sampling risk.
  A sampling approach that does not have characteristics (i) and (ii) is considered non-statistical sampling.

(h) Stratification – The process of dividing a population into sub-populations, each of which is a group of sampling units which have similar characteristics (often monetary value).

(i) Tolerable misstatement – A monetary amount set by the auditor in respect of which the auditor seeks to obtain an appropriate level of assurance that the monetary amount set by the auditor is not exceeded by the actual misstatement in the population. (Ref: Para A3)

(j) Tolerable rate of deviation – A rate of deviation from prescribed internal control procedures set by the auditor in respect of which the auditor seeks to obtain an appropriate level of assurance that the rate of deviation set by the auditor is not exceeded by the actual rate of deviation in the population.

# Requirements

## Sample Design, Size and Selection of Items for Testing

6  When designing an audit sample, the auditor shall consider the purpose of the audit procedure and the characteristics of the population from which the sample will be drawn. (Ref: Para. A4-A9)

7  The auditor shall determine a sample size sufficient to reduce sampling risk to an acceptably low level. (Ref: Para. A10-A11)

8  The auditor shall select items for the sample in such a way that each sampling unit in the population has a chance of selection. (Ref: Para. A12-A13)

## Performing Audit Procedures

9  The auditor shall perform audit procedures, appropriate to the purpose, on each item selected.

10  If the audit procedure is not applicable to the selected item, the auditor shall perform the procedure on a replacement item. (Ref: Para. A14)

11  If the auditor is unable to apply the designed audit procedures, or suitable alternative procedures, to a selected item, the auditor shall treat that item as a deviation from the prescribed control, in the case of tests of controls, or a misstatement, in the case of tests of details. (Ref: Para. A15-A16)

## Nature and Cause of Deviations and Misstatements

The auditor shall investigate the nature and cause of any deviations or misstatements    12
identified, and evaluate their possible effect on the purpose of the audit procedure
and on other areas of the audit. (Ref: Para. A17)

In the extremely rare circumstances when the auditor considers a misstatement or    13
deviation discovered in a sample to be an anomaly, the auditor shall obtain a high
degree of certainty that such misstatement or deviation is not representative of the
population. The auditor shall obtain this degree of certainty by performing additional audit procedures to obtain sufficient appropriate audit evidence that the
misstatement or deviation does not affect the remainder of the population.

## Projecting Misstatements

For tests of details, the auditor shall project misstatements found in the sample to the    14
population. (Ref: Para. A18-A20)

## Evaluating Results of Audit Sampling

The auditor shall evaluate:    15

(a)  The results of the sample; and (Ref: Para. A21-A22)
(b)  Whether the use of audit sampling has provided a reasonable basis for con-
     clusions about the population that has been tested. (Ref: Para. A23)

***

# Application and Other Explanatory Material

## Definitions

### *Non-Sampling Risk* (Ref: Para. 5(d))

Examples of non-sampling risk include use of inappropriate audit procedures, or    A1
misinterpretation of audit evidence and failure to recognize a misstatement or
deviation.

### *Sampling Unit* (Ref: Para. 5(f))

The sampling units might be physical items (for example, checks listed on deposit    A2
slips, credit entries on bank statements, sales invoices or debtors' balances) or
monetary units.

### *Tolerable Misstatement* (Ref: Para. 5(i))

When designing a sample, the auditor determines tolerable misstatement in order to    A3
address the risk that the aggregate of individually immaterial misstatements may
cause the financial statements to be materially misstated and provide a margin for
possible undetected misstatements. Tolerable misstatement is the application of
performance materiality, as defined in ISA (UK and Ireland) 320,[2] to a particular

---

[2] ISA (UK and Ireland) 320, *"Materiality in Planning and Performing an Audit,"* paragraph 9.

sampling procedure. Tolerable misstatement may be the same amount or an amount lower than performance materiality.

## Sample Design, Size and Selection of Items for Testing

*Sample Design* (Ref: Para. 6)

**A4**   Audit sampling enables the auditor to obtain and evaluate audit evidence about some characteristic of the items selected in order to form or assist in forming a conclusion concerning the population from which the sample is drawn. Audit sampling can be applied using either non-statistical or statistical sampling approaches.

**A5**   When designing an audit sample, the auditor's consideration includes the specific purpose to be achieved and the combination of audit procedures that is likely to best achieve that purpose. Consideration of the nature of the audit evidence sought and possible deviation or misstatement conditions or other characteristics relating to that audit evidence will assist the auditor in defining what constitutes a deviation or misstatement and what population to use for sampling. In fulfilling the requirement of paragraph 8 of ISA (UK and Ireland) 500, when performing audit sampling, the auditor performs audit procedures to obtain evidence that the population from which the audit sample is drawn is complete.

**A6**   The auditor's consideration of the purpose of the audit procedure, as required by paragraph 6, includes a clear understanding of what constitutes a deviation or misstatement so that all, and only, those conditions that are relevant to the purpose of the audit procedure are included in the evaluation of deviations or projection of misstatements. For example, in a test of details relating to the existence of accounts receivable, such as confirmation, payments made by the customer before the confirmation date but received shortly after that date by the client, are not considered a misstatement. Also, a misposting between customer accounts does not affect the total accounts receivable balance. Therefore, it may not be appropriate to consider this a misstatement in evaluating the sample results of this particular audit procedure, even though it may have an important effect on other areas of the audit, such as the assessment of the risk of fraud or the adequacy of the allowance for doubtful accounts.

**A7**   In considering the characteristics of a population, for tests of controls, the auditor makes an assessment of the expected rate of deviation based on the auditor's understanding of the relevant controls or on the examination of a small number of items from the population. This assessment is made in order to design an audit sample and to determine sample size. For example, if the expected rate of deviation is unacceptably high, the auditor will normally decide not to perform tests of controls. Similarly, for tests of details, the auditor makes an assessment of the expected misstatement in the population. If the expected misstatement is high, 100% examination or use of a large sample size may be appropriate when performing tests of details.

**A8**   In considering the characteristics of the population from which the sample will be drawn, the auditor may determine that stratification or value-weighted selection is appropriate. Appendix 1 provides further discussion on stratification and value-weighted selection.

**A9**   The decision whether to use a statistical or non-statistical sampling approach is a matter for the auditor's judgment; however, sample size is not a valid criterion to distinguish between statistical and non-statistical approaches.

*Sample Size* (Ref: Para. 7)

The level of sampling risk that the auditor is willing to accept affects the sample size required. The lower the risk the auditor is willing to accept, the greater the sample size will need to be.

**A10**

The sample size can be determined by the application of a statistically-based formula or through the exercise of professional judgment. Appendices 2 and 3 indicate the influences that various factors typically have on the determination of sample size. When circumstances are similar, the effect on sample size of factors such as those identified in Appendices 2 and 3 will be similar regardless of whether a statistical or non-statistical approach is chosen.

**A11**

*Selection of Items for Testing* (Ref: Para. 8)

With statistical sampling, sample items are selected in a way that each sampling unit has a known probability of being selected. With non-statistical sampling, judgment is used to select sample items. Because the purpose of sampling is to provide a reasonable basis for the auditor to draw conclusions about the population from which the sample is selected, it is important that the auditor selects a representative sample, so that bias is avoided, by choosing sample items which have characteristics typical of the population.

**A12**

The principal methods of selecting samples are the use of random selection, systematic selection and haphazard selection. Each of these methods is discussed in Appendix 4.

**A13**

## Performing Audit Procedures (Ref: Para. 10-11)

An example of when it is necessary to perform the procedure on a replacement item is when a voided check is selected while testing for evidence of payment authorization. If the auditor is satisfied that the check has been properly voided such that it does not constitute a deviation, an appropriately chosen replacement is examined.

**A14**

An example of when the auditor is unable to apply the designed audit procedures to a selected item is when documentation relating to that item has been lost.

**A15**

An example of a suitable alternative procedure might be the examination of subsequent cash receipts together with evidence of their source and the items they are intended to settle when no reply has been received in response to a positive confirmation request.

**A16**

## Nature and Cause of Deviations and Misstatements (Ref: Para. 12)

In analyzing the deviations and misstatements identified, the auditor may observe that many have a common feature, for example, type of transaction, location, product line or period of time. In such circumstances, the auditor may decide to identify all items in the population that possess the common feature, and extend audit procedures to those items. In addition, such deviations or misstatements may be intentional, and may indicate the possibility of fraud.

**A17**

**Projecting Misstatements** (Ref: Para. 14)

A18    The auditor is required to project misstatements for the population to obtain a broad view of the scale of misstatement but this projection may not be sufficient to determine an amount to be recorded.

A19    When a misstatement has been established as an anomaly, it may be excluded when projecting misstatements to the population. However, the effect of any such misstatement, if uncorrected, still needs to be considered in addition to the projection of the non-anomalous misstatements.

A20    For tests of controls, no explicit projection of deviations is necessary since the sample deviation rate is also the projected deviation rate for the population as a whole. ISA (UK and Ireland) 330[3] provides guidance when deviations from controls upon which the auditor intends to rely are detected.

**Evaluating Results of Audit Sampling** (Ref: Para. 15)

A21    For tests of controls, an unexpectedly high sample deviation rate may lead to an increase in the assessed risk of material misstatement, unless further audit evidence substantiating the initial assessment is obtained. For tests of details, an unexpectedly high misstatement amount in a sample may cause the auditor to believe that a class of transactions or account balance is materially misstated, in the absence of further audit evidence that no material misstatement exists.

A22    In the case of tests of details, the projected misstatement plus anomalous misstatement, if any, is the auditor's best estimate of misstatement in the population. When the projected misstatement plus anomalous misstatement, if any, exceeds tolerable misstatement, the sample does not provide a reasonable basis for conclusions about the population that has been tested. The closer the projected misstatement plus anomalous misstatement is to tolerable misstatement, the more likely that actual misstatement in the population may exceed tolerable misstatement. Also if the projected misstatement is greater than the auditor's expectations of misstatement used to determine the sample size, the auditor may conclude that there is an unacceptable sampling risk that the actual misstatement in the population exceeds the tolerable misstatement. Considering the results of other audit procedures helps the auditor to assess the risk that actual misstatement in the population exceeds tolerable misstatement, and the risk may be reduced if additional audit evidence is obtained.

A23    If the auditor concludes that audit sampling has not provided a reasonable basis for conclusions about the population that has been tested, the auditor may:

- Request management to investigate misstatements that have been identified and the potential for further misstatements and to make any necessary adjustments; or
- Tailor the nature, timing and extent of those further audit procedures to best achieve the required assurance. For example, in the case of tests of controls, the auditor might extend the sample size, test an alternative control or modify related substantive procedures.

---

[3] *ISA (UK and Ireland) 330, "The Auditor's Responses to Assessed Risks, paragraph 17.*

# Appendix 1 (Ref: Para. A8)

# Stratification and Value-Weighted Selection

In considering the characteristics of the population from which the sample will be drawn, the auditor may determine that stratification or value-weighted selection is appropriate. This Appendix provides guidance to the auditor on the use of stratification and value-weighted sampling techniques.

## Stratification

Audit efficiency may be improved if the auditor stratifies a population by dividing it into discrete sub-populations which have an identifying characteristic. The objective of stratification is to reduce the variability of items within each stratum and therefore allow sample size to be reduced without increasing sampling risk.

1

When performing tests of details, the population is often stratified by monetary value. This allows greater audit effort to be directed to the larger value items, as these items may contain the greatest potential misstatement in terms of overstatement. Similarly, a population may be stratified according to a particular characteristic that indicates a higher risk of misstatement, for example, when testing the allowance for doubtful accounts in the valuation of accounts receivable, balances may be stratified by age.

2

The results of audit procedures applied to a sample of items within a stratum can only be projected to the items that make up that stratum. To draw a conclusion on the entire population, the auditor will need to consider the risk of material misstatement in relation to whatever other strata make up the entire population. For example, 20% of the items in a population may make up 90% of the value of an account balance. The auditor may decide to examine a sample of these items. The auditor evaluates the results of this sample and reaches a conclusion on the 90% of value separately from the remaining 10% (on which a further sample or other means of gathering audit evidence will be used, or which may be considered immaterial).

3

If a class of transactions or account balance has been divided into strata, the misstatement is projected for each stratum separately. Projected misstatements for each stratum are then combined when considering the possible effect of misstatements on the total class of transactions or account balance.

4

## Value-Weighted Selection

When performing tests of details it may be efficient to identify the sampling unit as the individual monetary units that make up the population. Having selected specific monetary units from within the population, for example, the accounts receivable balance, the auditor may then examine the particular items, for example, individual balances, that contain those monetary units. One benefit of this approach to defining the sampling unit is that audit effort is directed to the larger value items because they have a greater chance of selection, and can result in smaller sample sizes. This approach may be used in conjunction with the systematic method of sample selection (described in Appendix 4) and is most efficient when selecting items using random selection.

5

**Appendix 2** (Ref: Para. A11)

# Examples of Factors Influencing Sample Size for Tests of Controls

The following are factors that the auditor may consider when determining the sample size for tests of controls. These factors, which need to be considered together, assume the auditor does not modify the nature or timing of tests of controls or otherwise modify the approach to substantive procedures in response to assessed risks.

| FACTOR | EFFECT ON SAMPLE SIZE | |
|---|---|---|
| 1. An increase in the extent to which the auditor's risk assessment takes into account relevant controls | Increase | The more assurance the auditor intends to obtain from the operating effectiveness of controls, the lower the auditor's assessment of the risk of material misstatement will be, and the larger the sample size will need to be. When the auditor's assessment of the risk of material misstatement at the assertion level includes an expectation of the operating effectiveness of controls, the auditor is required to perform tests of controls. Other things being equal, the greater the reliance the auditor places on the operating effectiveness of controls in the risk assessment, the greater is the extent of the auditor's tests of controls (and therefore, the sample size is increased). |
| 2. An increase in the tolerable rate of deviation | Decrease | The lower the tolerable rate of deviation, the larger the sample size needs to be. |
| 3. An increase in the expected rate of deviation of the population to be tested | Increase | The higher the expected rate of deviation, the larger the sample size needs to be so that the auditor is in a position to make a reasonable estimate of the actual rate of deviation. Factors relevant to the auditor's consideration of the expected rate of deviation include the auditor's understanding of the business (in particular, risk assessment procedures undertaken to obtain an understanding of internal control), changes in personnel or in internal control, the results of audit procedures applied in prior periods and the results of other audit procedures. High expected control deviation rates ordinarily warrant little, if any, reduction of the assessed risk of material misstatement. |

| FACTOR | EFFECT ON SAMPLE SIZE | |
|---|---|---|
| 4. An increase in the auditor's desired level of assurance that the tolerable rate of deviation is not exceeded by the actual rate of deviation in the population | Increase | The greater the level of assurance that the auditor desires that the results of the sample are in fact indicative of the actual incidence of deviation in the population, the larger the sample size needs to be. |
| 5. An increase in the number of sampling units in the population | Negligible effect | For large populations, the actual size of the population has little, if any, effect on sample size. For small populations however, audit sampling may not be as efficient as alternative means of obtaining sufficient appropriate audit evidence. |

## Appendix 3 (Ref: Para. A11)

## Examples of Factors Influencing Sample Size for Tests of Details

The following are factors that the auditor may consider when determining the sample size for tests of details. These factors, which need to be considered together, assume the auditor does not modify the approach to tests of controls or otherwise modify the nature or timing of substantive procedures in response to the assessed risks.

| FACTOR | EFFECT ON SAMPLE SIZE | |
|---|---|---|
| 1. An increase in the auditor's assessment of the risk of material misstatement | Increase | The higher the auditor's assessment of the risk of material misstatement, the larger the sample size needs to be. The auditor's assessment of the risk of material misstatement is affected by inherent risk and control risk. For example, if the auditor does not perform tests of controls, the auditor's risk assessment cannot be reduced for the effective operation of internal controls with respect to the particular assertion. Therefore, in order to reduce audit risk to an acceptably low level, the auditor needs a low detection risk and will rely more on substantive procedures. The more audit evidence that is obtained from tests of details (that is, the lower the detection risk), the larger the sample size will need to be |
| 2. An increase in the use of other substantive procedures directed at the same assertion | Decrease | The more the auditor is relying on other substantive procedures (tests of details or substantive analytical procedures) to reduce to an acceptable level the detection risk regarding a particular population, the less assurance the auditor will require from sampling and, therefore, the smaller the sample size can be |
| 3. An increase in the auditor's desired level of assurance that tolerable misstatement is not exceeded by actual misstatement in the population | Increase | The greater the level of assurance that the auditor requires that the results of the sample are in fact indicative of the actual amount of misstatement in the population, the larger the sample size needs to be. |

| FACTOR | EFFECT ON SAMPLE SIZE | |
|---|---|---|
| 4. An increase in tolerable misstatement | Decrease | The lower the tolerable misstatement, the larger the sample size needs to be |
| 5. An increase in the amount of misstatement the auditor expects to find in the population | Increase | The greater the amount of misstatement the auditor expects to find in the population, the larger the sample size needs to be in order to make a reasonable estimate of the actual amount of misstatement in the population. Factors relevant to the auditor's consideration of the expected misstatement amount include the extent to which item values are determined subjectively, the results of risk assessment procedures, the results of tests of control, the results of audit procedures applied in prior periods, and the results of other substantive procedures |
| 6. Stratification of the population when appropriate | Decrease | When there is a wide range (variability) in the monetary size of items in the population, it may be useful to stratify the population. When a population can be appropriately stratified, the aggregate of the sample sizes from the strata generally will be less than the sample size that would have been required to attain a given level of sampling risk, had one sample been drawn from the whole population |
| 7. The number of sampling units in the population | Negligible effect | For large populations, the actual size of the population has little, if any, effect on sample size. Thus, for small populations, audit sampling is often not as efficient as alternative means of obtaining sufficient appropriate audit evidence. (However, when using monetary unit sampling, an increase in the monetary value of the population increases sample size, unless this is offset by a proportional increase in materiality for the financial statements as a whole (and, if applicable, materiality level or levels for particular classes of transactions, account balances or disclosures.) |

# Appendix 4   (Ref: Para. A13)

# Sample Selection Methods

There are many methods of selecting samples. The principal methods are as follows:

(a) Random selection (applied through random number generators, for example, random number tables).

(b) Systematic selection, in which the number of sampling units in the population is divided by the sample size to give a sampling interval, for example 50, and having determined a starting point within the first 50, each 50th sampling unit thereafter is selected. Although the starting point may be determined haphazardly, the sample is more likely to be truly random if it is determined by use of a computerized random number generator or random number tables. When using systematic selection, the auditor would need to determine that sampling units within the population are not structured in such a way that the sampling interval corresponds with a particular pattern in the population.

(c) Monetary Unit Sampling is a type of value-weighted selection (as described in Appendix 1) in which sample size, selection and evaluation results in a conclusion in monetary amounts.

(d) Haphazard selection, in which the auditor selects the sample without following a structured technique. Although no structured technique is used, the auditor would nonetheless avoid any conscious bias or predictability (for example, avoiding difficult to locate items, or always choosing or avoiding the first or last entries on a page) and thus attempt to ensure that all items in the population have a chance of selection. Haphazard selection is not appropriate when using statistical sampling.

(e) Block selection involves selection of a block(s) of contiguous items from within the population. Block selection cannot ordinarily be used in audit sampling because most populations are structured such that items in a sequence can be expected to have similar characteristics to each other, but different characteristics from items elsewhere in the population. Although in some circumstances it may be an appropriate audit procedure to examine a block of items, it would rarely be an appropriate sample selection technique when the auditor intends to draw valid inferences about the entire population based on the sample.

# Addendum

*This addendum provides a summary of APB's rationale for retaining or excluding in the proposed clarified ISA (UK and Ireland) the supplementary requirements in the existing ISA (UK and Ireland). It also sets out the supplementary guidance material in the existing ISA (UK and Ireland) that APB considers is not necessary to retain in light of the improvements in the underlying Clarity ISAs issued by the IAASB as part of the Clarity Project. It is provided for information and does not form part of the proposed clarified ISA (UK and Ireland).*

*The Consultation Paper published with the exposure drafts explains the general approach used by the APB for determining whether current supplementary material should be proposed to be retained.*

### Analysis of proposed treatment of current APB supplementary material in current ISA (UK and Ireland) 530

<u>Requirements</u>

| APB supplementary requirements (*Italic text is from IAASB for context*) | Is it covered in substance in the Clarity ISA? | Should it be retained? |
|---|---|---|
| 31-1. **When designing an audit sample the auditor should also consider the sampling and selection methods.** | ✗ However, different sampling methods are addressed in the Application Material (e.g. A4 – A9 and Appendix 4). | ✗ |

<u>Guidance</u>

The following guidance in current ISA (UK and Ireland) 530 has not been carried forward to the proposed clarified standard.

| Current paragraph reference (*Italic text is from IAASB for context*) |
|---|
| 1-1.   This ISA (UK and Ireland) applies to any audit using sampling whether related to financial statements or not. Nothing contained in this statement is intended to preclude non-statistically based samples where there are reasonable grounds for believing that the results may be relied on for the purpose of the test. Statistically based sampling involves the use of techniques from which mathematically constructed conclusions about the population can be drawn. An auditor draws a judgmental opinion about the population from non-statistical methods |
| 1-2. – 1-5 [Description of management and those charged with governance] |

# Proposed Clarified International Standard on Auditing (UK and Ireland) 540

# Auditing accounting estimates, including fair value accounting estimates, and related disclosures

(Effective for audits of financial statements for periods ending on or after 15 December 2010)

# Contents

*Paragraph*

International Standard on Auditing (UK and Ireland) (ISA (UK and Ireland)) 540, "Auditing Accounting Estimates, Including Fair Value Accounting Estimates, and Related Disclosures" should be read in conjunction with ISA (UK and Ireland) 200, "Overall Objectives of the Independent Auditor and the Conduct of an Audit in Accordance with International Standards on Auditing (UK and Ireland)."

# Introduction

## Scope of this ISA (UK and Ireland)

1    This International Standard on Auditing (UK and Ireland) (ISA (UK and Ireland)) deals with the auditor's responsibilities relating to accounting estimates, including fair value accounting estimates, and related disclosures in an audit of financial statements. Specifically, it expands on how ISA (UK and Ireland) 315[1] and ISA (UK and Ireland) 330[2] and other relevant ISAs (UK and Ireland) are to be applied in relation to accounting estimates. It also includes requirements and guidance on misstatements of individual accounting estimates, and indicators of possible management bias.

## Nature of Accounting Estimates

2    Some financial statement items cannot be measured precisely, but can only be estimated. For purposes of this ISA (UK and Ireland), such financial statement items are referred to as accounting estimates. The nature and reliability of information available to management to support the making of an accounting estimate varies widely, which thereby affects the degree of estimation uncertainty associated with accounting estimates. The degree of estimation uncertainty affects, in turn, the risks of material misstatement of accounting estimates, including their susceptibility to unintentional or intentional management bias. (Ref: Para. A1-A11)

3    The measurement objective of accounting estimates can vary depending on the applicable financial reporting framework and the financial item being reported. The measurement objective for some accounting estimates is to forecast the outcome of one or more transactions, events or conditions giving rise to the need for the accounting estimate. For other accounting estimates, including many fair value accounting estimates, the measurement objective is different, and is expressed in terms of the value of a current transaction or financial statement item based on conditions prevalent at the measurement date, such as estimated market price for a particular type of asset or liability. For example, the applicable financial reporting framework may require fair value measurement based on an assumed hypothetical current transaction between knowledgeable, willing parties (sometimes referred to as "marketplace participants" or equivalent) in an arm's length transaction, rather than the settlement of a transaction at some past or future date.[3]

4    A difference between the outcome of an accounting estimate and the amount originally recognized or disclosed in the financial statements does not necessarily represent a misstatement of the financial statements. This is particularly the case for fair value accounting estimates, as any observed outcome is invariably affected by events or conditions subsequent to the date at which the measurement is estimated for purposes of the financial statements.

---

[1] *ISA (UK and Ireland) 315, "Identifying and Assessing the Risks of Material Misstatement through Understanding the Entity and Its Environment."*

[2] *ISA (UK and Ireland) 330, "The Auditor's Responses to Assessed Risks."*

[3] *Different definitions of fair value may exist among financial reporting frameworks.*

## Effective Date

This ISA (UK and Ireland) is effective for audits of financial statements for periods 5
ending on or after 15 December 2010.

## Objective

The objective of the auditor is to obtain sufficient appropriate audit evidence about 6
whether:

(a)  accounting estimates, including fair value accounting estimates, in the financial
     statements, whether recognized or disclosed, are reasonable; and
(b)  related disclosures in the financial statements are adequate,
     in the context of the applicable financial reporting framework.

## Definitions

For purposes of the ISAs (UK and Ireland), the following terms have the meanings 7
attributed below:

(a)  Accounting estimate – An approximation of a monetary amount in the absence
     of a precise means of measurement. This term is used for an amount measured
     at fair value where there is estimation uncertainty, as well as for other amounts
     that require estimation. Where this ISA (UK and Ireland) addresses only
     accounting estimates involving measurement at fair value, the term "fair value
     accounting estimates" is used.
(b)  Auditor's point estimate or auditor's range – The amount, or range of amounts,
     respectively, derived from audit evidence for use in evaluating management's
     point estimate.
(c)  Estimation uncertainty – The susceptibility of an accounting estimate and
     related disclosures to an inherent lack of precision in its measurement.
(d)  Management bias – A lack of neutrality by management in the preparation and
     presentation of information.
(e)  Management's point estimate – The amount selected by management[3a] for
     recognition or disclosure in the financial statements as an accounting estimate.
(f)  Outcome of an accounting estimate – The actual monetary amount which
     results from the resolution of the underlying transaction(s), event(s) or condi-
     tion(s) addressed by the accounting estimate.

## Requirements

### Risk Assessment Procedures and Related Activities

When performing risk assessment procedures and related activities to obtain an 8
understanding of the entity and its environment, including the entity's internal
control, as required by ISA (UK and Ireland) 315,[4] the auditor shall obtain an
understanding of the following in order to provide a basis for the identification and
assessment of the risks of material misstatement for accounting estimates: (Ref: Para.
A12)

---

[3a] *In the UK and Ireland those charged with governance are responsible for the preparation of the financial
statements.*

[4] *ISA (UK and Ireland) 315, paragraphs 5-6 and 11-12.*

(a) The requirements of the applicable financial reporting framework relevant to accounting estimates, including related disclosures. (Ref: Para. A13-A15)

(b) How management[3a] identifies those transactions, events and conditions that may give rise to the need for accounting estimates to be recognized or disclosed in the financial statements. In obtaining this understanding, the auditor shall make inquiries of management about changes in circumstances that may give rise to new, or the need to revise existing, accounting estimates. (Ref: Para. A16-A21)

(c) How management makes the accounting estimates, and an understanding of the data on which they are based, including: (Ref: Para. A22-A23)

    (i) The method, including where applicable the model, used in making the accounting estimate; (Ref: Para. A24-A26)

    (ii) Relevant controls; (Ref: Para. A27-A28)

    (iii) Whether management has used an expert; (Ref: Para. A29-A30)

    (iv) The assumptions underlying the accounting estimates; (Ref: Para. A31-A36)

    (v) Whether there has been or ought to have been a change from the prior period in the methods for making the accounting estimates, and if so, why; and (Ref: Para. A37)

    (vi) Whether and, if so, how management has assessed the effect of estimation uncertainty. (Ref: Para. A38)

9    The auditor shall review the outcome of accounting estimates included in the prior period financial statements, or, where applicable, their subsequent re-estimation for the purpose of the current period. The nature and extent of the auditor's review takes account of the nature of the accounting estimates, and whether the information obtained from the review would be relevant to identifying and assessing risks of material misstatement of accounting estimates made in the current period financial statements. However, the review is not intended to call into question the judgments made in the prior periods that were based on information available at the time. (Ref: Para. A39-A44)

## Identifying and Assessing the Risks of Material Misstatement

10    In identifying and assessing the risks of material misstatement, as required by ISA (UK and Ireland) 315,[5] the auditor shall evaluate the degree of estimation uncertainty associated with an accounting estimate. (Ref: Para. A45-A46)

11    The auditor shall determine whether, in the auditor's judgment, any of those accounting estimates that have been identified as having high estimation uncertainty give rise to significant risks. (Ref: Para. A47-A51)

## Responses to the Assessed Risks of Material Misstatement

12    Based on the assessed risks of material misstatement, the auditor shall determine: (Ref: Para. A52)

(a) Whether management has appropriately applied the requirements of the applicable financial reporting framework relevant to the accounting estimate; and (Ref: Para. A53-A56)

(b) Whether the methods for making the accounting estimates are appropriate and have been applied consistently, and whether changes, if any, in accounting

[5] *ISA (UK and Ireland) 315, paragraph 25.*

estimates or in the method for making them from the prior period are appropriate in the circumstances. (Ref: Para. A57-A58)

In responding to the assessed risks of material misstatement, as required by ISA (UK and Ireland) 330,[6] the auditor shall undertake one or more of the following, taking account of the nature of the accounting estimate: (Ref: Para. A59-A61) **13**

(a) Determine whether events occurring up to the date of the auditor's report provide audit evidence regarding the accounting estimate. (Ref: Para. A62-A67)
(b) Test how management made the accounting estimate and the data on which it is based. In doing so, the auditor shall evaluate whether: (Ref: Para. A68-A70)
  (i) The method of measurement used is appropriate in the circumstances; and (Ref: Para. A71-A76)
  (ii) The assumptions used by management are reasonable in light of the measurement objectives of the applicable financial reporting framework. (Ref: Para. A77-A83)
(c) Test the operating effectiveness of the controls over how management made the accounting estimate, together with appropriate substantive procedures. (Ref: Para. A84-A86)
(d) Develop a point estimate or a range to evaluate management's point estimate. For this purpose: (Ref: Para. A87-A91)
  (i) If the auditor uses assumptions or methods that differ from management's, the auditor shall obtain an understanding of management's assumptions or methods sufficient to establish that the auditor's point estimate or range takes into account relevant variables and to evaluate any significant differences from management's point estimate. (Ref: Para. A92)
  (ii) If the auditor concludes that it is appropriate to use a range, the auditor shall narrow the range, based on audit evidence available, until all outcomes within the range are considered reasonable. (Ref: Para. A93-A95)

In determining the matters identified in paragraph 12 or in responding to the assessed risks of material misstatement in accordance with paragraph 13, the auditor shall consider whether specialized skills or knowledge in relation to one or more aspects of the accounting estimates are required in order to obtain sufficient appropriate audit evidence. (Ref: Para. A96-A101) **14**

## Further Substantive Procedures to Respond to Significant Risks

### Estimation Uncertainty

For accounting estimates that give rise to significant risks, in addition to other substantive procedures performed to meet the requirements of ISA (UK and Ireland) 330,[7] the auditor shall evaluate the following: (Ref: Para. A102) **15**

(a) How management has considered alternative assumptions or outcomes, and why it has rejected them, or how management has otherwise addressed estimation uncertainty in making the accounting estimate. (Ref: Para. A103-A106)
(b) Whether the significant assumptions used by management are reasonable. (Ref: Para. A107-A109)
(c) Where relevant to the reasonableness of the significant assumptions used by management or the appropriate application of the applicable financial reporting

[6] ISA (UK and Ireland) 330, paragraph 5.

[7] ISA (UK and Ireland) 330, paragraph 18.

framework, management's intent to carry out specific courses of action and its ability to do so. (Ref: Para. A110)

**16** If, in the auditor's judgment, management has not adequately addressed the effects of estimation uncertainty on the accounting estimates that give rise to significant risks, the auditor shall, if considered necessary, develop a range with which to evaluate the reasonableness of the accounting estimate. (Ref: Para. A111-A112)

### *Recognition and Measurement Criteria*

**17** For accounting estimates that give rise to significant risks, the auditor shall obtain sufficient appropriate audit evidence about whether:

(a) management's[3a] decision to recognize, or to not recognize, the accounting estimates in the financial statements; and (Ref: Para. A113-A114)

(b) the selected measurement basis for the accounting estimates (Ref: Para. A115) are in accordance with the requirements of the applicable financial reporting framework.

## Evaluating the Reasonableness of the Accounting Estimates, and Determining Misstatements

**18** The auditor shall evaluate, based on the audit evidence, whether the accounting estimates in the financial statements are either reasonable in the context of the applicable financial reporting framework, or are misstated. (Ref: Para. A116-A119)

## Disclosures Related to Accounting Estimates

**19** The auditor shall obtain sufficient appropriate audit evidence about whether the disclosures in the financial statements related to accounting estimates are in accordance with the requirements of the applicable financial reporting framework. (Ref: Para. A120-A121)

**20** For accounting estimates that give rise to significant risks, the auditor shall also evaluate the adequacy of the disclosure of their estimation uncertainty in the financial statements in the context of the applicable financial reporting framework. (Ref: Para. A122-A123)

## Indicators of Possible Management Bias

21. The auditor shall review the judgments and decisions made by management in the making of accounting estimates to identify whether there are indicators of possible management bias. Indicators of possible management bias do not themselves constitute misstatements for the purposes of drawing conclusions on the reasonableness of individual accounting estimates. (Ref: Para. A124-A125)

## Written Representations

**22** The auditor shall obtain written representations from management and, where appropriate, those charged with governance whether they believe significant assumptions used by it in making accounting estimates are reasonable. (Ref: Para. A126-A127)

# Documentation

23. The auditor shall include in the audit documentation:[8]
(a) The basis for the auditor's conclusions about the reasonableness of accounting estimates and their disclosure that give rise to significant risks; and
(b) Indicators of possible management bias, if any. (Ref: Para. A128)

\*\*\*

# Application and Other Explanatory Material

## Nature of Accounting Estimates (Ref: Para. 2)

Because of the uncertainties inherent in business activities, some financial statement items can only be estimated. Further, the specific characteristics of an asset, liability or component of equity, or the basis of or method of measurement prescribed by the financial reporting framework, may give rise to the need to estimate a financial statement item. Some financial reporting frameworks prescribe specific methods of measurement and the disclosures that are required to be made in the financial statements, while other financial reporting frameworks are less specific. The Appendix to this ISA (UK and Ireland) discusses fair value measurements and disclosures under different financial reporting frameworks. **A1**

Some accounting estimates involve relatively low estimation uncertainty and may give rise to lower risks of material misstatements, for example: **A2**

- Accounting estimates arising in entities that engage in business activities that are not complex.
- Accounting estimates that are frequently made and updated because they relate to routine transactions.
- Accounting estimates derived from data that is readily available, such as published interest rate data or exchange-traded prices of securities. Such data may be referred to as "observable" in the context of a fair value accounting estimate.
- Fair value accounting estimates where the method of measurement prescribed by the applicable financial reporting framework is simple and applied easily to the asset or liability requiring measurement at fair value.
- Fair value accounting estimates where the model used to measure the accounting estimate is well-known or generally accepted, provided that the assumptions or inputs to the model are observable.

For some accounting estimates, however, there may be relatively high estimation uncertainty, particularly where they are based on significant assumptions, for example: **A3**

- Accounting estimates relating to the outcome of litigation.
- Fair value accounting estimates for derivative financial instruments not publicly traded.
- Fair value accounting estimates for which a highly specialized entity-developed model is used or for which there are assumptions or inputs that cannot be observed in the marketplace.

The degree of estimation uncertainty varies based on the nature of the accounting estimate, the extent to which there is a generally accepted method or model used to make the accounting estimate, and the subjectivity of the assumptions used to make **A4**

[8] *ISA (UK and Ireland) 230, "Audit Documentation," paragraphs 8-11, and paragraph A6.*

the accounting estimate. In some cases, estimation uncertainty associated with an accounting estimate may be so great that the recognition criteria in the applicable financial reporting framework are not met and the accounting estimate cannot be made.

**A5** Not all financial statement items requiring measurement at fair value, involve estimation uncertainty. For example, this may be the case for some financial statement items where there is an active and open market that provides readily available and reliable information on the prices at which actual exchanges occur, in which case the existence of published price quotations ordinarily is the best audit evidence of fair value. However, estimation uncertainty may exist even when the valuation method and data are well defined. For example, valuation of securities quoted on an active and open market at the listed market price may require adjustment if the holding is significant in relation to the market or is subject to restrictions in marketability. In addition, general economic circumstances prevailing at the time, for example, illiquidity in a particular market, may impact estimation uncertainty.

**A6** Additional examples of situations where accounting estimates, other than fair value accounting estimates, may be required include:

- Allowance for doubtful accounts.
- Inventory obsolescence.
- Warranty obligations.
- Depreciation method or asset useful life.
- Provision against the carrying amount of an investment where there is uncertainty regarding its recoverability.
- Outcome of long term contracts.
- Costs arising from litigation settlements and judgments.

**A7** Additional examples of situations where fair value accounting estimates may be required include:

- Complex financial instruments, which are not traded in an active and open market.
- Share-based payments.
- Property or equipment held for disposal.
- Certain assets or liabilities acquired in a business combination, including goodwill and intangible assets.
- Transactions involving the exchange of assets or liabilities between independent parties without monetary consideration, for example, a non-monetary exchange of plant facilities in different lines of business.

**A8** Estimation involves judgments based on information available when the financial statements are prepared. For many accounting estimates, these include making assumptions about matters that are uncertain at the time of estimation. The auditor is not responsible for predicting future conditions, transactions or events that, if known at the time of the audit, might have significantly affected management's actions or the assumptions used by management.

### Management Bias

**A9** Financial reporting frameworks often call for neutrality, that is, freedom from bias. Accounting estimates are imprecise, however, and can be influenced by management judgment. Such judgment may involve unintentional or intentional management bias (for example, as a result of motivation to achieve a desired result). The susceptibility of an accounting estimate to management bias increases with the subjectivity involved in making it. Unintentional management bias and the potential for intentional management bias are inherent in subjective decisions that are often required in making an accounting estimate. For continuing audits, indicators of possible management bias identified during the audit of the preceding periods influence the planning and risk identification and assessment activities of the auditor in the current period.

Management bias can be difficult to detect at an account level. It may only be **A10** identified when considered in the aggregate of groups of accounting estimates or all accounting estimates, or when observed over a number of accounting periods. Although some form of management bias is inherent in subjective decisions, in making such judgments there may be no intention by management to mislead the users of financial statements. Where, however, there is intention to mislead, management bias is fraudulent in nature.

### *Considerations Specific to Public Sector Entities*

Public sector entities may have significant holdings of specialized assets for which **A11** there are no readily available and reliable sources of information for purposes of measurement at fair value or other current value bases, or a combination of both. Often specialized assets held do not generate cash flows and do not have an active market. Measurement at fair value therefore ordinarily requires estimation and may be complex, and in some rare cases may not be possible at all.

## Risk Assessment Procedures and Related Activities (Ref: Para. 8)

The risk assessment procedures and related activities required by paragraph 8 of this **A12** ISA (UK and Ireland) assist the auditor in developing an expectation of the nature and type of accounting estimates that an entity may have. The auditor's primary consideration is whether the understanding that has been obtained is sufficient to identify and assess the risks of material misstatement in relation to accounting estimates, and to plan the nature, timing and extent of further audit procedures.

### *Obtaining an Understanding of the Requirements of the Applicable Financial Reporting Framework* (Ref: Para. 8(a))

Obtaining an understanding of the requirements of the applicable financial reporting **A13** framework assists the auditor in determining whether it, for example:

- Prescribes certain conditions for the recognition,[9] or methods for the measurement, of accounting estimates.
- Specifies certain conditions that permit or require measurement at a fair value, for example, by referring to management's intentions to carry out certain courses of action with respect to an asset or liability.
- Specifies required or permitted disclosures.
  Obtaining this understanding also provides the auditor with a basis for discussion with management about how management has applied those requirements relevant to the accounting estimate, and the auditor's determination of whether they have been applied appropriately.

---

[9] *Most financial reporting frameworks require incorporation in the balance sheet or income statement of items that satisfy their criteria for recognition. Disclosure of accounting policies or adding notes to the financial statements does not rectify a failure to recognize such items, including accounting estimates.*

**A14** Financial reporting frameworks may provide guidance for management on determining point estimates where alternatives exist. Some financial reporting frameworks, for example, require that the point estimate selected be the alternative that reflects management's judgment of the most likely outcome.[10] Others may require, for example, use of a discounted probability-weighted expected value. In some cases, management may be able to make a point estimate directly. In other cases, management may be able to make a reliable point estimate only after considering alternative assumptions or outcomes from which it is able to determine a point estimate.

**A15** Financial reporting frameworks may require the disclosure of information concerning the significant assumptions to which the accounting estimate is particularly sensitive. Furthermore, where there is a high degree of estimation uncertainty, some financial reporting frameworks do not permit an accounting estimate to be recognized in the financial statements, but certain disclosures may be required in the notes to the financial statements.

*Obtaining an Understanding of How Management Identifies the Need for Accounting Estimates* (Ref: Para. 8(b))

**A16** The preparation of the financial statements requires management[3a] to determine whether a transaction, event or condition gives rise to the need to make an accounting estimate, and that all necessary accounting estimates have been recognized, measured and disclosed in the financial statements in accordance with the applicable financial reporting framework.

**A17** Management's identification of transactions, events and conditions that give rise to the need for accounting estimates is likely to be based on:

- Management's knowledge of the entity's business and the industry in which it operates.
- Management's knowledge of the implementation of business strategies in the current period.
- Where applicable, management's[3a] cumulative experience of preparing the entity's financial statements in prior periods.

  In such cases, the auditor may obtain an understanding of how management identifies the need for accounting estimates primarily through inquiry of management. In other cases, where management's process is more structured, for example, when management has a formal risk management function, the auditor may perform risk assessment procedures directed at the methods and practices followed by management for periodically reviewing the circumstances that give rise to the accounting estimates and re-estimating the accounting estimates as necessary. The completeness of accounting estimates is often an important consideration of the auditor, particularly accounting estimates relating to liabilities.

**A18** The auditor's understanding of the entity and its environment obtained during the performance of risk assessment procedures, together with other audit evidence obtained during the course of the audit, assist the auditor in identifying circumstances, or changes in circumstances, that may give rise to the need for an accounting estimate.

[10] *Different financial reporting frameworks may use different terminology to describe point estimates determined in this way.*

Inquiries of management about changes in circumstances may include, for example, **A19** inquiries about whether:

- The entity has engaged in new types of transactions that may give rise to accounting estimates.
- Terms of transactions that gave rise to accounting estimates have changed.
- Accounting policies relating to accounting estimates have changed, as a result of changes to the requirements of the applicable financial reporting framework or otherwise.
- Regulatory or other changes outside the control of management have occurred that may require management to revise, or make new, accounting estimates.
- New conditions or events have occurred that may give rise to the need for new or revised accounting estimates.

During the audit, the auditor may identify transactions, events and conditions that **A20** give rise to the need for accounting estimates that management failed to identify. ISA (UK and Ireland) 315 deals with circumstances where the auditor identifies risks of material misstatement that management failed to identify, including determining whether there is a significant deficiency in internal control with regard to the entity's risk assessment processes.[11]

*Considerations Specific to Smaller Entities*

Obtaining this understanding for smaller entities is often less complex as their **A21** business activities are often limited and transactions are less complex. Further, often a single person, for example the owner-manager, identifies the need to make an accounting estimate and the auditor may focus inquiries accordingly.

**Obtaining an Understanding of How Management Makes the Accounting Estimates** (Ref: Para. 8(c))

The preparation of the financial statements also requires management[3a] to establish **A22** financial reporting processes for making accounting estimates, including adequate internal control. Such processes include the following:

- Selecting appropriate accounting policies and prescribing estimation processes, including appropriate estimation or valuation methods, including, where applicable, models.
- Developing or identifying relevant data and assumptions that affect accounting estimates.
- Periodically reviewing the circumstances that give rise to the accounting estimates and re-estimating the accounting estimates as necessary.

Matters that the auditor may consider in obtaining an understanding of how man- **A23** agement makes the accounting estimates include, for example:

- The types of accounts or transactions to which the accounting estimates relate (for example, whether the accounting estimates arise from the recording of routine and recurring transactions or whether they arise from non-recurring or unusual transactions).
- Whether and, if so, how management has used recognized measurement techniques for making particular accounting estimates.
- Whether the accounting estimates were made based on data available at an interim date and, if so, whether and how management has taken into account

[11] *ISA (UK and Ireland) 315, paragraph 16.*

the effect of events, transactions and changes in circumstances occurring between that date and the period end.

*Method of Measurement, Including the Use of Models (Ref: Para. 8(c)(i))*

A24   In some cases, the applicable financial reporting framework may prescribe the method of measurement for an accounting estimate, for example, a particular model that is to be used in measuring a fair value estimate. In many cases, however, the applicable financial reporting framework does not prescribe the method of measurement, or may specify alternative methods for measurement.

A25   When the applicable financial reporting framework does not prescribe a particular method to be used in the circumstances, matters that the auditor may consider in obtaining an understanding of the method or, where applicable the model, used to make accounting estimates include, for example:

●   How management considered the nature of the asset or liability being estimated when selecting a particular method.
●   Whether the entity operates in a particular business, industry or environment in which there are methods commonly used to make the particular type of accounting estimate.

A26   There may be greater risks of material misstatement, for example, in cases when management has internally developed a model to be used to make the accounting estimate or is departing from a method commonly used in a particular industry or environment.

*Relevant Controls (Ref: Para. 8(c)(ii))*

A27   Matters that the auditor may consider in obtaining an understanding of relevant controls include, for example, the experience and competence of those who make the accounting estimates, and controls related to:

●   How management determines the completeness, relevance and accuracy of the data used to develop accounting estimates.
●   The review and approval of accounting estimates, including the assumptions or inputs used in their development, by appropriate levels of management and, where appropriate, those charged with governance.
●   The segregation of duties between those committing the entity to the underlying transactions and those responsible for making the accounting estimates, including whether the assignment of responsibilities appropriately takes account of the nature of the entity and its products or services (for example, in the case of a large financial institution, relevant segregation of duties may include an independent function responsible for estimation and validation of fair value pricing of the entity's proprietary financial products staffed by individuals whose remuneration is not tied to such products).

A28   Other controls may be relevant to making the accounting estimates depending on the circumstances. For example, if the entity uses specific models for making accounting estimates, management may put into place specific policies and procedures around such models. Relevant controls may include, for example, those established over:

●   The design and development, or selection, of a particular model for a particular purpose.
●   The use of the model.
●   The maintenance and periodic validation of the integrity of the model.

*Management's Use of Experts (Ref: Para. 8(c)(iii))*

Management may have, or the entity may employ individuals with, the experience   **A29**
and competence necessary to make the required point estimates. In some cases,
however, management may need to engage an expert to make, or assist in making,
them. This need may arise because of, for example:

- The specialized nature of the matter requiring estimation, for example, the
  measurement of mineral or hydrocarbon reserves in extractive industries.
- The technical nature of the models required to meet the relevant requirements of
  the applicable financial reporting framework, as may be the case in certain
  measurements at fair value.
- The unusual or infrequent nature of the condition, transaction or event
  requiring an accounting estimate.

*Considerations specific to smaller entities*

In smaller entities, the circumstances requiring an accounting estimate often are such   **A30**
that the owner-manager is capable of making the required point estimate. In some
cases, however, an expert will be needed. Discussion with the owner-manager early in
the audit process about the nature of any accounting estimates, the completeness of
the required accounting estimates, and the adequacy of the estimating process may
assist the owner-manager in determining the need to use an expert.

*Assumptions (Ref: Para. 8(c)(iv))*

Assumptions are integral components of accounting estimates. Matters that the   **A31**
auditor may consider in obtaining an understanding of the assumptions underlying
the accounting estimates include, for example:

- The nature of the assumptions, including which of the assumptions are likely to
  be significant assumptions.
- How management assesses whether the assumptions are relevant and complete
  (that is, that all relevant variables have been taken into account).
- Where applicable, how management determines that the assumptions used are
  internally consistent.
- Whether the assumptions relate to matters within the control of management
  (for example, assumptions about the maintenance programs that may affect the
  estimation of an asset's useful life), and how they conform to the entity's
  business plans and the external environment, or to matters that are outside its
  control (for example, assumptions about interest rates, mortality rates, potential
  judicial or regulatory actions, or the variability and the timing of future cash
  flows).
- The nature and extent of documentation, if any, supporting the assumptions.
  Assumptions may be made or identified by an expert to assist management in
  making the accounting estimates. Such assumptions, when used by management, become management's assumptions.

In some cases, assumptions may be referred to as inputs, for example, where man-   **A32**
agement uses a model to make an accounting estimate, though the term inputs may
also be used to refer to the underlying data to which specific assumptions are applied.

Management may support assumptions with different types of information drawn   **A33**
from internal and external sources, the relevance and reliability of which will vary. In
some cases, an assumption may be reliably based on applicable information from
either external sources (for example, published interest rate or other statistical data)

or internal sources (for example, historical information or previous conditions experienced by the entity). In other cases, an assumption may be more subjective, for example, where the entity has no experience or external sources from which to draw.

A34   In the case of fair value accounting estimates, assumptions reflect, or are consistent with, what knowledgeable, willing arm's length parties (sometimes referred to as "marketplace participants" or equivalent) would use in determining fair value when exchanging an asset or settling a liability. Specific assumptions will also vary with the characteristics of the asset or liability being valued, the valuation method used (for example, a market approach, or an income approach) and the requirements of the applicable financial reporting framework.

A35   With respect to fair value accounting estimates, assumptions or inputs vary in terms of their source and bases, as follows:

(a)   Those that reflect what marketplace participants would use in pricing an asset or liability developed based on market data obtained from sources independent of the reporting entity (sometimes referred to as "observable inputs" or equivalent).

(b)   Those that reflect the entity's own judgments about what assumptions marketplace participants would use in pricing the asset or liability developed based on the best information available in the circumstances (sometimes referred to as "unobservable inputs" or equivalent).
      In practice, however, the distinction between (a) and (b) is not always apparent. Further, it may be necessary for management to select from a number of different assumptions used by different marketplace participants.

A36   The extent of subjectivity, such as whether an assumption or input is observable, influences the degree of estimation uncertainty and thereby the auditor's assessment of the risks of material misstatement for a particular accounting estimate.

*Changes in Methods for Making Accounting Estimates (Ref: Para. 8(c)(v))*

A37   In evaluating how management makes the accounting estimates, the auditor is required to understand whether there has been or ought to have been a change from the prior period in the methods for making the accounting estimates. A specific estimation method may need to be changed in response to changes in the environment or circumstances affecting the entity or in the requirements of the applicable financial reporting framework. If management has changed the method for making an accounting estimate, it is important that management can demonstrate that the new method is more appropriate, or is itself a response to such changes. For example, if management changes the basis of making an accounting estimate from a mark-to-market approach to using a model, the auditor challenges whether management's assumptions about the marketplace are reasonable in light of economic circumstances.

*Estimation Uncertainty (Ref: Para. 8(c)(vi))*

A38   Matters that the auditor may consider in obtaining an understanding of whether and, if so, how management has assessed the effect of estimation uncertainty include, for example:

●   Whether and, if so, how management has considered alternative assumptions or outcomes by, for example, performing a sensitivity analysis to determine the effect of changes in the assumptions on an accounting estimate.

- How management determines the accounting estimate when analysis indicates a number of outcome scenarios.
- Whether management monitors the outcome of accounting estimates made in the prior period, and whether management has appropriately responded to the outcome of that monitoring procedure.

*Reviewing Prior Period Accounting Estimates* (Ref: Para. 9)

The outcome of an accounting estimate will often differ from the accounting estimate recognized in the prior period financial statements. By performing risk assessment procedures to identify and understand the reasons for such differences, the auditor may obtain:

- Information regarding the effectiveness of management's prior period estimation process, from which the auditor can judge the likely effectiveness of management's current process.
- Audit evidence that is pertinent to the re-estimation, in the current period, of prior period accounting estimates.
- Audit evidence of matters, such as estimation uncertainty, that may be required to be disclosed in the financial statements.

A39

The review of prior period accounting estimates may also assist the auditor, in the current period, in identifying circumstances or conditions that increase the susceptibility of accounting estimates to, or indicate the presence of, possible management bias. The auditor's professional skepticism assists in identifying such circumstances or conditions and in determining the nature, timing and extent of further audit procedures.

A40

A retrospective review of management judgments and assumptions related to significant accounting estimates is also required by ISA (UK and Ireland) 240.[12] That review is conducted as part of the requirement for the auditor to design and perform procedures to review accounting estimates for biases that could represent a risk of material misstatement due to fraud, in response to the risks of management override of controls. As a practical matter, the auditor's review of prior period accounting estimates as a risk assessment procedure in accordance with this ISA (UK and Ireland) may be carried out in conjunction with the review required by ISA (UK and Ireland) 240.

A41

The auditor may judge that a more detailed review is required for those accounting estimates that were identified during the prior period audit as having high estimation uncertainty, or for those accounting estimates that have changed significantly from the prior period. On the other hand, for example, for accounting estimates that arise from the recording of routine and recurring transactions, the auditor may judge that the application of analytical procedures as risk assessment procedures is sufficient for purposes of the review.

A42

For fair value accounting estimates and other accounting estimates based on current conditions at the measurement date, more variation may exist between the fair value amount recognized in the prior period financial statements and the outcome or the amount re-estimated for the purpose of the current period. This is because the measurement objective for such accounting estimates deals with perceptions about value at a point in time, which may change significantly and rapidly as the environment in which the entity operates changes. The auditor may therefore focus the

A43

---

[12] ISA (UK and Ireland) 240, "The Auditor's Responsibilities Relating to Fraud in an Audit of Financial Statements," paragraph 32(b)(ii).

review on obtaining information that would be relevant to identifying and assessing risks of material misstatement. For example, in some cases obtaining an understanding of changes in marketplace participant assumptions which affected the outcome of a prior period fair value accounting estimate may be unlikely to provide relevant information for audit purposes. If so, then the auditor's consideration of the outcome of prior period fair value accounting estimates may be directed more towards understanding the effectiveness of management's prior estimation process, that is, management's track record, from which the auditor can judge the likely effectiveness of management's current process.

**A44**    A difference between the outcome of an accounting estimate and the amount recognized in the prior period financial statements does not necessarily represent a misstatement of the prior period financial statements. However, it may do so if, for example, the difference arises from information that was available to management when the prior period's financial statements were finalized, or that could reasonably be expected to have been obtained and taken into account in the preparation and presentation of those financial statements. Many financial reporting frameworks contain guidance on distinguishing between changes in accounting estimates that constitute misstatements and changes that do not, and the accounting treatment required to be followed.

## Identifying and Assessing the Risks of Material Misstatement

### *Estimation Uncertainty* (Ref: Para. 10)

**A45**    The degree of estimation uncertainty associated with an accounting estimate may be influenced by factors such as:

- The extent to which the accounting estimate depends on judgment.
- The sensitivity of the accounting estimate to changes in assumptions.
- The existence of recognized measurement techniques that may mitigate the estimation uncertainty (though the subjectivity of the assumptions used as inputs may nevertheless give rise to estimation uncertainty).
- The length of the forecast period, and the relevance of data drawn from past events to forecast future events.
- The availability of reliable data from external sources.
- The extent to which the accounting estimate is based on observable or unobservable inputs.
   The degree of estimation uncertainty associated with an accounting estimate may influence the estimate's susceptibility to bias.

**A46**    Matters that the auditor considers in assessing the risks of material misstatement may also include:

- The actual or expected magnitude of an accounting estimate.
- The recorded amount of the accounting estimate (that is, management's point estimate) in relation to the amount expected by the auditor to be recorded.
- Whether management has used an expert in making the accounting estimate.
- The outcome of the review of prior period accounting estimates.

### *High Estimation Uncertainty and Significant Risks* (Ref: Para. 11)

**A47**    Examples of accounting estimates that may have high estimation uncertainty include the following:

- Accounting estimates that are highly dependent upon judgment, for example, judgments about the outcome of pending litigation or the amount and timing of future cash flows dependent on uncertain events many years in the future.
- Accounting estimates that are not calculated using recognized measurement techniques.
- Accounting estimates where the results of the auditor's review of similar accounting estimates made in the prior period financial statements indicate a substantial difference between the original accounting estimate and the actual outcome.
- Fair value accounting estimates for which a highly specialized entity-developed model is used or for which there are no observable inputs.

A seemingly immaterial accounting estimate may have the potential to result in a material misstatement due to the estimation uncertainty associated with the estimation; that is, the size of the amount recognized or disclosed in the financial statements for an accounting estimate may not be an indicator of its estimation uncertainty. **A48**

In some circumstances, the estimation uncertainty is so high that a reasonable accounting estimate cannot be made. The applicable financial reporting framework may, therefore, preclude recognition of the item in the financial statements, or its measurement at fair value. In such cases, the significant risks relate not only to whether an accounting estimate should be recognized, or whether it should be measured at fair value, but also to the adequacy of the disclosures. With respect to such accounting estimates, the applicable financial reporting framework may require disclosure of the accounting estimates and the high estimation uncertainty associated with them (see paragraphs A120-A123). **A49**

If the auditor determines that an accounting estimate gives rise to a significant risk, the auditor is required to obtain an understanding of the entity's controls, including control activities.[13] **A50**

In some cases, the estimation uncertainty of an accounting estimate may cast significant doubt about the entity's ability to continue as a going concern. ISA (UK and Ireland) 570[14] establishes requirements and provides guidance in such circumstances. **A51**

## Responses to the Assessed Risks of Material Misstatement (Ref: Para. 12)

ISA (UK and Ireland) 330 requires the auditor to design and perform audit procedures whose nature, timing and extent are responsive to the assessed risks of material misstatement in relation to accounting estimates at both the financial statement and assertion levels.[15] Paragraphs A53-A115 focus on specific responses at the assertion level only. **A52**

### *Application of the Requirements of the Applicable Financial Reporting Framework* (Ref: Para. 12(a))

Many financial reporting frameworks prescribe certain conditions for the recognition of accounting estimates and specify the methods for making them and required **A53**

[13] *ISA (UK and Ireland) 315, paragraph 29.*

[14] *ISA (UK and Ireland) 570, "Going Concern."*

[15] *ISA (UK and Ireland) 330, paragraphs 5-6.*

disclosures. Such requirements may be complex and require the application of judgment. Based on the understanding obtained in performing risk assessment procedures, the requirements of the applicable financial reporting framework that may be susceptible to misapplication or differing interpretations become the focus of the auditor's attention.

A54   Determining whether management has appropriately applied the requirements of the applicable financial reporting framework is based, in part, on the auditor's understanding of the entity and its environment. For example, the measurement of the fair value of some items, such as intangible assets acquired in a business combination, may involve special considerations that are affected by the nature of the entity and its operations.

A55   In some situations, additional audit procedures, such as the inspection by the auditor of the current physical condition of an asset, may be necessary to determine whether management has appropriately applied the requirements of the applicable financial reporting framework.

A56   The application of the requirements of the applicable financial reporting framework requires management to consider changes in the environment or circumstances that affect the entity. For example, the introduction of an active market for a particular class of asset or liability may indicate that the use of discounted cash flows to estimate the fair value of such asset or liability is no longer appropriate.

*Consistency in Methods and Basis for Changes* (Ref: Para. 12(b))

A57   The auditor's consideration of a change in an accounting estimate, or in the method for making it from the prior period, is important because a change that is not based on a change in circumstances or new information is considered arbitrary. Arbitrary changes in an accounting estimate result in inconsistent financial statements over time and may give rise to a financial statement misstatement or be an indicator of possible management bias.

A58    Management often is able to demonstrate good reason for a change in an accounting estimate or the method for making an accounting estimate from one period to another based on a change in circumstances. What constitutes a good reason, and the adequacy of support for management's contention that there has been a change in circumstances that warrants a change in an accounting estimate or the method for making an accounting estimate, are matters of judgment.

*Responses to the Assessed Risks of Material Misstatements* (Ref: Para. 13)

A59   The auditor's decision as to which response, individually or in combination, in paragraph 13 to undertake to respond to the risks of material misstatement may be influenced by such matters as:

- The nature of the accounting estimate, including whether it arises from routine or non routine transactions.
- Whether the procedure(s) is expected to effectively provide the auditor with sufficient appropriate audit evidence.
- The assessed risk of material misstatement, including whether the assessed risk is a significant risk.

A60   For example, when evaluating the reasonableness of the allowance for doubtful accounts, an effective procedure for the auditor may be to review subsequent cash collections in combination with other procedures. Where the estimation uncertainty associated with an accounting estimate is high, for example, an accounting estimate based on a proprietary model for which there are unobservable inputs, it may be that a combination of the responses to assessed risks in paragraph 13 is necessary in order to obtain sufficient appropriate audit evidence.

Additional guidance explaining the circumstances in which each of the responses may be appropriate is provided in paragraphs A62-A95.  **A61**

*Events Occurring Up to the Date of the Auditor's Report (Ref: Para. 13(a))*

Determining whether events occurring up to the date of the auditor's report provide audit evidence regarding the accounting estimate may be an appropriate response when such events are expected to:  **A62**

- Occur; and
- Provide audit evidence that confirms or contradicts the accounting estimate.

Events occurring up to the date of the auditor's report may sometimes provide sufficient appropriate audit evidence about an accounting estimate. For example, sale of the complete inventory of a superseded product shortly after the period end may provide audit evidence relating to the estimate of its net realizable value. In such cases, there may be no need to perform additional audit procedures on the accounting estimate, provided that sufficient appropriate evidence about the events is obtained.  **A63**

For some accounting estimates, events occurring up to the date of the auditor's report are unlikely to provide audit evidence regarding the accounting estimate. For example, the conditions or events relating to some accounting estimates develop only over an extended period. Also, because of the measurement objective of fair value accounting estimates, information after the period-end may not reflect the events or conditions existing at the balance sheet date and therefore may not be relevant to the measurement of the fair value accounting estimate. Paragraph 13 identifies other responses to the risks of material misstatement that the auditor may undertake.  **A64**

In some cases, events that contradict the accounting estimate may indicate that management has ineffective processes for making accounting estimates, or that there is management bias in the making of accounting estimates.  **A65**

Even though the auditor may decide not to undertake this approach in respect of specific accounting estimates, the auditor is required to comply with ISA (UK and Ireland) 560.[16] The auditor is required to perform audit procedures designed to obtain sufficient appropriate audit evidence that all events occurring between the date of the financial statements and the date of the auditor's report that require adjustment of, or disclosure in, the financial statements have been identified[17] and appropriately reflected in the financial statements.[18] Because the measurement of many accounting estimates, other than fair value accounting estimates, usually depends on the outcome of future conditions, transactions or events, the auditor's work under ISA (UK and Ireland) 560 is particularly relevant.  **A66**

[16] ISA (UK and Ireland) 560, "Subsequent Events."

[17] ISA (UK and Ireland) 560, paragraph 6.

[18] ISA (UK and Ireland) 560, paragraph 7.

*Considerations specific to smaller entities*

**A67**   When there is a longer period between the balance sheet date and the date of the auditor's report, the auditor's review of events in this period may be an effective response for accounting estimates other than fair value accounting estimates. This may particularly be the case in some smaller owner-managed entities, especially when management does not have formalized control procedures over accounting estimates.

*Testing How Management Made the Accounting Estimate (Ref: Para. 13(b))*

**A68**   Testing how management made the accounting estimate and the data on which it is based may be an appropriate response when the accounting estimate is a fair value accounting estimate developed on a model that uses observable and unobservable inputs. It may also be appropriate when, for example:

- The accounting estimate is derived from the routine processing of data by the entity's accounting system.
- The auditor's review of similar accounting estimates made in the prior period financial statements suggests that management's current period process is likely to be effective.
- The accounting estimate is based on a large population of items of a similar nature that individually are not significant.

**A69**   Testing how management made the accounting estimate may involve, for example:

- Testing the extent to which data on which the accounting estimate is based is accurate, complete and relevant, and whether the accounting estimate has been properly determined using such data and management assumptions.
- Considering the source, relevance and reliability of external data or information, including that received from external experts engaged by management to assist in making an accounting estimate.
- Recalculating the accounting estimate, and reviewing information about an accounting estimate for internal consistency.
- Considering management's review and approval processes.

*Considerations specific to smaller entities*

**A70**   In smaller entities, the process for making accounting estimates is likely to be less structured than in larger entities. Smaller entities with active management involvement may not have extensive descriptions of accounting procedures, sophisticated accounting records, or written policies. Even if the entity has no formal established process, it does not mean that management is not able to provide a basis upon which the auditor can test the accounting estimate.

*Evaluating the method of measurement (Ref: Para. 13(b)(i))*

**A71**   When the applicable financial reporting framework does not prescribe the method of measurement, evaluating whether the method used, including any applicable model, is appropriate in the circumstances is a matter of professional judgment.

**A72**   For this purpose, matters that the auditor may consider include, for example, whether:

- Management's rationale for the method selected is reasonable.

- Management has sufficiently evaluated and appropriately applied the criteria, if any, provided in the applicable financial reporting framework to support the selected method.
- The method is appropriate in the circumstances given the nature of the asset or liability being estimated and the requirements of the applicable financial reporting framework relevant to accounting estimates.
- The method is appropriate in relation to the business, industry and environment in which the entity operates.

In some cases, management may have determined that different methods result in a range of significantly different estimates. In such cases, obtaining an understanding of how the entity has investigated the reasons for these differences may assist the auditor in evaluating the appropriateness of the method selected. **A73**

*Evaluating the use of models*

In some cases, particularly when making fair value accounting estimates, management may use a model. Whether the model used is appropriate in the circumstances may depend on a number of factors, such as the nature of the entity and its environment, including the industry in which it operates, and the specific asset or liability being measured. **A74**

The extent to which the following considerations are relevant depends on the circumstances, including whether the model is one that is commercially available for use in a particular sector or industry, or a proprietary model. In some cases, an entity may use an expert to develop and test a model. **A75**

Depending on the circumstances, matters that the auditor may also consider in testing the model include, for example, whether: **A76**

- The model is validated prior to usage, with periodic reviews to ensure it is still suitable for its intended use. The entity's validation process may include evaluation of:
  - The model's theoretical soundness and mathematical integrity, including the appropriateness of model parameters.
  - The consistency and completeness of the model's inputs with market practices.
  - The model's output as compared to actual transactions.
- Appropriate change control policies and procedures exist.
- The model is periodically calibrated and tested for validity, particularly when inputs are subjective.
- Adjustments are made to the output of the model, including in the case of fair value accounting estimates, whether such adjustments reflect the assumptions marketplace participants would use in similar circumstances.
- The model is adequately documented, including the model's intended applications and limitations and its key parameters, required inputs, and results of any validation analysis performed.

*Assumptions used by management (Ref: Para. 13(b)(ii))*

The auditor's evaluation of the assumptions used by management is based only on information available to the auditor at the time of the audit. Audit procedures dealing with management assumptions are performed in the context of the audit of the entity's financial statements, and not for the purpose of providing an opinion on assumptions themselves. **A77**

**A78**   Matters that the auditor may consider in evaluating the reasonableness of the assumptions used by management include, for example:

- Whether individual assumptions appear reasonable.
- Whether the assumptions are interdependent and internally consistent.
- Whether the assumptions appear reasonable when considered collectively or in conjunction with other assumptions, either for that accounting estimate or for other accounting estimates.
- In the case of fair value accounting estimates, whether the assumptions appropriately reflect observable marketplace assumptions.

**A79**   The assumptions on which accounting estimates are based may reflect what management expects will be the outcome of specific objectives and strategies. In such cases, the auditor may perform audit procedures to evaluate the reasonableness of such assumptions by considering, for example, whether the assumptions are consistent with:

- The general economic environment and the entity's economic circumstances.
- The plans of the entity.
- Assumptions made in prior periods, if relevant.
- Experience of, or previous conditions experienced by, the entity, to the extent this historical information may be considered representative of future conditions or events.
- Other assumptions used by management relating to the financial statements.

**A80**   The reasonableness of the assumptions used may depend on management's intent and ability to carry out certain courses of action. Management often documents plans and intentions relevant to specific assets or liabilities and the financial reporting framework may require it to do so. Although the extent of audit evidence to be obtained about management's intent and ability is a matter of professional judgment, the auditor's procedures may include the following:

- Review of management's history of carrying out its stated intentions.
- Review of written plans and other documentation, including, where applicable, formally approved budgets, authorizations or minutes.
- Inquiry of management about its reasons for a particular course of action.
- Review of events occurring subsequent to the date of the financial statements and up to the date of the auditor's report.
- Evaluation of the entity's ability to carry out a particular course of action given the entity's economic circumstances, including the implications of its existing commitments.
  Certain financial reporting frameworks, however, may not permit management's intentions or plans to be taken into account when making an accounting estimate. This is often the case for fair value accounting estimates because their measurement objective requires that assumptions reflect those used by marketplace participants.

**A81**   Matters that the auditor may consider in evaluating the reasonableness of assumptions used by management underlying fair value accounting estimates, in addition to those discussed above where applicable, may include, for example:

- Where relevant, whether and, if so, how management has incorporated market-specific inputs into the development of assumptions.
- Whether the assumptions are consistent with observable market conditions, and the characteristics of the asset or liability being measured at fair value.
- Whether the sources of market-participant assumptions are relevant and reliable, and how management has selected the assumptions to use when a number of different market participant assumptions exist.

- Where appropriate, whether and, if so, how management considered assumptions used in, or information about, comparable transactions, assets or liabilities.

Further, fair value accounting estimates may comprise observable inputs as well as unobservable inputs. Where fair value accounting estimates are based on unobservable inputs, matters that the auditor may consider include, for example, how management supports the following: **A82**

- The identification of the characteristics of marketplace participants relevant to the accounting estimate.
- Modifications it has made to its own assumptions to reflect its view of assumptions marketplace participants would use.
- Whether it has incorporated the best information available in the circumstances.
- Where applicable, how its assumptions take account of comparable transactions, assets or liabilities.
  If there are unobservable inputs, it is more likely that the auditor's evaluation of the assumptions will need to be combined with other responses to assessed risks in paragraph 13 in order to obtain sufficient appropriate audit evidence. In such cases, it may be necessary for the auditor to perform other audit procedures, for example, examining documentation supporting the review and approval of the accounting estimate by appropriate levels of management and, where appropriate, by those charged with governance.

In evaluating the reasonableness of the assumptions supporting an accounting estimate, the auditor may identify one or more significant assumptions. If so, it may indicate that the accounting estimate has high estimation uncertainty and may, therefore, give rise to a significant risk. Additional responses to significant risks are described in paragraphs A102-A115. **A83**

*Testing the Operating Effectiveness of Controls (Ref: Para. 13(c))*

Testing the operating effectiveness of the controls over how management made the accounting estimate may be an appropriate response when management's process has been well-designed, implemented and maintained, for example: **A84**

- Controls exist for the review and approval of the accounting estimates by appropriate levels of management and, where appropriate, by those charged with governance.
- The accounting estimate is derived from the routine processing of data by the entity's accounting system.

Testing the operating effectiveness of the controls is required when: **A85**

(a) The auditor's assessment of risks of material misstatement at the assertion level includes an expectation that controls over the process are operating effectively; or

(b) Substantive procedures alone do not provide sufficient appropriate audit evidence at the assertion level.[19]

*Considerations specific to smaller entities*

Controls over the process to make an accounting estimate may exist in smaller entities, but the formality with which they operate varies. Further, smaller entities **A86**

---

[19] *ISA (UK and Ireland) 330, paragraph 8.*

may determine that certain types of controls are not necessary because of active management involvement in the financial reporting process. In the case of very small entities, however, there may not be many controls that the auditor can identify. For this reason, the auditor's response to the assessed risks is likely to be substantive in nature, with the auditor performing one or more of the other responses in paragraph 13.

*Developing a Point Estimate or Range (Ref: Para. 13(d))*

**A87** Developing a point estimate or a range to evaluate management's point estimate may be an appropriate response where, for example:

- An accounting estimate is not derived from the routine processing of data by the accounting system.
- The auditor's review of similar accounting estimates made in the prior period financial statements suggests that management's current period process is unlikely to be effective.
- The entity's controls within and over management's processes for determining accounting estimates are not well designed or properly implemented.
- Events or transactions between the period end and the date of the auditor's report contradict management's point estimate.
- There are alternative sources of relevant data available to the auditor which can be used in making a point estimate or a range.

**A88** Even where the entity's controls are well designed and properly implemented, developing a point estimate or a range may be an effective or efficient response to the assessed risks. In other situations, the auditor may consider this approach as part of determining whether further procedures are necessary and, if so, their nature and extent.

**A89** The approach taken by the auditor in developing either a point estimate or a range may vary based on what is considered most effective in the circumstances. For example, the auditor may initially develop a preliminary point estimate, and then assess its sensitivity to changes in assumptions to ascertain a range with which to evaluate management's point estimate. Alternatively, the auditor may begin by developing a range for purposes of determining, where possible, a point estimate.

**A90** The ability of the auditor to make a point estimate, as opposed to a range, depends on several factors, including the model used, the nature and extent of data available and the estimation uncertainty involved with the accounting estimate. Further, the decision to develop a point estimate or range may be influenced by the applicable financial reporting framework, which may prescribe the point estimate that is to be used after consideration of the alternative outcomes and assumptions, or prescribe a specific measurement method (for example, the use of a discounted probability-weighted expected value).

**A91** The auditor may develop a point estimate or a range in a number of ways, for example, by:

- Using a model, for example, one that is commercially available for use in a particular sector or industry, or a proprietary or auditor-developed model.
- Further developing management's consideration of alternative assumptions or outcomes, for example, by introducing a different set of assumptions.
- Employing or engaging a person with specialized expertise to develop or execute the model, or to provide relevant assumptions.

- Making reference to other comparable conditions, transactions or events, or, where relevant, markets for comparable assets or liabilities.

*Understanding Management's Assumptions or Method (Ref: Para. 13(d)(i))*

When the auditor makes a point estimate or a range and uses assumptions or a method different from those used by management, paragraph 13(d)(i) requires the auditor to obtain a sufficient understanding of the assumptions or method used by management in making the accounting estimate. This understanding provides the auditor with information that may be relevant to the auditor's development of an appropriate point estimate or range. Further, it assists the auditor to understand and evaluate any significant differences from management's point estimate. For example, a difference may arise because the auditor used different, but equally valid, assumptions as compared with those used by management. This may reveal that the accounting estimate is highly sensitive to certain assumptions and therefore subject to high estimation uncertainty, indicating that the accounting estimate may be a significant risk. Alternatively, a difference may arise as a result of a factual error made by management. Depending on the circumstances, the auditor may find it helpful in drawing conclusions to discuss with management the basis for the assumptions used and their validity, and the difference, if any, in the approach taken to making the accounting estimate. **A92**

*Narrowing a Range (Ref: Para. 13(d)(ii))*

When the auditor concludes that it is appropriate to use a range to evaluate the reasonableness of management's point estimate (the auditor's range), paragraph 13(d)(ii) requires that range to encompass all "reasonable outcomes" rather than all possible outcomes. The range cannot be one that comprises all possible outcomes if it is to be useful, as such a range would be too wide to be effective for purposes of the audit. The auditor's range is useful and effective when it is sufficiently narrow to enable the auditor to conclude whether the accounting estimate is misstated. **A93**

Ordinarily, a range that has been narrowed to be equal to or less than performance materiality is adequate for the purposes of evaluating the reasonableness of management's point estimate. However, particularly in certain industries, it may not be possible to narrow the range to below such an amount. This does not necessarily preclude recognition of the accounting estimate. It may indicate, however, that the estimation uncertainty associated with the accounting estimate is such that it gives rise to a significant risk. Additional responses to significant risks are described in paragraphs A102-A115. **A94**

Narrowing the range to a position where all outcomes within the range are considered reasonable may be achieved by: **A95**

(a) Eliminating from the range those outcomes at the extremities of the range judged by the auditor to be unlikely to occur; and

(b) Continuing to narrow the range, based on audit evidence available, until the auditor concludes that all outcomes within the range are considered reasonable. In some rare cases, the auditor may be able to narrow the range until the audit evidence indicates a point estimate.

**Considering whether Specialized Skills or Knowledge Are Required** (Ref: Para. 14)

A96 In planning the audit, the auditor is required to ascertain the nature, timing and extent of resources necessary to perform the audit engagement.[20] This may include, as necessary, the involvement of those with specialized skills or knowledge. In addition, ISA (UK and Ireland) 220 requires the engagement partner to be satisfied that the engagement team, and any auditor's external experts who are not part of the engagement team, collectively have the appropriate competence and capabilities to perform the audit engagement.[21] During the course of the audit of accounting estimates the auditor may identify, in light of the experience of the auditor and the circumstances of the engagement, the need for specialized skills or knowledge to be applied in relation to one or more aspects of the accounting estimates.

A97 Matters that may affect the auditor's consideration of whether specialized skills or knowledge is required include, for example:

- The nature of the underlying asset, liability or component of equity in a particular business or industry (for example, mineral deposits, agricultural assets, complex financial instruments).
- A high degree of estimation uncertainty.
- Complex calculations or specialized models are involved, for example, when estimating fair values when there is no observable market.
- The complexity of the requirements of the applicable financial reporting framework relevant to accounting estimates, including whether there are areas known to be subject to differing interpretation or practice is inconsistent or developing.
- The procedures the auditor intends to undertake in responding to assessed risks.

A98 For the majority of accounting estimates, even when there is estimation uncertainty, it is unlikely that specialized skills or knowledge will be required. For example, it is unlikely that specialized skills or knowledge would be necessary for an auditor to evaluate an allowance for doubtful accounts.

A99 However, the auditor may not possess the specialized skills or knowledge required when the matter involved is in a field other than accounting or auditing and may need to obtain it from an auditor's expert. ISA (UK and Ireland) 620[22] establishes requirements and provides guidance in determining the need to employ or engage an auditor's expert and the auditor's responsibilities when using the work of an auditor's expert.

A100 Further, in some cases, the auditor may conclude that it is necessary to obtain specialized skills or knowledge related to specific areas of accounting or auditing. Individuals with such skills or knowledge may be employed by the auditor's firm or engaged from an external organization outside of the auditor's firm. Where such individuals perform audit procedures on the engagement, they are part of the engagement team and accordingly, they are subject to the requirements in ISA (UK and Ireland) 220.

A101 Depending on the auditor's understanding and experience of working with the auditor's expert or those other individuals with specialized skills or knowledge, the auditor may consider it appropriate to discuss matters such as the requirements of

---

[20] *ISA (UK and Ireland) 300, "Planning an Audit of Financial Statements," paragraph 8(e).*

[21] *ISA (UK and Ireland) 220, "Quality Control for an Audit of Financial Statements," paragraph 14.*

[22] *ISA (UK and Ireland) 620, "Using the Work of an Auditor's Expert."*

the applicable financial reporting framework with the individuals involved to establish that their work is relevant for audit purposes.

**Further Substantive Procedures to Respond to Significant Risks** (Ref: Para. 15)

In auditing accounting estimates that give rise to significant risks, the auditor's further substantive procedures are focused on the evaluation of: **A102**

(a) How management has assessed the effect of estimation uncertainty on the accounting estimate, and the effect such uncertainty may have on the appropriateness of the recognition of the accounting estimate in the financial statements; and
(b) The adequacy of related disclosures.

*Estimation Uncertainty*

*Management's Consideration of Estimation Uncertainty (Ref: Para. 15(a))*

Management may evaluate alternative assumptions or outcomes of the accounting estimates through a number of methods, depending on the circumstances. One possible method used by management is to undertake a sensitivity analysis. This might involve determining how the monetary amount of an accounting estimate varies with different assumptions. Even for accounting estimates measured at fair value there can be variation because different market participants will use different assumptions. A sensitivity analysis could lead to the development of a number of outcome scenarios, sometimes characterized as a range of outcomes by management, such as "pessimistic" and "optimistic" scenarios. **A103**

A sensitivity analysis may demonstrate that an accounting estimate is not sensitive to changes in particular assumptions. Alternatively, it may demonstrate that the accounting estimate is sensitive to one or more assumptions that then become the focus of the auditor's attention. **A104**

This is not intended to suggest that one particular method of addressing estimation uncertainty (such as sensitivity analysis) is more suitable than another, or that management's consideration of alternative assumptions or outcomes needs to be conducted through a detailed process supported by extensive documentation. Rather, it is whether management has assessed how estimation uncertainty may affect the accounting estimate that is important, not the specific manner in which it is done. Accordingly, where management has not considered alternative assumptions or outcomes, it may be necessary for the auditor to discuss with management, and request support for, how it has addressed the effects of estimation uncertainty on the accounting estimate. **A105**

*Considerations specific to smaller entities*

Smaller entities may use simple means to assess the estimation uncertainty. In addition to the auditor's review of available documentation, the auditor may obtain other audit evidence of management consideration of alternative assumptions or outcomes by inquiry of management. In addition, management may not have the expertise to consider alternative outcomes or otherwise address the estimation uncertainty of the accounting estimate. In such cases, the auditor may explain to management the process or the different methods available for doing so, and the **A106** documentation thereof. This would not, however, change the responsibilities of management[3a] for the preparation of the financial statements.

*Significant Assumptions (Ref: Para. 15(b))*

A107    An assumption used in making an accounting estimate may be deemed to be significant if a reasonable variation in the assumption would materially affect the measurement of the accounting estimate.

A108    Support for significant assumptions derived from management's knowledge may be obtained from management's continuing processes of strategic analysis and risk management. Even without formal established processes, such as may be the case in smaller entities, the auditor may be able to evaluate the assumptions through inquiries of and discussions with management, along with other audit procedures in order to obtain sufficient appropriate audit evidence.

A109    The auditor's considerations in evaluating assumptions made by management are described in paragraphs A77-A83.

*Management Intent and Ability (Ref: Para. 15(c))*

A110    The auditor's considerations in relation to assumptions made by management and management's intent and ability are described in paragraphs A13 and A80.

**Development of a Range** (Ref: Para. 16)

A111    In preparing the financial statements, management may be satisfied that it has adequately addressed the effects of estimation uncertainty on the accounting estimates that give rise to significant risks. In some circumstances, however, the auditor may view the efforts of management as inadequate. This may be the case, for example, where, in the auditor's judgment:

- Sufficient appropriate audit evidence could not be obtained through the auditor's evaluation of how management has addressed the effects of estimation uncertainty.
- It is necessary to explore further the degree of estimation uncertainty associated with an accounting estimate, for example, where the auditor is aware of wide variation in outcomes for similar accounting estimates in similar circumstances.
- It is unlikely that other audit evidence can be obtained, for example, through the review of events occurring up to the date of the auditor's report.
- Indicators of management bias in the making of accounting estimates may exist.

A112    The auditor's considerations in determining a range for this purpose are described in paragraphs A87-A95.

**Recognition and Measurement Criteria**

*Recognition of the Accounting Estimates in the Financial Statements (Ref: Para. 17(a))*

A113    Where management[3a] has recognized an accounting estimate in the financial statements, the focus of the auditor's evaluation is on whether the measurement of the accounting estimate is sufficiently reliable to meet the recognition criteria of the applicable financial reporting framework.

With respect to accounting estimates that have not been recognized, the focus of the **A114** auditor's evaluation is on whether the recognition criteria of the applicable financial reporting framework have in fact been met. Even where an accounting estimate has not been recognized, and the auditor concludes that this treatment is appropriate, there may be a need for disclosure of the circumstances in the notes to the financial statements. The auditor may also determine that there is a need to draw the reader's attention to a significant uncertainty by adding an Emphasis of Matter paragraph to the auditor's report. ISA (UK and Ireland) 706[23] establishes requirements and provides guidance concerning such paragraphs.

*Measurement Basis for the Accounting Estimates (Ref: Para. 17(b))*

With respect to fair value accounting estimates, some financial reporting frameworks **A115** presume that fair value can be measured reliably as a prerequisite to either requiring or permitting fair value measurements and disclosures. In some cases, this presumption may be overcome when, for example, there is no appropriate method or basis for measurement. In such cases, the focus of the auditor's evaluation is on whether management's basis for overcoming the presumption relating to the use of fair value set forth under the applicable financial reporting framework is appropriate.

**Evaluating the Reasonableness of the Accounting Estimates, and Determining Misstatements** (Ref: Para. 18)

Based on the audit evidence obtained, the auditor may conclude that the evidence **A116** points to an accounting estimate that differs from management's point estimate. Where the audit evidence supports a point estimate, the difference between the auditor's point estimate and management's point estimate constitutes a misstatement. Where the auditor has concluded that using the auditor's range provides sufficient appropriate audit evidence, a management point estimate that lies outside the auditor's range would not be supported by audit evidence. In such cases, the misstatement is no less than the difference between management's point estimate and the nearest point of the auditor's range.

Where management has changed an accounting estimate, or the method in making it, **A117** from the prior period based on a subjective assessment that there has been a change in circumstances, the auditor may conclude based on the audit evidence that the accounting estimate is misstated as a result of an arbitrary change by management, or may regard it as an indicator of possible management bias (see paragraphs A124-A125).

ISA (UK and Ireland) 450[24] provides guidance on distinguishing misstatements for **A118** purposes of the auditor's evaluation of the effect of uncorrected misstatements on the financial statements. In relation to accounting estimates, a misstatement, whether caused by fraud or error, may arise as a result of:

- Misstatements about which there is no doubt (factual misstatements).
- Differences arising from management's judgments concerning accounting estimates that the auditor considers unreasonable, or the selection or application of

---

[23] *ISA (UK and Ireland) 706, "Emphasis of Matter Paragraphs and Other Matter Paragraphs in the Independent Auditor's Report."*

[24] *ISA (UK and Ireland) 450, "Evaluation of Misstatements Identified during the Audit."*

accounting policies that the auditor considers inappropriate (judgmental misstatements).

- The auditor's best estimate of misstatements in populations, involving the projection of misstatements identified in audit samples to the entire populations from which the samples were drawn (projected misstatements).

  In some cases involving accounting estimates, a misstatement could arise as a result of a combination of these circumstances, making separate identification difficult or impossible.

A119   Evaluating the reasonableness of accounting estimates and related disclosures included in the notes to the financial statements, whether required by the applicable financial reporting framework or disclosed voluntarily, involves essentially the same types of considerations applied when auditing an accounting estimate recognized in the financial statements.

## Disclosures Related to Accounting Estimates

*Disclosures in Accordance with the Applicable Financial Reporting Framework* (Ref: Para. 19)

A120   The presentation of financial statements in accordance with the applicable financial reporting framework includes adequate disclosure of material matters. The applicable financial reporting framework may permit, or prescribe, disclosures related to accounting estimates, and some entities may disclose voluntarily additional information in the notes to the financial statements. These disclosures may include, for example:

- The assumptions used.
- The method of estimation used, including any applicable model.
- The basis for the selection of the method of estimation.
- The effect of any changes to the method of estimation from the prior period.
- The sources and implications of estimation uncertainty.

  Such disclosures are relevant to users in understanding the accounting estimates recognized or disclosed in the financial statements, and sufficient appropriate audit evidence needs to be obtained about whether the disclosures are in accordance with the requirements of the applicable financial reporting framework.

A121   In some cases, the applicable financial reporting framework may require specific disclosures regarding uncertainties. For example, some financial reporting frameworks prescribe:

- The disclosure of key assumptions and other sources of estimation uncertainty that have a significant risk of causing a material adjustment to the carrying amounts of assets and liabilities. Such requirements may be described using terms such as "Key Sources of Estimation Uncertainty" or "Critical Accounting Estimates."
- The disclosure of the range of possible outcomes, and the assumptions used in determining the range.
- The disclosure of information regarding the significance of fair value accounting estimates to the entity's financial position and performance.
- Qualitative disclosures such as the exposures to risk and how they arise, the entity's objectives, policies and procedures for managing the risk and the methods used to measure the risk and any changes from the previous period of these qualitative concepts.

- Quantitative disclosures such as the extent to which the entity is exposed to risk, based on information provided internally to the entity's key management personnel, including credit risk, liquidity risk and market risk.

***Disclosures of Estimation Uncertainty for Accounting Estimates that Give Rise to Significant Risks*** (Ref: Para. 20)

In relation to accounting estimates having significant risk, even where the disclosures are in accordance with the applicable financial reporting framework, the auditor may conclude that the disclosure of estimation uncertainty is inadequate in light of the circumstances and facts involved. The auditor's evaluation of the adequacy of disclosure of estimation uncertainty increases in importance the greater the range of possible outcomes of the accounting estimate is in relation to materiality (see related discussion in paragraph A94).      **A122**

In some cases, the auditor may consider it appropriate to encourage management[3a] to describe, in the notes to the financial statements, the circumstances relating to the estimation uncertainty. ISA (UK and Ireland) 705[25] provides guidance on the implications for the auditor's opinion when the auditor believes that management's disclosure of estimation uncertainty in the financial statements is inadequate or misleading.      **A123**

## Indicators of Possible Management Bias (Ref: Para. 21)

During the audit, the auditor may become aware of judgments and decisions made by management which give rise to indicators of possible management bias. Such indicators may affect the auditor's conclusion as to whether the auditor's risk assessment and related responses remain appropriate, and the auditor may need to consider the implications for the rest of the audit. Further, they may affect the auditor's evaluation of whether the financial statements as a whole are free from material misstatement, as discussed in ISA (UK and Ireland) 700.[26]      **A124**

Examples of indicators of possible management bias with respect to accounting estimates include:      **A125**

- Changes in an accounting estimate, or the method for making it, where management has made a subjective assessment that there has been a change in circumstances.
- Use of an entity's own assumptions for fair value accounting estimates when they are inconsistent with observable marketplace assumptions.
- Selection or construction of significant assumptions that yield a point estimate favorable for management objectives.
- Selection of a point estimate that may indicate a pattern of optimism or pessimism.

---

[25] *ISA (UK and Ireland) 705, "Modifications to the Opinion in the Independent Auditor's Report."*

[26] *ISA 700, "Forming an Opinion and Reporting on Financial Statements."*
*The APB has not promulgated ISA 700 as issued by the IAASB for application in the UK and Ireland. In the UK and Ireland the applicable auditing standard is ISA (UK and Ireland) 700, "The Auditor's Report on Financial Statements." Paragraph 8 of ISA (UK and Ireland) requires the auditor's evaluation of whether uncorrected misstatements are material. This evaluation is required to include consideration of possible indicators of management bias.*

**Written Representations** (Ref: Para. 22)

A126    ISA (UK and Ireland) 580[27] discusses the use of written representations. Depending on the nature, materiality and extent of estimation uncertainty, written representations about accounting estimates recognized or disclosed in the financial statements may include representations:

- About the appropriateness of the measurement processes, including related assumptions and models, used by management in determining accounting estimates in the context of the applicable financial reporting framework, and the consistency in application of the processes.
- That the assumptions appropriately reflect management's intent and ability to carry out specific courses of action on behalf of the entity, where relevant to the accounting estimates and disclosures.
- That disclosures related to accounting estimates are complete and appropriate under the applicable financial reporting framework.
- That no subsequent event requires adjustment to the accounting estimates and disclosures included in the financial statements.

A127    For those accounting estimates not recognized or disclosed in the financial statements, written representations may also include representations about:

- The appropriateness of the basis used by management for determining that the recognition or disclosure criteria of the applicable financial reporting framework have not been met (see paragraph A114).
- The appropriateness of the basis used by management to overcome the presumption relating to the use of fair value set forth under the entity's applicable financial reporting framework, for those accounting estimates not measured or disclosed at fair value (see paragraph A115).

**Documentation** (Ref: Para. 23)

A128    Documentation of indicators of possible management bias identified during the audit assists the auditor in concluding whether the auditor's risk assessment and related responses remain appropriate, and in evaluating whether the financial statements as a whole are free from material misstatement. See paragraph A125 for examples of indicators of possible management bias.

[27] *ISA (UK and Ireland) 580, "Written Representations."*

# **Appendix** (Ref: Para. A1)

## Fair Value Measurements and Disclosures under Different Financial Reporting Frameworks

The purpose of this appendix is only to provide a general discussion of fair value measurements and disclosures under different financial reporting frameworks, for background and context.

Different financial reporting frameworks require or permit a variety of fair value measurements and disclosures in financial statements. They also vary in the level of guidance that they provide on the basis for measuring assets and liabilities or the related disclosures. Some financial reporting frameworks give prescriptive guidance, others give general guidance, and some give no guidance at all. In addition, certain industry-specific measurement and disclosure practices for fair values also exist. **1**

In the UK and Ireland , specific accounting and disclosure requirements for fair value measurements and disclosures are established in accounting standards and in law and regulations. **1-1**

Definitions of fair value may differ among financial reporting frameworks, or for different assets, liabilities or disclosures within a particular framework. For example, International Accounting Standard (IAS) 39[28] defines fair value as "the amount for which an asset could be exchanged, or a liability settled, between knowledgeable, willing parties in an arm's length transaction." The concept of fair value ordinarily assumes a current transaction, rather than settlement at some past or future date. Accordingly, the process of measuring fair value would be a search for the estimated price at which that transaction would occur. Additionally, different financial reporting frameworks may use such terms as "entity-specific value," "value in use," or similar terms, but may still fall within the concept of fair value in this ISA (UK and Ireland). **2**

Financial reporting frameworks may treat changes in fair value measurements that occur over time in different ways. For example, a particular financial reporting framework may require that changes in fair value measurements of certain assets or liabilities be reflected directly in equity, while such changes might be reflected in income under another framework. In some frameworks, the determination of whether to use fair value accounting or how it is applied is influenced by management's intent to carry out certain courses of action with respect to the specific asset or liability. **3**

Different financial reporting frameworks may require certain specific fair value measurements and disclosures in financial statements and prescribe or permit them in varying degrees. The financial reporting frameworks may: **4**

- Prescribe measurement, presentation and disclosure requirements for certain information included in the financial statements or for information disclosed in notes to financial statements or presented as supplementary information;
- Permit certain measurements using fair values at the option of an entity or only when certain criteria have been met;

---

[28] *IAS 39, "Financial Instruments: Recognition and Measurement."*

- Prescribe a specific method for determining fair value, for example, through the use of an independent appraisal or specified ways of using discounted cash flows;
- Permit a choice of method for determining fair value from among several alternative methods (the criteria for selection may or may not be provided by the financial reporting framework); or
- Provide no guidance on the fair value measurements or disclosures of fair value other than their use being evident through custom or practice, for example, an industry practice.

5   Some financial reporting frameworks presume that fair value can be measured reliably for assets or liabilities as a prerequisite to either requiring or permitting fair value measurements or disclosures. In some cases, this presumption may be overcome when an asset or liability does not have a quoted market price in an active market and for which other methods of reasonably estimating fair value are clearly inappropriate or unworkable. Some financial reporting frameworks may specify a fair value hierarchy that distinguishes inputs for use in arriving at fair values ranging from those that involve clearly "observable inputs" based on quoted prices and active markets and those "unobservable inputs" that involve an entity's own judgments about assumptions that marketplace participants would use.

6   Some financial reporting frameworks require certain specified adjustments or modifications to valuation information, or other considerations unique to a particular asset or liability. For example, accounting for investment properties may require adjustments to be made to an appraised market value, such as adjustments for estimated closing costs on sale, adjustments related to the property's condition and location, and other matters. Similarly, if the market for a particular asset is not an active market, published price quotations may have to be adjusted or modified to arrive at a more suitable measure of fair value. For example, quoted market prices may not be indicative of fair value if there is infrequent activity in the market, the market is not well established, or small volumes of units are traded relative to the aggregate number of trading units in existence. Accordingly, such market prices may have to be adjusted or modified. Alternative sources of market information may be needed to make such adjustments or modifications. Further, in some cases, collateral assigned (for example, when collateral is assigned for certain types of investment in debt) may need to be considered in determining the fair value or possible impairment of an asset or liability.

7   In most financial reporting frameworks, underlying the concept of fair value measurements is a presumption that the entity is a going concern without any intention or need to liquidate, curtail materially the scale of its operations, or undertake a transaction on adverse terms. Therefore, in this case, fair value would not be the amount that an entity would receive or pay in a forced transaction, involuntary liquidation, or distress sale. On the other hand, general economic conditions or economic conditions specific to certain industries may cause illiquidity in the marketplace and require fair values to be predicated upon depressed prices, potentially significantly depressed prices. An entity, however, may need to take its current economic or operating situation into account in determining the fair values of its assets and liabilities if prescribed or permitted to do so by its financial reporting framework and such framework may or may not specify how that is done. For example, management's plan to dispose of an asset on an accelerated basis to meet specific business objectives may be relevant to the determination of the fair value of that asset.

## Prevalence of Fair Value Measurements

Measurements and disclosures based on fair value are becoming increasingly pre- **8**
valent in financial reporting frameworks. Fair values may occur in, and affect the
determination of, financial statements in a number of ways, including the measurement at fair value of the following:

- Specific assets or liabilities, such as marketable securities or liabilities to settle an
  obligation under a financial instrument, routinely or periodically "marked-to-
  market."
- Specific components of equity, for example when accounting for the recognition,
  measurement and presentation of certain financial instruments with equity
  features, such as a bond convertible by the holder into common shares of the
  issuer.
- Specific assets or liabilities acquired in a business combination. For example, the
  initial determination of goodwill arising on the purchase of an entity in a
  business combination usually is based on the fair value measurement of the
  identifiable assets and liabilities acquired and the fair value of the consideration
  given.
- Specific assets or liabilities adjusted to fair value on a one-time basis. Some
  financial reporting frameworks may require the use of a fair value measurement
  to quantify an adjustment to an asset or a group of assets as part of an asset
  impairment determination, for example, a test of impairment of goodwill
  acquired in a business combination based on the fair value of a defined operating entity or reporting unit, the value of which is then allocated among the
  entity's or unit's group of assets and liabilities in order to derive an implied
  goodwill for comparison to the recorded goodwill.
- Aggregations of assets and liabilities. In some circumstances, the measurement
  of a class or group of assets or liabilities calls for an aggregation of fair values of
  some of the individual assets or liabilities in such class or group. For example,
  under an entity's applicable financial reporting framework, the measurement of
  a diversified loan portfolio might be determined based on the fair value of some
  categories of loans comprising the portfolio.
- Information disclosed in notes to financial statements or presented as supplementary information, but not recognized in the financial statements.

# Addendum

*This addendum provides a summary of APB's rationale for retaining or excluding in the proposed clarified ISA (UK and Ireland) the supplementary requirements in the existing ISA (UK and Ireland). It also sets out the supplementary guidance material in the existing ISA (UK and Ireland) that APB considers is not necessary to retain in light of the improvements in the underlying Clarity ISAs issued by the IAASB as part of the Clarity Project. It is provided for information and does not form part of the proposed clarified ISA (UK and Ireland).*

*The Consultation Paper published with the exposure drafts explains the general approach used by the APB for determining whether current supplementary material should be proposed to be retained.*

### Analysis of proposed treatment of current APB supplementary material in current ISAs (UK and Ireland) 540 and 545

It should be noted that ISA 540 has been revised as well as clarified and ISA 545 has been subsumed into it.

### Requirements

There are no supplementary requirements in ISAs (UK and Ireland) 540 and 545.

### Guidance

The following guidance in current versions of ISAs (UK and Ireland) 540 and 545 has not been carried forward to the proposed clarified standard.

### ISA (UK and Ireland) 540

| Current paragraph reference (*Italic text is from IAASB for context*) |
| --- |
| 1-1. – 1-4. [Description of management and those charged with governance] |
| 4-1.  In addition, audit evidence obtained is generally less conclusive when accounting estimates are involved. Consequently, in assessing the sufficiency and appropriateness of audit evidence on which to base the audit opinion, the auditor is more likely to need to exercise judgment when considering accounting estimates than in other areas of the audit. |

## ISA (UK and Ireland) 545

| Current paragraph reference (*Italic text is from IAASB for context*) |
|---|
| 1-1. Many of the examples of accounting principles given in this ISA (UK and Ireland) are based on International Accounting Standards. If other accounting standards are used (e.g. Financial Reporting Standards issued by the UK Accounting Standards Board) the auditor recognizes that, whilst the accounting principles may differ, the audit principles remain the same. |
| 1-2. Paragraph 22 of ISA (UK and Ireland) 315 "Understanding the Entity and its Environment and Assessing the Risks of Material Misstatement" requires that "the auditor should obtain an understanding of ... the applicable financial reporting framework." That understanding includes the requirements of the particular accounting standards that the entity is required or chooses, where a choice is possible, to comply with. The auditor takes that understanding into account when complying with the requirements of this ISA (UK and Ireland). The auditor also takes into account requirements of legislation pertaining to fair value accounting (e.g. Schedule 4 of the UK Companies Act 1985 as amended by "The Companies Act 1985 (International Accounting Standards and Other Accounting Amendments) Regulations 2004". |
| 1-3. – 1-6. [Description of management and those charged with governance as in 200.] |

# Proposed Clarified International Standard on Auditing (UK and Ireland) 550

# Related parties

*(Effective for audits of financial statements for periods ending on or after 15 December 2010)*

## Contents

International Standard on Auditing (UK and Ireland) (ISA (UK and Ireland)) 550, "Related Parties" should be read in conjunction with ISA (UK and Ireland) 200, "Overall Objectives of the Independent Auditor and the Conduct of an Audit in Accordance with International Standards on Auditing (UK and Ireland)."

# Introduction

## Scope of this ISA (UK and Ireland)

1   This International Standard on Auditing (UK and Ireland) (ISA (UK and Ireland)) deals with the auditor's responsibilities relating to related party relationships and transactions in an audit of financial statements. Specifically, it expands on how ISA (UK and Ireland) 315,[1] ISA (UK and Ireland) 330,[2] and ISA (UK and Ireland) 240[3] are to be applied in relation to risks of material misstatement associated with related party relationships and transactions.

## Nature of Related Party Relationships and Transactions

2   Many related party transactions are in the normal course of business. In such circumstances, they may carry no higher risk of material misstatement of the financial statements than similar transactions with unrelated parties. However, the nature of related party relationships and transactions may, in some circumstances, give rise to higher risks of material misstatement of the financial statements than transactions with unrelated parties. For example:

- Related parties may operate through an extensive and complex range of relationships and structures, with a corresponding increase in the complexity of related party transactions.
- Information systems may be ineffective at identifying or summarizing transactions and outstanding balances between an entity and its related parties.
- Related party transactions may not be conducted under normal market terms and conditions; for example, some related party transactions may be conducted with no exchange of consideration.

## Responsibilities of the Auditor

3   Because related parties are not independent of each other, many financial reporting frameworks establish specific accounting and disclosure requirements for related party relationships, transactions and balances to enable users of the financial statements to understand their nature and actual or potential effects on the financial statements. Where the applicable financial reporting framework establishes such requirements[3a], the auditor has a responsibility to perform audit procedures to identify, assess and respond to the risks of material misstatement arising from the entity's failure to appropriately account for or disclose related party relationships, transactions or balances in accordance with the requirements of the framework.

4   Even if the applicable financial reporting framework establishes minimal or no related party requirements, the auditor nevertheless needs to obtain an understanding of the entity's related party relationships and transactions sufficient to be

---

[1] *ISA (UK and Ireland) 315, "Identifying and Assessing the Risks of Material Misstatement through Understanding the Entity and Its Environment."*

[2] *ISA (UK and Ireland) 330, "The Auditor's Responses to Assessed Risks."*

[3] *ISA (UK and Ireland) 240, "The Auditor's Responsibilities Relating to Fraud in an Audit of Financial Statements."*

[3a] *In the UK and Ireland, specific accounting and disclosure requirements for related party relationships, transactions and balances are established in accounting standards and in law and regulations.*

able to conclude whether the financial statements, insofar as they are affected by those relationships and transactions: (Ref: Para. A1)

(a)  Achieve fair presentation (for fair presentation frameworks); or (Ref: Para. A2)
(b)  Are not misleading (for compliance frameworks). (Ref: Para. A3)

In addition, an understanding of the entity's related party relationships and trans-   **5**
actions is relevant to the auditor's evaluation of whether one or more fraud risk
factors are present as required by ISA (UK and Ireland) 240,[4] because fraud may be
more easily committed through related parties.

Owing to the inherent limitations of an audit, there is an unavoidable risk that some   **6**
material misstatements of the financial statements may not be detected, even though
the audit is properly planned and performed in accordance with the ISAs (UK and
Ireland).[5] In the context of related parties, the potential effects of inherent limitations
on the auditor's ability to detect material misstatements are greater for such reasons
as the following:

- Management may be unaware of the existence of all related party relationships and transactions, particularly if the applicable financial reporting framework does not establish related party requirements.
- Related party relationships may present a greater opportunity for collusion, concealment or manipulation by management.

Planning and performing the audit with professional skepticism as required by ISA   **7**
(UK and Ireland) 200[6] is therefore particularly important in this context, given the
potential for undisclosed related party relationships and transactions. The requirements in this ISA (UK and Ireland) are designed to assist the auditor in identifying
and assessing the risks of material misstatement associated with related party relationships and transactions, and in designing audit procedures to respond to the
assessed risks.

## Effective Date

This ISA (UK and Ireland) is effective for audits of financial statements for periods   **8**
ending on or after 15 December 2010.

## Objectives

The objectives of the auditor are:   **9**

(a)  Irrespective of whether the applicable financial reporting framework establishes
related party requirements, to obtain an understanding of related party relationships and transactions sufficient to be able:
   (i)  To recognize fraud risk factors, if any, arising from related party relationships and transactions that are relevant to the identification and
assessment of the risks of material misstatement due to fraud; and

[4] *ISA (UK and Ireland) 240, paragraph 24.*

[5] *ISA (UK and Ireland) 200, "Overall Objectives of the Independent Auditor and the Conduct of an Audit in
Accordance with International Standards on Auditing," paragraph A52.*

[6] *ISA (UK and Ireland) 200, paragraph 15.*

    (ii)  To conclude, based on the audit evidence obtained, whether the financial statements, insofar as they are affected by those relationships and transactions:

        a.   Achieve fair presentation (for fair presentation frameworks); or

        b.   Are not misleading (for compliance frameworks); and

(b)  In addition, where the applicable financial reporting framework establishes related party requirements, to obtain sufficient appropriate audit evidence about whether related party relationships and transactions have been appropriately identified, accounted for and disclosed in the financial statements in accordance with the framework.

## Definitions

**10**    For purposes of the ISAs (UK and Ireland), the following terms have the meanings attributed below:

(a)  Arm's length transaction – A transaction conducted on such terms and conditions as between a willing buyer and a willing seller who are unrelated and are acting independently of each other and pursuing their own best interests.

(b)  Related party – A party that is either: (Ref: Para. A4-A7)

    (i)   A related party as defined in the applicable financial reporting framework; or

    (ii)  Where the applicable financial reporting framework establishes minimal or no related party requirements:

        a.   A person or other entity that has control or significant influence, directly or indirectly through one or more intermediaries, over the reporting entity;

        b.   Another entity over which the reporting entity has control or significant influence, directly or indirectly through one or more intermediaries; or

        c.   Another entity that is under common control with the reporting entity through having:

            i.   Common controlling ownership;

            ii.   Owners who are close family members; or

            iii.  Common key management.

            However, entities that are under common control by a state (i.e., a national, regional or local government) are not considered related unless they engage in significant transactions or share resources to a significant extent with one another.

## Requirements

**Risk Assessment Procedures and Related Activities**

**11**    As part of the risk assessment procedures and related activities that ISA (UK and Ireland) 315 and ISA (UK and Ireland) 240 require the auditor to perform during the audit,[7] the auditor shall perform the audit procedures and related activities set out in paragraphs 12-17 to obtain information relevant to identifying the risks of material misstatement associated with related party relationships and transactions. (Ref: Para. A8)

---

[7] *ISA (UK and Ireland) 315, paragraph 5; and ISA 240, paragraph 16.*

## Understanding the Entity's Related Party Relationships and Transactions

The engagement team discussion that ISA (UK and Ireland) 315 and ISA (UK and Ireland) 240 require[8] shall include specific consideration of the susceptibility of the financial statements to material misstatement due to fraud or error that could result from the entity's related party relationships and transactions. (Ref: Para. A9-A10)    **12**

The auditor shall inquire of management regarding:    **13**

(a)  The identity of the entity's related parties, including changes from the prior period; (Ref: Para. A11-A14)
(b)  The nature of the relationships between the entity and these related parties; and
(c)  Whether the entity entered into any transactions with these related parties during the period and, if so, the type and purpose of the transactions.

The auditor shall inquire of management and others within the entity, and perform other risk assessment procedures considered appropriate, to obtain an understanding of the controls, if any, that management has established to: (Ref: Para. A15-A20)    **14**

(a)  Identify, account for, and disclose related party relationships and transactions in accordance with the applicable financial reporting framework;
(b)  Authorize and approve significant transactions and arrangements with related parties; and (Ref: Para. A21)
(c)  Authorize and approve significant transactions and arrangements outside the normal course of business.

## Maintaining Alertness for Related Party Information When Reviewing Records or Documents

During the audit, the auditor shall remain alert, when inspecting records or documents, for arrangements or other information that may indicate the existence of related party relationships or transactions that management has not previously identified or disclosed to the auditor. (Ref: Para. A22-A23)    **15**

In particular, the auditor shall inspect the following for indications of the existence of related party relationships or transactions that management has not previously identified or disclosed to the auditor:

(a)  Bank and legal confirmations obtained as part of the auditor's procedures;
(b)  Minutes of meetings of shareholders and of those charged with governance; and
(c)  Such other records or documents as the auditor considers necessary in the circumstances of the entity.

If the auditor identifies significant transactions outside the entity's normal course of business when performing the audit procedures required by paragraph 15 or through other audit procedures, the auditor shall inquire of management about: (Ref: Para. A24-A25)    **16**

(a)  The nature of these transactions; and (Ref: Para. A26)
(b)  Whether related parties could be involved. (Ref: Para. A27)

## Sharing Related Party Information with the Engagement Team

The auditor shall share relevant information obtained about the entity's related parties with the other members of the engagement team. (Ref: Para. A28)    **17**

---

[8] *ISA (UK and Ireland) 315, paragraph 10; and ISA 240, paragraph 15.*

**Identification and Assessment of the Risks of Material Misstatement Associated with Related Party Relationships and Transactions**

18    In meeting the ISA (UK and Ireland) 315 requirement to identify and assess the risks of material misstatement,[9] the auditor shall identify and assess the risks of material misstatement associated with related party relationships and transactions and determine whether any of those risks are significant risks. In making this determination, the auditor shall treat identified significant related party transactions outside the entity's normal course of business as giving rise to significant risks.

19    If the auditor identifies fraud risk factors (including circumstances relating to the existence of a related party with dominant influence) when performing the risk assessment procedures and related activities in connection with related parties, the auditor shall consider such information when identifying and assessing the risks of material misstatement due to fraud in accordance with ISA (UK and Ireland) 240. (Ref: Para. A6 and A29-A30)

**Responses to the Risks of Material Misstatement Associated with Related Party Relationships and Transactions**

20    As part of the ISA (UK and Ireland) 330 requirement that the auditor respond to assessed risks,[10] the auditor designs and performs further audit procedures to obtain sufficient appropriate audit evidence about the assessed risks of material misstatement associated with related party relationships and transactions. These audit procedures shall include those required by paragraphs 21-24. (Ref: Para. A31-A34)

*Identification of Previously Unidentified or Undisclosed Related Parties or Significant Related Party Transactions*

21    If the auditor identifies arrangements or information that suggests the existence of related party relationships or transactions that management has not previously identified or disclosed to the auditor, the auditor shall determine whether the underlying circumstances confirm the existence of those relationships or transactions.

22    If the auditor identifies related parties or significant related party transactions that management has not previously identified or disclosed to the auditor, the auditor shall:

    (a)  Promptly communicate the relevant information to the other members of the engagement team; (Ref: Para. A35)

    (b)  Where the applicable financial reporting framework establishes related party requirements:

        (i)   Request management to identify all transactions with the newly identified related parties for the auditor's further evaluation; and

        (ii)  Inquire as to why the entity's controls over related party relationships and transactions failed to enable the identification or disclosure of the related party relationships or transactions;

    (c)  Perform appropriate substantive audit procedures relating to such newly identified related parties or significant related party transactions; (Ref: Para. A36)

---

[9] *ISA (UK and Ireland) 315, paragraph 25.*

[10] *ISA (UK and Ireland) 330, paragraphs 5-6.*

(d) Reconsider the risk that other related parties or significant related party transactions may exist that management has not previously identified or disclosed to the auditor, and perform additional audit procedures as necessary; and

(e) If the non-disclosure by management appears intentional (and therefore indicative of a risk of material misstatement due to fraud), evaluate the implications for the audit. (Ref: Para. A37)

## *Identified Significant Related Party Transactions outside the Entity's Normal Course of Business*

For identified significant related party transactions outside the entity's normal course of business, the auditor shall: **23**

(a) Inspect the underlying contracts or agreements, if any, and evaluate whether:
  (i) The business rationale (or lack thereof) of the transactions suggests that they may have been entered into to engage in fraudulent financial reporting or to conceal misappropriation of assets;[11] (Ref: Para. A38-A39)
  (ii) The terms of the transactions are consistent with management's explanations; and
  (iii) The transactions have been appropriately accounted for and disclosed in accordance with the applicable financial reporting framework; and

(b) Obtain audit evidence that the transactions have been appropriately authorized and approved. (Ref: Para. A40-A41)

## *Assertions That Related Party Transactions Were Conducted on Terms Equivalent to Those Prevailing in an Arm's Length Transaction*

If management has made an assertion in the financial statements to the effect that a related party transaction was conducted on terms equivalent to those prevailing in an arm's length transaction, the auditor shall obtain sufficient appropriate audit evidence about the assertion. (Ref: Para. A42-A45) **24**

## Evaluation of the Accounting for and Disclosure of Identified Related Party Relationships and Transactions

In forming an opinion on the financial statements in accordance with ISA (UK and Ireland) 700,[12] the auditor shall evaluate: (Ref: Para. A46) **25**

(a) Whether the identified related party relationships and transactions have been appropriately accounted for and disclosed in accordance with the applicable financial reporting framework; and (Ref: Para. A47 – A7-1)

(b) Whether the effects of the related party relationships and transactions:
  (i) Prevent the financial statements from achieving fair presentation (for fair presentation frameworks); or
  (ii) Cause the financial statements to be misleading (for compliance frameworks).

---

[11] *ISA (UK and Ireland) 240, paragraph 32(c).*

[12] *ISA 700, "Forming an Opinion and Reporting on Financial Statements," paragraphs 10-15.*
*The APB has not promulgated ISA 700 as issued by the IAASB for application in the UK and Ireland. In the UK and Ireland the applicable auditing standard is ISA (UK and Ireland) 700, "The Auditor's Report on Financial Statements." Paragraphs 8 – 11 of ISA (UK and Ireland) 700 establish requirements regarding forming an opinion on the financial statements.*

### Written Representations

26   Where the applicable financial reporting framework establishes related party requirements, the auditor shall obtain written representations from management and, where appropriate, those charged with governance that: (Ref: Para. A48-A49)

(a)   They have disclosed to the auditor the identity of the entity's related parties and all the related party relationships and transactions of which they are aware; and

(b)   They have appropriately accounted for and disclosed such relationships and transactions in accordance with the requirements of the framework.

### Communication with Those Charged with Governance

27   Unless all of those charged with governance are involved in managing the entity,[13] the auditor shall communicate with those charged with governance significant matters arising during the audit in connection with the entity's related parties. (Ref: Para. A50)

### Documentation

28   The auditor shall include in the audit documentation the names of the identified related parties and the nature of the related party relationships.[14]

\*\*\*

# Application and Other Explanatory Material

## Responsibilities of the Auditor

***Financial Reporting Frameworks That Establish Minimal Related Party Requirements*** (Ref: Para. 4)

A1   An applicable financial reporting framework that establishes minimal related party requirements is one that defines the meaning of a related party but that definition has a substantially narrower scope than the definition set out in paragraph 10(b)(ii) of this ISA (UK and Ireland), so that a requirement in the framework to disclose related party relationships and transactions would apply to substantially fewer related party relationships and transactions.

***Fair Presentation Frameworks*** (Ref: Para. 4(a))

A2   In the context of a fair presentation framework,[15] related party relationships and transactions may cause the financial statements to fail to achieve fair presentation if, for example, the economic reality of such relationships and transactions is not appropriately reflected in the financial statements. For instance, fair presentation may not be achieved if the sale of a property by the entity to a controlling shareholder at a price above or below fair market value has been accounted for as a

---

[13] *ISA (UK and Ireland) 260, "Communication with Those Charged with Governance," paragraph 13.*

[14] *ISA (UK and Ireland) 230, "Audit Documentation," paragraphs 8-11, and paragraph A6.*

[15] *ISA 200, paragraph 13(a), defines the meaning of fair presentation and compliance frameworks.*

transaction involving a profit or loss for the entity when it may constitute a contribution or return of capital or the payment of a dividend.

**Compliance Frameworks** (Ref: Para. 4(b))

In the context of a compliance framework, whether related party relationships and transactions cause the financial statements to be misleading as discussed in ISA (UK and Ireland) 700 depends upon the particular circumstances of the engagement. For example, even if non-disclosure of related party transactions in the financial statements is in compliance with the framework and applicable law or regulation, the financial statements could be misleading if the entity derives a very substantial portion of its revenue from transactions with related parties, and that fact is not disclosed. However, it will be extremely rare for the auditor to consider financial statements that are prepared and presented in accordance with a compliance framework to be misleading if in accordance with ISA (UK and Ireland) 210[16] the auditor determined that the framework is acceptable.[17]

**A3**

## Definition of a Related Party (Ref: Para. 10(b))

Many financial reporting frameworks discuss the concepts of control and significant influence. Although they may discuss these concepts using different terms, they generally explain that:

**A4**

(a)  Control is the power to govern the financial and operating policies of an entity so as to obtain benefits from its activities; and

(b)  Significant influence (which may be gained by share ownership, statute or agreement) is the power to participate in the financial and operating policy decisions of an entity, but is not control over those policies.

The existence of the following relationships may indicate the presence of control or significant influence:

**A5**

(a)  Direct or indirect equity holdings or other financial interests in the entity.

(b)  The entity's holdings of direct or indirect equity or other financial interests in other entities.

(c)  Being part of those charged with governance or key management (i.e., those members of management who have the authority and responsibility for planning, directing and controlling the activities of the entity).

(d)  Being a close family member of any person referred to in subparagraph (c).

(e)  Having a significant business relationship with any person referred to in subparagraph (c).

### Related Parties with Dominant Influence

Related parties, by virtue of their ability to exert control or significant influence, may be in a position to exert dominant influence over the entity or its management.

**A6**

---

[16] *ISA (UK and Ireland) 210, "Agreeing the Terms of Audit Engagements," paragraph 6(a).*

[17] *ISA 700, paragraph A12.*

*The APB has not promulgated ISA 700 as issued by the IAASB for application in the UK and Ireland. In the UK and Ireland the applicable auditing standard is ISA (UK and Ireland) 700, "The Auditor's Report on Financial Statements." Paragraph A12 of ISA 700 states "It will be extremely rare for the auditor to consider financial statements that are prepared in accordance with a compliance framework to be misleading if, in accordance with ISA 210, the auditor determined that the framework is acceptable."*

Consideration of such behavior is relevant when identifying and assessing the risks of material misstatement due to fraud, as further explained in paragraphs A29-A30.

### Special-Purpose Entities as Related Parties

A7    In some circumstances, a special-purpose entity[18] may be a related party of the entity because the entity may in substance control it, even if the entity owns little or none of the special-purpose entity's equity.

## Risk Assessment Procedures and Related Activities

### Risks of Material Misstatement Associated with Related Party Relationships and Transactions (Ref: Para. 11)

*Considerations Specific to Public Sector Entities*

A8    The public sector auditor's responsibilities regarding related party relationships and transactions may be affected by the audit mandate, or by obligations on public sector entities arising from law, regulation or other authority. Consequently, the public sector auditor's responsibilities may not be limited to addressing the risks of material misstatement associated with related party relationships and transactions, but may also include a broader responsibility to address the risks of non-compliance with law, regulation and other authority governing public sector bodies that lay down specific requirements in the conduct of business with related parties. Further, the public sector auditor may need to have regard to public sector financial reporting requirements for related party relationships and transactions that may differ from those in the private sector.

### Understanding the Entity's Related Party Relationships and Transactions

*Discussion among the Engagement Team (Ref: Para. 12)*

A9    Matters that may be addressed in the discussion among the engagement team include:

- The nature and extent of the entity's relationships and transactions with related parties (using, for example, the auditor's record of identified related parties updated after each audit).
- An emphasis on the importance of maintaining professional skepticism throughout the audit regarding the potential for material misstatement associated with related party relationships and transactions.
- The circumstances or conditions of the entity that may indicate the existence of related party relationships or transactions that management has not identified or disclosed to the auditor (e.g., a complex organizational structure, use of special-purpose entities for off-balance sheet transactions, or an inadequate information system).
- The records or documents that may indicate the existence of related party relationships or transactions.
- The importance that management and those charged with governance attach to the identification, appropriate accounting for, and disclosure of related party relationships and transactions (if the applicable financial reporting framework

---

[18] *ISA (UK and Ireland) 315, paragraphs A26-A27, provides guidance regarding the nature of a special-purpose entity.*

establishes related party requirements), and the related risk of management override of relevant controls.

In addition, the discussion in the context of fraud may include specific consideration of how related parties may be involved in fraud. For example:  **A10**

- How special-purpose entities controlled by management might be used to facilitate earnings management.
- How transactions between the entity and a known business partner of a key member of management could be arranged to facilitate misappropriation of the entity's assets.

*The Identity of the Entity's Related Parties (Ref: Para. 13(a))*

Where the applicable financial reporting framework establishes related party requirements, information regarding the identity of the entity's related parties is likely to be readily available to management because the entity's information systems will need to record, process and summarize related party relationships and transactions to enable the entity to meet the accounting and disclosure requirements of the framework. Management is therefore likely to have a comprehensive list of related parties and changes from the prior period. For recurring engagements, making the inquiries provides a basis for comparing the information supplied by management with the auditor's record of related parties noted in previous audits.  **A11**

However, where the framework does not establish related party requirements, the entity may not have such information systems in place. Under such circumstances, it is possible that management may not be aware of the existence of all related parties. Nevertheless, the requirement to make the inquiries specified by paragraph 13 still applies because management may be aware of parties that meet the related party definition set out in this ISA (UK and Ireland). In such a case, however, the auditor's inquiries regarding the identity of the entity's related parties are likely to form part of the auditor's risk assessment procedures and related activities performed in accordance with ISA (UK and Ireland) 315 to obtain information regarding:  **A12**

- The entity's ownership and governance structures;
- The types of investments that the entity is making and plans to make; and
- The way the entity is structured and how it is financed.

In the particular case of common control relationships, as management is more likely to be aware of such relationships if they have economic significance to the entity, the auditor's inquiries are likely to be more effective if they are focused on whether parties with which the entity engages in significant transactions, or shares resources to a significant degree, are related parties.

In the context of a group audit, ISA (UK and Ireland) 600 requires the group engagement team to provide each component auditor with a list of related parties prepared by group management and any other related parties of which the group engagement team is aware.[19] Where the entity is a component within a group, this information provides a useful basis for the auditor's inquiries of management regarding the identity of the entity's related parties.  **A13**

[19] *ISA (UK and Ireland) 600, "Special Considerations—Audits of Group Financial Statements (Including the Work of Component Auditors)," paragraph 40(e).*

**A14**    The auditor may also obtain some information regarding the identity of the entity's related parties through inquiries of management during the engagement acceptance or continuance process.

*The Entity's Controls over Related Party Relationships and Transactions (Ref: Para. 14)*

**A15**    Others within the entity are those considered likely to have knowledge of the entity's related party relationships and transactions, and the entity's controls over such relationships and transactions. These may include, to the extent that they do not form part of management:

- Those charged with governance;
- Personnel in a position to initiate, process, or record transactions that are both significant and outside the entity's normal course of business, and those who supervise or monitor such personnel;
- Internal auditors;
- In-house legal counsel; and
- The chief ethics officer or equivalent person.

**A16**    The audit is conducted on the premise that management and, where appropriate, those charged with governance have acknowledged and understand that they have responsibility for the preparation of the financial statements in accordance with the applicable financial reporting framework, including where relevant their fair presentation, and for such internal control as management and, where appropriate, those charged with governance determine is necessary to enable the preparation of financial statements that are free from material misstatement, whether due to fraud or error.[20] Accordingly, where the framework establishes related party requirements, the preparation of the financial statements requires management, with oversight from those charged with governance, to design, implement and maintain adequate controls over related party relationships and transactions so that these are identified and appropriately accounted for and disclosed in accordance with the framework. In their oversight role, those charged with governance monitor how management is discharging its responsibility for such controls. Regardless of any related party requirements the framework may establish, those charged with governance may, in their oversight role, obtain information from management to enable them to understand the nature and business rationale of the entity's related party relationships and transactions.

**A17**    In meeting the ISA (UK and Ireland) 315 requirement to obtain an understanding of the control environment,[21] the auditor may consider features of the control environment relevant to mitigating the risks of material misstatement associated with related party relationships and transactions, such as:

- Internal ethical codes, appropriately communicated to the entity's personnel and enforced, governing the circumstances in which the entity may enter into specific types of related party transactions.
- Policies and procedures for open and timely disclosure of the interests that management and those charged with governance have in related party transactions.
- The assignment of responsibilities within the entity for identifying, recording, summarizing, and disclosing related party transactions.

---

[20] *ISA (UK and Ireland) 200, paragraph A2.*

[21] *ISA (UK and Ireland) 315, paragraph 14.*

- Timely disclosure and discussion between management and those charged with governance of significant related party transactions outside the entity's normal course of business, including whether those charged with governance have appropriately challenged the business rationale of such transactions (for example, by seeking advice from external professional advisors).
- Clear guidelines for the approval of related party transactions involving actual or perceived conflicts of interest, such as approval by a subcommittee of those charged with governance comprising individuals independent of management.
- Periodic reviews by internal auditors, where applicable.
- Proactive action taken by management to resolve related party disclosure issues, such as by seeking advice from the auditor or external legal counsel.
- The existence of whistle-blowing policies and procedures, where applicable.

Controls over related party relationships and transactions within some entities may be deficient or non-existent for a number of reasons, such as: **A18**

- The low importance attached by management to identifying and disclosing related party relationships and transactions.
- The lack of appropriate oversight by those charged with governance.
- An intentional disregard for such controls because related party disclosures may reveal information that management considers sensitive, for example, the existence of transactions involving family members of management.
- An insufficient understanding by management of the related party requirements of the applicable financial reporting framework.
- The absence of disclosure requirements under the applicable financial reporting framework.
  Where such controls are ineffective or non-existent, the auditor may be unable to obtain sufficient appropriate audit evidence about related party relationships and transactions. If this were the case, the auditor would, in accordance with ISA (UK and Ireland) 705,[22] consider the implications for the audit, including the opinion in the auditor's report.

Fraudulent financial reporting often involves management override of controls that otherwise may appear to be operating effectively.[23] The risk of management override of controls is higher if management has relationships that involve control or significant influence with parties with which the entity does business because these relationships may present management with greater incentives and opportunities to perpetrate fraud. For example, management's financial interests in certain related parties may provide incentives for management to override controls by (a) directing the entity, against its interests, to conclude transactions for the benefit of these parties, or (b) colluding with such parties or controlling their actions. Examples of possible fraud include: **A19**

- Creating fictitious terms of transactions with related parties designed to misrepresent the business rationale of these transactions.
- Fraudulently organizing the transfer of assets from or to management or others at amounts significantly above or below market value.
- Engaging in complex transactions with related parties, such as special-purpose entities, that are structured to misrepresent the financial position or financial performance of the entity.

---

[22] *ISA (UK and Ireland) 705, "Modifications to the Opinion in the Independent Auditor's Report."*

[23] *ISA (UK and Ireland) 240, paragraphs 31 and A4.*

*Considerations specific to smaller entities*

**A20**  Control activities in smaller entities are likely to be less formal and smaller entities may have no documented processes for dealing with related party relationships and transactions. An owner-manager may mitigate some of the risks arising from related party transactions, or potentially increase those risks, through active involvement in all the main aspects of the transactions. For such entities, the auditor may obtain an understanding of the related party relationships and transactions, and any controls that may exist over these, through inquiry of management combined with other procedures, such as observation of management's oversight and review activities, and inspection of available relevant documentation.

*Authorization and approval of significant transactions and arrangements (Ref: Para. 14(b))*

**A21**  Authorization involves the granting of permission by a party or parties with the appropriate authority (whether management, those charged with governance or the entity's shareholders) for the entity to enter into specific transactions in accordance with pre-determined criteria, whether judgmental or not. Approval involves those parties' acceptance of the transactions the entity has entered into as having satisfied the criteria on which authorization was granted. Examples of controls the entity may have established to authorize and approve significant transactions and arrangements with related parties or significant transactions and arrangements outside the normal course of business include:

- Monitoring controls to identify such transactions and arrangements for authorization and approval.
- Approval of the terms and conditions of the transactions and arrangements by management, those charged with governance or, where applicable, shareholders.

**Maintaining Alertness for Related Party Information When Reviewing Records or Documents**

*Records or Documents That the Auditor May Inspect (Ref: Para. 15)*

**A22**  During the audit, the auditor may inspect records or documents that may provide information about related party relationships and transactions, for example:

- Third-party confirmations obtained by the auditor (in addition to bank and legal confirmations).
- Entity income tax returns.
- Information supplied by the entity to regulatory authorities.
- Shareholder registers to identify the entity's principal shareholders.
- Statements of conflicts of interest from management and those charged with governance.
- Records of the entity's investments and those of its pension plans.
- Contracts and agreements with key management or those charged with governance.
- Significant contracts and agreements not in the entity's ordinary course of business.
- Specific invoices and correspondence from the entity's professional advisors.
- Life insurance policies acquired by the entity.
- Significant contracts re-negotiated by the entity during the period.
- Internal auditors' reports.
- Documents associated with the entity's filings with a securities regulator (e.g., prospectuses).

*Arrangements that may indicate the existence of previously unidentified or undisclosed related party relationships or transactions*

An arrangement involves a formal or informal agreement between the entity and one or more other parties for such purposes as: **A23**

- The establishment of a business relationship through appropriate vehicles or structures.
- The conduct of certain types of transactions under specific terms and conditions.
- The provision of designated services or financial support.
  Examples of arrangements that may indicate the existence of related party relationships or transactions that management has not previously identified or disclosed to the auditor include:
- Participation in unincorporated partnerships with other parties.
- Agreements for the provision of services to certain parties under terms and conditions that are outside the entity's normal course of business.
- Guarantees and guarantor relationships.

*Identification of Significant Transactions outside the Normal Course of Business (Ref: Para. 16)*

Obtaining further information on significant transactions outside the entity's normal course of business enables the auditor to evaluate whether fraud risk factors, if any, are present and, where the applicable financial reporting framework establishes related party requirements, to identify the risks of material misstatement. **A24**

Examples of transactions outside the entity's normal course of business may include: **A25**

- Complex equity transactions, such as corporate restructurings or acquisitions.
- Transactions with offshore entities in jurisdictions with weak corporate laws.
- The leasing of premises or the rendering of management services by the entity to another party if no consideration is exchanged.
- Sales transactions with unusually large discounts or returns.
- Transactions with circular arrangements, for example, sales with a commitment to repurchase.
- Transactions under contracts whose terms are changed before expiry.

*Understanding the nature of significant transactions outside the normal course of business (Ref: Para. 16(a))*

Inquiring into the nature of the significant transactions outside the entity's normal course of business involves obtaining an understanding of the business rationale of the transactions, and the terms and conditions under which these have been entered into. **A26**

*Inquiring into whether related parties could be involved (Ref: Para. 16(b))*

A related party could be involved in a significant transaction outside the entity's normal course of business not only by directly influencing the transaction through being a party to the transaction, but also by indirectly influencing it through an intermediary. Such influence may indicate the presence of a fraud risk factor. **A27**

**Sharing Related Party Information with the Engagement Team** (Ref: Para. 17)

A28   Relevant related party information that may be shared among the engagement team members includes, for example:

- The identity of the entity's related parties.
- The nature of the related party relationships and transactions.
- Significant or complex related party relationships or transactions that may require special audit consideration, in particular transactions in which management or those charged with governance are financially involved.

## Identification and Assessment of the Risks of Material Misstatement Associated with Related Party Relationships and Transactions

**Fraud Risk Factors Associated with a Related Party with Dominant Influence** (Ref: Para. 19)

A29   Domination of management by a single person or small group of persons without compensating controls is a fraud risk factor.[24] Indicators of dominant influence exerted by a related party include:

- The related party has vetoed significant business decisions taken by management or those charged with governance.
- Significant transactions are referred to the related party for final approval.
- There is little or no debate among management and those charged with governance regarding business proposals initiated by the related party.
- Transactions involving the related party (or a close family member of the related party) are rarely independently reviewed and approved.
- Dominant influence may also exist in some cases if the related party has played a leading role in founding the entity and continues to play a leading role in managing the entity.

A30   In the presence of other risk factors, the existence of a related party with dominant influence may indicate significant risks of material misstatement due to fraud. For example:

- An unusually high turnover of senior management or professional advisors may suggest unethical or fraudulent business practices that serve the related party's purposes.
- The use of business intermediaries for significant transactions for which there appears to be no clear business justification may suggest that the related party could have an interest in such transactions through control of such intermediaries for fraudulent purposes.
- Evidence of the related party's excessive participation in or preoccupation with the selection of accounting policies or the determination of significant estimates may suggest the possibility of fraudulent financial reporting.

[24] *ISA (UK and Ireland) 240, Appendix 1.*

### Responses to the Risks of Material Misstatement Associated with Related Party Relationships and Transactions (Ref: Para. 20)

The nature, timing and extent of the further audit procedures that the auditor may select to respond to the assessed risks of material misstatement associated with related party relationships and transactions depend upon the nature of those risks and the circumstances of the entity.[25]     **A31**

Examples of substantive audit procedures that the auditor may perform when the auditor has assessed a significant risk that management has not appropriately accounted for or disclosed specific related party transactions in accordance with the applicable financial reporting framework (whether due to fraud or error) include:     **A32**

- Confirming or discussing specific aspects of the transactions with intermediaries such as banks, law firms, guarantors, or agents, where practicable and not prohibited by law, regulation or ethical rules.
- Confirming the purposes, specific terms or amounts of the transactions with the related parties (this audit procedure may be less effective where the auditor judges that the entity is likely to influence the related parties in their responses to the auditor).
- Where applicable, reading the financial statements or other relevant financial information, if available, of the related parties for evidence of the accounting of the transactions in the related parties' accounting records.

If the auditor has assessed a significant risk of material misstatement due to fraud as a result of the presence of a related party with dominant influence, the auditor may, in addition to the general requirements of ISA (UK and Ireland) 240, perform audit procedures such as the following to obtain an understanding of the business relationships that such a related party may have established directly or indirectly with the entity and to determine the need for further appropriate substantive audit procedures:     **A33**

- Inquiries of, and discussion with, management and those charged with governance.
- Inquiries of the related party.
- Inspection of significant contracts with the related party.
- Appropriate background research, such as through the Internet or specific external business information databases.
- Review of employee whistle-blowing reports where these are retained.

Depending upon the results of the auditor's risk assessment procedures, the auditor may consider it appropriate to obtain audit evidence without testing the entity's controls over related party relationships and transactions. In some circumstances, however, it may not be possible to obtain sufficient appropriate audit evidence from substantive audit procedures alone in relation to the risks of material misstatement associated with related party relationships and transactions. For example, where intra-group transactions between the entity and its components are numerous and a significant amount of information regarding these transactions is initiated, recorded, processed or reported electronically in an integrated system, the auditor may determine that it is not possible to design effective substantive audit procedures that by themselves would reduce the risks of material misstatement associated with these transactions to an acceptably low level. In such a case, in meeting the ISA (UK and Ireland) 330 requirement to obtain sufficient appropriate audit evidence as to the     **A34**

---

[25] *ISA (UK and Ireland) 330 provides further guidance on considering the nature, timing and extent of further audit procedures. ISA 240 establishes requirements and provides guidance on appropriate responses to assessed risks of material misstatement due to fraud.*

operating effectiveness of relevant controls,[26] the auditor is required to test the entity's controls over the completeness and accuracy of the recording of the related party relationships and transactions.

### *Identification of Previously Unidentified or Undisclosed Related Parties or Significant Related Party Transactions*

*Communicating Newly Identified Related Party Information to the Engagement Team (Ref: Para. 22(a))*

**A35**   Communicating promptly any newly identified related parties to the other members of the engagement team assists them in determining whether this information affects the results of, and conclusions drawn from, risk assessment procedures already performed, including whether the risks of material misstatement need to be reassessed.

*Substantive Procedures Relating to Newly Identified Related Parties or Significant Related Party Transactions (Ref: Para. 22(c))*

**A36**   Examples of substantive audit procedures that the auditor may perform relating to newly identified related parties or significant related party transactions include:

- Making inquiries regarding the nature of the entity's relationships with the newly identified related parties, including (where appropriate and not prohibited by law, regulation or ethical rules) inquiring of parties outside the entity who are presumed to have significant knowledge of the entity and its business, such as legal counsel, principal agents, major representatives, consultants, guarantors, or other close business partners.
- Conducting an analysis of accounting records for transactions with the newly identified related parties. Such an analysis may be facilitated using computer-assisted audit techniques.
- Verifying the terms and conditions of the newly identified related party transactions, and evaluating whether the transactions have been appropriately accounted for and disclosed in accordance with the applicable financial reporting framework.

*Intentional Non-Disclosure by Management (Ref: Para. 22(e))*

**A37**   The requirements and guidance in ISA (UK and Ireland) 240 regarding the auditor's responsibilities relating to fraud in an audit of financial statements are relevant where management appears to have intentionally failed to disclose related parties or significant related party transactions to the auditor. The auditor may also consider whether it is necessary to re-evaluate the reliability of management's responses to the auditor's inquiries and management's representations to the auditor.

---

[26] *ISA (UK and Ireland) 330, paragraph 8(b).*

**Identified Significant Related Party Transactions outside the Entity's Normal Course of Business**

*Evaluating the Business Rationale of Significant Related Party Transactions (Ref: Para. 23)*

In evaluating the business rationale of a significant related party transaction outside the entity's normal course of business, the auditor may consider the following:  **A38**

- Whether the transaction:
  - Is overly complex (e.g., it may involve multiple related parties within a consolidated group).
  - Has unusual terms of trade, such as unusual prices, interest rates, guarantees and repayment terms.
  - Lacks an apparent logical business reason for its occurrence.
  - Involves previously unidentified related parties.
  - Is processed in an unusual manner.
- Whether management has discussed the nature of, and accounting for, such a transaction with those charged with governance.
- Whether management is placing more emphasis on a particular accounting treatment rather than giving due regard to the underlying economics of the transaction.

If management's explanations are materially inconsistent with the terms of the related party transaction, the auditor is required, in accordance with ISA (UK and Ireland) 500,[27] to consider the reliability of management's explanations and representations on other significant matters.

The auditor may also seek to understand the business rationale of such a transaction  **A39** from the related party's perspective, as this may help the auditor to better understand the economic reality of the transaction and why it was carried out. A business rationale from the related party's perspective that appears inconsistent with the nature of its business may represent a fraud risk factor.

*Authorization and Approval of Significant Related Party Transactions (Ref: Para. 23(b))*

Authorization and approval by management, those charged with governance, or,  **A40** where applicable, the shareholders of significant related party transactions outside the entity's normal course of business may provide audit evidence that these have been duly considered at the appropriate levels within the entity and that their terms and conditions have been appropriately reflected in the financial statements. The existence of transactions of this nature that were not subject to such authorization and approval, in the absence of rational explanations based on discussion with management or those charged with governance, may indicate risks of material misstatement due to error or fraud. In these circumstances, the auditor may need to be alert for other transactions of a similar nature. Authorization and approval alone, however, may not be sufficient in concluding whether risks of material misstatement due to fraud are absent because authorization and approval may be ineffective if there has been collusion between the related parties or if the entity is subject to the dominant influence of a related party.

[27] *ISA (UK and Ireland) 500, "Audit Evidence," paragraph 11.*

*Considerations specific to smaller entities*

A41    A smaller entity may not have the same controls provided by different levels of authority and approval that may exist in a larger entity. Accordingly, when auditing a smaller entity, the auditor may rely to a lesser degree on authorization and approval for audit evidence regarding the validity of significant related party transactions outside the entity's normal course of business. Instead, the auditor may consider performing other audit procedures such as inspecting relevant documents, confirming specific aspects of the transactions with relevant parties, or observing the owner-manager's involvement with the transactions.

**Assertions That Related Party Transactions Were Conducted on Terms Equivalent to Those Prevailing in an Arm's Length Transaction** (Ref: Para. 24)

A42    Although audit evidence may be readily available regarding how the price of a related party transaction compares to that of a similar arm's length transaction, there are ordinarily practical difficulties that limit the auditor's ability to obtain audit evidence that all other aspects of the transaction are equivalent to those of the arm's length transaction. For example, although the auditor may be able to confirm that a related party transaction has been conducted at a market price, it may be impracticable to confirm whether other terms and conditions of the transaction (such as credit terms, contingencies and specific charges) are equivalent to those that would ordinarily be agreed between independent parties. Accordingly, there may be a risk that management's assertion that a related party transaction was conducted on terms equivalent to those prevailing in an arm's length transaction may be materially misstated.

A43    The preparation of the financial statements requires management to substantiate an assertion that a related party transaction was conducted on terms equivalent to those prevailing in an arm's length transaction. Management's support for the assertion may include:

- Comparing the terms of the related party transaction to those of an identical or similar transaction with one or more unrelated parties.
- Engaging an external expert to determine a market value and to confirm market terms and conditions for the transaction.
- Comparing the terms of the transaction to known market terms for broadly similar transactions on an open market.

A44    Evaluating management's support for this assertion may involve one or more of the following:

- Considering the appropriateness of management's process for supporting the assertion.
- Verifying the source of the internal or external data supporting the assertion, and testing the data to determine their accuracy, completeness and relevance.
- Evaluating the reasonableness of any significant assumptions on which the assertion is based.

A45    Some financial reporting frameworks require the disclosure of related party transactions not conducted on terms equivalent to those prevailing in arm's length transactions. In these circumstances, if management has not disclosed a related party transaction in the financial statements, there may be an implicit assertion that the transaction was conducted on terms equivalent to those prevailing in an arm's length transaction.

## Evaluation of the Accounting for and Disclosure of Identified Related Party Relationships and Transactions

*Materiality Considerations in Evaluating Misstatements* (Ref: Para. 25)

ISA (UK and Ireland) 450 requires the auditor to consider both the size and the nature of a misstatement, and the particular circumstances of its occurrence, when evaluating whether the misstatement is material.[28] The significance of the transaction to the financial statement users may not depend solely on the recorded amount of the transaction but also on other specific relevant factors, such as the nature of the related party relationship.

**A46**

*Evaluation of Related Party Disclosures* (Ref: Para. 25(a))

Evaluating the related party disclosures in the context of the disclosure requirements of the applicable financial reporting framework means considering whether the facts and circumstances of the entity's related party relationships and transactions have been appropriately summarized and presented so that the disclosures are understandable. Disclosures of related party transactions may not be understandable if:

**A47**

(a) The business rationale and the effects of the transactions on the financial statements are unclear or misstated; or
(b) Key terms, conditions, or other important elements of the transactions necessary for understanding them are not appropriately disclosed.

Accounting standards and corporate law applicable in the UK and Ireland include requirements for disclosures relating to control of the entity. The auditor may only be able to determine the name of the entity's ultimate controlling party through specific inquiry of management or those charged with governance. When the auditor considers it necessary, the auditor obtains corroboration from the ultimate controlling party confirming representations received in this regard.

**A47-1**

## Written Representations (Ref: Para. 26)

Circumstances in which it may be appropriate to obtain written representations from those charged with governance include:

**A48**

- When they have approved specific related party transactions that (a) materially affect the financial statements, or (b) involve management.
- When they have made specific oral representations to the auditor on details of certain related party transactions.
- When they have financial or other interests in the related parties or the related party transactions.

The auditor may also decide to obtain written representations regarding specific assertions that management may have made, such as a representation that specific related party transactions do not involve undisclosed side agreements.

**A49**

An entity may require its management and those charged with governance to sign individual declarations in relation to related party matters. It may be helpful if

**A49-1**

---

[28] *ISA (UK and Ireland) 450, "Evaluation of Misstatements Identified during the Audit," paragraph 11(a). Paragraph A16 of ISA 450 provides guidance on the circumstances that may affect the evaluation of a misstatement.*

any such declarations are addressed jointly to a designated official of the entity and also to the auditor. In other cases, the auditor may wish to obtain written representations directly from each of those charged with governance and from members of management.

## Communication with Those Charged with Governance (Ref: Para. 27)

A50   Communicating significant matters arising during the audit[29] in connection with the entity's related parties helps the auditor to establish a common understanding with those charged with governance of the nature and resolution of these matters. Examples of significant related party matters include:

- Non-disclosure (whether intentional or not) by management to the auditor of related parties or significant related party transactions, which may alert those charged with governance to significant related party relationships and transactions of which they may not have been previously aware.
- The identification of significant related party transactions that have not been appropriately authorized and approved, which may give rise to suspected fraud.
- Disagreement with management regarding the accounting for and disclosure of significant related party transactions in accordance with the applicable financial reporting framework.
- Non-compliance with applicable law or regulations prohibiting or restricting specific types of related party transactions.
- Difficulties in identifying the party that ultimately controls the entity.

---

[29] *ISA (UK and Ireland) 230, paragraph A8, provides further guidance on the nature of significant matters arising during the audit.*

# Addendum

*This addendum provides a summary of APB's rationale for retaining or excluding in the proposed clarified ISA (UK and Ireland) the supplementary requirements in the existing ISA (UK and Ireland). It also sets out the supplementary guidance material in the existing ISA (UK and Ireland) that APB considers is not necessary to retain in light of the improvements in the underlying Clarity ISAs issued by the IAASB as part of the Clarity Project. It is provided for information and does not form part of the proposed clarified ISA (UK and Ireland).*

*The Consultation Paper published with the exposure drafts explains the general approach used by the APB for determining whether current supplementary material should be proposed to be retained.*

## Analysis of proposed treatment of current APB supplementary material in current ISA (UK and Ireland) 550

There are two versions of the current ISA (UK and Ireland) – one for IAS 24 and one for FRS 8. The paragraphs reproduced here are in both versions unless specifically indicated otherwise.

It should be noted that ISA 550 has been revised as well as clarified. The revised ISA is framework neutral and it will not be necessary to have two versions for the UK and Ireland.

## Requirements

| APB supplementary requirements (*Italic text is from IAASB for context*) | Is it covered in substance in the Clarity ISA? | Should it be retained? |
|---|---|---|
| 6-3. **When planning the audit the auditor should assess the risk that material undisclosed related party transactions, or undisclosed outstanding balances between an entity and its related parties may exist.** | ✓  18 | ✗ |
| 7. *The auditor should review information provided by those charged with governance and management identifying the names of all known related parties and should perform the following audit procedures in respect of the completeness of this information: ...* | The revised ISA is less specific regarding documents required to be reviewed. (15) | |
| **(h) Review invoices and correspondence from lawyers for indications of the existence of related parties or related party transactions; and** | ✗  However, these are included in the Application Material. (A22) | ✗ |

| APB supplementary requirements (*Italic text is from IAASB for context*) | Is it covered in substance in the Clarity ISA? | Should it be retained? |
|---|---|---|
| (i) **Inquire of the names of all pension and other trusts established for the benefit of employees and the names of their management.** | ✗ The Application Material includes life insurance policies acquired by the entity and records of the entity's investments and those of its pension plans. (A22) | ✗ |
| **Disclosures Relating to Control of the Entity**<br>14-3. **The auditor should obtain sufficient appropriate audit evidence that disclosures in the financial statements relating to control of the entity are properly stated.** | ✗ However, there is a requirement to evaluate whether the identified related party relationships and transactions have been appropriately accounted for and disclosed in accordance with the applicable financial reporting framework. (25(a)) | ✗ But guidance has been added indicating that accounting standards and corporate law applicable in the UK and Ireland include requirements for disclosures relating to control of the entity. A47-1 |

## Guidance

The current ISAs (UK and Ireland) contain extensive guidance on the requirements in law and accounting standards in the UK and Ireland. It is proposed that such guidance no longer be provided auditors should have regard to the accounting standards themselves and relevant law and regulations rather than a summary in an auditing standard which is unlikely to be complete and may become out of date fairly quickly. A footnote has been added to paragraph 3 in the standard to indicate that in the UK and Ireland, specific accounting and disclosure requirements for related party relationships, transactions and balances are established in accounting standards and in law and regulations.

The following guidance in current versions of ISA (UK and Ireland) 550 has not been carried forward to the draft clarity version.

| |
|---|
| **Current paragraph reference (*Italic text is from IAASB for context*)** |
| 1-1.   In the UK and Ireland, for accounting periods commencing on or after 1 January 2005, the consolidated financial statements of listed companies must be prepared under EU adopted IFRS. From the same date other companies will be able, either to make an irrevocable election to prepare their financial statements under EU adopted IFRS, or to prepare their financial statements in accordance with UK and Irish accounting standards. Paragraphs 1 to 16-2 of this ISA (UK and Ireland) apply to financial statements prepared under EU adopted IFRS, including IAS 24. Paragraphs 101 to 116-2 of this ISA (UK and Ireland) apply to financial statements prepared under UK and Irish accounting standards, including FRS 8, "Related Party Disclosures". |
| *FRS 8*<br>101-1 In the UK and Ireland for accounting periods commencing on or after 1 January 2005, the following companies will continue to be able, if they wish, to prepare their financial statements in accordance with UK and Irish accounting standards;<br>   (a)   All companies within a listed group for their individual financial statements (and, where a consolidation is prepared by an unlisted subsidiary, for those consolidated financial statements);<br>   (b)   Unlisted companies; and<br>   (c)   Other entities, including many public benefit entities.<br>Paragraphs 101 to 116-2 apply to financial statements prepared under UK and Irish accounting standards, including FRS 8, "Related Party Disclosures". Paragraphs 1 to 16-2 of this ISA (UK and Ireland) apply to financial statements prepared under EU adopted IFRS, including IAS 24. |
| 1-2. – 1-5. [Description of management and those charged with governance] |
| 2.     *The auditor should perform audit procedures designed to obtain sufficient appropriate audit evidence regarding the identification and disclosure by management[1] of related parties and the effect of related party transactions that are material to the financial statements. ...*<br><br>[1] In the UK and Ireland those charged with governance are responsible for the preparation of the financial statements. |
| 4.     *Definitions regarding related parties are given in IAS 24 [FRS 8] and are adopted for the purposes of this ISA (UK and Ireland)[2]*<br><br>[2] Definitions from IAS 24 [FRS 8], "Related Party Disclosures," are set out in the Appendix. |
| 4-1.    IAS 24 [FRS 8] does not override the disclosure requirements of either companies legislation or listing rules. Similarly, the requirements of IAS 24 [FRS 8] do not override exemptions from disclosures given by law to, and utilized by, certain types of entity. For the purposes of this ISA (UK and Ireland) companies legislation is defined as:<br>   (a)   In Great Britain, the Companies Act 1985;<br>   (b)   In Northern Ireland, The Companies (Northern Ireland) Order 1986; and<br>   (c)   In the Republic of Ireland, the Companies Acts 1963 to 2003 and the European Communities (Companies: Group Accounts) Regulations 1992. |
| *FRS 8*<br>104-2 FRS 8 exempts the disclosure of certain related party transactions undertaken by an entity. In exceptional circumstances if an entity avails |

| Current paragraph reference (*Italic text is from IAASB for context*) |
|---|
| itself of an exemption contained in an accounting standard this may be inconsistent with the overriding requirement for the financial statements to give a true and fair view of the state of the entity's affairs. In the course of an audit the auditor may become aware of transactions that are exempt from disclosure under FRS 8. The auditor assesses whether such related party transactions need to be disclosed in order for the financial statements to give a true and fair view. |

| | |
|---|---|
| 5-1. | As transactions between related parties may not be on an arm's length basis and there may be an actual, or perceived, conflict of interest those charged with governance usually ensure that such transactions are subject to appropriate approval procedures. The approval of material related party transactions is often recorded in the minutes of meetings of those charged with governance. |
| 5-2. | In owner managed entities, as the risks associated with such transactions are the same, similar approval procedures would ideally apply. Often, however, procedures are less formalized because the owner manager is often personally aware of, and implicitly or explicitly approves, all such transactions. |
| 5-3. | The definition of a related party is complex and in part subjective and it may not always be self-evident to management whether a party is related. Furthermore, many information systems are not designed to either distinguish or summarize related party transactions and outstanding balances between an entity and its related parties. Management may, therefore, have to carry out additional analysis of the accounting records to identify related party transactions. Accordingly related party transactions are often inherently difficult for the auditor to detect. |

| |
|---|
| *FRS 8* |
| 105-4 These difficulties are heightened by the particular perspective to the concept of materiality introduced by FRS 8 which states: "The materiality of related party transactions is to be judged, not only in terms of their significance to the reporting entity, but also in relation to the other related party when that party is:<br>(a) A director, key manager or other individual in a position to influence, or accountable for stewardship of, the reporting entity; or<br>(b) A member of the close family of any individual mentioned in (a) above; or<br>(c) An entity controlled by any individual mentioned in (a) or (b) above".<br>Although the auditor designs audit procedures so as to have a reasonable expectation of detecting undisclosed related party transactions that are material to the reporting entity, an audit cannot necessarily be expected to detect all such transactions; nor can it be expected to detect transactions that are not material to the entity, even though they may be material to the other related party. |

| | |
|---|---|
| 6. | *The auditor needs to have a sufficient understanding of the entity and its environment to enable identification of the events, transactions and practices that may result in a risk of material misstatement regarding related parties and transactions with such parties. While the existence of related parties and transactions between such parties are considered ordinary features of business, the auditor needs to be aware of them because: ...*<br>(e) The entity may be engaged in transfers of goods and services with related parties in accordance with specified transfer pricing policies or under reciprocal trading arrangements, such as barter transactions, |

| **Current paragraph reference (*Italic text is from IAASB for context*)** |
|---|
| which may give rise to accounting recognition and measurement issues. In particular an entity may have received or provided management services at no charge. |
| 6-1.  The risk that undisclosed related party transactions, or outstanding balances between an entity and its related parties, will not be detected by the auditor is especially high when:<br>(a)  Related party transactions have taken place without charge;<br>(b)  Related party transactions are not self-evident to the auditor;<br>(c)  Transactions are with a party that the auditor could not reasonably be expected to know is a related party;<br>(d)  Transactions undertaken with a related party in an earlier period have remained unsettled for a considerable period of time; or<br>(e)  Active steps have been taken by those charged with governance or management to conceal either the full terms of a transaction or that a transaction is, in substance, with a related party. |
| 6-2.  Those charged with governance or management may wish to conceal the fact that a transaction, or an outstanding balance is with a related party because:<br>(a)  Its disclosure may be sensitive to the parties involved and they may be reticent about disclosing it; and<br>(b)  The transaction may be motivated by other than ordinary business considerations, for example to enhance the presentation of the financial statements (for example fraud or window dressing).<br>Related party transactions may be concealed in whole or in part from the auditor for fraudulent or other purposes. The likelihood of detecting fraudulent related party transactions depends upon the nature of the fraud and, in particular, the degree of collusion, the seniority of those involved and the level of deception concerned. ISA (UK and Ireland) 240 "The Auditor's responsibility to Consider Fraud in an Audit of Financial Statements" establishes the standards and provides the guidance on the auditor's responsibility to consider fraud in an audit of financial statements, including related party transactions. |
| 6-4.  The responsibility of those charged with governance to identify, approve and disclose related party transactions requires them to implement adequate information systems to identify related parties and internal control to ensure that related party transactions are appropriately identified in the accounting records and disclosed in the financial statements. As part of the risk assessment the auditor obtains an understanding of such information systems and internal control. |
| 6-5.  The extent to which formal policies and codes of conduct dealing with relationships with related parties are maintained normally depends on the significance of related parties and on the philosophy and operating style of the management of the entity and of those charged with governance. Such policies often cover the approval, recording and reporting of related party transactions entered into, on behalf of the entity, by employees and those charged with governance. |
| 6-6.  In respect of entities that do not have formal policies and codes of conduct concerning related party transactions, for example owner managed entities, the auditor may only be able to perform substantive procedures. If the auditor assesses the risk of undisclosed related party transactions as low such planned substantive procedures may not need to be extensive. |

| **Current paragraph reference (*Italic text is from IAASB for context*)** |
|---|
| 7-1. After evaluating the results of:<br>   (a) Determining the implementation of the entity's internal control with respect to related party transactions; and<br>   (b) The audit procedures described in the preceding paragraph<br>The auditor may determine that few additional substantive procedures are required to obtain sufficient appropriate audit evidence that no other material related party transactions have occurred. However, if the auditor assesses the controls with respect to related party transactions as weak, it may be necessary to perform additional substantive procedures to obtain reasonable assurance that no material undisclosed related party transactions have occurred. |
| 14. *Given the nature of related party relationships, audit evidence of a related party transaction may be limited, for example, regarding the existence of inventory held by a related party on consignment or an instruction from a parent company to a subsidiary to record a royalty expense. Because of the limited availability of appropriate audit evidence about such transactions, the auditor considers performing audit procedures such as:*<br>   • Discussing the purpose of the transaction with management or those charged with governance.<br>   • Corroborating with the related party the explanation of the purpose of the transaction and, if necessary, confirming that the transaction is bona fide.<br>   • Obtaining information from an unrelated third party. |
| *IAS 24*<br>14-1. IAS 24 requires that "an entity shall disclose the nature of the related party relationship as well as information about the transactions and outstanding balances necessary for an understanding of the potential effect of the relationship on the financial statements". An example of a disclosure falling within this requirement would be noting that the transfer of a major asset had taken place at an amount materially different from that obtainable on normal commercial terms. The auditor, therefore, is alert for related party transactions that have occurred on other than normal commercial terms. In particular, the auditor is alert for unrecorded transactions such as the receipt or provision of management services at no charge. |
| *FRS 8*<br>114-1 FRS 8 requires "disclosure of any other elements of the [related party] transactions necessary for an understanding of the financial statements. An example falling within this requirement would be the need to give an indication that the transfer of a major asset had taken place at an amount materially different from that obtainable on normal commercial terms". The auditor, therefore, is alert for related party transactions that have occurred on other than normal commercial terms. In particular, the auditor is alert for unrecorded transactions such as the receipt or provision of management services at no charge. |
| 14-2. The auditor considers the implications for other aspects of the audit if they identify material related party transactions not included in the information provided by management or those charged with governance. In particular, the auditor considers the impact on their assessment of audit risk and the reliance placed on other representations made by those charged with governance during the audit. |

| Current paragraph reference (*Italic text is from IAASB for context*) |
|---|
| *IAS 24*<br><br>14-4. IAS 24 requires "Relationships between parents and subsidiaries shall be disclosed irrespective of whether there have been transactions between those related parties. An entity shall disclose the name of the entity's parent and, if different, the ultimate controlling party. If neither the entity's parent nor the ultimate controlling party produces financial statements available for public use, the name of the next most senior parent that does so shall also be disclosed." Companies legislation contains additional detailed disclosures requirements relating to control of a company[3].<br><br>[3] In Great Britain these requirements are set out in S. 231 and Schedule 5 Parts I and II of the Companies Act 1985. In Northern Ireland these requirements are set out in Article 239 and Schedule 5 Parts I and II of the Companies (Northern Ireland) Order 1986. In the Republic of Ireland these requirements are set out in S 16 of the Companies (Amendment) Act 1986 and Regulations 36 and 44 of the European Communities (Companies: Group Accounts) Regulations 1992. |
| *FRS 8*<br><br>114-4 FRS 8 requires, "when the reporting entity is controlled by another party, there should be disclosure of the related party relationship and the name of that party and, if different, that of the ultimate controlling party. If the controlling party or ultimate controlling party of the entity is not known, that fact should be disclosed". Companies legislation contains additional detailed disclosures requirements relating to control of a company[3].<br><br>[3] In Great Britain these requirements are set out in S. 231 and Schedule 5 Parts I and II of the Companies Act 1985. In Northern Ireland these requirements are set out in Article 239 and Schedule 5 Parts I and II of the Companies (Northern Ireland) Order 1986. In the Republic of Ireland these requirements are set out in S 16 of the Companies (Amendment) Act 1986 and Regulations 36 and 44 of the European Communities (Companies: Group Accounts) Regulations 1992. |
| *IAS 24*<br><br>14-5. The next most senior parent is the first parent in the group above the immediate parent that produces consolidated financial statements available for public use. |
| *Management Representations*<br>15. *The auditor should obtain a written representation from management[4] concerning:* ...<br><br>[4] In the UK and Ireland the auditor obtains written representations from those charged with governance. |
| 15-1. The written representations obtained by the auditor include confirmation from those charged with governance that they (and any key managers or other individuals who are in a position to influence, or who are accountable for the stewardship of the reporting entity) have disclosed all transactions relevant to the entity and that they are not aware of any other such matters required to be disclosed in the financial statements, whether under IAS 24 [FRS 8] or other requirements. |
| 16-1. If the auditor is unable to obtain sufficient appropriate audit evidence concerning related party transactions and transactions with such parties, this is a limitation on the scope of the audit. Accordingly the auditor considers the need to issue either a qualified opinion or disclaimer of opinion in accordance with the requirements of ISA (UK and Ireland) 700, "The Auditor's Report on Financial Statements." |
| 16-2. If the auditor concludes that the disclosure of related party transactions is not adequate the auditor considers the need to issue either a qualified or |

| **Current paragraph reference (*Italic text is from IAASB for context*)** |
| --- |
| adverse opinion depending on the particular circumstances. Where the auditor is aware of material undisclosed related party transactions or an undisclosed control relationship, that in the auditor's opinion is required to be disclosed, the opinion section of the auditor's report, whenever practicable, includes the information that would have been included in the financial statements had the relevant requirements been followed. |
| Appendices – Set out the definitions in IAS 24 and FRS 8 of 'related party,' 'related party transaction,' 'close members of family,' 'control,' 'key management,' significant influence,' and 'persons acting in concert'. (Not reproduced here.) |

# Proposed Clarified International Standard on Auditing (UK and Ireland) 560
## Subsequent events

*(Effective for audits of financial statements for periods ending on or after 15 December 2010)*

## Contents

International Standard on Auditing (UK and Ireland) (ISA (UK and Ireland))
560,
"Subsequent Events" should be read in conjunction with ISA (UK and
Ireland) 200, "Overall Objectives of the Independent Auditor and the Conduct of
an Audit in Accordance with International Standards on Auditing (UK and
Ireland)."

# Introduction

## Scope of this ISA (UK and Ireland)

1   This International Standard on Auditing (UK and Ireland) (ISA (UK and Ireland)) deals with the auditor's responsibilities relating to subsequent events in an audit of financial statements.

## Subsequent Events

2   Financial statements may be affected by certain events that occur after the date of the financial statements. Many financial reporting frameworks specifically refer to such events.[1] Such financial reporting frameworks ordinarily identify two types of events:

(a) Those that provide evidence of conditions that existed at the date of the financial statements; and

(b) Those that provide evidence of conditions that arose after the date of the financial statements.

ISA (UK and Ireland) 700 explains that the date of the auditor's report informs the reader that the auditor has considered the effect of events and transactions of which the auditor becomes aware and that occurred up to that date.[2]

## Effective Date

3   This ISA (UK and Ireland) is effective for audits of financial statements for periods ending on or after 15 December 2010.

# Objectives

4   The objectives of the auditor are:

(a) To obtain sufficient appropriate audit evidence about whether events occurring between the date of the financial statements and the date of the auditor's report that require adjustment of, or disclosure in, the financial statements are appropriately reflected in those financial statements in accordance with the applicable financial reporting framework; and

(b) To respond appropriately to facts that become known to the auditor after the date of the auditor's report, that, had they been known to the auditor at that date, may have caused the auditor to amend the auditor's report.

---

[1] *For example, International Accounting Standard (IAS) 10, "Events After the Balance Sheet Date" deals with the treatment in financial statements of events, both favorable and unfavorable, that occur between the date of the financial statements (referred to as the "balance sheet date" in the IAS) and the date when the financial statements are authorized for issue.*

[2] *ISA (UK and Ireland) 700, "Forming an Opinion and Reporting on Financial Statements," paragraph A38. The APB has not promulgated ISA 700 as issued by the IAASB for application in the UK and Ireland. In the UK and Ireland the applicable auditing standard is ISA (UK and Ireland) 700, "The Auditor's Report on Financial Statements." Paragraph A15 of ISA (UK and Ireland) 700 explains that the date of the auditor's report informs the reader that the auditor has considered the effect of events and transactions of which the auditor becomes aware and that occurred up to that date.*

# Definitions

For purposes of the ISAs (UK and Ireland), the following terms have the meanings   **5**
attributed below:

(a)  Date of the financial statements – The date of the end of the latest period
covered by the financial statements.

(b)  Date of approval of the financial statements – The date on which all the
statements that comprise the financial statements, including the related notes,
have been prepared and those with the recognized authority have asserted that
they have taken responsibility for those financial statements. (Ref: Para. A2)

(c)  Date of the auditor's report – The date the auditor dates the report on the
financial statements in accordance with ISA (UK and Ireland) 700. (Ref: Para.
A3)

(d)  Date the financial statements are issued – The date that the auditor's report and
audited financial statements are made available to third parties. (Ref: Para. A4-
A5)

(e)  Subsequent events – Events occurring between the date of the financial statements and the date of the auditor's report, and facts that become known to the
auditor after the date of the auditor's report.

# Requirements

## Events Occurring between the Date of the Financial Statements and the Date of the Auditor's Report

The auditor shall perform audit procedures designed to obtain sufficient appropriate   **6**
audit evidence that all events occurring between the date of the financial statements
and the date of the auditor's report that require adjustment of, or disclosure in, the
financial statements have been identified. The auditor is not, however, expected to
perform additional audit procedures on matters to which previously applied audit
procedures have provided satisfactory conclusions. (Ref: Para. A6)

The auditor shall perform the procedures required by paragraph 6 so that they cover   **7**
the period from the date of the financial statements to the date of the auditor's
report, or as near as practicable thereto. The auditor shall take into account the
auditor's risk assessment in determining the nature and extent of such audit procedures, which shall include the following: (Ref: Para. A7-A8)

(a)  Obtaining an understanding of any procedures management has established to
ensure that subsequent events are identified.

(b)  Inquiring of management and, where appropriate, those charged with governance as to whether any subsequent events have occurred which might affect the
financial statements. (Ref: Para. A9)

(c)  Reading minutes, if any, of the meetings, of the entity's owners, management
and those charged with governance, that have been held after the date of the
financial statements and inquiring about matters discussed at any such meetings
for which minutes are not yet available. (Ref: Para. A10)

(d)  Reading the entity's latest subsequent interim financial statements, if any.

If, as a result of the procedures performed as required by paragraphs 6 and 7, the   **8**
auditor identifies events that require adjustment of, or disclosure in, the financial
statements, the auditor shall determine whether each such event is appropriately
reflected in those financial statements in accordance with the applicable financial
reporting framework.

**Written Representations**

9    The auditor shall request management and, where appropriate, those charged with governance, to provide a written representation in accordance with ISA (UK and Ireland) 580[3] that all events occurring subsequent to the date of the financial statements and for which the applicable financial reporting framework requires adjustment or disclosure have been adjusted or disclosed.

### Facts Which Become Known to the Auditor after the Date of the Auditor's Report but before the Date the Financial Statements Are Issued

10   The auditor has no obligation to perform any audit procedures regarding the financial statements after the date of the auditor's report. However, if, after the date of the auditor's report but before the date the financial statements are issued, a fact becomes known to the auditor that, had it been known to the auditor at the date of the auditor's report, may have caused the auditor to amend the auditor's report, the auditor shall: (Ref: Para. A11)

(a) Discuss the matter with management and, where appropriate, those charged with governance.
(b) Determine whether the financial statements need amendment and, if so,
(c) Inquire how management[3a] intends to address the matter in the financial statements.

11   If management[3a] amends the financial statements, the auditor shall:

(a) Carry out the audit procedures necessary in the circumstances on the amendment.
(b) Unless the circumstances in paragraph 12 apply:
   (i) Extend the audit procedures referred to in paragraphs 6 and 7 to the date of the new auditor's report; and
   (ii) Provide a new auditor's report on the amended financial statements. The new auditor's report shall not be dated earlier than the date of approval of the amended financial statements.

12   Where law, regulation or the financial reporting framework does not prohibit management[3a] from restricting the amendment of the financial statements to the effects of the subsequent event or events causing that amendment and those responsible for approving the financial statements are not prohibited from restricting their approval to that amendment, the auditor is permitted to restrict the audit procedures on subsequent events required in paragraph 11(b)(i) to that amendment. In such cases, the auditor shall either:

(a) Amend the auditor's report to include an additional date restricted to that amendment that thereby indicates that the auditor's procedures on subsequent events are restricted solely to the amendment of the financial statements described in the relevant note to the financial statements; or (Ref: Para. A12)
(b) Provide a new or amended auditor's report that includes a statement in an Emphasis of Matter paragraph[4] or Other Matter(s) paragraph that conveys that

---

[3] *ISA (UK and Ireland) 580, "Written Representations."*

[3a] *In the UK and Ireland the responsibility for amending the financial statements rests with those charged with governance.*

[4] *See ISA (UK and Ireland) 706, "Emphasis of Matter Paragraphs and Other Matter Paragraphs in the Independent Auditor's Report."*

the auditor's procedures on subsequent events are restricted solely to the amendment of the financial statements as described in the relevant note to the financial statements.

In some jurisdictions, management[3a] may not be required by law, regulation or the financial reporting framework to issue amended financial statements and, accordingly, the auditor need not provide an amended or new auditor's report. However, if management does not amend the financial statements in circumstances where the auditor believes they need to be amended, then: (Ref: Para. A13-A14)    **13**

(a) If the auditor's report has not yet been provided to the entity, the auditor shall modify the opinion as required by ISA (UK and Ireland) 705[5] and then provide the auditor's report; or

(b) If the auditor's report has already been provided to the entity, the auditor shall notify management and, unless all of those charged with governance are involved in managing the entity, those charged with governance, not to issue the financial statements to third parties before the necessary amendments have been made. If the financial statements are nevertheless subsequently issued without the necessary amendments, the auditor shall take appropriate action, to seek to prevent reliance on the auditor's report. (Ref. Para: A15-A16)

## Facts Which Become Known to the Auditor after the Financial Statements Have Been Issued

After the financial statements have been issued, the auditor has no obligation to perform any audit procedures regarding such financial statements. However, if, after the financial statements have been issued, a fact becomes known to the auditor that, had it been known to the auditor at the date of the auditor's report, may have caused the auditor to amend the auditor's report, the auditor shall:    **14**

(a) Discuss the matter with management and, where appropriate, those charged with governance.

(b) Determine whether the financial statements need amendment and, if so,

(c) Inquire how management intends to address the matter in the financial statements. (Ref: Para. A16-1 – A16-3)

If management[3a] amends the financial statements[5a], the auditor shall: (Ref: Para. A17)    **15**

(a) Carry out the audit procedures necessary in the circumstances on the amendment.

(b) Review the steps taken by management to ensure that anyone in receipt of the previously issued financial statements together with the auditor's report thereon is informed of the situation.

(c) Unless the circumstances in paragraph 12 apply:

   (i) Extend the audit procedures referred to in paragraphs 6 and 7 to the date of the new auditor's report, and date the new auditor's report no earlier than the date of approval of the amended financial statements; and

   (ii) Provide a new auditor's report on the amended financial statements.

(d) When the circumstances in paragraph 12 apply, amend the auditor's report, or provide a new auditor's report as required by paragraph 12.

---

[5] *ISA (UK and Ireland) 705, "Modifications to the Opinion in the Independent Auditor's Report."*

[5a] *In the UK the detailed regulations governing revised financial statements and directors' reports, where the revision is voluntary, are set out in section 454 of the Companies Act 2006. There are no provisions in the Companies Acts of the Republic of Ireland for revising financial statements.*

16    The auditor shall include in the new or amended auditor's report an Emphasis of Matter paragraph or Other Matter(s) paragraph referring to a note to the financial statements that more extensively discusses the reason for the amendment of the previously issued financial statements and to the earlier report provided by the auditor.

17    If management[5b] does not take the necessary steps to ensure that anyone in receipt of the previously issued financial statements is informed of the situation and does not amend the financial statements in circumstances where the auditor believes they need to be amended, the auditor shall notify management and, unless all of those charged with governance are involved in managing the entity[6], those charged with governance, that the auditor will seek to prevent future reliance on the auditor's report. If, despite such notification, management or those charged with governance do not take these necessary steps, the auditor shall take appropriate action to seek to prevent reliance on the auditor's report. (Ref: Para. A18 – A18-1)

*** 

# Application and Other Explanatory Material

## Scope of this ISA (UK and Ireland) (Ref: Para. 1)

A1    When the audited financial statements are included in other documents subsequent to the issuance of the financial statements, the auditor may have additional responsibilities relating to subsequent events that the auditor may need to consider, such as legal or regulatory requirements involving the offering of securities to the public in jurisdictions in which the securities are being offered. For example, the auditor may be required to perform additional audit procedures to the date of the final offering document. These procedures may include those referred to in paragraphs 6 and 7 performed up to a date at or near the effective date of the final offering document, and reading the offering document to assess whether the other information in the offering document is consistent with the financial information with which the auditor is associated.[7]

## Definitions

### *Date of Approval of the Financial Statements* (Ref: Para. 5(b))

A2    In some jurisdictions, law or regulation identifies the individuals or bodies (for example, management or those charged with governance) that are responsible for

---

[5b] *In the UK and Ireland, those charged with governance have responsibility for taking the steps referred to in paragraph 17.*

[6] *ISA (UK and Ireland) 260, "Communication with Those Charged with Governance," paragraph 13.*

[7] *See ISA (UK and Ireland) 200, "Overall Objectives of the Independent Auditor and the Conduct of an Audit in Accordance with International Standards on Auditing," paragraph 2.*
*Paragraph 2 of ISA (UK and Ireland) 200 includes the statement that "ISAs (UK and Ireland) do not address the responsibilities of the auditor that may exist in legislation, regulation or otherwise in connection with, for example, the offering of securities to the public. Such responsibilities may differ from those established in the ISAs (UK and Ireland). Accordingly, while the auditor may find aspects of the ISAs (UK and Ireland) helpful in such circumstances, it is the responsibility of the auditor to ensure compliance with all relevant legal, regulatory or professional obligations." In the UK and Ireland, standards and guidance for accountants engaged to prepare a report and/or letter for inclusion in, or in connection with, an investment circular are set out in APB's Statements of Investment Circular Reporting Standards (SIRS).*

concluding that all the statements that comprise the financial statements, including the related notes, have been prepared, and specifies the necessary approval process. In other jurisdictions, the approval process is not prescribed in law or regulation and the entity follows its own procedures in preparing and finalizing its financial statements in view of its management and governance structures. In some jurisdictions, final approval of the financial statements by shareholders is required. In these jurisdictions, final approval by shareholders is not necessary for the auditor to conclude that sufficient appropriate audit evidence on which to base the auditor's opinion on the financial statements has been obtained. The date of approval of the financial statements for purposes of the ISAs (UK and Ireland) is the earlier date on which those with the recognized authority determine that all the statements that comprise the financial statements, including the related notes, have been prepared and that those with the recognized authority have asserted that they have taken responsibility for those financial statements.

**Date of the Auditor's Report** (Ref: Para. 5(c))

The auditor's report cannot be dated earlier than the date on which the auditor has    A3
obtained sufficient appropriate audit evidence on which to base the opinion on the financial statements including evidence that all the statements that comprise the financial statements, including the related notes, have been prepared and that those with the recognized authority have asserted that they have taken responsibility for those financial statements.[8] Consequently, the date of the auditor's report cannot be earlier than the date of approval of the financial statements as defined in paragraph 5(b). A time period may elapse due to administrative issues between the date of the auditor's report as defined in paragraph 5(c) and the date the auditor's report is provided to the entity.

**Date the Financial Statements Are Issued** (Ref: Para. 5(d))

The date the financial statements are issued generally depends on the regulatory    A4
environment of the entity. In some circumstances, the date the financial statements are issued may be the date that they are filed with a regulatory authority. Since audited financial statements cannot be issued without an auditor's report, the date that the audited financial statements are issued must not only be at or later than the date of the auditor's report, but must also be at or later than the date the auditor's report is provided to the entity.

*Considerations Specific to Public Sector Entities*

In the case of the public sector, the date the financial statements are issued may be    A5
the date the audited financial statements and the auditor's report thereon are presented to the legislature or otherwise made public.

---

[8] *ISA 700, paragraph 41. In some cases, law or regulation also identifies the point in the financial statement reporting process at which the audit is expected to be complete.*

*The APB has not promulgated ISA 700 as issued by the IAASB for application in the UK and Ireland. In the UK and Ireland the applicable auditing standard is ISA (UK and Ireland) 700, "The Auditor's Report on Financial Statements." Paragraph 24 of ISA (UK and Ireland) 700 establishes requirements regarding dating of the auditor's report, including that this shall not be earlier than the date the auditor has considered all necessary available evidence.*

**Events Occurring between the Date of the Financial Statements and the Date of the Auditor's Report** (Ref: Para. 6-9)

A6   Depending on the auditor's risk assessment, the audit procedures required by paragraph 6 may include procedures, necessary to obtain sufficient appropriate audit evidence, involving the review or testing of accounting records or transactions occurring between the date of the financial statements and the date of the auditor's report. The audit procedures required by paragraphs 6 and 7 are in addition to procedures that the auditor may perform for other purposes that, nevertheless, may provide evidence about subsequent events (for example, to obtain audit evidence for account balances as at the date of the financial statements, such as cut-off procedures or procedures in relation to subsequent receipts of accounts receivable).

A7   Paragraph 7 stipulates certain audit procedures in this context that the auditor is required to perform pursuant to paragraph 6. The subsequent events procedures that the auditor performs may, however, depend on the information that is available and, in particular, the extent to which the accounting records have been prepared since the date of the financial statements. Where the accounting records are not up-to-date, and accordingly no interim financial statements (whether for internal or external purposes) have been prepared, or minutes of meetings of management or those charged with governance have not been prepared, relevant audit procedures may take the form of inspection of available books and records, including bank statements. Paragraph A8 gives examples of some of the additional matters that the auditor may consider in the course of these inquiries.

A8   In addition to the audit procedures required by paragraph 7, the auditor may consider it necessary and appropriate to:

- Read the entity's latest available budgets, cash flow forecasts and other related management reports for periods after the date of the financial statements;
- Inquire, or extend previous oral or written inquiries, of the entity's legal counsel concerning litigation and claims; or
- Consider whether written representations covering particular subsequent events may be necessary to support other audit evidence and thereby obtain sufficient appropriate audit evidence.

*Inquiry* (Ref. Para. 7(b))

A9   In inquiring of management and, where appropriate, those charged with governance, as to whether any subsequent events have occurred that might affect the financial statements, the auditor may inquire as to the current status of items that were accounted for on the basis of preliminary or inconclusive data and may make specific inquiries about the following matters:

- Whether new commitments, borrowings or guarantees have been entered into.
- Whether sales or acquisitions of assets have occurred or are planned.
- Whether there have been increases in capital or issuance of debt instruments, such as the issue of new shares or debentures, or an agreement to merge or liquidate has been made or is planned.
- Whether any assets have been appropriated by government or destroyed, for example, by fire or flood.
- Whether there have been any developments regarding contingencies.
- Whether any unusual accounting adjustments have been made or are contemplated.
- Whether any events have occurred or are likely to occur that will bring into question the appropriateness of accounting policies used in the financial

statements, as would be the case, for example, if such events call into question the validity of the going concern assumption.

* Whether any events have occurred that are relevant to the measurement of estimates or provisions made in the financial statements.
* Whether any events have occurred that are relevant to the recoverability of assets.

*Reading Minutes* (Ref. Para. 7(c))

*Considerations Specific to Public Sector Entities*

In the public sector, the auditor may read the official records of relevant proceedings of the legislature and inquire about matters addressed in proceedings for which official records are not yet available.                                                          **A10**

## Facts Which Become Known to the Auditor after the Date of the Auditor's Report but before the Date the Financial Statements Are Issued

*Management Responsibility towards Auditor* (Ref: Para. 10)

As explained in ISA (UK and Ireland) 210, the terms of the audit engagement include the agreement of management[8a] to inform the auditor of facts that may affect the financial statements, of which management may become aware during the period from the date of the auditor's report to the date the financial statements are issued.[9]                                        **A11**

*Dual Dating* (Ref: Para. 12(a))

When, in the circumstances described in paragraph 12(a), the auditor amends the auditor's report to include an additional date restricted to that amendment, the date of the auditor's report on the financial statements prior to their subsequent amendment by management[3a] remains unchanged because this date informs the reader as to when the audit work on those financial statements was completed. However, an additional date is included in the auditor's report to inform users that the auditor's procedures subsequent to that date were restricted to the subsequent amendment of the financial statements. The following is an illustration of such an additional date:                                                             **A12**

> "(Date of auditor's report), except as to Note Y, which is as of (date of completion of audit procedures restricted to amendment described in Note Y)."

*No Amendment of Financial Statements by Management* (Ref: Para. 13)

In some jurisdictions, management[3a] may not be required by law, regulation or the financial reporting framework to issue amended financial statements. This is often the case when issuance of the financial statements for the following period is imminent, provided appropriate disclosures are made in such statements.                      **A13**

---

[8a] *In the UK and Ireland the responsibility to inform the auditor of facts which may affect the financial statements rests with those charged with governance.*

[9] *ISA (UK and Ireland) 210, "Agreeing the Terms of Audit Engagements," paragraph A23.*

*Considerations Specific to Public Sector Entities*

A14    In the public sector, the actions taken in accordance with paragraph 13 when management does not amend the financial statements may also include reporting separately to the legislature, or other relevant body in the reporting hierarchy, on the implications of the subsequent event for the financial statements and the auditor's report.

***Auditor Action to Seek to Prevent Reliance on Auditor's Report*** (Ref: Para. 13(b))

A15    The auditor may need to fulfill additional legal obligations even when the auditor has notified management not to issue the financial statements and management has agreed to this request.

A16    Where management has issued the financial statements despite the auditor's notification not to issue the financial statements to third parties, the auditor's course of action to prevent reliance on the auditor's report on the financial statements depends upon the auditor's legal rights and obligations. Consequently, the auditor may consider it appropriate to seek legal advice.

**Facts Which Become Known to the Auditor after the Financial Statements Have Been Issued**

A16-1    When issuing a new report the auditor has regard to the regulations relating to reports on revised annual financial statements and directors' reports[5a].

A16-2    Where the auditor becomes aware of a fact relevant to the audited financial statements which did not exist at the date of the auditor's report there are no statutory provisions for revising financial statements. The auditor discusses with those charged with governance whether they should withdraw the financial statements and where those charged with governance decide not to do so the auditor may wish to take advice on whether it might be possible to withdraw their report. In both cases, other possible courses of action include the making of a statement by those charged with governance or the auditor at the annual general meeting. In any event legal advice may be helpful.

A16-3    In the UK or the Republic of Ireland the auditor has a statutory right to attend the AGM and be heard on any part of the business of the meeting which concerns them as auditor, including making a statement about facts discovered after the date of the auditor's report and this implies that where subsequent events come to the attention of the auditor, the auditor needs to consider what to do in relation to them.

***No Amendment of Financial Statements by Management*** (Ref: Para. 15)

*Considerations Specific to Public Sector Entities*

A17    In some jurisdictions, entities in the public sector may be prohibited from issuing amended financial statements by law or regulation. In such circumstances, the appropriate course of action for the auditor may be to report to the appropriate statutory body.

**Auditor Action to Seek to Prevent Reliance on Auditor's Report** (Ref: Para. 17)

Where the auditor believes that management, or those charged with governance, **A18** have failed to take the necessary steps to prevent reliance on the auditor's report on financial statements previously issued by the entity despite the auditor's prior notification that the auditor will take action to seek to prevent such reliance, the auditor's course of action depends upon the auditor's legal rights and obligations. Consequently, the auditor may consider it appropriate to seek legal advice.

Where the financial statements are issued but have not yet been laid before the **A18-1** members or equivalent, or if those charged with governance do not intend to make an appropriate statement at the annual general meeting, then the auditor may consider making an appropriate statement at the annual general meeting. The auditor does not have a statutory right to communicate directly in writing with the members although, if the auditor resigns or is removed or is not reappointed, the auditor has, for example, various duties under company law[9a].

---

[9a] *The auditor of a limited company in Great Britain who ceases to hold office as auditor is required to comply with the requirements of section 519 of the Companies Act 2006 regarding the statement to be made by the auditor in relation to ceasing to hold office. Equivalent requirements for the Republic of Ireland, are contained in section 185 of the Companies Act 1990.*

# Addendum

*This addendum provides a summary of APB's rationale for retaining or excluding in the proposed clarified ISA (UK and Ireland) the supplementary requirements in the existing ISA (UK and Ireland). It also sets out the supplementary guidance material in the existing ISA (UK and Ireland) that APB considers is not necessary to retain in light of the improvements in the underlying Clarity ISAs issued by the IAASB as part of the Clarity Project. It is provided for information and does not form part of the proposed clarified ISA (UK and Ireland).*

*The Consultation Paper published with the exposure drafts explains the general approach used by the APB for determining whether current supplementary material should be proposed to be retained.*

## Analysis of proposed treatment of current APB supplementary material in current ISA (UK and Ireland) 560

### Requirements

There are no supplementary requirements in the current ISA (UK and Ireland) 560.

### Guidance

The following guidance in current ISA (UK and Ireland) 560 has not been carried forward to the proposed clarified standard.

| Current paragraph reference (*Italic text is from IAASB for context*) |
| --- |
| 1-1. – 1-4. Definitions of management and those charged with governance.] |
| 1-5.   In the UK and Ireland the auditor has responsibility for three phases when considering subsequent events. The ISA (UK and Ireland) provides guidance on the auditor's responsibilities in relation to:<br>(a)  Events occurring between period end and the date of the auditor's report;<br>(b)  Facts discovered after the date of the auditor's report but before the financial statements are issued; and<br>(c)  Facts discovered after financial statements have been issued but before the laying of the financial statements before the members, or equivalent. |
| 1-6.   These three phases – and auditor's responsibilities in relation to them – leading to the laying of financial statements before members apply to all entities. However, in practice one or more of the phases may be so short as not to require separate consideration by the auditor, for example where the meeting at which those charged with governance of a small owner-managed entity approve the financial statements, and the auditor's report is signed, is immediately followed by the entity's annual general meeting. |
| 1-7.   Facts discovered after the laying of the financial statements before the members may result in those charged with governance issuing revised accounts as defined by relevant legislation. The auditor's considerations in relation to revised financial statements are covered in paragraphs 14 to 18 below. |

| **Current paragraph reference (*Italic text is from IAASB for context*)** |
|---|
| 5-1. In the UK and Ireland the auditor reviews procedures established by those charged with governance and inquires of those charged with governance as to whether any subsequent events have occurred which might affect the financial statements. |
| 9 *When, after the date of the auditor's report but before the financial statements are issued, the auditor becomes aware of a fact which may materially affect the financial statements, the auditor should consider whether the financial statements need amendment, should discuss the matter with management[2], and should take the action appropriate in the circumstances.* |
| [2] In the UK and Ireland the auditor discusses these matters with those charged with governance. Those charged with governance are responsible for the preparation of the financial statements. |

# Proposed Clarified International Standard on Auditing (UK and Ireland) 570
## Going concern

*(Effective for audits of financial statements for periods ending on or after 15 December 2010)*

## Contents

International Standard on Auditing (UK and Ireland) (ISA (UK and Ireland)) 570, "Going Concern" should be read in conjunction with ISA (UK and Ireland) 200, "Overall Objectives of the Independent Auditor and the Conduct of an Audit in Accordance with International Standards on Auditing (UK and Ireland)."

# Introduction

## Scope of this ISA (UK and Ireland)

This International Standard on Auditing (UK and Ireland) (ISA (UK and Ireland)) deals with the auditor's responsibilities in the audit of financial statements relating to management's use of the going concern assumption in the preparation of the financial statements.   **1**

## Going Concern Assumption

Under the going concern assumption, an entity is viewed as continuing in business   **2** for the foreseeable future. General purpose financial statements are prepared on a going concern basis, unless management either intends to liquidate the entity or to cease operations, or has no realistic alternative but to do so. Special purpose financial statements may or may not be prepared in accordance with a financial reporting framework for which the going concern basis is relevant (e.g., the going concern basis is not relevant for some financial statements prepared on a tax basis in particular jurisdictions). When the use of the going concern assumption is appropriate, assets and liabilities are recorded on the basis that the entity will be able to realize its assets and discharge its liabilities in the normal course of business. (Ref: Para. A1)

## Responsibility for Assessment of the Entity's Ability to Continue as a Going Concern

Some financial reporting frameworks contain an explicit requirement for manage-   **3** ment[1a] to make a specific assessment of the entity's ability to continue as a going concern, and standards regarding matters to be considered and disclosures to be made in connection with going concern. For example, International Accounting Standard (IAS) 1 requires management to make an assessment of an entity's ability to continue as a going concern.[1] The detailed requirements regarding management's responsibility to assess the entity's ability to continue as a going concern and related financial statement disclosures may also be set out in law or regulation.

In other financial reporting frameworks, there may be no explicit requirement for   **4** management to make a specific assessment of the entity's ability to continue as a going concern. Nevertheless, since the going concern assumption is a fundamental principle in the preparation of financial statements as discussed in paragraph 2, the preparation of the financial statements requires management to assess the entity's ability to continue as a going concern even if the financial reporting framework does not include an explicit requirement to do so.

Management's[1a] assessment of the entity's ability to continue as a going concern   **5** involves making a judgment, at a particular point in time, about inherently uncertain future outcomes of events or conditions. The following factors are relevant to that judgment:

- The degree of uncertainty associated with the outcome of an event or condition increases significantly the further into the future an event or condition or the

[1a] *In the UK and Ireland those charged with governance are responsible for the preparation of the financial statements and the assessment of the entity's ability to continue as a going concern.*

[1] *IAS 1, "Presentation of Financial Statements" as at 1 January 2009, paragraphs 25-26.*

outcome occurs. For that reason, most financial reporting frameworks that require an explicit management assessment specify the period for which management is required to take into account all available information.

- The size and complexity of the entity, the nature and condition of its business and the degree to which it is affected by external factors affect the judgment regarding the outcome of events or conditions.
- Any judgment about the future is based on information available at the time at which the judgment is made. Subsequent events may result in outcomes that are inconsistent with judgments that were reasonable at the time they were made.

### Responsibilities of the Auditor

6    The auditor's responsibility is to obtain sufficient appropriate audit evidence about the appropriateness of management's[1a] use of the going concern assumption in the preparation and presentation of the financial statements and to conclude whether there is a material uncertainty about the entity's ability to continue as a going concern. This responsibility exists even if the financial reporting framework used in the preparation of the financial statements does not include an explicit requirement for management to make a specific assessment of the entity's ability to continue as a going concern.

7    However, as described in ISA (UK and Ireland) 200,[2] the potential effects of inherent limitations on the auditor's ability to detect material misstatements are greater for future events or conditions that may cause an entity to cease to continue as a going concern. The auditor cannot predict such future events or conditions. Accordingly, the absence of any reference to going concern uncertainty in an auditor's report cannot be viewed as a guarantee as to the entity's ability to continue as a going concern.

### Effective Date

8    This ISA (UK and Ireland) is effective for audits of financial statements for periods ending on or after 15 December 2010.

# Objectives

9    The objectives of the auditor are:

(a)    To obtain sufficient appropriate audit evidence regarding the appropriateness of management's[1a] use of the going concern assumption in the preparation of the financial statements;

(b)    To conclude, based on the audit evidence obtained, whether a material uncertainty exists related to events or conditions that may cast significant doubt on the entity's ability to continue as a going concern; and

(c)    To determine the implications for the auditor's report.

---

[2] ISA (UK and Ireland) 200, "Overall Objectives of the Independent Auditor and the Conduct of an Audit in Accordance with International Standards on Auditing."

# Requirements

## Risk Assessment Procedures and Related Activities

When performing risk assessment procedures as required by ISA (UK and Ireland) 315,[3] the auditor shall consider whether there are events or conditions that may cast significant doubt on the entity's ability to continue as a going concern. In so doing, the auditor shall determine whether management[1a] has already performed a preliminary assessment of the entity's ability to continue as a going concern, and: (Ref: Para. A2-A5)   **10**

(a) If such an assessment has been performed, the auditor shall discuss the assessment with management and determine whether management has identified events or conditions that, individually or collectively, may cast significant doubt on the entity's ability to continue as a going concern and, if so, management's plans to address them; or

(b) If such an assessment has not yet been performed, the auditor shall discuss with management the basis for the intended use of the going concern assumption, and inquire of management whether events or conditions exist that, individually or collectively, may cast significant doubt on the entity's ability to continue as a going concern.

The auditor shall remain alert throughout the audit for audit evidence of events or conditions that may cast significant doubt on the entity's ability to continue as a going concern. (Ref: Para. A6)   **11**

## Evaluating Management's Assessment

The auditor shall evaluate management's[1a] assessment of the entity's ability to continue as a going concern. (Ref: Para. A7-A9; A11-A12)   **12**

In evaluating management's[1a] assessment of the entity's ability to continue as a going concern, the auditor shall cover the same period as that used by management to make its assessment as required by the applicable financial reporting framework, or by law or regulation if it specifies a longer period. If management's assessment of the entity's ability to continue as a going concern covers less than twelve months from the date of the financial statements as defined in ISA 560,[4] the auditor shall request management to extend its assessment period to at least twelve months from that date. (Ref: Para. A10-A12)   **13**

In the UK and Ireland the period used by the those charged with governance in making their assessment is usually at least one year from the date of approval of the financial statements[4a].   **13-1**

---

[3] ISA (UK and Ireland) 315, "Identifying and Assessing the Risks of Material Misstatement through Understanding the Entity and Its Environment," paragraph 5.

[4] ISA (UK and Ireland) 560, "Subsequent Events," paragraph 5(a).

[4a] Guidance issued by the FRC for directors of listed companies in "An Update for Directors of Listed Companies: Going Concern and Liquidity Risk" (November 2008) states that "Where the period considered by the directors has been limited, for example to a period of less than twelve months from the date of the approval of the annual report and accounts, the directors need to consider whether additional disclosures are necessary to explain adequately the assumptions that underlie the adoption of the going concern basis." Companies complying with UK Financial Reporting Standard 18, "Accounting Policies," are required to make disclosure if the period considered by the directors is less than twelve months from the date of approval of the financial statements.

**13-2**   Having regard to the future period to which those charged with governance have paid particular attention in assessing going concern, the auditor shall plan and perform procedures specifically designed to identify any material matters which could indicate concern about the entity's ability to continue as a going concern. (Ref: Para. A10-1 – A10-6)

**14**   In evaluating management's[1a] assessment, the auditor shall consider whether management's assessment includes all relevant information of which the auditor is aware as a result of the audit.

### Period beyond Management's[1a] Assessment

**15**   The auditor shall inquire of management as to its knowledge of events or conditions beyond the period of management's[1a] assessment that may cast significant doubt on the entity's ability to continue as a going concern. (Ref: Para. A13-A14)

### Additional Audit Procedures When Events or Conditions Are Identified

**16**   If events or conditions have been identified that may cast significant doubt on the entity's ability to continue as a going concern, the auditor shall obtain sufficient appropriate audit evidence to determine whether or not a material uncertainty exists through performing additional audit procedures, including consideration of mitigating factors. These procedures shall include: (Ref: Para. A15)

(a)   Where management[1a] has not yet performed an assessment of the entity's ability to continue as a going concern, requesting management to make its assessment.

(b)   Evaluating management's[1a] plans for future actions in relation to its going concern assessment, whether the outcome of these plans is likely to improve the situation and whether management's plans are feasible in the circumstances. (Ref: Para. A16)

(c)   Where the entity has prepared a cash flow forecast, and analysis of the forecast is a significant factor in considering the future outcome of events or conditions in the evaluation of management's[1a] plans for future action: (Ref: Para. A17-A18)

(i)   Evaluating the reliability of the underlying data generated to prepare the forecast; and

(ii)   Determining whether there is adequate support for the assumptions underlying the forecast.

(d)   Considering whether any additional facts or information have become available since the date on which management made its assessment.

(e)   Requesting written representations from management and, where appropriate, those charged with governance, regarding their plans for future action and the feasibility of these plans[1a].

### Audit Conclusions and Reporting

**17**   Based on the audit evidence obtained, the auditor shall conclude whether, in the auditor's judgment, a material uncertainty exists related to events or conditions that, individually or collectively, may cast significant doubt on the entity's ability to continue as a going concern. A material uncertainty exists when the magnitude of its potential impact and likelihood of occurrence is such that, in the auditor's judgment, appropriate disclosure of the nature and implications of the uncertainty is necessary for:

(a) In the case of a fair presentation financial reporting framework, the fair presentation of the financial statements, or

(b) In the case of a compliance framework, the financial statements not to be misleading. (Ref: Para. A19)

| | |
|---|---|
| The auditor shall document the extent of the auditor's concern (if any) about the entity's ability to continue as a going concern. | **17-1** |
| If the period to which those charged with governance have paid particular attention in assessing going concern is less than one year from the date of approval of the financial statements, and those charged with governance have not disclosed that fact, the auditor shall do so within the auditor's report[4b]. (Ref: Para A19-1) | **17-2** |

## Use of Going Concern Assumption Appropriate but a Material Uncertainty Exists

If the auditor concludes that the use of the going concern assumption is appropriate in the circumstances but a material uncertainty exists, the auditor shall determine whether the financial statements: **18**

(a) Adequately describe the principal events or conditions that may cast significant doubt on the entity's ability to continue as a going concern and management's[1a] plans to deal with these events or conditions; and

(b) Disclose clearly that there is a material uncertainty related to events or conditions that may cast significant doubt on the entity's ability to continue as a going concern and, therefore, that it may be unable to realize its assets and discharge its liabilities in the normal course of business. (Ref: Para. A20)

If adequate disclosure is made in the financial statements, the auditor shall express an unmodified opinion and include an Emphasis of Matter paragraph in the auditor's report to: **19**

(a) Highlight the existence of a material uncertainty relating to the event or condition that may cast significant doubt on the entity's ability to continue as a going concern; and to

(b) Draw attention to the note in the financial statements that discloses the matters set out in paragraph 18. (See ISA (UK and Ireland) 706.[5]) (Ref: Para. A21-A22)

If adequate disclosure is not made in the financial statements, the auditor shall express a qualified opinion or adverse opinion, as appropriate, in accordance with ISA (UK and Ireland) 705.[6]) The auditor shall state in the auditor's report that there is a material uncertainty that may cast significant doubt about the entity's ability to continue as a going concern. (Ref: Para. A23-A24) **20**

---

[4b] *If the non-disclosure of the fact in the financial statements is a departure from the requirements of the applicable financial reporting framework, the auditor would give a qualified opinion ("except for").*

[5] ISA (UK and Ireland) 706, "Emphasis of Matter Paragraphs and Other Matter Paragraphs in the Independent Auditor's Report."

[6] ISA (UK and Ireland) 705, "Modifications to the Opinion in the Independent Auditor's Report."

## Use of Going Concern Assumption Inappropriate

21   If the financial statements have been prepared on a going concern basis but, in the auditor's judgment, management's[1a] use of the going concern assumption in the financial statements is inappropriate, the auditor shall express an adverse opinion. (Ref: Para. A25-A26)

## Management Unwilling to Make or Extend Its Assessment

22   If management[1a] is unwilling to make or extend its assessment when requested to do so by the auditor, the auditor shall consider the implications for the auditor's report. (Ref: Para. A27)

## Communication with Those Charged with Governance

23   Unless all those charged with governance are involved in managing the entity[7], the auditor shall communicate with those charged with governance events or conditions identified that may cast significant doubt on the entity's ability to continue as a going concern. Such communication with those charged with governance shall include the following:

(a)   Whether the events or conditions constitute a material uncertainty;
(b)   Whether the use of the going concern assumption is appropriate in the preparation and presentation of the financial statements; and
(c)   The adequacy of related disclosures in the financial statements.

## Significant Delay in the Approval of Financial Statements

24   If there is significant delay in the approval of the financial statements by management or those charged with governance after the date of the financial statements, the auditor shall inquire as to the reasons for the delay. If the auditor believes that the delay could be related to events or conditions relating to the going concern assessment, the auditor shall perform those additional audit procedures necessary, as described in paragraph 16, as well as consider the effect on the auditor's conclusion regarding the existence of a material uncertainty, as described in paragraph 17.

\*\*\*

# Application and Other Explanatory Material

## Going Concern Assumption (Ref: Para. 2)

### *Considerations Specific to Public Sector Entities*

A1   Management's[1a] use of the going concern assumption is also relevant to public sector entities. For example, International Public Sector Accounting Standard (IPSAS) 1 addresses the issue of the ability of public sector entities to continue as going concerns.[8] Going concern risks may arise, but are not limited to, situations where public sector entities operate on a for-profit basis, where government support may be reduced or withdrawn, or in the case of privatization. Events or conditions that may

---

[7] *ISA (UK and Ireland) 260, "Communication with Those Charged with Governance," paragraph 13.*

[8] *IPSAS 1, "Presentation of Financial Statements" as at 1 January 2007, paragraphs 38-41.*

cast significant doubt on an entity's ability to continue as a going concern in the public sector may include situations where the public sector entity lacks funding for its continued existence or when policy decisions are made that affect the services provided by the public sector entity.

## Risk Assessment Procedures and Related Activities

*Events or Conditions That May Cast Doubt about Going Concern Assumption* (Ref: Para. 10)

The following are examples of events or conditions that, individually or collectively, **A2** may cast significant doubt about the going concern assumption. This listing is not all-inclusive nor does the existence of one or more of the items always signify that a material uncertainty exists.

Financial

- Net liability or net current liability position.
- Fixed-term borrowings approaching maturity without realistic prospects of renewal or repayment; or excessive reliance on short-term borrowings to finance long-term assets.
- Indications of withdrawal of financial support by creditors.
- Negative operating cash flows indicated by historical or prospective financial statements.
- Adverse key financial ratios.
- Substantial operating losses or significant deterioration in the value of assets used to generate cash flows.
- Arrears or discontinuance of dividends.
- Inability to pay creditors on due dates.
- Inability to comply with the terms of loan agreements.
- Change from credit to cash-on-delivery transactions with suppliers.
- Inability to obtain financing for essential new product development or other essential investments.

Operating

- Management intentions to liquidate the entity or to cease operations.
- Loss of key management without replacement.
- Loss of a major market, key customer(s), franchise, license, or principal supplier(s).
- Labor difficulties.
- Shortages of important supplies.
- Emergence of a highly successful competitor.
Other
- Non-compliance with capital or other statutory requirements.
- Pending legal or regulatory proceedings against the entity that may, if successful, result in claims that the entity is unlikely to be able to satisfy.
- Changes in law or regulation or government policy expected to adversely affect the entity.
- Uninsured or underinsured catastrophes when they occur.
The significance of such events or conditions often can be mitigated by other factors. For example, the effect of an entity being unable to make its normal debt repayments may be counterbalanced by management's plans to maintain adequate cash flows by alternative means, such as by disposing of assets, rescheduling loan repayments, or obtaining additional capital. Similarly, the

loss of a principal supplier may be mitigated by the availability of a suitable alternative source of supply.

**A3** The risk assessment procedures required by paragraph 10 help the auditor to determine whether management's use of the going concern assumption is likely to be an important issue and its impact on planning the audit. These procedures also allow for more timely discussions with management, including a discussion of management's[1a] plans and resolution of any identified going concern issues.

*Considerations Specific to Smaller Entities*

**A4** The size of an entity may affect its ability to withstand adverse conditions. Small entities may be able to respond quickly to exploit opportunities, but may lack reserves to sustain operations.

**A5** Conditions of particular relevance to small entities include the risk that banks and other lenders may cease to support the entity, as well as the possible loss of a principal supplier, major customer, key employee, or the right to operate under a license, franchise or other legal agreement.

**Remaining Alert throughout the Audit for Audit Evidence about Events or Conditions** (Ref: Para. 11)

**A6** ISA (UK and Ireland) 315 requires the auditor to revise the auditor's risk assessment and modify the further planned audit procedures accordingly when additional audit evidence is obtained during the course of the audit that affects the auditor's assessment of risk.[9] If events or conditions that may cast significant doubt on the entity's ability to continue as a going concern are identified after the auditor's risk assessments are made, in addition to performing the procedures in paragraph 16, the auditor's assessment of the risks of material misstatement may need to be revised. The existence of such events or conditions may also affect the nature, timing and extent of the auditor's further procedures in response to the assessed risks. ISA (UK and Ireland) 330[10] establishes requirements and provides guidance on this issue.

**Evaluating Management's[1a] Assessment**

**Management's[1a] Assessment and Supporting Analysis and the Auditor's Evaluation** (Ref: Para. 12)

**A7** Management's[1a] assessment of the entity's ability to continue as a going concern is a key part of the auditor's consideration of management's use of the going concern assumption.

**A8** It is not the auditor's responsibility to rectify the lack of analysis by management[1a]. In some circumstances, however, the lack of detailed analysis by management to support its assessment may not prevent the auditor from concluding whether management's use of the going concern assumption is appropriate in the circumstances. For example, when there is a history of profitable operations and a ready access to financial resources, management may make its assessment without detailed analysis. In this case, the auditor's evaluation of the appropriateness of management's

---

[9] *ISA (UK and Ireland) 315, paragraph 31.*

[10] *ISA (UK and Ireland) 330, "The Auditor's Responses to Assessed Risks."*

assessment may be made without performing detailed evaluation procedures if the auditor's other audit procedures are sufficient to enable the auditor to conclude whether management's use of the going concern assumption in the preparation of the financial statements is appropriate in the circumstances.

In other circumstances, evaluating management's[1a] assessment of the entity's ability to continue as a going concern, as required by paragraph 12, may include an evaluation of the process management followed to make its assessment, the assumptions on which the assessment is based and management's plans for future action and whether management's plans are feasible in the circumstances.  **A9**

### The Period of Management's[1a] Assessment (Ref: Para. 13)

Most financial reporting frameworks requiring an explicit management[1a] assessment specify the period for which management is required to take into account all available information.[11]  **A10**

In assessing going concern, those charged with governance take account of all relevant information of which they are aware at the time. The nature of the exercise entails that those charged with governance look forward, and there will be some future period to which they will pay particular attention in assessing going concern. It is not possible to specify a minimum length for this period: it is recognized in any case that any such period would be artificial and arbitrary since in reality there is no 'cut off point' after which there should be a sudden change in the approach adopted by those charged with governance. The length of the period is likely to depend upon such factors as:  **A10-1**

* The entity's reporting and budgeting systems; and
* The nature of the entity, including its size or complexity.

Where the period considered by those charged with governance has been limited, for example, to a period of less than one year from the date of approval of the financial statements, those charged with governance will have determined whether, in its opinion, the financial statements require any additional disclosure to explain adequately the assumptions that underlie the adoption of the going concern basis.

A determination of the sufficiency of the evidence supplied to the auditor by those charged with governance will depend on the particular circumstances. However, to be sufficient the evidence may not require formal cash flow forecasts and budgets to have been prepared for the period ending one year from the date of approval of the financial statements. Although such forecasts and budgets are likely to provide the most persuasive evidence, alternative sources of evidence may also be acceptable. Often, the auditor through discussion with those charged with governance of their plans and expectations for that period may be able to obtain satisfaction that those charged with governance have in fact paid particular attention to a period of one year from the date of approval of the financial statements.  **A10-2**

---

[11] *For example, IAS 1 defines this as a period that should be at least, but is not limited to, twelve months from the balance sheet date.*

*FRS 18 does not specify this period but does require that where the foreseeable future considered by the directors has been limited to a period of less than one year from the date of approval of the financial statements, that fact should be disclosed in the financial statements.*

**A10-3**   If the future period to which those charged with governance have paid particular attention is, as described in paragraph A10-2, not very long, those charged with governance will have determined whether, in their opinion, the financial statements require any additional disclosures to explain adequately the assumptions that underlie the adoption of the going concern basis. The auditor assesses whether to concur with the judgments of those charged with governance regarding the need for additional disclosures and their adequacy. Disclosure, however, does not eliminate the need to make appropriate judgments about the suitability of the future period as an adequate basis for assessing the position.

### Procedures to Identify Material Matters Indicating Concern

**A10-4**   The basis for the auditor's procedures to identify any material matters which could indicate concern about the entity's ability to continue as a going concern is the information upon which those charged with governance have based their assessment and the reasoning of those charged with governance. The auditor assesses whether this constitutes sufficient appropriate audit evidence for the purpose of the audit and whether the auditor concurs with the judgment of those charged with governance about the need for additional disclosures.

**A10-5**   The following factors in particular may affect the information available to the auditor, and whether the auditor considers this information constitutes sufficient audit evidence for the purpose of the audit.

(a) *The nature of the entity (its size and the complexity of its circumstances, for instance).* This ISA (UK and Ireland) applies to the audits of the financial statements of all sizes of entity. The larger or more complex the entity the more sophisticated is likely to be the information available and needed to support the assessment of whether it is appropriate to adopt the going concern basis.

(b) *Whether the information relates to future events, and if so how far into the future those events lie.* The information relating to the period falling after one year from the balance sheet date is often prepared in far less detail and subject to a greater degree of estimation than the information relating to periods ending on or before one year from the balance sheet date.

**A10-6**   The extent of the procedures is influenced primarily by the excess of the financial resources available to the entity over the financial resources that it requires. The entity's procedures (and the auditor's procedures) need not always be elaborate in order to provide sufficient appropriate audit evidence. For example, the auditor may not always need to examine budgets and forecasts for this purpose. This is particularly likely to be the case in respect of entities with uncomplicated circumstances. Many smaller companies fall into this category.

### Considerations Specific to Smaller Entities (Ref: Para. 12-13)

**A11**   In many cases, the management[1a] of smaller entities may not have prepared a detailed assessment of the entity's ability to continue as a going concern, but instead may rely on in-depth knowledge of the business and anticipated future prospects. Nevertheless, in accordance with the requirements of this ISA (UK and Ireland), the auditor needs to evaluate management's assessment of the entity's ability to continue as a going concern. For smaller entities, it may be appropriate to discuss the medium and long-term financing of the entity with management, provided that management's contentions can be corroborated by sufficient documentary evidence and are not inconsistent with the auditor's understanding of the entity. Therefore, the requirement in paragraph 13 for the auditor to request management to extend its assessment may, for example, be satisfied by discussion, inquiry and inspection of supporting documentation, for example, orders received for future supply, evaluated as to their feasibility or otherwise substantiated.

Continued support by owner-managers is often important to smaller entities' ability to continue as a going concern. Where a small entity is largely financed by a loan from the owner-manager, it may be important that these funds are not withdrawn. For example, the continuance of a small entity in financial difficulty may be dependent on the owner-manager subordinating a loan to the entity in favor of banks or other creditors, or the owner manager supporting a loan for the entity by providing a guarantee with his or her personal assets as collateral. In such circumstances the auditor may obtain appropriate documentary evidence of the subordination of the owner-manager's loan or of the guarantee. Where an entity is dependent on additional support from the owner-manager, the auditor may evaluate the owner-manager's ability to meet the obligation under the support arrangement. In addition, the auditor may request written confirmation of the terms and conditions attaching to such support and the owner-manager's intention or understanding.    **A12**

## Period beyond Management's[1a] Assessment (Ref: Para. 15)

As required by paragraph 11, the auditor remains alert to the possibility that there may be known events, scheduled or otherwise, or conditions that will occur beyond the period of assessment used by management[1a] that may bring into question the appropriateness of management's use of the going concern assumption in preparing the financial statements. Since the degree of uncertainty associated with the outcome of an event or condition increases as the event or condition is further into the future, in considering events or conditions further in the future, the indications of going concern issues need to be significant before the auditor needs to consider taking further action. If such events or conditions are identified, the auditor may need to request management to evaluate the potential significance of the event or condition on its assessment of the entity's ability to continue as a going concern. In these circumstances the procedures in paragraph 16 apply.    **A13**

Other than inquiry of management, the auditor does not have a responsibility to perform any other audit procedures to identify events or conditions that may cast significant doubt on the entity's ability to continue as a going concern beyond the period assessed by management[1a], which, as discussed in paragraph 13, would be at least twelve months from the date of the financial statements.    **A14**

## Additional Audit Procedures When Events or Conditions Are Identified (Ref: Para. 16)

Audit procedures that are relevant to the requirement in paragraph 16 may include the following:    **A15**

- Analyzing and discussing cash flow, profit and other relevant forecasts with management.
- Analyzing and discussing the entity's latest available interim financial statements.
- Reading the terms of debentures and loan agreements and determining whether any have been breached.
- Reading minutes of the meetings of shareholders, those charged with governance and relevant committees for reference to financing difficulties.

- Inquiring of the entity's legal counsel regarding the existence of litigation and claims and the reasonableness of management's[1a] assessments of their outcome and the estimate of their financial implications.
- Confirming the existence, legality and enforceability of arrangements to provide or maintain financial support with related and third parties and assessing the financial ability of such parties to provide additional funds.
- Evaluating the entity's plans to deal with unfilled customer orders.
- Performing audit procedures regarding subsequent events to identify those that either mitigate or otherwise affect the entity's ability to continue as a going concern.
- Confirming the existence, terms and adequacy of borrowing facilities.
- Obtaining and reviewing reports of regulatory actions.
- Determining the adequacy of support for any planned disposals of assets.

***Evaluating Management's Plans for Future Actions*** (Ref: Para. 16(b))

A16   Evaluating management's[1a] plans for future actions may include inquiries of management as to its plans for future action, including, for example, its plans to liquidate assets, borrow money or restructure debt, reduce or delay expenditures, or increase capital.

***The Period of Management's[1a] Assessment*** (Ref: Para. 16(c))

A17   In addition to the procedures required in paragraph 16(c), the auditor may compare:
- The prospective financial information for recent prior periods with historical results; and
- The prospective financial information for the current period with results achieved to date.

A18   Where management's[1a] assumptions include continued support by third parties, whether through the subordination of loans, commitments to maintain or provide additional funding, or guarantees, and such support is important to an entity's ability to continue as a going concern, the auditor may need to consider requesting written confirmation (including of terms and conditions) from those third parties and to obtain evidence of their ability to provide such support.

## Audit Conclusions and Reporting (Ref: Para. 17)

A19   The phrase "material uncertainty" is used in IAS 1 in discussing the uncertainties related to events or conditions which may cast significant doubt on the entity's ability to continue as a going concern that should be disclosed in the financial statements. In some other financial reporting frameworks the phrase "significant uncertainty" is used in similar circumstances.

A19-1   Where, in forming their opinion, the auditor's assessment of going concern is based on a period to which those charged with governance have paid particular attention which is less than one year from the date of approval of the financial statements, it is appropriate for the auditor to disclose that fact within the basis of the audit opinion, unless it is disclosed in the financial statements or accompanying information (for example, an Operating and Financial Review). In deciding whether to disclose the fact, the auditor assesses whether the evidence supplied by those charged with governance is sufficient to demonstrate that those charged with governance have, in assessing going concern, paid particular attention to a period of one year from the date of approval of the financial statements.

## Use of Going Concern Assumption Appropriate but a Material Uncertainty Exists

### *Adequacy of Disclosure of Material Uncertainty* (Ref: Para. 18)

The determination of the adequacy of the financial statement disclosure may involve    **A20**
determining whether the information explicitly draws the reader's attention to the possibility that the entity may be unable to continue realizing its assets and discharging its liabilities in the normal course of business.

### *Audit Reporting When Disclosure of Material Uncertainty Is Adequate* (Ref: Para. 19)

The following is an illustration of an Emphasis of Matter paragraph when the    **A21**
auditor is satisfied as to the adequacy of the note disclosure:

*Emphasis of Matter*

Without qualifying our opinion, we draw attention to Note X in the financial statements which indicates that the Company incurred a net loss of ZZZ during the year ended December 31, 20X1 and, as of that date, the Company's current liabilities exceeded its total assets by YYY. These conditions, along with other matters as set forth in Note X, indicate the existence of a material uncertainty that may cast significant doubt about the Company's ability to continue as a going concern.

With respect to companies, illustrative examples of auditor's reports tailored for use with audits conducted in accordance with ISAs (UK and Ireland) are given in the most recent versions of the APB Bulletins, "Auditor's Reports on Financial Statements in the United Kingdom"/"Auditor's Reports on Financial Statements in the Republic of Ireland." Illustrative examples for various other entities are give in other Bulletins and Practice Notes issued by the APB.

In situations involving multiple material uncertainties that are significant to the    **A22**
financial statements as a whole, the auditor may consider it appropriate in extremely rare cases to express a disclaimer of opinion instead of adding an Emphasis of Matter paragraph. ISA (UK and Ireland) 705 provides guidance on this issue.

### *Audit Reporting When Disclosure of Material Uncertainty Is Inadequate* (Ref: Para. 20)

The following is an illustration of the relevant paragraphs when a qualified opinion is    **A23**
to be expressed:

*Basis for Qualified Opinion*

The Company's financing arrangements expire and amounts outstanding are payable on March 19, 20X1. The Company has been unable to re-negotiate or obtain replacement financing. This situation indicates the existence of a material uncertainty that may cast significant doubt on the Company's ability to continue as a going concern and therefore the Company may be unable to realize its assets and discharge its liabilities in the normal course of business. The financial statements (and notes thereto) do not fully disclose this fact.

*Qualified Opinion*

In our opinion, except for the incomplete disclosure of the information referred to in the Basis for Qualified Opinion paragraph, the financial statements present fairly, in all material respects (or "give a true and fair view of") the financial position of the Company at December 31, 20X0 and of its financial performance and its cash flows for the year then ended in accordance with ...

With respect to companies, illustrative examples of auditor's reports tailored for use with audits conducted in accordance with ISAs (UK and Ireland) are given in the most recent versions of the APB Bulletins, "Auditor's Reports on Financial Statements in the United Kingdom"/"Auditor's Reports on Financial Statements in the Republic of Ireland." Illustrative examples for various other entities are give in other Bulletins and Practice Notes issued by the APB.

A24    The following is an illustration of the relevant paragraphs when an adverse opinion is to be expressed:

*Basis for Adverse Opinion*

The Company's financing arrangements expired and the amount outstanding was payable on December 31, 20X0. The Company has been unable to re-negotiate or obtain replacement financing and is considering filing for bankruptcy. These events indicate a material uncertainty that may cast significant doubt on the Company's ability to continue as a going concern and therefore it may be unable to realize its assets and discharge its liabilities in the normal course of business. The financial statements (and notes thereto) do not disclose this fact.

*Adverse Opinion*

In our opinion, because of the omission of the information mentioned in the Basis for Adverse Opinion paragraph, the financial statements do not present fairly (or "give a true and fair view of") the financial position of the Company as at December 31, 20X0, and of its financial performance and its cash flows for the year then ended in accordance with...

With respect to companies, illustrative examples of auditor's reports tailored for use with audits conducted in accordance with ISAs (UK and Ireland) are given in the most recent versions of the APB Bulletins, "Auditor's Reports on Financial Statements in the United Kingdom"/"Auditor's Reports on Financial Statements in the Republic of Ireland." Illustrative examples for various other entities are give in other Bulletins and Practice Notes issued by the APB.

## Use of Going Concern Assumption Inappropriate (Ref: Para. 21)

A25    If the financial statements have been prepared on a going concern basis but, in the auditor's judgment, management's use of the going concern assumption in the financial statements is inappropriate, the requirement of paragraph 21 for the auditor to express an adverse opinion applies regardless of whether or not the financial statements include disclosure of the inappropriateness of management's[1a] use of the going concern assumption.

If the entity's management[1a] is required, or elects, to prepare financial statements **A26**
when the use of the going concern assumption is not appropriate in the circumstances, the financial statements are prepared on an alternative basis (e.g., liquidation
basis). The auditor may be able to perform an audit of those financial statements
provided that the auditor determines that the alternative basis is an acceptable
financial reporting framework in the circumstances. The auditor may be able to
express an unmodified opinion on those financial statements, provided there is
adequate disclosure therein but may consider it appropriate or necessary to include
an Emphasis of Matter paragraph in the auditor's report to draw the user's attention
to that alternative basis and the reasons for its use.

## Management[1a] Unwilling to Make or Extend Its Assessment (Ref: Para. 22)

In certain circumstances, the auditor may believe it necessary to request manage- **A27**
ment[1a] to make or extend its assessment. If management is unwilling to do so, a
qualified opinion or a disclaimer of opinion in the auditor's report may be appropriate, because it may not be possible for the auditor to obtain sufficient appropriate
audit evidence regarding the use of the going concern assumption in the preparation
of the financial statements, such as audit evidence regarding the existence of plans
management has put in place or the existence of other mitigating factors.

### Regulated Entities

When the auditor of a regulated financial entity considers that it might be **A27-1**
necessary to either qualify the audit opinion or add an explanatory paragraph to
the audit report, the auditor may have a duty to inform the appropriate regulator
at an early stage in the audit. In such cases the regulator might, if it has not
already done so, specify corrective action to be taken by the entity. At the time at
which the auditor formulates the audit report, the auditor takes account of
matters such as:

- Any views expressed by the regulator.
- Any legal advice obtained by those charged with governance.
- The actual and planned corrective action.

# Addendum

*This addendum provides a summary of APB's rationale for retaining or excluding in the proposed clarified ISA (UK and Ireland) the supplementary requirements in the existing ISA (UK and Ireland). It also sets out the supplementary guidance material in the existing ISA (UK and Ireland) that APB considers is not necessary to retain in light of the improvements in the underlying Clarity ISAs issued by the IAASB as part of the Clarity Project. It is provided for information and does not form part of the proposed clarified ISA (UK and Ireland).*

*The Consultation Paper published with the exposure drafts explains the general approach used by the APB for determining whether current supplementary material should be proposed to be retained.*

## Analysis of proposed treatment of current APB supplementary material in current ISA (UK and Ireland) 570

### Requirements

| APB supplementary material (*Italic text is from IAASB for context*) | Is it covered in substance in the Clarity ISA? | Should it be retained? |
|---|---|---|
| 2-1.   The auditor should consider any relevant disclosures in the financial statements. | ✓ There are requirements to determine whether disclosure in the financial statements is adequate. | ✗ |
| 17-1.   The auditor should assess the adequacy of the means by which the those charged with governance have satisfied themselves that: <br>(a) It is appropriate for them to adopt the going concern basis in preparing the financial statements; and | ✓ The ISA is less detailed, but does require an evaluation of management's assessment of the entity's ability to continue as a going concern (12). An elevated requirement is included to consider whether management's assessment includes all relevant information of which the auditor is aware as a result of the audit (14). | ✗ re (a) |
| (b) The financial statements include such disclosures, if any, relating to going concern as are necessary for them to give a true and fair view. | ✓ There are requirements relating to whether disclosure is necessary for the fair presentation of the financial statements (17(a)) and whether adequate disclosure is made of an uncertainty (18). | ✗ re (b) |

| APB supplementary material (*Italic text is from IAASB for context*) | Is it covered in substance in the Clarity ISA? | Should it be retained? |
|---|---|---|
| For this purpose:<br>(i) The auditor should make enquiries of those charged with governance and examine appropriate available financial information; and | – There is a requirement to communicate with TCWG re significant doubts about going concern (23). The guidance identifies factors that may give rise to concern (A2). | ✗ re (i) |
| (ii) Having regard to the future period to which those charged with governance have paid particular attention in assessing going concern (see paragraphs 18 and 18-1 below), the auditor should plan and perform procedures specifically designed to identify any material matters which could indicate concern about the entity's ability to continue as a going concern. | ✗ | ✓ re (ii) (Audit Quality) 13-2 |
| 26. *When events or conditions have been identified which may cast significant doubt on the entity's ability to continue as a going concern, the auditor should: ...*<br>*(c) Seek written representations from management⁵ regarding its plans for future action.*<br><sup>5</sup> In the UK and Ireland the auditor obtains written representations from those charged with governance. | ✓ 16(e) "where appropriate" | ✗ |
| 26-1. The auditor should consider the need to obtain written confirmations of representations from those charged with governance regarding:<br>(a) The assessment of those charged with governance that the company is a going concern; | ✗ However, there is a requirement to request written representations about plans for future action (and an elevated requirement to include the feasibility of these plans). (16(e)) | ✗ |

| APB supplementary material (*Italic text is from IAASB for context*) | Is it covered in substance in the Clarity ISA? | Should it be retained? |
|---|---|---|
| (b) **Any relevant disclosures in the financial statements.** | – ISA 580.10 requires that the auditor shall request management to provide a written representation that it has fulfilled its responsibility for the preparation of the financial statements in accordance with the applicable financial reporting framework, including where relevant their fair presentation, as set out in the terms of the audit engagement. | ✗ |
| 30-1. **The auditor should document the extent of the auditor's concern (if any) about the entity's ability to continue as a going concern.** | ✗ There are no specific documentation requirements in ISA 570. | ✓ (Audit Quality) **17-1** |
| 31-1. **The auditor should consider whether the financial statements are required to include disclosures relating to going concern in order to give a true and fair view.** | ✓ 17(a) | ✗ |
| 31-4. **If the period to which those charged with governance have paid particular attention in assessing going concern is less than one year from the date of approval of the financial statements, and those charged with governance have not disclosed that fact, the auditor should do so within the section of the auditor's report setting out the basis of the audit opinion, unless the fact is clear from any other references in the auditor's report[6].**<br><br>[6] If the non-disclosure of the fact in the financial statements is a departure from the requirements of the applicable financial reporting framework, the auditor would give a qualified opinion ("except for"). | ✗ The auditor is required to cover the same period as that used by management to make its assessment as required by the applicable financial reporting framework, or by law or regulation if it specifies a longer period. If management's assessment of the entity's ability to continue as a going concern covers less than twelve months from the date of the financial statements as defined in ISA 560 (Redrafted), the auditor shall request management to extend its assessment period to at least twelve months from that date. (13) | ✓<br><br>(Regulatory) **17-2** |

| APB supplementary material (*Italic text is from IAASB for context*) | Is it covered in substance in the Clarity ISA? | Should it be retained? |
|---|---|---|
| 36-1. **In rare circumstances, in order to give a true and fair view, those charged with governance may have prepared the financial statements on a basis other than that of going concern. If the auditor considers this other basis to be appropriate in the specific circumstances, and if the financial statements contain the necessary disclosures, the auditor should not qualify the auditor's report in this respect.** | ✗ However, this is covered in the Application Material. (A26) | ✗ |

## Guidance

The following guidance in current ISA 570 has not been carried forward to the draft clarity version.

| Current paragraph reference (*Italic text is from IAASB for context*) |
|---|
| 1-2. – 1-5. [Definitions of management and those charged with governance.] |
| **1-1.** This ISA (UK and Ireland) contains standards and guidance for the auditor in relation to the going concern basis that is generally presumed in financial statements which are required to be properly prepared in accordance with the Act[1b], and to give a true and fair view. In the absence of specific legal or other provisions to the contrary, the principles and procedures embodied in the ISA (UK and Ireland) apply also to the audit of the financial statements of other entities. This ISA (UK and Ireland) does not establish standards nor provide guidance about going concern in any other context, such as that of an engagement to report on an entity's future viability.<br><br>[1b] For Great Britain, 'the Act' refers to the Companies Act 1985. For Northern Ireland, the equivalent legislation is provided by the Companies (Northern Ireland) Order 1986 and for the Republic of Ireland by the Companies Acts 1963 to 2003. |
| **4-1.** Appendix 1 to this ISA (UK and Ireland) summarizes, in relation to going concern, the legal and professional accounting requirements in the UK and Ireland with which those charged with governance comply in preparing financial statements. |
| **4-2.** An important consequence of the legal and professional accounting requirements in the UK and Ireland is that, when preparing financial statements, those charged with governance should satisfy themselves as to whether the going concern basis is appropriate. Even if it is appropriate, it may still be necessary for the financial statements to contain additional disclosures, for instance relating to the adoption of that basis, in order to give a true and fair view. |
| **8.** *Examples of events or conditions, which may give rise to business risks, that individually or collectively may cast significant doubt about the going concern assumption are set out below. ...*<br>*Financial*<br>• Necessary borrowing facilities have not been agreed.<br>• Major debt repayment falling due where refinancing is necessary to the entity's continued existence.<br>• Major restructuring of debt<br>• Major losses or cash flow problems which have arisen since the balance sheet date.<br>• Reduction in normal terms of trade credit by suppliers.<br>• Substantial sales of fixed assets not intended to be replaced.<br>*Operating*<br>• Loss of key staff without replacement.<br>• Fundamental changes in the market or technology to which the entity is unable to adapt adequately.<br>• Excessive dependence on a few product lines where the market is depressed.<br>• Technical developments which render a key product obsolete. |

| Current paragraph reference (*Italic text is from IAASB for context*) |
|---|
| *Other* <br> • Issues which involve a range of possible outcomes so wide that an unfavorable result could affect the appropriateness of the going concern basis. |
| 9-1.  The auditor also considers whether there are adequate disclosures regarding the going concern basis in the financial statements in order that they give a true and fair view. |
| 9-2.  The auditor's procedures necessarily involve a consideration of the entity's ability to continue in operational existence for the foreseeable future. In turn, that necessitates consideration both of the current and the possible future circumstances of the business and the environment in which it operates. |
| 19.  *Management's[1a] assessment of the entity's ability to continue as a going concern is a key part of the auditor's consideration of the going concern assumption. As noted in paragraph 7, most financial reporting frameworks requiring an explicit management assessment specify the period for which management is required to take into account all available information.[4]* <br><br> [4] *For example, IAS 1 defines this as a period that should be at least, but is not limited to, twelve months from the balance sheet date.* <br><br> FRS 18 does not specify this period but does require that where the foreseeable future considered by the directors has been limited to a period of less than one year from the date of approval of the financial statements, that fact should be disclosed in the financial statements. |
| 20-1.  The auditor may need to consider some or all of the following matters: <br> • Whether the period to which those charged with governance have paid particular attention in assessing going concern is reasonable in the entity's circumstances and in the light of the need for those charged with governance to consider the ability of the entity to continue in operational existence for the foreseeable future. <br> • The systems, or other means (formal or informal), for timely identification of warnings of future risks and uncertainties the entity might face. <br> • Budget and/or forecast information (cash flow information in particular) produced by the entity, and the quality of the systems (or other means, formal or informal) in place for producing this information and keeping it up to date. <br> • Whether the key assumptions underlying the budgets and/or forecasts appear appropriate in the circumstances. <br> • The sensitivity of budgets and/or forecasts to variable factors both within the control of those charged with governance and outside their control. <br> • Any obligations, undertakings or guarantees arranged with other entities (in particular, lenders, suppliers and group companies) for the giving or receiving of support. <br> • The existence, adequacy and terms of borrowing facilities, and supplier credit. <br> • The plans of those charged with governance for resolving any matters giving rise to the concern (if any) about the appropriateness of the going concern basis. In particular, the auditor may need to consider whether the plans are realistic, whether there is a reasonable |

| **Current paragraph reference** (*Italic text is from IAASB for context*) |
|---|
| expectation that the plans are likely to resolve any problems foreseen and whether those charged with governance are likely to put the plans into practice effectively. |
| The Auditor's Examination of Borrowing Facilities<br>21-1. In examining borrowing facilities the auditor could decide, for example, that it is necessary:<br>   (a) To obtain confirmations of the existence and terms of bank facilities; and<br>   (b) To make an own assessment of the intentions of the bankers relating thereto.<br>The latter assessment could involve the auditor examining written evidence or making notes of meetings which the auditor would hold with those charged with governance and, occasionally, with those charged with governance and the entity's bankers. In making an assessment of the bankers' intentions the auditor ascertains, normally through enquiries of those charged with governance, whether the bankers are aware of the matters that are causing the auditor to decide that such an assessment is necessary. It is also important that the relationships between the auditor, those charged with governance and the bankers are clarified and understood. |
| 21-2. The auditor might be more likely to decide that it is necessary to obtain confirmations of the existence and terms of bank facilities, and to make an independent assessment of the intentions of the bankers relating thereto, in cases where, for example:<br>  • There is a low margin of financial resources available to the entity.<br>  • The entity is dependent on borrowing facilities shortly due for renewal.<br>  • Correspondence between the bankers and the entity reveals that the last renewal of facilities was agreed with difficulty, or that, since the last review of facilities, the bankers have imposed additional conditions as a prerequisite for continued lending.<br>  • A significant deterioration in cash flow is projected.<br>  • The value of assets granted as security for the borrowings is declining.<br>  • The entity has breached the terms of borrowing covenants, or there are indications of potential breaches. |
| 21-3. The auditor considers whether any inability to obtain sufficient appropriate audit evidence regarding the existence and terms of borrowing facilities and the intentions of the lender relating thereto, and/or the factors giving rise to this inability, need to be:<br>  • Disclosed in the financial statements in order that they give a true and fair view; and/or<br>  • Referred to (by way of an explanatory paragraph or a qualified opinion) in the auditor's report. |
| 26-2. Such written confirmations are necessary in respect of matters material to the financial statements when those representations are critical to obtaining sufficient appropriate audit evidence. In view of their importance, it is appropriate for such confirmations to be provided by those charged with governance, rather than other levels of the entity's management. |
| 26-3. If they are unable to obtain such written confirmations of representations as they consider necessary from those charged with governance, the auditor considers whether:<br>  • There is a limitation on the scope of the auditor's work which requires a qualified opinion or disclaimer of opinion; or |

| Current paragraph reference (*Italic text is from IAASB for context*) |
|---|
| • The failure of those charged with governance to provide the written confirmations could indicate that there is concern. |
| 30-2. The auditor might be more likely to conclude that there is a significant level of concern about the entity's ability to continue as a going concern if, for example, indications such as those in paragraph 8 are present. However, where such indications are present, the auditor may have obtained sufficient appropriate evidence causing the auditor to conclude that there is not a significant level of concern about the entity's ability to continue as a going concern. |
| 30-3. The auditor could consider that there is a significant level of concern about the entity's ability to continue as a going concern, or the auditor could disagree with the preparation of the financial statements on the going concern basis. In such cases (whether or not this is because of potential insolvency) the auditor might decide to write to those charged with governance drawing their attention to the need to consider taking suitable advice. In particular, those charged with governance of an entity may need to obtain advice from specialist accountants or lawyers on the appropriateness and implications of continuing to trade while they know, or ought to know, that the entity is insolvent. |
| 31-3. To avoid repetition, the text in the financial statements might refer readers to specific disclosures located elsewhere in the annual report (for instance in the Operating and Financial Review). The auditor takes account of such specified disclosures in considering the adequacy of disclosures in the financial statements. |
| 31-6. The auditor qualifies the audit opinion if the auditor considers that those charged with governance have not taken adequate steps to satisfy themselves that it is appropriate for them to adopt the going concern basis. This might arise, for example, when the auditor does not consider that the future period to which those charged with governance have paid particular attention in assessing going concern is reasonable in the entity's circumstances. This is a limitation on the scope of the auditor's work, as the auditor is unable to obtain all the information and explanations which they consider necessary for the purpose of their audit. |
| 33-1. The emphasis of matter paragraph describes clearly the nature of the matters giving rise to the auditor's concern and refers to the relevant disclosures in the financial statements. The auditor uses judgment to decide the extent to which it is necessary for the description in the auditor's report to repeat information taken from the notes to the financial statements. The extent of the auditor's concern is one factor affecting the nature and extent of the description in the auditor's report. The prime consideration is clarity of communication. The description is normally identified within the auditor's report through the use of the sub-heading 'Going concern'. |
| 33-2. The auditor might have concluded that there is a significant level of concern about the entity's ability to continue as a going concern. In these cases the auditor does not normally regard the disclosures as adequate unless (in addition to any disclosures otherwise required, for example by accounting standards) the following matters are included in the financial statements:<br>(a) A statement that the financial statements have been prepared on the going concern basis;<br>(b) A statement of the pertinent facts;<br>(c) The nature of the concern; |

| Current paragraph reference (*Italic text is from IAASB for context*) |
|---|
| (d) A statement of the assumptions adopted by those charged with governance, which should be clearly distinguishable from the pertinent facts; <br> (e) (Where appropriate and practicable) a statement regarding the plans of those charged with governance for resolving the matters giving rise to the concern; and <br> (f) Details of any relevant actions by those charged with governance. <br> The guidance above regarding disclosures in the financial statements does not constitute an accounting standard. |
| 36-2. Some enterprises are formed for a specific purpose, such as a joint venture to undertake a construction project, and are wound up or dissolved when the purpose is achieved. Under these circumstances the financial statements may be prepared on a basis that reflects the fact that assets may need to be realized other than in the ordinary course of operations. In these circumstances the auditor may wish, without qualifying the audit opinion, to refer in the auditor's report to the basis on which the financial statements are prepared; the auditor may do this in the introductory paragraph of the report. |
| Application to Groups <br> 39-1. The principles and procedures set out in this ISA (UK and Ireland) apply also to the audit of consolidated financial statements. |
| 39-2. It may be appropriate, on the grounds of materiality, for the group financial statements to be prepared on the going concern basis even though it is inappropriate for the individual financial statements of one or more members of the group to be prepared on the going concern basis. |
| Appendices – see below <br> 1    Summary of legal and professional requirements <br> 2    Illustrative examples of auditors' assessments |

# ISA (UK and Ireland) 570

## Appendix 1

### Preparation of the Financial Statements: Note on Legal and Professional Requirements

#### Company Law and Accounting Standards

The UK Companies Act 1985 specifies certain accounting principles which should    1
normally be adopted in preparing the financial statements of a company. One of
these principles is that:

> 'the company shall be presumed to be carrying on business as a going concern'
> (paragraph 10 of Schedule 4 to the Act)[12].
> However such a presumption is not conclusive and may be disregarded if the
> facts of the particular situation so require. The term 'going concern' is not
> defined in the Act but, as discussed below, is explained in International
> Accounting Standard (IAS) 1 'Presentation of Financial Statements' and
> Financial Reporting Standard (FRS) 18 'Accounting Policies'.

Paragraph 15 of Schedule 4 to the UK Companies Act 1985 states that departures    2
from the Act's accounting principles *may* be made if it appears to the directors that
there are 'special reasons' for doing so[13]. The financial statements must disclose any
such departure, the reasons for it and its effect. 'Special reasons' would include
circumstances where the directors conclude, on the basis of the facts as they appear
to them, that it is appropriate to depart from the going concern presumption.

Furthermore, in addition to that particular provision of the UK Companies Act    3
1985, section 226 of the Act contains an overriding requirement for directors to
prepare financial statements which give a true and fair view of the state of affairs of
the company as at the end of the financial year and of its profit or loss for the
financial year[14].

If compliance with the provisions of the Act would not be *sufficient* to give a true and    4
fair view, the Act requires the directors to give the necessary additional information
in the financial statements. If, in 'special circumstances', compliance with the provisions of the Act is *inconsistent* with the requirement to give a true and fair view, the
Act requires the directors to depart from the particular provision to the extent
necessary to give a true and fair view. The financial statements must disclose the
particulars of any such departure, the reasons for it and its effect.

Accordingly, directors cannot assume that preparing the financial statements on the    5
going concern basis and in accordance with the other provisions of the Act will
necessarily result in the financial statements giving a true and fair view. Whilst, in
general, compliance with accounting standards is also necessary to meet the
requirement to prepare financial statements giving a true and fair view, such compliance is not of itself sufficient to ensure that a true and fair view is given in all cases.

---

[12] *In the Republic of Ireland the equivalent is Section 5(a), Companies (Amendment) Act, 1986.*

[13] *In the Republic of Ireland the equivalent is Section 6, Companies (Amendment) Act 1986.*

[14] *In the Republic of Ireland the equivalent is Section 3(b), Companies (Amendment) Act 1986.*

## Accounting Standards and the Definition of 'Going Concern'

**6**   FRS 18 states that "The information provided by financial statements is usually most relevant if prepared on the hypothesis that the entity is able to continue in existence for the foreseeable future. This hypothesis is commonly referred to as the going concern assumption."

**7**   FRS 18 requires that:

"An entity should prepare its financial statements on a going concern basis, unless
(a)   the entity is being liquidated or has ceased trading, or
(b)   the directors have no realistic alternative but to liquidate the entity or to cease trading,
in which circumstances the entity may, if appropriate, prepare its financial statements on a basis other than that of going concern."

**8**   FRS 18 also requires that "When preparing financial statements, directors should assess whether there are significant doubts about an entity's ability to continue as a going concern." and, in relation to that assessment, the following information should be disclosed in the financial statements:

"(a)   any material uncertainties of which the directors are aware in making their assessment, related to events or conditions that may cast significant doubt upon the entity's ability to continue as a going concern.
(b)   where the foreseeable future considered by the directors has been limited to a period of less than one year from the date of approval of the financial statements, that fact.
(c)   when the financial statements are not prepared on a going concern basis, that fact, together with the basis on which the financial statements are prepared and the reason why the entity is not regarded as a going concern."

**9**   The requirements of IAS 1 are consistent with those of FRS 18 with the exception that, if the foreseeable future considered by the directors has been limited to a period of less than one year from the date of approval of the financial statements, IAS 1 does not require disclosure of that fact. IAS 1 states that "In assessing whether the going concern assumption is appropriate, management takes into account all available information about the future, which is at least, but not limited to, twelve months from the balance sheet date.

# Appendix 2

**Illustrative Examples of the Auditor's Assessment of Whether Evidence Provided by Those Charged With Governance, Concerning the Attention They Have Paid to the Period One Year From the Date of Approval of the Financial Statements, is Sufficient**

*The appendix is illustrative only and does not form part of the Auditing Standards. The purpose of the appendix is to illustrate the application of the Auditing Standards to assist in clarifying their meaning in a number of commercial situations. The examples focus on particular aspects of the situations illustrated and are not intended to be a comprehensive discussion of all the relevant factors that might influence either the directors' or auditor's assessment of the appropriateness of the going concern basis. As the auditor would need to exercise judgment in the circumstances described it is possible that different auditors may arrive at different conclusions. This does not, however, detract from the examples which demonstrate thought process and the implications for an audit report once certain conclusions have been reached by the auditor. These examples neither modify nor override the Auditing Standards.*

## Example 1 – A small company producing specialized computer application software

### *Extract from the auditor's risk assessment*

This owner managed company employs a few highly trained and highly paid computer system designers to design application software for use by transportation enterprises, such as airlines and bus companies, in preparing their timetables and fare structures. Few companies are engaged in this field and the supply of suitably trained staff is limited. The system designers, who met at University, have been with the company since its formation. They all have an equity interest in the company.

Although the company has only been in existence for five years it has established a reputation for excellence in its field. Its reputation derives from the skill and expertise of its individual employees rather than from anything attaching to the company itself.

A significant amount of time is spent by the designers in pure research activities developing new products. In addition the time needed to develop individual systems relating to an established product can be considerable. In addition to design of new systems the company maintains those systems it has installed on a contractual basis and undertakes training courses in the use of the systems for the employees of its customers.

The company is thinly capitalized and relies primarily on advances from its customers supplemented by short term bank borrowings for its day to day cash requirements.

The company employs a part time book-keeper to prepare the financial statements, cash flow forecasts and maintain the books of account.

The company has usually been in a position to choose which contracts it accepts and has not had difficulty in recovering its costs. The company is not economically dependent on any one transportation enterprise.

The company updates each month a rolling cash flow projection with a six month time horizon. The company does not prepare projections for a longer period as it perceives its management need is to be able to manage effectively its short term cash flow. The company has negotiated a line of credit with its bankers which it would be able to utilize to overcome short term cash shortages.

### *Assessment by the auditor of whether there is sufficient evidence that the directors have paid particular attention to a period of twelve months*

When the auditor assesses whether the directors have, in assessing going concern, paid particular attention to a period of one year from the expected date of approval of the financial statements the auditor:

(a) Reviews the cash flow forecasts for the six month period from the expected date of approval of the financial statements; and

(b) Then enquires of the directors the steps they have taken to assess the appropriateness of the going concern basis for the subsequent six month period.

The directors inform the auditor that they do not consider there is any need for cash flow forecasts to be prepared beyond six months because:

- The cash flow forecasts show a net cash inflow for the period;
- They have reviewed in detail the assumptions implicit in the forecast with the bookkeeper and concur with them;
- The company has a significant back-log of orders which will occupy half of the designers for at least the next year;
- The company is actively tendering for both systems design and maintenance contracts in the United Kingdom and Europe and is considering expanding into the Americas;
- The company has recently renewed its arrangements with its bankers for a further year;
- The design employees seem to be settled and stimulated and there is no reason to believe that they will leave the company in the foreseeable future; and
- In the unlikely event that the company did not win many of the tenders it could modify its existing expansion plans which have been necessitated by an increase in maintenance contracts. Rather than employ new staff to undertake this work existing staff could be reassigned to it.

The auditor concludes that the directors have paid particular attention to the period ending one year after their approval of the financial statements.

## Example 2 – An enterprise in the fashion industry

### *Extract from the auditor's risk assessment*

This company employing 1,000 people designs and manufactures ladies fashion wear. Its business is seasonal and it presents two major collections per year: one in the spring and one in the autumn.

The company has attracted established designers and they are regarded as one of the leading manufacturers.

Almost all of the company's sales orders are received from the major retailers when they show their collections. Although some of the garments are manufactured prior to the showing of the collection the majority of them will be manufactured in the four months immediately following the showing.

The company's finance director is a qualified accountant with a staff of 6. Because of the seasonal nature of the business the company prepares its detailed budgets and cash flow forecasts until the end of the next season. The company's year end is 30 June and the directors expect to approve the financial statements during October. Detailed cash flow forecasts are only available to the end of February in the following year a period of only four months from the approval of the financial statements.

The company which has been marginally profitable over the last few years has a small line of credit with its bank but is financed primarily through the factoring of its debtors.

***Assessment by the auditor of whether there is sufficient evidence that the directors have paid particular attention to a period of twelve months***

When the auditor assesses whether the directors have, in assessing going concern, paid particular attention to a period of one year from the expected date of approval of the financial statements the auditor would:

(a) Review the cash flow forecasts for the four month period from the expected date of approval of the financial statements; and
(b) Then enquire of the directors the steps they have taken to assess the appropriateness of the going concern basis for the subsequent eight month period.

The directors inform the auditor that they do not consider there is any need for additional cash flow forecasts to be prepared beyond the end of February in the following year because:

- The cash flow forecasts show a net cash inflow for the period and the present cash position is strong because of a recent sale of debtors from the present collection;
- The directors have reviewed in detail the assumptions implicit in the forecast and concur with them;
- The designers are working on the next collection and they believe, based on discussions with some of the retailers, that they have some good general ideas which will appeal to their customers if translated into imaginative detailed designs;
- Discussions with the major retailers indicate that they expect demand to be high next season;
- The company's relationship with its factor is good and they do not expect any difficulties in selling their debtors in the future;
- The company anticipates no major capital expenditures in the next twelve months. Most of the machinery is less than five years old and in any event is financed by lease arrangements rather than by purchase; and
- The company has recently renewed its arrangements with its bankers for a further year.

The auditor concludes that the directors have paid particular attention to the period ending one year after their approval of the financial statements.

**The auditor's options when the auditor concludes that the directors have not paid particular attention to the period ending one year after the approval of the financial statements**

The two examples above illustrate that the auditor may conclude that the directors have paid particular attention, to the period ending one year after the approval of the financial statements, even though they have not prepared cash flow forecasts for that period.

The auditor may conclude in slightly different situations that the directors have not paid particular attention to the period ending one year after the approval of the financial statements. If this is the case the auditor needs to consider the impact on the auditor's report which may be either:

(a) The auditor may conclude that there is a significant level of concern about the entity's ability to continue as a going concern (but the auditor does not disagree with the use of the going concern basis). In which case the directors include a note to the financial statements and the auditor includes an emphasis of matter paragraph when setting out the basis of their opinion (in accordance with paragraph 33 of the ISA (UK and Ireland)); or, less probably;

(b) The auditor may conclude that the directors have not paid particular attention to the period ending one year from the date of approval of the financial statements but there is no significant level of concern. Then if the directors:

(i) Refer to the period paid particular attention to, in the annual report, the auditor need not refer to the period in the basis of opinion (in accordance with paragraph 31-5 of the ISA (UK and Ireland)); however

(ii) If the directors do not refer to the period paid particular attention to, the auditor would do so in the auditor's report in accordance with paragraph 31-4 of the ISA (UK and Ireland)[15]; or

(c) The auditor may conclude that the directors have not taken adequate steps to satisfy themselves that it is appropriate to adopt the going concern basis. Accordingly, there is a limitation of scope which gives rise to a qualified auditor's report (in accordance with paragraph 31-6 of the ISA (UK and Ireland)).

---

[15] *If the non-disclosure in the financial statements of the period paid particular attention to is a departure from the requirements of the applicable financial reporting framework, the auditor would give a qualified opinion ("except for").*

# Proposed Clarified International Standard on Auditing (UK and Ireland) 580

# Written representations

*(Effective for audits of financial statements for periods ending on or after 15 December 2010)*

## Contents

International Standard on Auditing (UK and Ireland) (ISA (UK and Ireland)) 580, "Written Representations" should be read in conjunction with ISA (UK and Ireland) 200, "Overall Objectives of the Independent Auditor and the Conduct of an Audit in Accordance with International Standards on Auditing (UK and Ireland)."

# Introduction

## Scope of this ISA (UK and Ireland)

1    This International Standard on Auditing (UK and Ireland) (ISA (UK and Ireland)) deals with the auditor's responsibility to obtain written representations from management and, where appropriate, those charged with governance in an audit of financial statements.

2    Appendix 1 lists other ISAs (UK and Ireland) containing subject-matter specific requirements for written representations. The specific requirements for written representations of other ISAs (UK and Ireland) do not limit the application of this ISA (UK and Ireland).

## Written Representations as Audit Evidence

3    Audit evidence is the information used by the auditor in arriving at the conclusions on which the auditor's opinion is based.[1] Written representations are necessary information that the auditor requires in connection with the audit of the entity's financial statements. Accordingly, similar to responses to inquiries, written representations are audit evidence. (Ref: Para. A1)

4    Although written representations provide necessary audit evidence, they do not provide sufficient appropriate audit evidence on their own about any of the matters with which they deal. Furthermore, the fact that management has provided reliable written representations does not affect the nature or extent of other audit evidence that the auditor obtains about the fulfillment of management's responsibilities, or about specific assertions.

## Effective Date

5    This ISA (UK and Ireland) is effective for audits of financial statements for periods ending on or after 15 December 2010.

# Objectives

6    The objectives of the auditor are:

(a)    To obtain written representations from management and, where appropriate, those charged with governance that they believe that they have fulfilled their responsibility for the preparation of the financial statements and for the completeness of the information provided to the auditor;

(b)    To support other audit evidence relevant to the financial statements or specific assertions in the financial statements by means of written representations if determined necessary by the auditor or required by other ISAs (UK and Ireland); and

(c)    To respond appropriately to written representations provided by management and, where appropriate, those charged with governance, or if management or, where appropriate, those charged with governance do not provide the written representations requested by the auditor.

---

[1] ISA (UK and Ireland) 500, "Audit Evidence," paragraph 5(c).

# Definitions

For purposes of the ISAs (UK and Ireland), the following term has the meaning attributed below:   **7**

> Written representation – A written statement by management provided to the auditor to confirm certain matters or to support other audit evidence. Written representations in this context do not include financial statements, the assertions therein, or supporting books and records.

For purposes of this ISA (UK and Ireland), references to "management" should be read as "management and, where appropriate, those charged with governance." Furthermore, in the case of a fair presentation framework, management is responsible for the preparation and *fair* presentation of the financial statements in accordance with the applicable financial reporting framework; or the preparation of financial statements *that give a true and fair view* in accordance with the applicable financial reporting framework.   **8**

# Requirements

## Management from whom Written Representations Requested

The auditor shall request written representations from management with appropriate responsibilities for the financial statements and knowledge of the matters concerned. (Ref: Para. A2-A6)   **9**

## Written Representations about Management's Responsibilities

### Preparation of the Financial Statements

The auditor shall request management to provide a written representation that it has fulfilled its responsibility for the preparation of the financial statements in accordance with the applicable financial reporting framework, including where relevant their fair presentation, as set out in the terms of the audit engagement.[2] (Ref: Para. A7-A9, A14, A22)   **10**

### Information Provided and Completeness of Transactions

The auditor shall request management to provide a written representation that:   **11**

(a) It has provided the auditor with all relevant information and access as agreed in the terms of the audit engagement,[3] and
(b) All transactions have been recorded and are reflected in the financial statements. (Ref: Para. A7-A9, A14, A22 – A22-1)

Management may include in the written representations required by paragraphs 10 and 11 qualifying language to the effect that the representations are made to the best of its knowledge and belief. Such qualifying language does not cause paragraph 20 to apply if, during the audit, the auditor found no evidence that the representations are incorrect. (Ref: Para A5, A8-1)   **11-1**

[2] ISA (UK and Ireland) 210, "Agreeing the Terms of Audit Engagements," paragraph 6(b)(i).

[3] ISA (UK and Ireland) 210, paragraph 6(b)(ii).

### Description of Management's Responsibilities in the Written Representations

12    Management's responsibilities shall be described in the written representations required by paragraphs 10 and 11 in the manner in which these responsibilities are described in the terms of the audit engagement.

## Other Written Representations

13    Other ISAs (UK and Ireland) require the auditor to request written representations. If, in addition to such required representations, the auditor determines that it is necessary to obtain one or more written representations to support other audit evidence relevant to the financial statements or one or more specific assertions in the financial statements, the auditor shall request such other written representations. (Ref: Para. A10-A13, A14, A22 – A22-1)

## Date of and Period(s) Covered by Written Representations

14    The date of the written representations shall be as near as practicable to, but not after, the date of the auditor's report on the financial statements. The written representations shall be for all financial statements and period(s) referred to in the auditor's report. (Ref: Para. A15-A18)

## Form of Written Representations

15    The written representations shall be in the form of a representation letter addressed to the auditor. If law or regulation requires management to make written public statements about its responsibilities, and the auditor determines that such statements provide some or all of the representations required by paragraphs 10 or 11, the relevant matters covered by such statements need not be included in the representation letter. (Ref: Para. A19-A21)

## Doubt as to the Reliability of Written Representations and Requested Written Representations Not Provided

### Doubt as to the Reliability of Written Representations

16    If the auditor has concerns about the competence, integrity, ethical values or diligence of management, or about its commitment to or enforcement of these, the auditor shall determine the effect that such concerns may have on the reliability of representations (oral or written) and audit evidence in general. (Ref: Para. A24-A25)

17    In particular, if written representations are inconsistent with other audit evidence, the auditor shall perform audit procedures to attempt to resolve the matter. If the matter remains unresolved, the auditor shall reconsider the assessment of the competence, integrity, ethical values or diligence of management, or of its commitment to or enforcement of these, and shall determine the effect that this may have on the reliability of representations (oral or written) and audit evidence in general. (Ref: Para. A23)

18    If the auditor concludes that the written representations are not reliable, the auditor shall take appropriate actions, including determining the possible effect on the

opinion in the auditor's report in accordance with ISA (UK and Ireland) 705,[4] having regard to the requirement in paragraph 20 of this ISA (UK and Ireland).

### Requested Written Representations Not Provided

If management does not provide one or more of the requested written representa- **19** tions, the auditor shall:

(a) Discuss the matter with management;
(b) Reevaluate the integrity of management and evaluate the effect that this may have on the reliability of representations (oral or written) and audit evidence in general; and
(c) Take appropriate actions, including determining the possible effect on the opinion in the auditor's report in accordance with ISA (UK and Ireland) 705, having regard to the requirement in paragraph 20 of this ISA (UK and Ireland).

### Written Representations about Management's Responsibilities

The auditor shall disclaim an opinion on the financial statements in accordance with **20** ISA (UK and Ireland) 705 if: (Ref: Para. A26-A27)

(a) The auditor concludes that there is sufficient doubt about the integrity of management such that the written representations required by paragraphs 10 and 11 are not reliable; or
(b) Management does not provide the written representations required by paragraphs 10 and 11.

\*\*\*

# Application and Other Explanatory Material

### Written Representations as Audit Evidence (Ref: Para. 3)

Written representations are an important source of audit evidence. If management **A1** modifies or does not provide the requested written representations, it may alert the auditor to the possibility that one or more significant issues may exist. Further, a request for written, rather than oral, representations in many cases may prompt management to consider such matters more rigorously, thereby enhancing the quality of the representations.

### Management from whom Written Representations Requested (Ref: Para. 9)

Written representations are requested from those responsible for the preparation and **A2** presentation of the financial statements. Those individuals may vary depending on the governance structure of the entity, and relevant law or regulation; however, management (rather than those charged with governance) is often the responsible party. Written representations may therefore be requested from the entity's chief executive officer and chief financial officer, or other equivalent persons in entities that do not use such titles. In some circumstances, however, other parties, such as those charged with governance, are also responsible for the preparation and presentation of the financial statements[4a].

---

[4] *ISA (UK and Ireland) 705, "Modifications to the Opinion in the Independent Auditor's Report."*

[4a] *In the UK and Ireland, those charged with governance are responsible for the preparation of the financial statements.*

**A2-1** In view of their importance, it is appropriate for written representations that are critical to obtaining sufficient appropriate audit evidence to be provided by those charged with governance rather than the entity's management.

**A3** Due to its responsibility for the preparation and presentation of the financial statements, and its responsibilities for the conduct of the entity's business, management would be expected to have sufficient knowledge of the process followed by the entity in preparing and presenting the financial statements and the assertions therein on which to base the written representations.

**A4** In some cases, however, management may decide to make inquiries of others who participate in preparing and presenting the financial statements and assertions therein, including individuals who have specialized knowledge relating to the matters about which written representations are requested. Such individuals may include:

- An actuary responsible for actuarially determined accounting measurements.
- Staff engineers who may have responsibility for and specialized knowledge about environmental liability measurements.
- Internal counsel who may provide information essential to provisions for legal claims.

**A5** In some cases, management may include in the written representations qualifying language to the effect that representations are made to the best of its knowledge and belief. It is reasonable for the auditor to accept such wording if the auditor is satisfied that the representations are being made by those with appropriate responsibilities and knowledge of the matters included in the representations.

**A6** To reinforce the need for management to make informed representations, the auditor may request that management include in the written representations confirmation that it has made such inquiries as it considered appropriate to place it in the position to be able to make the requested written representations. It is not expected that such inquiries would usually require a formal internal process beyond those already established by the entity.

**Written Representations about Management's Responsibilities** (Ref: Para. 10-11)

**A7** Audit evidence obtained during the audit that management has fulfilled the responsibilities referred to in paragraphs 10 and 11 is not sufficient without obtaining confirmation from management that it believes that it has fulfilled those responsibilities. This is because the auditor is not able to judge solely on other audit evidence whether management has prepared and presented the financial statements and provided information to the auditor on the basis of the agreed acknowledgement and understanding of its responsibilities. For example, the auditor could not conclude that management has provided the auditor with all relevant information agreed in the terms of the audit engagement without asking it whether, and receiving confirmation that, such information has been provided.

**A7-1** A signed copy of the financial statements for a company may be sufficient evidence of the directors' acknowledgement of their collective responsibility for the preparation of the financial statements where it incorporates a statement to that effect. A signed copy of the financial statements, however, is not, by itself, sufficient appropriate evidence to confirm other representations given to the auditor as it does not, ordinarily, clearly identify and explain the specific separate representations.

The written representations required by paragraphs 10 and 11 draw on the agreed acknowledgement and understanding of management of its responsibilities in the terms of the audit engagement by requesting confirmation that it has fulfilled them. The auditor may also ask management to reconfirm its acknowledgement and understanding of those responsibilities in written representations. This is common in certain jurisdictions, but in any event may be particularly appropriate when:  **A8**

- Those who signed the terms of the audit engagement on behalf of the entity no longer have the relevant responsibilities;
- The terms of the audit engagement were prepared in a previous year;
- There is any indication that management misunderstands those responsibilities; or
- Changes in circumstances make it appropriate to do so.

   Consistent with the requirement of ISA (UK and Ireland) 210,[5] such reconfirmation of management's acknowledgement and understanding of its responsibilities is not made subject to the best of management's knowledge and belief (as discussed in paragraph A5 of this ISA (UK and Ireland)).

Although reconfirmation of management's acknowledgement and understanding of its responsibilities is not made subject to the best of management's knowledge and belief, as discussed in paragraph A8, this does not prevent management from stating that the written representations required by paragraphs 10 and 11 relating to the fulfillment of its responsibilities are given to the best of its knowledge and belief.  **A8-1**

### *Considerations Specific to Public Sector Entities*

The mandates for audits of the financial statements of public sector entities may be broader than those of other entities. As a result, the premise, relating to management's responsibilities, on which an audit of the financial statements of a public sector entity is conducted may give rise to additional written representations. These may include written representations confirming that transactions and events have been carried out in accordance with law, regulation or other authority.  **A9**

## Other Written Representations (Ref: Para. 13)

### *Additional Written Representations about the Financial Statements*

In addition to the written representation required by paragraph 10, the auditor may consider it necessary to request other written representations about the financial statements. Such written representations may supplement, but do not form part of, the written representation required by paragraph 10. They may include representations about the following:  **A10**

- Whether the selection and application of accounting policies are appropriate; and

---

[5] *ISA (UK and Ireland) 210, paragraph 6(b).*

- Whether matters such as the following, where relevant under the applicable financial reporting framework, have been recognized, measured, presented or disclosed in accordance with that framework:
  - Plans or intentions that may affect the carrying value or classification of assets and liabilities;
  - Liabilities, both actual and contingent;
  - Title to, or control over, assets, the liens or encumbrances on assets, and assets pledged as collateral; and
  - Aspects of laws, regulations and contractual agreements that may affect the financial statements, including non-compliance.

### *Additional Written Representations about Information Provided to the Auditor*

A11   In addition to the written representation required by paragraph 11, the auditor may consider it necessary to request management to provide a written representation that it has communicated to the auditor all deficiencies in internal control of which management is aware.

### *Written Representations about Specific Assertions*

A12   When obtaining evidence about, or evaluating, judgments and intentions, the auditor may consider one or more of the following:

- The entity's past history in carrying out its stated intentions.
- The entity's reasons for choosing a particular course of action.
- The entity's ability to pursue a specific course of action.
- The existence or lack of any other information that might have been obtained during the course of the audit that may be inconsistent with management's judgment or intent.

A13   In addition, the auditor may consider it necessary to request management to provide written representations about specific assertions in the financial statements; in particular, to support an understanding that the auditor has obtained from other audit evidence of management's judgment or intent in relation to, or the completeness of, a specific assertion. For example, if the intent of management is important to the valuation basis for investments, it may not be possible to obtain sufficient appropriate audit evidence without a written representation from management about its intentions. Although such written representations provide necessary audit evidence, they do not provide sufficient appropriate audit evidence on their own for that assertion.

### Communicating a Threshold Amount (Ref: Para. 10-11, 13)

A14   ISA (UK and Ireland) 450 requires the auditor to accumulate misstatements identified during the audit, other than those that are clearly trivial.[6] The auditor may determine a threshold above which misstatements cannot be regarded as clearly trivial. In the same way, the auditor may consider communicating to management a threshold for purposes of the requested written representations.

---

[6] *ISA (UK and Ireland) 450, "Evaluation of Misstatements Identified during the Audit," paragraph 5.*

**Date of and Period(s) Covered by Written Representations** (Ref: Para. 14)

Because written representations are necessary audit evidence, the auditor's opinion **A15** cannot be expressed, and the auditor's report cannot be dated, before the date of the written representations. Furthermore, because the auditor is concerned with events occurring up to the date of the auditor's report that may require adjustment to or disclosure in the financial statements, the written representations are dated as near as practicable to, but not after, the date of the auditor's report on the financial statements.

In some circumstances it may be appropriate for the auditor to obtain a written **A16** representation about a specific assertion in the financial statements during the course of the audit. Where this is the case, it may be necessary to request an updated written representation.

The written representations are for all periods referred to in the auditor's report **A17** because management needs to reaffirm that the written representations it previously made with respect to the prior periods remain appropriate. The auditor and management may agree to a form of written representation that updates written representations relating to the prior periods by addressing whether there are any changes to such written representations and, if so, what they are.

Situations may arise where current management were not present during all periods **A18** referred to in the auditor's report. Such persons may assert that they are not in a position to provide some or all of the written representations because they were not in place during the period. This fact, however, does not diminish such persons' responsibilities for the financial statements as a whole. Accordingly, the requirement for the auditor to request from them written representations that cover the whole of the relevant period(s) still applies.

**Form of Written Representations** (Ref: Para. 15)

Written representations are required to be included in a representation letter **A19** addressed to the auditor. In some jurisdictions, however, management may be required by law or regulation to make a written public statement about its responsibilities. Although such statement is a representation to the users of the financial statements, or to relevant authorities, the auditor may determine that it is an appropriate form of written representation in respect of some or all of the representations required by paragraph 10 or 11. Consequently, the relevant matters covered by such statement need not be included in the representation letter. Factors that may affect the auditor's determination include:

- Whether the statement includes confirmation of the fulfillment of the responsibilities referred to in paragraphs 10 and 11.
- Whether the statement has been given or approved by those from whom the auditor requests the relevant written representations.
- Whether a copy of the statement is provided to the auditor as near as practicable to, but not after, the date of the auditor's report on the financial statements (see paragraph 14).

A formal statement of compliance with law or regulation, or of approval of the **A20** financial statements, would not contain sufficient information for the auditor to be satisfied that all necessary representations have been consciously made. The expression of management's responsibilities in law or regulation is also not a substitute for the requested written representations.

**A21**    Appendix 2 provides an illustrative example of a representation letter.

## Communication with Those Charged with Governance (Ref: Para. 10-11, 13)

**A22**    ISA (UK and Ireland) 260 requires the auditor to communicate with those charged with governance the written representations which the auditor has requested from management.[7]

**A22-1**    In the UK and Ireland these communications are made before those charged with governance approve the financial statements, to ensure that they are aware of the representations on which the auditor intends to rely in expressing the auditor's opinion on those financial statements. For the audit of statutory financial statements, the auditor may also wish to consider whether to take the opportunity to remind the directors that it is an offence to mislead the auditor[7a].

## Doubt as to the Reliability of Written Representations and Requested Written Representations Not Provided

### *Doubt as to the Reliability of Written Representations* (Ref: Para. 16-17)

**A23**    In the case of identified inconsistencies between one or more written representations and audit evidence obtained from another source, the auditor may consider whether the risk assessment remains appropriate and, if not, revise the risk assessment and determine the nature, timing and extent of further audit procedures to respond to the assessed risks.

**A24**    Concerns about the competence, integrity, ethical values or diligence of management, or about its commitment to or enforcement of these, may cause the auditor to conclude that the risk of management misrepresentation in the financial statements is such that an audit cannot be conducted. In such a case, the auditor may consider withdrawing from the engagement, where withdrawal is possible under applicable law or regulation, unless those charged with governance put in place appropriate corrective measures. Such measures, however, may not be sufficient to enable the auditor to issue an unmodified audit opinion.

**A25**    ISA (UK and Ireland) 230 requires the auditor to document significant matters arising during the audit, the conclusions reached thereon, and significant professional judgments made in reaching those conclusions.[8] The auditor may have identified significant issues relating to the competence, integrity, ethical values or diligence of management, or about its commitment to or enforcement of these, but concluded that the written representations are nevertheless reliable. In such a case, this significant matter is documented in accordance with ISA (UK and Ireland) 230.

### *Written Representations about Management's Responsibilities* (Ref: Para. 20)

**A26**    As explained in paragraph A7, the auditor is not able to judge solely on other audit evidence whether management has fulfilled the responsibilities referred to in paragraphs 10 and 11. Therefore, if, as described in paragraph 20(a), the auditor

---

[7] *ISA (UK and Ireland) 260, "Communication with Those Charged with Governance," paragraph 16(c)(ii).*

[7a] *In the UK: Section 501 of the Companies Act 2006; In Ireland: Section 197(i), Companies Act, 1990.*

[8] *ISA (UK and Ireland) 230, "Audit Documentation," paragraphs 8(c) and 10.*

concludes that the written representations about these matters are unreliable, or if management does not provide those written representations, the auditor is unable to obtain sufficient appropriate audit evidence. The possible effects on the financial statements of such inability are not confined to specific elements, accounts or items of the financial statements and are hence pervasive. ISA (UK and Ireland) 705 requires the auditor to disclaim an opinion on the financial statements in such circumstances.[9]

A written representation that has been modified from that requested by the auditor does not necessarily mean that management did not provide the written representation. However, the underlying reason for such modification may affect the opinion in the auditor's report. For example: **A27**

- The written representation about management's fulfillment of its responsibility for the preparation and presentation of the financial statements may state that management believes that, except for material non-compliance with a particular requirement of the applicable financial reporting framework, the financial statements are prepared and presented in accordance with that framework. The requirement in paragraph 20 does not apply because the auditor concluded that management has provided reliable written representations. However, the auditor is required to consider the effect of the non-compliance on the opinion in the auditor's report in accordance with ISA (UK and Ireland) 705.
- The written representation about the responsibility of management to provide the auditor with all relevant information agreed in the terms of the audit engagement may state that management believes that, except for information destroyed in a fire, it has provided the auditor with such information. The requirement in paragraph 20 does not apply because the auditor concluded that management has provided reliable written representations. However, the auditor is required to consider the effects of the pervasiveness of the information destroyed in the fire on the financial statements and the effect thereof on the opinion in the auditor's report in accordance with ISA (UK and Ireland) 705.

- The written representation that all transactions have been recorded and are reflected in the financial statements may be modified, for example to refer a threshold amount agreed with the auditor (see paragraph A14) or to state that all transactions that may have a material effect on the financial statements have been recorded.

# Appendix 1 (Ref: Para. 2)

## List of ISAs (UK and Ireland) Containing Requirements for Written Representations

This appendix identifies paragraphs in other ISAs (UK and Ireland) in effect for audits of financial statements for periods ending on or after 15 December 2010 that require subject- matter specific written representations. The list is not a substitute for considering the requirements and related application and other explanatory material in ISAs (UK and Ireland).

- ISA 240 (UK and Ireland), "The Auditor's Responsibilities Relating to Fraud in an Audit of Financial Statements" – paragraph 39
- ISA 250 (UK and Ireland), "Consideration of Laws and Regulations in an Audit of Financial Statements" – paragraph 16
- ISA 450 (UK and Ireland), "Evaluation of Misstatements Identified during the Audit" – paragraph 14 and paragraph 14-1
- ISA 501 (UK and Ireland), "Audit Evidence—Specific Considerations for Selected Items" – paragraph 12
- ISA 540 (UK and Ireland), "Auditing Accounting Estimates, Including Fair Value Accounting Estimates, and Related Disclosures" – paragraph 22
- ISA 550 (UK and Ireland), "Related Parties" – paragraph 26
- ISA 560 (UK and Ireland), "Subsequent Events" – paragraph 9
- ISA 570 (UK and Ireland), "Going Concern" – paragraph 16(e)
- ISA 710 (UK and Ireland), "Comparative Information—Corresponding Figures and Comparative Financial Statements" – paragraph 9

# Appendix 2 (Ref: Para. A21)

This illustrative representation letter has not been tailored for the UK and Ireland. For example, when describing the responsibilities of management and those charged with governance for the financial statements and providing information to the auditor, the auditor has regard to manner in which those responsibilities are described in the terms of the audit engagement (see ISA (UK and Ireland) 210).

## Illustrative Representation Letter

The following illustrative letter includes written representations that are required by this and other ISAs in effect for audits of financial statements for periods ending on or after 15 December 2010. It is assumed in this illustration that the applicable financial reporting framework is International Financial Reporting Standards; the requirement of ISA 570[10] to obtain a written representation is not relevant; and that there are no exceptions to the requested written representations. If there were exceptions, the representations would need to be modified to reflect the exceptions.

(Entity Letterhead)

(To Auditor)                                                                                          (Date)

This representation letter is provided in connection with your audit of the financial statements of ABC Company for the year ended December 31, 20XX[11] for the purpose of expressing an opinion as to whether the financial statements are presented fairly, in all material respects, (or *give a true and fair view*) in accordance with International Financial Reporting Standards.

We confirm that (*, to the best of our knowledge and belief, having made such inquiries as we considered necessary for the purpose of appropriately informing ourselves*):

### Financial Statements

- We have fulfilled our responsibilities, as set out in the terms of the audit engagement dated [insert date], for the preparation of the financial statements in accordance with International Financial Reporting Standards; in particular the financial statements are fairly presented (or *give a true and fair view*) in accordance therewith.
- Significant assumptions used by us in making accounting estimates, including those measured at fair value, are reasonable. (ISA 540)
- Related party relationships and transactions have been appropriately accounted for and disclosed in accordance with the requirements of International Financial Reporting Standards. (ISA 550)
- All events subsequent to the date of the financial statements and for which International Financial Reporting Standards require adjustment or disclosure have been adjusted or disclosed. (ISA 560)

---

[10] *ISA 570, "Going Concern."*

[11] *Where the auditor reports on more than one period, the auditor adjusts the date so that the letter pertains to all periods covered by the auditor's report.*

- The effects of uncorrected misstatements are immaterial, both individually and in the aggregate, to the financial statements as a whole. A list of the uncorrected misstatements is attached to the representation letter. (ISA 450)
- [Any other matters that the auditor may consider appropriate (see paragraph A12 of this ISA).]

### Information Provided

- We have provided you with:
  - Access to all information of which we are aware that is relevant to the preparation of the financial statements such as records, documentation and other matters;
  - Additional information that you have requested from us for the purpose of the audit; and
  - Unrestricted access to persons within the entity from whom you determined it necessary to obtain audit evidence.
- All transactions have been recorded in the accounting records and are reflected in the financial statements.
- We have disclosed to you the results of our assessment of the risk that the financial statements may be materially misstated as a result of fraud. (ISA 240)
- We have disclosed to you all information in relation to fraud or suspected fraud that we are aware of and that affects the entity and involves:
  - Management;
  - Employees who have significant roles in internal control; or
  - Others where the fraud could have a material effect on the financial statements. (ISA 240)
- We have disclosed to you all information in relation to allegations of fraud, or suspected fraud, affecting the entity's financial statements communicated by employees, former employees, analysts, regulators or others. (ISA 240)
- We have disclosed to you all known instances of non-compliance or suspected non-compliance with laws and regulations whose effects should be considered when preparing financial statements. (ISA 250)
- We have disclosed to you the identity of the entity's related parties and all the related party relationships and transactions of which we are aware. 550)
- [Any other matters that the auditor may consider necessary (see paragraph A13 of this ISA).]

---

Management                    Management

# Addendum

*This addendum provides a summary of APB's rationale for retaining or excluding in the proposed clarified ISA (UK and Ireland) the supplementary requirements in the existing ISA (UK and Ireland). It also sets out the supplementary guidance material in the existing ISA (UK and Ireland) that APB considers is not necessary to retain in light of the improvements in the underlying Clarity ISAs issued by the IAASB as part of the Clarity Project. It is provided for information and does not form part of the proposed clarified ISA (UK and Ireland).*

*The Consultation Paper published with the exposure drafts explains the general approach used by the APB for determining whether current supplementary material should be proposed to be retained.*

## Analysis of proposed treatment of current APB supplementary material in current ISA (UK and Ireland) 580

It should be noted that ISA 580 has been revised as well as clarified.

### Requirements

| APB supplementary requirements (*Italic text is from IAASB for context*) | Is it covered in substance in the Clarity ISA? | Should it be retained? |
|---|---|---|
| 2-1. **Written confirmation of appropriate representations from management, as required by paragraph 4 below, should be obtained before the audit report is issued.** | ✓ 9, 14 | ✗ |
| 3-1. **In the UK and Ireland, the auditor should obtain evidence that those charged with governance acknowledge their collective responsibility for the preparation of the financial statements and have approved the financial statements.** | ✓ This is addressed in ISAs 210 and 700. They do not refer to "collective responsibility" – however that is not a term ordinarily used in engagement letters and audit reports. | ✗ |

### Guidance

During development of the revised ISA APB was concerned with the interaction between the 'automatic disclaimer' required by paragraph 20(b) and the absolute nature of the written representations required by paragraphs 10 and 11 about management's fulfillment of its responsibilities. To help address this, 'essential explanatory guidance' has been added in paragraph 11-1 to emphasise that management may include qualifying language to the effect that these representations are made to the best of its knowledge and belief.

The following guidance in current ISA (UK and Ireland) 580 has not been carried forward to the proposed clarified standard.

| Current paragraph reference (*Italic text is from IAASB for context*) |
|---|
| Definitions of management and those charged with governance. |
| 3. *The auditor should obtain audit evidence that management[1a] acknowledges its responsibility for the fair presentation of the financial statements in accordance with the applicable financial reporting framework, and has approved the financial statements.* ... |
| [1a] In the UK and Ireland, those charged with governance are responsible for the preparation of the financial statements. |
| 3-2. In the UK and Ireland, the directors of a company have a legal collective responsibility to prepare company and, where appropriate, group financial statements that give a true and fair view. |
| 3-3. When the auditor has responsibility for reporting on the financial statements of a group of companies, acknowledgement by the directors of their responsibility for the financial statements applies to both the group financial statements and the financial statements of the parent undertaking. |
| 4. *The auditor should obtain written representations from management on matters material to the financial statements when other sufficient appropriate audit evidence cannot reasonably be expected to exist.* ... *Matters which might be included in a letter from management or in a confirmatory letter to management are contained in the example of a management representation letter in the Appendix to this ISA (UK and Ireland)[1b].* |
| [1b] The example letter does not include all management representations that ISAs (UK and Ireland) require the auditor to obtain. Appendix 2 gives a summary of the management representations the auditor is required by other ISAs (UK and Ireland) to obtain as at 15 December 2004. |
| 4-1. It is advisable for the auditor to discuss the relevant matters with those responsible for giving written representations before they sign them to ensure that they understand what it is that they are being asked to confirm. |
| 8-1. In some exceptional cases, the matter may be of such significance the auditor refers to the representations in the auditor's report as being relevant to an understanding of the basis of the audit opinion. |
| 8-2. When the auditor has responsibility for reporting on group financial statements, where appropriate the auditor obtains written confirmation of representations relating to specific matters regarding both the group financial statements and the financial statements of the parent undertaking. The means by which the auditor obtains these representations depends on the group's methods of delegation of management control and authority. The auditor may be able to obtain the required representations regarding the group financial statements from the management of the parent undertaking because of the level of their involvement in the management of the group. Alternatively, the auditor may obtain certain representations regarding matters material to the group financial statements directly from the management of the subsidiary undertakings, or by seeing relevant representations by management to the auditors of those subsidiary undertakings, in addition to those obtained from the management of the parent undertaking. |
| 9-1 The investigation of apparently contradictory audit evidence regarding a representation received usually begins with further enquiries of management, to ascertain whether the representation has been misunderstood or whether the other audit evidence has been misinterpreted, |

| Current paragraph reference (*Italic text is from IAASB for context*) |
|---|
| followed by corroboration of management's responses. If management is unable to provide an explanation or if the explanation is not considered adequate, further audit procedures may be required to resolve the matter. |
| 13-1. Written representations required as audit evidence are obtained before the audit report is issued. |
| Appendix<br><br>"This example letter does not include all representations that ISAs (UK and Ireland) require the auditor to obtain. A summary of such representations as at 15 December 2004 is included in Appendix 2. Additionally, in the UK and Ireland representations from those charged with governance would include acknowledgment of any responsibilities they may have in law in relation to the preparation of financial statements and providing information to the auditor. An example of such a representation for directors of a UK company incorporated under the Companies Act 1985 is:<br><br>"We acknowledge as directors our responsibilities under the Companies Act 1985 for preparing financial statements which give a true and fair view and for making accurate representations to you. All the accounting records have been made available to you for the purpose of your audit and all the transactions undertaken by the company have been properly reflected and recorded in the accounting records. All other records and related information, including minutes of all management and shareholders meetings, have been made available to you."<br><br>In the Republic of Ireland reference would be made to the Companies Acts 1963 – 2003."<br><br><br>[A simpler statement has been added to make clear the example letter in the clarified ISA has not been tailored for the UK and Ireland.] |

# Proposed Clarified International Standard on Auditing (UK and Ireland) 600
# Special considerations—audits of group financial statements (including the work of component auditors)

*(Effective for audits of group financial statements for periods ending on or after 15 December 2010)*

## Contents

---

International Standard on Auditing (UK and Ireland) (ISA (UK and Ireland))
600, "Special Considerations—Audits of Group Financial Statements (Including
the Work of Component Auditors)" should be read in conjunction with ISA (UK
and Ireland) 200, "Overall Objectives of the Independent Auditor and the Conduct of an Audit in Accordance with International Standards on Auditing (UK
and Ireland)."

---

# Introduction

## Scope of this ISA (UK and Ireland)

1    The International Standards on Auditing (UK and Ireland) (ISAs (UK and Ireland)) apply to group audits. This ISA (UK and Ireland) deals with special considerations that apply to group audits, in particular those that involve component auditors.

2    An auditor may find this ISA (UK and Ireland), adapted as necessary in the circumstances, useful when that auditor involves other auditors in the audit of financial statements that are not group financial statements. For example, an auditor may involve another auditor to observe the inventory count or inspect physical fixed assets at a remote location.

3    A component auditor may be required by statute, regulation or for another reason, to express an audit opinion on the financial statements of a component. The group engagement team may decide to use the audit evidence on which the audit opinion on the financial statements of the component is based to provide audit evidence for the group audit, but the requirements of this ISA (UK and Ireland) nevertheless apply. (Ref: Para. A1)

4    In accordance with ISA (UK and Ireland) 220,[1] the group engagement partner is required to be satisfied that those performing the group audit engagement, including component auditors, collectively have the appropriate competence and capabilities. The group engagement partner is also responsible for the direction, supervision and performance of the group audit engagement.

5    The group engagement partner applies the requirements of ISA (UK and Ireland) 220 regardless of whether the group engagement team or a component auditor performs the work on the financial information of a component. This ISA (UK and Ireland) assists the group engagement partner to meet the requirements of ISA (UK and Ireland) 220 where component auditors perform work on the financial information of components.

6    Audit risk is a function of the risk of material misstatement of the financial statements and the risk that the auditor will not detect such misstatements.[2] In a group audit, this includes the risk that the component auditor may not detect a misstatement in the financial information of the component that could cause a material misstatement of the group financial statements, and the risk that the group engagement team may not detect this misstatement. This ISA (UK and Ireland) explains the matters that the group engagement team considers when determining the nature, timing and extent of its involvement in the risk assessment procedures and further audit procedures performed by the component auditors on the financial information of the components. The purpose of this involvement is to obtain sufficient appropriate audit evidence on which to base the audit opinion on the group financial statements.

---

[1] ISA (UK and Ireland) 220, "Quality Control for an Audit of Financial Statements," paragraphs 14 and 15.

[2] ISA (UK and Ireland) 200, "Overall Objectives of the Independent Auditor and the Conduct of an Audit in Accordance with International Standards on Auditing (UK and Ireland)," paragraph A32.

## Effective Date

This ISA (UK and Ireland) is effective for audits of group financial statements for periods ending on or after 15 December 2010.   7

## Objectives

The objectives of the auditor are:   8

(a) To determine whether to act as the auditor of the group financial statements; and
(b) If acting as the auditor of the group financial statements:
   (i) To communicate clearly with component auditors about the scope and timing of their work on financial information related to components and their findings; and
   (ii) To obtain sufficient appropriate audit evidence regarding the financial information of the components and the consolidation process to express an opinion on whether the group financial statements are prepared, in all material respects, in accordance with the applicable financial reporting framework.

## Definitions

For purposes of the ISAs (UK and Ireland), the following terms have the meanings attributed below:   9

(a) Component – An entity or business activity for which group or component management prepares financial information that should be included in the group financial statements. (Ref: Para. A2-A4)
(b) Component auditor – An auditor who, at the request of the group engagement team, performs work on financial information related to a component for the group audit. (Ref: Para. A7)
(c) Component management – Management responsible for preparing the financial information of a component.
(d) Component materiality – The materiality for a component determined by the group engagement team.
(e) Group – All the components whose financial information is included in the group financial statements. A group always has more than one component.
(f) Group audit – The audit of group financial statements.
(g) Group audit opinion – The audit opinion on the group financial statements.
(h) Group engagement partner – The partner or other person in the firm who is responsible for the group audit engagement and its performance, and for the auditor's report on the group financial statements that is issued on behalf of the firm. Where joint auditors conduct the group audit, the joint engagement partners and their engagement teams collectively constitute the group engagement partner and the group engagement team. This ISA (UK and Ireland) does not, however, deal with the relationship between joint auditors or the work that one joint auditor performs in relation to the work of the other joint auditor.
(i) Group engagement team – Partners, including the group engagement partner, and staff who establish the overall group audit strategy, communicate with component auditors, perform work on the consolidation process, and evaluate the conclusions drawn from the audit evidence as the basis for forming an opinion on the group financial statements.

(j)  Group financial statements – Financial statements that include the financial information of more than one component. The term "group financial statements" also refers to combined financial statements aggregating the financial information prepared by components that have no parent but are under common control.

(k)  Group management – Management responsible for preparing and presenting the group financial statements.

(l)  Group-wide controls – Controls designed, implemented and maintained by group management over group financial reporting.

(m)  Significant component – A component identified by the group engagement team (i) that is of individual financial significance to the group, or (ii) that, due to its specific nature or circumstances, is likely to include significant risks of material misstatement of the group financial statements. (Ref: Para. A5-A6)

10    Reference to "the applicable financial reporting framework" means the financial reporting framework that applies to the group financial statements. Reference to "the consolidation process" includes:

(a)  The recognition, measurement, presentation, and disclosure of the financial information of the components in the group financial statements by way of consolidation, proportionate consolidation, or the equity or cost methods of accounting; and

(b)  The aggregation in combined financial statements of the financial information of components that have no parent but are under common control.

# Requirements

## Responsibility

11    The group engagement partner is responsible for the direction, supervision and performance of the group audit engagement in compliance with professional standards and applicable legal and regulatory requirements, and whether the auditor's report that is issued is appropriate in the circumstances.[3] As a result, the auditor's report on the group financial statements shall not refer to a component auditor, unless required by law or regulation to include such reference. If such reference is required by law or regulation, the auditor's report shall indicate that the reference does not diminish the group engagement partner's or the group engagement partner's firm's responsibility for the group audit opinion. (Ref: Para. A8-A9)

## Acceptance and Continuance

12    In applying ISA (UK and Ireland) 220, the group engagement partner shall determine whether sufficient appropriate audit evidence can reasonably be expected to be obtained in relation to the consolidation process and the financial information of the components on which to base the group audit opinion. For this purpose, the group engagement team shall obtain an understanding of the group, its components, and their environments that is sufficient to identify components that are likely to be significant components. Where component auditors will perform work on the financial information of such components, the group engagement partner shall evaluate whether the group engagement team will be able to be involved in the work of those component auditors to the extent necessary to obtain sufficient appropriate audit evidence. (Ref: Para. A10-A12)

---

[3] ISA (UK and Ireland) 220, paragraph 15.

If the group engagement partner concludes that: **13**

(a) it will not be possible for the group engagement team to obtain sufficient appropriate audit evidence due to restrictions imposed by group management; and

(b) the possible effect of this inability will result in a disclaimer of opinion on the group financial statements),[4]
the group engagement partner shall either:

- in the case of a new engagement, not accept the engagement, or, in the case of a continuing engagement, withdraw from the engagement, where withdrawal is possible under applicable law or regulation; or

- where law or regulation prohibits an auditor from declining an engagement or where withdrawal from an engagement is not otherwise possible, having performed the audit of the group financial statements to the extent possible, disclaim an opinion on the group financial statements. (Ref: Para. A13-A19)

*Terms of Engagement*

The group engagement partner shall agree on the terms of the group audit engagement in accordance with ISA (UK and Ireland) 210.[5] (Ref: Para. A20-A21) **14**

## Overall Audit Strategy and Audit Plan

The group engagement team shall establish an overall group audit strategy and shall develop a group audit plan in accordance with ISA (UK and Ireland) 300.[6] **15**

The group engagement partner shall review the overall group audit strategy and group audit plan. (Ref: Para. A22) **16**

## Understanding the Group, Its Components and Their Environments

The auditor is required to identify and assess the risks of material misstatement through obtaining an understanding of the entity and its environment.[7] The group engagement team shall: **17**

(a) Enhance its understanding of the group, its components, and their environments, including group-wide controls, obtained during the acceptance or continuance stage; and

(b) Obtain an understanding of the consolidation process, including the instructions issued by group management to components. (Ref: Para. A23-A29)

The group engagement team shall obtain an understanding that is sufficient to: **18**

(a) Confirm or revise its initial identification of components that are likely to be significant; and

---

[4] *ISA (UK and Ireland) 705, "Modifications to the Opinion in the Independent Auditor's Report."*

[5] *ISA (UK and Ireland) 210, "Agreeing the Terms of Audit Engagements."*

[6] *ISA (UK and Ireland) 300, "Planning an Audit of Financial Statements," paragraphs 7-12.*

[7] *ISA (UK and Ireland) 315, "Identifying and Assessing the Risks of Material Misstatement through Understanding the Entity and Its Environment."*

(b) Assess the risks of material misstatement of the group financial statements, whether due to fraud or error.[8] (Ref: Para. A30-A31)

## Understanding the Component Auditor

19   If the group engagement team plans to request a component auditor to perform work on the financial information of a component, the group engagement team shall obtain an understanding of the following: (Ref: Para. A32-A35)

(a) Whether the component auditor understands and will comply with the ethical requirements that are relevant to the group audit and, in particular, is independent. (Ref: Para. A37)
(b) The component auditor's professional competence. (Ref: Para. A38)
(c) Whether the group engagement team will be able to be involved in the work of the component auditor to the extent necessary to obtain sufficient appropriate audit evidence.
(d) Whether the component auditor operates in a regulatory environment that actively oversees auditors. (Ref: Para. A36)

20   If a component auditor does not meet the independence requirements that are relevant to the group audit, or the group engagement team has serious concerns about the other matters listed in paragraph 19(a)-(c), the group engagement team shall obtain sufficient appropriate audit evidence relating to the financial information of the component without requesting that component auditor to perform work on the financial information of that component. (Ref: Para. A39-A41)

## Materiality

21   The group engagement team shall determine the following: (Ref: Para. A42)

(a) Materiality for the group financial statements as a whole when establishing the overall group audit strategy.
(b) If, in the specific circumstances of the group, there are particular classes of transactions, account balances or disclosures in the group financial statements for which misstatements of lesser amounts than materiality for the group financial statements as a whole could reasonably be expected to influence the economic decisions of users taken on the basis of the group financial statements, the materiality level or levels to be applied to those particular classes of transactions, account balances or disclosures.
(c) Component materiality for those components where component auditors will perform an audit or a review for purposes of the group audit. To reduce to an appropriately low level the probability that the aggregate of uncorrected and undetected misstatements in the group financial statements exceeds materiality for the group financial statements as a whole, component materiality shall be lower than materiality for the group financial statements as a whole. (Ref: Para. A43-A44)
(d) The threshold above which misstatements cannot be regarded as clearly trivial to the group financial statements. (Ref: Para. A45)

22   Where component auditors will perform an audit for purposes of the group audit, the group engagement team shall evaluate the appropriateness of performance materiality determined at the component level. (Ref: Para. A46)

[8] *ISA (UK and Ireland) 315.*

If a component is subject to audit by statute, regulation or other reason, and the group engagement team decides to use that audit to provide audit evidence for the group audit, the group engagement team shall determine whether:    **23**

(a) materiality for the component financial statements as a whole; and
(b) performance materiality at the component level
    meet the requirements of this ISA (UK and Ireland).

## Responding to Assessed Risks

The auditor is required to design and implement appropriate responses to address the assessed risks of material misstatement of the financial statements.[9] The group engagement team shall determine the type of work to be performed by the group engagement team, or the component auditors on its behalf, on the financial information of the components (see paragraphs 26-29). The group engagement team shall also determine the nature, timing and extent of its involvement in the work of the component auditors (see paragraphs 30-31).    **24**

If the nature, timing and extent of the work to be performed on the consolidation process or the financial information of the components are based on an expectation that group-wide controls are operating effectively, or if substantive procedures alone cannot provide sufficient appropriate audit evidence at the assertion level, the group engagement team shall test, or request a component auditor to test, the operating effectiveness of those controls.    **25**

### *Determining the Type of Work to Be Performed on the Financial Information of Components*

#### *Significant Components*

For a component that is significant due to its individual financial significance to the group, the group engagement team, or a component auditor on its behalf, shall perform an audit of the financial information of the component using component materiality.    **26**

For a component that is significant because it is likely to include significant risks of material misstatement of the group financial statements due to its specific nature or circumstances, the group engagement team, or a component auditor on its behalf, shall perform one or more of the following:    **27**

(a) An audit of the financial information of the component using component materiality.
(b) An audit of one or more account balances, classes of transactions or disclosures relating to the likely significant risks of material misstatement of the group financial statements. (Ref: Para. A48)
(c) Specified audit procedures relating to the likely significant risks of material misstatement of the group financial statements. (Ref: Para. A49)

#### *Components that Are Not Significant Components*

For components that are not significant components, the group engagement team shall perform analytical procedures at group level. (Ref: Para. A50)    **28**

---

[9] *ISA (UK and Ireland) 330, "The Auditor's Responses to Assessed Risks."*

**29**   If the group engagement team does not consider that sufficient appropriate audit evidence on which to base the group audit opinion will be obtained from:

(a)   the work performed on the financial information of significant components;

(b)   the work performed on group-wide controls and the consolidation process; and

(c)   the analytical procedures performed at group level,

the group engagement team shall select components that are not significant components and shall perform, or request a component auditor to perform, one or more of the following on the financial information of the individual components selected: (Ref: Para. A51-A53)

- An audit of the financial information of the component using component materiality.
- An audit of one or more account balances, classes of transactions or disclosures.
- A review of the financial information of the component using component materiality.
- Specified procedures.

The group engagement team shall vary the selection of components over a period of time.

***Involvement in the Work Performed by Component Auditors*** (Ref: Para. A54-A55)

*Significant Components—Risk Assessment*

**30**   If a component auditor performs an audit of the financial information of a significant component, the group engagement team shall be involved in the component auditor's risk assessment to identify significant risks of material misstatement of the group financial statements. The nature, timing and extent of this involvement are affected by the group engagement team's understanding of the component auditor, but at a minimum shall include:

(a)   Discussing with the component auditor or component management those of the component's business activities that are significant to the group;

(b)   Discussing with the component auditor the susceptibility of the component to material misstatement of the financial information due to fraud or error; and

(c)   Reviewing the component auditor's documentation of identified significant risks of material misstatement of the group financial statements. Such documentation may take the form of a memorandum that reflects the component auditor's conclusion with regard to the identified significant risks.

*Identified Significant Risks of Material Misstatement of the Group Financial Statements—Further Audit Procedures*

**31**   If significant risks of material misstatement of the group financial statements have been identified in a component on which a component auditor performs the work, the group engagement team shall evaluate the appropriateness of the further audit procedures to be performed to respond to the identified significant risks of material misstatement of the group financial statements. Based on its understanding of the component auditor, the group engagement team shall determine whether it is necessary to be involved in the further audit procedures.

## Consolidation Process

**32**   In accordance with paragraph 17, the group engagement team obtains an understanding of group-wide controls and the consolidation process, including the instructions issued by group management to components. In accordance with paragraph 25, the group engagement team, or component auditor at the request of the group engagement team, tests the operating effectiveness of group-wide controls if the nature, timing and extent of the work to be performed on the consolidation process are based on an expectation that group-wide controls are operating effectively, or if substantive procedures alone cannot provide sufficient appropriate audit evidence at the assertion level.

The group engagement team shall design and perform further audit procedures on the consolidation process to respond to the assessed risks of material misstatement of the group financial statements arising from the consolidation process. This shall include evaluating whether all components have been included in the group financial statements. **33**

The group engagement team shall evaluate the appropriateness, completeness and accuracy of consolidation adjustments and reclassifications, and shall evaluate whether any fraud risk factors or indicators of possible management bias exist. (Ref: Para. A56) **34**

If the financial information of a component has not been prepared in accordance with the same accounting policies applied to the group financial statements, the group engagement team shall evaluate whether the financial information of that component has been appropriately adjusted for purposes of preparing and presenting the group financial statements. **35**

The group engagement team shall determine whether the financial information identified in the component auditor's communication (see paragraph 41(c)) is the financial information that is incorporated in the group financial statements. **36**

If the group financial statements include the financial statements of a component with a financial reporting period-end that differs from that of the group, the group engagement team shall evaluate whether appropriate adjustments have been made to those financial statements in accordance with the applicable financial reporting framework. **37**

## Subsequent Events

Where the group engagement team or component auditors perform audits on the financial information of components, the group engagement team or the component auditors shall perform procedures designed to identify events at those components that occur between the dates of the financial information of the components and the date of the auditor's report on the group financial statements, and that may require adjustment to or disclosure in the group financial statements. **38**

Where component auditors perform work other than audits of the financial information of components, the group engagement team shall request the component auditors to notify the group engagement team if they become aware of subsequent events that may require an adjustment to or disclosure in the group financial statements. **39**

## Communication with the Component Auditor

The group engagement team shall communicate its requirements to the component auditor on a timely basis. This communication shall set out the work to be performed, the use to be made of that work, and the form and content of the component **40** auditor's communication with the group engagement team. (Ref: Para. A57, A58, A60) It shall also include the following:

(a)   A request that the component auditor, knowing the context in which the group engagement team will use the work of the component auditor, confirms that the component auditor will cooperate with the group engagement team. (Ref: Para. A59)

(b)   The ethical requirements that are relevant to the group audit and, in particular, the independence requirements.

(c)   In the case of an audit or review of the financial information of the component, component materiality (and, if applicable, the materiality level or levels for particular classes of transactions, account balances or disclosures) and the threshold above which misstatements cannot be regarded as clearly trivial to the group financial statements.

(d)   Identified significant risks of material misstatement of the group financial statements, due to fraud or error, that are relevant to the work of the component auditor. The group engagement team shall request the component auditor to communicate on a timely basis any other identified significant risks of material misstatement of the group financial statements, due to fraud or error, in the component, and the component auditor's responses to such risks.

(e)   A list of related parties prepared by group management, and any other related parties of which the group engagement team is aware. The group engagement team shall request the component auditor to communicate on a timely basis related parties not previously identified by group management or the group engagement team. The group engagement team shall determine whether to identify such additional related parties to other component auditors.

**41**   The group engagement team shall request the component auditor to communicate matters relevant to the group engagement team's conclusion with regard to the group audit. Such communication shall include: (Ref: Para. A60)

(a)   Whether the component auditor has complied with ethical requirements that are relevant to the group audit, including independence and professional competence;

(b)   Whether the component auditor has complied with the group engagement team's requirements;

(c)   Identification of the financial information of the component on which the component auditor is reporting;

(d)   Information on instances of non-compliance with laws or regulations that could give rise to a material misstatement of the group financial statements;

(e)   A list of uncorrected misstatements of the financial information of the component (the list need not include misstatements that are below the threshold for clearly trivial misstatements communicated by the group engagement team (see paragraph 40(c));

(f)   Indicators of possible management bias;

(g)   Description of any identified significant deficiencies in internal control at the component level;

(h)   Other significant matters that the component auditor communicated or expects to communicate to those charged with governance of the component, including fraud or suspected fraud involving component management, employees who have significant roles in internal control at the component level or others where the fraud resulted in a material misstatement of the financial information of the component;

(i)   Any other matters that may be relevant to the group audit, or that the component auditor wishes to draw to the attention of the group engagement team, including exceptions noted in the written representations that the component auditor requested from component management; and

(j)   The component auditor's overall findings, conclusions or opinion.

## Evaluating the Sufficiency and Appropriateness of Audit Evidence Obtained

*Evaluating the Component Auditor's Communication and Adequacy of their Work*

The group engagement team shall evaluate the component auditor's communication **42** (see paragraph 41). The group engagement team shall:

(a)   Discuss significant matters arising from that evaluation with the component auditor, component management or group management, as appropriate; and
(b)   Determine whether it is necessary to review other relevant parts of the component auditor's audit documentation. (Ref: Para. A61)

If the group engagement team concludes that the work of the component auditor is **43** insufficient, the group engagement team shall determine what additional procedures are to be performed, and whether they are to be performed by the component auditor or by the group engagement team.

*Sufficiency and Appropriateness of Audit Evidence*

The auditor is required to obtain sufficient appropriate audit evidence to reduce **44** audit risk to an acceptably low level and thereby enable the auditor to draw reasonable conclusions on which to base the auditor's opinion.[10] The group engagement team shall evaluate whether sufficient appropriate audit evidence has been obtained from the audit procedures performed on the consolidation process and the work performed by the group engagement team and the component auditors on the financial information of the components, on which to base the group audit opinion. (Ref: Para. A62)

The group engagement partner shall evaluate the effect on the group audit opinion of **45** any uncorrected misstatements (either identified by the group engagement team or communicated by component auditors) and any instances where there has been an inability to obtain sufficient appropriate audit evidence. (Ref: Para. A63)

## Communication with Group Management and Those Charged with Governance of the Group

*Communication with Group Management*

The group engagement team shall determine which identified deficiencies in internal **46** control to communicate to those charged with governance and group management in accordance with ISA (UK and Ireland) 265[11]. In making this determination, the group engagement team shall consider:

(a)   Deficiencies in group-wide internal control that the group engagement team has identified;
(b)   Deficiencies in internal control that the group engagement team has identified in internal controls at components; and

---

[10] *ISA (UK and Ireland) 200, paragraph 17.*

[11] *ISA (UK and Ireland) 265, "Communicating Deficiencies in Internal Control to Those Charged with Governance and Management."*

(c) Deficiencies in internal control that component auditors have brought to the attention of the group engagement team.

**47** If fraud has been identified by the group engagement team or brought to its attention by a component auditor (see paragraph 41(h)), or information indicates that a fraud may exist, the group engagement team shall communicate this on a timely basis to the appropriate level of group management in order to inform those with primary responsibility for the prevention and detection of fraud of matters relevant to their responsibilities. (Ref. Para. A64)

**48** A component auditor may be required by statute, regulation or for another reason, to express an audit opinion on the financial statements of a component. In that case, the group engagement team shall request group management to inform component management of any matter of which the group engagement team becomes aware that may be significant to the financial statements of the component, but of which component management may be unaware. If group management refuses to communicate the matter to component management, the group engagement team shall discuss the matter with those charged with governance of the group. If the matter remains unresolved, the group engagement team, subject to legal and professional confidentiality considerations, shall consider whether to advise the component auditor not to issue the auditor's report on the financial statements of the component until the matter is resolved. (Ref: Para. A65)

### Communication with Those Charged with Governance of the Group

**49** The group engagement team shall communicate the following matters with those charged with governance of the group, in addition to those required by ISA (UK and Ireland) 260[12] and other ISAs (UK and Ireland): (Ref: Para. A66)

(a) An overview of the type of work to be performed on the financial information of the components.
(b) An overview of the nature of the group engagement team's planned involvement in the work to be performed by the component auditors on the financial information of significant components.
(c) Instances where the group engagement team's evaluation of the work of a component auditor gave rise to a concern about the quality of that auditor's work.
(d) Any limitations on the group audit, for example, where the group engagement team's access to information may have been restricted.
(e) Fraud or suspected fraud involving group management, component management, employees who have significant roles in group-wide controls or others where the fraud resulted in a material misstatement of the group financial statements.

### Documentation

**50** The group engagement team shall include in the audit documentation the following matters:[13]

(a) An analysis of components, indicating those that are significant, and the type of work performed on the financial information of the components.
(b) The nature, timing and extent of the group engagement team's involvement in the work performed by the component auditors on significant components

[12] ISA (UK and Ireland) 260, "Communication with Those Charged with Governance."

[13] ISA (UK and Ireland) 230, "Audit Documentation," paragraphs 8-11, and paragraph A6.

including, where applicable, the group engagement team's review of relevant parts of the component auditors' audit documentation and conclusions thereon. (Ref: Para. A66-1)

(c) Written communications between the group engagement team and the component auditors about the group engagement team's requirements.

\*\*\*

# Application and Other Explanatory Material

## Components Subject to Audit by Statute, Regulation or Other Reason (Ref: Para. 3)

Factors that may affect the group engagement team's decision whether to use an audit required by statute, regulation or for another reason to provide audit evidence for the group audit include the following:  **A1**

- Differences in the financial reporting framework applied in preparing the financial statements of the component and that applied in preparing the group financial statements.
- Differences in the auditing and other standards applied by the component auditor and those applied in the audit of the group financial statements.
- Whether the audit of the financial statements of the component will be completed in time to meet the group reporting timetable.

### Considerations Specific to Public Sector Entities

In certain parts of the public sector where the responsibilities of principal and other auditors are governed by statutory provisions, these override the provisions of this ISA (UK and Ireland).  **A1-1**

## Definitions

### Component (Ref: Para. 9(a))

The structure of a group affects how components are identified. For example, the group financial reporting system may be based on an organizational structure that provides for financial information to be prepared by a parent and one or more subsidiaries, joint ventures, or investees accounted for by the equity or cost methods of accounting; by a head office and one or more divisions or branches; or by a combination of both. Some groups, however, may organize their financial reporting system by function, process, product or service (or by groups of products or services), or geographical locations. In these cases, the entity or business activity for which group or component management prepares financial information that is included in the group financial statements may be a function, process, product or service (or group of products or services), or geographical location.  **A2**

Various levels of components may exist within the group financial reporting system, in which case it may be more appropriate to identify components at certain levels of aggregation rather than individually.  **A3**

Components aggregated at a certain level may constitute a component for purposes of the group audit; however, such a component may also prepare group financial statements that incorporate the financial information of the components it  **A4** encompasses (i.e., a subgroup). This ISA (UK and Ireland) may therefore be applied by different group engagement partners and teams for different subgroups within a larger group.

### *Significant Component* (Ref: Para. 9(m))

**A5**    As the individual financial significance of a component increases, the risks of material misstatement of the group financial statements ordinarily increase. The group engagement team may apply a percentage to a chosen benchmark as an aid to identify components that are of individual financial significance. Identifying a benchmark and determining a percentage to be applied to it involve the exercise of professional judgment. Depending on the nature and circumstances of the group, appropriate benchmarks might include group assets, liabilities, cash flows, profit or turnover. For example, the group engagement team may consider that components exceeding 15% of the chosen benchmark are significant components. A higher or lower percentage may, however, be deemed appropriate in the circumstances.

**A6**    The group engagement team may also identify a component as likely to include significant risks of material misstatement of the group financial statements due to its specific nature or circumstances (i.e., risks that require special audit consideration[14]). For example, a component could be responsible for foreign exchange trading and thus expose the group to a significant risk of material misstatement, even though the component is not otherwise of individual financial significance to the group.

### *Component Auditor* (Ref: Para. 9(b))

**A7**    A member of the group engagement team may perform work on the financial information of a component for the group audit at the request of the group engagement team. Where this is the case, such a member of the engagement team is also a component auditor.

### **Responsibility** (Ref: Para. 11)

**A8**    Although component auditors may perform work on the financial information of the components for the group audit and as such are responsible for their overall findings, conclusions or opinions, the group engagement partner or the group engagement partner's firm is responsible for the group audit opinion.

**A9**    When the group audit opinion is modified because the group engagement team was unable to obtain sufficient appropriate audit evidence in relation to the financial information of one or more components, the Basis for Modification paragraph in the auditor's report on the group financial statements describes the reasons for that inability without referring to the component auditor, unless such a reference is necessary for an adequate explanation of the circumstances.[15]

---

[14] *ISA (UK and Ireland) 315, paragraphs 28-29.*

[15] *ISA (UK and Ireland) 705, paragraph 20.*

## Acceptance and Continuance

### *Obtaining an Understanding at the Acceptance or Continuance Stage* (Ref: Para. 12)

In the case of a new engagement, the group engagement team's understanding of the group, its components, and their environments may be obtained from:    **A10**

- Information provided by group management;
- Communication with group management; and
- Where applicable, communication with the previous group engagement team, component management, or component auditors.

The group engagement team's understanding may include matters such as the following:    **A11**

- The group structure, including both the legal and organizational structure (i.e., how the group financial reporting system is organized).
- Components' business activities that are significant to the group, including the industry and regulatory, economic and political environments in which those activities take place.
- The use of service organizations, including shared service centers.
- A description of group-wide controls.
- The complexity of the consolidation process.
- Whether component auditors that are not from the group engagement partner's firm or network will perform work on the financial information of any of the components, and group management's rationale for appointing more than one auditor.
- Whether the group engagement team:
  - Will have unrestricted access to those charged with governance of the group, group management, those charged with governance of the component, component management, component information, and the component auditors (including relevant audit documentation sought by the group engagement team); and
  - Will be able to perform necessary work on the financial information of the components.

In the case of a continuing engagement, the group engagement team's ability to obtain sufficient appropriate audit evidence may be affected by significant changes, for example:    **A12**

- Changes in the group structure (e.g., acquisitions, disposals, reorganizations, or changes in how the group financial reporting system is organized).
- Changes in components' business activities that are significant to the group.
- Changes in the composition of those charged with governance of the group, group management, or key management of significant components.
- Concerns the group engagement team has with regard to the integrity and competence of group or component management.
- Changes in group-wide controls.
- Changes in the applicable financial reporting framework.

### *Expectation to Obtain Sufficient Appropriate Audit Evidence* (Ref: Para. 13)

A group may consist only of components not considered significant components. In these circumstances, the group engagement partner can reasonably expect to obtain sufficient appropriate audit evidence on which to base the group audit opinion if the group engagement team will be able to:    **A13**

(a) Perform the work on the financial information of some of these components; and

(b) Be involved in the work performed by component auditors on the financial information of other components to the extent necessary to obtain sufficient appropriate audit evidence.

### *Access to Information* (Ref: Para. 13)

**A14** The group engagement team's access to information may be restricted by circumstances that cannot be overcome by group management, for example, laws relating to confidentiality and data privacy, or denial by the component auditor of access to relevant audit documentation sought by the group engagement team. It may also be restricted by group management.

**A14-1** In the UK and Ireland there are statutory obligations on corporate subsidiary undertakings, and, and their auditors and other parties, in the UK and Ireland to provide the auditor of a corporate parent undertaking with such information and explanations as that auditor may reasonably require for the purposes of the audit[15a]. Where there is no such statutory obligation (e.g. for non corporate entities and overseas subsidiary undertakings), permission may be needed by the auditors of the subsidiary undertakings, from those charged with governance of the subsidiary undertakings, to disclose the contents of any communication to them to the auditor of the parent undertaking and also for the auditor of the parent undertaking to pass those disclosures onto those charged with governance of the parent undertaking. The auditor of the parent undertaking seeks to ensure that appropriate arrangements are made at the planning stage for these disclosures. Normally, such arrangements for groups are recorded in the instructions to the auditors of subsidiary undertakings and relevant engagement letters.

**A15** Where access to information is restricted by circumstances, the group engagement team may still be able to obtain sufficient appropriate audit evidence; however, this is less likely as the significance of the component increases. For example, the group engagement team may not have access to those charged with governance, management, or the auditor (including relevant audit documentation sought by the group engagement team) of a component that is accounted for by the equity method of accounting. If the component is not a significant component, and the group engagement team has a complete set of financial statements of the component, including the auditor's report thereon, and has access to information kept by group management in relation to that component, the group engagement team may

---

[15a] *In the UK, Section 499 of the Companies Act 2006 specifies that the auditor of a company may require any subsidiary undertaking of the company which is a body corporate incorporated in the UK, and any officer, employee or auditor of any such subsidiary undertaking or any person holding or accountable for any books, accounts or vouchers of any such subsidiary undertaking, to provide him with such information or explanations as he thinks necessary for the performance of his duties as auditor. (Similar obligations regarding companies incorporated in the Republic of Ireland are set out in Section 196, Companies Act 1990.) If a parent company has a subsidiary undertaking that is not a body corporate incorporated in the UK, Section 500 of the Companies Act 2006 specifies that the auditor of the parent company may require it to take all such steps as are reasonably open to it to obtain from the subsidiary undertaking, any officer, employee or auditor of the undertaking, or any person holding or accountable for any of the undertaking's books, accounts or vouchers, such information and explanations as he may reasonably require for the purposes of his duties as auditor.*
*Schedule 10, paragraph 10A, to the Companies Act 2006 includes provisions relating to arrangements to enable Recognised Supervisory Bodies and other bodies involved in monitoring audits to have access to the audit documentation of certain other auditors involved in the group audit. These provisions are addressed in audit regulations not in ISAs (UK and Ireland). [footnote 1 to para 15-1 in current ISA (UK and Ireland) 600]*

conclude that this information constitutes sufficient appropriate audit evidence in relation to that component. If the component is a significant component, however, the group engagement team will not be able to comply with the requirements of this ISA (UK and Ireland) relevant in the circumstances of the group audit. For example, the group engagement team will not be able to comply with the requirement in paragraphs 30-31 to be involved in the work of the component auditor. The group engagement team will not, therefore, be able to obtain sufficient appropriate audit evidence in relation to that component. The effect of the group engagement team's inability to obtain sufficient appropriate audit evidence is considered in terms of ISA (UK and Ireland) 705.

The group engagement team will not be able to obtain sufficient appropriate audit **A16** evidence if group management restricts the access of the group engagement team or a component auditor to the information of a significant component.

Although the group engagement team may be able to obtain sufficient appropriate **A17** audit evidence if such restriction relates to a component considered not a significant component, the reason for the restriction may affect the group audit opinion. For example, it may affect the reliability of group management's responses to the group engagement team's inquiries and group management's representations to the group engagement team.

Law or regulation may prohibit the group engagement partner from declining or **A18** withdrawing from an engagement. For example, in some jurisdictions the auditor is appointed for a specified period of time and is prohibited from withdrawing before the end of that period. Also, in the public sector, the option of declining or withdrawing from an engagement may not be available to the auditor due to the nature of the mandate or public interest considerations. In these circumstances, this ISA (UK and Ireland) still applies to the group audit, and the effect of the group engagement team's inability to obtain sufficient appropriate audit evidence is considered in terms of ISA (UK and Ireland) 705.

Appendix 1 contains an example of an auditor's report containing a qualified opi- **A19** nion based on the group engagement team's inability to obtain sufficient appropriate audit evidence in relation to a significant component accounted for by the equity method of accounting, but where, in the group engagement team's judgment, the effect is material but not pervasive.

With respect to companies, illustrative examples of auditor's reports tailored for use with audits conducted in accordance with ISAs (UK and Ireland) are given in the most recent versions of the APB Bulletins, "Auditor's Reports on Financial Statements in the United Kingdom"/"Auditor's Reports on Financial Statements in the Republic of Ireland." Illustrative examples for various other entities are give in other Bulletins and Practice Notes issued by the APB.

*Terms of Engagement* (Ref: Para. 14)

The terms of engagement identify the applicable financial reporting framework.[16] **A20** Additional matters may be included in the terms of a group audit engagement, such as the fact that:

---

[16] *ISA (UK and Ireland) 210, paragraph [8].*

- The communication between the group engagement team and the component auditors should be unrestricted to the extent possible under law or regulation;
- Important communications between the component auditors, those charged with governance of the component, and component management, including communications on significant deficiencies in internal control, should be communicated as well to the group engagement team;
- Important communications between regulatory authorities and components related to financial reporting matters should be communicated to the group engagement team; and
- To the extent the group engagement team considers necessary, it should be permitted:
  - Access to component information, those charged with governance of components, component management, and the component auditors (including relevant audit documentation sought by the group engagement team); and
  - To perform work or request a component auditor to perform work on the financial information of the components.

A21   Restrictions imposed on:

- the group engagement team's access to component information, those charged with governance of components, component management, or the component auditors (including relevant audit documentation sought by the group engagement team); or
- the work to be performed on the financial information of the components

after the group engagement partner's acceptance of the group audit engagement, constitute an inability to obtain sufficient appropriate audit evidence that may affect the group audit opinion. In exceptional circumstances it may even lead to withdrawal from the engagement where withdrawal is possible under applicable law or regulation.

**Overall Audit Strategy and Audit Plan** (Ref: Para. 16)

A22   The group engagement partner's review of the overall group audit strategy and group audit plan is an important part of fulfilling the group engagement partner's responsibility for the direction of the group audit engagement.

**Understanding the Group, Its Components and Their Environments**

*Matters about Which the Group Engagement Team Obtains an Understanding* (Ref: Para. 17)

A23   ISA (UK and Ireland) 315 contains guidance on matters the auditor may consider when obtaining an understanding of the industry, regulatory, and other external factors that affect the entity, including the applicable financial reporting framework; the nature of the entity; objectives and strategies and related business risks; and measurement and review of the entity's financial performance.[17] Appendix 2 of this ISA (UK and Ireland) contains guidance on matters specific to a group, including the consolidation process.

---

[17] *ISA (UK and Ireland) 315, paragraphs A17-A41.*

**Instructions Issued by Group Management to Components** (Ref: Para. 17)

To achieve uniformity and comparability of financial information, group manage- **A24**
ment ordinarily issues instructions to components. Such instructions specify the
requirements for financial information of the components to be included in the group
financial statements and often include financial reporting procedures manuals and a
reporting package. A reporting package ordinarily consists of standard formats for
providing financial information for incorporation in the group financial statements.
Reporting packages generally do not, however, take the form of complete financial
statements prepared and presented in accordance with the applicable financial
reporting framework.

The instructions ordinarily cover:                                              **A25**

- The accounting policies to be applied;
- Statutory and other disclosure requirements applicable to the group financial
  statements, including:
  - The identification and reporting of segments;
  - Related party relationships and transactions;
  - Intra-group transactions and unrealized profits;
  - Intra-group account balances; and
- A reporting timetable.

The group engagement team's understanding of the instructions may include the     **A26**
following:

- The clarity and practicality of the instructions for completing the reporting
  package.
- Whether the instructions:
  - Adequately describe the characteristics of the applicable financial reporting
    framework;
  - Provide for disclosures that are sufficient to comply with the requirements
    of the applicable financial reporting framework, for example, disclosure of
    related party relationships and transactions, and segment information;
  - Provide for the identification of consolidation adjustments, for example,
    intra-group transactions and unrealized profits, and intra-group account
    balances; and
  - Provide for the approval of the financial information by component
    management.

**Fraud** (Ref: Para. 17)

The auditor is required to identify and assess the risks of material misstatement of   **A27**
the financial statements due to fraud, and to design and implement appropriate
responses to the assessed risks.[18] Information used to identify the risks of material
misstatement of the group financial statements due to fraud may include the
following:

- Group management's assessment of the risks that the group financial statements
  may be materially misstated as a result of fraud.
- Group management's process for identifying and responding to the risks of
  fraud in the group, including any specific fraud risks identified by group management, or account balances, classes of transactions, or disclosures for which a
  risk of fraud is likely.

---

[18] *ISA (UK and Ireland) 240, "The Auditor's Responsibilities Relating to Fraud in an Audit of Financial
Statements."*

- Whether there are particular components for which a risk of fraud is likely.
- How those charged with governance of the group monitor group management's processes for identifying and responding to the risks of fraud in the group, and the controls group management has established to mitigate these risks.
- Responses of those charged with governance of the group, group management, internal audit (and if considered appropriate, component management, the component auditors, and others) to the group engagement team's inquiry whether they have knowledge of any actual, suspected, or alleged fraud affecting a component or the group.

### Discussion among Group Engagement Team Members and Component Auditors Regarding the Risks of Material Misstatement of the Group Financial Statements, Including Risks of Fraud (Ref: Para. 17)

A28　The key members of the engagement team are required to discuss the susceptibility of an entity to material misstatement of the financial statements due to fraud or error, specifically emphasizing the risks due to fraud. In a group audit, these discussions may also include the component auditors.[19] The group engagement partner's determination of who to include in the discussions, how and when they occur, and their extent, is affected by factors such as prior experience with the group.

A29　The discussions provide an opportunity to:

- Share knowledge of the components and their environments, including group-wide controls.
- Exchange information about the business risks of the components or the group.
- Exchange ideas about how and where the group financial statements may be susceptible to material misstatement due to fraud or error, how group management and component management could perpetrate and conceal fraudulent financial reporting, and how assets of the components could be misappropriated.
- Identify practices followed by group or component management that may be biased or designed to manage earnings that could lead to fraudulent financial reporting, for example, revenue recognition practices that do not comply with the applicable financial reporting framework.
- Consider known external and internal factors affecting the group that may create an incentive or pressure for group management, component management, or others to commit fraud, provide the opportunity for fraud to be perpetrated, or indicate a culture or environment that enables group management, component management, or others to rationalize committing group fraud.
- Consider the risk that group or component management may override controls.
- Consider whether uniform accounting policies are used to prepare the financial information of the components for the group financial statements and, where not, how differences in accounting policies are identified and adjusted (where required by the applicable financial reporting framework).
- Discuss fraud that has been identified in components, or information that indicates existence of a fraud in a component.
- Share information that may indicate non-compliance with national laws or regulations, for example, payments of bribes and improper transfer pricing practices.

[19] *ISA (UK and Ireland) 240, paragraph 15, and ISA 315, paragraph 10.*

***Risk Factors*** (Ref: Para. 18)

Appendix 3 sets out examples of conditions or events that, individually or together, may indicate risks of material misstatement of the group financial statements, including risks due to fraud.                      **A30**

***Risk Assessment*** (Ref: Para. 18)

The group engagement team's assessment at group level of the risks of material     **A31** misstatement of the group financial statements is based on information such as the following:

- Information obtained from the understanding of the group, its components, and their environments, and of the consolidation process, including audit evidence obtained in evaluating the design and implementation of group-wide controls and controls that are relevant to the consolidation.
- Information obtained from the component auditors.

## Understanding the Component Auditor (Ref: Para. 19-20)

The group engagement team obtains an understanding of a component auditor only     **A32** when it plans to request the component auditor to perform work on the financial information of a component for the group audit. For example, it will not be necessary to obtain an understanding of the auditors of those components for which the group engagement team plans to perform analytical procedures at group level only.

***Group Engagement Team's Procedures to Obtain an Understanding of the Component Auditor and Sources of Audit Evidence*** (Ref: Para. 19)

The nature, timing and extent of the group engagement team's procedures to obtain     **A33** an understanding of the component auditor are affected by factors such as previous experience with or knowledge of the component auditor, and the degree to which the group engagement team and the component auditor are subject to common policies and procedures, for example:

- Whether the group engagement team and a component auditor share:
  - Common policies and procedures for performing the work (e.g., audit methodologies);
  - Common quality control policies and procedures; or
  - Common monitoring policies and procedures.
- The consistency or similarity of:
  - Laws and regulations or legal system;
  - Professional oversight, discipline, and external quality assurance;
  - Education and training;
  - Professional organizations and standards; or
  - Language and culture.

These factors interact and are not mutually exclusive. For example, the extent of the     **A34** group engagement team's procedures to obtain an understanding of Component Auditor A, who consistently applies common quality control and monitoring policies and procedures and a common audit methodology or operates in the same jurisdiction as the group engagement partner, may be less than the extent of the group engagement team's procedures to obtain an understanding of Component Auditor B, who is not consistently applying common quality control and monitoring policies and procedures and a common audit methodology or operates in a foreign jurisdiction. The nature of the procedures performed in relation to Component Auditors A and B may also be different.

**A35**    The group engagement team may obtain an understanding of the component auditor in a number of ways. In the first year of involving a component auditor, the group engagement team may, for example:

- Evaluate the results of the quality control monitoring system where the group engagement team and component auditor are from a firm or network that operates under and complies with common monitoring policies and procedures;[20]
- Visit the component auditor to discuss the matters in paragraph 19(a)-(c);
- Request the component auditor to confirm the matters referred to in paragraph 19(a)-(c) in writing. Appendix 4 contains an example of written confirmations by a component auditor;
- Request the component auditor to complete questionnaires about the matters in paragraph 19(a)-(c);
- Discuss the component auditor with colleagues in the group engagement partner's firm, or with a reputable third party that has knowledge of the component auditor; or
- Obtain confirmations from the professional body or bodies to which the component auditor belongs, the authorities by which the component auditor is licensed, or other third parties.
  In subsequent years, the understanding of the component auditor may be based on the group engagement team's previous experience with the component auditor. The group engagement team may request the component auditor to confirm whether anything in relation to the matters listed in paragraph 19(a)-(c) has changed since the previous year.

**A36**    Where independent oversight bodies have been established to oversee the auditing profession and monitor the quality of audits, awareness of the regulatory environment may assist the group engagement team in evaluating the independence and competence of the component auditor. Information about the regulatory environment may be obtained from the component auditor or information provided by the independent oversight bodies.

*Ethical Requirements that Are Relevant to the Group Audit* (Ref: Para. 19(a))

**A37**    When performing work on the financial information of a component for a group audit, the component auditor is subject to ethical requirements that are relevant to the group audit. Such requirements may be different or in addition to those applying to the component auditor when performing a statutory audit in the component auditor's jurisdiction. The group engagement team therefore obtains an understanding whether the component auditor understands and will comply with the ethical requirements that are relevant to the group audit, sufficient to fulfill the component auditor's responsibilities in the group audit.

---

[20] *As required by ISQC (UK and Ireland) 1, "Quality Control for Firms that Perform Audits and Reviews of Financial Statements, and Other Assurance and Related Services Engagements," paragraph 54, or national requirements that are at least as demanding.*

*The Component Auditor's Professional Competence* (Ref: Para. 19(b))

The group engagement team's understanding of the component auditor's profes- **A38**
sional competence may include whether the component auditor:

- Possesses an understanding of auditing and other standards applicable to the
group audit that is sufficient to fulfill the component auditor's responsibilities in
the group audit;

- Has sufficient resources (e.g. personnel with the necessary capabilities) to
perform the work on the financial information of the particular component;

- Possesses the special skills (e.g., industry specific knowledge) necessary to perform the work on the financial information of the particular component; and
- Where relevant, possesses an understanding of the applicable financial reporting
framework that is sufficient to fulfill the component auditor's responsibilities in
the group audit (instructions issued by group management to components often
describe the characteristics of the applicable financial reporting framework).

*Application of the Group Engagement Team's Understanding of a Component Auditor*
(Ref: Para. 20)

The group engagement team cannot overcome the fact that a component auditor is **A39**
not independent by being involved in the work of the component auditor or by
performing additional risk assessment or further audit procedures on the financial
information of the component.

However, the group engagement team may be able to overcome less than serious **A40**
concerns about the component auditor's professional competency (e.g., lack of
industry specific knowledge), or the fact that the component auditor does not operate
in an environment that actively oversees auditors, by being involved in the work of
the component auditor or by performing additional risk assessment or further audit
procedures on the financial information of the component.

Where law or regulation prohibits access to relevant parts of the audit documenta- **A41**
tion of the component auditor, the group engagement team may request the
component auditor to overcome this by preparing a memorandum that covers the
relevant information.

## Materiality (Ref: Para. 21-23)

The auditor is required:[21] **A42**

(a) When establishing the overall audit strategy, to determine:
  (i) Materiality for the financial statements as a whole; and
  (ii) If, in the specific circumstances of the entity, there are particular classes of
  transactions, account balances or disclosures for which misstatements of
  lesser amounts than materiality for the financial statements as a whole
  could reasonably be expected to influence the economic decisions of users
  taken on the basis of the financial statements, the materiality level or levels
  to be applied to those particular classes of transactions, account balances or
  disclosures; and

---

[21] *ISA (UK and Ireland) 320, "Materiality in Planning and Performing an Audit," paragraph 10.*

(b)  To determine performance materiality.

In the context of a group audit, materiality is established for both the group financial statements as a whole, and for the financial information of the components. Materiality for the group financial statements as a whole is used when establishing the overall group audit strategy.

**A43**  To reduce to an appropriately low level the probability that the aggregate of uncorrected and undetected misstatements in the group financial statements exceeds materiality for the group financial statements as a whole, component materiality is set lower than materiality for the group financial statements as a whole. Different component materiality may be established for different components. Component materiality need not be an arithmetical portion of the materiality for the group financial statements as a whole and, consequently, the aggregate of component materiality for the different components may exceed the materiality for the group financial statements as a whole. Component materiality is used when establishing the overall audit strategy for a component.

**A44**  Component materiality is determined for those components whose financial information will be audited or reviewed as part of the group audit in accordance with paragraphs 26, 27(a) and 29. Component materiality is used by the component auditor to evaluate whether uncorrected detected misstatements are material, individually or in the aggregate.

**A45**  A threshold for misstatements is determined in addition to component materiality. Misstatements identified in the financial information of the component that are above the threshold for misstatements are communicated to the group engagement team.

**A46**  In the case of an audit of the financial information of a component, the component auditor (or group engagement team) determines performance materiality at the component level. This is necessary to reduce to an appropriately low level the probability that the aggregate of uncorrected and undetected misstatements in the financial information of the component exceeds component materiality. In practice, the group engagement team may set component materiality at this lower level. Where this is the case, the component auditor uses component materiality for purposes of assessing the risks of material misstatement of the financial information of the component and to design further audit procedures in response to assessed risks as well as for evaluating whether detected misstatements are material individually or in the aggregate.

## Responding to Assessed Risks

***Determining the Type of Work to Be Performed on the Financial Information of Components*** (Ref: Para. 26-27)

**A47**  The group engagement team's determination of the type of work to be performed on the financial information of a component and its involvement in the work of the component auditor is affected by:

(a)  The significance of the component;
(b)  The identified significant risks of material misstatement of the group financial statements;
(c)  The group engagement team's evaluation of the design of group-wide controls and determination whether they have been implemented; and
(d)  The group engagement team's understanding of the component auditor.

The diagram shows how the significance of the component affects the group engagement team's determination of the type of work to be performed on the financial information of the component.

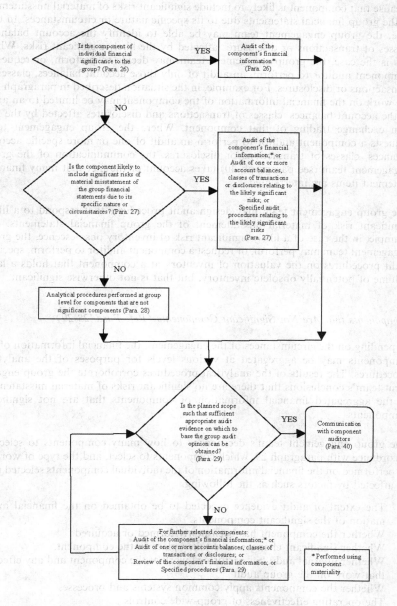

*Significant Components (Ref: Para. 27(b)-(c))*

A48 The group engagement team may identify a component as a significant component because that component is likely to include significant risks of material misstatement of the group financial statements due to its specific nature or circumstances. In that case, the group engagement team may be able to identify the account balances, classes of transactions or disclosures affected by the likely significant risks. Where this is the case, the group engagement team may decide to perform, or request a component auditor to perform, an audit of only those account balances, classes of transactions or disclosures. For example, in the situation described in paragraph A6, the work on the financial information of the component may be limited to an audit of the account balances, classes of transactions and disclosures affected by the foreign exchange trading of that component. Where the group engagement team requests a component auditor to perform an audit of one or more specific account balances, classes of transactions or disclosures, the communication of the group engagement team (see paragraph 40) takes account of the fact that many financial statement items are interrelated.

A49 The group engagement team may design audit procedures that respond to a likely significant risk of material misstatement of the group financial statements. For example, in the case of a likely significant risk of inventory obsolescence, the group engagement team may perform, or request a component auditor to perform, specified audit procedures on the valuation of inventory at a component that holds a large volume of potentially obsolete inventory, but that is not otherwise significant.

*Components that Are Not Significant Components (Ref: Para. 28-29)*

A50 Depending on the circumstances of the engagement, the financial information of the components may be aggregated at various levels for purposes of the analytical procedures. The results of the analytical procedures corroborate the group engagement team's conclusions that there are no significant risks of material misstatement of the aggregated financial information of components that are not significant components.

A51 The group engagement team's decision as to how many components to select in accordance with paragraph 29, which components to select, and the type of work to be performed on the financial information of the individual components selected may be affected by factors such as the following:

- The extent of audit evidence expected to be obtained on the financial information of the significant components.
- Whether the component has been newly formed or acquired.
- Whether significant changes have taken place in the component.
- Whether internal audit has performed work at the component and any effect of that work on the group audit.
- Whether the components apply common systems and processes.
- The operating effectiveness of group-wide controls.
- Abnormal fluctuations identified by analytical procedures performed at group level.
- The individual financial significance of, or the risk posed by, the component in comparison with other components within this category.
- Whether the component is subject to audit required by statute, regulation or for another reason.
  Including an element of unpredictability in selecting components in this category may increase the likelihood of identifying material misstatement of the

components' financial information. The selection of components is often varied on a cyclical basis.

A review of the financial information of a component may be performed in accor- **A52** dance with International Standard on Review Engagements (ISRE) 2400[22] or ISRE (UK and Ireland) 2410,[23] adapted as necessary in the circumstances. The group engagement team may also specify additional procedures to supplement this work.

As explained in paragraph A13, a group may consist only of components that are not **A53** significant components. In these circumstances, the group engagement team can obtain sufficient appropriate audit evidence on which to base the group audit opinion by determining the type of work to be performed on the financial information of the components in accordance with paragraph 29. It is unlikely that the group engagement team will obtain sufficient appropriate audit evidence on which to base the group audit opinion if the group engagement team, or a component auditor, only tests group-wide controls and performs analytical procedures on the financial information of the components.

### Involvement in the Work Performed by Component Auditors (Ref: Para. 30-31)

Factors that may affect the group engagement team's involvement in the work of the **A54** component auditor include:

(a) The significance of the component;
(b) The identified significant risks of material misstatement of the group financial statements; and
(c) The group engagement team's understanding of the component auditor.
 In the case of a significant component or identified significant risks, the group engagement team performs the procedures described in paragraphs 30-31. In the case of a component that is not a significant component, the nature, timing and extent of the group engagement team's involvement in the work of the component auditor will vary based on the group engagement team's understanding of that component auditor. The fact that the component is not a significant component becomes secondary. For example, even though a component is not considered a significant component, the group engagement team nevertheless may decide to be involved in the component auditor's risk assessment, because it has less than serious concerns about the component auditor's professional competency (e.g., lack of industry specific knowledge), or the component auditor does not operate in an environment that actively oversees auditors.

Forms of involvement in the work of a component auditor other than those **A55** described in paragraphs 30-31 and 42 may, based on the group engagement team's understanding of the component auditor, include one or more of the following:

(a) Meeting with component management or the component auditors to obtain an understanding of the component and its environment.
(b) Reviewing the component auditors' overall audit strategy and audit plan.
(c) Performing risk assessment procedures to identify and assess the risks of material misstatement at the component level. These may be performed with the component auditors, or by the group engagement team.

[22] *ISRE 2400, "Engagements to Review Financial Statements."*
*ISRE 2400 has not been promulgated by APB for application in the UK and Ireland.*

[23] *ISRE (UK and Ireland) 2410, "Review of Interim Financial Information Performed by the Independent Auditor of the Entity."*

(d) Designing and performing further audit procedures. These may be designed and performed with the component auditors, or by the group engagement team.

(e) Participating in the closing and other key meetings between the component auditors and component management.

(f) Reviewing other relevant parts of the component auditors' audit documentation.

## Consolidation Process

### *Consolidation Adjustments and Reclassifications* (Ref: Para. 34)

**A56**    The consolidation process may require adjustments to amounts reported in the group financial statements that do not pass through the usual transaction processing systems, and may not be subject to the same internal controls to which other financial information is subject. The group engagement team's evaluation of the appropriateness, completeness and accuracy of the adjustments may include:

- Evaluating whether significant adjustments appropriately reflect the events and transactions underlying them;
- Determining whether significant adjustments have been correctly calculated, processed and authorized by group management and, where applicable, by component management;
- Determining whether significant adjustments are properly supported and sufficiently documented; and
- Checking the reconciliation and elimination of intra-group transactions and unrealized profits, and intra-group account balances.

## Communication with the Component Auditor (Ref: Para. 40-41)

**A57**    If effective two-way communication between the group engagement team and the component auditors does not exist, there is a risk that the group engagement team may not obtain sufficient appropriate audit evidence on which to base the group audit opinion. Clear and timely communication of the group engagement team's requirements forms the basis of effective two-way communication between the group engagement team and the component auditor.

**A58**    The group engagement team's requirements are often communicated in a letter of instruction. Appendix 5 contains guidance on required and additional matters that may be included in such a letter of instruction. The component auditor's communication with the group engagement team often takes the form of a memorandum or report of work performed. Communication between the group engagement team and the component auditor, however, may not necessarily be in writing. For example, the group engagement team may visit the component auditor to discuss identified significant risks or review relevant parts of the component auditor's audit documentation. Nevertheless, the documentation requirements of this and other ISAs (UK and Ireland) apply.

**A59**    In cooperating with the group engagement team, the component auditor, for example, would provide the group engagement team with access to relevant audit documentation if not prohibited by law or regulation.

**A60**    Where a member of the group engagement team is also a component auditor, the objective for the group engagement team to communicate clearly with the component auditor can often be achieved by means other than specific written communication. For example:

- Access by the component auditor to the overall audit strategy and audit plan may be sufficient to communicate the group engagement team's requirements set out in paragraph 40; and
- A review of the component auditor's audit documentation by the group engagement team may be sufficient to communicate matters relevant to the group engagement team's conclusion set out in paragraph 41.

## Evaluating the Sufficiency and Appropriateness of Audit Evidence Obtained

### *Reviewing the Component Auditor's Audit Documentation* (Ref: Para. 42(b))

What parts of the audit documentation of the component auditor will be relevant to the group audit may vary depending on the circumstances. Often the focus is on audit documentation that is relevant to the significant risks of material misstatement of the group financial statements. The extent of the review may be affected by the fact that the component auditor's audit documentation has been subjected to the component auditor's firm's review procedures.   **A61**

### *Sufficiency and Appropriateness of Audit Evidence* (Ref: Para. 44-45)

If the group engagement team concludes that sufficient appropriate audit evidence on which to base the group audit opinion has not been obtained, the group engagement team may request the component auditor to perform additional procedures. If this is not feasible, the group engagement team may perform its own procedures on the financial information of the component.   **A62**

The group engagement partner's evaluation of the aggregate effect of any misstatements (either identified by the group engagement team or communicated by component auditors) allows the group engagement partner to determine whether the group financial statements as a whole are materially misstated.   **A63**

## Communication with Group Management and Those Charged with Governance of the Group

### *Communication with Group Management* (Ref: Para. 46-48)

ISA (UK and Ireland) 240 contains requirements and guidance on communication of fraud to management and, where management may be involved in the fraud, to those charged with governance.[24]   **A64**

Group management may need to keep certain material sensitive information confidential. Examples of matters that may be significant to the financial statements of the component of which component management may be unaware include the following:   **A65**

- Potential litigation.
- Plans for abandonment of material operating assets.
- Subsequent events.

---

[24] *ISA (UK and Ireland) 240, paragraphs 40-42.*

- Significant legal agreements.

**A65-1**    Information that group management has determined needs to be kept confidential would ordinarily be known to those charged with governance of the group[24a].

*Communication with Those Charged with Governance of the Group* (Ref: Para. 49)

**A66**    The matters the group engagement team communicates to those charged with governance of the group may include those brought to the attention of the group engagement team by component auditors that the group engagement team judges to be significant to the responsibilities of those charged with governance of the group. Communication with those charged with governance of the group takes place at various times during the group audit. For example, the matters referred to in paragraph 49(a)-(b) may be communicated after the group engagement team has determined the work to be performed on the financial information of the components. On the other hand, the matter referred to in paragraph 49(c) may be communicated at the end of the audit, and the matters referred to in paragraph 49(d)-(e) may be communicated when they occur.

## Documentation (Ref: Para. 50(b))

**A66-1**    In the UK legislation[24b] has been enacted to implement Article 27(b) of the Statutory Audit Directive which requires that group auditors:

(a)  review for the purposes of a group audit the audit work conducted by other persons, and

(b)  record that review.

Accordingly, the documentation of the group engagement team's involvement in the work performed by the component auditors includes any review that the group engagement team undertook, for the purpose of the group audit, of the audit work conducted by component auditors.

---

[24a] *ISA (UK and Ireland) 260, paragraph 16(c), requires that, unless all of those charged with governance are involved in managing the entity, the auditor shall communicate with those charged with governance significant matters, if any, arising from the audit that were discussed, or subject to correspondence with management.*

[24b] *UK Companies Act 2006, Schedule 10, paragraph 10A(1).*

## Appendix 1 (Ref: Para. A19)

This example has not been tailored for the UK and Ireland. With respect to companies, illustrative examples of auditor's reports tailored for use with audits conducted in accordance with ISAs (UK and Ireland) are given in the most recent versions of the APB Bulletins, "Auditor's Reports on Financial Statements in the United Kingdom"/"Auditor's Reports on Financial Statements in the Republic of Ireland." Illustrative examples for various other entities are give in other Bulletins and Practice Notes issued by the APB.

### Example of a Qualified Opinion Where the Group Engagement Team Is Not Able to Obtain Sufficient Appropriate Audit Evidence on Which to Base the Group Audit Opinion

In this example, the group engagement team is unable to obtain sufficient appropriate audit evidence relating to a significant component accounted for by the equity method (recognized at $15 million in the balance sheet, which reflects total assets of $60 million) because the group engagement team did not have access to the accounting records, management, or auditor of the component.

The group engagement team has read the audited financial statements of the component as of December 31, 20X1, including the auditor's report thereon, and considered related financial information kept by group management in relation to the component.

In the group engagement partner's judgment, the effect on the group financial statements of this inability to obtain sufficient appropriate audit evidence is material but not pervasive.

### INDEPENDENT AUDITOR'S REPORT

[Appropriate Addressee]

#### Report on the Consolidated Financial Statements[25]

We have audited the accompanying consolidated financial statements of ABC Company and its subsidiaries, which comprise the consolidated balance sheet as at December 31, 20X1, and the consolidated income statement, statement of changes in equity and cash flow statement for the year then ended, and a summary of significant accounting policies and other explanatory information.

*Management's[26] Responsibility for the Consolidated Financial Statements*

Management is responsible for the preparation and fair presentation of these consolidated financial statements in accordance with International Financial Reporting Standards,[27] and for such internal control as management determines is necessary to enable the preparation of consolidated financial statements that are free from material misstatement, whether due to fraud or error.

---

[25] *The sub-title, "Report on the Consolidated Financial Statements" is unnecessary in circumstances when the second sub-title, "Report on Other Legal and Regulatory Requirements" is not applicable.*

[26] *Or other term that is appropriate in the context of the legal framework in the particular jurisdiction.*

[27] *Where management's responsibility is to prepare consolidated financial statements that give a true and fair view, this may read: "Management is responsible for the preparation of consolidated financial statements that give a true and fair view in accordance with International Financial Reporting Standards, and for such ..."*

*Auditor's Responsibility*

Our responsibility is to express an opinion on these consolidated financial statements based on our audit. We conducted our audit in accordance with International Standards on Auditing. Those standards require that we comply with ethical requirements and plan and perform the audit to obtain reasonable assurance about whether the consolidated financial statements are free from material misstatement.

An audit involves performing procedures to obtain audit evidence about the amounts and disclosures in the consolidated financial statements. The procedures selected depend on the auditor's judgment, including the assessment of the risks of material misstatement of the consolidated financial statements, whether due to fraud or error. In making those risk assessments, the auditor considers internal control relevant to the entity's preparation and fair presentation[28] of the consolidated financial statements in order to design audit procedures that are appropriate in the circumstances, but not for the purpose of expressing an opinion on the effectiveness of the entity's internal control.[29] An audit also includes evaluating the appropriateness of accounting policies used and the reasonableness of accounting estimates made by management, as well as evaluating the overall presentation of the consolidated financial statements.

We believe that the audit evidence we have obtained is sufficient and appropriate to provide a basis for our qualified audit opinion.

*Basis for Qualified Opinion*

ABC Company's investment in XYZ Company, a foreign associate acquired during the year and accounted for by the equity method, is carried at $15 million on the consolidated balance sheet as at December 31, 20X1, and ABC's share of XYZ's net income of $1 million is included in the consolidated income statement for the year then ended. We were unable to obtain sufficient appropriate audit evidence about the carrying amount of ABC's investment in XYZ as at December 31, 20X1 and ABC's share of XYZ's net income for the year because we were denied access to the financial information, management, and the auditors of XYZ. Consequently, we were unable to determine whether any adjustments to these amounts were necessary.

*Qualified Opinion*

In our opinion, except for the possible effects of the matter described in the Basis for Qualified Opinion paragraph, the consolidated financial statements present fairly, in all material respects, *(or give a true and fair view of)* the financial position of ABC Company and its subsidiaries as at December 31, 20X1, and *(of)* their financial performance and cash flows for the year then ended in accordance with International Financial Reporting Standards.

---

[28] *In the case of footnote 27, this may read: "In making those risk assessments, the auditor considers internal control relevant to the entity's preparation of consolidated financial statements that give a true and fair view in order to design audit procedures that are appropriate in the circumstances, but not for the purpose of expressing an opinion on the effectiveness of the entity's internal control."*

[29] *In circumstances when the auditor also has responsibility to express an opinion on the effectiveness of internal control in conjunction with the audit of the consolidated financial statements, this sentence would be worded as follows: "In making those risk assessments, the auditor considers internal control relevant to the entity's preparation and fair presentation of the consolidated financial statements in order to design audit procedures that are appropriate in the circumstances." In the case of footnote 27, this may read: "In making those risk assessments, the auditor considers internal control relevant to the entity's preparation of consolidated financial statements that give a true and fair view in order to design audit procedures that are appropriate in the circumstances."*

**Report on Other Legal and Regulatory Requirements**

[Form and content of this section of the auditor's report will vary depending on the nature of the auditor's other reporting responsibilities.]

[Auditor's signature]

[Date of the auditor's report]

[Auditor's address]

If, in the group engagement partner's judgment, the effect on the group financial statements of the inability to obtain sufficient appropriate audit evidence is material and pervasive, the group engagement partner would disclaim an opinion in accordance with ISA (UK and Ireland) 705.

**Appendix 2** (Ref: Para. A23)

## Examples of Matters about Which the Group Engagement Team Obtains an Understanding

The examples provided cover a broad range of matters; however, not all matters are relevant to every group audit engagement and the list of examples is not necessarily complete.

### Group-Wide Controls

1   Group-wide controls may include a combination of the following:

- Regular meetings between group and component management to discuss business developments and to review performance.
- Monitoring of components' operations and their financial results, including regular reporting routines, which enables group management to monitor components' performance against budgets, and to take appropriate action.
- Group management's risk assessment process, i.e., the process for identifying, analyzing and managing business risks, including the risk of fraud, that may result in material misstatement of the group financial statements.
- Monitoring, controlling, reconciling, and eliminating intra-group transactions and unrealized profits, and intra-group account balances at group level.
- A process for monitoring the timeliness and assessing the accuracy and completeness of financial information received from components.
- A central IT system controlled by the same general IT controls for all or part of the group.
- Control activities within an IT system that is common for all or some components.
- Monitoring of controls, including activities of internal audit and self-assessment programs.
- Consistent policies and procedures, including a group financial reporting procedures manual.
- Group-wide programs, such as codes of conduct and fraud prevention programs.
- Arrangements for assigning authority and responsibility to component management.

2   Internal audit may be regarded as part of group-wide controls, for example, when the internal audit function is centralized. ISA (UK and Ireland) 610[30] deals with the group engagement team's evaluation of the competence and objectivity of the internal auditors where it plans to use their work.

### Consolidation Process

3   The group engagement team's understanding of the consolidation process may include matters such as the following:

Matters relating to the applicable financial reporting framework:

- The extent to which component management has an understanding of the applicable financial reporting framework.
- The process for identifying and accounting for components in accordance with the applicable financial reporting framework.

---

[30] ISA (UK and Ireland) 610, *"Using the Work of Internal Auditors,"* paragraph 9.

- The process for identifying reportable segments for segment reporting in accordance with the applicable financial reporting framework.
- The process for identifying related party relationships and related party transactions for reporting in accordance with the applicable financial reporting framework.
- The accounting policies applied to the group financial statements, changes from those of the previous financial year, and changes resulting from new or revised standards under the applicable financial reporting framework.
- The procedures for dealing with components with financial year-ends different from the group's year-end.

Matters relating to the consolidation process:

- Group management's process for obtaining an understanding of the accounting policies used by components, and, where applicable, ensuring that uniform accounting policies are used to prepare the financial information of the components for the group financial statements, and that differences in accounting policies are identified, and adjusted where required in terms of the applicable financial reporting framework. Uniform accounting policies are the specific principles, bases, conventions, rules, and practices adopted by the group, based on the applicable financial reporting framework, that the components use to report similar transactions consistently. These policies are ordinarily described in the financial reporting procedures manual and reporting package issued by group management.
- Group management's process for ensuring complete, accurate and timely financial reporting by the components for the consolidation.
- The process for translating the financial information of foreign components into the currency of the group financial statements.
- How IT is organized for the consolidation, including the manual and automated stages of the process, and the manual and programmed controls in place at various stages of the consolidation process.
- Group management's process for obtaining information on subsequent events.

Matters relating to consolidation adjustments:

- The process for recording consolidation adjustments, including the preparation, authorization and processing of related journal entries, and the experience of personnel responsible for the consolidation.
- The consolidation adjustments required by the applicable financial reporting framework.
- Business rationale for the events and transactions that gave rise to the consolidation adjustments.
- Frequency, nature and size of transactions between components.
- Procedures for monitoring, controlling, reconciling and eliminating intra-group transactions and unrealized profits, and intra-group account balances.
- Steps taken to arrive at the fair value of acquired assets and liabilities, procedures for amortizing goodwill (where applicable), and impairment testing of goodwill, in accordance with the applicable financial reporting framework.
- Arrangements with a majority owner or minority interests regarding losses incurred by a component (for example, an obligation of the minority interest to make good such losses).

## Appendix 3 (Ref: Para. A30)

## Examples of Conditions or Events that May Indicate Risks of Material Misstatement of the Group Financial Statements

The examples provided cover a broad range of conditions or events; however, not all conditions or events are relevant to every group audit engagement and the list of examples is not necessarily complete.

- A complex group structure, especially where there are frequent acquisitions, disposals or reorganizations.
- Poor corporate governance structures, including decision-making processes, that are not transparent.
- Non-existent or ineffective group-wide controls, including inadequate group management information on monitoring of components' operations and their results.
- Components operating in foreign jurisdictions that may be exposed to factors such as unusual government intervention in areas such as trade and fiscal policy, and restrictions on currency and dividend movements; and fluctuations in exchange rates.
- Business activities of components that involve high risk, such as long-term contracts or trading in innovative or complex financial instruments.
- Uncertainties regarding which components' financial information require incorporation in the group financial statements in accordance with the applicable financial reporting framework, for example, whether any special-purpose entities or non-trading entities exist and require incorporation.
- Unusual related party relationships and transactions.
- Prior occurrences of intra-group account balances that did not balance or reconcile on consolidation.
- The existence of complex transactions that are accounted for in more than one component.
- Components' application of accounting policies that differ from those applied to the group financial statements.
- Components with different financial year-ends, which may be utilized to manipulate the timing of transactions.
- Prior occurrences of unauthorized or incomplete consolidation adjustments.
- Aggressive tax planning within the group, or large cash transactions with entities in tax havens.
- Frequent changes of auditors engaged to audit the financial statements of components.

# **Appendix 4** (Ref: Para. A35)

# **Examples of a Component Auditor's Confirmations**

The following is not intended to be a standard letter. Confirmations may vary from one component auditor to another and from one period to the next.

Confirmations often are obtained before work on the financial information of the component commences.

[Component Auditor Letterhead]

[Date]

[To Group Engagement Partner]

This letter is provided in connection with your audit of the group financial statements of [name of parent] for the year ended [date] for the purpose of expressing an opinion on whether the group financial statements present fairly, in all material respects (give a true and fair view of) the financial position of the group as of [date] and of its financial performance and cash flows for the year then ended in accordance with [indicate applicable financial reporting framework].

We acknowledge receipt of your instructions dated [date], requesting us to perform the specified work on the financial information of [name of component] for the year ended [date].

We confirm that:

1    We will be able to comply with the instructions. / We advise you that we will not be able to comply with the following instructions [specify instructions] for the following reasons [specify reasons].
2    The instructions are clear and we understand them. / We would appreciate it if you could clarify the following instructions [specify instructions].
3    We will cooperate with you and provide you with access to relevant audit documentation.

We acknowledge that:

1    The financial information of [name of component] will be included in the group financial statements of [name of parent].
2    You may consider it necessary to be involved in the work you have requested us to perform on the financial information of [name of component] for the year ended [date].
3    You intend to evaluate and, if considered appropriate, use our work for the audit of the group financial statements of [name of parent].

In connection with the work that we will perform on the financial information of [name of component], a [describe component, e.g., wholly-owned subsidiary, subsidiary, joint venture, investee accounted for by the equity or cost methods of accounting] of [name of parent], we confirm the following:

1    We have an understanding of [indicate relevant ethical requirements] that is sufficient to fulfill our responsibilities in the audit of the group financial statements, and will comply therewith. In particular, and with respect to [name of parent] and the other components in the group, we are independent within the meaning of [indicate relevant ethical requirements] and comply with the

applicable requirements of [refer to rules] promulgated by [name of regulatory agency].

2   We have an understanding of International Standards on Auditing and [indicate other national standards applicable to the audit of the group financial statements] that is sufficient to fulfill our responsibilities in the audit of the group financial statements and will conduct our work on the financial information of [name of component] for the year ended [date] in accordance with those standards.

3   We possess the special skills (e.g., industry specific knowledge) necessary to perform the work on the financial information of the particular component.

4   We have an understanding of [indicate applicable financial reporting framework or group financial reporting procedures manual] that is sufficient to fulfill our responsibilities in the audit of the group financial statements.

We will inform you of any changes in the above representations during the course of our work on the financial information of [name of component].

[Auditor's signature]

[Date]

[Auditor's address]

**Appendix 5** (Ref: Para. A58)

# Required and Additional Matters Included in the Group Engagement Team's Letter of Instruction

*Matters required by this ISA (UK and Ireland) to be communicated to the component auditor are shown in italicized text.*

Matters that are relevant to the planning of the work of the component auditor:

- *A request for the component auditor, knowing the context in which the group engagement team will use the work of the component auditor, to confirm that the component auditor will cooperate with the group engagement team.*
- The timetable for completing the audit.
- Dates of planned visits by group management and the group engagement team, and dates of planned meetings with component management and the component auditor.
- A list of key contacts.
- *The work to be performed by the component auditor, the use to be made of that work,* and arrangements for coordinating efforts at the initial stage of and during the audit, including the group engagement team's planned involvement in the work of the component auditor.
- *The ethical requirements that are relevant to the group audit and, in particular, the independence requirements.*
- *In the case of an audit or review of the financial information of the component, component materiality (and, if applicable, the materiality level or levels for particular classes of transactions, account balances or disclosures), and the threshold above which misstatements cannot be regarded as clearly trivial to the group financial statements.*
- *A list of related parties prepared by group management, and any other related parties that the group engagement team is aware of, and a request that the component auditor communicates on a timely basis to the group engagement team related parties not previously identified by group management or the group engagement team.*
- Work to be performed on intra-group transactions and unrealized profits and intra-group account balances.
- Guidance on other statutory reporting responsibilities, for example, reporting on group management's assertion on the effectiveness of internal control.
- Where time lag between completion of the work on the financial information of the components and the group engagement team's conclusion on the group financial statements is likely, specific instructions for a subsequent events review.

Matters that are relevant to the conduct of the work of the component auditor

- The findings of the group engagement team's tests of control activities of a processing system that is common for all or some components, and tests of controls to be performed by the component auditor.
- *Identified significant risks of material misstatement of the group financial statements, due to fraud or error, that are relevant to the work of the component auditor, and a request that the component auditor communicates on a timely basis any other significant risks of material misstatement of the group financial statements, due to fraud or error, identified in the component and the component auditor's response to such risks.*
- The findings of internal audit, based on work performed on controls at or relevant to components.
- A request for timely communication of audit evidence obtained from performing work on the financial information of the components that contradicts

the audit evidence on which the group engagement team originally based the risk assessment performed at group level.
- A request for a written representation on component management's compliance with the applicable financial reporting framework, or a statement that differences between the accounting policies applied to the financial information of the component and those applied to the group financial statements have been disclosed.
- Matters to be documented by the component auditor.

Other information

- A request that the following be reported to the group engagement team on a timely basis:
- Significant accounting, financial reporting and auditing matters, including accounting estimates and related judgments.
- Matters relating to the going concern status of the component.
- Matters relating to litigation and claims.
- Significant deficiencies in internal control that the component auditor has identified during the performance of the work on the financial information of the component, and information that indicates the existence of fraud.
- A request that the group engagement team be notified of any significant or unusual events as early as possible.
- *A request that the matters listed in paragraph 41 be communicated to the group engagement team when the work on the financial information of the component is completed.*

# Addendum

*This addendum provides a summary of APB's rationale for retaining or excluding in the proposed clarified ISA (UK and Ireland) the supplementary requirements in the existing ISA (UK and Ireland). It also sets out the supplementary guidance material in the existing ISA (UK and Ireland) that APB considers is not necessary to retain in light of the improvements in the underlying Clarity ISAs issued by the IAASB as part of the Clarity Project. It is provided for information and does not form part of the proposed clarified ISA (UK and Ireland).*

*The Consultation Paper published with the exposure drafts explains the general approach used by the APB for determining whether current supplementary material should be proposed to be retained.*

## Analysis of proposed treatment of current APB supplementary material in current ISA (UK and Ireland) 600

It should be noted that ISA 600 has been revised as well as clarified.

## Requirements

| APB supplementary requirements (*Italic text is from IAASB for context*) | Is it covered in substance in the Clarity ISA? | Should it be retained? |
|---|---|---|
| 7-1. **In the UK and Ireland, when planning to use the work of another auditor, the principal auditor's consideration of the professional competence of the other auditor should include consideration of the professional qualifications, experience and resources of the other auditor in the context of the specific assignment.** | ✓ Re competence. (19(b))<br><br>✗ Re qualifications experience and resources. However, the Application Material (A38) refers to possession of necessary special skills (e.g. industry specific knowledge). | ✗<br>But guidance has been added to refer to consideration of resources. **A38** |
| 14-1. **In the UK and Ireland, the principal auditor should document any review that it undertakes, for the purpose of the group audit, of the audit work conducted by other auditors.** | – The ISA requires documentation of "The nature, timing and extent of the group engagement team's involvement in the work performed by the component auditors on significant components including, where applicable, the group engagement team's review of relevant parts of the component auditors' audit documentation and | ✗<br>But guidance has been added indicating the UK legal requirements in this area. **A66-1** |

| APB supplementary requirements (*Italic text is from IAASB for context*) | Is it covered in substance in the Clarity ISA? | Should it be retained? |
|---|---|---|
| | conclusions thereon." 50(b) | |

### Guidance

The following guidance in current ISA (UK and Ireland) 600 has not been carried forward to the proposed clarified standard.

| Current paragraph reference (*Italic text is from IAASB for context*) |
|---|
| 1-1.   The statutory requirements relating to companies incorporated in the UK and Ireland for other auditors to co-operate with principal auditors are explained in more detail in paragraphs 15-1 to 15-5 below and in the attached Appendix. This ISA (UK and Ireland) does not deal with those instances where two or more auditors are appointed as joint auditors nor does it deal with the auditor's relationship with predecessor auditors. |
| 5-1. – 5-4. [Description of management and those charged with governance.] |
| 6.   ***The auditor should consider whether the auditor's own participation is sufficient to be able to act as the principal auditor.*** *For this purpose the principal auditor would consider: ...*<br>(e)   The nature of the principal auditor's relationship with the firm acting as other auditor. |
| 7-2.   The principal auditor considers the standing of any firm with which the other auditor is affiliated and also considers making reference to the other auditor's professional organization. The principal auditor's assessment may be influenced by the review of the previous work of the other auditor. |
| 13-1.   In the UK and Ireland, the principal auditor may also consider it appropriate to discuss with those charged with governance of the component the audit findings or other matters affecting the financial information of the component. The principal auditor may consider it appropriate to request copies of reports to management or those charged with governance issued by the other auditor. |

| Current paragraph reference (*Italic text is from IAASB for context*) |
|---|
| 15-1. In the UK and Ireland, the other auditor carries out the audit work in the knowledge that the financial information on which the other auditor reports is to be included within the financial statements which are reported on by the principal auditor. In many circumstances when the component is a subsidiary undertaking, there is a statutory obligation on the other auditor, and the component which the other auditor audits, to give the principal auditor such information and explanations as the principal auditor may reasonably require for the purpose of the principal auditor's audit. Where there is no statutory obligation on the other auditor and the principal auditor advises that the principal auditor intends to use the other auditor's work, the other auditor may require permission from the component to communicate with the principal auditor on matters pertaining to the component's audit. If the component refuses such permission, the other auditor brings this to the attention of the principal auditor so that the principal auditor can discuss and agree an appropriate course of action with those charged with governance of the entity which they audit. [1] |

[1] Schedule 10, paragraph 10A, to the Companies Act 2006 includes provisions relating to arrangements to enable Recognised Supervisory Bodies and other bodies involved in monitoring audits to have access to the audit documentation of certain other auditors involved in the group audit. These provisions are addressed in audit regulations not in ISAs (UK and Ireland).

| |
|---|
| 15-2. If the other auditor identifies a matter which the other auditor considers likely to be relevant to the principal auditor's work, the other auditor may communicate directly with the principal auditor, providing consent is obtained by the component or there exists a statutory obligation, or it may require reference to the matter to be made within the other auditor's audit report. |
| 15-3. In the UK and Ireland the other auditor has sole responsibility for the other auditor's audit opinion on the financial statements of the component which the other auditor audits. Accordingly, the other auditor plans and executes the audit in a manner which enables the other auditor to report on the component without placing reliance on the principal auditor necessarily informing the other auditor of matters which have come to the principal auditor's attention and which may have an important bearing on the financial statements of the component. This may involve the other auditor seeking representations directly from the management or those charged with governance of the entity audited by the principal auditor. |
| 15-4. In the UK and Ireland there is no obligation, statutory or otherwise, on the principal auditor to provide information to the other auditor. However, in undertaking the audit work the principal auditor may identify matters which the principal auditor considers to be relevant to the other auditor's work. In these circumstances, the principal auditor discusses and agrees an appropriate course of action with those charged with governance of the entity which they audit. |
| 15-5. The course of action agreed with those charged with governance may involve the principal auditor communicating directly with the other auditor, or those charged with governance informing the component or the other auditor. However, there may be circumstances where sensitive commercial considerations dictate that information cannot be passed on to the component or the other auditor. In this event, the principal auditor is not required to take further action as to do so would be in breach of the principle of client confidentiality. |

| Current paragraph reference (*Italic text is from IAASB for context*) |
|---|
| 17-1. When the principal auditor is satisfied that the work of the other auditors is adequate for the purposes of the audit, no reference to the other auditors is made in the principal auditor's report. |
| 18-1. In the UK and Ireland the principal auditor has sole responsibility for the principal auditor's audit opinion and a reference to the other auditor in the principal auditor's report may be misunderstood and interpreted as a qualification of the principal auditor's opinion or a division of responsibility, which is not acceptable. |
| Appendix – Statutory Framework – see below |

# ISA 600 – Appendix

This Appendix provides a summary of the legal rights of parent company auditors to obtain information from subsidiary undertakings and the auditors of those undertakings. It is not intended to be an authoritative guide to all of the legal provisions relevant to auditors' rights to information. For complete guidance reference should be made to the relevant legislation.

## *Statutory Framework at 15 December 2004*[31]

1   If a parent company and its subsidiary undertaking are companies incorporated in Great Britain, section 389A(3) of the Companies Act 1985 imposes a duty on the subsidiary undertaking and its auditors to 'give to the auditors of any parent company of the undertaking such information and explanations as they may reasonably require for the purposes of their duties as auditors of that company'. Similar obligations regarding companies incorporated in Northern Ireland and the Republic of Ireland are set out in Article 397A(3) of the Companies (Northern Ireland) Order 1986 and section 196(1) of the Companies Act 1990 respectively.

2   Where a parent company is incorporated in Great Britain but its subsidiary undertaking is not, section 389A(4) of the Companies Act 1985 imposes a duty on the parent company, if required by its auditors to do so, to 'take all such steps as are reasonably open to it to obtain from the subsidiary undertaking such information and explanations as they may reasonably require for the purposes of their duties as auditors of that company'. Similar obligations on parent companies incorporated in Northern Ireland and the Republic of Ireland are set out in Article 397A(4) of the Companies (Northern Ireland) Order 1986 and section 196(2) of the Companies Act 1990 respectively.

## Companies Act 2006

3   Under the UK Companies Act 2006, the auditor's rights to information are addressed in sections 499 and 500.

4   Section 499 addresses the auditor's general right to information and identifies persons the auditor of a company may require to "provide him with such information or explanations as he thinks necessary for the performance of his duties as auditor." These persons include:

[31] *A revision of section 389A of the UK Companies Act 1985 came into effect in 2005 which strengthened the rights of auditors to obtain information and explanations from other parties as well as subsidiary undertakings and their auditors.*

- any subsidiary undertaking of the company which is a body corporate incorporated in the United Kingdom; and
- any officer, employee or auditor of any such subsidiary undertaking or any person holding or accountable for any books, accounts or vouchers of any such subsidiary undertaking,

  including any persons who fell in these categories at a time to which the information required by the auditor relates or relate.

Section 500 addresses the auditor's rights to information from overseas subsidiaries. It provides that where a parent company has a subsidiary undertaking that is not a body corporate incorporated in the United Kingdom, the auditor of the parent company may require it to "take all such steps as are reasonably open to it" to obtain such information or explanations from particular persons as the parent company auditor may reasonably require for the purposes of his duties as auditor. Those persons are:  **5**

(a) the undertaking;
(b) any officer, employee or auditor of the undertaking;
(c) any person holding or accountable for any of the undertaking's books, accounts or vouchers;
(d) any person who fell within paragraph (b) or (c) at a time to which the information or explanations relates or relate.

The rights to information provided for in sections 499 and 500 are subject to any restrictions imposed by rights to legal privilege.  **6**

# Proposed Clarified International Standard on Auditing (UK and Auditing) 610
# Using the work of internal auditors

*(Effective for audits of financial statements for periods ending on or after 15 December 2010)*

## Contents

International Standard on Auditing (UK and Ireland) (ISA (UK and Ireland)) 610, "Using the Work of Internal Auditors" should be read in conjunction with ISA (UK and Ireland) 200, "Overall Objectives of the Independent Auditor and the Conduct of an Audit in Accordance with International Standards on Auditing (UK and Ireland)."

# Introduction

## Scope of this ISA (UK and Ireland)

This International Standard on Auditing (UK and Ireland) (ISA (UK and Ireland)) **1** deals with the external auditor's responsibilities relating to the work of internal auditors when the external auditor has determined, in accordance with ISA (UK and Ireland) 315,[1] that the internal audit function is likely to be relevant to the audit. (Ref: Para. A1-A2)

This ISA (UK and Ireland) ~~does not deal with~~ provides guidance on instances when **2** individual internal auditors provide direct assistance to the external auditor in carrying out audit procedures. (Ref: Para. A6-1)

## Relationship between the Internal Audit Function and the External Auditor

The objectives of the internal audit function are determined by management and, **3** where applicable, those charged with governance[1a]. While the objectives of the internal audit function and the external auditor are different, some of the ways in which the internal audit function and the external auditor achieve their respective objectives may be similar. (Ref: Para. A3)

Irrespective of the degree of autonomy and objectivity of the internal audit function, **4** such function is not independent of the entity as is required of the external auditor when expressing an opinion on financial statements. The external auditor has sole responsibility for the audit opinion expressed, and that responsibility is not reduced by the external auditor's use of the work of the internal auditors.

## Effective Date

This ISA (UK and Ireland) is effective for audits of financial statements for periods **5** ending on or after 15 December 2010.

# Objectives

The objectives of the external auditor, where the entity has an internal audit function **6** that the external auditor has determined is likely to be relevant to the audit, are:

(a) To determine whether, and to what extent, to use specific work of the internal auditors; and
(b) If using the specific work of the internal auditors, to determine whether that work is adequate for the purposes of the audit.

---

[1] *ISA (UK and Ireland) 315, "Identifying and Assessing the Risks of Material Misstatement through Understanding the Entity and Its Environment," paragraph 23.*

[1a] *For Listed Companies in the UK and Ireland, "The Combined Code on Corporate Governance" (published by the FRC) contains guidance to assist company boards in making suitable arrangements for their audit committees.*

# Definitions

7    For purposes of the ISAs (UK and Ireland), the following terms have the meanings attributed below:

(a) Internal audit function – An appraisal activity established or provided as a service to the entity. Its functions include, amongst other things, examining, evaluating and monitoring the adequacy and effectiveness of internal control.

(b) Internal auditors – Those individuals who perform the activities of the internal audit function. Internal auditors may belong to an internal audit department or equivalent function.

# Requirements

## Determining Whether and to What Extent to Use the Work of the Internal Auditors

8    The external auditor shall determine:

(a) Whether the work of the internal auditors is likely to be adequate for purposes of the audit; and

(b) If so, the planned effect of the work of the internal auditors on the nature, timing or extent of the external auditor's procedures.

9    In determining whether the work of the internal auditors is likely to be adequate for purposes of the audit, the external auditor shall evaluate:

(a) The objectivity of the internal audit function;

(b) The technical competence of the internal auditors;

(c) Whether the work of the internal auditors is likely to be carried out with due professional care; and

(d) Whether there is likely to be effective communication between the internal auditors and the external auditor. (Ref: Para. A4)

10    In determining the planned effect of the work of the internal auditors on the nature, timing or extent of the external auditor's procedures, the external auditor shall consider:

(a) The nature and scope of specific work performed, or to be performed, by the internal auditors;

(b) The assessed risks of material misstatement at the assertion level for particular classes of transactions, account balances, and disclosures; and

(c) The degree of subjectivity involved in the evaluation of the audit evidence gathered by the internal auditors in support of the relevant assertions. (Ref: Para. A5)

## Using Specific Work of the Internal Auditors

11    In order for the external auditor to use specific work of the internal auditors, the external auditor shall evaluate and perform audit procedures on that work to determine its adequacy for the external auditor's purposes. (Ref: Para. A6 – A6-1)

12    To determine the adequacy of specific work performed by the internal auditors for the external auditor's purposes, the external auditor shall evaluate whether:

(a) The work was performed by internal auditors having adequate technical training and proficiency;

(b) The work was properly supervised, reviewed and documented;

(c) Adequate audit evidence has been obtained to enable the internal auditors to draw reasonable conclusions;

(d) Conclusions reached are appropriate in the circumstances and any reports prepared by the internal auditors are consistent with the results of the work performed; and

(e) Any exceptions or unusual matters disclosed by the internal auditors are properly resolved.

## Documentation

If the external auditor uses specific work of the internal auditors, the external auditor shall include in the audit documentation the conclusions reached regarding the evaluation of the adequacy of the work of the internal auditors, and the audit procedures performed by the external auditor on that work, in accordance with paragraph 11.[2]

**13**

\*\*\*

# Application and Other Explanatory Material

### Scope of this ISA (UK and Ireland) (Ref: Para. 1)

As described in ISA (UK and Ireland) 315,[3] the entity's internal audit function is likely to be relevant to the audit if the nature of the internal audit function's responsibilities and activities are related to the entity's financial reporting, and the auditor expects to use the work of the internal auditors to modify the nature or timing, or reduce the extent, of audit procedures to be performed.

**A1**

Carrying out procedures in accordance with this ISA (UK and Ireland) may cause the external auditor to re-evaluate the external auditor's assessment of the risks of material misstatement. Consequently, this may affect the external auditor's determination of the relevance of the internal audit function to the audit. Similarly, the external auditor may decide not to otherwise use the work of the internal auditors to affect the nature, timing or extent of the external auditor's procedures. In such circumstances, the external auditor's further application of this ISA (UK and Ireland) may not be necessary.

**A2**

### Objectives of the Internal Audit Function (Ref: Para. 3)

The objectives of internal audit functions vary widely and depend on the size and structure of the entity and the requirements of management and, where applicable, those charged with governance. The activities of the internal audit function may include one or more of the following:

**A3**

● Monitoring of internal control. The internal audit function may be assigned specific responsibility for reviewing controls, monitoring their operation and recommending improvements thereto.

[2] *ISA (UK and Ireland) 230, "Audit Documentation," paragraphs 8-11, and paragraph A6.*

[3] *ISA (UK and Ireland) 315, paragraph A101.*

- Examination of financial and operating information. The internal audit function may be assigned to review the means used to identify, measure, classify and report financial and operating information, and to make specific inquiry into individual items, including detailed testing of transactions, balances and procedures.
- Review of operating activities. The internal audit function may be assigned to review the economy, efficiency and effectiveness of operating activities, including non-financial activities of an entity.
- Review of compliance with laws and regulations. The internal audit function may be assigned to review compliance with laws, regulations and other external requirements, and with management policies and directives and other internal requirements.
- Risk management. The internal audit function may assist the organization by identifying and evaluating significant exposures to risk and contributing to the improvement of risk management and control systems.
- Governance. The internal audit function may assess the governance process in its accomplishment of objectives on ethics and values, performance management and accountability, communicating risk and control information to appropriate areas of the organization and effectiveness of communication among those charged with governance, external and internal auditors, and management.

## Determining Whether and to What Extent to Use the Work of the Internal Auditors

*Whether the Work of the Internal Auditors Is Likely to Be Adequate for Purposes of the Audit* (Ref: Para. 9)

A4 Factors that may affect the external auditor's determination of whether the work of the internal auditors is likely to be adequate for the purposes of the audit include:

Objectivity

- The status of the internal audit function within the entity and the effect such status has on the ability of the internal auditors to be objective.
- Whether the internal audit function reports to those charged with governance or an officer with appropriate authority, and whether the internal auditors have direct access to those charged with governance.
- Whether the internal auditors are free of any conflicting responsibilities.
- Whether those charged with governance oversee employment decisions related to the internal audit function.
- Whether there are any constraints or restrictions placed on the internal audit function by management or those charged with governance.
- Whether, and to what extent, management acts on the recommendations of the internal audit function, and how such action is evidenced.

Technical competence

- Whether the internal auditors are members of relevant professional bodies.
- Whether the internal auditors have adequate technical training and proficiency as internal auditors.
- Whether there are established policies for hiring and training internal auditors. Due professional care
- Whether activities of the internal audit function are properly planned, supervised, reviewed and documented.
- The existence and adequacy of audit manuals or other similar documents, work programs and internal audit documentation.

Communication

Communication between the external auditor and the internal auditors may be most effective when the internal auditors are free to communicate openly with the external auditors, and:

- Meetings are held at appropriate intervals throughout the period;
- The external auditor is advised of and has access to relevant internal audit reports and is informed of any significant matters that come to the attention of the internal auditors when such matters may affect the work of the external auditor; and
- The external auditor informs the internal auditors of any significant matters that may affect the internal audit function.

**Planned Effect of the Work of the Internal Auditors on the Nature, Timing or Extent of the External Auditor's Procedures** (Ref: Para. 10)

Where the work of the internal auditors is to be a factor in determining the nature, **A5** timing or extent of the external auditor's procedures, it may be useful to agree in advance the following matters with the internal auditors:

- The timing of such work;
- The extent of audit coverage;
- Materiality for the financial statements as a whole (and, if applicable, materiality level or levels for particular classes of transactions, account balances or disclosures), and performance materiality;
- Proposed methods of item selection;
- Documentation of the work performed; and
- Review and reporting procedures.

## Using Specific Work of the Internal Auditors (Ref: Para. 11 – 12)

The nature, timing and extent of the audit procedures performed on specific work of **A6** the internal auditors will depend on the external auditor's assessment of the risk of material misstatement, the evaluation of the internal audit function, and the evaluation of the specific work of the internal auditors. Such audit procedures may include:

- Examination of items already examined by the internal auditors;
- Examination of other similar items; and
- Observation of procedures performed by the internal auditors.

In addition to using specific work of an internal audit function, the external **A6-1** auditor may obtain direct assistance from individuals from the internal audit function. In addition to the considerations set out in paragraphs 12 and A6, when direct assistance is provided by individuals from the internal audit function, the external auditor:

(a) obtains a written confirmation from such individuals that they agree to follow the instructions of staff of the audit firm in relation to the work performed and that, where applicable, they will keep confidential specific matters as instructed by the audit team;

(b) directly supervises, reviews and evaluates the work performed;

(c) ensures that such individuals are only involved in work where self-review or judgment is not an important part of the audit procedure; and

(d) communicates the details of the planned arrangements with those charged with governance at the planning stage of the audit, so as to agree this approach, as described in paragraph 11-9 of ISA (UK and Ireland) 260.

# Addendum

*This addendum provides a summary of APB's rationale for retaining or excluding in the proposed clarified ISA (UK and Ireland) the supplementary requirements in the existing ISA (UK and Ireland). It also sets out the supplementary guidance material in the existing ISA (UK and Ireland) that APB considers is not necessary to retain in light of the improvements in the underlying Clarity ISAs issued by the IAASB as part of the Clarity Project. It is provided for information and does not form part of the proposed clarified ISA (UK and Ireland).*

*The Consultation Paper published with the exposure drafts explains the general approach used by the APB for determining whether current supplementary material should be proposed to be retained.*

## Analysis of proposed treatment of current APB supplementary material in current ISA (UK and Ireland) 610

### Requirements

There are no supplementary requirements in the current ISA (UK and Ireland) 610.

### Guidance

The scope of the guidance provided in the proposed clarified standard has been extended to cover instances when individual internal auditors provide direct assistance to the external auditor (see paragraphs 2 and A6-1). The new guidance was issued for consultation by APB in March 2009 (Consultation Paper: Revised Draft Ethical Standards for Auditor). If necessary, the guidance in the final clarified standard will be amended to reflect APB's conclusions in light of responses received to the consultation.

The following guidance in current ISA (UK and Ireland) 610 has not been carried forward to the proposed clarified standard.

| Current paragraph reference (*Italic text is from IAASB for context*) |
| --- |
| 1-1. – 1-4. [Description of management and those charged with governance] |
| 5     *The scope and objectives of internal auditing vary widely and depend on the size and structure of the entity and the requirements of its management. Ordinarily, internal auditing activities include one or more of the following: ...*<br>      • Special investigations into particular areas, for example, suspected fraud. |
| 6.     *The role of internal auditing is determined by management[1], and its objectives differ from those of the external auditor who is appointed to report independently on the financial statements. The internal audit function's objectives vary according to management's requirements. The external auditor's primary concern is whether the financial statements are free of material misstatements.* |

[1] In the UK and Ireland those charged with governance, rather than management, are usually responsible for determining the role of internal auditing.

| Current paragraph reference (*Italic text is from IAASB for context*) |
|---|
| 10-1. The effectiveness of internal auditing may be an important factor in the external auditor's evaluation of the control environment and assessment of audit risk. |
| 18-1. In the event that the external auditor concludes that the work of internal auditing is not adequate for the external auditor's purposes, the external auditor extends the audit procedures beyond those originally planned to ensure that sufficient appropriate audit evidence is obtained to support the conclusions reached. |
| 19-1. The auditor considers whether amendments to the external audit program are required as a result of matters identified by internal auditing. |

# Proposed Clarified International Standard on Auditing (UK and Ireland) 620

# Using the work of an auditor's expert

*(Effective for audits of financial statements for periods ending on or after 15 December 2010)*

# Contents

---

International Standard on Auditing (UK and Ireland) (ISA (UK and Ireland)) 620, "Using the Work of an Auditor's Expert" should be read in conjunction with ISA (UK and Ireland) 200, "Overall Objectives of the Independent Auditor and the Conduct of an Audit in Accordance with International Standards on Auditing (UK and Ireland)."

# Introduction

## Scope of this ISA (UK and Ireland)

1   This International Standard on Auditing (UK and Ireland) (ISA (UK and Ireland)) deals with the auditor's responsibilities relating to the work of an individual or organization in a field of expertise other than accounting or auditing, when that work is used to assist the auditor in obtaining sufficient appropriate audit evidence.

2   This ISA (UK and Ireland) does not deal with:

(a) Situations where the engagement team includes a member, or consults an individual or organization, with expertise in a specialized area of accounting or auditing, which are dealt with in ISA (UK and Ireland) 220;[1] or

(b) The auditor's use of the work of an individual or organization possessing expertise in a field other than accounting or auditing, whose work in that field is used by the entity to assist the entity in preparing the financial statements (a management's expert), which is dealt with in ISA (UK and Ireland) 500.[2]

## The Auditor's Responsibility for the Audit Opinion

3   The auditor has sole responsibility for the audit opinion expressed, and that responsibility is not reduced by the auditor's use of the work of an auditor's expert. Nonetheless, if the auditor using the work of an auditor's expert, having followed this ISA (UK and Ireland), concludes that the work of that expert is adequate for the auditor's purposes, the auditor may accept that expert's findings or conclusions in the expert's field as appropriate audit evidence.

## Effective Date

4   This ISA (UK and Ireland) is effective for audits of financial statements for periods ending on or after 15 December 2010.

# Objectives

5   The objectives of the auditor are:

(a) To determine whether to use the work of an auditor's expert; and

(b) If using the work of an auditor's expert, to determine whether that work is adequate for the auditor's purposes.

# Definitions

6   For purposes of the ISAs (UK and Ireland), the following terms have the meanings attributed below:

(a) Auditor's expert – An individual or organization possessing expertise in a field other than accounting or auditing, whose work in that field is used by the auditor to assist the auditor in obtaining sufficient appropriate audit evidence.

---

[1] *ISA (UK and Ireland) 220, "Quality Control for an Audit of Financial Statements," paragraphs A10, A20-A22.*

[2] *ISA (UK and Ireland) 500, "Audit Evidence," paragraphs A34-A48.*

An auditor's expert may be either an auditor's internal expert (who is a partner[3] or staff, including temporary staff, of the auditor's firm or a network firm), or an auditor's external expert. (Ref: Para. A1-A3)
(b) Expertise – Skills, knowledge and experience in a particular field.
(c) Management's expert – An individual or organization possessing expertise in a field other than accounting or auditing, whose work in that field is used by the entity to assist the entity in preparing the financial statements.

# Requirements

### Determining the Need for an Auditor's Expert

If expertise in a field other than accounting or auditing is necessary to obtain sufficient appropriate audit evidence, the auditor shall determine whether to use the work of an auditor's expert. (Ref: Para. A4-A9)   **7**

### Nature, Timing and Extent of Audit Procedures

The nature, timing and extent of the auditor's procedures with respect to the requirements in paragraphs 9-13 of this ISA (UK and Ireland) will vary depending on the circumstances. In determining the nature, timing and extent of those procedures, the auditor shall consider matters including: (Ref: Para. A10)   **8**

(a) The nature of the matter to which that expert's work relates;
(b) The risks of material misstatement in the matter to which that expert's work relates;
(c) The significance of that expert's work in the context of the audit;
(d) The auditor's knowledge of and experience with previous work performed by that expert; and
(e) Whether that expert is subject to the auditor's firm's quality control policies and procedures. (Ref: Para. A11-A13)

### The Competence, Capabilities and Objectivity of the Auditor's Expert

The auditor shall evaluate whether the auditor's expert has the necessary competence, capabilities and objectivity for the auditor's purposes. In the case of an auditor's external expert, the evaluation of objectivity shall include inquiry regarding interests and relationships that may create a threat to that expert's objectivity. (Ref: Para. A14-A20)   **9**

### Obtaining an Understanding of the Field of Expertise of the Auditor's Expert

The auditor shall obtain a sufficient understanding of the field of expertise of the auditor's expert to enable the auditor to: (Ref: Para. A21-A22)   **10**

(a) Determine the nature, scope and objectives of that expert's work for the auditor's purposes; and
(b) Evaluate the adequacy of that work for the auditor's purposes.

---

[3] *"Partner" and "firm" should be read as referring to their public sector equivalents where relevant.*

## Agreement with the Auditor's Expert

11   The auditor shall agree, in writing when appropriate, on the following matters with the auditor's expert: (Ref: Para. A23-A26)

(a)   The nature, scope and objectives of that expert's work; (Ref: Para. A27)
(b)   The respective roles and responsibilities of the auditor and that expert; (Ref: Para. A28-A29)
(c)   The nature, timing and extent of communication between the auditor and that expert, including the form of any report to be provided by that expert; and (Ref: Para. A30)
(d)   The need for the auditor's expert to observe confidentiality requirements. (Ref: Para. A31)

## Evaluating the Adequacy of the Auditor's Expert's Work

12   The auditor shall evaluate the adequacy of the auditor's expert's work for the auditor's purposes, including: (Ref: Para. A32)

(a)   The relevance and reasonableness of that expert's findings or conclusions, and their consistency with other audit evidence; (Ref: Para. A33-A34)
(b)   If that expert's work involves use of significant assumptions and methods, the relevance and reasonableness of those assumptions and methods in the circumstances; and (Ref: Para. A35-A37)
(c)   If that expert's work involves the use of source data that is significant to that expert's work, the relevance, completeness, and accuracy of that source data. (Ref: Para. A38-A39)

13   If the auditor determines that the work of the auditor's expert is not adequate for the auditor's purposes, the auditor shall: (Ref: Para. A40)

(a)   Agree with that expert on the nature and extent of further work to be performed by that expert; or
(b)   Perform additional audit procedures appropriate to the circumstances.

## Reference to the Auditor's Expert in the Auditor's Report

14   The auditor shall not refer to the work of an auditor's expert in an auditor's report containing an unmodified opinion unless required by law or regulation to do so. If such reference is required by law or regulation, the auditor shall indicate in the auditor's report that the reference does not reduce the auditor's responsibility for the auditor's opinion. (Ref: Para. A41)

15   If the auditor makes reference to the work of an auditor's expert in the auditor's report because such reference is relevant to an understanding of a modification to the auditor's opinion, the auditor shall indicate in the auditor's report that such reference does not reduce the auditor's responsibility for that opinion. (Ref: Para. A42)

\*\*\*

# Application and Other Explanatory Material

## Definition of an Auditor's Expert (Ref: Para. 6(a))

Expertise in a field other than accounting or auditing may include expertise in relation to such matters as: **A1**

- The valuation of complex financial instruments, land and buildings, plant and machinery, jewelry, works of art, antiques, intangible assets, assets acquired and liabilities assumed in business combinations and assets that may have been impaired.
- The actuarial calculation of liabilities associated with insurance contracts or employee benefit plans.
- The estimation of oil and gas reserves.
- The valuation of environmental liabilities, and site clean-up costs.
- The interpretation of contracts, laws and regulations.
- The analysis of complex or unusual tax compliance issues.

In many cases, distinguishing between expertise in accounting or auditing, and expertise in another field, will be straightforward, even where this involves a specialized area of accounting or auditing. For example, an individual with expertise in applying methods of accounting for deferred income tax can often be easily distinguished from an expert in taxation law. The former is not an expert for the purposes of this ISA (UK and Ireland) as this constitutes accounting expertise; the latter is an expert for the purposes of this ISA (UK and Ireland) as this constitutes legal expertise. Similar distinctions may also be able to be made in other areas, for example, between expertise in methods of accounting for financial instruments, and expertise in complex modeling for the purpose of valuing financial instruments. In some cases, however, particularly those involving an emerging area of accounting or auditing expertise, distinguishing between specialized areas of accounting or auditing, and expertise in another field, will be a matter of professional judgment. Applicable professional rules and standards regarding education and competency requirements for accountants and auditors may assist the auditor in exercising that judgment.[4] **A2**

It is necessary to apply judgment when considering how the requirements of this ISA (UK and Ireland) are affected by the fact that an auditor's expert may be either an individual or an organization. For example, when evaluating the competence, capabilities and objectivity of an auditor's expert, it may be that the expert is an organization the auditor has previously used, but the auditor has no prior experience of the individual expert assigned by the organization for the particular engagement; or it may be the reverse, that is, the auditor may be familiar with the work of an individual expert but not with the organization that expert has joined. In either case, both the personal attributes of the individual and the managerial attributes of the organization (such as systems of quality control the organization implements) may be relevant to the auditor's evaluation. **A3**

## Determining the Need for an Auditor's Expert (Ref: Para. 7)

An auditor's expert may be needed to assist the auditor in one or more of the following: **A4**

[4] *For example, International Education Standard 8, "Competence Requirements for Audit Professionals" may be of assistance.*

- Obtaining an understanding of the entity and its environment, including its internal control.
- Identifying and assessing the risks of material misstatement.
- Determining and implementing overall responses to assessed risks at the financial statement level.
- Designing and performing further audit procedures to respond to assessed risks at the assertion level, comprising tests of controls or substantive procedures.
- Evaluating the sufficiency and appropriateness of audit evidence obtained in forming an opinion on the financial statements.

A5    The risks of material misstatement may increase when expertise in a field other than accounting is needed for management[4a] to prepare the financial statements, for example, because this may indicate some complexity, or because management may not possess knowledge of the field of expertise. If in preparing the financial statements management does not possess the necessary expertise, a management's expert may be used in addressing those risks. Relevant controls, including controls that relate to the work of a management's expert, if any, may also reduce the risks of material misstatement.

A6    If the preparation of the financial statements involves the use of expertise in a field other than accounting, the auditor, who is skilled in accounting and auditing, may not possess the necessary expertise to audit those financial statements. The engagement partner is required to be satisfied that the engagement team, and any auditor's experts who are not part of the engagement team, collectively have the appropriate competence and capabilities to perform the audit engagement.[5] Further, the auditor is required to ascertain the nature, timing and extent of resources necessary to perform the engagement.[6] The auditor's determination of whether to use the work of an auditor's expert, and if so when and to what extent, assists the auditor in meeting these requirements. As the audit progresses, or as circumstances change, the auditor may need to revise earlier decisions about using the work of an auditor's expert.

A7    An auditor who is not an expert in a relevant field other than accounting or auditing may nevertheless be able to obtain a sufficient understanding of that field to perform the audit without an auditor's expert. This understanding may be obtained through, for example:

- Experience in auditing entities that require such expertise in the preparation of their financial statements.
- Education or professional development in the particular field. This may include formal courses, or discussion with individuals possessing expertise in the relevant field for the purpose of enhancing the auditor's own capacity to deal with matters in that field. Such discussion differs from consultation with an auditor's expert regarding a specific set of circumstances encountered on the engagement where that expert is given all the relevant facts that will enable the expert to provide informed advice about the particular matter.[7]
- Discussion with auditors who have performed similar engagements.

---

[4a] *In the UK and Ireland those charged with governance are responsible for the preparation of the financial statements.*

[5] *ISA (UK and Ireland) 220, paragraph 14.*

[6] *ISA (UK and Ireland) 300, "Planning an Audit of Financial Statements," paragraph 7(e).*

[7] *ISA (UK and Ireland) 220, paragraph A21.*

In other cases, however, the auditor may determine that it is necessary, or may **A8** choose, to use an auditor's expert to assist in obtaining sufficient appropriate audit evidence. Considerations when deciding whether to use an auditor's expert may include:

- Whether management[4a] has used a management's expert in preparing the financial statements (see paragraph A9).
- The nature and significance of the matter, including its complexity.
- The risks of material misstatement in the matter.
- The expected nature of procedures to respond to identified risks, including: the auditor's knowledge of and experience with the work of experts in relation to such matters; and the availability of alternative sources of audit evidence.

When management has used a management's expert in preparing the financial **A9** statements, the auditor's decision on whether to use an auditor's expert may also be influenced by such factors as:

- The nature, scope and objectives of the management's expert's work.
- Whether the management's expert is employed by the entity, or is a party engaged by it to provide relevant services.
- The extent to which management can exercise control or influence over the work of the management's expert.
- The management's expert's competence and capabilities.
- Whether the management's expert is subject to technical performance standards or other professional or industry requirements
- Any controls within the entity over the management's expert's work.
  ISA (UK and Ireland) 500[8] includes requirements and guidance regarding the effect of the competence, capabilities and objectivity of management's experts on the reliability of audit evidence.

## Nature, Timing and Extent of Audit Procedures (Ref: Para. 8)

The nature, timing and extent of audit procedures with respect to the requirements in **A10** paragraphs 9-13 of this ISA (UK and Ireland) will vary depending on the circumstances. For example, the following factors may suggest the need for different or more extensive procedures than would otherwise be the case:

- The work of the auditor's expert relates to a significant matter that involves subjective and complex judgments.
- The auditor has not previously used the work of the auditor's expert, and has no prior knowledge of that expert's competence, capabilities and objectivity.
- The auditor's expert is performing procedures that are integral to the audit, rather than being consulted to provide advice on an individual matter.
- The expert is an auditor's external expert and is not, therefore, subject to the firm's quality control policies and procedures.

### *The Auditor's Firm's Quality Control Policies and Procedures* (Ref: Para. 8(e))

An auditor's internal expert may be a partner or staff, including temporary staff, of **A11** the auditor's firm, and therefore subject to the quality control policies and procedures of that firm in accordance with ISQC (UK and Ireland) 1[9] or national

---

[8] *ISA (UK and Ireland) 500, paragraph 8.*

[9] *ISQC (UK and Ireland) 1, "Quality Control for Firms that Perform Audits and Reviews of Financial Statements, and Other Assurance and Related Services Engagements," paragraph 12(f).*

requirements that are at least as demanding.[10] Alternatively, an auditor's internal expert may be a partner or staff, including temporary staff, of a network firm, which may share common quality control policies and procedures with the auditor's firm.

A12    An auditor's external expert is not a member of the engagement team and is not subject to quality control policies and procedures in accordance with ISQC (UK and Ireland) 1.[11] In some jurisdictions, however, law or regulation may require that an auditor's external expert be treated as a member of the engagement team, and may therefore be subject to relevant ethical requirements, including those pertaining to independence, and other professional requirements, as determined by that law or regulation.

A13    Engagement teams are entitled to rely on the firm's system of quality control, unless information provided by the firm or other parties suggests otherwise.[12] The extent of that reliance will vary with the circumstances, and may affect the nature, timing and extent of the auditor's procedures with respect to such matters as:

- Competence and capabilities, through recruitment and training programs.
- Objectivity. Auditor's internal experts are subject to relevant ethical requirements, including those pertaining to independence.
- The auditor's evaluation of the adequacy of the auditor's expert's work. For example, the firm's training programs may provide auditor's internal experts with an appropriate understanding of the interrelationship of their expertise with the audit process. Reliance on such training and other firm processes, such as protocols for scoping the work of auditor's internal experts, may affect the nature, timing and extent of the auditor's procedures to evaluate the adequacy of the auditor's expert's work.
- Adherence to regulatory and legal requirements, through monitoring processes.
- Agreement with the auditor's expert.
  Such reliance does not reduce the auditor's responsibility to meet the requirements of this ISA (UK and Ireland).

## The Competence, Capabilities and Objectivity of the Auditor's Expert (Ref: Para. 9)

A14    The competence, capabilities and objectivity of an auditor's expert are factors that significantly affect whether the work of the auditor's expert will be adequate for the auditor's purposes. Competence relates to the nature and level of expertise of the auditor's expert. Capability relates to the ability of the auditor's expert to exercise that competence in the circumstances of the engagement. Factors that influence capability may include, for example, geographic location, and the availability of time and resources. Objectivity relates to the possible effects that bias, conflict of interest, or the influence of others may have on the professional or business judgment of the auditor's expert.

A15    Information regarding the competence, capabilities and objectivity of an auditor's expert may come from a variety of sources, such as:

- Personal experience with previous work of that expert.
- Discussions with that expert.

[10] See ISA (UK and Ireland) 220, paragraph 2.

[11] ISQC (UK and Ireland) 1, paragraph 12(f).

[12] ISA (UK and Ireland) 220, paragraph 4.

- Discussions with other auditors or others who are familiar with that expert's work.
- Knowledge of that expert's qualifications, membership of a professional body or industry association, license to practice, or other forms of external recognition.
- Published papers or books written by that expert.
- The auditor's firm's quality control policies and procedures (see paragraphs A11-A13)

Matters relevant to evaluating the competence, capabilities and objectivity of the auditor's expert include whether that expert's work is subject to technical performance standards or other professional or industry requirements, for example, ethical standards and other membership requirements of a professional body or industry association, accreditation standards of a licensing body, or requirements imposed by law or regulation.   **A16**

Other matters that may be relevant include:   **A17**

- The relevance of the auditor's expert's competence to the matter for which that expert's work will be used, including any areas of specialty within that expert's field. For example, a particular actuary may specialize in property and casualty insurance, but have limited expertise regarding pension calculations.
- The auditor's expert's competence with respect to relevant accounting and auditing requirements, for example, knowledge of assumptions and methods, including models where applicable, that are consistent with the applicable financial reporting framework.
- Whether unexpected events, changes in conditions, or the audit evidence obtained from the results of audit procedures indicate that it may be necessary to reconsider the initial evaluation of the competence, capabilities and objectivity of the auditor's expert as the audit progresses.

A broad range of circumstances may threaten objectivity, for example, self-interest threats, advocacy threats, familiarity threats, self-review threats, and intimidation threats. Safeguards may eliminate or reduce such threats, and may be created by external structures (for example, the auditor's expert's profession, legislation or regulation), or by the auditor's expert's work environment (for example, quality control policies and procedures). There may also be safeguards specific to the audit engagement.   **A18**

The evaluation of the significance of threats to objectivity and of whether there is a need for safeguards may depend upon the role of the auditor's expert and the significance of the expert's work in the context of the audit. There may be some circumstances in which safeguards cannot reduce threats to an acceptable level, for example, if a proposed auditor's expert is an individual who has played a significant role in preparing the information that is being audited, that is, if the auditor's expert is a management's expert.   **A19**

When evaluating the objectivity of an auditor's external expert, it may be relevant to:   **A20**

(a) Inquire of the entity about any known interests or relationships that the entity has with the auditor's external expert that may affect that expert's objectivity.
(b) Discuss with that expert any applicable safeguards, including any professional requirements that apply to that expert; and evaluate whether the safeguards are adequate to reduce threats to an acceptable level. Interests and relationships that it may be relevant to discuss with the auditor's expert include:
  - Financial interests.
  - Business and personal relationships.

- Provision of other services by the expert, including by the organization in the case of an external expert that is an organization.

In some cases, it may also be appropriate for the auditor to obtain a written representation from the auditor's external expert about any interests or relationships with the entity of which that expert is aware.

## Obtaining an Understanding of the Field of Expertise of the Auditor's Expert (Ref: Para. 10)

A21 The auditor may obtain an understanding of the auditor's expert's field of expertise through the means described in paragraph A7, or through discussion with that expert.

A22 Aspects of the auditor's expert's field relevant to the auditor's understanding may include:

- Whether that expert's field has areas of specialty within it that are relevant to the audit (see paragraph A17).
- Whether any professional or other standards, and regulatory or legal requirements apply.
- What assumptions and methods, including models where applicable, are used by the auditor's expert, and whether they are generally accepted within that expert's field and appropriate for financial reporting purposes.
- The nature of internal and external data or information the auditor's expert uses.

## Agreement with the Auditor's Expert (Ref: Para. 11)

A23 The nature, scope and objectives of the auditor's expert's work may vary considerably with the circumstances, as may the respective roles and responsibilities of the auditor and the auditor's expert, and the nature, timing and extent of communication between the auditor and the auditor's expert. It is therefore required that these matters are agreed between the auditor and the auditor's expert regardless of whether the expert is an auditor's external expert or an auditor's internal expert.

A24 The matters noted in paragraph 8 may affect the level of detail and formality of the agreement between the auditor and the auditor's expert, including whether it is appropriate that the agreement be in writing. For example, the following factors may suggest the need for more a detailed agreement than would otherwise be the case, or for the agreement to be set out in writing:

- The auditor's expert will have access to sensitive or confidential entity information.
- The respective roles or responsibilities of the auditor and the auditor's expert are different from those normally expected.
- Multi-jurisdictional legal or regulatory requirements apply.
- The matter to which the auditor's expert's work relates is highly complex.
- The auditor has not previously used work performed by that expert.
- The greater the extent of the auditor's expert's work, and its significance in the context of the audit.

A25 The agreement between the auditor and an auditor's external expert is often in the form of an engagement letter. The Appendix lists matters that the auditor may consider for inclusion in such an engagement letter, or in any other form of agreement with an auditor's external expert.

When there is no written agreement between the auditor and the auditor's expert,   **A26**
evidence of the agreement may be included in, for example:

- Planning memoranda, or related working papers such as the audit program.
- The policies and procedures of the auditor's firm. In the case of an auditor's internal expert, the established policies and procedures to which that expert is subject may include particular policies and procedures in relation to that expert's work. The extent of documentation in the auditor's working papers depends on the nature of such policies and procedures. For example, no documentation may be required in the auditor's working papers if the auditor's firm has detailed protocols covering the circumstances in which the work of such an expert is used.

### *Nature, Scope and Objectives of Work* (Ref: Para. 11(a))

It may often be relevant when agreeing on the nature, scope and objectives of the   **A27**
auditor's expert's work to include discussion of any relevant technical performance standards or other professional or industry requirements that the expert will follow.

### *Respective Roles and Responsibilities* (Ref: Para. 11(b))

Agreement on the respective roles and responsibilities of the auditor and the audi-   **A28**
tor's expert may include:

- Whether the auditor or the auditor's expert will perform detailed testing of source data.
- Consent for the auditor to discuss the auditor's expert's findings or conclusions with the entity and others, and to include details of that expert's findings or conclusions in the basis for a modified opinion in the auditor's report, if necessary (see paragraph A42).
- Any agreement to inform the auditor's expert of the auditor's conclusions concerning that expert's work.

### *Working Papers*

Agreement on the respective roles and responsibilities of the auditor and the audi-   **A29**
tor's expert may also include agreement about access to, and retention of, each other's working papers. When the auditor's expert is a member of the engagement team, that expert's working papers form part of the audit documentation. Subject to any agreement to the contrary, auditor's external experts' working papers are their own and do not form part of the audit documentation.

### *Communication* (Ref: Para. 11(c))

Effective two-way communication facilitates the proper integration of the nature,   **A30**
timing and extent of the auditor's expert's procedures with other work on the audit, and appropriate modification of the auditor's expert's objectives during the course of the audit. For example, when the work of the auditor's expert relates to the auditor's conclusions regarding a significant risk, both a formal written report at the conclusion of that expert's work, and oral reports as the work progresses, may be appropriate. Identification of specific partners or staff who will liaise with the auditor's expert, and procedures for communication between that expert and the entity, assists timely and effective communication, particularly on larger engagements.

*Confidentiality* (Ref: Para. 11(d))

A31   It is necessary for the confidentiality provisions of relevant ethical requirements that apply to the auditor also to apply to the auditor's expert. Additional requirements may be imposed by law or regulation. The entity may also have requested that specific confidentiality provisions be agreed with auditor's external experts.

## Evaluating the Adequacy of the Auditor's Expert's Work (Ref: Para. 12)

A32   The auditor's evaluation of the auditor's expert's competence, capabilities and objectivity, the auditor's familiarity with the auditor's expert's field of expertise, and the nature of the work performed by the auditor's expert affect the nature, timing and extent of audit procedures to evaluate the adequacy of that expert's work for the auditor's purposes.

### *The Findings and Conclusions of the Auditor's Expert* (Ref: Para. 12(a))

A33   Specific procedures to evaluate the adequacy of the auditor's expert's work for the auditor's purposes may include:

- Inquiries of the auditor's expert.
- Reviewing the auditor's expert's working papers and reports.
- Corroborative procedures, such as:
  - Observing the auditor's expert's work;
  - Examining published data, such as statistical reports from reputable, authoritative sources;
  - Confirming relevant matters with third parties;
  - Performing detailed analytical procedures; and
  - Reperforming calculations.
- Discussion with another expert with relevant expertise when, for example, the findings or conclusions of the auditor's expert are not consistent with other audit evidence.
- Discussing the auditor's expert's report with management[12a].

A34   Relevant factors when evaluating the relevance and reasonableness of the findings or conclusions of the auditor's expert, whether in a report or other form, may include whether they are:

- Presented in a manner that is consistent with any standards of the auditor's expert's profession or industry;
- Clearly expressed, including reference to the objectives agreed with the auditor, the scope of the work performed and standards applied;
- Based on an appropriate period and take into account subsequent events, where relevant;
- Subject to any reservation, limitation or restriction on use, and if so, whether this has implications for the auditor; and
- Based on appropriate consideration of errors or deviations encountered by the auditor's expert.

---

[12a] *In the UK and Ireland these discussions may be with those charged with governance where appropriate*

## Assumptions, Methods and Source Data

*Assumptions and Methods (Ref: Para. 12(b))*

When the auditor's expert's work is to evaluate underlying assumptions and methods, including models where applicable, used by management in developing an accounting estimate, the auditor's procedures are likely to be primarily directed to evaluating whether the auditor's expert has adequately reviewed those assumptions and methods. When the auditor's expert's work is to develop an auditor's point estimate or an auditor's range for comparison with management's point estimate, the auditor's procedures may be primarily directed to evaluating the assumptions and methods, including models where appropriate, used by the auditor's expert. **A35**

ISA (UK and Ireland) 540[13] discusses the assumptions and methods used by management in making accounting estimates, including the use in some cases of highly specialized, entity-developed models. Although that discussion is written in the context of the auditor obtaining sufficient appropriate audit evidence regarding management's assumptions and methods, it may also assist the auditor when evaluating an auditor's expert's assumptions and methods. **A36**

When an auditor's expert's work involves the use of significant assumptions and methods, factors relevant to the auditor's evaluation of those assumptions and methods include whether they are: **A37**

* Generally accepted within the auditor's expert's field;
* Consistent with the requirements of the applicable financial reporting framework;
* Dependent on the use of specialized models; and
* Consistent with those of management, and if not, the reason for, and effects of, the differences.

*Source Data Used by the Auditor's Expert (Ref: Para. 12(c))*

When an auditor's expert's work involves the use of source data that is significant to that expert's work, procedures such as the following may be used to test that data: **A38**

* Verifying the origin of the data, including obtaining an understanding of, and where applicable testing, the internal controls over the data and, where relevant, its transmission to the expert.
* Reviewing the data for completeness and internal consistency.

In many cases, the auditor may test source data. However, in other cases, when the nature of the source data used by an auditor's expert is highly technical in relation to the expert's field, that expert may test the source data. If the auditor's expert has tested the source data, inquiry of that expert by the auditor, or supervision or review of that expert's tests may be an appropriate way for the auditor to evaluate that data's relevance, completeness, and accuracy. **A39**

## Inadequate Work (Ref: Para. 13)

If the auditor concludes that the work of the auditor's expert is not adequate for the auditor's purposes and the auditor cannot resolve the matter through the additional audit procedures required by paragraph 13, which may involve further work being **A40**

---

[13] *ISA (UK and Ireland) 540, "Auditing Accounting Estimates, Including Fair Value Accounting Estimates, and Related Disclosures," paragraphs 8, 13 and 15.*

performed by both the expert and the auditor, or include employing or engaging another expert, it may be necessary to express a modified opinion in the auditor's report in accordance with ISA (UK and Ireland) 705 because the auditor has not obtained sufficient appropriate audit evidence.[14]

## Reference to the Auditor's Expert in the Auditor's Report (Ref: Para. 14-15)

A41   In some cases, law or regulation may require a reference to the work of an auditor's expert, for example, for the purposes of transparency in the public sector.

A42   It may be appropriate in some circumstances to refer to the auditor's expert in an auditor's report containing a modified opinion, to explain the nature of the modification. In such circumstances, the auditor may need the permission of the auditor's expert before making such a reference.

---

[14] *ISA (UK and Ireland) 705, "Modifications to the Opinion in the Independent Auditor's Report," paragraph 6(b).*

# Appendix (Ref: Para. A25)

# Considerations for Agreement between the Auditor and an Auditor's External Expert

This Appendix lists matters that the auditor may consider for inclusion in any agreement with an auditor's external expert. The following list is illustrative and is not exhaustive; it is intended only to be a guide that may be used in conjunction with the considerations outlined in this ISA (UK and Ireland). Whether to include particular matters in the agreement depends on the circumstances of the engagement. The list may also be of assistance in considering the matters to be included in an agreement with an auditor's internal expert.

## Nature, Scope and Objectives of the Auditor's External Expert's Work

- The nature and scope of the procedures to be performed by the auditor's external expert.
- The objectives of the auditor's external expert's work in the context of materiality and risk considerations concerning the matter to which the auditor's external expert's work relates, and, when relevant, the applicable financial reporting framework.
- Any relevant technical performance standards or other professional or industry requirements the auditor's external expert will follow.
- The assumptions and methods, including models where applicable, the auditor's external expert will use, and their authority.
- The effective date of, or when applicable the testing period for, the subject matter of the auditor's external expert's work, and requirements regarding subsequent events.

## The Respective Roles and Responsibilities of the Auditor and the Auditor's External Expert

- Relevant auditing and accounting standards, and relevant regulatory or legal requirements.
- The auditor's external expert's consent to the auditor's intended use of that expert's report, including any reference to it, or disclosure of it, to others, for example reference to it in the basis for a modified opinion in the auditor's report, if necessary, or disclosure of it to management or an audit committee.
- The nature and extent of the auditor's review of the auditor's external expert's work.
- Whether the auditor or the auditor's external expert will test source data.
- The auditor's external expert's access to the entity's records, files, personnel and to experts engaged by the entity.
- Procedures for communication between the auditor's external expert and the entity.
- The auditor's and the auditor's external expert's access to each other's working papers.
- Ownership and control of working papers during and after the engagement, including any file retention requirements.
- The auditor's external expert's responsibility to perform work with due skill and care.
- The auditor's external expert's competence and capability to perform the work.
- The expectation that the auditor's external expert will use all knowledge that expert has that is relevant to the audit or, if not, will inform the auditor.

- Any restriction on the auditor's external expert's association with the auditor's report.
- Any agreement to inform the auditor's external expert of the auditor's conclusions concerning that expert's work

## Communications and Reporting

- Methods and frequency of communications, including:
  - How the auditor's external expert's findings or conclusions will be reported (written report, oral report, ongoing input to the engagement team, etc.).
  - Identification of specific persons within the engagement team who will liaise with the auditor's external expert.
- When the auditor's external expert will complete the work and report findings or conclusions to the auditor.
- The auditor's external expert's responsibility to communicate promptly any potential delay in completing the work, and any potential reservation or limitation on that expert's findings or conclusions.
- The auditor's external expert's responsibility to communicate promptly instances in which the entity restricts that expert's access to records, files, personnel or experts engaged by the entity.
- The auditor's external expert's responsibility to communicate to the auditor all information that expert believes may be relevant to the audit, including any changes in circumstances previously communicated.
- The auditor's external expert's responsibility to communicate circumstances that may create threats to that expert's objectivity, and any relevant safeguards that may eliminate or reduce such threats to an acceptable level.

## Confidentiality

- The need for the auditor's expert to observe confidentiality requirements, including:
  - The confidentiality provisions of relevant ethical requirements that apply to the auditor.
  - Additional requirements that may be imposed by law or regulation, if any.
  - Specific confidentiality provisions requested by the entity, if any.

# Addendum

*This addendum provides a summary of APB's rationale for retaining or excluding in the proposed clarified ISA (UK and Ireland) the supplementary requirements in the existing ISA (UK and Ireland). It also sets out the supplementary guidance material in the existing ISA (UK and Ireland) that APB considers is not necessary to retain in light of the improvements in the underlying Clarity ISAs issued by the IAASB as part of the Clarity Project. It is provided for information and does not form part of the proposed clarified ISA (UK and Ireland).*

*The Consultation Paper published with the exposure drafts explains the general approach used by the APB for determining whether current supplementary material should be proposed to be retained.*

## Analysis of proposed treatment of current APB supplementary material in current ISA (UK and Ireland) 620

It should be noted that ISA 620 has been revised as well as clarified.

## Requirements

| APB supplementary requirements (*Italic text is from IAASB for context*) | Is it covered in substance in the Clarity ISA? | Should it be retained? |
|---|---|---|
| 8-1. **In the UK and Ireland, when planning to use the work of an expert the auditor should assess the professional qualifications, experience and resources of the expert.** | – The ISA refers to competence, capabilities and, objectivity (9). However, resources and qualifications are referred to in the Application Material (A14, A15). | ✗ |

## Guidance

The following guidance in current ISA (UK and Ireland) 620 has not been carried forward to the proposed clarified standard.

| **Current paragraph reference (*Italic text is from IAASB for context*)** |
|---|
| 1-1. – 1-4. [Description of management and those charged with governance as in 200.] |
| 5-1.    If the auditor determines that it is appropriate to seek to use the work of an expert, the auditor considers whether an appropriate expert is already employed by the auditor or the entity. If neither the auditor or the entity employ an appropriate expert, the auditor considers asking those charged with governance to engage an appropriate expert subject to the auditor being satisfied as to the expert's competence and objectivity (see paragraphs 8 to 10-1 below). If those charged with governance are unable or unwilling to engage an expert, the auditor may consider engaging an expert or whether sufficient appropriate audit evidence can be obtained from other sources. If unable to obtain sufficient appropriate audit evidence, the auditor considers the possible need to modify the auditor's report. |
| 5-2.    Although the auditor may use the work of an expert, the auditor has sole responsibility for the audit opinion. |
| 10-1.   If the auditor is unable to obtain sufficient appropriate audit evidence concerning the work of an expert, the auditor considers the possible need to modify the auditor's report. |
| 12     ***The auditor should evaluate the appropriateness of the expert's work as audit evidence regarding the assertion being considered.*** *This will involve evaluation of whether the substance of the expert's findings is properly reflected in the financial statements or supports the assertions, and consideration of: ...*<br>   •   When the expert carried out the work. |

# Proposed International Standard on Auditing (UK and Ireland) 700

# The auditor's report on financial statements

*(Effective for audits of financial statements for periods ending on or after 15 December 2010)*

## Contents

International Standard on Auditing (UK and Ireland) (ISA (UK and Ireland) 700, "The Auditor's Report on Financial Statements" (Revised and Redrafted) should be read in conjunction with ISA (UK and Ireland) 200, "Overall Objectives of the Independent Auditor and the Conduct of an Audit in Accordance with International Standards on Auditing (UK and Ireland)."

*NOTE: APB has not at this time adopted ISA 700 "Forming an Opinion and Reporting on Financial Statements". APB has instead issued ISA (UK and Ireland) 700 "The Auditor's Report on Financial Statements". The main effect of this is that the form of UK and Ireland auditor's report may not be exactly aligned with the precise format required by ISA 700 issued by the IAASB. However, ISA (UK and Ireland) 700 has been drafted such that compliance with it will not preclude the auditor from being able to assert compliance with the ISAs issued by the IAASB.*

# Introduction

## Scope of this ISA (UK and Ireland)

1    This International Standard on Auditing (UK and Ireland) (ISA (UK and Ireland) establishes standards and provides guidance on the form and content of the auditor's report issued as a result of an audit performed by an independent auditor of the financial statements.

2    This ISA (UK and Ireland) is written to address both "true and fair frameworks[1]" and "compliance frameworks". A "true and fair framework" is one that requires compliance with the framework but which acknowledges that to achieve a true and fair view:

(a)  It may be necessary to provide disclosures additional to those specifically required by the framework[2]; and

(b)  It may be necessary to depart from a requirement of the framework[3].

A "compliance framework" is one that requires compliance with the framework and does not contain the acknowledgements in (a) or (b) above.

3    With respect to companies, illustrative examples of auditor's reports tailored for use with audits conducted in accordance with ISAs (UK and Ireland) are given in the most recent versions of the APB Bulletins, "Auditor's Reports on Financial Statements in the United Kingdom"/"Auditor's Reports on Financial Statements in the Republic of Ireland." Illustrative examples for various other entities are give in other Bulletins and Practice Notes issued by the APB.

4    ISA 705 (UK and Ireland) and ISA 706 (UK and Ireland) deal with how the form and content of the auditor's report are affected when the auditor expresses a modified opinion or includes an Emphasis of Matter paragraph or an Other Matter paragraph in the auditor's report.

## Status of this ISA (UK and Ireland)

5    Paragraph 43 of ISA 700, "Forming an opinion and reporting on financial statements," as issued by the IAASB specifies the minimum elements of auditor's reports where the regulation of a specific jurisdiction specify wording of the auditor's report. Reports prepared in accordance with ISA (UK and Ireland) 700 contain those minimum elements and consequently compliance with this ISA (UK and Ireland) does not preclude the auditor from being able to assert compliance with International Standards on Auditing issued by the IAASB.

---

[1] *True and fair frameworks are sometimes referred to as "fair presentation frameworks".*

[2] *In the IFRS Framework this is acknowledged in paragraph 17(c) of IAS 1. In UK GAAP this is acknowledged in Sections 396(4) and 404(4) of the Companies Act 2006. In Ireland equivalent acknowledgements are contained in Section 3 Companies (amendment) Act 1986 and Regulation 14 of the European Communities (Companies: Group Accounts) Regulations 1992.*

[3] *This is sometimes referred to as the "true and fair override". In the IFRS Framework this is acknowledged in paragraph 19 of IAS 1. In UK GAAP this is acknowledged in Sections 396(5) and 404(5) of the Companies Act 2006.*

## Effective Date

This ISA (UK and Ireland) is effective for audits for periods ending on or after 15 December 2010.    6

# Objectives

The objectives of the auditor are to:    7

(a) Form an opinion on the financial statements based on an evaluation of the conclusions drawn from the audit evidence obtained; and
(b) Express clearly that opinion through a written report that also describes the basis for the opinion.

# Requirements

## Forming an Opinion on the Financial Statements

The auditor's report on the financial statements shall contain a clear written expression of opinion on the financial statements taken as a whole, based on the auditor evaluating the conclusions drawn from the audit evidence obtained, including evaluating whether:    8

(a) Sufficient appropriate audit evidence as to whether the financial statements as a whole are free from material misstatement, whether due to fraud or error has been obtained;
(b) Uncorrected misstatements are material, individually or in aggregate. This evaluation shall include consideration of the qualitative aspects of the entity's accounting practices, including indicators of possible bias in management's judgments; (Ref: Para. A1-A3)
(c) In respect of a true and fair framework, the financial statements, including the related notes, give a true and fair view; and
(d) In respect of all frameworks the financial statements have been prepared in all material respects in accordance with the framework, including the requirements of applicable law.

In particular, the auditor shall evaluate whether:    9

(a) The financial statements adequately refer to or describe the relevant financial reporting framework;
(b) The financial statements adequately disclose the significant accounting policies selected and applied;
(c) The accounting policies selected and applied are consistent with the applicable financial reporting framework, and are appropriate in the circumstances;
(d) Accounting estimates are reasonable;
(e) The information presented in the financial statements is relevant, reliable, comparable and understandable;
(f) The financial statements provide adequate disclosures to enable the intended users to understand the effect of material transactions and events on the information conveyed in the financial statements; and
(g) The terminology used in the financial statements, including the title of each financial statement, is appropriate.

**10**    With respect to compliance frameworks an unqualified opinion on the financial statements shall be expressed only when the auditor concludes that they have been prepared in accordance with the identified financial reporting framework, including the requirements of applicable law.

**11**    With respect to true and fair frameworks an unqualified opinion on the financial statements shall be expressed only when the auditor concludes that they have been prepared in accordance with the identified financial reporting framework, including the requirements of applicable law, and the financial statements give a true and fair view.

## Auditor's Report

### Title

**12**    The auditor's report shall have an appropriate title. (Ref: Para A4)

### Addressee

**13**    The auditor's report shall be appropriately addressed as required by the circumstances of the engagement. (Ref: Para A5)

### Introductory Paragraph

**14**    The auditor's report shall identify the financial statements of the entity that have been audited, including the date of, and period covered by, the financial statements.

### Respective Responsibilities of Those Charged with Governance and Auditors

**15**    The auditor's report shall include a statement that those charged with governance are responsible for the preparation of the financial statements and a statement that the responsibility of the auditor is to audit and express an opinion on the financial statements in accordance with applicable legal requirements and International Standards on Auditing (UK and Ireland). The report shall also state that those standards require the auditor to comply with the APB's Ethical Standards for Auditors. (Ref: Para A6 – A7)

### Scope of the Audit of the Financial Statements

**16**    The auditor's report shall either:

(a)  Cross refer to a "Statement of the Scope of an Audit" that is maintained on the APB's web-site; or

(b)  Cross refer to a "Statement of the Scope of an Audit" that is included elsewhere within the Annual Report; or

(c)  Include the following description of the scope of an audit.

"An audit involves obtaining evidence about the amounts and disclosures in the financial statements sufficient to give reasonable assurance that the financial statements are free from material misstatement, whether caused by fraud or error. This includes an assessment of: whether the accounting policies are appropriate to the *[describe nature of entity]* circumstances and have been consistently applied and adequately disclosed; the reasonableness of significant accounting estimates made by *[describe those charged with governance]*; and the overall presentation of the financial statements". (Ref: Para A8 – A9)

### Opinion on the financial statements

The opinion paragraph of the auditor's report shall clearly state the auditor's opinion as required by the relevant financial reporting framework used to prepare the financial statements, including applicable law.

**17**

When expressing an unqualified opinion on financial statements prepared in accordance with a true and fair framework the opinion paragraph shall clearly state that the financial statements give a true and fair view. It is not sufficient for the auditor to conclude that the financial statements give a true and fair view solely on the basis that the financial statements were prepared in accordance with accounting standards and any other applicable legal requirements. (Ref: Para A10 – A12)

**18**

### Opinion in respect of an additional financial reporting framework

When an auditor is engaged to issue an opinion on the compliance of the financial statements with an additional financial reporting framework the second opinion shall be clearly separated from the first opinion on the financial statements, by use of an appropriate heading. (Ref: Para A13)

**19**

### Requirement specific to public sector entities where an opinion on regularity is given.

The auditor shall address other reporting responsibilities in [a] separate section[s] of the auditor's report following the opinion[s] on the financial statements and, where there is one, the opinion on regularity. (Ref: Para A14)

**20**

### Opinion on other matters

When the auditor addresses other reporting responsibilities within the auditor's report on the financial statements, the opinion arising from such other responsibilities shall be set out in a separate section of the auditor's report following the opinion[s] on the financial statements or, where there is one, the opinion on regularity. (Ref: Para A15 – A16)

**21**

If the auditor is required to report on certain matters by exception the auditor shall describe its responsibilities under the heading "Matters on which we are required to report by exception" and incorporate a suitable conclusion in respect of such matters. (Ref: Para A17 – A18)

**22**

### Date of Report

23    The date of an auditor's report on a reporting entity's financial statements shall be the date on which the auditor signed the report expressing an opinion on those financial statements. (Ref. Para A19)

24    The auditor shall not sign, and hence date, the report earlier than the date on which all other information contained in a report of which the audited financial statements form a part have been approved by those charged with governance and the auditor has considered all necessary available evidence. (Ref. Para A20 – A23)

### Location of Auditor's Office

25    The report shall name the location of the office where the auditor is based.

### Auditor's Signature

26    The auditor's report shall state the name of the auditor and be signed and dated. (Ref. Para A24)

\*\*\*

# Application and Other Explanatory Material

## Qualitative Aspects of the Entity's Accounting Practices (Ref: Para 8)

A1    Management makes a number of judgments about the amounts and disclosures in the financial statements.

A2    ISA (UK and Ireland) 260 contains a discussion of the qualitative aspects of accounting practices.[4] In considering the qualitative aspects of the entity's accounting practices, the auditor may become aware of possible bias in management's judgments. The auditor may conclude that the cumulative effect of a lack of neutrality, together with the effect of uncorrected misstatements, causes the financial statements as a whole to be materially misstated. Indicators of a lack of neutrality that may affect the auditor's evaluation of whether the financial statements as a whole are materially misstated include the following:

- The selective correction of misstatements brought to management's attention during the audit (e.g., correcting misstatements with the effect of increasing reported earnings, but not correcting misstatements that have the effect of decreasing reported earnings).
- Possible management bias in the making of accounting estimates.

A3    ISA (UK and Ireland) 540 addresses possible management bias in making accounting estimates.[5] Indicators of possible management bias do not constitute misstatements for purposes of drawing conclusions on the reasonableness of individual accounting estimates. They may, however, affect the auditor's

---

[4] *ISA (UK and Ireland) 260, "Communication with Those Charged with Governance," Appendix 2.*

[5] *ISA (UK and Ireland) 540, " Auditing Accounting Estimates, Including Fair Value Accounting Estimates, and Related Disclosures," paragraph 21.*

evaluation of whether the financial statements as a whole are free from material misstatement.

## Auditor's Report

*Title* (Ref: Para 12)

The term "Independent Auditor" is usually used in the title in order to distinguish the auditor's report from reports that might be issued by others, such as by those charged with governance, or from the reports of other auditors who may not have to comply with the APB's Ethical Standards for Auditors.

**A4**

*Addressee* (Ref: Para 13)

The Companies Acts[6] require the auditor to report to the company's members because the audit is undertaken on their behalf. Such auditor's reports are, therefore, typically addressed to either the members or the shareholders of the company. The auditor's report on financial statements of other types of reporting entity is addressed to the appropriate person or persons, as defined by statute or by the terms of the individual engagement.

**A5**

*Respective Responsibilities of Those Charged with Governance and Auditors* (Ref: Para 15)

An appreciation of the interrelationship between the responsibilities of those who prepare financial statements and those who audit them facilitates an understanding of the nature and context of the opinion expressed by the auditor.

**A6**

The preparation of financial statements requires those charged with governance to make significant accounting estimates and judgments, as well as to determine the appropriate accounting principles and methods used in preparation of the financial statements. This determination will be made in the context of the financial reporting framework that those charged with governance choose, or are required, to use. In contrast, the auditor's responsibility is to audit the financial statements in order to express an opinion on them.

**A7**

*Scope of the Audit* (Ref: Para 16)

The APB maintains on its web site[7] example descriptions of the scope of an audit of the financial statements of various categories of United Kingdom company.

**A8**

Where the scope of the audit is described within the Annual Report but not in the auditor's report, such description includes the prescribed text set out in paragraph 16 above. The content of the description of the scope of the audit is determined by the auditor regardless of whether it is incorporated into the auditor's report or published as a separate statement elsewhere in the annual report.

**A9**

---

[6] *In the United Kingdom the Companies Act 2006 establishes this requirement. In the Republic of Ireland the Companies Acts 1963 to 2006 establish this requirement.*

[7] *With respect to a UK publicly traded company the web-site reference is www.frc.org.uk/apb/scope/UKP. With respect to a UK non-publicly traded company the web-site reference is www.frc.org.uk/apb/scope/UKNP.*

**Opinion on the financial statements** (Ref: Para 18)

A10   Although the "true and fair" concept has been central to accounting and auditing practice in the UK and Ireland for many years it is not defined in legislation. In 2008, the Financial Reporting Council published a legal opinion, that it had commissioned, entitled "The true and fair requirement revisited" (The Opinion)[8]. The Opinion confirms the overarching nature of the true and fair requirement to the preparation of financial statements in the United K ingdom, whether they are prepared in accordance with international or national accounting standards.

A11   The Opinion states that "The preparation of financial statements is not a mechanical process where compliance with relevant accounting standards will automatically ensure that those financial statements show a true and fair view, or a fair presentation. Such compliance may be highly likely to produce such an outcome; but it does not guarantee it".

A12   To advise the reader of the context in which the auditor's opinion is expressed, the auditor's opinion indicates the financial reporting framework upon which the financial statements are based. In the UK and Ireland, subject to certain restrictions, these normally comprise:

- "International Financial Reporting Standards (IFRSs) as adopted by the European Union", and the national law that is applicable when using IFRSs and, in the case of consolidated financial; statements of publicly traded companies[9], Article 4 of the IAS Regulation (1606/2002/EC); or
- "UK Generally Accepted Accounting Practice", which comprises applicable UK company law and UK Accounting Standards as issued by the Accounting Standards Board (ASB); or
- "Generally Accepted Accounting Practice in Ireland", which comprises applicable Irish company law and the Accounting Standards issued by the ASB and promulgated by the Institute of Chartered Accountants in Ireland.

**Opinion in respect of an additional financial reporting framework** (Ref: Para 19)

A13   The financial statements of some entities may comply with two financial reporting frameworks (for example "IFRSs as issued by the IASB" and "IFRSs as adopted by the European Union" and those charged with governance may engage the auditor to express an opinion in respect of both frameworks. Once the auditor is satisfied that there are no differences between the two financial reporting frameworks that affect the financial statements being reported on, the auditor states a second separate opinion with regard to the other financial reporting framework.

[8] *The opinion can be downloaded from the FRC web site at http://www.frc.org.uk/about/trueandfair.cfm*

[9] *A publicly traded company is one whose securities are admitted to trading on a regulated market in any Member State in the European Union.*

***Requirement specific to public sector entities where an opinion on regularity is given.***
(Ref: Para 20)

For the audit of certain public sector entities the audit mandate may require the auditor to express an opinion on regularity[10]. Regularity is the requirement that financial transactions are in accordance with the legislation authorising them.

**A14**

***Opinion on other matters*** (Ref: Para 21 – 22)

The auditor sets out its opinion[s] on these other reporting responsibilities in [a] separate section[s] of the report in order to clearly distinguish it from the auditor's opinion[s] on the financial statements.

**A15**

Other reporting responsibilities may be determined by specific statutory requirements applicable to the reporting entity, or, in some circumstances, by the terms of the auditor's engagement[11]. Such matters may be required to be dealt with by either:

**A16**

(a) a positive statement in the auditor's report; or
(b) by exception.
    An example of (a) arises in the United Kingdom where the auditor of a company is required to state whether, in the auditor's opinion, the information given in the directors' report for the financial year for which the accounts are prepared is consistent with those accounts[12]. An example of (b) arises in the United Kingdom where company legislation requires the auditor of a company to report when a company has not maintained adequate accounting records[13].

Where the auditor has discharged such responsibilities and has nothing to report in respect of them, the conclusion could be expressed in the form of the following phrase: "We have nothing to report in respect of the following".

**A17**

Where the auditor expresses a modified conclusion in respect of other reporting responsibilities (including those on which they are required to report by exception) this may give rise to a modification of the auditor's opinion on the financial statements. For example, if adequate accounting records have not been maintained and as a result it proves impracticable for the auditor to obtain sufficient appropriate evidence concerning material matters in the financial statements, the

**A18**

---

[10] *Guidance for auditors of public sector bodies in the UK and Ireland is given in Practice Note 10 "Audit of Financial Statements of Public Sector Bodies in the United Kingdom (Revised)" and Practice Note 10 (I) "Audit of Central Government Financial Statements in the Republic of Ireland".*

[11] *An example of a reporting responsibility determined by the terms of the auditor's engagement is where the directors of a listed company are required by the rules of a Listing Authority to ensure that the auditor reviews certain statements made by the directors before the annual report is published.*

[12] *Section 496 of the Companies Act 2006*

[13] *Section 498(2) of the Companies Act 2006*

auditor's report on the financial statements includes a qualified opinion or disclaimer of opinion arising from that limitation.[14]

***Date of Report*** (Ref: Para 23 – 24)

A19    This informs the reader that the auditor has considered the effect on the financial statements and on the auditor's report of events and transactions of which the auditor became aware and that occurred up to that date.

A20    The auditor is not in a position to form the opinion until the financial statements (and any other information contained in a report of which the audited financial statements form a part) have been approved by those charged with governance and the auditor has completed the assessment of all the evidence the auditor considers necessary for the opinion or opinions to be given in the auditor's report. This assessment includes events occurring up to the date the opinion is expressed. The auditor, therefore, plans the conduct of the audit to take account of the need to ensure, before expressing an opinion on financial statements, that those charged with governance have approved the financial statements and any accompanying other information and that the auditor has completed a sufficient review of post balance sheet events.

A21    The date of the auditor's report is, therefore, the date on which the auditor signs the auditor's report expressing an opinion on the financial statemenst for distribution with those financial statements, following:

(a)    Receipt of the financial statements and accompanying documents in the form approved by those charged with governance for release;

(b)    Review of all documents which the auditor is required to consider in addition to the financial statements (for example the directors' report, chairman's statement or other review of an entity's affairs which will accompany the financial statements); and

(c)    Completion of all procedures necessary to form an opinion on the financial statements (and any other opinions required by law or regulation) including a review of post balance sheet events,

A22    The form of the financial statements and other information approved by those charged with governance, and considered by the auditor when signing a report expressing the auditor's opinion, may be in the form of final drafts from which printed documents will be prepared. Subsequent production of printed copies of the financial statements and the auditor's report does not constitute the creation of a new document. Copies of the report produced for circulation to shareholders or others may, therefore, reproduce a printed version of the auditor's signature showing the date of actual signature.

A23    If the date on which the auditor signs the report is later than that on which those charged with governance approved the financial statements, the auditor takes such steps as are appropriate:

---

[14] *International Standard on Auditing (UK and Ireland) 705 "Modifications to the opinion in the independent auditor's report" sets out the requirements relating to qualified opinions and disclaimer of opinions on financial statements.*

(a) To obtain assurance that those charged with governance would have approved the financial statements on that later date (for example, by obtaining confirmation form specified individual members of the Board to whom authority has been delegated for this purpose); and

(b) To ensure that their procedures for reviewing subsequent events cover the period up to that date.

**Auditor's Signature** (Ref: Para 26)

The report is signed in the name of the audit firm, the personal name of the auditor or both, as required by law. In the case of a UK company, where the auditor is an individual the report is required to be signed by the individual. Where the auditor of a UK company is a firm the report is signed by the senior statutory auditor[15] in his or her own name, for and on behalf of the auditor.

A24

---

[15] See Bulletin 2008/6 "The "Senior Statutory Auditor" under the United Kingdom Companies Act 2006". That Bulletin at paragraphs 8-10 also explains the meaning of "signing the auditor's report" in a UK context.

# Addendum

*This addendum is provided for information and does not form part of the proposed clarified ISA (UK and Ireland) 700.*

*APB is not proposing to adopt ISA 700, "Forming an Opinion and Reporting on Financial Statements," as issued by the IAASB. It is instead proposing to issue a clarified version of the recently revised ISA (UK and Ireland) 700, "The Auditor's Report on Financial Statements," which addresses the requirements of company law and also provide for a more concise auditor's report, reflecting feedback to APB consultations. The main effect of this is that the form of UK and Ireland auditor's reports may not be exactly aligned with the precise format of auditor's reports required by ISA 700 issued by the IAASB. However, ISA (UK and Ireland) 700 has been designed to ensure that compliance with it will not preclude the auditor from being able to assert compliance with the ISAs issued by the IAASB (see paragraph 5 of proposed clarified ISA (UK and Ireland) 700).*

*The APB does propose to adopt ISAs 705 and 706 which address modified auditor's reports.*

# Proposed Clarified International Standard on Auditing (UK and Ireland) 705

# Modifications to the opinion in the independent auditor's report

*(Effective for audits of financial statements for periods ending on or after 15 December 2010)*

## Contents

International Standard on Auditing (UK and Ireland) (ISA (UK and Ireland)) 705, "Modifications to the Opinion in the Independent Auditor's Report" should be read in conjunction with ISA (UK and Ireland) 200, "Overall Objectives of the Independent Auditor and the Conduct of an Audit in Accordance with International Standards on Auditing (UK and Ireland)."

# Introduction

## Scope of this ISA (UK and Ireland)

1   This International Standard on Auditing (UK and Ireland) (ISA (UK and Ireland)) deals with the auditor's responsibility to issue an appropriate report in circumstances when, in forming an opinion in accordance with ISA (UK and Ireland) 700,[1] the auditor concludes that a modification to the auditor's opinion on the financial statements is necessary.

## Types of Modified Opinions

2   This ISA (UK and Ireland) establishes three types of modified opinions, namely, a qualified opinion, an adverse opinion, and a disclaimer of opinion. The decision regarding which type of modified opinion is appropriate depends upon: (Ref: Para. A1)

(a)   The nature of the matter giving rise to the modification, that is, whether the financial statements are materially misstated or, in the case of an inability to obtain sufficient appropriate audit evidence, may be materially misstated; and

(b)   The auditor's judgment about the pervasiveness of the effects or possible effects of the matter on the financial statements.

## Effective Date

3   This ISA (UK and Ireland) is effective for audits of financial statements for periods ending on or after 15 December 2010.

# Objective

4   The objective of the auditor is to express clearly an appropriately modified opinion on the financial statements that is necessary when:

(a)   The auditor concludes, based on the audit evidence obtained, that the financial statements as a whole are not free from material misstatement; or

(b)   The auditor is unable to obtain sufficient appropriate audit evidence to conclude that the financial statements as a whole are free from material misstatement.

# Definitions

5   For purposes of the ISAs (UK and Ireland), the following terms have the meanings attributed below:

(a)   Pervasive – A term used, in the context of misstatements, to describe the effects on the financial statements of misstatements or the possible effects on the financial statements of misstatements, if any, that are undetected due to an inability to obtain sufficient appropriate audit evidence. Pervasive effects on the financial statements are those that, in the auditor's judgment:

   (i)   Are not confined to specific elements, accounts or items of the financial statements;

   (ii)   If so confined, represent or could represent a substantial proportion of the financial statements; or

---

[1] *ISA (UK and Ireland) 700, "Forming an Opinion and Reporting on Financial Statements."*

(iii) In relation to disclosures, are fundamental to users' understanding of the financial statements.

(b) Modified opinion – A qualified opinion, an adverse opinion or a disclaimer of opinion.

# Requirements

## Circumstances When a Modification to the Auditor's Opinion Is Required

The auditor shall modify the opinion in the auditor's report when:  6

(a) The auditor concludes that, based on the audit evidence obtained, the financial statements as a whole are not free from material misstatement; or (Ref: Para. A2-A7)

(b) The auditor is unable to obtain sufficient appropriate audit evidence to conclude that the financial statements as a whole are free from material misstatement. (Ref: Para. A8-A12)

## Determining the Type of Modification to the Auditor's Opinion

### Qualified Opinion

The auditor shall express a qualified opinion when:  7

(a) The auditor, having obtained sufficient appropriate audit evidence, concludes that misstatements, individually or in the aggregate, are material, but not pervasive, to the financial statements; or

(b) The auditor is unable to obtain sufficient appropriate audit evidence on which to base the opinion, but the auditor concludes that the possible effects on the financial statements of undetected misstatements, if any, could be material but not pervasive.

### Adverse Opinion

The auditor shall express an adverse opinion when the auditor, having obtained  8
sufficient appropriate audit evidence, concludes that misstatements, individually or in the aggregate, are both material and pervasive to the financial statements.

### Disclaimer of Opinion

The auditor shall disclaim an opinion when the auditor is unable to obtain sufficient  9
appropriate audit evidence on which to base the opinion, and the auditor concludes that the possible effects on the financial statements of undetected misstatements, if any, could be both material and pervasive.

The auditor shall disclaim an opinion when, in extremely rare circumstances invol-  10
ving multiple uncertainties, the auditor concludes that, notwithstanding having obtained sufficient appropriate audit evidence regarding each of the individual uncertainties, it is not possible to form an opinion on the financial statements due to the potential interaction of the uncertainties and their possible cumulative effect on the financial statements.

### Consequence of an Inability to Obtain Sufficient Appropriate Audit Evidence Due to a Management-Imposed Limitation after the Auditor Has Accepted the Engagement

11    If, after accepting the engagement, the auditor becomes aware that management has imposed a limitation on the scope of the audit that the auditor considers likely to result in the need to express a qualified opinion or to disclaim an opinion on the financial statements, the auditor shall request that management remove the limitation.

12    If management refuses to remove the limitation referred to in paragraph 11, the auditor shall communicate the matter to those charged with governance, unless all of those charged with governance are involved in managing the entity,[2] and determine whether it is possible to perform alternative procedures to obtain sufficient appropriate audit evidence.

13    If the auditor is unable to obtain sufficient appropriate audit evidence, the auditor shall determine the implications as follows:

    (a)  If the auditor concludes that the possible effects on the financial statements of undetected misstatements, if any, could be material but not pervasive, the auditor shall qualify the opinion; or

    (b)  If the auditor concludes that the possible effects on the financial statements of undetected misstatements, if any, could be both material and pervasive so that a qualification of the opinion would be inadequate to communicate the gravity of the situation, the auditor shall: (Ref: Para. A13-A14)

        (i)  Withdraw from the audit, where practicable and possible under applicable law or regulation; or

        (ii)  If withdrawal from the audit before issuing the auditor's report is not practicable or possible, disclaim an opinion on the financial statements.

14    If the auditor withdraws as contemplated by paragraph 13(b)(i), before withdrawing, the auditor shall communicate to those charged with governance any matters regarding misstatements identified during the audit that would have given rise to a modification of the opinion. (Ref: Para. A15 – A15-1)

### Other Considerations Relating to an Adverse Opinion or Disclaimer of Opinion

15    When the auditor considers it necessary to express an adverse opinion or disclaim an opinion on the financial statements as a whole, the auditor's report shall not also include an unmodified opinion with respect to the same financial reporting framework on a single financial statement or one or more specific elements, accounts or items of a financial statement. To include such an unmodified opinion in the same report[3] in these circumstances would contradict the auditor's adverse opinion or disclaimer of opinion on the financial statements as a whole. (Ref: Para. A16)

---

[2] *ISA (UK and Ireland) 260, "Communication with Those Charged with Governance," paragraph 13.*

[3] *ISA 805, "Special Considerations—Audits of Single Financial Statements and Specific Elements, Accounts or Items of a Financial Statement" deals with circumstances where the auditor is engaged to express a separate opinion on one or more specific elements, accounts or items of a financial statement.* ISA 805 has not been promulgated by the APB for application in the UK and Ireland.

# Form and Content of the Auditor's Report When the Opinion Is Modified

## Basis for Modification Paragraph

When the auditor modifies the opinion on the financial statements, the auditor shall, in addition to the specific elements required by ISA (UK and Ireland) 700, include a paragraph in the auditor's report that provides a description of the matter giving rise to the modification. The auditor shall place this paragraph immediately before the opinion paragraph in the auditor's report and use the heading "Basis for Qualified Opinion," "Basis for Adverse Opinion," or "Basis for Disclaimer of Opinion," as appropriate. (Ref: Para. A17) **16**

If there is a material misstatement of the financial statements that relates to specific amounts in the financial statements (including quantitative disclosures), the auditor shall include in the basis for modification paragraph a description and quantification of the financial effects of the misstatement, unless impracticable. If it is not practicable to quantify the financial effects, the auditor shall so state in the basis for modification paragraph. (Ref: Para. A18) **17**

If there is a material misstatement of the financial statements that relates to narrative disclosures, the auditor shall include in the basis for modification paragraph an explanation of how the disclosures are misstated. **18**

If there is a material misstatement of the financial statements that relates to the non-disclosure of information required to be disclosed, the auditor shall: **19**

(a) Discuss the non-disclosure with those charged with governance;
(b) Describe in the basis for modification paragraph the nature of the omitted information; and
(c) Unless prohibited by law or regulation, include the omitted disclosures, provided it is practicable to do so and the auditor has obtained sufficient appropriate audit evidence about the omitted information. (Ref: Para. A19)

If the modification results from an inability to obtain sufficient appropriate audit evidence, the auditor shall include in the basis for modification paragraph the reasons for that inability. **20**

Even if the auditor has expressed an adverse opinion or disclaimed an opinion on the financial statements, the auditor shall describe in the basis for modification paragraph the reasons for any other matters of which the auditor is aware that would have required a modification to the opinion, and the effects thereof. (Ref: Para. A20) **21**

## Opinion Paragraph

When the auditor modifies the audit opinion, the auditor shall use the heading "Qualified Opinion," "Adverse Opinion," or "Disclaimer of Opinion," as appropriate, for the opinion paragraph. (Ref: Para. A21, A23-A24) **22**

When the auditor expresses a qualified opinion due to a material misstatement in the financial statements, the auditor shall state in the opinion paragraph that, in the auditor's opinion, except for the effects of the matter(s) described in the Basis for Qualified Opinion paragraph: **23**

(a) The financial statements present fairly, in all material respects (or give a true and fair view) in accordance with the applicable financial reporting framework when reporting in accordance with a fair presentation framework; or

(b)  The financial statements have been prepared, in all material respects, in accordance with the applicable financial framework when reporting in accordance with a compliance framework.

When the modification arises from an inability to obtain sufficient appropriate audit evidence, the auditor shall use the corresponding phrase "except for the possible effects of the matter(s) ..." for the modified opinion. (Ref: Para. A22)

**24**  When the auditor expresses an adverse opinion, the auditor shall state in the opinion paragraph that, in the auditor's opinion, because of the significance of the matter(s) described in the Basis for Adverse Opinion paragraph:

(a)  The financial statements do not present fairly (or give a true and fair view) in accordance with the applicable financial reporting framework when reporting in accordance with a fair presentation framework; or

(b)  The financial statements have not been prepared, in all material respects, in accordance with the applicable financial reporting framework when reporting in accordance with a compliance framework.

**25**  When the auditor disclaims an opinion due to an inability to obtain sufficient appropriate audit evidence, the auditor shall state in the opinion paragraph that:

(a)  because of the significance of the matter(s) described in the Basis for Disclaimer of Opinion paragraph, the auditor has not been able to obtain sufficient appropriate audit evidence to provide a basis for an audit opinion; and, accordingly,

(b)  the auditor does not express an opinion on the financial statements.

### Description of Auditor's Responsibility When the Auditor Expresses a Qualified or Adverse Opinion

**26**  When the auditor expresses a qualified or adverse opinion, the auditor shall amend the description of the auditor's responsibility to state that the auditor believes that the audit evidence the auditor has obtained is sufficient and appropriate to provide a basis for the auditor's modified audit opinion.

### Description of Auditor's Responsibility When the Auditor Disclaims an Opinion

27.  When the auditor disclaims an opinion due to an inability to obtain sufficient appropriate audit evidence, the auditor shall amend the introductory paragraph of the auditor's report to state that the auditor was engaged to audit the financial statements. The auditor shall also amend the description of the auditor's responsibility and the description of the scope of the audit to state only the following: "Our responsibility is to express an opinion on the financial statements based on conducting the audit in accordance with International Standards on Auditing. Because of the matter(s) described in the Basis for Disclaimer of Opinion paragraph, however, we were not able to obtain sufficient appropriate audit evidence to provide a basis for an audit opinion."

## Communication with Those Charged with Governance

**28**  When the auditor expects to modify the opinion in the auditor's report, the auditor shall communicate with those charged with governance the circumstances that led to the expected modification and the proposed wording of the modification. (Ref: Para. A25)

***

# Application and Other Explanatory Material

## Types of Modified Opinions (Ref: Para. 2)

The table below illustrates how the auditor's judgment about the nature of the matter **A1** giving rise to the modification, and the pervasiveness of its effects or possible effects on the financial statements, affects the type of opinion to be expressed.

| | *Auditor's Judgment about the Pervasiveness of the Effects or Possible Effects on the Financial Statements* | |
|---|---|---|
| *Nature of Matter Giving Rise to the Modification* | *Material but Not Pervasive* | *Material and Pervasive* |
| Financial statements are materially misstated | Qualified opinion | Adverse opinion |
| Inability to obtain sufficient appropriate audit evidence | Qualified opinion | Disclaimer of opinion |

## Nature of Material Misstatements (Ref: Para. 6(a))

ISA (UK and Ireland) 700 requires the auditor, in order to form an opinion on the **A2** financial statements, to conclude as to whether reasonable assurance has been obtained about whether the financial statements as a whole are free from material misstatement.[4] This conclusion takes into account the auditor's evaluation of uncorrected misstatements, if any, on the financial statements in accordance with ISA (UK and Ireland) 450.[5]

ISA (UK and Ireland) 450 defines a misstatement as a difference between the **A3** amount, classification, presentation, or disclosure of a reported financial statement item and the amount, classification, presentation, or disclosure that is required for the item to be in accordance with the applicable financial reporting framework. Accordingly, a material misstatement of the financial statements may arise in relation to:

(a) The appropriateness of the selected accounting policies;
(b) The application of the selected accounting policies; or
(c) The appropriateness or adequacy of disclosures in the financial statements.

### *Appropriateness of the Selected Accounting Policies*

In relation to the appropriateness of the accounting policies management has **A4** selected, material misstatements of the financial statements may arise when:

- The selected accounting policies are not consistent with the applicable financial reporting framework; or
- The financial statements, including the related notes, do not represent the underlying transactions and events in a manner that achieves fair presentation.

---

[4] *ISA 700, paragraph 11.*

*The APB has not promulgated ISA 700 as issued by the IAASB for application in the UK and Ireland. In the UK and Ireland the applicable auditing standard is ISA (UK and Ireland) 700, "The Auditor's Report on Financial Statements." Paragraph 8 of ISA (UK and Ireland) 700 requires evaluation of whether sufficient appropriate audit evidence has been obtained.*

[5] *ISA (UK and Ireland) 450, "Evaluation of Misstatements Identified during the Audit," paragraph 4(a).*

**A5**   Financial reporting frameworks often contain requirements for the accounting for, and disclosure of, changes in accounting policies. Where the entity has changed its selection of significant accounting policies, a material misstatement of the financial statements may arise when the entity has not complied with these requirements.

### Application of the Selected Accounting Policies

**A6**   In relation to the application of the selected accounting policies, material misstatements of the financial statements may arise:

- When management has not applied the selected accounting policies consistently with the financial reporting framework, including when management has not applied the selected accounting policies consistently between periods or to similar transactions and events (consistency in application); or
- Due to the method of application of the selected accounting policies (such as an unintentional error in application).

### Appropriateness or Adequacy of Disclosures in the Financial Statements

**A7**   In relation to the appropriateness or adequacy of disclosures in the financial statements, material misstatements of the financial statements may arise when:

(a)  The financial statements do not include all of the disclosures required by the applicable financial reporting framework;

(b)  The disclosures in the financial statements are not presented in accordance with the applicable financial reporting framework; or

(c)  The financial statements do not provide the disclosures necessary to achieve fair presentation.

### Nature of an Inability to Obtain Sufficient Appropriate Audit Evidence (Ref: Para. 6(b))

**A8**   The auditor's inability to obtain sufficient appropriate audit evidence (also referred to as a limitation on the scope of the audit) may arise from:

(a)  Circumstances beyond the control of the entity;

(b)  Circumstances relating to the nature or timing of the auditor's work; or

(c)  Limitations imposed by management.

**A9**   An inability to perform a specific procedure does not constitute a limitation on the scope of the audit if the auditor is able to obtain sufficient appropriate audit evidence by performing alternative procedures. If this is not possible, the requirements of paragraphs 7(b) and 10 apply as appropriate. Limitations imposed by management may have other implications for the audit, such as for the auditor's assessment of fraud risks and consideration of engagement continuance.

**A10**   Examples of circumstances beyond the control of the entity include when:

- The entity's accounting records have been destroyed.
- The accounting records of a significant component have been seized indefinitely by governmental authorities.

**A11**   Examples of circumstances relating to the nature or timing of the auditor's work include when:

- The entity is required to use the equity method of accounting for an associated entity, and the auditor is unable to obtain sufficient appropriate audit evidence about the latter's financial information to evaluate whether the equity method has been appropriately applied.

- The timing of the auditor's appointment is such that the auditor is unable to observe the counting of the physical inventories.
- The auditor determines that performing substantive procedures alone is not sufficient, but the entity's controls are not effective.

Examples of an inability to obtain sufficient appropriate audit evidence arising from a limitation on the scope of the audit imposed by management include when:                **A12**

- Management prevents the auditor from observing the counting of the physical inventory.
- Management prevents the auditor from requesting external confirmation of specific account balances.

## Consequence of an Inability to Obtain Sufficient Appropriate Audit Evidence Due to a Management-Imposed Limitation after the Auditor Has Accepted the Engagement (Ref: Para. 13(b)-14)

The practicality of withdrawing from the audit may depend on the stage of completion of the engagement at the time that management imposes the scope limitation. If the auditor has substantially completed the audit, the auditor may decide to complete the audit to the extent possible, disclaim an opinion and explain the scope limitation in the Basis for Disclaimer of Opinion paragraph prior to withdrawing.                **A13**

In certain circumstances, withdrawal from the audit may not be possible if the auditor is required by law or regulation to continue the audit engagement. This may be the case for an auditor that is appointed to audit the financial statements of public sector entities. It may also be the case in jurisdictions where the auditor is appointed to audit the financial statements covering a specific period, or appointed for a specific period and is prohibited from withdrawing before the completion of the audit of those financial statements or before the end of that period, respectively. The auditor may also consider it necessary to include an Other Matter paragraph in the auditor's report.[6]                **A14**

When the auditor concludes that withdrawal from the audit is necessary because of a scope limitation, there may be a professional, legal or regulatory requirement for the auditor to communicate matters relating to the withdrawal from the engagement to regulators or the entity's owners.                **A15**

### Statement by Auditor on Ceasing to Hold Office

The auditor of a limited company in the UK who ceases to hold office as auditor is required to comply with the requirements of sections 519 and 521 of the Companies Act 2006 regarding the statement to be made by the auditor in relation to ceasing to hold office. For the Republic of Ireland, equivalent requirements are contained in section 185 of the Companies Act 1990. In addition, in the UK the auditor may need to notify the appropriate audit authority in accordance with section 522 of the Companies Act 2006.                **A15-1**

---

[6] *ISA (UK and Ireland) 706, "Emphasis of Matter Paragraphs and Other Matter Paragraphs in the Independent Auditor's Report," paragraph A5.*

**Other Considerations Relating to an Adverse Opinion or Disclaimer of Opinion** (Ref: Para. 15)

A16   The following are examples of reporting circumstances that would not contradict the auditor's adverse opinion or disclaimer of opinion:

● The expression of an unmodified opinion on financial statements prepared under a given financial reporting framework and, within the same report, the expression of an adverse opinion on the same financial statements under a different financial reporting framework.[7]

● The expression of a disclaimer of opinion regarding the results of operations, and cash flows, where relevant, and an unmodified opinion regarding the financial position (see ISA (UK and Ireland) 510[8]). In this case, the auditor has not expressed a disclaimer of opinion on the financial statements as a whole.

## Form and Content of the Auditor's Report When the Opinion Is Modified

*Basis for Modification Paragraph* (Ref: Para. 16-17, 19(b), 21)

A17   Consistency in the auditor's report helps to promote users' understanding and to identify unusual circumstances when they occur. Accordingly, although uniformity in the wording of a modified opinion and in the description of the basis for the modification may not be possible, consistency in both the form and content of the auditor's report is desirable.

A18   An example of the financial effects of material misstatements that the auditor may describe in the basis for modification paragraph in the auditor's report is the quantification of the effects on income tax, income before taxes, net income and equity if inventory is overstated.

A19   Disclosing the omitted information in the basis for modification paragraph would not be practicable if:

(a) The disclosures have not been prepared by management or the disclosures are otherwise not readily available to the auditor; or

(b) In the auditor's judgment, the disclosures would be unduly voluminous in relation to the auditor's report.

A20   An adverse opinion or a disclaimer of opinion relating to a specific matter described in the basis for qualification paragraph does not justify the omission of a description of other identified matters that would have otherwise required a modification of the auditor's opinion. In such cases, the disclosure of such other matters of which the auditor is aware may be relevant to users of the financial statements.

*Opinion Paragraph* (Ref: Para. 22-23)

A21   Inclusion of this paragraph heading makes it clear to the user that the auditor's opinion is modified and indicates the type of modification.

---

[7] *See paragraph A32 of ISA 700 for a description of this circumstance.*
*The APB has not promulgated ISA 700 as issued by the IAASB for application in the UK and Ireland. In the UK and Ireland the applicable auditing standard is ISA (UK and Ireland) 700, "The Auditor's Report on Financial Statements." Paragraph A13 of ISA (UK and Ireland) 700 provides guidance on expressing an opinion in respect of an additional financial reporting framework.*

[8] *ISA (UK and Ireland) 510, "Initial Audit Engagements—Opening Balances," paragraph 10.*

When the auditor expresses a qualified opinion, it would not be appropriate to use phrases such as "with the foregoing explanation" or "subject to" in the opinion paragraph as these are not sufficiently clear or forceful.  **A22**

*Illustrative Auditors' Reports*

With respect to companies, illustrative examples of auditor's reports tailored for use with audits conducted in accordance with ISAs (UK and Ireland) are given in the most recent versions of the APB Bulletins, "Auditor's Reports on Financial Statements in the United Kingdom"/"Auditor's Reports on Financial Statements in the Republic of Ireland." Illustrative examples for various other entities are give in other Bulletins and Practice Notes issued by the APB.

Illustrations 1 and 2 in the Appendix contain auditors' reports with qualified and adverse opinions, respectively, as the financial statements are materially misstated.  **A23**

Illustration 3 in the Appendix contains an auditor's report with a qualified opinion as the auditor is unable to obtain sufficient appropriate audit evidence. Illustration 4 contains a disclaimer of opinion due to an inability to obtain sufficient appropriate audit evidence about a single element of the financial statements. Illustration 5 contains a disclaimer of opinion due to an inability to obtain sufficient appropriate audit evidence about multiple elements of the financial statements. In each of the latter two cases, the possible effects on the financial statements of the inability are both material and pervasive.  **A24**

## Communication with Those Charged with Governance (Ref: Para. 28)

Communicating with those charged with governance the circumstances that lead to an expected modification to the auditor's opinion and the proposed wording of the modification enables:  **A25**

(a)  The auditor to give notice to those charged with governance of the intended modification(s) and the reasons (or circumstances) for the modification(s);

(b)  The auditor to seek the concurrence of those charged with governance regarding the facts of the matter(s) giving rise to the expected modification(s), or to confirm matters of disagreement with management as such; and

(c)  Those charged with governance to have an opportunity, where appropriate, to provide the auditor with further information and explanations in respect of the matter(s) giving rise to the expected modification(s).

## Appendix (Ref: Para. A23-24)

The examples in the Appendix have not been tailored for the UK and Ireland. With respect to companies, illustrative examples of auditor's reports tailored for use with audits conducted in accordance with ISAs (UK and Ireland) are given in the most recent versions of the APB Bulletins, "Auditor's Reports on Financial Statements in the United Kingdom"/"Auditor's Reports on Financial Statements in the Republic of Ireland." Illustrative examples for various other entities are give in other Bulletins and Practice Notes issued by the APB.

## Illustrations of Auditors' Reports with Modifications to the Opinion

- Illustration 1: An auditor's report containing a qualified opinion due to a material misstatement of the financial statements.
- Illustration 2: An auditor's report containing an adverse opinion due to a material misstatement of the financial statements.
- Illustration 3: An auditor's report containing a qualified opinion due to the auditor's inability to obtain sufficient appropriate audit evidence.
- Illustration 4: An auditor's report containing a disclaimer of opinion due to the auditor's inability to obtain sufficient appropriate audit evidence about a single element of the financial statements.
- Illustration 5: An auditor's report containing a disclaimer of opinion due to the auditor's inability to obtain sufficient appropriate audit evidence about multiple elements of the financial statements.

---

**Illustration 1:**

**Circumstances include the following:**

- **Audit of a complete set of general purpose financial statements prepared by management of the entity in accordance with International Financial Reporting Standards.**
- **The terms of the audit engagement reflect the description of management's responsibility for the financial statements in ISA 210.[9]**
- **Inventories are misstated. The misstatement is deemed to be material but not pervasive to the financial statements.**
- **In addition to the audit of the financial statements, the auditor has other reporting responsibilities required under local law.**

---

INDEPENDENT AUDITOR'S REPORT

[Appropriate Addressee]

**Report on the Financial Statements[10]**

We have audited the accompanying financial statements of ABC Company, which comprise the balance sheet as at December 31, 20X1, and the income statement,

[9] *ISA 210, "Agreeing the Terms of Audit Engagements."*

[10] *The sub-title "Report on the Financial Statements" is unnecessary in circumstances when the second sub-title "Report on Other Legal and Regulatory Requirements" is not applicable.*

statement of changes in equity and cash flow statement for the year then ended, and a summary of significant accounting policies and other explanatory information.

## *Management's*[11] *Responsibility for the Financial Statements*

Management is responsible for the preparation and fair presentation of these financial statements in accordance with International Financial Reporting Standards,[12] and for such internal control as management determines is necessary to enable the preparation of financial statements that are free from material misstatement, whether due to fraud or error.

## *Auditor's Responsibility*

Our responsibility is to express an opinion on these financial statements based on our audit. We conducted our audit in accordance with International Standards on Auditing. Those standards require that we comply with ethical requirements and plan and perform the audit to obtain reasonable assurance about whether the financial statements are free from material misstatement.

An audit involves performing procedures to obtain audit evidence about the amounts and disclosures in the financial statements. The procedures selected depend on the auditor's judgment, including the assessment of the risks of material misstatement of the financial statements, whether due to fraud or error. In making those risk assessments, the auditor considers internal control relevant to the entity's preparation and fair presentation[13] of the financial statements in order to design audit procedures that are appropriate in the circumstances, but not for the purpose of expressing an opinion on the effectiveness of the entity's internal control.[14] An audit also includes evaluating the appropriateness of accounting policies used and the reasonableness of accounting estimates made by management, as well as evaluating the overall presentation of the financial statements.

We believe that the audit evidence we have obtained is sufficient and appropriate to provide a basis for our qualified audit opinion.

---

[11] *Or other term that is appropriate in the context of the legal framework in the particular jurisdiction.*

[12] *Where management's responsibility is to prepare financial statements that give a true and fair view, this may read: "Management is responsible for the preparation of financial statements that give a true and fair view in accordance with International Financial Reporting Standards, and for such ..."*

[13] *In the case of footnote 12, this may read: "In making those risk assessments, the auditor considers internal control relevant to the entity's preparation of financial statements that give a true and fair view in order to design audit procedures that are appropriate in the circumstances, but not for the purpose of expressing an opinion on the effectiveness of the entity's internal control."*

[14] *In circumstances when the auditor also has responsibility to express an opinion on the effectiveness of internal control in conjunction with the audit of the financial statements, this sentence would be worded as follows: "In making those risk assessments, the auditor considers internal control relevant to the entity's preparation and fair presentation of the financial statements in order to design audit procedures that are appropriate in the circumstances." In the case of footnote 12, this may read: "In making those risk assessments, the auditor considers internal control relevant to the entity's preparation of financial statements that give a true and fair view in order to design audit procedures that are appropriate in the circumstances."*

### Basis for Qualified Opinion

The company's inventories are carried in the balance sheet at xxx. Management has not stated the inventories at the lower of cost and net realizable value but has stated them solely at cost, which constitutes a departure from International Financial Reporting Standards. The company's records indicate that had management stated the inventories at the lower of cost and net realizable value, an amount of xxx would have been required to write the inventories down to their net realizable value. Accordingly, cost of sales would have been increased by xxx, and income tax, net income and shareholders' equity would have been reduced by xxx, xxx and xxx, respectively.

### Qualified Opinion

In our opinion, except for the effects of the matter described in the Basis for Qualified Opinion paragraph, the financial statements present fairly, in all material respects, (or *give a true and fair view of*) the financial position of ABC Company as at December 31, 20X1, and (*of*) its financial performance and its cash flows for the year then ended in accordance with International Financial Reporting Standards.

## Report on Other Legal and Regulatory Requirements

[Form and content of this section of the auditor's report will vary depending on the nature of the auditor's other reporting responsibilities.]

[Auditor's signature]

[Date of the auditor's report]

[Auditor's address]

---

**Illustration 2:**

**Circumstances include the following:**

- Audit of consolidated general purpose financial statements prepared by management of the parent in accordance with International Financial Reporting Standards.
- The terms of the audit engagement reflect the description of management's responsibility for the financial statements in ISA 210.
- The financial statements are materially misstated due to the non-consolidation of a subsidiary. The material misstatement is deemed to be pervasive to the financial statements. The effects of the misstatement on the financial statements have not been determined because it was not practicable to do so.
- In addition to the audit of the consolidated financial statements, the auditor has other reporting responsibilities required under local law.

---

## INDEPENDENT AUDITOR'S REPORT

[Appropriate Addressee]

### Report on the Consolidated Financial Statements[15]

We have audited the accompanying consolidated financial statements of ABC Company and its subsidiaries, which comprise the consolidated balance sheet as at December 31, 20X1, and the consolidated income statement, statement of changes in equity and cash flow statement for the year then ended, and a summary of significant accounting policies and other explanatory information.

### *Management's*[16] *Responsibility for the Financial Statements*

Management is responsible for the preparation and fair presentation of these consolidated financial statements in accordance with International Financial Reporting Standards,[17] and for such internal control as management determines is necessary to enable the preparation of financial statements that are free from material misstatement, whether due to fraud or error.

### *Auditor's Responsibility*

Our responsibility is to express an opinion on these consolidated financial statements based on our audit. We conducted our audit in accordance with International Standards on Auditing. Those standards require that we comply with ethical requirements and plan and perform the audit to obtain reasonable assurance about whether the consolidated financial statements are free from material misstatement.

An audit involves performing procedures to obtain audit evidence about the amounts and disclosures in the consolidated financial statements. The procedures

---

[15] *The sub-title "Report on the Consolidated Financial Statements" is unnecessary in circumstances when the second sub-title "Report on Other Legal and Regulatory Requirements" is not applicable.*

[16] *Or other term that is appropriate in the context of the legal framework in the particular jurisdiction.*

[17] *Where management's responsibility is to prepare consolidated financial statements that give a true and fair view, this may read: "Management is responsible for the preparation of consolidated financial statements that give a true and fair view in accordance with International Financial Reporting Standards, and for such ..."*

selected depend on the auditor's judgment, including the assessment of the risks of material misstatement of the financial statements, whether due to fraud or error. In making those risk assessments, the auditor considers internal control relevant to the entity's preparation and fair presentation[18] of the consolidated financial statements in order to design audit procedures that are appropriate in the circumstances, but not for the purpose of expressing an opinion on the effectiveness of the entity's internal control.[19] An audit also includes evaluating the appropriateness of accounting policies used and the reasonableness of accounting estimates made by management, as well as evaluating the overall presentation of the consolidated financial statements.

We believe that the audit evidence we have obtained is sufficient and appropriate to provide a basis for our adverse audit opinion.

### Basis for Adverse Opinion

As explained in Note X, the company has not consolidated the financial statements of subsidiary XYZ Company it acquired during 20X1 because it has not yet been able to ascertain the fair values of certain of the subsidiary's material assets and liabilities at the acquisition date. This investment is therefore accounted for on a cost basis. Under International Financial Reporting Standards, the subsidiary should have been consolidated because it is controlled by the company. Had XYZ been consolidated, many elements in the accompanying financial statements would have been materially affected. The effects on the financial statements of the failure to consolidate have not been determined.

### Adverse Opinion

In our opinion, because of the significance of the matter discussed in the Basis for Adverse Opinion paragraph, the consolidated financial statements do not present fairly (or *do not give a true and fair view of*) the financial position of ABC Company and its subsidiaries as at December 31, 20X1, and (*of*) their financial performance and cash flows for the year then ended in accordance with International Financial Reporting Standards.

## Report on Other Legal and Regulatory Requirements

[Form and content of this section of the auditor's report will vary depending on the nature of the auditor's other reporting responsibilities.]

[Auditor's signature]

[Date of the auditor's report]

[Auditor's address]

---

[18] *In the case of footnote 17, this may read: "In making those risk assessments, the auditor considers internal control relevant to the entity's preparation of consolidated financial statements that give a true and fair view in order to design audit procedures that are appropriate in the circumstances, but not for the purpose of expressing an opinion on the effectiveness of the entity's internal control."*

[19] *In circumstances when the auditor also has responsibility to express an opinion on the effectiveness of internal control in conjunction with the audit of the consolidated financial statements, this sentence would be worded as follows: "In making those risk assessments, the auditor considers internal control relevant to the entity's preparation and fair presentation of the financial statements in order to design audit procedures that are appropriate in the circumstances." In the case of footnote 17, this may read: "In making those risk assessments, the auditor considers internal control relevant to the entity's preparation of financial statements that give a true and fair view in order to design audit procedures that are appropriate in the circumstances."*

**Illustration 3:**

**Circumstances include the following:**

- Audit of a complete set of general purpose financial statements prepared by management of the entity in accordance with International Financial Reporting Standards.
- The terms of the audit engagement reflect the description of management's responsibility for the financial statements in ISA 210.
- The auditor was unable to obtain sufficient appropriate audit evidence regarding an investment in a foreign affiliate. The possible effects of the inability to obtain sufficient appropriate audit evidence are deemed to be material but not pervasive to the financial statements.
- In addition to the audit of the financial statements, the auditor has other reporting responsibilities required under local law.

## INDEPENDENT AUDITOR'S REPORT

[Appropriate Addressee]

## Report on the Financial Statements[20]

We have audited the accompanying financial statements of ABC Company, which comprise the balance sheet as at December 31, 20X1, and the income statement, statement of changes in equity and cash flow statement for the year then ended, and a summary of significant accounting policies and other explanatory information.

### *Management's[21] Responsibility for the Financial Statements*

Management is responsible for the preparation and fair presentation of these financial statements in accordance with International Financial Reporting Standards,[22] and for such internal control as management determines is necessary to enable the preparation of financial statements that are free from material misstatement, whether due to fraud or error.

### *Auditor's Responsibility*

Our responsibility is to express an opinion on these financial statements based on our audit. We conducted our audit in accordance with International Standards on Auditing. Those standards require that we comply with ethical requirements and plan and perform the audit to obtain reasonable assurance about whether the financial statements are free from material misstatement.

An audit involves performing procedures to obtain audit evidence about the amounts and disclosures in the financial statements. The procedures selected depend on the auditor's judgment, including the assessment of the risks of material

---

[20] *The sub-title "Report on the Financial Statements" is unnecessary in circumstances when the second sub-title "Report on Other Legal and Regulatory Requirements" is not applicable.*

[21] *Or other term that is appropriate in the context of the legal framework in the particular jurisdiction.*

[22] *Where management's responsibility is to prepare financial statements that give a true and fair view, this may read: "Management is responsible for the preparation of financial statements that give a true and fair view in accordance with International Financial Reporting Standards, and for such ..."*

misstatement of the financial statements, whether due to fraud or error. In making those risk assessments, the auditor considers internal control relevant to the entity's preparation and fair presentation[23] of the financial statements in order to design audit procedures that are appropriate in the circumstances, but not for the purpose of expressing an opinion on the effectiveness of the entity's internal control.[24] An audit also includes evaluating the appropriateness of accounting policies used and the reasonableness of accounting estimates made by management, as well as evaluating the overall presentation of the financial statements.

We believe that the audit evidence we have obtained is sufficient and appropriate to provide a basis for our qualified audit opinion.

### Basis for Qualified Opinion

ABC Company's investment in XYZ Company, a foreign associate acquired during the year and accounted for by the equity method, is carried at xxx on the balance sheet as at December 31, 20X1, and ABC's share of XYZ's net income of xxx is included in ABC's income for the year then ended. We were unable to obtain sufficient appropriate audit evidence about the carrying amount of ABC's investment in XYZ as at December 31, 20X1 and ABC's share of XYZ's net income for the year because we were denied access to the financial information, management, and the auditors of XYZ. Consequently, we were unable to determine whether any adjustments to these amounts were necessary.

### Qualified Opinion

In our opinion, except for the possible effects of the matter described in the Basis for Qualified Opinion paragraph, the financial statements present fairly, in all material respects, (or *give a true and fair view of*) the financial position of ABC Company as at December 31, 20X1, and (*of*) its financial performance and its cash flows for the year then ended in accordance with International Financial Reporting Standards.

## Report on Other Legal and Regulatory Requirements

[Form and content of this section of the auditor's report will vary depending on the nature of the auditor's other reporting responsibilities.]

[Auditor's signature]

[Date of the auditor's report]

[Auditor's address]

---

[23] *In the case of footnote 22, this may read: "In making those risk assessments, the auditor considers internal control relevant to the entity's preparation of financial statements that give a true and fair view in order to design audit procedures that are appropriate in the circumstances, but not for the purpose of expressing an opinion on the effectiveness of the entity's internal control."*

[24] *In circumstances when the auditor also has responsibility to express an opinion on the effectiveness of internal control in conjunction with the audit of the financial statements, this sentence would be worded as follows: "In making those risk assessments, the auditor considers internal control relevant to the entity's preparation and fair presentation of the financial statements in order to design audit procedures that are appropriate in the circumstances." In the case of footnote 22, this may read: "In making those risk assessments, the auditor considers internal control relevant to the entity's preparation of financial statements that give a true and fair view in order to design audit procedures that are appropriate in the circumstances."*

---

**Illustration 4:**

**Circumstances include the following:**

● Audit of a complete set of general purpose financial statements prepared by management of the entity in accordance with International Financial Reporting Standards.

● The terms of the audit engagement reflect the description of management's responsibility for the financial statements in ISA 210.

● The auditor was unable to obtain sufficient appropriate audit evidence about a single element of the financial statements. That is, the auditor was also unable to obtain audit evidence about the financial information of a joint venture investment that represents over 90% of the company's net assets. The possible effects of this inability to obtain sufficient appropriate audit evidence are deemed to be both material and pervasive to the financial statements.

● In addition to the audit of the financial statements, the auditor has other reporting responsibilities required under local law.

---

INDEPENDENT AUDITOR'S REPORT

[Appropriate Addressee]

## Report on the Financial Statements[25]

We were engaged to audit the accompanying financial statements of ABC Company, which comprise the balance sheet as at December 31, 20X1, and the income statement, statement of changes in equity and cash flow statement for the year then ended, and a summary of significant accounting policies and other explanatory information.

### Management's[26] Responsibility for the Financial Statements

Management is responsible for the preparation and fair presentation of these financial statements in accordance with International Financial Reporting Standards,[27] and for such internal control as management determines is necessary to enable the preparation of financial statements that are free from material misstatement, whether due to fraud or error.

### Auditor's Responsibility

Our responsibility is to express an opinion on these financial statements based on conducting the audit in accordance with International Standards on Auditing. Because of the matter described in the Basis for Disclaimer of Opinion paragraph, however, we were not able to obtain sufficient appropriate audit evidence to provide a basis for an audit opinion.

---

[25] *The sub-title "Report on the Financial Statements" is unnecessary in circumstances when the second sub-title "Report on Other Legal and Regulatory Requirements" is not applicable.*

[26] *Or other term that is appropriate in the context of the legal framework in the particular jurisdiction.*

[27] *Where management's responsibility is to prepare financial statements that give a true and fair view, this sentence may read: "Management is responsible for the preparation of financial statements that give a true and fair view in accordance with International Financial Reporting Standards."*

*Basis for Disclaimer of Opinion*

The company's investment in its joint venture XYZ (Country X) Company is carried at xxx on the company's balance sheet, which represents over 90% of the company's net assets as at December 31, 20X1. We were not allowed access to the management and the auditors of XYZ, including XYZ's auditors' audit documentation. As a result, we were unable to determine whether any adjustments were necessary in respect of the company's proportional share of XYZ's assets that it controls jointly, its proportional share of XYZ's liabilities for which it is jointly responsible, its proportional share of XYZ's income and expenses for the year, and the elements making up the statement of changes in equity and cash flow statement.

*Disclaimer of Opinion*

Because of the significance of the matter described in the Basis for Disclaimer of Opinion paragraph, we have not been able to obtain sufficient appropriate audit evidence to provide a basis for an audit opinion. Accordingly, we do not express an opinion on the financial statements.

## Report on Other Legal and Regulatory Requirements

[Form and content of this section of the auditor's report will vary depending on the nature of the auditor's other reporting responsibilities.]

[Auditor's signature]

[Date of the auditor's report]

[Auditor's address]

> **Illustration 5:**
>
> **Circumstances include the following:**
>
> - Audit of a complete set of general purpose financial statements prepared by management of the entity in accordance with International Financial Reporting Standards.
> - The terms of the audit engagement reflect the description of management's responsibility for the financial statements in ISA 210.
> - The auditor was unable to obtain sufficient appropriate audit evidence about multiple elements of the financial statements. That is, the auditor was unable to obtain audit evidence about the entity's inventories and accounts receivable. The possible effects of this inability to obtain sufficient appropriate audit evidence are deemed to be both material and pervasive to the financial statements.
> - In addition to the audit of the financial statements, the auditor has other reporting responsibilities required under local law.

## INDEPENDENT AUDITOR'S REPORT

[Appropriate Addressee]

**Report on the Financial Statements[28]**

We were engaged to audit the accompanying financial statements of ABC Company, which comprise the balance sheet as at December 31, 20X1, and the income statement, statement of changes in equity and cash flow statement for the year then ended, and a summary of significant accounting policies and other explanatory information.

*Management's[29] Responsibility for the Financial Statements*

Management is responsible for the preparation and fair presentation of these financial statements in accordance with International Financial Reporting Standards,[30] and for such internal control as management determines is necessary to enable the preparation of financial statements that are free from material misstatement, whether due to fraud or error.

*Auditor's Responsibility*

Our responsibility is to express an opinion on these financial statements based on conducting the audit in accordance with International Standards on Auditing. Because of the matters described in the Basis for Disclaimer of Opinion paragraph, however, we were not able to obtain sufficient appropriate audit evidence to provide a basis for an audit opinion.

[28] *The sub-title "Report on the Financial Statements" is unnecessary in circumstances when the second sub-title "Report on Other Legal and Regulatory Requirements" is not applicable.*

[29] *Or other term that is appropriate in the context of the legal framework in the particular jurisdiction.*

[30] *Where management's responsibility is to prepare financial statements that give a true and fair view, this may read: "Management is responsible for the preparation and presentation of financial statements that give a true and fair view in accordance with International Financial Reporting Standards."*

### Basis for Disclaimer of Opinion

We were not appointed as auditors of the company until after December 31, 20X1 and thus did not observe the counting of physical inventories at the beginning and end of the year. We were unable to satisfy ourselves by alternative means concerning the inventory quantities held at December 31, 20X0 and 20X1 which are stated in the balance sheet at xxx and xxx, respectively. In addition, the introduction of a new computerized accounts receivable system in September 20X1 resulted in numerous errors in accounts receivable. As of the date of our audit report, management was still in the process of rectifying the system deficiencies and correcting the errors. We were unable to confirm or verify by alternative means accounts receivable included in the balance sheet at a total amount of xxx as at December 31, 20X1. As a result of these matters, we were unable to determine whether any adjustments might have been found necessary in respect of recorded or unrecorded inventories and accounts receivable, and the elements making up the income statement, statement of changes in equity and cash flow statement.

### Disclaimer of Opinion

Because of the significance of the matters described in the Basis for Disclaimer of Opinion paragraph, we have not been able to obtain sufficient appropriate audit evidence to provide a basis for an audit opinion. Accordingly, we do not express an opinion on the financial statements.

## Report on Other Legal and Regulatory Requirements

[Form and content of this section of the auditor's report will vary depending on the nature of the auditor's other reporting responsibilities.]

[Auditor's signature]

[Date of the auditor's report]

[Auditor's address]

# Addendum

*This addendum is provided for information and does not form part of the proposed clarified ISA (UK and Ireland) 705.*

*Proposed ISA (UK and Ireland) 705 addresses matters that are currently covered in ISA (UK and Ireland) 700. The APB is not proposing to add any supplementary requirements but is proposing a small amount of supplementary guidance, primarily to draw attention to the auditor's legal obligations with regard to making a statement when ceasing to hold office (see paragraph A15-1).*

# Proposed Clarified International Standard on Auditing (UK and Ireland) 706

## Emphasis of matter paragraphs and other matter paragraphs in the independent auditor's report

*(Effective for audits of financial statements for periods ending on or after 15 December 2010)*

## Contents

*Paragraph*

> International Standard on Auditing (UK and Ireland) (ISA (UK and Ireland))
> 706, "Emphasis of Matter Paragraphs and Other Matter Paragraphs in the
> Independent Auditor's Report" should be read in conjunction with ISA (UK and
> Ireland) 200, "Overall Objectives of the Independent Auditor and the Conduct of
> an Audit in Accordance with International Standards on Auditing (UK and
> Ireland)."

# Introduction

## Scope of this ISA (UK and Ireland)

This International Standard on Auditing (UK and Ireland) (ISA (UK and Ireland)) **1** deals with additional communication in the auditor's report when the auditor considers it necessary to:

(a) Draw users' attention to a matter or matters presented or disclosed in the financial statements that are of such importance that they are fundamental to users' understanding of the financial statements; or

(b) Draw users' attention to any matter or matters other than those presented or disclosed in the financial statements that are relevant to users' understanding of the audit, the auditor's responsibilities or the auditor's report.

Appendices 1 and 2 identify ISAs (UK and Ireland) that contain specific require- **2** ments for the auditor to include Emphasis of Matter paragraphs or Other Matter paragraphs in the auditor's report. In those circumstances, the requirements in this ISA regarding the form and placement of such paragraphs apply.

## Effective Date

This ISA (UK and Ireland) is effective for audits of financial statements for periods **3** ending on or after 15 December 2010.

# Objective

The objective of the auditor, having formed an opinion on the financial statements, is **4** to draw users' attention, when in the auditor's judgment it is necessary to do so, by way of clear additional communication in the auditor's report, to:

(a) A matter, although appropriately presented or disclosed in the financial statements, that is of such importance that it is fundamental to users' understanding of the financial statements; or

(b) As appropriate, any other matter that is relevant to users' understanding of the audit, the auditor's responsibilities or the auditor's report.

# Definitions

For the purposes of the ISAs (UK and Ireland), the following terms have the **5** meanings attributed below:

(a) Emphasis of Matter paragraph – A paragraph included in the auditor's report that refers to a matter appropriately presented or disclosed in the financial statements that, in the auditor's judgment, is of such importance that it is fundamental to users' understanding of the financial statements.

(b) Other Matter paragraph – A paragraph included in the auditor's report that refers to a matter other than those presented or disclosed in the financial statements that, in the auditor's judgment, is relevant to users' understanding of the audit, the auditor's responsibilities or the auditor's report.

# Requirements

## Emphasis of Matter Paragraphs in the Auditor's Report

6   If the auditor considers it necessary to draw users' attention to a matter presented or disclosed in the financial statements that, in the auditor's judgment, is of such importance that it is fundamental to users' understanding of the financial statements, the auditor shall include an Emphasis of Matter paragraph in the auditor's report provided the auditor has obtained sufficient appropriate audit evidence that the matter is not materially misstated in the financial statements[1a]. Such a paragraph shall refer only to information presented or disclosed in the financial statements. (Ref: Para. A1-A2)

7   When the auditor includes an Emphasis of Matter paragraph in the auditor's report, the auditor shall:

   (a)   Include it immediately after the Opinion on financial statements paragraph in the auditor's report;
   (b)   Use the heading "Emphasis of Matter," or other appropriate heading;
   (c)   Include in the paragraph a clear reference to the matter being emphasized and to where relevant disclosures that fully describe the matter can be found in the financial statements; and
   (d)   Indicate that the auditor's opinion is not modified in respect of the matter emphasized. (Ref: Para. A3-A4)

## Other Matter Paragraphs in the Auditor's Report

8   If the auditor considers it necessary to communicate a matter other than those that are presented or disclosed in the financial statements that, in the auditor's judgment, is relevant to users' understanding of the audit, the auditor's responsibilities or the auditor's report and this is not prohibited by law or regulation, the auditor shall do so in a paragraph in the auditor's report, with the heading "Other Matter," or other appropriate heading. The auditor shall include this paragraph immediately after the Opinion on financial statements paragraph and any Emphasis of Matter paragraph, or elsewhere in the auditor's report if the content of the Other Matter paragraph is relevant to the Other Reporting Responsibilities section. (Ref: Para. A5-A11)

## Communication with Those Charged with Governance

9   If the auditor expects to include an Emphasis of Matter or an Other Matter paragraph in the auditor's report, the auditor shall communicate with those charged with governance regarding this expectation and the proposed wording of this paragraph. (Ref: Para. A12)

\*\*\*

---

[1a] *Paragraph 19 of ISA (UK and Ireland) 570, "Going Concern," requires, where adequate disclosure is made in the financial statements, the auditor always include an Emphasis of Matter paragraph in the auditor's report to highlight the existence of a material uncertainty relating to an event or condition that may cast significant doubt on the entity's ability to continue as a going concern.*

# Application and Other Explanatory Material

## Emphasis of Matter Paragraphs in the Auditor's Report

*Circumstances in Which an Emphasis of Matter Paragraph May Be Necessary* (Ref: Para. 6)

Examples of circumstances where the auditor may consider it necessary to include an   **A1**
Emphasis of Matter paragraph are:

- An uncertainty relating to the future outcome of exceptional litigation or regulatory action.
- Early application (where permitted) of a new accounting standard (for example, a new International Financial Reporting Standard) that has a pervasive effect on the financial statements in advance of its effective date.
- A major catastrophe that has had, or continues to have, a significant effect on the entity's financial position.

A widespread use of Emphasis of Matter paragraphs diminishes the effectiveness of   **A2**
the auditor's communication of such matters. Additionally, to include more information in an Emphasis of Matter paragraph than is presented or disclosed in the financial statements may imply that the matter has not been appropriately presented or disclosed; accordingly, paragraph 6 limits the use of an Emphasis of Matter paragraph to matters presented or disclosed in the financial statements.

*Including an Emphasis of Matter Paragraph in the Auditor's Report* (Ref: Para. 7)

The inclusion of an Emphasis of Matter paragraph in the auditor's report does not   **A3**
affect the auditor's opinion. An Emphasis of Matter paragraph is not a substitute for either:

(a) The auditor expressing a qualified opinion or an adverse opinion, or disclaiming an opinion, when required by the circumstances of a specific audit engagement (see ISA (UK and Ireland) 705[1]); or
(b) Disclosures in the financial statements that the applicable financial reporting framework requires management to make.

The illustrative report in Appendix 3 includes an Emphasis of Matter paragraph in   **A4**
an auditor's report that contains a qualified opinion.

> With respect to companies, illustrative examples of auditor's reports tailored for use with audits conducted in accordance with ISAs (UK and Ireland) are given in the most recent versions of the APB Bulletins, "Auditor's Reports on Financial Statements in the United Kingdom"/"Auditor's Reports on Financial Statements in the Republic of Ireland." Illustrative examples for various other entities are give in other Bulletins and Practice Notes issued by the APB.

---

[1] *ISA (UK and Ireland) 705, "Modifications to the Opinion in the Independent Auditor's Report."*

## Other Matter Paragraphs in the Auditor's Report (Ref: Para. 8)

### *Circumstances in Which an Other Matter Paragraph May Be Necessary*

*Relevant to Users' Understanding of the Audit*

**A5**    In the rare circumstance where the auditor is unable to withdraw from an engagement even though the possible effect of an inability to obtain sufficient appropriate audit evidence due to a limitation on the scope of the audit imposed by management is pervasive,[2] the auditor may consider it necessary to include an Other Matter paragraph in the auditor's report to explain why it is not possible for the auditor to withdraw from the engagement.

*Relevant to Users' Understanding of the Auditor's Responsibilities or the Auditor's Report*

**A6**    Law, regulation or generally accepted practice in a jurisdiction may require or permit the auditor to elaborate on matters that provide further explanation of the auditor's responsibilities in the audit of the financial statements or of the auditor's report thereon. Where relevant, one or more sub-headings may be used that describe the content of the Other Matter paragraph.

**A7**    An Other Matter paragraph does not deal with circumstances where the auditor has other reporting responsibilities that are in addition to the auditor's responsibility under the ISAs (UK and Ireland) to report on the financial statements (see "Other Reporting Responsibilities" section in ISA (UK and Ireland) 700[3]), or where the auditor has been asked to perform and report on additional specified procedures, or to express an opinion on specific matters.

*Reporting on more than one set of financial statements*

**A8**    An entity may prepare one set of financial statements in accordance with a general purpose framework (e.g., the national framework) and another set of financial statements in accordance with another general purpose framework (e.g., International Financial Reporting Standards), and engage the auditor to report on both sets of financial statements. If the auditor has determined that the frameworks are acceptable in the respective circumstances, the auditor may include an Other Matter paragraph in the auditor's report, referring to the fact that another set of financial statements has been prepared by the same entity in accordance with another general purpose framework and that the auditor has issued a report on those financial statements.

**A8-1**    The situation described in paragraph A8 is differentiated from the requirement in paragraph 19 of ISA (UK and Ireland) 700 in that, in the latter case, the auditor is engaged to express in the same auditor's report an opinion on the compliance of the financial statements with an additional financial reporting framework. This latter situation only arises if the auditor is satisfied that there are no differences

---

[2] *See paragraph 13(b)(ii) of ISA (UK and Ireland) 705 for a discussion of this circumstance.*

[3] *ISA 700, "Forming an Opinion and Reporting on Financial Statements," paragraphs 38-39.*
*The APB has not promulgated ISA 700 as issued by the IAASB for application in the UK and Ireland. In the UK and Ireland the applicable auditing standard is ISA (UK and Ireland) 700, "The Auditor's Report on Financial Statements." Paragraphs 21 and 22 of ISA (UK and Ireland) 700 are the equivalent paragraphs to 38 -39 of ISA 700.*

between the two financial reporting frameworks that affect the financial statements being reported on.

*Restriction on distribution or use of the auditor's report*

Financial statements prepared for a specific purpose may be prepared in accordance with a general purpose framework because the intended users have determined that such general purpose financial statements meet their financial information needs. Since the auditor's report is intended for specific users, the auditor may consider it necessary in the circumstances to include an Other Matter paragraph, stating that the auditor's report is intended solely for the intended users, and should not be distributed to or used by other parties.   **A9**

### *Including an Other Matter Paragraph in the Auditor's Report*

The content of an Other Matter paragraph reflects clearly that such other matter is not required to be presented and disclosed in the financial statements. An Other Matter paragraph does not include information that the auditor is prohibited from providing by law, regulation or other professional standards, for example, ethical standards relating to confidentiality of information. An Other Matter paragraph also does not include information that is required to be provided by management.   **A10**

The placement of an Other Matter paragraph depends on the nature of the information to be communicated. When an Other Matter paragraph is included to draw users' attention to a matter relevant to their understanding of the audit of the financial statements, the paragraph is included immediately after the Opinion paragraph and any Emphasis of Matter paragraph. When an Other Matter paragraph is included to draw users' attention to a matter relating to Other Reporting Responsibilities addressed in the auditor's report, the paragraph may be included in the section sub-titled "Report on Other Legal and Regulatory Requirements." Alternatively, when relevant to all the auditor's responsibilities or users' understanding of the auditor's report, the Other Matter paragraph may be included as a separate section following the Report on the Financial Statements and the Report on Other Legal and Regulatory Requirements.   **A11**

## Communication with Those Charged with Governance (Ref. Para. 9)

Such communication enables those charged with governance to be made aware of the nature of any specific matters that the auditor intends to highlight in the auditor's report, and provides them with an opportunity to obtain further clarification from the auditor where necessary. Where the inclusion of an Other Matter paragraph on a particular matter in the auditor's report recurs on each successive engagement, the auditor may determine that it is unnecessary to repeat the communication on each engagement.   **A12**

## Appendix 1 (Ref: Para. 2)

## List of ISAs (UK and Ireland) Containing Requirements for Emphasis of Matter Paragraphs

This appendix identifies paragraphs in other ISAs (UK and Ireland) in effect for audits of financial statements for periods ending on or after 15 December 2010 that require the auditor to include an Emphasis of Matter paragraph in the auditor's report in certain circumstances. The list is not a substitute for considering the requirements and related application and other explanatory material in ISAs.

ISA (UK and Ireland) 210, "Agreeing the Terms of Audit Engagements" – paragraph 19(b)

ISA (UK and Ireland) 560, "Subsequent Events" – paragraphs 12(b) and 16

ISA (UK and Ireland) 570, "Going Concern" – paragraph 19

ISA 800[3a], "Special Considerations—Audits of Financial Statements Prepared in Accordance with Special Purpose Frameworks" – paragraph 14

---

[3a] *ISA 800 has not been promulgated by the APB for application in the UK and Ireland.*

## Appendix 2 (Ref: Para. 2)
# List of ISAs (UK and Ireland) Containing Requirements for Other Matter Paragraphs

This appendix identifies paragraphs in other ISAs (UK and Ireland) in effect for audits of financial statements for periods ending on or after 15 December 2010 that require the auditor to include an Other Matter paragraph in the auditor's report in certain circumstances. The list is not a substitute for considering the requirements and related application and other explanatory material in ISAs.

ISA (UK and Ireland) 560, "Subsequent Events" – paragraphs 12(b) and 16

ISA (UK and Ireland) 710, "Comparative Information—Corresponding Figures and Comparative Financial Statements" – paragraphs 13-14, 16-17 and 19

ISA (UK and Ireland) 720 Section A, "The Auditor's Responsibilities Relating to Other Information in Documents Containing Audited Financial Statements" – paragraph 10(a)

## Appendix 3 (Ref: Para. A4)

The examples in this Appendix have not been tailored for the UK and Ireland. With respect to companies, illustrative examples of auditor's reports tailored for use with audits conducted in accordance with ISAs (UK and Ireland) are given in the most recent versions of the APB Bulletins, "Auditor's Reports on Financial Statements in the United Kingdom"/"Auditor's Reports on Financial Statements in the Republic of Ireland." Illustrative examples for various other entities are give in other Bulletins and Practice Notes issued by the APB.

## Illustration of an Auditor's Report that Includes an Emphasis of Matter Paragraph

Circumstances include the following:

- **Audit of a complete set of general purpose financial statements prepared by management of the entity in accordance with International Financial Reporting Standards.**
- **The terms of the audit engagement reflect the description of management's responsibility for the financial statements in ISA 210.[4]**
- **There is uncertainty relating to a pending exceptional litigation matter.**
- **A departure from the applicable financial reporting framework resulted in a qualified opinion.**
- **In addition to the audit of the financial statements, the auditor has other reporting responsibilities required under local law.**

INDEPENDENT AUDITOR'S REPORT

[Appropriate Addressee]

**Report on the Financial Statements[5]**

We have audited the accompanying financial statements of ABC Company, which comprise the balance sheet as at December 31, 20X1, and the income statement, statement of changes in equity and cash flow statement for the year then ended, and a summary of significant accounting policies and other explanatory information.

*Management's[6] Responsibility for the Financial Statements*

Management is responsible for the preparation and fair presentation of these financial statements in accordance with International Financial Reporting Standards,[7] and for such internal control as management determines is necessary to

---

[4] *ISA 210, "Agreeing the Terms of Audit Engagements."*

[5] *The subtitle "Report on the Financial Statements" is unnecessary in circumstances when the second subtitle "Report on Other Legal and Regulatory Requirements" is not applicable.*

[6] *Or other term that is appropriate in the context of the legal framework in the particular jurisdiction.*

[7] *Where management's responsibility is to prepare financial statements that give a true and fair view, this may read: "Management is responsible for the preparation of financial statements that give a true and fair view in accordance with International Financial Reporting Standards, and for such ..."*

enable the preparation of financial statements that are free from material misstatement, whether due to fraud or error.

### Auditor's Responsibility

Our responsibility is to express an opinion on these financial statements based on our audit. We conducted our audit in accordance with International Standards on Auditing. Those standards require that we comply with ethical requirements and plan and perform the audit to obtain reasonable assurance about whether the financial statements are free from material misstatement.

An audit involves performing procedures to obtain audit evidence about the amounts and disclosures in the financial statements. The procedures selected depend on the auditor's judgment, including the assessment of the risks of material misstatement of the financial statements, whether due to fraud or error. In making those risk assessments, the auditor considers internal control relevant to the entity's preparation and fair presentation[8] of the financial statements in order to design audit procedures that are appropriate in the circumstances, but not for the purpose of expressing an opinion on the effectiveness of the entity's internal control.[9] An audit also includes evaluating the appropriateness of accounting policies used and the reasonableness of accounting estimates made by management, as well as evaluating the overall presentation of the financial statements.

We believe that the audit evidence that we have obtained is sufficient and appropriate to provide a basis for our qualified audit opinion.

### Basis for Qualified Opinion

The company's short-term marketable securities are carried in the balance sheet at xxx. Management has not marked these securities to market but has instead stated them at cost, which constitutes a departure from International Financial Reporting Standards. The company's records indicate that had management marked the marketable securities to market, the company would have recognized an unrealized loss of xxx in the income statement for the year. The carrying amount of the securities in the balance sheet would have been reduced by the same amount at December 31, 20X1, and income tax, net income and shareholders' equity would have been reduced by xxx, xxx and xxx, respectively.

### Qualified Opinion

In our opinion, except for the effects of the matter described in the Basis for Qualified Opinion paragraph, the financial statements present fairly, in all material respects (or *give a true and fair view of*) the financial position of ABC Company as at

---

[8] *In the case of footnote 7, this sentence may read: "In making those risk assessments, the auditor considers internal control relevant to the entity's preparation of financial statements that give a true and fair view in order to design audit procedures that are appropriate in the circumstances, but nor for the purpose of expressing an opinion on the effectiveness of the entity's internal control."*

[9] *In circumstances when the auditor also has responsibility to express an opinion on the effectiveness of internal control in conjunction with the audit of the financial statements, this sentence would be worded as follows: "In making those risk assessments, the auditor considers internal control relevant to the entity's preparation and fair presentation of the financial statements in order to design audit procedures that are appropriate in the circumstances." In the case of footnote 7, this may read: "In making those risk assessments, the auditor considers internal control relevant to the entity's preparation of financial statements that give a true and fair view in order to design audit procedures that are appropriate in the circumstances."*

December 31, 20X1, and (*of*) its financial performance and its cash flows for the year then ended in accordance with International Financial Reporting Standards.

### Emphasis of Matter

We draw attention to Note X to the financial statements which describes the uncertainty[10] related to the outcome of the lawsuit filed against the company by XYZ Company. Our opinion is not qualified in respect of this matter.

## Report on Other Legal and Regulatory Requirements

[Form and content of this section of the auditor's report will vary depending on the nature of the auditor's other reporting responsibilities.]

[Auditor's signature]

[Date of the auditor's report]

[Auditor's address]

---

[10] *In highlighting the uncertainty, the auditor uses the same terminology that is used in the note to the financial statements.*

# Addendum

*This addendum is provided for information and does not form part of the proposed clarified ISA (UK and Ireland) 706.*

*Proposed ISA (UK and Ireland) 706 addresses matters that are currently covered in ISA (UK and Ireland) 700. The APB is not proposing to add any supplementary requirements but is proposing a small amount of supplementary guidance, primarily to differentiate between the situation described in paragraph A8 and the requirement in paragraph 19 of proposed clarified ISA (UK and Ireland) 700 (see paragraph A8-1).*

# Proposed Clarified International Standard on Auditing (UK and Ireland) 710

## Comparative information – corresponding figures and comparative financial statements

*(Effective for audits of financial statements for periods ending on or after 15 December 2010)*

# Contents

International Standard on Auditing (UK and Ireland) (ISA (UK and Ireland)) 710, "Comparative Information—Corresponding Figures and Comparative Financial Statements" should be read in conjunction with ISA (UK and Ireland) 200, "Overall Objectives of the Independent Auditor and the Conduct of an Audit in Accordance with International Standards on Auditing (UK and Ireland)."

# Introduction

## Scope of this ISA (UK and Ireland)

This International Standard on Auditing (UK and Ireland) (ISA (UK and Ireland)) deals with the auditor's responsibilities relating to comparative information in an audit of financial statements. When the financial statements of the prior period have been audited by a predecessor auditor or were not audited, the requirements and guidance in ISA (UK and Ireland) 510[1] regarding opening balances also apply.   **1**

> ISA (UK and Ireland) 510 "Opening Balances" establishes standards and guidance regarding opening balances, including when the financial statements are audited by a continuing auditor.   **1-1**

## The Nature of Comparative Information

The nature of the comparative information that is presented in an entity's financial statements depends on the requirements of the applicable financial reporting framework. There are two different broad approaches to the auditor's reporting responsibilities in respect of such comparative information: corresponding figures and comparative financial statements. The approach to be adopted is often specified by law or regulation but may also be specified in the terms of engagement.   **2**

> In the UK and Ireland the corresponding figures method of presentation is usually required.   **2-1**

The essential audit reporting differences between the approaches are:   **3**

(a) For corresponding figures, the auditor's opinion on the financial statements refers to the current period only; whereas
(b) For comparative financial statements, the auditor's opinion refers to each period for which financial statements are presented.

This ISA (UK and Ireland) addresses separately the auditor's reporting requirements for each approach.

## Effective Date

This ISA (UK and Ireland) is effective for audits of financial statements for periods ending on or after 15 December 2010.   **4**

## Objectives

The objectives of the auditor are:   **5**

(a) To obtain sufficient appropriate audit evidence about whether the comparative information included in the financial statements has been presented, in all material respects, in accordance with the requirements for comparative information in the applicable financial reporting framework; and
(b) To report in accordance with the auditor's reporting responsibilities.

---

[1] *ISA (UK and Ireland) 510, "Initial Audit Engagements—Opening Balances."*

# Definitions

**6**    For purposes of the ISAs (UK and Ireland), the following terms have the meanings attributed below:

(a)   Comparative information – The amounts and disclosures included in the financial statements in respect of one or more prior periods in accordance with the applicable financial reporting framework.

(b)   Corresponding figures – Comparative information where amounts and other disclosures for the prior period are included as an integral part of the current period financial statements, and are intended to be read only in relation to the amounts and other disclosures relating to the current period (referred to as "current period figures"). The level of detail presented in the corresponding amounts and disclosures is dictated primarily by its relevance to the current period figures.

(c)   Comparative financial statements – Comparative information where amounts and other disclosures for the prior period are included for comparison with the financial statements of the current period but, if audited, are referred to in the auditor's opinion. The level of information included in those comparative financial statements is comparable with that of the financial statements of the current period.

For purposes of this ISA (UK and Ireland), references to "prior period" should be read as "prior periods" when the comparative information includes amounts and disclosures for more than one period.

# Requirements

## Audit Procedures

**7**    The auditor shall determine whether the financial statements include the comparative information required by the applicable financial reporting framework and whether such information is appropriately classified. For this purpose, the auditor shall evaluate whether:

(a)   The comparative information agrees with the amounts and other disclosures presented in the prior period or, when appropriate, have been restated; and

(b)   The accounting policies reflected in the comparative information are consistent with those applied in the current period or, if there have been changes in accounting policies, whether those changes have been properly accounted for and adequately presented and disclosed.

**8**    If the auditor becomes aware of a possible material misstatement in the comparative information while performing the current period audit, the auditor shall perform such additional audit procedures as are necessary in the circumstances to obtain sufficient appropriate audit evidence to determine whether a material misstatement exists. If the auditor had audited the prior period's financial statements, the auditor shall also follow the relevant requirements of ISA (UK and Ireland) 560.[2] If the prior period financial statements are amended, the auditor shall determine that the comparative information agrees with the amended financial statements.

**9**    As required by ISA (UK and Ireland) 580,[3] the auditor shall request written representations for all periods referred to in the auditor's opinion. The auditor shall also

---

[2] *ISA (UK and Ireland) 560, "Subsequent Events," paragraphs 14-17.*

[3] *ISA (UK and Ireland) 580, "Written Representations," paragraph 14.*

obtain a specific written representation regarding any restatement made to correct a material misstatement in prior period financial statements that affect the comparative information. (Ref: Para. A1)

## Audit Reporting

### *Corresponding Figures*

When corresponding figures are presented, the auditor's opinion shall not refer to the corresponding figures except in the circumstances described in paragraphs 11, 12, and 14. (Ref: Para. A2)   **10**

If the auditor's report on the prior period, as previously issued, included a qualified opinion, a disclaimer of opinion, or an adverse opinion and the matter which gave rise to the modification is unresolved, the auditor shall modify the auditor's opinion on the current period's financial statements. In the Basis for Modification paragraph in the auditor's report, the auditor shall either:   **11**

(a)  Refer to both the current period's figures and the corresponding figures in the description of the matter giving rise to the modification when the effects or possible effects of the matter on the current period's figures are material; or
(b)  In other cases, explain that the audit opinion has been modified because of the effects or possible effects of the unresolved matter on the comparability of the current period's figures and the corresponding figures. (Ref: Para. A3-A5)

If the auditor obtains audit evidence that a material misstatement exists in the prior period financial statements on which an unmodified opinion has been previously issued, and the corresponding figures have not been properly restated or appropriate disclosures have not been made, the auditor shall express a qualified opinion or an adverse opinion in the auditor's report on the current period financial statements, modified with respect to the corresponding figures included therein. (Ref: Para. A6)   **12**

### *Prior Period Financial Statements Audited by a Predecessor Auditor*

If the financial statements of the prior period were audited by a predecessor auditor and the auditor is not prohibited by law or regulation from referring to the predecessor auditor's report on the corresponding figures and decides to do so, the auditor shall state in an Other Matter paragraph in the auditor's report:   **13**

(a)  That the financial statements of the prior period were audited by the predecessor auditor;
(b)  The type of opinion expressed by the predecessor auditor and, if the opinion was modified, the reasons therefore; and
(c)  The date of that report. (Ref: Para. A7 – A7-2)

### *Prior Period Financial Statements Not Audited*

If the prior period financial statements were not audited, the auditor shall state in an Other Matter paragraph in the auditor's report that the corresponding figures are unaudited. Such a statement does not, however, relieve the auditor of the requirement to obtain sufficient appropriate audit evidence that the opening balances do not contain misstatements that materially affect the current period's financial statements.[4]   **14**

---

[4] *ISA (UK and Ireland) 510, paragraph 6.*

### Comparative Financial Statements

15    When comparative financial statements are presented, the auditor's opinion shall refer to each period for which financial statements are presented and on which an audit opinion is expressed. (Ref: Para. A8-A9)

16    When reporting on prior period financial statements in connection with the current period's audit, if the auditor's opinion on such prior period financial statements differs from the opinion the auditor previously expressed, the auditor shall disclose the substantive reasons for the different opinion in an Other Matter paragraph in accordance with ISA (UK and Ireland) 706.[5] (Ref: Para. A10)

### Prior Period Financial Statements Audited by a Predecessor Auditor

17    If the financial statements of the prior period were audited by a predecessor auditor, in addition to expressing an opinion on the current period's financial statements, the auditor shall state in an Other Matter paragraph:

(a)   That the financial statements of the prior period were audited by a predecessor auditor;

(b)   The type of opinion expressed by the predecessor auditor and, if the opinion was modified, the reasons therefore; and

(c)   The date of that report,
      unless the predecessor auditor's report on the prior period's financial statements is reissued with the financial statements.

18    If the auditor concludes that a material misstatement exists that affects the prior period financial statements on which the predecessor auditor had previously reported without modification, the auditor shall communicate the misstatement with the appropriate level of management and, unless all of those charged with governance are involved in managing the entity,[6] those charged with governance and request that the predecessor auditor be informed. If the prior period financial statements are amended, and the predecessor auditor agrees to issue a new auditor's report on the amended financial statements of the prior period, the auditor shall report only on the current period. (Ref: Para. A11)

### Prior Period Financial Statements Not Audited

19    If the prior period financial statements were not audited, the auditor shall state in an Other Matter paragraph that the comparative financial statements are unaudited. Such a statement does not, however, relieve the auditor of the requirement to obtain sufficient appropriate audit evidence that the opening balances do not contain misstatements that materially affect the current period's financial statements.[7]

***

[5] ISA (UK and Ireland) 706, "Emphasis of Matter Paragraphs and Other Matter Paragraphs in the Independent Auditor's Report," paragraph 8.

[6] ISA (UK and Ireland) 260, "Communication with Those Charged with Governance," paragraph 13.

[7] ISA (UK and Ireland) 510, paragraph 6.

# Application and Other Explanatory Material

## Audit Procedures

### Written Representations (Ref: Para. 9)

In the case of comparative financial statements, the written representations are **A1** requested for all periods referred to in the auditor's opinion because management needs to reaffirm that the written representations it previously made with respect to the prior period remain appropriate. In the case of corresponding figures, the written representations are requested for the financial statements of the current period only because the auditor's opinion is on those financial statements, which include the corresponding figures. However, the auditor requests a specific written representation regarding any restatement made to correct a material misstatement in the prior period financial statements that affect the comparative information.

## Audit Reporting

### Corresponding Figures

#### No Reference in Auditor's Opinion (Ref: Para. 10)

The auditor's opinion does not refer to the corresponding figures because the **A2** auditor's opinion is on the current period financial statements as a whole, including the corresponding figures.

#### Modification in Auditor's Report on the Prior Period Unresolved (Ref: Para. 11)

When the auditor's report on the prior period, as previously issued, included a **A3** qualified opinion, a disclaimer of opinion, or an adverse opinion and the matter which gave rise to the modified opinion is resolved and properly accounted for or disclosed in the financial statements in accordance with the applicable financial reporting framework, the auditor's opinion on the current period need not refer to the previous modification.

In some circumstances the auditor may consider it appropriate to qualify the **A3-1** audit opinion on the current period's financial statements. For example, if a provision which the auditor considered should have been made in the previous period is made in the current period.

When the auditor's opinion on the prior period, as previously expressed, was **A4** modified, the unresolved matter that gave rise to the modification may not be relevant to the current period figures. Nevertheless, a qualified opinion, a disclaimer of opinion, or an adverse opinion (as applicable) may be required on the current period's financial statements because of the effects or possible effects of the unresolved matter on the comparability of the current and corresponding figures.

Illustrative examples of the auditor's report if the auditor's report on the prior period **A5** included a modified opinion and the matter giving rise to the modification is unresolved are contained in Examples A and B of the Appendix.

With respect to companies, illustrative examples of auditor's reports tailored for use with audits conducted in accordance with ISAs (UK and Ireland) are given in the most recent versions of the APB Bulletins, "Auditor's Reports on Financial Statements in the United Kingdom"/"Auditor's Reports on Financial Statements in the Republic of Ireland." Illustrative examples for various other entities are give in other Bulletins and Practice Notes issued by the APB.

*Misstatement in Prior Period Financial Statements (Ref: Para. 12)*

**A6**   When the prior period financial statements that are misstated have not been amended and an auditor's report has not been reissued, but the corresponding figures have been properly restated or appropriate disclosures have been made in the current period financial statements, the auditor's report may include an Emphasis of Matter paragraph describing the circumstances and referring to, where relevant, disclosures that fully describe the matter that can be found in the financial statements (see ISA (UK and Ireland) 706).

*Prior Period Financial Statements Audited by a Predecessor Auditor* (Ref: Para. 13)

**A7**   An illustrative example of the auditor's report if the prior period financial statements were audited by a predecessor auditor and the auditor is not prohibited by law or regulation from referring to the predecessor auditor's report on the corresponding figures is contained in Example C of the Appendix.

With respect to companies, illustrative examples of auditor's reports tailored for use with audits conducted in accordance with ISAs (UK and Ireland) are given in the most recent versions of the APB Bulletins, "Auditor's Reports on Financial Statements in the United Kingdom"/"Auditor's Reports on Financial Statements in the Republic of Ireland." Illustrative examples for various other entities are give in other Bulletins and Practice Notes issued by the APB.

**A7-1**   In the UK and Ireland the incoming auditor does not refer to the predecessor auditor's report on the corresponding figures in the incoming auditor's report for the current period. The incoming auditor assumes audit responsibility for the corresponding figures only in the context of the financial statements as a whole. The incoming auditor reads the preceding period's financial statements and, using the knowledge gained during the current audit, considers whether they have been properly reflected as corresponding figures in the current period's financial statements.

**A7-2**   Although the incoming auditor is not required to re-audit the financial statements of the preceding period, if the incoming auditor becomes aware of a possible material misstatement of corresponding figures, the requirement and guidance in paragraphs 12 and A6 apply.

### Comparative Financial Statements

*Reference in Auditor's Opinion (Ref: Para. 15)*

**A8**   Because the auditor's report on comparative financial statements applies to the financial statements for each of the periods presented, the auditor may express a qualified opinion or an adverse opinion, disclaim an opinion, or include an Emphasis of Matter paragraph with respect to one or more periods, while expressing a different auditor's opinion on the financial statements of the other period.

An illustrative example of the auditor's report if the auditor is required to report on both the current and the prior period financial statements in connection with the current year's audit and the prior period included a modified opinion and the matter giving rise to the modification is unresolved, is contained in Example D of the Appendix. **A9**

> With respect to companies, illustrative examples of auditor's reports tailored for use with audits conducted in accordance with ISAs (UK and Ireland) are given in the most recent versions of the APB Bulletins, "Auditor's Reports on Financial Statements in the United Kingdom"/"Auditor's Reports on Financial Statements in the Republic of Ireland." Illustrative examples for various other entities are give in other Bulletins and Practice Notes issued by the APB.

*Opinion on Prior Period Financial Statements Different from Previous Opinion (Ref: Para. 16)*

When reporting on the prior period financial statements in connection with the current period's audit, the opinion expressed on the prior period financial statements may be different from the opinion previously expressed if the auditor becomes aware of circumstances or events that materially affect the financial statements of a prior period during the course of the audit of the current period. In some jurisdictions, the auditor may have additional reporting responsibilities designed to prevent future reliance on the auditor's previously issued report on the prior period financial statements. **A10**

*Prior Period Financial Statements Audited by a Predecessor Auditor (Ref: Para. 18)*

The predecessor auditor may be unable or unwilling to reissue the auditor's report on the prior period financial statements. An Other Matter paragraph of the auditor's report may indicate that the predecessor auditor reported on the financial statements of the prior period before amendment. In addition, if the auditor is engaged to audit and obtains sufficient appropriate audit evidence to be satisfied as to the appropriateness of the amendment, the auditor's report may also include the following paragraph: **A11**

> As part of our audit of the 20X2 financial statements, we also audited the adjustments described in Note X that were applied to amend the 20X1 financial statements. In our opinion, such adjustments are appropriate and have been properly applied. We were not engaged to audit, review, or apply any procedures to the 20X1 financial statements of the company other than with respect to the adjustments and, accordingly, we do not express an opinion or any other form of assurance on the 20X1 financial statements taken as a whole.

# Appendix

# Example Auditors' Reports

These examples have not been tailored for the UK and Ireland. With respect to companies, illustrative examples of auditor's reports tailored for use with audits conducted in accordance with ISAs (UK and Ireland) are given in the most recent versions of the APB Bulletins, "Auditor's Reports on Financial Statements in the United Kingdom"/"Auditor's Reports on Financial Statements in the Republic of Ireland." Illustrative examples for various other entities are give in other Bulletins and Practice Notes issued by the APB.

## Example A – Corresponding Figures (Ref: Para. A5)

Report illustrative of the circumstances described in paragraph 11(a), as follows:

- The auditor's report on the prior period, as previously issued, included a qualified opinion.
- The matter giving rise to the modification is unresolved.
- The effects or possible effects of the matter on the current period's figures are material and require a modification to the auditor's opinion regarding the current period figures.

INDEPENDENT AUDITOR'S REPORT

[Appropriate Addressee]

## Report on the Financial Statements[8]

We have audited the accompanying financial statements of ABC Company, which comprise the balance sheet as at December 31, 20X1, and the income statement, statement of changes in equity and cash flow statement for the year then ended, and a summary of significant accounting policies and other explanatory information.

### *Management's[9] Responsibility for the Financial Statements*

Management is responsible for the preparation and fair presentation of these financial statements in accordance with International Financial Reporting Standards,[10] and for such internal control as management determines is necessary to enable the preparation of financial statements that are free from material misstatement, whether due to fraud or error.

---

[8] *The sub-title "Report on the Financial Statements" is unnecessary in circumstances when the second sub-title "Report on Other Legal and Regulatory Requirements" is not applicable.*

[9] *Or other term that is appropriate in the context of the legal framework in the particular jurisdiction.*

[10] *Where management's responsibility is to prepare financial statements that give a true and fair view, this may read: "Management is responsible for the preparation of financial statements that give a true and fair view in accordance with International Financial Reporting Standards, and for such ..."*

## Auditor's Responsibility

Our responsibility is to express an opinion on these financial statements based on our audit. We conducted our audit in accordance with International Standards on Auditing. Those standards require that we comply with ethical requirements and plan and perform the audit to obtain reasonable assurance about whether the financial statements are free from material misstatement.

An audit involves performing procedures to obtain audit evidence about the amounts and disclosures in the financial statements. The procedures selected depend on the auditor's judgment, including the assessment of the risks of material misstatement of the financial statements, whether due to fraud or error. In making those risk assessments, the auditor considers internal control relevant to the entity's preparation and fair presentation[11] of the financial statements in order to design audit procedures that are appropriate in the circumstances, but not for the purpose of expressing an opinion on the effectiveness of the entity's internal control.[12] An audit also includes evaluating the appropriateness of accounting policies used and the reasonableness of accounting estimates made by management, as well as evaluating the overall presentation of the financial statements.

We believe that the audit evidence we have obtained is sufficient and appropriate to provide a basis for our qualified audit opinion.

## Basis for Qualified Opinion

As discussed in Note X to the financial statements, no depreciation has been provided in the financial statements, which constitutes a departure from International Financial Reporting Standards. This is the result of a decision taken by management at the start of the preceding financial year and caused us to qualify our audit opinion on the financial statements relating to that year. Based on the straight-line method of depreciation and annual rates of 5% for the building and 20% for the equipment, the loss for the year should be increased by xxx in 20X1 and xxx in 20X0, property, plant and equipment should be reduced by accumulated depreciation of xxx in 20X1 and xxx in 20X0, and the accumulated loss should be increased by xxx in 20X1 and xxx in 20X0.

## Qualified Opinion

In our opinion, except for the effects of the matter described in the Basis for Qualified Opinion paragraph, the financial statements present fairly, in all material respects, (or *give a true and fair view of*) the financial position of ABC Company as at December 31, 20X1, and (*of*) its financial performance and its cash flows for the year then ended in accordance with International Financial Reporting Standards.

[11] *In the case of footnote 10, this may read: "In making those risk assessments, the auditor considers internal control relevant to the entity's preparation of financial statements that give a true and fair view in order to design audit procedures that are appropriate in the circumstances, but not for the purpose of expressing an opinion on the effectiveness of the entity's internal control."*

[12] *In circumstances when the auditor also has responsibility to express an opinion on the effectiveness of internal control in conjunction with the audit of the financial statements, this sentence would be worded as follows: "In making those risk assessments, the auditor considers internal control relevant to the entity's preparation and fair presentation of the financial statements in order to design audit procedures that are appropriate in the circumstances." In the case of footnote 10, this may read: "In making those risk assessments, the auditor considers internal control relevant to the entity's preparation of financial statements that give a true and fair view in order to design audit procedures that are appropriate in the circumstances."*

**Report on Other Legal and Regulatory Requirements**

[Form and content of this section of the auditor's report will vary depending on the nature of the auditor's other reporting responsibilities.]

[Auditor's signature]

[Date of the auditor's report]

[Auditor's address]

## Example B – Corresponding Figures (Ref: Para. A5)

---

**Report illustrative of the circumstances described in paragraph 11(b), as follows:**

- The auditor's report on the prior period, as previously issued, included a qualified opinion.
- The matter giving rise to the modification is unresolved.
- The effects or possible effects of the matter on the current period's figures are immaterial but require a modification to the auditor's opinion because of the effects or possible effects of the unresolved matter on the comparability of the current period's figures and the corresponding figures.

---

### INDEPENDENT AUDITOR'S REPORT

[Appropriate Addressee]

#### Report on the Financial Statements[13]

We have audited the accompanying financial statements of ABC Company, which comprise the balance sheet as at December 31, 20X1, and the income statement, statement of changes in equity and cash flow statement for the year then ended, and a summary of significant accounting policies and other explanatory information.

#### *Management's[14] Responsibility for the Financial Statements*

Management is responsible for the preparation and fair presentation of these financial statements in accordance with International Financial Reporting Standards,[15] and for such internal control as management determines is necessary to enable the preparation of financial statements that are free from material misstatement, whether due to fraud or error.

#### *Auditor's Responsibility*

Our responsibility is to express an opinion on these financial statements based on our audit. We conducted our audit in accordance with International Standards on Auditing. Those standards require that we comply with ethical requirements and plan and perform the audit to obtain reasonable assurance about whether the financial statements are free from material misstatement.

An audit involves performing procedures to obtain audit evidence about the amounts and disclosures in the financial statements. The procedures selected depend on the auditor's judgment, including the assessment of the risks of material

---

[13] *The sub-title "Report on the Financial Statements" is unnecessary in circumstances when the second sub-title "Report on Other Legal and Regulatory Requirements" is not applicable.*

[14] *Or other term that is appropriate in the context of the legal framework in the particular jurisdiction.*

[15] *Where management's responsibility is to prepare financial statements that give a true and fair view, this may read: "Management is responsible for the preparation of financial statements that give a true and fair view in accordance with International Financial Reporting Standards, and for such ..."*

misstatement of the financial statements, whether due to fraud or error. In making those risk assessments, the auditor considers internal control relevant to the entity's preparation and fair presentation[16] of the financial statements in order to design audit procedures that are appropriate in the circumstances, but not for the purpose of expressing an opinion on the effectiveness of the entity's internal control.[17] An audit also includes evaluating the appropriateness of accounting policies used and the reasonableness of accounting estimates made by management, as well as evaluating the overall presentation of the financial statements.

We believe that the audit evidence we have obtained is sufficient and appropriate to provide a basis for our qualified audit opinion.

### Basis for Qualified Opinion

Because we were appointed auditors of ABC Company during 20X0, we were not able to observe the counting of the physical inventories at the beginning of that period or satisfy ourselves concerning those inventory quantities by alternative means. Since opening inventories affect the determination of the results of operations, we were unable to determine whether adjustments to the results of operations and opening retained earnings might be necessary for 20X0. Our audit opinion on the financial statements for the period ended December 31, 20X0 was modified accordingly. Our opinion on the current period's financial statements is also modified because of the possible effect of this matter on the comparability of the current period's figures and the corresponding figures.

### Qualified Opinion

In our opinion, except for the possible effects on the corresponding figures of the matter described in the Basis for Qualified Opinion paragraph, the financial statements present fairly, in all material respects, (or *give a true and fair view of*) the financial position of ABC Company as at December 31, 20X1, and (*of*) its financial performance and its cash flows for the year then ended in accordance with International Financial Reporting Standards.

## Report on Other Legal and Regulatory Requirements

[Form and content of this section of the auditor's report will vary depending on the nature of the auditor's other reporting responsibilities.]

[Auditor's signature]

[Date of the auditor's report]

[Auditor's address]

---

[16] *In the case of footnote 15, this may read: "In making those risk assessments, the auditor considers internal control relevant to the entity's preparation of financial statements that give a* true and fair view in order to design audit procedures that are appropriate in the circumstances, but not for the purpose of expressing an opinion on the effectiveness of the entity's internal control."

[17] *In circumstances when the auditor also has responsibility to express an opinion on the effectiveness of internal control in conjunction with the audit of the financial statements, this sentence would be worded as follows: "In making those risk assessments, the auditor considers internal control relevant to the entity's preparation and fair presentation of the financial statements in order to design audit procedures that are appropriate in the circumstances." In the case of footnote 15, this may read: "In making those risk assessments, the auditor considers internal control relevant to the entity's preparation of financial statements that give a true and fair view in order to design audit procedures that are appropriate in the circumstances."*

## Example C – Corresponding Figures: (Ref: Para. A7)

> **Report illustrative of the circumstances described in paragraph 13, as follows:**
> - **The prior period's financial statements were audited by a predecessor auditor.**
> - **The auditor is not prohibited by law or regulation from referring to the predecessor auditor's report on the corresponding figures and decides to do so.**

INDEPENDENT AUDITOR'S REPORT

[Appropriate Addressee]

### Report on the Financial Statements[18]

We have audited the accompanying financial statements of ABC Company, which comprise the balance sheet as at December 31, 20X1, and the income statement, statement of changes in equity and cash flow statement for the year then ended, and a summary of significant accounting policies and other explanatory information.

### Management's[19] Responsibility for the Financial Statements

Management is responsible for the preparation and fair presentation of these financial statements in accordance with International Financial Reporting Standards,[20] and for such internal control as management determines is necessary to enable the preparation of financial statements that are free from material misstatement, whether due to fraud or error.

### Auditor's Responsibility

Our responsibility is to express an opinion on these financial statements based on our audit. We conducted our audit in accordance with International Standards on Auditing. Those standards require that we comply with ethical requirements and plan and perform the audit to obtain reasonable assurance about whether the financial statements are free from material misstatement.

An audit involves performing procedures to obtain audit evidence about the amounts and disclosures in the financial statements. The procedures selected depend on the auditor's judgment, including the assessment of the risks of material misstatement of the financial statements, whether due to fraud or error. In making those risk assessments, the auditor considers internal control relevant to the entity's preparation and fair presentation[21] of the financial statements in order to design audit procedures that are appropriate in the circumstances, but not for the purpose of

---

[18] *The sub-title "Report on the Financial Statements" is unnecessary in circumstances when the second sub-title "Report on Other Legal and Regulatory Requirements" is not applicable.*

[19] *Or other term that is appropriate in the context of the legal framework in the particular jurisdiction.*

[20] *Where management's responsibility is to prepare financial statements that give a true and fair view, this may read: "Management is responsible for the preparation of financial statements that give a true and fair view in accordance with International Financial Reporting Standards, and for such ..."*

[21] *In the case of footnote 20, this may read: "In making those risk assessments, the auditor considers internal control relevant to the entity's preparation of financial statements that give a true and fair view in order to design audit procedures that are appropriate in the circumstances, but not for the purpose of expressing an opinion on the effectiveness of the entity's internal control."*

expressing an opinion on the effectiveness of the entity's internal control.[22] An audit also includes evaluating the appropriateness of accounting policies used and the reasonableness of accounting estimates made by management, as well as evaluating the overall presentation of the financial statements.

We believe that the audit evidence we have obtained is sufficient and appropriate to provide a basis for our audit opinion.

### Opinion

In our opinion, the financial statements present fairly, in all material respects, (or *give a true and fair view of*) the financial position of ABC Company as at December 31, 20X1, and (*of*) its financial performance and its cash flows for the year then ended in accordance with International Financial Reporting Standards.

### Other Matter

The financial statements of ABC Company for the year ended December 31, 20X0, were audited by another auditor who expressed an unmodified opinion on those statements on March 31, 20X1.

## Report on Other Legal and Regulatory Requirements

[Form and content of this section of the auditor's report will vary depending on the nature of the auditor's other reporting responsibilities.]

[Auditor's signature]

[Date of the auditor's report]

[Auditor's address]

---

[22] *In circumstances when the auditor also has responsibility to express an opinion on the effectiveness of internal control in conjunction with the audit of the financial statements, this sentence would be worded as follows: "In making those risk assessments, the auditor considers internal control relevant to the entity's preparation and fair presentation of the financial statements in order to design audit procedures that are appropriate in the circumstances." In the case of footnote 20, this may read: "In making those risk assessments, the auditor considers internal control relevant to the entity's preparation and presentation of financial statements that give a true and fair view in order to design audit procedures that are appropriate in the circumstances."*

## Example D – Comparative Financial Statements: (Ref: Para. A9)

> **Report illustrative of the circumstances described in paragraph 15, as follows:**
>
> - **Auditor is required to report on both the current period financial statements and the prior period financial statements in connection with the current year's audit.**
> - **The auditor's report on the prior period, as previously issued, included a qualified opinion.**
> - **The matter giving rise to the modification is unresolved.**
> - **The effects or possible effects of the matter on the current period's figures are material to both the current period financial statements and prior period financial statements and require a modification to the auditor's opinion.**

INDEPENDENT AUDITOR'S REPORT

[Appropriate Addressee]

### Report on the Financial Statements[23]

We have audited the accompanying financial statements of ABC Company, which comprise the balance sheets as at December 31, 20X1 and 20X0, and the income statements, statements of changes in equity and cash flow statements for the years then ended, and a summary of significant accounting policies and other explanatory information.

### *Management's[24] Responsibility for the Financial Statements*

Management is responsible for the preparation and fair presentation of these financial statements in accordance with International Financial Reporting Standards,[25] and for such internal control as management determines is necessary to enable the preparation of financial statements that are free from material misstatement, whether due to fraud or error.

### *Auditor's Responsibility*

Our responsibility is to express an opinion on these financial statements based on our audits. We conducted our audits in accordance with International Standards on Auditing. Those standards require that we comply with ethical requirements and plan and perform the audit to obtain reasonable assurance about whether the financial statements are free from material misstatement.

An audit involves performing procedures to obtain audit evidence about the amounts and disclosures in the financial statements. The procedures selected depend on the auditor's judgment, including the assessment of the risks of material misstatement of the financial statements, whether due to fraud or error. In making those risk assessments, the auditor considers internal control relevant to the entity's

---

[23] *The sub-title "Report on the Financial Statements" is unnecessary in circumstances when the second sub-title "Report on Other Legal and Regulatory Requirements" is not applicable.*

[24] *Or other term that is appropriate in the context of the legal framework in the particular jurisdiction.*

[25] *Where management's responsibility is to prepare financial statements that give a true and fair view, this may read: "Management is responsible for the preparation of financial statements that give a true and fair view in accordance with International Financial Reporting Standards, and for such ..."*

preparation and fair presentation[26] of the financial statements in order to design audit procedures that are appropriate in the circumstances, but not for the purpose of expressing an opinion on the effectiveness of the entity's internal control.[27] An audit also includes evaluating the appropriateness of accounting policies used and the reasonableness of accounting estimates made by management, as well as evaluating the overall presentation of the financial statements.

We believe that the audit evidence we have obtained in our audits is sufficient and appropriate to provide a basis for our qualified audit opinion.

### Basis for Qualified Opinion

As discussed in Note X to the financial statements, no depreciation has been provided in the financial statements, which constitutes a departure from International Financial Reporting Standards. Based on the straight-line method of depreciation and annual rates of 5% for the building and 20% for the equipment, the loss for the year should be increased by xxx in 20X1 and xxx in 20X0, property, plant and equipment should be reduced by accumulated depreciation of xxx in 20X1 and xxx in 20X0, and the accumulated loss should be increased by xxx in 20X1 and xxx in 20X0.

### Qualified Opinion

In our opinion, except for the effects of the matter described in the Basis for Qualified Opinion paragraph, the financial statements present fairly, in all material respects, (or *give a true and fair view of*) the financial position of ABC Company as at December 31, 20X1 and 20X0 and (*of*) its financial performance and its cash flows for the years then ended in accordance with International Financial Reporting Standards.

## Report on Other Legal and Regulatory Requirements

[Form and content of this section of the auditor's report will vary depending on the nature of the auditor's other reporting responsibilities.]

[Auditor's signature]

[Date of the auditor's report]

[Auditor's address]

---

[26] In the case of footnote 25, this sentence may read: "In making those risk assessments, the auditor considers internal control relevant to the entity's preparation of financial statements that give a true and fair view in order to design audit procedures that are appropriate in the circumstances, but not for the purpose of expressing an opinion on the effectiveness of the entity's internal control."

[27] In circumstances when the auditor also has responsibility to express an opinion on the effectiveness of internal control in conjunction with the audit of the financial statements, this sentence would be worded as follows: "In making those risk assessments, the auditor considers internal control relevant to the entity's preparation and fair presentation of the financial statements in order to design audit procedures that are appropriate in the circumstances." In the case of footnote 25, this sentence may read: "In making those risk assessments, the auditor considers internal control relevant to the entity's preparation of financial statements that give a true and fair view in order to design audit procedures that are appropriate in the circumstances."

# Addendum

*This addendum provides a summary of APB's rationale for retaining or excluding in the proposed clarified ISA (UK and Ireland) the supplementary requirements in the existing ISA (UK and Ireland). It also sets out the supplementary guidance material in the existing ISA (UK and Ireland) that APB considers is not necessary to retain in light of the improvements in the underlying Clarity ISAs issued by the IAASB as part of the Clarity Project. It is provided for information and does not form part of the proposed clarified ISA (UK and Ireland).*

*The Consultation Paper published with the exposure drafts explains the general approach used by the APB for determining whether current supplementary material should be proposed to be retained.*

## Analysis of proposed treatment of current APB supplementary material in current ISA (UK and Ireland) 710

## Requirements

| APB supplementary requirements (*Italic text is from IAASB for context*) | Is it covered in substance in the Clarity ISA? | Should it be retained? |
|---|---|---|
| 2-1. **The auditor should obtain sufficient appropriate audit evidence that amounts derived from the preceding period's financial statements are free from material misstatements and are appropriately incorporated in the financial statements for the current period.** | ✓ This is covered by the objective of the standard (5(a)). <br><br> Further, the scope of proposed clarified ISA (UK and Ireland) 510 has been extended to all audits (as for the current ISA (UK and Ireland) 510) to require the auditor to obtain sufficient appropriate evidence in relation to opening balances. | ✗ |
| 6-1. **In the UK and Ireland, the auditor should obtain sufficient appropriate audit evidence that:** | The ISA requirement is to "determine" whether information required by the framework is included appropriately by "evaluating" particular matters. | |
| (a) **The accounting policies used for the corresponding amounts are consistent with those of the current period and appropriate adjustments and disclosures have been made where this is not the case;** | ✓ 7(b), 8 | ✗ |

| APB supplementary requirements (*Italic text is from IAASB for context*) | Is it covered in substance in the Clarity ISA? | Should it be retained? |
|---|---|---|
| (b) The corresponding amounts agree with the amounts and other disclosures presented in the preceding period and are free from errors in the context of the financial statements of the current period; and | ✓ 7(a), 8 | ✗ |
| (c) Where corresponding amounts have been adjusted as required by relevant legislation and accounting standards, appropriate disclosures have been made. | ✓ 7(b) | ✗ |

## Guidance

The following guidance in current ISA (UK and Ireland) 710 has not been carried forward to the proposed clarified standard.

| Current paragraph reference (*Italic text is from IAASB for context*) |
|---|
| 1-1. – 1-4. [Definitions of management and those charged with governance.] |
| [Prior period qualified, matter unresolved but does not affect current period] 12-1. With respect to situations described in 12(b), if corresponding amounts are required by law or regulation, the reference is in the form of a qualification on the grounds of non-compliance with that requirement. If corresponding amounts are presented solely as good practice, the reference is made in the auditor's report in the form of an explanatory paragraph |
| [Prior period not audited] 18-1. If the auditor is not able to obtain sufficient appropriate audit evidence regarding the corresponding figures, or if there is not adequate disclosure, the auditor considers the implications for the auditor's report. |
| 19. *In situations where the incoming auditor identifies that the corresponding figures are materially misstated, the auditor should request management[1a] to revise the corresponding figures or if management refuses to do so, appropriately modify the report.* |

[1a] In The UK and Ireland, those charged with governance are responsible for the preparation of the financial statements.

# Proposed Clarified International Standard on Auditing (UK and Ireland) 720

## Section A – The auditor's responsibilities relating to other information in documents containing audited financial statements

*(Effective for audits of financial statements for periods ending on or after 15 December 2010)*

## Contents

International Standard on Auditing (UK and Ireland) (ISA (UK and Ireland)) 720 Section A, "The Auditor's Responsibilities Relating to Other Information in Documents Containing Audited Financial Statements" should be read in conjunction with ISA (UK and Ireland) 200, "Overall Objectives of the Independent Auditor and the Conduct of an Audit in Accordance with International Standards on Auditing (UK and Ireland)."

# Introduction

### Scope of this ISA (UK and Ireland)

1   This International Standard on Auditing (UK and Ireland) (ISA (UK and Ireland)) deals with the auditor's responsibilities relating to other information in documents containing audited financial statements and the auditor's report thereon. In the absence of any separate requirement in the particular circumstances of the engagement, the auditor's opinion does not cover other information and the auditor has no specific responsibility for determining whether or not other information is properly stated. However, the auditor reads the other information because the credibility of the audited financial statements may be undermined by material inconsistencies between the audited financial statements and other information. (Ref: Para. A1)

1-1   The standards and guidance in this Section apply to all other information included in documents containing audited financial statements, including the directors' report. Further standards and guidance on the auditor's statutory reporting obligations in relation to directors' reports are set out in Section B.

2   In this ISA (UK and Ireland) "documents containing audited financial statements" refers to annual reports (or similar documents), that are issued to owners (or similar stakeholders), containing audited financial statements and the auditor's report thereon. This ISA (UK and Ireland) may also be applied, adapted as necessary in the circumstances, to other documents containing audited financial statements, such as those used in securities offerings.[1] (Ref: Para. A2)

### Effective Date

3   This ISA (UK and Ireland) is effective for audits of financial statements for periods ending on or after 15 December 2010

# Objective

4   The objective of the auditor is to respond appropriately when documents containing audited financial statements and the auditor's report thereon include other information that could undermine the credibility of those financial statements and the auditor's report.

---

[1] See ISA (UK and Ireland) 200, "Overall Objectives of the Independent Auditor and the Conduct of an Audit in Accordance with International Standards on Auditing," paragraph 2.
Paragraph 2 of ISA (UK and Ireland) 200 includes the statement that "ISAs (UK and Ireland) do not address the responsibilities of the auditor that may exist in legislation, regulation or otherwise in connection with, for example, the offering of securities to the public. Such responsibilities may differ from those established in the ISAs (UK and Ireland). Accordingly, while the auditor may find aspects of the ISAs (UK and Ireland) helpful in such circumstances, it is the responsibility of the auditor to ensure compliance with all relevant legal, regulatory or professional obligations." Guidance on other information issued with investment circulars is covered in the APB's Statement of Investment Reporting Standard (SIR) 1000. Accordingly, the guidance in this ISA (UK and Ireland) is limited to Annual Reports and statutory audits.

# Definitions

For purposes of the ISAs (UK and Ireland) the following terms have the meanings attributed below:    **5**

(a) Other information – Financial and non-financial information (other than the financial statements and the auditor's report thereon) which is included, either by law, regulation or custom, in a document containing audited financial statements and the auditor's report thereon. (Ref: Para. A3-A4)
(b) Inconsistency – Other information that contradicts information contained in the audited financial statements. A material inconsistency may raise doubt about the audit conclusions drawn from audit evidence previously obtained and, possibly, about the basis for the auditor's opinion on the financial statements.
(c) Misstatement of fact – Other information that is unrelated to matters appearing in the audited financial statements that is incorrectly stated or presented. A material misstatement of fact may undermine the credibility of the document containing audited financial statements.

# Requirements

## Reading Other Information

The auditor shall read the other information to identify material inconsistencies, if any, with the audited financial statements. (Ref: Para. A4-1 – A4-2)    **6**

The auditor shall make appropriate arrangements with management or those charged with governance to obtain the other information prior to the date of the auditor's report. If it is not possible to obtain all the other information prior to the date of the auditor's report, the auditor shall read such other information as soon as practicable[1a]. (Ref: Para. A5)    **7**

## Material Inconsistencies

If, on reading the other information, the auditor identifies a material inconsistency, the auditor shall determine whether the audited financial statements or the other information needs to be revised.    **8**

### Material Inconsistencies Identified in Other Information Obtained Prior to the Date of the Auditor's Report

If revision of the audited financial statements is necessary and management[1b] refuses to make the revision, the auditor shall modify the opinion in the auditor's report in accordance with ISA (UK and Ireland) 705.[2]    **9**

---

[1a] *ISA (UK and Ireland) 700 requires that "The auditor shall not sign, and hence date, the report earlier than the date on which all other information contained in a report of which the audited financial statements form a part have been approved by those charged with governance and the auditor has considered all necessary available evidence."*

[1b] *In the UK and Ireland those charged with governance are responsible for the preparation of the financial statements.*

[2] *ISA (UK and Ireland) 705, "Modifications to the Opinion in the Independent Auditor's Report."*

**10**   If revision of the other information is necessary and management refuses to make the revision, the auditor shall communicate this matter to those charged with governance, unless all of those charged with governance are involved in managing the entity[3]; and

   (a)   Include in the auditor's report an Other Matter(s) paragraph describing the material inconsistency in accordance with ISA (UK and Ireland) 706;[4] or
   (b)   Withhold the auditor's report; or
   (c)   Withdraw from the engagements, where withdrawal is possible under applicable law or regulation. (Ref: Para. A6-A7)

*Material Inconsistencies Identified in Other Information Obtained Subsequent to the Date of the Auditor's Report*

> *Paragraphs 11 to 13 deal with other information obtained subsequent to the date of the auditor's report. These are not applicable in an audit conducted in accordance with ISAs (UK and Ireland) because ISA (UK and Ireland) 700, "The Auditor's Report on Financial Statements" requires that "The auditor shall not sign, and hence date, the report earlier than the date on which all other information contained in a report of which the audited financial statements forma part have been approved by those charged with governance and the auditor has considered all necessary available evidence."*

**11**   *If revision of the audited financial statements is necessary, the auditor shall follow the relevant requirements in ISA (UK and Ireland) 560.[5]*

**12**   *If revision of the other information is necessary and management agrees to make the revision, the auditor shall carry out the procedures necessary under the circumstances. (Ref: Para. A8)*

**13**   *If revision of the other information is necessary, but management refuses to make the revision, the auditor shall notify those charged with governance, unless all of those charged with governance are involved in managing the entity, of the auditor's concern regarding the other information and take any further appropriate action. (Ref: Para. A9)*

## Material Misstatements of Fact

**14**   If, on reading the other information for the purpose of identifying material inconsistencies, the auditor becomes aware of an apparent material misstatement of fact, the auditor shall discuss the matter with management. (Ref: Para. A10)

**15**   If, following such discussions, the auditor still considers that there is an apparent material misstatement of fact, the auditor shall request management to consult with a qualified third party, such as the entity's legal counsel, and the auditor shall consider the advice received.

[3] *ISA (UK and Ireland) 260, "Communication with Those Charged with Governance," paragraph 13.*

[4] *ISA (UK and Ireland) 706, "Emphasis of Matter Paragraphs and Other Matter Paragraphs in the Independent Auditor's Report," paragraph 8.*

[5] *ISA (UK and Ireland) 560, "Subsequent Events," paragraphs 10-17.*

If the auditor concludes that there is a material misstatement of fact in the other information which management refuses to correct, the auditor shall notify those charged with governance, unless all of those charged with governance are involved in managing the entity, of the auditor's concern regarding the other information and take any further appropriate action. (Ref: Para. A11) **16**

> If an amendment is necessary in the other information and the entity refuses to make the amendment, the auditor shall consider including in the auditor's report an "Other Matters" paragraph describing the material misstatement. **16-1**

***

## Application and Other Explanatory Material

### Scope of this ISA (UK and Ireland)

*Additional Responsibilities, through Statutory or Other Regulatory Requirements, in Relation to Other Information* (Ref: Para. 1)

The auditor may have additional responsibilities, through statutory or other regulatory requirements, in relation to other information that are beyond the scope of this ISA (UK and Ireland). For example, some jurisdictions may require the auditor to apply specific procedures to certain of the other information such as required supplementary data or to express an opinion on the reliability of performance indicators described in the other information. Where there are such obligations, the auditor's additional responsibilities are determined by the nature of the engagement and by law, regulation and professional standards. If such other information is omitted or contains deficiencies, the auditor may be required by law or regulation to refer to the matter in the auditor's report. **A1**

> In the UK and Ireland an example of an auditor's additional responsibilities for a listed company would include the auditor's review of whether the Corporate Governance Statement reflects the company's compliance with the provisions of the Combined Code specified by the Listing Rules for review by the auditor. **A1-1**

*Documents Containing Audited Financial Statements* (Ref: Para. 2)

*Considerations Specific to Smaller Entities*

Unless required by law or regulation, smaller entities are less likely to issue documents containing audited financial statements. However, an example of such a document would be where a legal requirement exists for an accompanying report by those charged with governance. Examples of other information that may be included in a document containing the audited financial statements of a smaller entity are a detailed income statement and a management report. **A2**

### Definition of Other Information (Ref: Para. 5(a))

Other information may comprise, for example: **A3**

- A report by management or those charged with governance on operations.

- Financial summaries or highlights.
- Employment data.
- Planned capital expenditures.
- Financial ratios.
- Names of officers and directors.
- Selected quarterly data.

A3-1    Further examples relevant in the UK and Ireland are a directors' report required by statute (see Section B), statements relating to corporate governance, as required by the Listing Rules, a chairman's statement, a voluntary Operating and Financial Review and non-statutory financial information included within the annual report[5a].

A4    For purposes of the ISAs (UK and Ireland), other information does not encompass, for example:

- A press release or a transmittal memorandum, such as a covering letter, accompanying the document containing audited financial statements and the auditor's report thereon.
- Information contained in analyst briefings.
- Information contained on the entity's website.

## Reading Other Information (Ref: Para. 6-7)

A4-1    When the auditor reads the other information, the auditor does so in the light of the knowledge the auditor has acquired during the audit. The auditor is not expected to verify any of the other information. The audit engagement partner (and, where appropriate, other senior members of the engagement team who can reasonably be expected to be aware of the more important matters arising during the audit and to have a general understanding of the entity's affairs), reads the other information with a view to identifying significant misstatements therein or matters which are inconsistent with the financial statements.

A4-2    If the auditor believes that the other information contains a material misstatement of fact, is materially inconsistent with the financial statements, or is otherwise misleading, and the auditor is unable to resolve the matter with management and those charged with governance, the auditor considers the implications for the auditor's report and what further actions may be appropriate. The auditor has regard to the guidance in paragraphs A11-1 and A11-2 below.

A5    Obtaining the other information prior to the date of the auditor's report enables the auditor to resolve possible material inconsistencies and apparent material misstatements of fact with management on a timely basis. An agreement with management as

---

[5a] *The APB recognises that in some circumstances the presentation of non-statutory financial information and associated narrative explanations with the statutory results may help shareholders understand better the financial performance of a company. However, the APB is concerned that in other circumstances such non-statutory information in annual reports has the potential to be misleading and shareholders may sometimes be misinformed by the manner in which non-statutory information is presented. The APB believes that the potential for non-statutory information to be misleading is considerable when undue and inappropriate prominence is given to the non-statutory information, when there is no description of the non-statutory information and, where appropriate, the adjusted numbers are not reconciled to the statutory financial information.*

to when the other information will be available may be helpful.

> Guidance to auditors in the UK and Ireland on the consideration of other information where the annual financial statements accompanied by the auditor's report are published on an entity's website, or in the UK where companies can meet their statutory reporting obligations to shareholders by distributing annual financial statements and certain other reports electronically, is given in the Appendix to this Section[sb].

**A5-2**

## Material Inconsistencies

*Material Inconsistencies Identified in Other Information Obtained Prior to the Date of the Auditor's Report* (Ref: Para. 10)

When management refuses to revise the other information, the auditor may base any decision on what further action to take on advice from the auditor's legal counsel.

**A6**

> If the auditor concludes that the other information contains inconsistencies with the financial statements, and the auditor is unable to resolve them through discussion with those charged with governance, the auditor considers requesting those charged with governance to consult with a qualified third party, such as the entity's legal counsel and considers the advice received.

**A6-1**

*Considerations Specific to Public Sector Entities*

In the public sector, withdrawal from the engagement or withholding the auditor's report may not be options. In such cases the auditor may issue a report to the appropriate statutory body giving details of the inconsistency.

**A7**

*Material Inconsistencies Identified in Other Information Obtained Subsequent to the Date of the Auditor's Report* (Ref: Para. 12-13)

When management agrees to revise the other information, the auditor's procedures may include reviewing the steps taken by management to ensure that individuals in receipt of the previously issued financial statements, the auditor's report thereon, and the other information are informed of the revision.

**A8**

A9. *When management refuses to make the revision of such other information that the auditor concludes is necessary, appropriate further actions by the auditor may include obtaining advice from the auditor's legal counsel.*

## Material Misstatements of Fact (Ref: Para. 14-16)

When discussing an apparent material misstatement of fact with management, the auditor may not be able to evaluate the validity of some disclosures included within the other information and management's responses to the auditor's inquiries, and

**A10**

---

[sb] *In the UK, the Companies Act 2006 enables companies, subject to certain conditions set out in Schedule 5 thereto, to make communications in electronic form, including by means of a website. Further, section 430 of the Companies Act 2006 requires that a quoted company must ensure that its annual accounts and reports are made available on a website.*

may conclude that valid differences of judgment or opinion exist.

A10-1   A material misstatement of fact in other information would potentially include an inconsistency between information obtained by the auditor during the audit (such as information obtained as part of the planning process or analytical procedures, or as written representations) and information which is included in the other information.

A10-2   The auditor has regard to the nature of the inconsistency or misstatement that in the auditor's opinion exists. A distinction may be drawn between a matter of fact and one of judgment. It is generally more difficult for the auditor to take issue with a matter of judgment (such as the view of those charged with governance of the likely out-turn for the following year) than a factual error. Although an auditor does not substitute the auditor's judgment for that of management and those charged with governance in such matters, there may be circumstances in which the auditor is aware that the expressed view of management and those charged with governance is significantly at variance with the entity's internal assessment or is so unreasonable as not to be credible to someone with the auditor's knowledge.

A11   When the auditor concludes that there is a material misstatement of fact that management refuses to correct, appropriate further actions by the auditor may include obtaining advice from the auditor's legal counsel.

### Further Actions Available to the Auditor

A11-1   The auditor of a limited company in the United Kingdom or the Republic of Ireland may use the auditor's right to be heard at any general meeting of the members on any part of the business of the meeting which concerns the auditor as auditor[5c].

A11-2   The auditor may also consider resigning from the audit engagement. In the case of auditors of limited companies in the United Kingdom or the Republic of Ireland, the requirements for the auditor to make a statement on ceasing to hold office as auditor apply[5d]. When making a statement in these circumstances, the considerations set out in paragraph A10-1 above would normally be applicable. In addition, in the UK the auditor may need to notify the relevant audit authority.

---

[5c] *The relevant reference for the UK is section 502 of the Companies Act 2006, and for the Republic of Ireland is section 193(5) of the Companies Act 1990.*

[5d] *The relevant reference for the UK is section 519 of the Companies Act 2006, and for the Republic of Ireland is section 185 of the Companies Act 1990.*

# Appendix

# Electronic Publication of the Auditor's Report

## Introduction

In the UK, section 430 of the Companies Act 2006 requires that a quoted company must ensure that its annual accounts and reports are made available on a website. The Companies Act 2006 also enables all companies, subject to certain conditions set out in Schedule 5 thereto, to make communications in electronic form, including by means of a website.  **1**

Various types of financial information can be found on websites including information that has been audited (for example the annual financial statements), information which the auditor may have reviewed (for example interim financial information) and information with which the auditor has had no direct involvement, such as financial highlights from a company's Annual Report or may never have seen, such as presentations for analysts. In addition, websites typically contain a considerable amount of non-financial information.  **2**

The purpose of this Appendix is to provide guidance to auditors on the consideration of other information in situations where the annual financial statements accompanied by the auditor's report are published on an entity's website[5e].  **3**

# The Auditor's Consideration of Other Information Issued with the Annual Report

## Checking Information Presented Electronically

When companies include the annual financial statements and the auditor's report on their website or, in the UK, decide to distribute annual financial statements to their shareholders electronically, the auditor:  **4**

(a) Reviews the process by which the financial statements to be published electronically are derived from the financial information contained in the manually signed accounts;
(b) Checks that the proposed electronic version is identical in content with the manually signed accounts; and
(c) Checks that the conversion of the manually signed accounts into an electronic format has not distorted the overall presentation of the financial information, for example, by highlighting certain information so as to give it greater prominence.

It is recommended that the auditor retains a printout or disk of the final electronic version for future reference if necessary.  **5**

---

[5e] *This guidance is generally applicable both to auditors in the UK (where the provisions of the Companies Act 2006 apply) and the Republic of Ireland (where they do not).*

**Auditor's Report Wording**

6    The auditor considers whether the wording of the auditor's report is suitable for electronic distribution. Issues include:

- Identifying the financial statements that have been audited and the information that has been reviewed, or read, by the auditor.
- Limiting the auditor's association with any other information distributed with the Annual Report.

**Identification of the Financial Statements That Have Been Audited**

7    In Annual Reports produced in a hard copy format, the auditor's report usually identifies the financial statements which have been audited by reference to page numbers. The use of page numbers is often not a suitable method of identifying particular financial information presented on a website[5f]. The auditor's report therefore needs to specify in another way the location and description of the information that has been audited.

8    The APB recommends that the auditor's report describes, by name, the primary statements that comprise the financial statements. The same technique can also be used to specify the information that has been reviewed or, because it is included in the Annual Report, read by the auditor.

9    The auditor ensures that the auditor's statutory report on the full financial statements is not associated with extracts from, or summaries of, those audited financial statements.

**Identification of the Nationality of the Accounting and Auditing Standards Applied**

10   Auditor's reports on websites will be accessible internationally, and it is therefore important that the auditor's report indicates clearly the nationality of the accounting standards used in the preparation of the financial statements and the nationality of the auditing standards applied. For the same reason, the auditor ensures that the auditor's report discloses sufficient of the auditor's address to enable readers to understand in which country the auditor is located.

## Limitation of the Auditor's Association With any Other Information Distributed With the Annual Report

11   In addition to the Annual Report many companies publish on their websites a considerable volume of financial and non-financial information. This information could take the form of additional analyses or alternative presentations of audited financial information. Users of the website are likely to find it difficult to distinguish financial information which the auditor has audited, or read, from other data. This issue is exacerbated when there are hyperlinks which allow users to move easily from one area of the website to another.

---

[5f] *The audited financial statements can be presented on the website using a variety of webfile formats. As at the date of this Bulletin, examples of these are the Portable Document Format (PDF) or Hypertext Mark-up Language (HTML). Page numbers generally continue to be an effective referencing mechanism for PDF files but this is not always the case when data is represented 'in HTML.*

The auditor gives careful consideration to the use of hyperlinks between the audited financial statements and information contained on the website that has not been subject to audit or 'reading' by the auditor ('other information'). To avoid possible misunderstandings concerning the scope of the audit, the auditor requests those charged with governance to ensure that hyperlinks contain warnings that the linkage is from audited to unaudited information.

12

Sometimes audited information is not included in the financial statements themselves (e.g. certain information relating to directors' remuneration may be set out as part of a company's corporate governance disclosures). The APB is of the view that companies should be encouraged to make disclosures that are required to be audited, as part of the financial statements or included in the Annual Report in such a way that it is clear which elements of it have been audited. In other circumstances the auditor assesses whether the scope of the audit will be capable of being clearly described. If this cannot be achieved to the satisfaction of the auditor it may be necessary to describe the particulars that have been audited within the auditor's report.

13

The auditor is concerned to establish that the auditor's report on the financial statements is not inappropriately associated with other information. The auditor takes steps to satisfy themselves that information that they have audited or, because it is included in the Annual Report, read, is distinguished from other information in a manner appropriate to the electronic format used by the entity. Techniques that can be used to differentiate material within a website include

14

- Icons or watermarks.
- Colour borders.
- Labels/banners such as 'annual report' or 'audited financial statements'. The appropriate mode of differentiation between audited and unaudited information will be dependent on the electronic format selected, and the nature and extent of other information presented on the website. The method of differentiation would normally also be clearly stated in an introduction page within the website.

During the course of the audit, the auditor discusses with the those charged with governance or, where appropriate, the audit committee how the financial statements and auditor's report will be presented on the entity's website with a view to minimizing the possibility that the auditor's report is inappropriately associated with other information. If the auditor is not satisfied with the proposed electronic presentation of the audited financial statements and auditor's report, the auditor requests that the presentation be amended. If the presentation is not amended the auditor will, in accordance with the terms of the engagement, not give consent for the electronic release of the audit opinion.

15

If the auditor's report is used without the auditor's consent, and the auditor has concerns about the electronic presentation of the audited financial statements or the auditor's report and appropriate action is not taken by those charged with governance, the auditor seeks legal advice as necessary. The auditor also considers whether it would be appropriate to resign.

16

# Addendum

*This addendum provides a summary of APB's rationale for retaining or excluding in the proposed clarified ISA (UK and Ireland) the supplementary requirements in the existing ISA (UK and Ireland). It also sets out the supplementary guidance material in the existing ISA (UK and Ireland) that APB considers is not necessary to retain in light of the improvements in the underlying Clarity ISAs issued by the IAASB as part of the Clarity Project. It is provided for information and does not form part of the proposed clarified ISA (UK and Ireland).*

*The Consultation Paper published with the exposure drafts explains the general approach used by the APB for determining whether current supplementary material should be proposed to be retained.*

**Analysis of proposed treatment of current APB supplementary material in current ISA (UK and Ireland) 720 Section A**

<u>Requirements</u>

| APB supplementary requirements (*Italic text is from IAASB for context*) | Is it covered in substance in the Clarity ISA? | Should it be retained? |
|---|---|---|
| 2-1. **If, as a result of reading the other information, the auditor becomes aware of any apparent misstatements therein, or identifies any material inconsistencies with the audited financial statements, the auditor should seek to resolve them.** | ✓ The objective of the ISA is for the auditor to respond appropriately when documents containing audited financial statements and the auditor's report thereon include other information that could undermine the credibility of those financial statements and the auditor's report.<br><br>Whilst the ISA does not include any explicit requirements to "resolve" such matters, this is clearly the spirit of the standard and is referred to in the Application Material which states "Obtaining the other information prior to the date of the auditor's report enables the auditor to resolve possible material inconsistencies and apparent material misstatements of fact | ✗ |

| APB supplementary requirements (*Italic text is from IAASB for context*) | Is it covered in substance in the Clarity ISA? | Should it be retained? |
|---|---|---|
| | with management on a timely basis." (A5) | |
| 11-1. **If the auditor identifies a material inconsistency the auditor should seek to resolve the matter through discussion with those charged with governance.** | ✓ As in the current ISA, the auditor is required to determine whether the audited financial statements or the other information needs to be revised (8). There is a new requirement to communicate with TCWG that when management refuses to make a change to the other information, that the auditor considers necessary (10). | ✗ |
| 16-1. **The auditor should consider whether the other information requires to be amended.** | ✓ However, as in the current ISA, this is implied. | ✗ Adding the plus identified below re para 18-2 should be sufficient. |
| 18-2. **If an amendment is necessary in the other information and the entity refuses to make the amendment, the auditor should consider including in the auditor's report an emphasis of matter paragraph describing the material misstatement.** | ✗ The ISA requires notification of TCWG and taking any further appropriate action (e.g. obtaining legal advice). (15, 16, A11) | ✓ (Audit Quality **16-1** |

## Guidance

The following guidance in current ISA (UK and Ireland) 720 Section A has not been carried forward to the proposed clarified standard.

| Current paragraph reference (*Italic text is from IAASB for context*) |
|---|
| 1-2.  This ISA (UK and Ireland) is primarily directed towards the auditor's consideration of other information contained in an entity's published annual report. It is not intended to address issues which may arise if financial information is extracted from the document. |
| 1-3. – 1-6. [Definitions of management and those charged with governance.] |
| 6-1.  The credibility of the audited financial statements may also be undermined by misstatements within the other information. |
| 13-1.  In circumstances where the auditor has no issues with the financial statements themselves, and the emphasis of matter is being used to report on matters other than those affecting the financial statements, an emphasis of matter paragraph in relation to a material inconsistency does not give rise to a qualified audit opinion. |
| 16.  *If the auditor becomes aware that the other information appears to include a material misstatement of fact, the auditor should discuss the matter with the entity's management[6]. ....* <br><br> [6] In the UK and Ireland the auditor discusses such matters with, and obtains responses from, those charged with governance. |
| 17.  *When the auditor still considers that there is an apparent misstatement of fact, the auditor should request management[7] to consult with a qualified third party, such as the entity's legal counsel and should consider the advice received.* <br><br> [7] In the UK and Ireland the auditor requests those charged with governance to consult with a qualified third party. |
| 18-1.  In the UK and Ireland the auditor requests those charged with governance to correct any material misstatements of fact in the other information. |
| 18-3.  In circumstances where the auditor has no issues with the financial statements, and the emphasis of matter is being used to report on matters other than those affecting the financial statements, an emphasis of matter paragraph in relation to a material misstatement of fact in the other information does not give rise to a qualified audit opinion. |

# Proposed Clarified International Standard on Auditing (UK and Ireland) 720

## Section B – The auditor's statutory reporting responsibility in relation to directors' reports

*(Effective for audits of financial statements for periods ending on or after 15 December 2010)*

## Contents

International Standard on Auditing (UK and Ireland) (ISA (UK and Ireland)) 720 Section B, "The Auditor's Statutory Reporting Responsibility in Relation to Directors' Reports" should be read in conjunction with ISA (UK and Ireland) 200, "Overall Objectives of the Independent Auditor and the Conduct of an Audit in Accordance with International Standards on Auditing (UK and Ireland)."

# Introduction

## Scope of this Section

1    This Section of International Standard on Auditing (UK and Ireland) (ISA (UK and Ireland)) 720 deals with the auditor's statutory reporting responsibility in relation to directors' reports.

2    In the United Kingdom and the Republic of Ireland, legislation[1] requires the auditor of a company to state in the auditor's report whether, in the auditor's opinion, the information given in the directors' report is consistent with the financial statements.

3    "Information given in the directors' report" includes information that is included by way of cross reference to other information presented separately from the directors' report. For example, a UK company may decide to present a voluntary Operating and Financial Review (OFR) which includes some or all of the matters required for the Business Review section of the directors' report. Rather than duplicate the information, the company may cross refer from the Business Review section in the directors' report to the relevant information provided in the OFR.

4    The auditor is not required to verify, or report on, the completeness of the information in the directors' report. If, however, the auditor becomes aware that information that is required by law or regulations to be in the directors' report has been omitted the auditor communicates the matter to those charged with governance. This communication includes situations where the required information is presented separately from the directors' report without appropriate cross references.

5    Illustrative examples of wording to include auditor's reports tailored for use with audits conducted in accordance with ISAs (UK and Ireland) are provided in the most recent versions of the APB Bulletins, "Auditor's Reports on Financial Statements in the United Kingdom"/"Auditor's Reports on Financial Statements in the Republic of Ireland".

## Effective Date

6    This Section of ISA (UK and Ireland) 720 is effective for audits of financial statements for periods ending on or after 15 December 2010.

# Objective

7    The objective of the auditor is to form an opinion on whether the information given in the directors' report is consistent with the financial statements and to respond appropriately if it is not consistent.

---

[1] *Relevant legislation includes:*
- *In the UK, Section 496 of the Companies Act 2006*
- *In the Republic of Ireland, Section 15 of the Companies (Amendment) Act 1986.*

# Requirements

## Reading the Directors' Report

The auditor shall read the information in the directors' report and assess whether it is consistent with the financial statements. (Ref: Para. A1) — 8

## Inconsistencies

If the auditor identifies any inconsistencies between the information in the directors' report and the financial statements the auditor shall seek to resolve them. (Ref: Para. A2) — 9

If the auditor is of the opinion that the information in the directors' report is materially inconsistent[2] with the financial statements, and has been unable to resolve the inconsistency, the auditor shall state that opinion and describe the inconsistency in the auditor's report. — 10

If an amendment is necessary to the financial statements and management and those charged with governance refuse to make the amendment, the auditor shall express a qualified or adverse opinion on the financial statements. — 11

## Documentation

The auditor shall document: — 12

(a) The results of those procedures performed to assess whether the information in the directors' report is consistent with the financial statements, including details of any material inconsistencies identified and how they were resolved; and

(b) The conclusion reached as to whether the information in the directors' report is consistent with the financial statements.

***

# Application and Other Explanatory Material

## Reading the Directors' Report (Ref: Para. 8)

Much of the information in the directors' report is likely to be extracted or directly derived from the financial statements and will therefore be directly comparable with them. Some financial information may, however, be more detailed or prepared on a different basis from that in the financial statements. Where the financial information is more detailed, the auditor agrees the information to the auditor's working papers or the entity's accounting records. Where the financial information has been prepared on a different basis, the auditor considers whether there is adequate disclosure of the differences in the bases of preparation to enable an understanding of the differences in the information, and checks the reconciliation of the information to the financial statements. — A1

[2] *Materiality is addressed in ISA (UK and Ireland) 320 "Audit Materiality". An inconsistency is "material" if it could influence the economic decisions of users.*

**Inconsistencies** (Ref: Para. 9)

A2   Inconsistencies include:

- Differences between amounts or narrative appearing in the financial statements and the directors' report.
- Differences between the bases of preparation of related items appearing in the financial statements and the directors' report, where the figures themselves are not directly comparable and the different bases are not disclosed.
- Contradictions between figures contained in the financial statements and narrative explanations of those figures in the directors' report.

The auditor ordinarily seeks to resolve inconsistencies through discussion with management and those charged with governance.

# Addendum

*This addendum is provided for information and does not form part of proposed clarified ISA (UK and Ireland) 720 Section B.*

*ISA (UK and Ireland) 720 Section B is, in effect, a complete supplementary standard addressing legal and regulatory requirements. The proposed clarified standard has been reformatted to match the Clarity format (i.e. stating an objective and having separate sections for requirements and application material). However, present tense guidance in the current standard has not been eliminated.*

*The illustrative wording for auditor's reports given in the Appendix to the current ISA (UK and Ireland) 720 Section B has not been included in the proposed clarified standard. Illustrative examples of wording to include auditor's reports tailored for use with audits conducted in accordance with ISAs (UK and Ireland) are provided in the most recent versions of the APB Bulletins, "Auditor's Reports on Financial Statements in the United Kingdom"/"Auditor's Reports on Financial Statements in the Republic of Ireland".*